The
Social Work Skills
WORKBOOK 8e

Barry R. Cournoyer

Emeritus Professor of Social Work, Indiana University

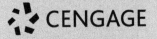
CENGAGE

Australia • Brazil • Canada • Mexico • Singapore • United Kingdom • United States

The Social Work Skills Workbook, **Eighth Edition**

Barry R. Cournoyer

Product Director: Jon Goodspeed

Product Manager: Julie Martinez

Content Developer: Jennifer Risden

Product Assistant: Stephen Lagos

Content Project Manager: Carol Samet

Art Director: Vernon Boes

Manufacturing Planner: Judy Inouye

Compositor and Production Service: MPS Limited

Text Researcher: Lumina Datamatics Ltd.

Cover and Text Designer: Cheryl Carrington

Art Stylist: Lisa Torri

Cover Image Credit: Watercolor background: RDC_designs/iStock/Getty Images Plus/Getty Images Caring hand/Artishokcs/iStock/Getty Images Plus/Getty Images

For product information and technology assistance, contact us at
Cengage Customer & Sales Support, 1-800-354-9706

For permission to use material from this text or product,
submit all requests online at **www.cengage.com/permissions**
Further permissions questions can be e-mailed to
permissionrequest@cengage.com

Library of Congress Control Number: 2016933683

ISBN: 978-1-305-63378-0

Loose-leaf Edition:
ISBN: 978-1-305-86631-7

Cengage
200 Pier 4 Boulevard
Boston, MA 02210
USA

Cengage is a leading provider of customized learning solutions with employees residing in nearly 40 different countries and sales in more than 125 countries around the world. Find your local representative at: **www.cengage.com**

To learn more about Cengage platforms and services, register or access your online learning solution, or purchase materials for your course, visit **www.cengage.com**.

Printed at CLDPC, USA, 03-21

CHAPTER 4

Diversity and Difference; Human Rights; Social, Economic, and Environmental Justice; and Policy–Practice   93

CHAPTER 5

Social Work Values and Ethical Decision Making   157

PART 2   Social Work Skills   205

CHAPTER 6
Talking and Listening: The Basic Interpersonal Skills   207

CHAPTER **7**

Preparing

CHAPTER **8**

Beginning

CHAPTER 9

Exploring

CHAPTER 10

Assessing

CHAPTER 13

Ending   499

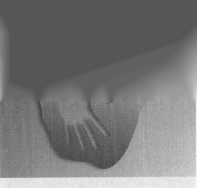

The original impetus for creating *The Social Work Skills Workbook* began with observations and, yes, complaints from students that social work professors and their textbooks tend to "talk about practice rather than help us learn what to do and how to do it." This was a typical comment: "In the classroom, the professors talk at such abstract levels that when I'm with clients, I don't really know what I'm supposed to do." Clearly, we needed more practical and applied learning materials.

The eighth edition of *The Social Work Skills Workbook* addresses these needs and provides opportunities for you to gain proficiency in essential social work skills. While maintaining the general organizational structure of earlier editions, several changes enhance support for the social, economic, and environmental justice mission of the profession and the nature and scope of contemporary social work practice. The integration of the social work skills and the competencies identified in the 2015 iteration of the Educational Policy and Accreditation Standards (EPAS) of the Council on Social Work Education (CSWE) remain evident, as do many of the abilities addressed in social work licensing examinations sponsored by the Association of Social Work Boards (ASWB). Indeed, each social work skill supports one or more of the 43 knowledge and value statements (KVs) and the 31 **practice behaviors (PBs)** which elaborate the nine core competencies presented in the EPAS. They also address knowledge, skills and abilities (KSAs) contained in the ASWB exams. However, the skills workbook should not be viewed as a manual for the CSWE endorsed EPAS competencies or as a study guide for the ASWB sponsored licensing examinations. The social work skills incorporated here are consistent with the purposes of the profession, its core values and ethics, and findings from the professional literature and scholarly research studies.

Consistent with social work's *person-in-environment* perspective, studies that highlight the "power of context" serve to inform the selection of case examples and exercises included in this edition. This edition reflects increased attention to policy–practice and social action, and maintains its focus upon scientific inquiry, critical thought, and

Goals

Following completion of *The Social Work Skills Workbook*, you should be able to:

- Apply the dimensions of professionalism in social work practice.
- Think critically in professional contexts and throughout the phases and processes of social work.
- Engage in scientific inquiry and lifelong learning to seek, discover, evaluate, and apply relevant knowledge in professional practice.
- Access a place of peace, engage diversity and difference, and accept others in a culturally sensitive and respectful manner.
- Consider core social work values, ethics, and relevant legal obligations in making ethical decisions and taking ethical action.
- Demonstrate oral and written communication skills in working with individuals, families, groups, organizations, communities, and societies.
- Apply the skills of preparing, beginning, exploring, assessing, contracting, working and evaluating, and ending in your work with and on behalf of individuals, families, groups, organizations, and communities.
- Engage in policy-practice and social action to advocate for human rights; social, economic, and environmental justice; and social well-being.
- Assess and evaluate one's proficiency in the social work skills.
- Prepare a Social Work Skills Learning Portfolio to plan, integrate, synthesize, and document lifelong learning for your career in social work.

incorporation of research-based knowledge in collaborative decision making with clients and others. Such emphases reflect current political and socioeconomic conditions as well as contemporary views of evidence-based and outcome-informed practice. Clearly, social workers are guided by practice-relevant, credible research findings. However, we also recognize our human tendencies toward self-affirmation and confirmation bias. Therefore, we consistently seek evidence of progress toward those collaboratively established goals that clients, social workers, and other stakeholders pursue. We engage in continuous evaluation of our work with individuals, families, groups, organizations, and communities to improve outcomes as well as enhance the quality of our service to others.

This edition of *The Social Work Skills Workbook* may be used (1) as the primary text for social work practice and social work skills laboratory courses (which might be titled "interviewing skills," "interpersonal skills," "professional skills," "interactional skills," "interpersonal communication skills," "microskills," "practice skills," or "helping skills" labs); (2) as a text for introductory, "immersion," or professional socialization seminars or modules; (3) as a workbook for social work practice courses; (4) by social work students and field instructors during practicum experiences; and (5) by professional social workers seeking to enhance their professionalism and their proficiency in essential social work skills.

New to the Eighth Edition

- Fully integrated with the most recent (2015) iteration of the Educational Policy and Educational Standards (EPAS) of the Council on Social Work Education (CSWE).
- Enhanced integration with online resources through MindTap.
- More colorful and attractive style, and improved readability.
- Increased exploration of social, economic, and environmental justice—including contemporary forms of racism and related topics such as mass incarceration, police misconduct, increasing income and wealth inequality, and political and financial corruption and oppression.
- Added emphasis to social and political action, policy-practice, and cause and class advocacy.
- Major new case illustration and analysis for the purposes of ethical analysis and decision making.
- New, revised, and updated in-chapter and end-of chapter exercises.
- Revised assessment content, processes, and skills.
- Improved and more detailed guidelines for the five-session experiential learning exercise with a practice client.
- The Self-Appraisal of Proficiency of EPAS Competency-Based Knowledge and Values, and Practice Behaviors—Updated and revised.
- The Social Work Skills Test—Updated and revised.

Social work programs may use the skills workbook in courses over two terms in their BSW or MSW foundation curriculums. This approach allows students additional time to complete and reflect upon the numerous skill-building exercises, and to refine materials included within their Social Work Skills Learning Portfolios (see Appendix 1) that result from completion of chapter exercises. To facilitate such an option, this edition is organized into two major parts. *Part 1: Professionalism* introduces students to the values, culture, and context of social work. It contains an introduction and four chapters that address 10 dimensions of professionalism: integrity; self-understanding and self-control; knowledge, expertise, and self-efficacy; social support and well-being; critical thinking and scientific inquiry; lifelong learning; diversity and difference; human rights and social, economic, and environmental justice; policy–practice; and ethical decision making. The exercises contained in Part 1 emphasize these aspects of professionalism and involve scientific inquiry, critical thought and reflection, independent learning, and preparation of several written documents.

Part 2: Social Work Skills emphasizes skills needed for contemporary practice. Part 2 begins with a review of the basic skills of talking and listening followed by chapters that address skills associated with seven phases of practice: (1) preparing, (2) beginning, (3) exploring, (4) assessing, (5) contracting, (6) working and evaluating, and (7) ending. The exercises in Part 2 are competency-based and focus on the development of proficiency in the social work skills.

The Council on Social Work expects programs to assess students' progress toward the achievement of competencies. Furthermore, programs must use the results of such assessments to improve program quality and educational outcomes. Typically, social work programs expect their students to demonstrate proficiency in most or all of the social work skills reflected in this book. Because each of the social work skills supports one or more of the EPAS competencies, the Social Work Skills Self-Appraisal Questionnaire (Appendix 3); the Self-Appraisal of Proficiency: EPAS Competency-Based Knowledge and Values, and Practice Behaviors (Appendix 13), and items from The Social Work Skills Test (Appendix 2)—especially when used in "before" and "after" fashion—can contribute data for student learning outcome assessment of individual students, student cohorts, and the program as a whole.

The Social Work Skills Test may be used to advance individual student learning or for social work program evaluation. Students may complete some or all test items at the beginning of a course or program of study and then again at the end to provide a direct indication of learning progress. Professors may find students' responses to the first test administration helpful in determining which skills to emphasize or reinforce during the learning experience.

The Social Work Skills Test contains two major parts. Part 1 includes 140 true-false and multiple-choice items that refer directly to descriptive content contained within the book. These items are written primarily at the comprehension level of intellectual development. In order to answer such items correctly, you must have read, understood, and remembered material presented in the book. Part 2 includes 50 short-answer items through which you apply what you have learned to practice scenarios. More intellectually challenging than Part 1, these items are framed at the application, analysis, synthesis, and evaluation levels of intellectual development. Many of these items approximate contexts and exchanges that commonly occur in social work practice. You must invest considerable thought, judgment, and care in responding to items in Part 2 of The Social Work Skills Test.

Many of the end-of-chapter exercises result in word-processed documents for inclusion in the Social Work Skills Learning Portfolio. As a result, learners naturally create additional relevant information for potential use in outcome assessment—whether that involves self-assessment by learners themselves, or evaluation by their professors, advisers, or the school, department, or educational program. The documents are stored in a designated portion of an electronic storage medium such as a computer hard drive or removable disk. Prepared in word-processed format, the learning portfolio provides ready access to documentary evidence of progress in developing proficiency in the social work skills. The Social Work Skills Learning Portfolio may also be used for self-assessment purposes or by professors to evaluate individual student learning. Social work schools and departments may use the portfolios of student cohorts (or samples thereof) to evaluate the general effectiveness of a course or educational program. Educators may use the assessments and evaluations *formatively* to identify additional individual or group learning needs, or *summatively* to determine a rank, status, or grade. When collated and aggregated by class or cohort, responses to self-appraisal questions and test items, and the numerous documents produced for the Social Work Skills Learning Portfolio can help social work programs evaluate progress toward the achievement of their educational goals, objectives, and competencies as part of their effort to improve learning outcomes and meet CSWE accreditation standards.

Some skill-building exercises involve resources available through the Internet, whereas others require personal reflection, self-analysis, or some form of critical thinking and scholarly inquiry. Certain exercises may provoke discomfort as students begin to question or challenge strongly held personal beliefs, attitudes, and ideologies. Indeed, some discomfort may stimulate you to think skeptically and critically about your own ideas and those of others. You might even change your mind about some things you now assume to be true. As social workers, we routinely face extraordinarily difficult and highly stressful situations that challenge our personal views, values, and expectations. We must learn to cope with and manage considerable individual, interpersonal, and social distress as well as a great deal of intellectual ambiguity so that we can maintain primary focus on our clients' needs and goals, on human rights and social justice, and on our own professional responsibilities.

Please use the exercises in this book to explore and indeed question your assumptions about humans and human behavior, about fairness and justice, and about life and living. *Don't believe everything you think.* Appreciate that social work commonly involves complex, deep thinking about personal and social phenomena that often trigger powerful emotions and attitudes. As you use this book, I hope you learn to examine and analyze the underlying assumptions and the nature, source, and quality of the evidence that support the values and ideas that guide your approach to others and the world around you.

The individuals, families, groups, organizations, communities, and societies that social workers serve differ in various ways. As you proceed through the skills book, you will explore problems, issues, and scenarios that reflect diversity and difference as well as some that reveal profound commonalities within our human family. Many exercises address aspects of culture, status, and difference as they relate to policies and practices that affect human rights and social, economic, and environmental justice.

Completion of the learning exercises leads to the preparation of two "case records." Based on self-understanding gained through various exercises, you prepare the description and assessment sections of your own personal case record. In addition, you produce a more complete and more formal case record in the course of conducting five interviews with a "practice client." The five interviews provide an opportunity for you to simulate all phases of the working relationship (preparing, beginning, exploring, assessing, contracting, working and evaluating, and ending). In addition to the description, assessment, and contract sections, you also prepare progress notes and a closing summary as you engage a practice client in this intensive practice exercise. Both "case records" represent important written products for inclusion in the Social Work Skills Learning Portfolio.

The cases and situations used as illustrative examples and incorporated within learning exercises come from a variety of service settings and circumstances. Although many of the case vignettes involve interaction with individuals, families, and groups, several relate to work with organizations and communities. The significance of social and environmental factors is reflected as are the interrelationships between people and the environment. Several examples of extra-client systems (for example, referral sources, community resources, or related social systems) are incorporated, and case vignettes are chosen with a view toward diversity of age, gender, sexual orientation, and racial, ethnic, cultural, and socioeconomic status.

Professors who employ the workbook in their social work courses may use the exercises in a variety of ways. As part of a homework or in-class assignment, they might ask students to respond to selected exercises and then call on students to share their responses and discuss the characteristics that account for proficiency. Alternately, professors may assign certain exercises as written homework for evaluation. Numerous opportunities stimulate evaluation processes of various kinds, including self-assessments, peer assessments, and appraisals by instructors. Indeed, professors may use aggregated assessment data to highlight skill areas that need further collective attention or move more quickly through skill areas where proficiency is already high. Similarly, students and professors may periodically review the Social Work Skills Learning Portfolios for formative or summative assessment purposes.

During classroom meetings, professors may ask students to form pairs, triads, or small groups to carry out selected learning exercises. Role plays in which learners alternately assume the part of client and social worker can be especially effective learning experiences—particularly when there is timely and constructive feedback from the professor. In general, professors should recognize that we use the social work skills in the context of helping people. Therefore, learning processes that approximate the actual doing with opportunities for evaluative feedback are preferred. "Talking about" topics can lead to considerable insight. However, when skills and competencies are involved, doing, applying, and practicing tend to yield a much greater return on our educational investment.

In addition to appendices that pertain to self-appraisal and evaluation tools, other appendices contain materials to support your learning. Within the appendices you will find an interview rating form for clients; guidelines and forms for the multiweek experiential interviewing exercise; an alphabetized vocabulary of English "feeling" words; an example of the Description, Assessment, and Contract (DAC) portions of a case record; a form for assessing skills performance during interviews with simulated or actual clients; a table of social work skills; and a table that links skills to the knowledge and values, and practice behaviors that support the nine core EPAS competencies.

In addition to the appendices, ancillary learning resources are available through the book's companion website—accessible via the Cengage Learning portal at www.cengage.com.

■ Ancillaries

MindTap

The Social Work Skills Workbook comes with MindTap, an online learning solution created to harness the power of technology to drive student success. This cloud-based platform integrates a number of learning applications ("apps") into an easy to use and easy to access tool that supports a personalized learning experience. MindTap combines student learning tools—readings, multimedia, activities, and assessments—into a singular Learning Path that guides students through the course.

Online Instructor's Manual

The Instructor's Manual (IM) contains a variety of resources to aid instructors in preparing and presenting text material in a manner that meets their personal preferences and course needs. It presents chapter-by-chapter suggestions and resources to enhance and facilitate learning. *Available on the instructor companion site.*

Online Test Bank

For supplementary assessment support, the updated test bank includes true/false, multiple-choice, matching, short answer, and essay questions for each chapter. *Available on the instructor companion site.*

Online PowerPoint Lecture Slides

These vibrant Microsoft® PowerPoint® lecture slides for each chapter assist instructors with their lectures by providing concept coverage using images, figures, and tables directly from the textbook. *Available on the instructor companion site.*

■ Acknowledgments

The eighth edition of *The Social Work Skills Workbook* reflects the experience of some 40 years of social work practice and more than 35 years of university teaching. Over the years, clients and students have consistently been cherished advisors. I am most appreciative of my physically challenged students and clients. Time and time again, they forgave my mistakes, encouraged growth, and inspired awe and reverence.

I am especially indebted to those clients and students who allowed me a glimpse into their worlds. Their life stories are remarkable. I feel privileged to have participated with them in their heroic journeys. Indeed, students in my social work courses have been my most gifted teachers. If they learned half of what I learned from them, I will feel satisfied. I also appreciate the letters and e-mail messages from social work students and professors. I treasure their suggestions for improving the book.

I would also like to recognize those social workers whose teachings and writings have affected me professionally and contributed to the approach taken in this workbook. Dr. Eldon Marshall, my former professor and current friend and colleague, was the first to introduce me to the interpersonal helping skills. I shall never forget his class or the impact of my first videotaped interview. Dr. Dean Hepworth, through both his teaching and writing, furthered the skills emphasis begun during my master's education. My former colleague, the late Dr. Beulah Compton, also deserves much credit. Her clear conception of fundamental social work processes has served me well indeed. I shall long remember our sometimes heated but always stimulating conversations about social work practice.

I am also grateful to my colleagues at the Indiana University School of Social Work. An extraordinary group of professionals, their dedication to student learning continues to inspire.

I wish to express my appreciation to the reviewers whose suggestions led to improvements in this and earlier editions:

Carolyn Ericson, George Mason University
Kathi Trawver, University of Alaska, Anchorage
Melissa Green, Clark Atlanta University
Debbie Gioia, University of Maryland, Baltimore
Carla Fagan, Methodist University
Antrina Bell, Alcorn State University
Amy Crossland, Lipscomb University
Michele Kelly, University of Mississippi

Finally, I want to thank my mother, Marjorie Murphy Cournoyer, for her love and compassion for others; my late father, Armand Cournoyer, for his courage, determination, and resilience; Karma Hughes and the late Grant Hughes for their unflagging support; and, most importantly, to my loving partner, Catherine Hughes Cournoyer, and our children, John Paul and Michael. Catherine is the most generous person I have ever met and without question the best social worker. Each day, she and the boys continue to make me more and better than I could possibly be without them.

Dedication

I want to dedicate this edition to Native Americans, African Americans, Hispanic Americans, Japanese Americans, immigrants, women, children, and to gay, lesbian, transgender, and all other persons who have been subject to unjustified and inexcusable human rights violations at the hands of dominant forces within the United States. We must make amends for the harm done, and the violence, oppression, incarceration, and abuse must stop!

On a more personal note, I would also like to dedicate this edition to our grandson, Zeke Armand Cournoyer. May his future be characterized by kindness and compassion rather than meanness and judgment; by cooperation more than competition; by peace rather than violence; and by genuine respect for mother earth and the wonderfully diverse forms of life that share her bounties.

Barry R. Cournoyer
Emeritus Professor of Social Work
Indiana University

Other Books by Barry R. Cournoyer

Cournoyer, Barry R., & Stanley, Mary J. (2002). *The Social Work Portfolio: Planning, Assessing and Documenting Lifelong Learning in a Dynamic Profession*. Pacific Grove, CA: Brooks/Cole.

Cournoyer, Barry R. (2004). *The Evidence-Based Social Work Skills Book*. Boston: Allyn & Bacon.

Compton, Beulah R., Galaway, Burt, & Cournoyer, Barry R. (2005). *Social Work Processes* (7th ed.). Pacific Grove, CA: Brooks/Cole.

Professionalism

Introduction

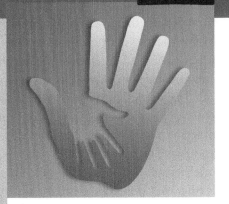

Welcome to the exciting and challenging world of social work! As a social worker, you may serve individuals, families, groups, organizations, and communities in all kinds of situations. You may do so in direct collaboration with others or indirectly through the development and implementation of policies and programs; organization of groups and communities; leadership of organizations; the design and conduct of socially relevant research studies and evaluation projects; or participation in major social movements intended to resist oppression, safeguard endangered human rights, or advance social, economic, or environmental justice. The range of settings in which you might function is wide and varied. The contexts for social work practice are often complex, usually demanding, and always challenging. Despite the extraordinary demands,

(Continued)

Chapter Goals

Following completion of this chapter, you should be able to:

- Describe the mission and purposes of the social work profession.

- Discuss the concepts of social work skills and competencies.

- Identify the phases or processes of social work practice.

- Identify the dimensions of professionalism addressed in *The Social Work Skills Workbook*.

Core Competencies

The content addressed in this chapter supports the following core EPAS competencies:

- Competency 1: Demonstrate Ethical and Professional Behavior

- Competency 2: Engage Diversity and Difference in Practice

- Competency 3: Advance Human Rights and Social, Economic, and Environmental Justice

- Competency 4: Engage in Practice-Informed Research and Research-Informed Practice

- Competency 5: Engage in Policy–Practice

service as a social worker remains a satisfying and personally rewarding endeavor. Social workers often attribute their satisfaction to factors such as the variety of work challenges, the creativity needed to address those challenges, the opportunity to work closely with and on behalf of people—especially people in need—and, importantly, high-quality supervision and positive relationships within their service organizations (Smith & Shields, 2013).

The demands, challenges, and responsibilities of social work service are sometimes daunting. To serve competently in such circumstances, social workers today need to be knowledgeable, thoughtful, ethical, accountable, and proficient. In this chapter, we introduce you to the mission of the social work profession and to our conception of social work skills; outline the phases of practice; and briefly outline the qualities and characteristics of professionalism needed for ethical, effective social work practice in our complex, ever-changing, contemporary society.

The overall purpose of *The Social Work Skills Workbook* is to help learners develop a strong sense of professionalism and gain proficiency in skills needed for ethical and effective social work practice. These skills are consistent with the raison d'être of the social work profession, its aims, and its values and ethics. Of course, we could not include every one of the various skills that might potentially have relevance for some social workers on certain occasions in some situations. Rather, we address those skills that are (1) most applicable to the social work profession's mission, purposes, and scope; (2) compatible with and supportive of the phases or processes of contemporary social work practice; (3) representative of the dimensions of professionalism; (4) consistent with social work values, ethics, and obligations; (5) supported by research-based knowledge; and (6) consistent with the competencies, knowledge, values, and practice behaviors identified in the Educational Policy and Accreditation Standards (EPAS) of the Council on Social Work Education (2015) as well as knowledge, skills, and abilities addressed in social work licensing examinations.

The social work skills are organized and presented to coincide with the phases or processes of contemporary social work practice. Of course, any phase-to-phase or stage-to-stage approach runs the risk of suggesting that service to all client systems follows the same linear sequence and that the characteristics and skills relevant to one phase are distinctly different from those of another. This is not the case. Sometimes work usually undertaken in one phase emerges in another, or the sequence must change to address urgent circumstances. In work with a particular client system, many of the dynamics, tasks, functions, and skills applicable to one phase are evident in other phases as well. We typically use certain skills (for example, empathic reflection, questioning, and seeking feedback) repeatedly throughout the course of our efforts with and on behalf of people we serve. Many skills are applied in similar fashion in work with individuals, dyads, families, groups, organizations, and communities. Others must be adapted somewhat to accommodate the size and composition of the client system, or when we are engaged in policy–practice and advocacy. Indeed, reflective thought and sound judgment are vital in the selection and application of skills throughout all phases of practice.

Professionalism is essential precisely because the social work skills cannot and should not be applied mechanically or bureaucratically without careful consideration of the people and contexts involved. Aspects of professionalism, such as integrity, knowledge, critical thinking and scientific inquiry, ethical decision making, recognition of human rights, respect for diversity, and the promotion of social, economic, and environmental justice, serve as the basic foundation and context within which the social work skills emerge (see Figure 1.1). Without such a professional foundation, the skills could easily be used in an insensitive, shallow, inappropriate, untimely, and ultimately damaging manner.

At some point in your career as a social worker, you might serve in a child-protection capacity, responding to indications that a child may be at risk of abuse or neglect. You may

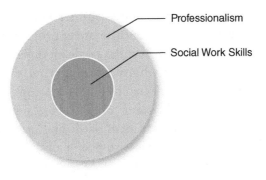

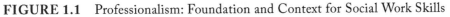

FIGURE 1.1 Professionalism: Foundation and Context for Social Work Skills

help families improve their child-caring capabilities or serve in the emergency room of a hospital, intervening with people and families in crises. You might lead groups for sexually victimized children or provide education and counseling to abusive or incarcerated adults. You could aid couples in strained relationships or help single parents who seek guidance and support in rearing their children. You may serve people who misuse alcohol and drugs or help family members affected by the substance abuse of a parent, child, spouse, or sibling. You might work in a residential setting for youthful offenders, a prison for adults, or a psychiatric institution.

You might serve in a university counseling center, working with college students, faculty members, and other campus employees. You could help people challenged in some way—perhaps physically or mentally, or both. You might serve in a school system or perhaps as a consultant to a local police department or a state or national agency. You might serve as a member of the armed services— helping soldiers, sailors, marines, airmen, or members of the coast guard and their families. You could work in a mayor's office, serve on the staff of a state legislator, or perhaps even become a member of Congress yourself.

You may function in a crisis intervention capacity for a suicide prevention service. You could work for a health maintenance organization (HMO), a managed health care system, or an employee assistance program (EAP). As a social worker, you might act as an advocate for people who have experienced discrimination, oppression, or exploitation, perhaps because of racism, sexism, ageism, or dogmatic ideology. For example, you might help lesbian, bisexual, gay, transgendered, intersexed, or asexual people assert their human rights in a hostile social environment. You might take action to prevent human sex trafficking—one of the contemporary forms of slavery. You might organize groups or communities, perhaps help workers create or join labor unions, or lead a social action movement. For example, you might take action to strengthen women's human rights or perhaps the rights of our descendants to an environmentally secure planet. You could challenge extreme social and economic inequality, protest the militarization of local police departments (Balko, 2013; Balko & Cato, 2006) and police misconduct, or challenge political and financial corruption. You could publicly disagree with certain policies of your government and promote alternative approaches. For example, you might object to the extraordinary rendition of international suspects, the torture of prisoners, the premature use of deadly military force against people who may or may not represent a potential danger to your country at some point in the future, or the use of the death penalty as a form of punishment.

You might engage in social entrepreneurship and create social programs designed to aid people or groups in need. You might analyze policies, conduct research related to various social problems, or evaluate the effectiveness and outcomes of intervention programs and practices. You might work with homeless families, runaway youth, or street people struggling to survive through panhandling or prostitution. You might work with people victimized by crime or perhaps with those who previously engaged in criminal activity. You might serve in a domestic violence program, providing social services to people affected by child abuse, spouse abuse, or elder abuse; or you might help those affected by war and violent conflicts. For example, you might help injured or traumatized soldiers recover from the horrors of battle and provide needed support to their families. You could provide psychosocial services to people dealing with a physical illness, such as cancer, kidney failure, Alzheimer's disease, HIV/AIDS, or Ebola, and help their families cope with the myriad psychosocial effects of such conditions. You might work in a hospice, helping people with a terminal illness prepare for their own death or that of a family member. You could help unemployed and underemployed people find employment or locate needed services and resources by providing information and arranging referrals, or by promoting the creation of additional employment opportunities. You might serve documented or undocumented immigrants, refugees, transients, or migrant workers. You might counsel individuals suffering from a serious mental illness, such as schizophrenia or bipolar disorder, and provide support and education to their families. You could work in an assisted care facility for aged people, leading groups for residents or counseling family members. You might serve in a halfway house, work with foster care providers, or perhaps provide information and support to teenage parents. You might serve active or retired military personnel and their families or work in industry, consulting with employers and employees about problems and issues that affect their well-being during times of economic instability.

In conjunction with affected individuals and groups, you might engage in the design, development, and establishment of organizations that promote social well-being among vulnerable populations and struggling communities. You might consult with or help to facilitate the creation of social or political advocacy groups that promote social and economic justice, or participate in those that need additional support.

The range of settings where you might work and the variety of functions that you could fulfill are mind-boggling. Such breadth, diversity, and complexity can be overwhelming. You may ask yourself, "Can I possibly learn what I need to so that I can serve competently as a social worker in all those places, serving such different people, and helping them to address such complex issues?" The answer to that question is certainly NO!

We could never become truly competent in all the arenas where social workers practice because it would require a greater breadth and depth of knowledge and expertise than any one person could ever acquire. Indeed, social workers need a specialized body of knowledge and skill for each practice setting, each special population group, and each social problem. You cannot know everything, do everything, or be competent in helping people struggling with every one of the enormous array of psychosocial issues. However, you can acquire expertise in those skills that are common to social work practice with all population groups and all problems in all settings. These common social work skills bring coherence to the profession, despite its extraordinary variety and complexity.

A Social Work Profession

In addition to applying a common set of skills, social workers tend to approach clients from a similar perspective—one that is reflected in a set of core values and a distinctive language, and epitomized in the name of our profession. Our profession is "social work" and we call ourselves "social workers." We do not attach "ist" to the end of our name, as do our sister helping professionals in psychology and psychiatry. Rather, we identify ourselves as "workers." In so do-ing, we establish a view of ourselves as equal rather than superior to others; that we work with and on behalf of people; and that we do much more than think, study, and advise—we also take action.

In this context, the terms *profession, professional,* and *professionalism* warrant some clar-ification. A **profession** is a "vocation or calling, especially one that involves some branch of advanced learning or science" as, for example, the medical profession (*The Oxford English Dictionary* [Online], 2014). For many of us, social work is both a vocation and a calling. We sin-cerely want to help others and are motivated by more than money and status to do so. Although the term **professional** as used, for example, in the sentence, "She is a professional," connotes a relatively high social status—as would befit those with advanced learning—many social work-ers use the term to refer to qualities such as integrity, competence, and conscientiousness rather than as a sign of rank or privilege. In this sense, we distinguish those who have earned a college diploma or advanced degree, or hold a license to practice a profession from those who both pos-sess the relevant educational and legal credentials *and* regularly perform in a respectful, caring, competent, and ethical manner. The former may be members of a profession while the latter are professional indeed.

Social workers usually refer to the people we serve as *clients, consumers,* or *people* rather than *patients, subjects,* or *cases.* Social workers also favor the word *assessment* over *diagnosis, study, examination,* or *investigation.* Furthermore, we tend to look for *strengths, assets, resources, resiliencies, competencies,* and *abilities* rather than attending exclusively to *problems, obstacles, deficiencies,* or *pathologies.* We also commonly adopt helping processes that involve *cooperation, collaboration, mutuality, shared decision making,* and *joint action* rather than *prescription, direction,* or *coercion.* In addition, we use language that is easily understood by all. Eschewing esoteric ter-minology, such as is often associated with the legal, medical, and psychology professions, we at-tempt to speak the "language of the people." In so doing, we may downplay our special, advanced knowledge and expertise; and underplay our social status to promote a sense of collaboration, equal participation, and mutual respect with clients and other constituents. The active encour-agement of equal status with others, reflected in our identity as social workers and our use of the people's language, is characteristic of most contemporary social workers regardless of practice setting.

Professional social workers have earned a baccalaureate, master's, or doctoral degree in social work. Usually, we are licensed or certified to practice social work in our locale. We adopt certain common values that pervade all aspects of our helping activities, pledge adherence to a social work code of ethics, and tend to view social work in a manner similar to that reflected in the Global Definition of Social Work of the International Federation of Social Workers (IFSW):

> Social work is a practice-based profession and an academic discipline that promotes social change and development, social cohesion, and the empowerment and liberation of people. Principles of social justice, human rights, collective responsibility and respect for diversities are central to social work. Underpinned by theories of social work, social sciences, humanities and indigenous knowledge, social work engages people and structures to address life challenges and enhance well-being. (2014, para. 1)

While our specialized education, subscription to a code of ethics, and public endorsement in the form of legal certification or licensure are similar to that of medical doctors and lawyers, the **social work mission** is quite different from those professions. Rather than maintaining the status quo, social workers actively seek to "promote social change ... and the empowerment and liberation of people" (International Federation of Social Workers, 2014, para. 1). These are radical and, in some contexts, revolutionary aspirations. In their pursuit, we often risk our jobs and social status, and sometimes even our lives.

Regardless of our practice setting or position, social workers tend to view person-in-environment, person-and-environment, or person-in-context[1] as the basic unit of attention. This too is a radical notion, especially in North America where individuals are commonly viewed iconically as autonomous, independent, and completely free-willed creatures who can readily choose to become whatever and whomever they wish to become, regardless of current or past circumstances. Social workers recognize that the past and present physical and social environments profoundly affect people by influencing their development, their thinking processes and belief systems, their habits and behavior toward others, and their subjective experience. We understand that hurricanes or tsunamis, tornadoes, earthquakes, floods or droughts; war, civil conflict, acts of terror, or crimes of violence; political, cultural, and economic conditions; access to food, clean air, water, and opportunities for training and education impact humans and their thoughts, emotions, and actions. We recognize that the "playing field" is not level and the concept of "equal opportunity" is mythical (Stiglitz, 2013, Feb. 16). In addition, social workers realize that many communities are predisposed to react favorably or unfavorably to individual characteristics clearly beyond anyone's personal control. Each of us is born with certain genitalia and a particular skin tone. We cannot easily change those; nor can we readily alter our DNA or that of our ancestors. Humans can relocate but we can never change the time and place of our birth nor the communities and cultures of our childhood. We cannot choose to have been born in a time and place of peace when we were not, into a dominant and privileged class when we were not, nor physically beautiful when we were not. As infants, we could not decide upon our ethnicity, religious or nonreligious affiliation, and language, dialect, or accent; nor could we determine how the people around us would respond to our presence. Others might love and cherish us or treat us with disgust and disdain. Their attitudes and behavior were beyond our influence. Many of us were unfortunate and grew up unwanted and unloved in violent, chaotic times and places. Some of us survived and a few thrived. While we celebrate survivors' resilience and capacity to overcome obstacles and transcend limitations, we recognize that peaceful, loving, resource-rich environments containing wide-ranging opportunities enable people to more readily maximize their potential and fulfill their aspirations than do conflicted, unloving, resource-scarce settings. Social workers resist temptations to blame people—and especially so for circumstances beyond their control.

Recognizing the power of context (Gershoff, Mistry, & Crosby, 2014), social workers consider the **enhancement of social functioning** and the promotion or restoration of "a mutually beneficial interaction between individuals and society to improve the quality of life for everyone" (Minahan, 1981, p. 6) as an overriding purpose of practice. This consistent **dual focus** on people and environment leads social workers to consider multiple systems—even when an individual person or family is formally the "client." Indeed, social workers always consider and usually involve other people or other social systems in the helping process.

In the Preamble to its Code of Ethics, the National Association of Social Workers (NASW) states that:

A historic and defining feature of social work is the profession's focus on individual well-being in a social context and the well-being of society. Fundamental to social work is attention to the

[1] In this book, we use the term *person* or *people* in the same manner we use the term *client* or *clients*. We recognize that a client may be an individual person or many people. A client might be a dyad, family, group, organization, community, or even a society with which a social worker has an agreement to provide services. Furthermore, in the spirit of the concept *person-in-environment*, we always consider clients, indeed all people, within the context of their situation and circumstances.

environmental forces that create, contribute to, and address problems in living. Social workers promote social justice and social change with and on behalf of clients…. Social workers are sensitive to cultural and ethnic diversity and strive to end discrimination, oppression, poverty, and other forms of social injustice. (2008)

In its EPAS, the Council on Social Work Education (CSWE) indicates that:

The purpose of the social work profession is to promote human and community well-being. Guided by a person-in-environment framework, a global perspective, respect for human diversity, and knowledge based on scientific inquiry, the purpose of social work is actualized through its quest for social and economic justice, the prevention of conditions that limit human rights, the elimination of poverty, and the enhancement of the quality of life for all persons, locally and globally. (2015, para. 1)

Notice that the NASW and the CSWE, like the IFSW, endorse a social change–oriented conception of the profession. These organizations suggest that social work's mission involves the promotion of social, economic, and environmental justice; the enhancement of social well-being and quality of life; and the elimination of "discrimination, oppression, poverty, and other forms of social injustice" (National Association of Social Workers, 2008, Preamble). Such aspirations do not appear in the mission statements or ethical codes of other professions. Social work alone dares to endorse publicly such potentially controversial ideas and to establish them as central to its professional identity, purpose, and raison d'être.

Given our focus on social change, social workers tend to conceive of people and situations as dynamic and as having the potential for planned change. We view professional practice as predominantly for clients: the individuals, families, groups, organizations, communities, and societies that we serve. Whatever personal benefit we might gain is secondary; the notion of service to others is foremost. The primacy of service in social work is reflected through a special sensitivity to those living in poverty; unemployed and underemployed people; vulnerable populations and at-risk individuals; and oppressed peoples. Indeed, people with the lowest status, the fewest resources, and the least power constitute social work's most cherished constituency.

Many social workers address the most urgent social, economic, and environmental problems facing individuals, families, and communities throughout North America and the world. These include the devastating consequences of apparently endless war (Risen, 2014); state and non-state sponsored international violence—including the use of assassination, preemptive military strikes, extraordinary rendition, and torture of prisoners (Senate Select Committee on Intelligence, 2014); militarization of domestic police forces, the rise of the "warrior cop" (Balko, 2013), and frequent incidents of police misconduct—especially toward African American, Hispanic, and other "profiled" minorities (Johnson, Hoyer, & Heath, 2014, May 8; Lee, 2014, Aug. 15), and persons affected by mental illness and other disabilities (Mizner, 2015, Jan. 8); disproportionately high rates of incarceration—especially among racial and ethnic minority groups (Alexander, 2010; Henrichson & Delaney, 2012, Jan.); high levels of homelessness (Homelessness Research Institute, 2014); widespread political and financial corruption (Taibbi, 2011); and rising income and wealth inequality along with diminished economic opportunity and decreasing socioeconomic mobility (Krugman, 2014, May 8; Piketty, 2014). Other problems addressed include increased expense and decreased value of several forms of higher education (Arum & Roksa, 2011); apparently increasing self-admiration, narcissism, and materialism among many populations (Campbell, Bush, Brunell, & Shelton, 2005; Twenge, 2006; Twenge & Campbell, 2009); pervasive incivility toward and intolerance of "others" (Bey, 2012, Mar. 2); extensive and growing medicalization of personal and social problems (Szasz, 2007; Whitaker, 2010); deleterious effects of increasing rates of climate and oceanic change (Hönisch et al., 2012); continued adoption of ideological dogma, violence, and oppression as "acceptable" means to control and subordinate people—especially women and children (Heimlich, 2011); pervasive dissemination of religious, political, and commercial propaganda that distort or oversimplify complex issues (Larsen, 2006; Postman, 1985); and an apparent willingness among many to accept superstitious or opinionated statements and logically irrational arguments as true and factually correct (Jacoby, 2008).

In such perilous times, social workers increasingly recognize the need for social and political action, community organization, and participation in major social movements to address widespread systemic and structural injustice in social, environmental, and economic spheres. And we do so with a growing sense of urgency (Bulletin of the Atomic Scientists, 2015).

There are some signs that "enough is enough." These include the popular demonstrations of the Arab Spring, which began in Tunisia in December 2011, continued in Cairo, and then spread throughout much of the world (Schiffrin & Kircher-Allen, 2012); the Occupy movements that began in Wall Street's Zuccotti Park on Constitution Day (September 17) in 2011 (Blumenkranz, 2011); the outrage, emergence of the #BlackLivesMatter movement, and the large demonstrations throughout the United States in response to disproportionate police reactions leading to the deaths of several unarmed African American men (Lee, 2014, Aug. 15); worldwide popular demonstrations in reaction to the killing of 12 people in the January 7, 2015, attack on the Paris headquarters of the satirical magazine *Charlie Hebdo*; and the nationwide outcry following the June 17, 2015, massacre of nine African Americans in a historic Charleston, South Carolina, church by a 21-year-old proponent of white supremacist ideology (Mazza, Walker, & Chen, 2015, June 17).

Social movements are especially important in light of a growing body of research findings that confirm and illuminate the powerful influence of situational and contextual factors in understanding human experience and motivating human behavior (DeSteno & Valdesolo, 2011; Sommers, 2011). Consistent with social work's "person-in-environment" perspective, studies that highlight the "power of context," the "power of place," and the "power of the social" encourage us to collaborate with others in our pursuit of social change and community well-being. Our consistent use of a **person-in-environment perspective**, with strong emphasis on the environment, helps social workers avoid the seductive trap of explaining social problems by referencing the individual characteristics or traits of people directly affected by those problems—a phenomenon called **blaming the victim** (Ryan, 1971, 1976; Savani, Stephens, & Markus, 2011; Valor-Segura, Exposito, & Moya, 2011; Van Prooijen & Van den Bos, 2009).

In service and advocacy activities, we call upon our strengths in scientific inquiry, critical thought, and knowledge of nomothetic[2] and ideographic[3] research-based findings in collaborative decision making with clients. Despite our knowledge and expertise, however, social workers maintain a strong sense of humility. We recognize that interventions and activities that help many people are sometimes ineffective with a particular person. Therefore, we evaluate progress throughout the course of our work to determine the effectiveness of our collaborative efforts with client systems. Indeed, systematic evaluation of service impact represents a hallmark of professionalism and, when evaluative feedback is shared and discussed with clients, powerfully contributes

---

[2] The term *nomothetic* refers to research studies that relate to or contribute to general scientific knowledge. In our context, the term applies to research studies that involve groups of participants, often randomly selected and sometimes compared with members of control groups, so that the results or findings may be generalized to a larger population.

[3] The term *ideographic* (or *idiographic*) refers to studies that pertain to scientific knowledge of a particular or specific kind. In our context, ideographic studies often involve the systematic evaluation of a client system's progress toward problem resolution or goal attainment. In social work, the most common forms of ideographic research are single-system or N-of-1 studies.

to favorable outcomes (Anker, Duncan, & Sparks, 2009; Lambert, 2010a, 2010b; Miller, Duncan, Brown, Sorrell, & Chalk, 2006; Probst, Lambert, Dahlbender, Loew, & Tritt, 2014).

Especially when combined with lack of critical thought, insufficient knowledge about safe and effective services can result in damage to individuals, families, groups, organizations, communities, and societies. Social workers who think in a naïve, thoughtless, ignorant, egocentric, ethnocentric, xenophobic, or superstitious manner are frequently ineffective and sometimes harmful to others. During an era when personal opinions, popular myths, and "truthiness" are commonly confused with facts, truth, and validity, and ideology is frequently presented as "knowledge," scientific inquiry and critical thought are vitally important. We desperately need scholarly, rational, reflective, and indeed skeptical social workers to recognize unsubstantiated claims, falsehoods, shams, scams, cons, and quackery—many of which are inflicted upon desperate and highly vulnerable populations. As professional helpers who often serve people and groups on the margins of society, social workers must be adept at scientific inquiry, critical thinking, and lifelong learning—not only for our own welfare but also for the well-being of our clients and communities.

Social workers recognize that professional service to others often involves powerful interpersonal and social processes that have considerable potential for harm as well as for good. We realize that competent practice requires exceptional personal and professional integrity, a highly developed understanding of ourselves, and extraordinary personal discipline and self-control. In particular, social workers must be expert critical thinkers and energetic lifelong learners to make sense of the ever-increasing glut of information—much of it false, misleading, and nonsensical.

A great deal more than good intentions, admirable personal qualities, and compassionate feelings are required. Indeed, as you probably already realize, good intentions can sometimes cause the most catastrophic of consequences (Coyne, 2013). As social workers, we must base our words and actions on professional knowledge; critical thought; social work values, ethics, and obligations; and, of course, the analogous knowledge, thoughts, values, and aspirations of the people with whom we are so fortunate to work.

Social Work Skills

The terms *skill* and **competency** have become extremely popular in social work and other helping professions during the past half century. In addition to the emphasis on competencies suggested by the EPAS (Council on Social Work Education, 2015), several social work textbooks incorporate the word *skills* in their titles (Hepworth, Rooney, Rooney, & Strom-Gottfried, 2013; Ruffolo, Perron, & Voshel, 2015; Shulman, 2012).

Henry (1981) suggests that skills are "finite and discrete sets of behaviors or tasks employed by a worker at a given time, for a given purpose, in a given manner" (p. vii). She (1992) also cites Phillips (1957), who characterizes skill as "knowledge in action" (p. 20). Middleman and Goldberg (1990) describe skill as "the production of specific behaviors under the precise conditions designated for their use" (p. 12).

Notice that these descriptions and definitions refer to action and behaviors. The CSWE adopts a similar approach in their specification of nine core **competencies** needed by professional social workers. Incorporated in the EPAS (Council on Social Work Education, 2015) graduates of accredited social work programs should be able to:

1. Demonstrate Ethical and Professional Behavior.
2. Engage Diversity and Difference in Practice.
3. Advance Human Rights and Social, Economic, and Environmental Justice.

4. Engage in Practice-Informed Research and Research-Informed Practice.
5. Engage in Policy–Practice.
6. Engage with Individuals, Families, Groups, Organizations, and Communities.
7. Assess Individuals, Families, Groups, Organizations, and Communities.
8. Intervene with Individuals, Families, Groups, Organizations, and Communities.
9. Evaluate Practice with Individuals, Families, Groups, Organizations, and Communities. (p. 8)

Notice how each of the nine competencies begins with an action verb (for example, engage, assess, intervene, or evaluate). The EPAS competencies and the knowledge and values, and the practice behaviors that explicate them, provide a fundamental standard for social work professionals. All accredited BSW and MSW educational programs infuse these competencies throughout their curriculums. In addition, programs may and usually do identify additional competencies to reflect the unique characteristics of their educational missions, the populations and social problems they address, and the social and environmental contexts in which their students and graduates function.

As cognitive and interpersonal practice behaviors, the skills addressed in this book support the competencies, knowledge and values, and the practice behaviors specified in the EPAS. They reflect our fundamental social work values and principles. Although they are usually associated with particular phases or processes of practice, we never view the social work skills as technical activities to complete, robotlike, at exactly the same relative time and in precisely the same way with all clients and all situations. Rather, we select, combine, and adapt specific social work skills to suit the particular needs and characteristics of the person-in-environment. This requires advanced knowledge, professional expertise, and sophisticated judgment. Indeed, social workers think carefully about timing and context as they decide which skills to use and when and how to use them.

The range and scope of skills that social workers might use in the context of service are wide and varied. A "social worker's skills include being proficient in communication, assessing problems and client workability, matching needs with resources, developing resources, and changing social structures" (Barker, 2014, p. 393).

In addition to supporting the EPAS competencies, the skills addressed in this workbook are also consistent with the most important qualities that employers of college graduates seek in their prospective employees. These include the abilities to "work in a team structure," "make decisions and solve problems," "plan, organize, and prioritize work," "verbally communicate with persons inside and outside the organization," "obtain and process information," "analyze quantitative data," "create and/or edit written reports," and "influence others." Employers also prefer candidates who possess "technical knowledge related to the job" and "proficiency with computer software programs" (National Association of Colleges and Employers, 2014).

More specifically, however, the skills addressed in this book serve the tasks associated with seven commonly identified **phases of social work practice**, and the dimensions of professionalism. As shown in Figure 1.2, these seven phases extend the four outlined in the EPAS: *engage, assess, intervene,* and *evaluate* (Council on Social Work Education, 2015).

The preparing, beginning, and exploring skills support the *engagement* and some of the *assessment* competencies; the assessing and contracting skills support the *assessment* competency; and the working and evaluating, and the ending skills support the *intervention* and *evaluation* competencies. Furthermore, the skills addressed in this text are applicable to work with individuals, families, groups, organizations, communities, and societies at the micro, mezzo, and macro levels of practice.

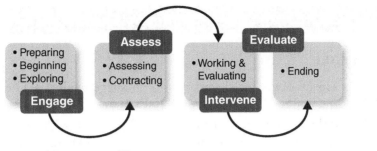

FIGURE 1.2 Phases and Processes of Practice

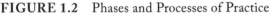

We separate the discrete behaviors associated with each phase or process into small, manageable units of thought and action that are consistent with the dimensions of professionalism. Integrated and synthesized in this fashion, they form the social work skills.

For the purposes of teaching and learning, we define **social work skill** as follows:

A social work skill is a circumscribed set of discrete cognitive and behavioral actions that are consistent and congruent with (1) social work values, ethics, and obligations; (2) research-based knowledge; (3) the dimensions of professionalism; and (4) a legitimate social work purpose within the context of a phase or process of practice.

We also integrate the following **dimensions of professionalism** in our work with others:

- Integrity
- Self-understanding and self-control
- Knowledge, expertise, and self-efficacy
- Social support and well-being
- Critical thinking and scientific inquiry
- Lifelong learning
- Diversity and difference
- Human rights and social, economic, and environmental justice
- Policy–practice
- Social work values and ethics, and ethical decision making

Each of these dimensions requires integrated knowledge of the values, ethics, and legal obligations that inform our professional decisions and actions. Indeed, the values of the social work profession permeate all aspects of our service.

SUMMARY

Social work has a change-oriented mission that includes promoting social, economic, and environmental justice, enhancing social well-being and quality of life, and eliminating discrimination, oppression, and poverty. In pursuit of these aspirations, effective social workers consistently exhibit professionalism throughout the entire helping process—from preparing and beginning on through to the conclusion of work. They appear in our exchanges with other members of client systems, colleagues, referral sources, various stakeholders and constituents, and the public at large.

CHAPTER 1 Summary Exercises

Reflective Exercise

1. Review the core aspects of the social work mission as suggested by the Global Definition of Social Work (International Federation of Social Workers, 2014), the Preamble to the Code of Ethics of the National Association of Social Workers (2008), and the Educational Policy and Accreditation Standards of the Council on Social Work Education (2015). Use your word-processing program to prepare a brief one- to two-page (250–500 words) report in which you discuss what the following passages mean to you as a person, a student, and a future social worker:

   a. social workers "promote social change ... and the empowerment and liberation of people" (International Federation of Social Workers, 2014, para. 1);

   b. social workers pay "attention to the environmental forces that create, contribute to, and address problems in living ... (and) promote social justice ... (and) ... strive to end discrimination, oppression, poverty, and other forms of social injustice" (National Association of Social Workers, 2008); and

   c. social workers seek "human and community well-being ... social and economic justice, the prevention of conditions that limit human rights, the elimination of poverty, and the enhancement of the quality of life for all persons, locally and globally" (Council on Social Work Educcation, 2015, para. 1).

   Be sure to discuss how these aspects of the social work mission coincide or conflict with your view of the profession and your aspirations as a social worker. Title the report "Reflections on the Social Work Mission." Save it as "SWK_Mission_Reflections" and store it in a folder of your electronic Social Work Skills Learning Portfolio.

Write-Now Exercises

Use the space below each of the following write-now exercises to record your responses.

1. Reflect upon the various social, economic, and environmental problems that people will face during the next 50 years or so. Identify those that you consider most urgent (that is, those that represent the greatest threat to life and well-being). Select one for each of the three domains (social, economic, and environmental) and provide a brief one-sentence rationale for each of your three selections.

2. What do you see as the advantages and disadvantages of identifying yourself as a "social worker" rather than, say, a "therapist" or a "counselor"?

CHAPTER 1 Self-Appraisal

As you finish this chapter, please reflect on your learning by using the following space to identify any ideas, terms, or concepts addressed in Chapter 1 that remain confusing or unclear to you:

Next, respond to the following items by carefully reading each statement. Please use a 1-to-10-point rating scale (where *1 = strongly disagree* and *10 = strongly agree*) to indicate the degree to which you agree or disagree with each statement. Place a check mark at the point that best reflects your view at this particular point in time. If you are truly *undecided*, place your check at the mid-point (5.5) mark.

1. I can describe the mission and purposes of the social work profession.

1   2   3   4   5   6   7   8   9   10

2. I can discuss the concepts of social work skills and competencies.

1   2   3   4   5   6   7   8   9   10

3. I can identify the phases or processes of social work practice.

1   2   3   4   5   6   7   8   9   10

4. I can identify the dimensions of professionalism addressed in *The Social Work Skills Workbook*.

1   2   3   4   5   6   7   8   9   10

Introduction to Professionalism

Society entrusts social workers with the status, authority, and responsibility for promoting human rights; pursuing social, economic, and environmental justice; and helping people address personal and social problems in living. In this chapter, we begin to explore the first four of 10 dimensions of professionalism. We will address the others in the following three chapters. Each of the four chapters contains learning exercises to help you explore these interrelated dimensions of professionalism. You also create materials for inclusion in your Social Work Skills Learning Portfolio.

Core Competencies

The content addressed in this chapter supports the following core EPAS competencies:

- Competency 1: Demonstrate Ethical and Professional Behavior
- Competency 2: Engage Diversity and Difference in Practice
- Competency 3: Advance Human Rights and Social, Economic, and Environmental Justice
- Competency 4: Engage In Practice-Informed Research and Research-Informed Practice
- Competency 5: Engage in Policy Practice
- Competency 6: Engage with Individuals, Families, Groups, Organizations, and Communities
- Competency 7: Assess Individuals, Families, Groups, Organizations, and Communities
- Competency 8: Intervene with Individuals, Families, Groups, Organizations, and Communities
- Competency 9: Evaluate Practice with Individuals, Families, Groups, Organizations, and Communities

Chapter Goals

Following completion of this chapter, you should be able to reflect upon and discuss:

- Professionalism within the context of social work practice.
- Integrity.
- Self-understanding and self-control.
- Knowledge, expertise, and self-efficacy.
- Social support and well-being.

■ Professionalism

Membership in the community of professional helpers involves considerable status, power, and prestige. A **professional** is one who "has or displays ... skill, knowledge, experience, standards, or expertise ... [and is] ... competent, efficient" ("professional," 2014). In the case of social work, however, professionalism goes well beyond knowledge, competence, and expertise to incorporate qualities of honesty, honor, and humility; dedication, commitment, and altruism; and, importantly, adherence to a core set of values and a code of ethics. Our conception of professionalism in social work includes the dimensions of (1) personal and professional integrity; (2) self-understanding and self-control; (3) advanced knowledge, expertise, and self-efficacy; (4) social support and well-being; (5) critical thinking and scientific inquiry; (6) lifelong learning; (7) diversity and difference; (8) human rights and social, economic, and environmental justice; (9) policy–practice; and (10) social work values and ethical decision making (see Figure 2.1).

Notice that the terms *status* and *licensed* do not appear in the illustration. Although social workers certainly do benefit from our status and authority as licensed professionals, the fundamental aspects of professionalism involve our knowledge, attitudes, ideals, expertise, and actions rather than our social position, educational achievements, or prestige. Indeed, our privileged status as professionals may sometimes leave us hesitant to take action against discrimination, oppression, inequality, and other forms of injustice. Perhaps because we have studied so long and hard to become professionals, we might fear the loss of our social status—and perhaps our employment—if we were to actively advocate against certain unjust practices. Such ambivalence is hardly surprising.

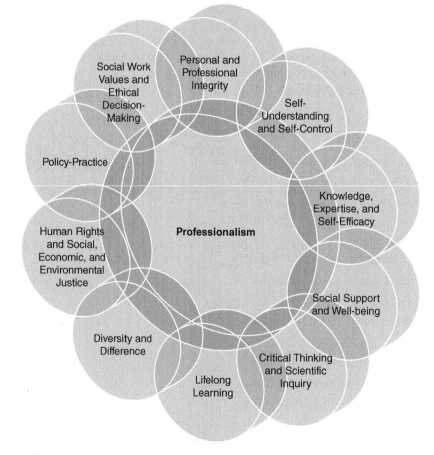

FIGURE 2.1 Professionalism: A Conceptual Framework

Risk of diminished status or threat of job loss tends to promote an establishmentarian orientation that favors the social, political, and economic status quo and may interfere with our mission as a social-change-focused profession.

Although social work's mission clearly involves advocacy for human rights, elimination of discrimination and oppression, an end to poverty, promotion of social and economic and environmental justice, and the enhancement of all persons' quality of life, social workers sometimes reflect cautious and bureaucratic tendencies—even when current conditions reflect obvious and pervasive injustice. Despite our understandable hesitation and inertia, however, let's be courageous. Let's engage in active, conscientious attempts to transcend our own self-interest and safety concerns as we learn how to pursue social work's mission and help clients address issues, achieve their goals, and enhance the quality of their lives while also working to eliminate poverty and promote social, economic, and environmental justice.

Social workers affect people in profound ways—often for the better, but sometimes for the worse. Given the large number of social workers and the nature and scope of the services we provide, the importance of professionalism cannot be overemphasized. When social workers are competent and trustworthy, our clients feel satisfied and society as a whole benefits. The overall reputation of social workers and our profession improves. However, when social workers lack professionalism, many people suffer. Clients or others affected by our policies, programs, and practices may be harmed. Indeed, lives can, and sometimes are, lost due to social workers' negligence or incompetence. When some social workers lack professionalism, employers may become reluctant to hire others. The stature of the profession may decline, and funding sources may become less inclined to support social services in general.

The stakes are so high that social workers are obligated—personally, morally, ethically, and legally—to reflect high standards of professionalism in all aspects of our service activities. Fortunately, most of us are committed to providing ethical and effective services to our clients and promoting a better quality of life for all people. Most social workers are knowledgeable in their areas of practice and honest and trustworthy in their relations with others. Most social workers sincerely try to demonstrate understanding, respect, compassion, and competence in their efforts to provide high-quality services. Many of us try to keep current with advances in professional knowledge. We also recognize that personal behavior in our private lives may affect both our professional reputation and the quality of our professional performance. Indeed, most social workers fully realize that a positive professional reputation among colleagues and constituents results primarily from conscientious attention and consistent adherence to the dimensions of professionalism.

Integrity

Personal and professional integrity are essential aspects of professionalism. Within the context of social work service, **integrity** suggests honesty, truthfulness, sincerity, humility, and trustworthiness. In its Code of Ethics, the NASW (2008) states that "Social workers should not participate in, condone, or be associated with dishonesty, fraud, or deception" (Section 4.04). However, in social work, integrity goes well beyond the simple avoidance or absence of misbehavior. Rather, we pursue professional integrity with conviction, dedication, and enthusiasm.

As a social worker, you demonstrate integrity when you share information that is supported by valid and reliable evidence, and, conversely, when you refrain from repeating gossip, rumors, and other forms of invalid and unreliable information. You reflect integrity when you publicly acknowledge others' contributions and credit sources of information used to support your statements and positions. You demonstrate integrity when you openly state that you are sharing a personal opinion rather than a professional recommendation or admit ignorance when you do not know the answer to a particular question. You exemplify integrity when you manage your own personal or religious beliefs in order to better serve clients who hold different views. You show integrity when you resist temptations to cheat, lie, or misrepresent facts; and when you recognize that your immediate thoughts and emotional reactions may not always serve as a valid basis for professional action. You reflect integrity when you keep your promises and fulfill your commitments. You display integrity when you willingly acknowledge mistakes and errors in your own thoughts, words, and deeds; and change your mind when credible evidence challenges your previously held beliefs.

You manifest integrity when you report a colleague who exploited a client, cheated on an exam, or plagiarized a report; or, when you admit that you have done so. You reflect integrity when you reveal that your organization intentionally defrauds its funding sources by billing for services it does not provide; and perhaps lose your job when you do so. Despite laws intended to protect honest whistleblowers from retaliation, the consequences of trying to right wrongs and combat injustice can be painful indeed (Devine & Maassarani, 2011; Kohn, 2011; Press, 2012). Unfortunately, direct or indirect punishment sometimes results from "doing the right thing." Integrity can be costly indeed.

The NASW Code of Ethics includes integrity as one of its core values and describes the related ethical principle as follows:

Value: Integrity

Ethical Principle: Social workers behave in a trustworthy manner.

Social workers are continually aware of the profession's mission, values, ethical principles, and ethical standards and practice in a manner consistent with them. Social workers act honestly and responsibly and promote ethical practices on the part of the organizations with which they are affiliated. (2008, Ethical Principles Section, para. 6)

Adherence to the values and ethics of the profession and to fundamental moral principles such as sincerity, fairness, truthfulness, reliability, dedication, and loyalty is central to professional integrity. However, integrity goes beyond the sum of these virtues to include a general sense of coherence, wholeness, and harmony with social work roles, responsibilities, and expectations. Involving authenticity and sincerity, professional integrity is a matter of personal honor.

Consider, for example, the notions of trust and credibility. Clients tend to seek help from social workers because they assume they will receive honest, fair, responsible, and competent service. Indeed, first meetings often reflect an initial trust that may continue throughout the entire course of the relationship. However, clients tend to notice when a professional's words or actions suggest insincerity, irresponsibility, unfairness, incompetence, or dishonesty. Lapses of integrity jeopardize the assumption of goodwill and may leave clients disappointed and their friends and family members reluctant to trust other social workers in the future.

In some instances, these losses may be permanent as clients conclude "I'll never go back to that place" or "Social workers are useless" or even "I guess it's hopeless." Relationships with colleagues, employers, and community members are similar in this regard. Lapses in integrity can, in short order, destroy personal, family, friendship, and professional relationships. Once damaged, our personal and professional reputations are extremely difficult to restore.

Some social workers have neglected to fulfill fundamental responsibilities such as regularly checking on the welfare of abused or neglected children under their supervision (Kaufman & Jones, 2003; McCoy & Phillips, 2008, July 31; The Associated Press, 2009, June 9; Wynn, 2012, May 23). When violations such as these occur, the consequences may be profound. Trust in social workers erodes and regard for the child welfare system declines. Relatives, neighbors, and other citizens may fail to report suspicions of child neglect or abuse out of fear that children could be worse off in the care of the system than they would be if left alone. As a result, children may go without needed protective services and some may suffer severe injuries or die.

Some organizations and some social workers have systematically defrauded public and private insurance services by assigning medical or psychiatric diagnoses that do not actually apply to their clients (Reamer, 2008b). Others have falsified documents to suggest that they completed work or provided services they did not actually perform (Snider, 2012, Apr. 19; Spears, 2012, July 24; Ujifusa, 2008, July 30). When questioned about such practices, some have obstructed judicial process—perhaps by rewriting or destroying client records (Reuters News Service, 2009, Apr. 21; Wynn, 2012, May 23).

In addition, some social workers have exploited clients for their own personal satisfaction or financial benefit (Clarridge, 2009, May 9; Shifrel, 2009, June 25). Indeed, sexual relations with clients—expressly forbidden by social work's ethical code—remain a common form of client exploitation (Berkman, Turner, Cooper, Polnerow, & Swartz, 2000). Some social workers have enriched their own bank accounts by embezzling funds from their agencies; by billing clients or third-party insurers for unnecessary services; or by stealing money from foster children (The Associated Press, 2000) or from elderly or disabled clients (WSLS-TV Staff Reports, 2010, Oct. 27). Violations such as these affect many lives. Clients and their loved ones are often directly injured and, of course, the offending social workers often lose their jobs, their licenses, and their careers. Some are heavily fined, and a few go to jail. In addition, the reputations of social workers in general and the profession as a whole are damaged.

In contemporary life, social workers' reputations may also be affected—often quite unfairly—by the incredible memory capacity of our digital devices and the insidious presence of the Internet. Once recorded—whether via a cell phone or laptop camera, an audio or video recorder, or in computer memory—a more or less permanent artifact remains available, perhaps forever. Indeed, we should probably presume that most things transmitted or posted electronically remain somewhere in cyberspace. Messages sent via e-mail, instant message, or Twitter; postings on Facebook or other social-networking websites; or statements made in blogs or electronic forums can become quite embarrassing at points in our careers. Those pictures taken during spring break vacations can come back to haunt us!

Many employers now regularly search the Internet for information about and digital artifacts related to job applicants (de la Llama, Trueba, Voges, Barreto, & Park, 2012). As part of the application process, some now ask prospective employees to permit them access to their personal Facebook pages. Even when the reality is entirely understandable and quite innocent, the appearance of personal impropriety can negatively affect our professional reputation, our ability to obtain or maintain a position, and our opportunity to help people in need.

As helping professionals, we tend to benefit from a presumption of integrity. What an extraordinary gift! Involving exceptional power and influence, it carries enormous moral responsibility. Cherish it and consider your personal and professional integrity and reputation among your most valuable assets. Keep your promises. Maintain a sense of humility. Sincerely acknowledge your mistakes. Be forthcoming about your level of knowledge, skills, and areas of competence. Tell your clients and colleagues the truth. Be transparent about your work. Furthermore, and perhaps most importantly, be brutally honest with yourself. Adopt an extreme attitude in this regard. Among helping professionals, self-deception is a most dangerous conceit.

Self-Understanding and Self-Control

In addition to integrity, professionalism also involves a sophisticated level of **self-understanding** and **self-control**. Because social work practice involves the conscious and deliberate use of various facets of yourself, you become the medium through which to convey knowledge, attitudes, and skill. Therefore, you need a truly extraordinary depth of self-awareness and a well-developed ability to access different aspects of yourself in your efforts to serve others. Without self-understanding and self-control, integrity would be virtually impossible. You could, and indeed most likely would, repeat your own personal patterns of thinking, feeling, and behavior with clients, colleagues, or others. You might sometimes act out unresolved personal issues in professional settings or behave inappropriately without understanding why. You might act on the basis of your personal or religious beliefs rather than on the basis of professional knowledge, values, and ethics. Despite the most noble and idealistic of motives, and a determined intention to help others, if you lack self-awareness or self-control you may unwittingly enact ingrained emotional, or behavioral patterns that damage the very people you hope to help (Caplan & Caplan, 2001; Keith-Lucas, 1972).

Self-understanding and self-control are not products or outcomes that can be completed and then set aside. Rather, they reflect ongoing processes of maturity through which we grow personally and professionally. Effective service requires that you recognize how you think about things, how you react to stress or conflict, how you deal with ambiguity, how you address problems and obstacles, how you present yourself, how you appear to others, and what mannerisms you commonly exhibit. Acknowledge your ideological and cultural preferences and recognize which issues cause you anxiety or uneasiness; which topics trigger emotional reactivity; what kinds of people, problems, or events elicit fear or anger; and which patterns of personal interaction you prefer or dislike. Of course, such a level of self-understanding does not occur through a single set of exercises, a course, or a complete program of university study. It certainly does not accompany a bachelor's (BSW), master's (MSW), or doctoral degree (DSW or PhD) in social work. Rather, sophisticated self-understanding is an ongoing endeavor that continues throughout life.

At a minimum, social workers must appreciate how our personal beliefs, attitudes, and ideologies might influence or interfere with our professional activities. Appreciate how your cultural background, family history, and current social and environmental circumstances affect your personal views as well as your psychosocial functioning and relationship patterns (Kondrat, 1999). Recognize the impact of significant life events, and identify your personality characteristics and qualities. Learn about your preferred relational styles including how you typically seek, receive, and give social support. Become aware of your own biases, stereotypes, prejudices, and tendencies to discriminate for or against certain people, as well as the ways you express genuine acceptance of others. Identify how different situations and contexts affect you, your mood, attitudes, and actions. Examine how you respond to uncertainty and frustration. Based on your enhanced self-understanding, develop ways and means to calm yourself. Then, learn how to redirect your attention to your primary professional purposes. Typically, that involves focusing less on ourselves and more upon others.

As is the case with most worthwhile endeavors, self-awareness and consciousness-raising activities involve certain risks. You may discover aspects of yourself that you have not previously recognized or considered. For example, you may learn that you have a strong need for power, control, and predictability in relationships. You may crave certainty and become uneasy in novel or chaotic situations. You may find that you relate to women with less interest, energy, or attention than you do to men; or to low-income people with less enthusiasm than to those of high economic status. You could realize that your personal belief systems (that is, religious, spiritual, or philosophical) prevent you from gaining a scientific understanding of various phenomena. You may realize that you have not fully examined the potential implications of a physical challenge that you personally face (for example, vision or hearing loss) for clients you serve. You may become aware of fixed racial or ethnic stereotypes that interfere with genuine engagement and objective assessment of individual members of certain groups. You might become aware of unmet childhood needs for acceptance and approval that lead you to avoid confrontation or withdraw from conflict. You may find that you experience heightened anxiety when you are in the presence of authority figures. You may discover that you have problems with alcohol or drugs; that you suffer from occasional periods of depression or carry substantial unresolved rage; or that you are unsuited for a career in the profession of social work.

The processes of self-discovery may give rise to disturbing thoughts, feelings, or sensations. You may even find yourself reconsidering significant life choices. Indeed, numerous dangers are inherent in any serious process of self-examination. However, as a social worker, the pursuit of self-understanding is usually well worth the costs. Ignorance or distortions in self-awareness may put you and the people you serve at considerable risk.

As you gain self-understanding, you may recognize a parallel need for self-control and self-discipline. As professional social workers, we must manage our thoughts, feelings, words, gestures, and behavior. We regulate our reactions, and do so under conditions where other people might well be overwhelmed by powerful emotions and impulses. We maturely choose our words and actions in accord with our professional purpose, knowledge, values, ethics, and the agreed-upon goals for service. Social workers carefully select our nonverbal as well as our verbal expressions. We manage our overt and covert communications by adjusting our body movements, gestures, eye contact, and facial expressions, and by modulating our voice and speech.

At times, it may even be necessary to regulate our inner thoughts and feelings to better serve clients and advocate on their behalf. Self-control is one of the true hallmarks of professionalism. It distinguishes a professional social worker from a friendly person with good intentions. For example, suppose you happen to be a highly extroverted, talkative, or even garrulous person. You would have to recognize and manage how much you talk so that clients have a genuine opportunity to share information about themselves, their concerns, and their situations. Conversely, if you are shy, introverted, and reluctant to express yourself, challenge the pattern so that clients and members of the public can benefit from your professional knowledge and expertise.

Address your fears, anxieties, and compulsive habits that might negatively influence your professional performance. Excessive eating, dieting, exercising, television watching, texting, or computer gaming can indirectly interfere with effective social work practice. Substance misuse can easily impair judgment. Procrastination may be a problem, as might issues with authority, a quick temper, or other forms of impulsivity. Narrow, fixed beliefs and ideologies, and strong needs for certainty can impede our helpfulness. Similarly, some interpersonal or interactional social patterns may become compulsive and interfere with professional functioning. For example, some of us might use sex or pornography in a compulsive manner while others may be excessively dependent upon social approval and acceptance.

Self-understanding and self-control are continuous processes that you may advance through personal counseling, individual or group psychotherapy, consultation or supervision by experienced social workers, and participation in professional workshops and training institutes. If you are open to it, self-awareness may also improve as a natural outgrowth of mindful interaction with peers, clients, friends, and family members. Strengthening self-control, however, requires an active approach—one that involves frequent, systematic practice. Like a muscle in the body, development of self-control requires that we engage in regular, vigorous exercise for quite some time before it becomes a personal asset that we can rely upon in times of distress and temptation.

Environmental and Cultural Contexts

The environmental and cultural contexts in which we live affect us all. We are influenced by past and present circumstances as well as by expectations for our future. Places (Gallagher, 1993) and situations matter; and they do so in powerful ways (Sommers, 2011). Circumstances influence humans' health, longevity, and our thoughts, emotional feelings, bodily sensations, and behavioral actions. Of course, social workers are also affected by these factors. Indeed, our past and current social and ecological systems are quite likely to influence our professional experience and performance as social workers. And, the nature and speed of environmental change affect our lives and functioning as well as the lives of future generations.

For our purposes, let's consider the term **environment** to be a broad concept that includes the natural physical environment (geography, atmosphere, water, soil, climate), the "built" or human-made[1] physical environment (architecture, transportation structures and systems, energy systems, communication and information systems, food production and distribution systems), and the social environment (the social structures and processes, and cultures that surround the living organisms that exist within the environment). In technical terms, **ecology** is "the study of the relationships among organisms as well as the relationships between them and their physical environment" (Collin, 2004, p. 69). In social work, however, we sometimes use the term environment and ecology as synonyms; and do so in a way that includes both the physical dimensions of our surroundings, the organisms that live within them, and the social systems and social processes created and maintained by those living organisms. Our world is a large, interactive and interdependent ecosystem in which virtually everything affects and is affected by everything else. Social workers recognize that human activity can and does affect plant and animal life and aspects of the environment such as air and water quality; and that ecological changes, in turn, affect us. Such awareness is fundamental to our person-in-environment perspective and to our pursuit of environmental justice.

As an illustration, let's consider air quality and ready access to clean water as aspects of our environment. Without them and sunlight, humans would not long survive. When clean water is not easily available or can be obtained only by privileged groups, the consequences can be severe. In addition to the obvious complications of thirst, malnutrition, food scarcity, and reduced air quality, insufficient or contaminated water supplies are associated with a range of negative health effects, including higher infant mortality rates, increased incidence of cardiopulmonary illness, and heightened risk of infectious disease. Communities are often displaced and conflicts sometimes erupt as populations search and compete for water and food (Sena, Barcellos, Freitas, & Corvalan, 2014; Stanke, Kerac, Prudhomme, Medlock, & Murray, 2013). The reverse is also true, as violent conflict and war erupt, food, water, and places of refuge become scarce.

The presence of toxic chemicals in our air, water, and soil affects plants and animals—including human animals. You may know that the distribution of toxic waste dumps in the United States and the presence of damaging chemicals in the surrounding environment falls disproportionately on low-income and minority groups (Lenhardt & Ogneva-Himmelberger, 2013). Furthermore, when animal populations such as salmon, honey bees, chickens, or livestock are "farmed" the risk of "new" diseases not usually found in the "wild" may increase.[2]

Consider the case of mad cow disease. Formally called bovine spongiform encephalopathy (BSE), it is a degenerative brain disease that affects cattle—apparently through feed that contains animal parts, including parts from other cows (Grady, 2004, Feb. 6). As herbivores, cows prefer vegetation and eat large quantities of various grasses. Commercially produced animal feed may contain corn, alfalfa, or a host of by-products such as soy meal, cottonseed, citrus pulp, and waste from various food production processes. Despite federal restrictions, animal parts are sometimes included in the feed; some cows become infected; and occasionally—as they ingest

---

[1] In addition to humans, other species also create physical structures. For example, bees build hives, spiders spin webs, beavers construct dams, birds build nests, and moles bore tunnels. The terms *built* and *human-made* are used here because of Homo sapiens' dominance in the construction of physical structures and objects.

[2] The dramatic loss of honey bee colonies in many parts of the world is probably the result of toxic chemicals such as insecticides and herbicides. The fact that huge numbers of honey bees are "farmed" leave entire colonies especially susceptible.

meat from BSE infected cattle—some humans become infected as well. A few may die (Stone, 2014, June 4).

As Jared Diamond (1998, 2005, 2012) has eloquently observed, our surroundings and the environmental resources available to us powerfully affect the quality of our lives; and, potentially, the lives of others with whom we have contact. In the past, human societies with plentiful water supplies, arable land, and access to fish, wildlife, minerals, and other natural resources generated surpluses that could be used for exchange or invested in commercial enterprises or exploration.

Excess wealth in China during the first half of the 15th century and in Europe during the second half permitted extensive and expensive explorations to other parts of the world (Menzies, 2003, 2008). Although China discontinued their worldwide adventures and became more insulated, European nations expanded their influence through intensive and extensive colonization. European explorers and settlers used advanced weapons and, unwittingly, their own germs to dominate and sometimes eliminate aboriginal populations (Diamond, 1998). Their beliefs about themselves as superior, their views and attitudes that "others" were inferior, and their assumptions about property, possession, and ownership also contributed to the cultural subjugation and sometimes genocide of native peoples.

Human behavior with and toward other humans, other life forms, and the planet earth is a part of what we call **culture**. Social workers tend to adopt an anthropological or sociological view of the term *culture*—although there are similarities with what happens in scientific laboratories when a virus or bacterium is "cultured" or on farms when seedlings are "cultivated." All three involve the facilitation of growth. In our personal lives, culture may refer to the "arts" or "fashion" or to levels of aesthetic knowledge or achievement. Not so in our professional lives. Rather, we understand that all people reflect cultures, that no one culture is necessarily superior to another, and that no one person is more or less "cultured" than any other.

A specific, universal definition of culture does not exist—perhaps because language and its usage are fundamental aspects of culture; and cultures tend to have their own languages, symbols, and meanings. Despite the loss of hundreds of discrete languages over the past century (Davis, Harrison, & Howell, 2007; Harrison, 2007) as many as 7,000 remain (Davis, 2009). Language and its nonverbal correlates are central aspects of culture, representing as they do, the major pathways for socialization of the young; the processes by which interpretative meanings are shared, disputed, and revised; and a means for rewarding and punishing social behavior.

Although the nature of the term remains fluid, we can say that that culture involves, in addition to language and symbols, shared beliefs about the world and how the world should and does operate. Culture includes music; art; cuisine; social customs; private and public celebrations and ceremonies; religious beliefs, practices, and rituals; views about what constitutes acceptable thoughts and behavior; processes for judging sin or crime; and punishments for deviance. Resulting from the socialization of its members, culture is "the collective programming of the mind that distinguishes the members of one group or category of people from another" (Hofstede, Hofstede, & Minkov, 2010, p. 6). Members of cultural groups share an identity. Furthermore, each of us may be part of and subject to the cultural norms and sanctions of one or more larger cultures and several smaller ones. We simultaneously belong to numerous cultures. For instance, one person might be a citizen of the United States and part of its national culture and at the same time belong to Spanish-speaking, secular–humanist, political, bisexual, and neighborhood subcultures; and serve as a leading member of a local Star Trek fan club.

As children, we possess little control over several aspects of our cultures. Infants are not "free" to choose, for example, the languages they absorb or the metaphysical beliefs they acquire. Children who are born to English-speaking parents in an English-speaking culture speak English rather than Portuguese, and those who grow up in a Mormon family in a Mormon community assume the religious beliefs of the Church of Latter Day Saints rather than those of Hinduism. In this sense, we acquire many cultural characteristics without choosing to do so. Indeed, in some cultures, individual choice—even for adults—is socially unacceptable. In other cultures, individualism is valued and people sometimes depart from their cultural heritage to learn a new language, and enroll in a different religion or adopt agnostic or atheistic beliefs. At least in theory, humans may be able to exercise some control over many cultural and subcultural aspects of their lives; and, of course, our cultures also change over the course of time. Rapid transportation, mass media, and Internet communications, in particular, have made certain cultural phenomena virtually contagious. The term *meme* and the phrase "It has gone viral" capture the power of modern technology to change social attitudes and behavior. And, as a source of great influence, quick and widely disseminated information can be used for both beneficial and harmful purposes.

In the United States especially, mass advertising and, to a much lesser extent, public service announcements, affect what and how much we purchase and consume. We are bombarded with advertisements for clothes, cosmetics, cars, prescription drugs, and food! In general, food products are plentiful in the United States, and advertising for them is virtually constant. In our "food environment," however, most products are highly processed with added salts, sugars, fats, and various preservatives to increase shelf life and enhance flavor. Humans are especially attracted to such ingredients—especially sugars and refined carbohydrates that readily convert to sugar within the body. Unfortunately, sugars have addictive properties and are directly linked to weight gain, obesity, and metabolic diseases such as Type 2 diabetes (Wang, Beydoun, Liang, Caballero, & Kumanyika, 2008). Indeed, several research studies suggest that intensely sweet sugars and sugar substitutes may be as or more addictive than drugs such as cocaine (Lenoir, Serre, Cantin, & Ahmed, 2007; Schulte, Avena, & Gearhardt, 2015). In the United States, approximately "75% of all foods and beverages contain added sugar in a large array of forms. Consumption of soft drinks has increased fivefold since 1950. Meta-analyses suggest that consumption of sugar-sweetened beverages (SSBs) is related to the risk of diabetes, the metabolic syndrome, and cardiovascular disease. Drinking two 16-ounce SSBs per day for 6 months induced features of the metabolic syndrome and fatty liver" (Bray & Popkin, 2014, para. 1).[3]

Most breakfast cereals also contain large quantities of sugar—many exceeding the amounts in candy or other desserts. Consumers are hard-pressed to locate products that contain fiber rich whole grains without added sugars. The high fiber content in many unprocessed grains, fruits, and vegetables effectively neutralizes the negative metabolic effects of their natural sugars. For example, an 8 ounce serving of processed orange juice (with the fibrous pulp and pith removed) contains about 24 grams of sugars but less than 0.1 gram of fiber. When ingested, the juice functions like other sugary drinks by stimulating a large spike in pancreatic insulin production. Eating a medium-size naval orange, however, causes only a minimal increase in insulin because it contains less than half as much sugar as the juice and about 31 times the amount of fiber. The pith and pulp mitigate the sugar rush and, of course, contribute vitamins and nutrients that are absent from its processed juice counterpart (Kaufman, 2005).

Based in part upon the globalization of the American diet, obesity and diabetes among children and adults throughout the world have reached epidemic proportions. This combination of diabetes and obesity is sometimes called "diabesity" (Farag & Gaballa, 2011; Kaufman, 2005). About 12.3 percent of the U.S. population of persons 20 years of age and older have the disease and another 86 million are prediabetic (Centers for Disease Control and Prevention, 2014). Worldwide, more than

---

[3] See the documentary films *Lunch, Fed Up,* and *Carb-Loaded: A Culture Dying to Eat* (Bonequi & Richards, 2010; Marson, 2014; Poland, 2014) for information about the relationship between the food industry and health.

350 million people have diabetes—90 percent of which is of the Type 2 form. Not surprisingly, the continued high rates of diabetes are associated with similarly high rates of overweight, obesity, and physical inactivity (World Health Organization, 2015b). In the United States, some 16.9 percent of children and youth and 34.9 percent of adults were obese in 2011–2012 (Ogden, Carroll, Kit, & Flegal, 2014).

Many argue that individuals can and should exercise personal willpower to adopt healthy eating behavior. However, the food environment and eating culture are extraordinarily powerful. They combine to elicit and then sustain our addictions to sugar, salt, and fat-enhanced diets. The advertising environment first stimulates our addictive cravings and then the food distribution system satisfies us with processed foods that contain the desired ingredients. Except for the fact that they do not contain warning labels, the most widely advertised and readily available food products do not appear that much different than cigarettes or other addictive drugs. When available, many of us will consume them, and do so again and again and again. The parallel epidemics of obesity and diabetes are clearly associated with these habit-forming food products. Although the U.S. food industry and its associated lobbyists argue that all calories are the same, they certainly are not. In particular, calories from processed carbohydrates and added sugars are different. Sugars not only negatively impact our bodies by spiking insulin production, they also turn us into food junkies (Bray & Popkin, 2014; Malik, Schulze, & Hu, 2006; Payne, Chassard, & Lacroix, 2012; Schulze et al., 2004; Sylvetsky, Welsh, Brown, & Vos, 2012; World Health Organization, 2015a).

Our social and physical environments not only affect what, when, how, and where we eat; they also influence almost all other aspects of our lives as well. As children, most of us absorb the "outside" so that it becomes part of our "inside." As grown-ups, and especially as social workers, let's be alert to the influence and impact of our environments and cultures and do what we can to create contexts that promote health, justice, and well-being for people in general, and particularly for those most adversely affected by the world around them.

The Family Context

Although mass and social media are growing in influence, human families continue to function as the major social system through which children are socialized, language learned, and cultures transmitted. Our families profoundly affect our attitudes, beliefs, values, personality characteristics, and behavioral patterns. They are the context in which we acquire our first identities and learn our earliest roles. We quickly come to know what is acceptable and what is not. We learn how to think (and how to avoid thinking); how and what to feel (and how not to feel); how to make decisions (and how to postpone them); how to respond to (and how to ignore) unexpected events; and how to relate to (and how to shun) other people. In a sense, we psychologically internalize our experiences so that each family member is imprinted within us. Most of us have internalized parental parts that guide, judge, sanction, or nurture us; childlike parts that encourage us to play or create and to feel various emotions such as joy or shame; and adult or "grown-up" parts that enable us to think rationally, analyze multiple factors, and regulate the parental and childlike parts—much as a chairperson might do with a committee (Berne, 1961; Harris, 1969).

All families exhibit internal structures, subsystems, and communication and relationship processes of one kind or another. Some families reflect a hierarchical organizational structure; others are more collegial, cooperative, and democratic. Some display high levels of warmth, acceptance, inclusion, and affection; others are more cool, detached, and distant with one another. Some are peaceful; others are violent. In some families, roles and the expectations that accompany them are firm and fixed, and the penalties for performance lapses sometimes severe. In other families, roles are flexible and the consequence for mistakes lenient. Regardless of the nature of the structure, processes, roles, and rules, families play an extraordinarily powerful part in both the socialization of children as well as the stability of the larger community and society.

We might, for example, expect that all social systems would or should reflect similar rules, structures, and processes as those experienced in our own family. For example, if you came from a family with a hierarchical power structure, you might anticipate that other groups and systems would "naturally" be organized in a similar top-down fashion. Leaderless groups and cooperative organizations might well seem "strange." In like fashion, if in your family men and boys were accorded greater status, authority, and prestige than women and girls, you could view male privilege as "natural" and perhaps judge systems where women and girls are privileged as "unnatural." If your family considered heterosexuality as "normal" and homosexuality as sinful, criminal, or "sick," then you might reflect similar views. If your family expressed opinions or took action suggesting that one "race" is superior to others, it is quite conceivable that you might hold comparable views and take like action, perhaps in the form of micro-aggressions that occur outside your own awareness (Nadal et al., 2015; Owen, Tao, Imel, Wampold, & Rodolfa, 2014; Sue, 2010b).

In many respects, our families represent microcosms of the larger society and cultures within which they function. What we observe and experience in our own families is often reflected within the social environment; and, conversely the "outside" is often reflected both within our own families and "inside" ourselves. The structures, assumptions, rules, and processes often parallel each other.[4]

Unless you are keenly aware of the power and influence of your family, you may inadvertently or unconsciously play out a family role or an interpersonal pattern in your work with clients and colleagues. Among the common family roles that social workers sometimes assume include rescuer, peacemaker, hero, and parental child (Satir, 1972; Wegscheider-Cruse, 1985). Other family roles include the lost child, mascot, and scapegoat (Sanders, Szymanski, & Fiori, 2014). Of course, sometimes it is entirely proper to use a part of your family-based self in social work practice. In all such cases, however, it should be consciously planned and adopted for a clearly identified social work purpose.

Personal Factors

Helping professionals frequently use the term **personality** but many of us are not quite clear about its meaning. Magill (1998) suggests that a majority of personality "theorists agree that people have an internal 'essence' that determines who they are and that guides their behavior, but the nature of that essence differs from theory to theory" (p. 453). Some personality theorists focus upon instinctual urges, others highlight motivational factors, and still others emphasize internal conflicts. Some reflect their strong interest in human developmental processes, others in internal or external expectations, and still others in enduring types, characteristics, or traits. These diverse theoretical approaches to personality may be categorized into (1) type, (2) trait, (3) psychodynamic/psychoanalytic, (4) behavioral, (5) social learning/social cognitive, and (6) humanistic theories (Roeckelein, 1998, pp. 374–375).

As you might imagine, various personality researchers have developed assessment instruments that correspond to different theoretical perspectives. Currently, one of the most popular trait approaches to personality assessment involves attention to the following "big five" or OCEAN personality factors: *openness, conscientiousness, extraversion, agreeableness,* and *neuroticism* (Benet-Martinez & John, 1998; Digman, 1990; John, 2007–2009; John, Donahue, & Kentle, 1991; John, Naumann, & Soto, 2008; John & Srivastava, 1999; Srivastava, John, Gosling, & Potter, 2003).[5]

---

[4] We discuss the phenomenon of parallel processes in subsequent chapters.

[5] For a more detailed description of these factors, see the "Preliminary Definitions" section (page 30) of John and Srivastava's paper "The Big-Five Trait Taxonomy: History, Measurement, and Theoretical Perspectives" (1999) available at http://pages .uoregon.edu/sanjay/pubs/bigfive.pdf.

"Big five" and other personality indices may be useful to social workers and clients in some circumstances. However, because of our core professional values and our emphasis on the person-in-environment, we recognize that situations, circumstances, and environments strongly influence human experience and action. Indeed, social workers understand that situational factors may override personal characteristics so that even strongly moral and conscientious people sometimes take immoral or illegal action (Zimbardo, 2007). Conversely, those who routinely engage in morally reprehensible behavior occasionally behave in incredibly generous and honorable ways. Through our recognition of the power of social circumstances and environmental factors—external to the person—social workers may be better suited to counter the prevailing popular tendency to overestimate biological and psychological factors in attempting to explain or understand human phenomena. The overvaluing of personal (internal) and the undervaluing of social and environmental (external) factors is known as the **fundamental attribution error** (Ross, 1977).

Interestingly, when people attempt to explain their own lapses of judgment or their own misbehavior, they often mention external factors such as other people or circumstances. For example: "I was late because my alarm clock didn't go off." Or, "I lost my temper because he behaved so despicably." Conversely, when explaining the misbehavior of others—perhaps especially those who differ in some way—people often refer to individual traits, dispositions, or personality characteristics. For example: "He got into the auto accident because he's an alcoholic." "He steals because he's a sociopath." Or, "He's probably guilty because he's black."[6]

As you consider individual characteristics or traits, temperament, or personality, keep the fundamental attribution error in mind. Situations strongly influence our thoughts, feelings, sensations, and behavior. Even personality characteristics—such as introversion and extraversion—are influenced by circumstances. The shy introvert may become the life of the party when she is with her closest friends while the gregarious extrovert may become the quiet wallflower in the company of experts outside his field. In sum, personality helps us to understand some human phenomena at certain times in some circumstances. However, personality-based explanations that fail to consider and include contextual factors often convey an incomplete picture at best.

Knowledge, Expertise, and Self-Efficacy

Advanced professional knowledge and expertise are, of course, essential for ethical and effective social work practice. In social work, the particular knowledge required varies considerably according to the characteristics of the setting, the issues for work, the populations served, and the roles assumed. However, a common base of knowledge exists for all social workers. For instance, educational programs accredited by the CSWE (2015) offer curriculums that address at least nine core competencies. Graduates of accredited programs should be able to demonstrate understanding of the knowledge base as well as proficiency in measurable practice behaviors that support each of the nine competencies. The targeted professional behaviors may be exhibited and evaluated in classroom, skills laboratory, or field practicum contexts. Some field practicum settings enable students to apply professional knowledge and demonstrate practice expertise in supervised practice contexts. In such settings, students learn through doing, and refine skills and competencies that would be difficult to develop in any other way.

---

[6] The "ultimate attribution error" and "blaming the victim" processes involve tendencies to view misbehavior by low-status or "undesirable" people as a result of their "common, negative" traits (for example, "they are all greedy," "they are less intelligent," or "they can't control their impulses"). It also includes the corollary view that "their" positive behavior is the result of contextual or situational factors and special circumstances. In other words, "they" cause (and are responsible for) their mistakes and failures but do not cause (and not personally credited with) successes and achievements. On the other hand, "we" cause our own successes and achievements but do not cause (and are not responsible for) our mistakes and failures.

TABLE 2.1	Content Areas: ASWB Sponsored Bachelor's and Master's Examinations			
	Bachelor's Examination	**Percent of Exam**	**Master's Examination**	**Percent of Exam**
I.	Human development, diversity, and behavior in the environment	27%	Human development, diversity, and behavior in the environment	28%
II.	Assessment	28%	Assessment and intervention planning	24%
III.	Direct and indirect practice	26%	Direct and indirect practice	21%
IV.	Professional relationships, values, and ethics	19%	Professional relationships, values, and ethics	27%
		100.00%		**100.00%**

Adapted from Association of Social Work Boards, 2011.

Although they may vary in specific information and emphasis, all CSWE accredited social work programs provide educational experiences that address a common, profession-wide, knowledge base. The CSWE expectations are also congruent with the content addressed in the Association of Social Work Boards (ASWB) sponsored nationally standardized social work licensing examinations currently used in all 50 states[7], the District of Columbia, the U.S. Virgin Islands, and several Canadian provinces (Association of Social Work Boards, 2013a, About the exams, para. 2).

The major content areas addressed in the ASWB Bachelor's and Master's level examinations include those contained in Table 2.1 (Association of Social Work Boards, 2013b). The ASWB also sponsors Advanced Generalist and Clinical Examinations. These nationally standardized social work examinations ensure that reasonably equivalent standards exist throughout most of North America. They, along with the policies of NASW and CSWE, help to establish a common social work knowledge base.[8]

Social workers must not only possess sophisticated knowledge and expertise; we must also *expect* that we can make a difference as well. Just as clients benefit when they anticipate the goodwill, integrity, and competence of social workers, social workers profit from self-confidence as well. Supported by knowledge and expertise, we need attitudes of hope, optimism, and self-efficacy.

For social workers, **self-efficacy** involves the "confidence in their ability to execute specific skills in a particular set of circumstances and thereby achieve a successful outcome" (Holden, Meenaghan, Anastas, & Metrey, 2001, p. 116). Without knowledge-based self-efficacy, social workers would likely be relatively inactive, passive observers rather than energetic, collaborative agents of change. Gary Holden, in particular, has contributed greatly to the development of specialized self-efficacy assessment instruments for use in social work practice and education (Holden, 1991; Holden, Barker, Rosenberg, & Onghena, 2008; Holden, Cuzzi, Rutter, Chernack, & Rosenberg, 1997; Holden, Cuzzi, Rutter, Rosenberg, & Chernack, 1996; Holden, Cuzzi, Spitzer et al., 1997; Holden, Meenaghan, & Anastas, 2003). In addition to specific forms of self-efficacy, people tend to benefit from a generalized belief in their own ability to effect change in themselves and their lives (Bandura, 1977, 1992, 1995a, 1997).

---

[7] As of January 2016, California began to use the ASWB-sponsored Clinical Examination.

[8] You may access the Association of Social Work Boards at **www.aswb.org**, the Council on Social Work Education at **www.cswe.org**, and the National Association of Social Workers at **www.socialworkers.org**.

People make causal contributions to their own psychosocial functioning through mechanisms of personal agency. Among the mechanisms of agency, none is more central or pervasive than people's beliefs of personal efficacy. Perceived self-efficacy refers to beliefs in one's capabilities to organize and execute the courses of action required to manage prospective situations. Efficacy beliefs influence how people think, feel, motivate themselves, and act. (Bandura, 1995a, p. 2)

As the 21st century continues to unfold, social workers and the social work profession face extraordinary, and probably unprecedented, challenges (Austin, 1997). A broad and deep base of current, valid, and reliable knowledge and a correspondingly strong sense of self-efficacy are required for ethical and effective social work practice in the often unpredictable, contemporary world.

In addition to the CSWE (2015), the NASW (2015e), and the ASWB (2011), eminent social workers (Bartlett, 1958, 1970; Minahan, 1981) have also helped to clarify the general parameters of a common social work knowledge base. In actual practice, however, social workers also require a great deal of specialized knowledge that applies to the unique characteristics of the clientele and communities we serve.

Suppose, for example, that you provide social work services to women physically abused in domestic violence circumstances. Just imagine what and how much you would need to know to serve your clients and community effectively!

You would have to be well acquainted with the current theoretical and research literature concerning the nature and outcome of social services for domestically abused women, and those for abusive men and children exposed to such violence as well. You would need to know the factors that contribute to domestic violence, as well as those that tend to reduce its likelihood. You should understand the range of risks facing women in such circumstances and know how to assess the risk of injury or death; and what to do when risk is high, moderate, or low; and how to help clients consider the risk–benefit ratio of various courses of action.

In approaching service from a person-in-environment perspective, you would need to know how to identify, assess, and intervene in primary and secondary social systems. Familiarity with the racial and ethnic cultures of your community would help. Knowledge about and skill in determining the biopsychosocial needs of children affected by domestic violence could apply in many circumstances. Expertise in assessing the strengths and potentials of all members of the primary social system—including people suspected of initiating violence—could help to further understanding and identify possible solutions. You would need to know the laws and regulations of the locale where you serve and the professional values and ethics that might apply. Familiarity with actual and potential resources—locally, nationally, and, sometimes, internationally—that might become needed at various times in the process could be vital.

In addition, you would also need knowledge about and expertise in relationships. Regardless of the specific nature of the issue, whether it involves intimate violence, homelessness, racial discrimination, or something else, social workers require advanced skills in making relationships work. Fortunately, we have access to a substantial research base about positive and effective working relationships between helping professionals and their clients. We can organize that information into two interrelated conceptual dimensions: **common factors** and **facilitative conditions**.

Common Factors

As early as the 1930s, helping professionals (Rosenzweig, 1936) discussed the presence of implicit common factors in diverse therapeutic approaches. Findings from numerous research studies confirm that certain common factors present in helping relationships account for many of the beneficial outcomes (Asay & Lambert, 1999; Barth et al., 2012; Hoffart, Borge, Sexton, &

Clark, 2008; Laska, Gurman, & Wampold, 2014; Murphy, 1999; Scovern, 1999; Sparks & Duncan, 2010; Wampold, 2010). These **common factors** are separate from the effects of specific intervention approaches and techniques.[9] In other words, they are common to most helping endeavors and are not specific or exclusive to any particular model or approach. The following common factors are associated with favorable outcomes in counseling and psychotherapy (Lambert, 1992; Lambert & Bergin, 1994; Lambert & Cattani-Thompson, 1996; Sprenkle, Blow, & Dickey, 1999):

Client Factors and Situational Factors: The strengths, assets, resources, challenges, and limitations within the client, the client's social situation, economic circumstances, and the physical environment are strongly associated with service outcomes. Clients' stage of change and degree of motivation are also relevant (Prochaska, 1999; Prochaska & Norcross, 2007; Prochaska, Norcross, & DiClemente, 1994). Not surprisingly, the internal and external assets and liabilities that clients bring to the relationship with a helping professional generally have more of an influence than any other single element (Asay & Lambert, 1999; Bohart & Tallman, 2010; Lambert, 1992; Miller, Wampold, & Varhely, 2008; Tallman & Bohart, 1999; Wampold, 2001, 2010). Within the context of counseling and psychotherapy, as much as 87 percent (Wampold, 2001) of the variability in therapeutic outcomes is associated with client and external or situational factors. Social work's emphasis on "starting where the client is" and our focus on the person-in-environment correspond to this finding. By incorporating client strengths and ecosystem assets, and by addressing environmental limitations and obstacles, social workers can supplement our otherwise relatively modest 13 percent impact on client outcomes. One of social work's greatest strengths is our attention to the social and physical environments within which people function. Through systematic inclusion of the environmental context in our helping efforts, we become dramatically more effective agents of social change than we would be if we focused on the person alone.

Helper and Relationship Factors: As social workers, our personal characteristics and the quality of our relationships with others also influence client outcomes (Asay & Lambert, 1999; Lambert, 1992). In the counseling and psychotherapy literature, this is often discussed as the "therapeutic alliance." Involving "three components: (a) bond between therapist and patient, (b) agreement about the goals of therapy, and (c) agreement about the tasks of therapy" (Laska et al., 2014, p. 471), a positive alliance contributes to positive therapeutic outcomes. These processes also occur within groups, organizations, communities, and societies as well. The term *group cohesion* reflects the quality of relationships among group members. *Organizational climate* does the same for organizations and *solidarity* for large social movements.

Social workers have long recognized the importance of our personal qualities and our relationship with clients and other constituents (Perlman, 1979). Your dedication, integrity, concern for others, and your proficiency in the social work skills can help you establish positive working relationships with the people you serve.

Hope and Expectancy Factors: When clients anticipate that your work together will be effective, they tend to experience better outcomes (Lambert, 1992). In other words, we are more effective when clients have "hope," when they expect favorable results. It also helps when social workers expect success, when we believe we can make a positive impact, and when we feel self-efficacious. Social workers commonly encourage hope and serve as examples to others through our optimistic

---

[9] In addition to "common factors" there also seem to be "common practice elements" associated with favorable outcomes in counseling and therapy. These include specific intervention activities from across various models or approaches that are empirically associated with effective results. See Barth et al. (2012) and Chorpita et al. (2005; Chorpita & Weisz, 2009).

attitude, energy, and enthusiasm. However, we do so in a direct, open, and realistic fashion. Social workers eschew false promises and excessive bravado as we maximize the power of hope, anticipation, and positive expectations. We remain honest and honorable (Perlman, 1969).

Technique and Allegiance Factors: The theoretical approaches or models, change strategies, intervention techniques, and practice protocols we adopt in the process of helping affect client outcomes. Helpers' allegiance to the approaches adopted or interventions undertaken also contribute. By **allegiance**, we mean the degree to which helpers believe in the value and effectiveness of what they do and how they do it. Furthermore, the client's belief in the chosen approach is probably just as important and perhaps even more so than the helper's. In this sense, improved outcomes are likely when both the client and the worker agree with the ideas, concepts, and hypotheses used to explain problems and formulate goals, and to prepare plans to reach those goals (Imel & Wampold, 2008). When combined, the hope and expectancy, and the model or technique and allegiance factors account for about the same amount of client outcome impact as do relationship factors (Asay & Lambert, 1999; Lambert, 1992).

Other scholars have reached similar conclusions about common factors. In addition to the quality of the working relationship and client expectancies, Weinberger (1993, 1995, 2003) emphasizes the importance of (1) exposure to and exploration of problem issues, (2) practice in coping with or mastering aspects of the problematic issues, and (3) development of a conceptual means[10] or framework to understand and explain why and how the problems occur and how they can be managed.

Evaluative Feedback Factors: Previously underappreciated, **systematic evaluative feedback** from clients has gained increasing recognition as a powerful factor associated with better outcomes. Indeed, the quality and the effectiveness of the helping process tends to improve when clients provide regular, formalized evaluative feedback about the helper, the helping relationship, the service approach, and progress toward desired goals; and when the helper regularly inquires about and tabulates results, and then uses those findings to make adjustments in approach or style (Crits-Christoph et al., 2012; Hawkins, Lambert, Vermeersch, Slade, & Tuttle, 2004; Lambert, 2010b; Lambert & Shimokawa, 2011; Lambert, Whipple, Vermeersch, Smart, & Hawkins, 2002; Slade, Lambert, Harmon, Smart, & Bailey, 2008; Whipple & Lambert, 2011). Regardless of intervention approach or model, the routine use of brief evaluation instruments (Campbell & Hemsley, 2009; Duncan et al., 2003; Luborsky, 1996) tends to increase the probability of service success and decrease the likelihood of failure (Anker et al., 2009; Miller et al., 2006; Miller, Duncan, Sorrell, & Brown, 2005). Regular use of evaluative tools also improves client satisfaction and, importantly, enhances the quality of the worker–client relationship.

The Facilitative Conditions

Recognition of the significance of relationship factors and helper characteristics has encouraged researchers to explore personal qualities that might be associated with better client outcomes. Qualities such as empathy, caring, personal warmth, acceptance, affirmation, sincerity, and encouragement are frequently included among the characteristics of effective helpers (Duncan, Miller, Wampold, & Hubble, 2010; Hubble, Duncan, & Miller, 1999). When social workers reflect these **facilitative conditions**, we tend to foster:

a cooperative working endeavor in which the client's increased sense of trust, security, and safety, along with decreases in tension, threat, and anxiety, lead to changes in conceptualizing his

---

[10] We consider the topic of "conceptual means" in a later chapter when we discuss the explanatory and change-oriented hypotheses that clients and workers adopt during the course of their work together.

or her problems and ultimately in acting differently by reframing fears, taking risks, and working through problems in interpersonal relationships (i.e., clients confront and cope with reality in more effective ways). (Lambert & Cattani-Thompson, 1996, p. 603)

When social workers consistently demonstrate the core or the **facilitative conditions**, we contribute to the development and maintenance of a special connection with our clients (Carkhuff & Truax, 1965; Rogers, 1951, 1957, 1961, 1975; Truax & Carkhuff, 1967). Various authors refer to this special relationship as the helping relationship, the working relationship, the therapeutic alliance, professional rapport, or the working alliance. Perlman (1979) suggested that we can distinguish the professional working relationship between social worker and client from other relationships by the following characteristics:

- It is formed for a recognized and agreed-upon purpose.
- It is time-bound.
- It is *for* the client.
- It carries authority.
- It is a controlled relationship. (pp. 48–77)

The nature and quality of working relationships are affected by the facilitative conditions, the common factors, and the degree of agreement about what to do and how to do it. When social workers and clients agree on the problems or issues to address in their work together, the goals to pursue, the plan and methods to pursue those goals, and the means to evaluate progress, the likelihood of success improves. Disagreements on one or more of these aspects can strain, damage, or even rupture the working alliance; and lead to diminished hope and motivation, and decreased goal-oriented activity. In many instances, disagreements about problems, goals, and plans emerge in first meetings and become so troublesome that clients do not return for a subsequent visit.

Obviously, the quality of the working relationship is powerfully affected by social workers' attitudes toward and behavior with clients. Consensus about problems, goals, and plans is more easily reached when we consistently reflect the essential facilitative qualities. Under such conditions, the risk of harm tends to decrease and the likelihood of benefit tends to increase. Indeed, a positive working alliance is clearly associated with favorable outcomes in work with individuals, couples, families, groups, and organizations (Anker, Owen, Duncan, & Sparks, 2010; Escudero, Heatherington, & Friedlander, 2010; Fluckiger, Del Re, Wampold, Symonds, & Horvath, 2012; Horvath & Bedi, 2002; Horvath, Symonds, & Tapia, 2010; Martin, Garske, & Davis, 2000; Meier, Barrowclough, & Donmall, 2005; Muran & Barber, 2010; Owen, Rhoades, Stanley, & Markman, 2011; Piper & Ogrodniczuk, 2010; Safran & Muran, 2000; Watson & Kalogerakos, 2010). However, demonstrating these qualities alone is rarely enough to enable clients to reach agreed-upon goals. Social workers nearly always need to add expert knowledge and skills to help clients progress toward goal attainment; and, together with our clients, we commonly seek situational, social, or environmental change as well. Furthermore, social workers must apply the facilitative conditions differentially according to the individual and cultural characteristics of each client. Some clients feel quite uneasy when social workers are frequently and intensively empathic. They might prefer a formal encounter in which we provide direct advice and guidance in a businesslike fashion. Others seem to benefit from an emotionally close and intimate relationship where both the client and the worker share personal thoughts and feelings. Obviously, client characteristics play a powerful role in both the process and outcomes of the working relationship. Motivated clients who participate actively in the process tend to benefit from competent, relevant services. Clients who are ambivalent or pessimistic and those who passively or reluctantly engage in the process tend to experience less favorable outcomes. Of course, social workers' and clients' attitudes may vary during an encounter, sometimes from moment to moment. Many clients seem to follow certain stages of change (Prochaska, 1999; Prochaska & Norcross, 2007; Prochaska et al., 1994; Prochaska & Velicera, 1998). Indeed, some people first contact social workers well before they are ready or motivated to engage actively in plans for change. A caring, involved, and encouraging worker may help to increase a client's hope and optimism and thus help the client become a more active and involved participant. Conversely, a motivated, energetic, hard-working client may encourage a social worker to become more understanding, supportive, and hopeful.

Identifying and measuring all the potential factors that affect the outcome of helping processes are complicated undertakings. The picture is especially complex for social workers who focus on the environment as well as the person and fulfill disparate professional functions in varied settings with a wide range of populations confronting extremely challenging social issues. Different social workers in different contexts assume quite different roles and responsibilities. Indeed, a single social worker may emphasize certain characteristics at various times. The social worker serving parents and siblings of babies in the neonatal care unit of a children's hospital emphasizes different qualities than does the worker who serves people long addicted to heroin or crack cocaine. Similarly, the social worker who advocates for fair banking practices or a ban on capital punishment may adopt other qualities. Even when advocating in an assertive manner, however, we remain empathic, respectful, and authentic. When these dimensions accompany them, assertive expressions are likely to be especially impactful.

Despite the breadth and diversity inherent in social work and the evolutionary nature of relevant research findings, certain aspects of the worker–client experience appear related to client satisfaction and effective outcomes. Krill (1986) suggests that the relationship between a social worker and a client is more likely to be productive if:

- The participants like and respect each other.
- The client is clearly told what to expect and how to contribute to the helping process.
- The worker is warm, genuine, and sincere and regularly expresses empathy about the client's experience.
- The worker and client engage in goal-directed activities such as practice, in-session tasks, or between-session action steps.
- The social worker actively seeks to involve significant people in the client's life in the helping process. (p. xi)

In sum, effective helpers tend to reflect certain facilitative conditions in our service to others. Social workers express these qualities differentially according to individual clients' stage of change, the unique circumstances of the person-in-environment, the nature of the social worker's role, and the phase of service. Nonetheless, as a general guide, social workers consistently reflect the following essential facilitative conditions in virtually all of their relationships with others: (1) empathy, (2) respect, and (3) authenticity.

Empathy: The term **empathy** (Altmann, 1973; Bohart & Greenberg, 1997a, 1997b; Bozarth, 1997; Breithaupt, 2012a, 2012b; Keefe, 1976; Pinderhughes, 1979; Rogers, 1975) is widely used in social work and other helping professions. Derived from the Greek word *empatheia*, empathy may be described as a process of joining in the feelings of another, of feeling how and what another person experiences, of feeling with someone, or of "suffering with" another.

Scholars in the areas of neuroscience, social psychology, philosophy, and anthropology have approached the study of empathy from different perspectives. Some researchers focus on "how" people come to understand what others are thinking, feeling, or experiencing. Others study those factors that lead people to respond to others' distress with care, compassion, and understanding. Researchers may use the concept of empathy to refer to the experience of (1) recognizing the thoughts, feelings, and internal subjective experience of someone else; (2) feeling personally distressed when observing another person's misery or feeling the emotions that another person appears to feel; (3) adopting another's perspective and imagining how she or he might be thinking and feeling; (4) matching the body position, movements, and mannerisms of someone; (5) imagining oneself in another person's place or circumstances and identifying what one would think and feel; and (6) feeling sympathy for a distressed other (Batson, 2009).

Frans de Waal (2009) also suggests that empathy is multilayered and involves three core elements along with multiple subordinate capacities. The core three include (1) the ability to adopt another's perspective or point of view; (2) concern for others—often manifested through expressions and acts of consolation, that is, seeking to comfort or console another; and (3) feeling what the other is feeling or matching the emotional state or expression of the other.

Empathy may indeed appear in several forms. For example, when we interact with someone who feels distress and we both feel her or his distress and show our concern, we engage in *proximal empathy*. When we become concerned about people outside our immediate vicinity—perhaps those in another part of our community or in a distant corner of the world—we reflect *altruistic empathy*. When we say or do something that contributes to others' discomfort and then, upon noticing their reaction, express our awareness and show our concern—perhaps by acknowledging the impact of our own actions through an expression of remorse—we engage in *self-corrective empathy* (Quann & Wien, 2006, July).

Certainly, a capacity and willingness to take on others' perspectives; to imagine being in their circumstances; and to feel what they feel are fundamental to most moral philosophies. Stotland (2001) concludes that "the key antecedent condition for empathy appears to be the empathizer's imagining himself or herself as having the same experience as the other—thus imaginatively taking the role of the other" (Empathy section, para. 6). In effect, empathy involves the proverbial "putting oneself in another's shoes." Indeed, empathic imagination is reflected in both the Golden and Silver Rules which hold, respectively, that we should (1) treat others as we would like to be treated and (2) not treat others in ways that we would not like to be treated.

Along with several other species, *Homo sapiens* seem to possess an innate capacity for empathy. Among most human children, empathic reactions first become obvious in the 1-to-2-year age range, overlapping with the period known as the "terrible twos." In social contexts, toddlers readily display empathic responses to others' expressions of distress or discomfort. In effect, they are empathic "mind-readers" (Ickes, 2003) who routinely perceive and experience what others are experiencing (Iacoboni, 2008).

Unless socialized out of us, most humans possess an ability to transcend our selfish tendencies to recognize that we are part of a greater community—a larger whole or "hive" (Haidt, Seder, & Kesebir, 2008)—and connect empathically with other members (Trout, 2009). Roman Krznaric uses the term *outrospection* (2012) to encourage humans to focus less on our own experience and more on the thoughts, feelings, and circumstances of others. He concludes that, individually and collectively, many of us are becoming so self-oriented and self-centered that our empathic abilities are beginning to atrophy. He urges us to become more other-focused or *outrospective*.

Considerable scholarship suggests that a key foundation for human morality involves this extraordinary capacity for empathy (Carter, Harris, & Porges, 2009). If so, individuals and groups that highly value empathy would likely be more kind, moral, and altruistic than those that devalue and discourage empathic involvement with others. Indeed, tolerance, acceptance, compassion, and generosity toward others—especially others who are "different" in some way—require considerable levels of empathy.

Unfortunately, empathic interest in the experiences of others may diminish as children grow into adulthood—especially in social contexts that place great importance on the individual; value self-interest; emphasize adversarial conflict and competition; and promote extreme notions of personal autonomy and individual responsibility. Indeed, some cultures tend to emphasize the "self" much more than the "other"; and the "I" or "me" much more than the "you," "we," or "us." In such contexts, individuals may focus primarily on themselves; their own thoughts, feelings, and experiences; and their own appearance, status, possessions, and wealth. Conversely, they may ignore or discount people outside their primary kinship group and social circle, perhaps especially those who differ from themselves. In some sociopolitical and economic contexts, self-centeredness and self-admiration may be promoted as a high moral value. Indeed, greed and the accumulation and display of material wealth may be equated with goodness.

The Latin phrase *caveat emptor* (let the buyer beware) captures an ethos in which benefiting oneself at the expense of another is viewed as legitimate and, indeed, desirable. The burden of responsibility is placed upon consumers to be knowledgeable, vigilant, and self-disciplined in their resistance to sellers' deception, distortion, pressure, and manipulation. Sellers who intentionally disregard predictable negative consequences to consumers and profit greatly from such exchanges tend to increase their wealth and status, and enhance their reputation as valued members of a community. Empathic feelings for exploited consumers are suppressed while the benefits to oneself and one's kin are emphasized.

Obviously, greed and selfishness are hardly limited to the economic sphere. Self-centeredness and self-admiration, perhaps to the extent of narcissism, may be endemic in some societies and some cultures (Twenge & Campbell, 2009; Twenge, Konrath, Foster, Campbell, & Bushman, 2008). Interestingly, a preoccupation with oneself may run counter to humans' evolution as highly social mammals (Aronson & Aronson, 2012). Despite a prevailing view that humans are basically selfish creatures, much evidence suggests that we are quite cooperative and collaborative in nature. Humans actually tend to be extraordinarily "groupish" in our social behavior (Christakis & Fowler, 2009; Haidt et al., 2008; McTaggart, 2011; Montagu & Matson, 1979). Somewhat like bees in a hive, we tend to thrive in most social contexts and decline in solitary environments. Is it any wonder that severe punishments often involve banishment from one's community or imprisonment in solitary confinement?

Social workers in particular tend to recognize the importance of the social dimensions of human experience. We seek to transcend the powerful cultural and economic forces that promote excessive egocentricity by developing strength and skill in empathic understanding, communication, and connectedness. We recognize that our efforts to help others address problems and pursue goals become more effective when we genuinely experience and convey authentic empathy. Simply stated, our sincerely experienced and accurately demonstrated expression of empathy substantially increases our effectiveness and improves client outcomes (Bohart & Greenberg, 1997a, 1997b; Breggin, 1997; Patterson, 1984).

In social work, we make a distinction between empathy and several related emotional responses. Social workers tend to view **empathy** as a conscious and intentional joining with others in their subjective experience. It involves being intellectually and emotionally present, attentive, and responsive in relationships. However, empathy is not an expression of *feeling for* or *feeling toward* as we might if we pity another person. Nor is it a diagnostic or evaluative appraisal (Hammond, Hepworth, & Smith, 1977, p. 3). Rather, empathy involves thinking and feeling *as* and *with another*.

Naturally, there are limits to anyone's ability and willingness to feel with and feel as another does. In fact, as a professional social worker, you must always retain a portion of yourself for your professional responsibilities. Be careful not to over identify. Clients retain ultimate ownership of their thoughts and feelings. They are not yours to take, absorb, or keep. Indeed, if you completely assumed clients' feelings as your own, you might well become paternalistic or maternalistic in your approach.

Empathy helps us gain an understanding of, appreciation for, and sensitivity to the people we serve. Through empathic connection with your clients and other constituents, you increase the probability of developing rapport and maintaining productive working relationships, and, partly as a result, improve the chances for an effective outcome.

Respect: Integrally related to empathy is the facilitative quality of **respect** (Hammond et al., 1977, pp. 170–203). Respect suggests an attitude of noncontrolling, warm, caring, and nonpossessive acceptance of other people. Involving aspects of awe or reverence, wonder, and curiosity, respect includes the demonstration of unconditional positive regard (Rogers, 1957, 1961) and recognition of the unique experience of each individual person. In intercultural contexts, respect also includes the genuine acceptance of difference and recognition of the value of diversity. Respect of this nature goes far beyond basic tolerance to include appreciation for the beneficial impact of diversity and difference in human communities and throughout the biological and ecological environment as well.

We humans tend to spend most of our time with people like ourselves, who live and work in similar circumstances, have comparable incomes and social status, hold views that resemble our own, and express interest in and affection toward us. Conversely, we tend to spend less time with people unlike ourselves, who live and work in different circumstances, have much higher or lower incomes and social status, espouse views that differ from our own, and are unfriendly or disinterested in us. Very few of us actively seek out and engage people who differ from ourselves and even fewer of us seem willing to consider the relevance, utility, or reasonableness of points of view that conflict with our own.

Some of us frequently engage in a "let's blame them" form of thinking in which we view "others" as the primary cause for problems in the world or in our own lives. We tend to blame people we call *them* as distinguished from people we call *us*. This kind of thinking is often linked to scapegoating and sometimes to hatred, discrimination, persecution, and genocide. There are numerous examples throughout the course of human history. What often happens is that a particular group, usually one having greater numbers or possessing greater wealth, status, and physical power, holds another group—usually one that is smaller in size or possessing less wealth, status, or power—responsible for past or current social or economic problems. In recent and contemporary history, humans have blamed members of other religious faiths or nonbelievers, other racial or ethnic groups, and people in different circumstances or statuses. For example, immigrants, welfare recipients, women, union members, and persons who are gay or lesbian have been blamed for a myriad of social and economic problems. Obviously, views that certain others are less human or less worthy than we are and the cause of our problems contributes to an "us" versus "them" form of thinking which, in turn, fosters various forms of prejudice, discrimination, segregation, and oppression. Such thinking is apparent throughout all spheres of society—from the international and societal levels to the family, neighborhood, and organizational levels. Indeed, individuals and groups within school communities commonly engage in various kinds of bullying—sometimes by students toward other students, sometimes by students toward adults, sometimes by adults toward students, and sometimes by adults toward other adults.

Despite these human tendencies to judge, divide, and separate, we social workers routinely work with people who differ from ourselves, often in multiple ways. As a social worker, you will serve those who are very much unlike yourself in personal, familial, philosophical, religious, or political views. And, sometimes, you will serve clients who are extremely similar to yourself.

At times, you may find that you do not personally like certain clients, and some clients will dislike you. You may disagree with the beliefs, attitudes, and actions of many others. Nonetheless, as a social worker, you maintain respect for and caring acceptance of the people you engage and serve.

Social workers aspire to view each person as unique and inherently valuable, and as an important member of the human community. We convey our respect and regard by prizing and cherishing the personhood of all clients, regardless of the nature of their racial or ethnic backgrounds, gender, sexual orientation, age, ability, appearance, status, views, actions, or circumstances. Although we may personally disapprove of some clients' words or deeds, we continue to care about and accept them as unique people of dignity and worth. Furthermore, we recognize the fundamental right of clients to make their own decisions. This ability to respect clients neither because of nor in spite of their views, attributes, behaviors, or circumstances is an essential facilitative condition in social work practice.

Caring for clients as valuable human beings, however, does not preclude you from formulating professional hypotheses and assessments. Nor does it prevent you from sharing knowledge or offering suggestions and advice. You need not turn off your brain to demonstrate positive regard for others. Furthermore, respect for clients does not mean that you neglect other people, groups, or communities in the process. A person-in-environment perspective suggests that you always consider people and social systems affecting and affected by the clients you serve.

Authenticity: **Authenticity** refers to the genuineness and sincerity of a person's manner of relating. Reflecting fundamental honesty, an authentic social worker is natural, real, and personable. The presentation is congruent, so that verbal, nonverbal, and behavioral expressions reflect synchronicity. Words and deeds match. The genuine social worker is nondefensive; open to others' ideas, suggestions, and feedback; and forthright in sharing thoughts and feelings. "An authentic person relates to others personally, so that expressions do not seem rehearsed or contrived" (Hammond et al., 1977, p. 7).

Earlier, we discussed the significance of regularly and systematically seeking evaluative feedback from clients. Such processes involve aspects of authenticity in that social workers strive to transcend preconceived notions and biases, and use client feedback to reduce the likelihood that our service might be ineffective or harmful, and increase the probability that it might actually help.

Certainly, various psychological and social services have the capacity to and often do benefit consumers. Indeed, our professional efforts often dramatically enhance the lives of the individuals, families, groups, organizations, and communities we serve. Unfortunately, however, we can also do much damage. Studies suggest that between 9 and 14 percent of clients are detrimentally affected by counseling and psychotherapy services. In other words, a substantial number of clients are worse off than they would be had they not sought professional help. At least as disturbing as these figures, and perhaps more so, is the fact that many and perhaps most helping professionals cannot accurately identify which of their clients are deteriorating (Lambert & Shimokawa, 2011).

As do most other humans, social workers reflect a tendency to ignore information that challenges our view of ourselves as "good people, doing good work." We tend to believe that we would certainly recognize it if any of our clients failed to benefit or worsened during our service to them. However, Lambert and his colleagues' research studies (Crits-Christoph et al., 2012; Hawkins et al., 2004; Lambert, 2010a, 2010b; Lambert & Shimokawa, 2011; Lambert et al., 2002; Slade et al., 2008) suggest that unless our clients provide us with regular, formal, and systematic evaluative feedback, and unless we use that feedback to assess the quality of our services, we will probably also fail to notice when our clients do not progress or begin to worsen. Authentic social workers actively attempt to seek evaluative feedback from clients.

Genuineness, congruence, transparency, or authenticity (Rogers, 1961) may sometimes seem contrary to the notion of the professional social worker as cool, calm, and collected. However, professionalism in social work does not mean adopting a stiffly formal or overly controlled attitude. As a social worker, you need not and should not present yourself as an unfeeling, detached, computer-like technician. People seeking social services almost always prefer to talk with a knowledgeable and competent professional who comes across as a living, breathing, feeling human being—not as someone playing a canned role, spouting clichés, or repeating the same phrases again and again.

This emphasis on authenticity or genuineness in the working relationship, however, does not grant social workers a license to say or do anything or everything we think or feel at a particular moment in time. Remember that the helping relationship is fundamentally *for* clients. It is not primarily for us. Expression of our own thoughts and feelings for any other purpose than serving the client and working toward mutually agreed-upon goals is, at best, inefficient and, at worst, harmful.

Social Support and Well-Being

Social workers are dedicated to the resolution of social problems and the enhancement of social functioning and social well-being. We could not possibly provide effective service if we operated in isolation. Rather, we are grounded in a person-in-environment perspective and remain deeply involved with others. The nature of the work requires regular collaboration and cooperation, ongoing supervision or consultation, and a great deal of social support. In the absence of energy-enhancing support and reality-testing feedback, social workers would quickly deplete our personal resources and increase the likelihood of improperly meeting some of our own psychosocial needs and personal wants through our relationships with clients. Indeed, if social workers are isolated and lack strong, positive personal and professional social networks, we become quite vulnerable to numerous temptations. We need substantial social support and a solid sense of well-being.

As social mammals, human infants require an enormous amount of postpartum parenting and an extensive developmental "nest" or "external womb" (Lancy, 2008). At the time of (full-term) birth, human babies require at least another year or so of "exterior gestation" before autonomous survival would be even remotely conceivable. Many other animals can ambulate and forage for food shortly after birth. Human babies cannot. They must be fed, warmed, and comforted by others. They need a great deal of eye-to-eye and skin-to-skin contact for optimal development. Throughout most of our species' evolutionary history, this occurred more or less naturally as babies nursed at their mothers' breasts for about four years—about the same as other great apes. In contemporary times, however, most human infants are weaned from breast milk in much less time (Trevathan & McKenna, 1994). Many are also placed alone for long periods in plastic containers called cribs, car seats, or strollers. Detached from the close human contact and touch that characterizes an ideal "pouch" or external womb, their development may be affected. Fortunately, some babies are kept in close proximity to a nurturing caregiver; carried around in human arms or a cloth sling; and touched, caressed, looked at, spoken too, and breast-fed for a year or more.

Humans are extremely vulnerable to predators during infancy and childhood. Parents and adult caregivers provide essential protection and increase the probability of survival. Dependable social relationships are associated with a greater chance of individual and species longevity (Lumsden & Wilson, 1981; Wright, 1995). During adolescence and adulthood, human primary and secondary groups also become important for our well-being (Lang, 2002; Lincoln, 2000; Sinha, Nayyar, & Sinha, 2002; Turner & Marino, 1994; Whitfield & Wiggins, 2003). Our brains are undoubtedly affected by our relationships with other people (Siegel, 2008, 2012a, 2012b). Indeed, the human drive for social connection may be genetically hard-wired and incorporated within our biochemistry. Because of their importance, social support and well-being represent especially relevant themes for social workers—personally as well as professionally. **Social support** includes those "formal and informal activities and relationships that provide for the needs of humans in their efforts to live in society. These needs include . . . a network of other individuals and groups who offer encouragement, access, empathy, role models, and social identity" (Barker, 2014, p. 401).

Social support involves several dimensions. As a social worker, you may help clients identify sources of social support that are satisfying or energizing—because they represent strengths within their social world. You might help clients take steps to increase the size or enhance the quality of their social networks and relationships. Sometimes a client's family members and friends might join you and your client in meetings intended to further such goals. At other times, you and a client may determine that certain people or groups are not now and are unlikely to become future sources of support. In such contexts, your client may decide to reconfigure or restructure selected social networks. Efforts such as these may help clients enhance their social functioning and improve the overall quality of their lives.

Of course, social relationships and social networks also influence social workers. Indeed, the nature and extent of our own social support and personal well-being undoubtedly affect the quality of our professional work, as well as the satisfaction we experience in providing service. The interpersonal and emotional demands of professional social work practice can be exhausting. Social workers who feel personally and professionally supported in their networks and personal relationships are better prepared to cope effectively with the inevitable stress and the numerous temptations that accompany professional practice. For example, suppose you are a social worker who feels lonely, isolated, and largely unsupported by your family members and friends. Might you be tempted to seek some support from one or more of your clients—just as they seek support from you?

Especially when faced with multiple demands of a highly stressful nature, social workers can indeed be affected by our own social circumstances. As social workers steeped in the person-in-environment perspective, we recognize the importance of the social world for our clients' well-being. Let's not underestimate its importance for our own.

Personal and social **well-being** involve health and longevity, knowledge and education, and decent living standards. However, other, less tangible dimensions are also relevant. Our experience of life satisfaction, subjective well-being, and happiness involve genetic, physiological, psychological, and social aspects. Interest in these interrelated topics has grown enormously over the past half century. Several scholars and organizations are engaged in ongoing research related to these factors. At this time, there seems to be emerging consensus around several points. For instance, it seems clear that genetics and biology play a powerful role in individual and family happiness. Both serotonin and dopamine levels in the brain are associated with experience of subjective well-being (Canli et al., 2005; Ebstein, Novick, Umansky, Priel, & Osher, 1996; Fox, Ridgewell, & Ashwin, 2009). Numerous twin studies suggest that a great deal of individual happiness is genetically based (Lykken & Tellegen, 1996; Lyubomirsky, Sheldon, & Schkade, 2005)—perhaps in the form of temperamental characteristics or traits. Indeed, recognition that individual happiness tends to remain moderately stable over time leads to the hypothesis that each person has a kind of a "happiness set-point." Based on their studies, Lyubomirsky (2006) suggests that much of the variation "among people's happiness levels are explained by their immutable genetically-determined set points . . . like genes for intelligence or cholesterol, the set point that a person inherits has a substantial influence on how happy he or she will be" (p. 54). Other research findings, however, raise questions about the strength of the happiness set point notion—for both individuals and populations. Although genetics certainly play a part, it is now clear that many people can and do increase their happiness level and maintain it on a long-lasting basis (Diener, Lucas, & Scollon, 2006; Fujita & Diener, 2005; Inglehart, Foa, Peterson, & Welzel, 2008).

According to Lyubomirsky (2006), life circumstances (for example, health, wealth, marriage, death of loved ones, injury and disability, natural and human-made disasters, war, civil conflict) play a notable role in happiness. However, she also points out that most people show remarkable resilience and, in time, return to or close to their previous happiness levels. This phenomenon is commonly explained by the "adaptation theory of well-being" (Brickman & Campbell, 1971). That is, through habituation, people tend to adapt to changes in their circumstances and regain a sense of equilibrium. In addition, people tend to adjust their aspirations to current conditions. For example, within a few years many lottery winners, at least those who do not spend everything, adapt to their newfound lifestyle and adjust their aspirations upward—so that the "gap" between what is and what they aspire to (that is, their happiness) remains about the same. Brickman and Campbell (1971) refer to this as the "hedonic treadmill."

Like the happiness set point, however, the notion of a hedonic treadmill has also been scientifically questioned. It appears that some people, in fact, are able to step off the treadmill and maintain higher levels of life satisfaction for many years thereafter (Diener, 2006, Feb. 13).

The remaining portion of Lyubomirsky's happiness paradigm involves our intentional activities—that is, how people think and act. According to her, much of our happiness results from our cognitions and behavior. This suggests that we can take action to become much happier than the concepts of "happiness set-point" and "hedonic treadmill" would suggest. Indeed, Diener, Lucas, and Scollon (2006) demonstrate that people can and do influence their own happiness and sense of well-being. Furthermore, it appears that skills associated with optimism and resilience can be taught and learned (American Psychological Association, 2009a).

Despite the relatively large size of the biological and intentional activities portions of Lyubomirsky's proposed happiness paradigm, logic and empirical data suggest that life circumstances—including social, economic, and environmental justice—do, after all, play a substantial role in the well-being of both individuals and societies. For example, Inglehart and colleagues (2008) found that a positive rate of economic development, an increase in per capita gross domestic product (GDP), greater freedom of choice and more opportunities for self-expression, and increasing tolerance toward outgroups were strongly associated with growth in social well-being.

It appears that when societies develop economically, tensions between survival and self-expression values emerge. When a large "share of the population has grown up taking survival for granted . . . [priorities shift] . . . from an overwhelming emphasis on economic and physical security toward an increasing emphasis on subjective well-being, self-expression and quality of life" (Inglehart, 2006, para. 4).

In looking at the social well-being of nations, the United Nations Development Programme (UNDP) incorporates several related indicators in their **Human Development Index (HDI).** The HDI is a composite index of three dimensions and four indicators associated with human development. The dimensions include (1) *health*—as indicated or measured by life expectancy at birth; (2) *education*—as indicated by expected years of schooling and the average years of schooling; and (3) *living standards*—as measured by the gross national income per capita (United Nations Development Programme, 2011).

In 2013, the United States ranked 5th among the 187 surveyed nations on the Human Development Index, neighboring Canada 8th, and Mexico 71st. In 2013, all 10 of the lowest ranked nations were located in Africa. The United States scored lower than the top four HDI ranked nations of Norway, Australia, Switzerland, and the Netherlands primarily because of two major factors: life expectancy at birth and health care. At 78.9 years, the U.S. life expectancy was 3.6 and 3.7 years shorter than, for example, Australia and Switzerland, respectively (United Nations Development Programme, 2014). The U.S. health care system, although by far the most expensive in the world, performs poorly when compared to those of 10 other rich nations: Australia, Canada, France, Germany, the Netherlands, New Zealand, Norway, Sweden, Switzerland, and the United Kingdom. In terms of health care, the United States ranked last overall and "last or near last on dimensions of access, efficiency, and equity" (Davis, Stremikis, Schoen, & Squires, 2014, June, para. 1).

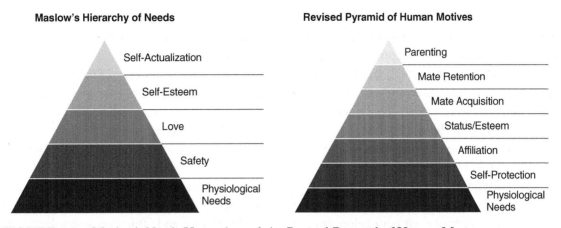

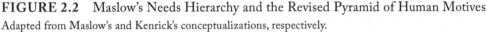

FIGURE 2.2 Maslow's Needs Hierarchy and the Revised Pyramid of Human Motives
Adapted from Maslow's and Kenrick's conceptualizations, respectively.

In addition to health, social well-being is positively associated with income and wealth. However, there is a point of diminishing returns. In other words, once people acquire a certain level of surplus wealth, additional income does not contribute to greater happiness or well-being. Furthermore, at some point, additional money seems to lose its power as an incentive for increased productivity or performance. Executives who make 100 times the income of the average company employee do not improve their performance by 25 percent when the board of directors increases their salary packages by that much. There are many reasons why the incomes of business executives, hedge fund operators, professional athletes, and college administrators grow so much faster and higher than those of regular workers. However, it is definitely not because large increases result in improved work quality, productivity, or performance. When people are already extraordinarily rich, becoming even more so does not make them better at what they are paid to do, and it certainly does not lead to greater personal or social well-being. The richest people are not necessarily the happiest, and the richest nations do not necessarily reflect the highest social well-being (Inglehart et al., 2008).

Inglehart's findings (2004, 2006; Inglehart et al., 2008; Inglehart & Welzel, 2005) may help social workers in our efforts to promote social well-being among the people and communities we serve. It seems reasonable to hypothesize, as Abraham Maslow (1943, 1968) did in his "hierarchy of needs," that satisfaction of basic survival needs (that is, physiological, safety, and social needs) generally takes precedence over higher order needs such as self-esteem and self-actualization or, to use Inglehart and Welzel's (2005) term, "self-expression."

Based upon an analysis of data from evolutionary biology, Kenrick and colleagues (2010) propose a renovation of Maslow's hierarchy of needs[11] in the form of a "Revised Pyramid of Human Motives." Their model of motives proceeds hierarchically as follows: Physiological Needs, Self-Protection, Affiliation, Status/Esteem, Mate Acquisition, Mate Retention, and Parenting. Notice the comparatively greater emphasis on the social and relationship aspects of human life and lesser emphasis on the "self." In Maslow's view, individually focused self-actualization represents the highest level (see Figure 2.2). The revised pyramid reflects the motives of humans as a species. Despite the fact that some of us cannot and some of us do not want to "mate" and have and raise children, survival of the human species requires that many of us do so. Therefore, Kenrick and colleagues

---

[11] Other scholars have discussed human needs and introduced lists (see, for example, Braybrooke, 1987; Doyal & Gough, 1991; Gough, 2003, Mar.); and some view needs more as capabilities (see, for example, Nussbaum & Glover, 1995; Nussbaum & Sen, 1993; Sen, 2009).

(2010) consider parenting—which includes teaching, socializing, guiding, mentoring, nurturing, and supporting others—at the highest level of human motives. In a genuine sense, we can "parent" others whether or not we produce biological children of our own.

Both Maslow (1943, 1968) and Kenrick et al. (2010) recognize the primacy of the basic survival needs (food, water, shelter, and safety). If they are correct, we can expect higher average levels of subjective well-being among peoples who are economically, environmentally, politically, and socially secure than among those who lack security in these areas. The evidence generally supports such a thesis. However, even among the developed or rich nations, there is considerable variation in levels of social well-being (Inglehart et al., 2008).

Such differences may be viewed from a human needs and motives perspective. As intrinsically social animals, we require interaction with other humans. Societies and cultures that provide for the basic survival needs of their population, encourage social exchange and affiliation, and tolerate the free expression of ideas and feelings provide a context for human well-being.

It is now clear that several factors contribute to social well-being. A leader in the positive psychology movement, Seligman (2002) suggests that personal happiness involves three different dimensions (see Figure 2.3): (1) a more or less pleasant life that includes considerably more positive than negative emotional experiences; (2) an engaged life in which one becomes challenged by and invested in activities such as work, recreation, and love; and (3) a meaningful life in which one uses her or his assets, talents, and strengths with others in purposeful endeavors that contribute to something greater than oneself. For Seligman (2002), Lyubomirsky and colleagues (2005), Maslow (1943, 1968), and Kenrick et al. (2010) happiness involves much more than pleasurable experience alone. All recognize the limits of hedonism in their views of sustained well-being. Active engagement with others, meaningful pursuits, and acts of kindness, generosity, and gratitude contribute to lasting happiness as well.

As the study of human well-being has evolved, the relevant theoretical models and evaluation measures have become more sophisticated. They have also become less discipline specific. In early studies, psychologists focused on mental phenomena and individual behavior; sociologists concentrated on social structures and interactions; economists attended to measures of income, wealth, and inequality; epidemiologists examined health, mortality, and longevity; and political scientists explored governing structures and processes. Interdisciplinary investigations were relatively rare and, perhaps as a consequence, measures were often unidimensional in nature. In recognition of these

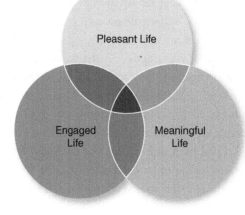

FIGURE 2.3 Seligman's Dimensions of Happiness
Adapted from Seligman's conceptualization.

gaps, the Gallup and Healthways organizations collaborated in the development of an updated, multidimensional survey instrument. The Gallup-Healthways Well-Being 5™ survey addresses five important dimensions of individual human well-being. Each dimension is scored on a scale from 0 to 10. The five elements include:

- *Purpose*: Liking what you do each day and being motivated to achieve your goals.
- *Social*: Having supportive relationships and love in your life.
- *Financial*: Managing your economic life to reduce stress and increase security.
- *Community*: Liking where you live, feeling safe and having pride in your community.
- *Physical*: Having good health and enough energy to get things done daily. (Gallup-Healthways, 2015, para. 2)

These five dimensions seem reasonable. However, let's revise the financial dimension somewhat to recognize that excellent money management skills cannot compensate for insufficient income, savings, and insurance. An enormous burden of worry and stress disappears when a family has a modest surplus of income, some savings, and adequate insurance coverage so that unexpected events do not throw them into deficit spending. Many families live paycheck to paycheck—one crisis away from financial disaster. For example, the loss of employment or a medical emergency can quickly eliminate savings and credit. In 2007, at least 62.1 percent of all bankruptcies in the United States resulted from the costs associated with medical illness or injury (Himmelstein, Thorne, Warren, & Woolhandler, 2009).

Once we adjust the description of the financial aspect, social workers may find the Gallup-Healthways five-dimensional approach to human well-being as useful as those of Seligman, Lyubomirsky, and Kenrick for our work with individuals, families, groups, organizations, and communities. The various conceptions may be especially applicable as we engage clients in exploring life domains, in goal setting and intervention planning, in social and program development activities, and perhaps especially in policy–practice intended to promote social well-being. In our efforts, however, let's continue to recognize the power of circumstances and contexts by maintaining our person-in-environment perspective. Well-being is more likely among people who are relatively safe from violence, possess at least a basic level of food and economic security, and live in societies where human rights, free expression, and opportunities for affectionate affiliation are respected and valued.

As social workers pursue our mission of promoting social, economic, and environmental justice, eliminating poverty, and helping others with social problems, let's also keep our own well-being in mind. As satisfying and personally rewarding as our helping activities often are, we frequently observe and commonly experience the profound pain and suffering of others. Sometimes our efforts seem all too feeble in comparison to the magnitude of contemporary social problems. Faced with our limitations, we may become frustrated, depressed, or even hopeless. The quality of our work can suffer and our sense of well-being can decrease. Because social workers expend so much energy in our work, we must find ways to replenish our resources. To "take care of others," we must "take care of ourselves." However, let's base our choices for restorative activities on our knowledge base rather than on popular cultural or commercially induced pastimes. The scientific evidence is now fairly clear: self-centered, hedonistic activities—often in the form of overconsumption, addictive substances, or addictive behaviors—tend to exhaust rather than regenerate our personal resources. Instead, let's maintain a strong and active social life; participate with others in the community; spend time with happy, supportive people; and frequently engage in physical movement of some kind. A brisk "walk and talk" with a close friend can often revive even the most depleted among us.

SUMMARY

Social workers come from all sorts of backgrounds. We exhibit a wide range of personality profiles and social lifestyles. We are attracted to the profession for many different reasons. Our motivations for service vary. Some of us have a strong sense of altruism—a desire to give of ourselves to others. Others have a philosophical commitment to social justice or a better world. Some are motivated by outrage about corruption or violence or crimes against humanity. Some of us are proponents of a particular cause that we hope to promote through a career in social work. Others follow in the footsteps of a relative or other significant person who served as a social worker. Some see social work as a way to continue in a family role, such as caretaker, with which we are personally familiar, whereas others see social work as a way to become a counselor or psychotherapist.

Some of us choose educational programs in social work because we think admission requirements are lower, course work less challenging, and professors less rigorous than in certain other schools or departments. Still others have personal or social problems that we believe might be resolved through social work education and through service to others, or perhaps we have been clients ourselves and identified with the social workers who served us.

In this chapter, you explored several dimensions of professionalism. At this point, you can probably recognize the significance of integrity, self-understanding and self-control, knowledge—including the common factors and facilitative conditions—and self-efficacy, and social support and well-being as they pertain to your own personal and professional lives as well as to those of the people and communities you hope to serve.

CHAPTER 2   Summary Exercises

Reflective Exercises

1. According to the counseling and psychotherapy effectiveness research, the overall impact of counselors and psychotherapists on outcomes is relatively modest when compared with the power of personal, social, economic, and environmental factors outside the confines of the interview room. Use your word-processing program to prepare a brief one-page (250 words) report in which you discuss what social workers could do to increase our effectiveness in our work with and on behalf of clients. Title the report "How We Could Do Better." Save your document file as "Better_SWK" and include it in your Social Work Skills Learning Portfolio.

2. Go to Appendix 13 and complete the Self-Appraisal of Proficiency: EPAS Competency-Based Knowledge, Values, and Practice Behaviors. Then go to Appendix 14 or 15 (depending on whether you are in a BSW or MSW program) and complete the Self-Appraisal of Proficiency in the ASWB Knowledge, Skills, and Abilities. When complete, review and summarize your ratings to both instruments. Recognizing the limitations of these two self-report instruments, word-process a brief one-page summary outline of your areas of strength and weakness. Title the report "Preliminary Self-Appraisal of Social Work Knowledge and Abilities." Save the document as "Prelim_Self-Eval_K_and_A" and include it in your Social Work Skills Learning Portfolio.

3. Let's assume that most humans—including those of us who aspire to be ethical and effective social workers—reflect major gaps in self-understanding and lapses in self-control. Think about how those lapses in self-regulation might affect your performance as a social worker. Then, in a brief one-page (250 words) word-processed report, generate hypotheses about how and why those lapses continue, and then propose steps to strengthen your ability to regulate your

thoughts, feelings, and actions. Title the report "Self-Regulation for Social Work." Save the document as "Self-Reg_for_SWK" and include it in your Social Work Skills Learning Portfolio.

Write-Now Exercises

Use the space below each of the following write-now exercises to record your responses.

1. The facilitative conditions of empathy, respect, and authenticity appear fundamental to the development and maintenance of positive relationships of all kinds—professional and non-professional alike. With whom and in what contexts have you found it difficult to be genuine, convey respect, and experience and express empathy? What could you do to demonstrate these qualities when it is challenging for you to do so?

2. Integrity is an especially critical aspect of professionalism. In what circumstances as a social work student might you find it challenging to maintain your personal or professional integrity? How about when you have graduated and are serving in a professional social work role?

3. Consider the core beliefs about people and the world as reflected in your past and current cultural contexts. Identify three such beliefs that conflict with the mission and values of the social work professional culture. Briefly discuss how you might address these cultural conflicts.

4. As social animals, we humans think, feel, and perform better when we inhabit safe and resource-rich environments, belong to intimate social groups, have regular and reliable sources of social support, and have a strong sense of social well-being. As social workers, we expend large quantities of energy managing our emotions, controlling impulses, thinking deeply, and exercising professional judgment. To balance such energy costs, we require energy assets in the form of social supports and connections. Briefly outline up to three

completely reliable sources of unconditional social support in your contemporary life. Then, identify how you might improve the depth and quality of your current social supports and improve your social well-being.

CHAPTER 2   Self-Appraisal

As you finish this chapter, please reflect on your learning by using the following space to identify any ideas, terms, or concepts addressed in Chapter 2 that remain confusing or unclear to you:

Next, respond to the following items by carefully reading each statement. Please use a 1-to-10-point rating scale (where *1 = strongly disagree* and *10 = strongly agree*) to indicate the degree to which you agree or disagree with each statement. Place a check mark at the point that best reflects your view at this particular point in time. If you're truly *undecided*, place your check at the midpoint (5.5) mark.

1. I can discuss the topic of professionalism within the context of social work practice.

    1   2   3   4   5   6   7   8   9   10

2. I can discuss integrity as an integral aspect of professionalism.

    1   2   3   4   5   6   7   8   9   10

3. I can discuss self-understanding and self-control as essential for professionalism.

    1   2   3   4   5   6   7   8   9   10

4. I can discuss knowledge, expertise, and self-efficacy as important aspects of professionalism within social work.

    1   2   3   4   5   6   7   8   9   10

5. I can discuss the relationship of social support and well-being to professionalism in social work.

    1   2   3   4   5   6   7   8   9   10

Critical Thinking, Scientific Inquiry, and Lifelong Learning

Social workers must possess an extraordinary breadth and depth of knowledge, have access to even more, and be able to understand and analyze a massive amount of emerging information to provide effective, up-to-date services to people facing difficult challenges. The intellectual demands faced by social workers in contemporary practice are daunting. To meet them, we need highly developed skills in critical thinking, scientific inquiry, and lifelong learning. Indeed, the Council on Social Work Education (2015) expects graduates of both undergraduate and master's programs to

(Continued)

Core Competencies

The content addressed in this chapter supports the following core EPAS competencies:

- Competency 1: Demonstrate Ethical and Professional Behavior
- Competency 4: Engage in Practice-Informed Research and Research-Informed Practice
- Competency 5: Engage in Policy Practice
- Competency 6: Engage with Individuals, Families, Groups, Organizations, and Communities
- Competency 7: Assess Individuals, Families, Groups, Organizations, and Communities
- Competency 8: Intervene with Individuals, Families, Groups, Organizations, and Communities
- Competency 9: Evaluate Practice with Individuals, Families, Groups, Organizations, and Communities

Chapter Goals

Following completion of this chapter, you should be able to:

- Discuss the processes of critical thinking, scientific inquiry, and lifelong learning.
- Use critical thinking skills to assess the credibility of a claim, conclusion, or argument; and to evaluate the quality of a research study.
- Recognize logical fallacies in your own and in others' written and verbal communications.
- Use scientific inquiry skills to formulate a precise question and search for, discover, and analyze research studies related to a practice or policy-relevant topic.
- Incorporate the universal intellectual virtues in scholarly and professional activities.
- Assess lifelong learning needs, establish learning goals, prepare learning plans, and document learning progress.

"apply critical thinking," "critically evaluate," "critically choose," "critically analyze," "use and translate research evidence," participate in "scientific inquiry," and regularly engage in "life-long learning" to update their knowledge and skills (Council on Social Work Education, 2015, pp. 7–9).

In this chapter, we explore critical thinking and scientific inquiry, and lifelong learning as additional aspects of professionalism to complement those addressed in Chapters 2, 4, and 5.

▮ Critical Thinking and Scientific Inquiry

Critical thinking involves "the propensity and skill to use reflective skepticism when engaged in some specific activity" (McPeck, 1990, p. 3). Involving "the careful examination and evaluation of beliefs and actions" (Gibbs & Gambrill, 1996, p. 3), critical thinking is "the art of thinking about your thinking while you are thinking in order to make your thinking better: more clear, more accurate, or more defensible" (Paul, 1993, p. 462).

Scientific inquiry:

> involves making observations; posing questions; examining books and other sources of information to see what is already known; planning investigations; reviewing what is already known in light of experimental evidence; using tools to gather, analyze, and interpret data; proposing answers, explanations, and predictions; and communicating the results. Inquiry requires identification of assumptions, use of critical and logical thinking, and consideration of alternative explanations. (National Research Council, 1996, p. 23)

Obviously, scientific inquiry and critical thinking are inseparable. Membership in a profession requires advanced, specialized "knowledge of some subject, field, or science . . . [gained through] . . . prolonged training and a formal qualification" ("profession," 2014). The National Research Council (NRC) recognizes the importance of science and scientific inquiry in the complex and ever-changing world of the 21st century. The NRC (2012) suggests that students in grades K–12 should develop increasing proficiency in the following eight scientific practices:

1. Asking questions . . . and defining problems . . .
2. Developing and using models
3. Planning and carrying out investigations
4. Analyzing and interpreting data
5. Using mathematics and computational thinking
6. Constructing explanations . . . and designing solutions . . .
7. Engaging in argument from evidence
8. Obtaining, evaluating, and communicating information. (p. 49)

Truly professional social workers engage in scientific inquiry and critical thought about all aspects of their work—including the selection and application of theories and research findings that inform our knowledge base and guide our decisions and actions. Furthermore, in our collaborative work with clients, we regularly monitor, assess, and evaluate progress toward goal achievement and use those findings to make adjustments in plans and action steps.

As helping professionals, we have, in effect, agreed to a "social contract" with society and the people we serve. Our knowledge and expertise must be based on more than good intentions or on the opinions of colleagues, supervisors, professors, or textbook authors. As professionals, we must be rational and thoughtful in our pursuit, discovery, analysis, and application of knowledge for use in service to others. The evidence we select cannot derive from personal or ideological bias, prejudice, or superstition. Rather, our evidence base is built upon and supported by findings from research studies and sophisticated logical analyses, empirical results from our work with clients and, of course, direct feedback from clients themselves. We engage in strong critical thinking and consider such findings in light of universal intellectual standards or "intellectual virtues" (Paul & Elder, 2010, Oct., 2012). We must be scientifically minded and critically thoughtful because the validity and relevance of our knowledge base, the quality of our analyses, and the nature of our judgments profoundly affect people's lives.

Most of us recognize that knowledge alone does not necessarily lead to good decisions. Social workers must ask questions about the validity, reliability, and relevance of information that might guide the nature and quality of our service. It probably comes as no surprise to you that the degree of confidence humans have in our own conclusions bears little relationship to the likelihood that those conclusions are correct. Let's repeat that in other words: The certainty that our thoughts are true is not indicative of the truth of those thoughts. We can be 100 percent sure and 100 percent wrong!

"Confidence is a feeling, one determined mostly by the coherence of the story and by the ease with which it comes to mind, even when the evidence for the story is sparse and unreliable. . . . An individual who expresses high confidence probably has a good story, which may or may not be true" (Kahneman, 2011, Oct. 19, para. 13).

Social workers realize that our ideas, beliefs, or judgments are subject to error. We cannot always "believe what we think" (Kida, 2006). Indeed, our brains often "lie to us" (Aamodt & Wang, 2008; Gilboa et al., 2006; Heidler, 2014). As social workers, we must conscientiously remain open to credible evidence that calls our "beliefs" and our "truths" into question. We have to think deeply (LeGault, 2006) and remain open to the possibility of changing our minds (Brockman, 2009) as we carefully consider factors such as risk of harm, efficiency, probability of success, and sometimes cost-effectiveness. We also consider legal and ethical dimensions, and consciously reflect upon the cultural implications of the words we might use and the actions we could take.

In considering the value of information, critical thinkers tend to be adept at:

- Distinguishing between verifiable facts and value claims.
- Distinguishing relevant from irrelevant information, claims, or reasons.
- Determining the factual accuracy of a statement.
- Determining the credibility of a source.
- Identifying ambiguous claims or arguments.
- Identifying unstated assumptions.
- Detecting bias.
- Identifying logical fallacies.
- Recognizing logical inconsistencies in a line of reasoning.
- Determining the strength of an argument or claim. (Beyer, 1988)

Thoughtful reflection and analysis are necessary throughout all phases, aspects, and forms of professional social work. Particularly because social workers commonly address unstructured issues that do not have easy "right" or "wrong," "true" or "false," or "multiple-choice" solutions, we generally engage in complex rather than dichotomous thinking (Berlin, 1990). Ideally, we also engage in "strong" rather than "weak" forms of thought (Paul & Elder, 2012). As humans, we are extremely

TABLE 3.1	Weak and Strong Thinking: Our Own and Conflicting Beliefs	
	Our Own Beliefs	**Conflicting Beliefs**
Weak Thinking	We immediately (almost automatically) recognize and celebrate the strengths of our own beliefs but ignore their weaknesses.	We immediately (almost automatically) recognize the weaknesses of conflicting beliefs but ignore their strengths.
Strong Thinking	In a thoughtful, considered manner, we recognize both the strengths and weaknesses of our own beliefs.	In a thoughtful, considered manner, we recognize both the strengths and the weaknesses of beliefs that conflict with our own.

likely to adopt thinking strategies that confirm our own beliefs.[1] We are unlikely to critique our own views or to see value in those who take opposing or conflicting positions (see Table 3.1).

The notions of **weak and strong thinking** are somewhat analogous to the **System 1 thinking** (fast) and **System 2 thinking** (slow) forms of intellectual processing made famous by Daniel Kahneman (2011).

> *System 1* operates automatically and quickly, with little or no effort and no sense of voluntary control.[2]
> *System 2* allocates attention to the effortful mental activities that demand it, including complex computations. The operations of System 2 are often associated with the subjective experience of agency, choice, and concentration. (Kahneman, 2011, p. 22)

Proficiency in strong and slow forms of critical thinking requires considerable intellectual prowess. Social workers must think clearly, logically, deeply, and creatively to adapt effectively to the wide range of people, issues, and contexts we face. The stakes are extremely high. Social work practice is complex, multidimensional, multisystemic, and extraordinarily challenging. There are few simple issues and fewer easy solutions. Social workers proficient in critical thinking skills are better able to address complex issues and more likely to benefit others. Those of us who do not think critically represent a genuine risk of harm to our clients, our colleagues, and ourselves.

Especially when we feel frustrated, overwhelmed, and ineffective in the face of obstacles, we may be tempted to just "try something" and do so on the basis of weak or fast thinking. We might take some action—perhaps any action—to reduce our own feelings of stress, confusion, and powerlessness; and we may do so without seriously considering the consequences. At other times, we might feel an impulse to respond to a client in a certain way because of our own strongly held personal beliefs, our own passion, or our own individual experiences. Occasionally, we might be tempted to react to a client as we might to one of our own family members—perhaps as a parent might react to a child or sometimes as a child to a parent. Critical thinking skills can provide balance, rationality, and sometimes restraint in such contexts.

---

[1] This process is called "confirmation bias" and often contributes to fallacious thinking and mistaken conclusions. Confirmation bias is common in weak and fast thinking.

[2] In addition to confirmation bias, fast thinking is also associated with our implicit biases—including our attitudes toward those who differ from us in terms of skin color, sexual orientation, or attractiveness. Our implicit attitudes include those that are just beneath the surface of consciousness and play a strong role in fast (System 1) thinking. For example, based on data from Project Implicit, "Most white Americans demonstrate bias against blacks, even if they're not aware of or able to control it" (Mooney, 2014, Dec. 8, para. 1).

Similarly, we may find ourselves attracted to information presented on television, in popular magazines, or on the Internet. We might think, "I could try this with my clients." Be extremely careful. Think critically and inquire scientifically before taking action based on such material. Although some popular information may be accurate, pertinent, and useful, much is untested, unexamined, and false. Critical thinking skills are essential to determine the relative validity, reliability, and relevance of information for professional social work service.

Although all human beings engage in various "thinking" activities, it appears that relatively few of us are highly skilled in critical thinking, and fewer still regularly engage in "thinking practice" in an effort to improve. Paul and Elder (2012) describe six stages of **critical thinking development** that proceed in this fashion: (1) *unreflective* (lacks awareness of thinking problems), (2) *challenged* (aware of thinking problems but takes no action to improve), (3) *beginning* (episodic attempts to improve thinking quality), (4) *practicing* (regular efforts to improve thinking quality), (5) *advanced* (noticeable improvement as efforts to do so become more systematic), and (6) *accomplished* (skillful thinking becomes second nature).

Paul and Elder's critical thinking stages reflect some similarities to **Perry's model of intellectual development**. Perry (1970) suggests that during their educational experience, college students tend to adopt positions within four categories of intellectual development: (1) *dualism*, (2) *multiplicity*, (3) *contextual relativism*, and (4) *committed relativism* (Battaglini & Schenkat, 1987; Belenky, Clinchy, Goldberger, & Tarule, 1986; Moore, 2003, Oct.; Perry, 1970, 1981).

College students often begin their education as dualistic thinkers, whose thinking occurs in simplistic and dichotomous fashion. Things are either "good or bad," "correct or incorrect," "right or wrong," or "true or false." **Dualistic thinkers** often assume that absolute truth exists; there is a valid source for that knowledge (for example, a supernatural being or force, a sacred or authoritative text, or a superior authority); and someone (for example, a professor, parent, employer, or a political or religious leader) has extraordinary access to and special understanding of that valid source. Dualistic thinkers often make claims without providing evidence or arguments to substantiate them, or by referring to authorities or authoritative sources as if they were infallible.

Unfortunately, life does not present in a true–false, right–wrong, or good–bad fashion. Many issues and situations are complex and dynamic. When we approach life's challenges in simplistic, dualistic fashion, we usually overlook potentially useful perspectives and fail to consider innovative solutions. Furthermore, such a lens seriously interferes with our ability to appreciate, understand, and empathize with others.

During their college experience, students often begin to realize that there are, indeed, many different points of view and frames of reference. Dualistic thinking may give way to an open appreciation of multiple perspectives because "anything could be true" or "your opinion is just as good as anybody else's." **Multiplistic thinkers** often make claims based upon an assumption that perspectives cannot, and perhaps should not, be judged by others or by external standards. Furthermore, "everyone has a right to his or her point of view." When making claims, multiplistic thinkers may provide support in the form of statements such as, "That's my view. I have a right to my opinion—just as you have a right to yours."

A major problem with multiplistic thinking is that opinions, positions, claims, and arguments are not all equally valid, reasonable, or relevant. Some claims have such a low probability of validity that we can readily see them as erroneous, irrational, unreasonable, unlikely, or untrue. Indeed, some clearly false views (for example, notions of racial or national superiority) routinely contribute to much human suffering. By accepting all ideas as valid and legitimate, multiplistic thinkers could easily tolerate ludicrous, superstitious, dangerous, or even genocidal positions.

Whereas dualistic thinkers believe they know absolutely what is right and wrong and can readily take action based upon such certainty, multiplistic thinkers may be unable to assess various positions from a rational or scientific perspective and, as a result, may become indecisive and passive. Dualistic thinking in the form of national, racial, tribal, or religious bigotry and hatred can contribute to attempts to eliminate undesired peoples from existence. We can easily recognize such thinking in the Holocaust and the genocides in Armenia, Cambodia, Darfur, East Timor, Rwanda and Burundi, Kosovo, Macedonia, and Sierra Leone. Unfortunately, multiplistic thinking can lead to passivity and indecision in the face of complex and competing viewpoints, and when horrendous crimes against humanity occur. As Edmund Burke reputedly said, "All that is necessary for the triumph of evil is that good people do nothing." Inaction may contribute to rather than ameliorate danger when human beings are at risk.

In contrast to multiplistic thinkers, **contextually relativistic thinkers** realize that different points of view or frames of reference vary in terms of their value or utility vis-à-vis the situation or circumstance. The context influences the relativistic thinker's perspective and judgment. As social workers, we often engage in this kind of thinking when we attempt to understand clients from a person-in-environment perspective. Seeking to understand and empathize, we find value in the experiences and viewpoints of people from various cultures and circumstances. The combination of attention to context and empathic understanding without judgment often contributes greatly to our ability to develop strong working relationships and alliances with people confronting challenging issues as well as those who differ from us in some way. Contextual considerations are crucial to genuine respect and understanding. However, if we remain exclusively focused on the particular people and the immediate situation, we may fail to consider transcendent factors (for example, human rights, social and economic justice, the safety and well-being of children, the rights of minorities, and the ecological health of planet earth) and the long-term consequences of our actions.

As you might infer, one problem with situational or contextually relativistic thinking is its inconsistent and amorphous quality. If we consider ideas and phenomena exclusively in personal and situational terms, others may find it difficult to trust us because we seem to change so much. Indeed, interactions with a situational thinker often lead to a sense of ambiguity about that person's identity. The person seems to change in accord with changing circumstances. In the extreme, there is a chameleon-like quality. We cannot know whether the situational thinker will keep a promise or maintain a position in the face of challenge or during times of stress and change. He or she might readily neglect a commitment, alter a position, or reverse a decision because of changing circumstances. The situational thinker often lacks a general sense of continuity and congruence in the form of a personal or professional identity and a philosophical perspective from which to address the inevitable tensions associated with multiple viewpoints, various and dynamic circumstances, and changing demands. Situational thinkers often find it extremely difficult and sometimes quite frightening to make final decisions and firm commitments, or to take strong intellectual positions. After all, circumstances might change.

In contrast to situational thinkers, **committed relativistic thinkers** adopt a general philosophy with a set of values or guiding principles through which to approach life and consider various points of view. Committed thinkers reflect a coherent identity and a tangible sense of "self." Well-conceived values and principles complement multiplistic and situational thinking and contribute to the development of logically coherent positions on complex issues. By applying transcendent values and principles such as human rights and social justice to ideas, positions, proposals, and intellectual dilemmas, committed thinkers can prioritize, reach conclusions, make decisions, and take action. In committed thinking, value-based principles, the particulars of the situation, and various perspectives are all considered. When conflicts among these aspects arise, committed thinkers apply their philosophically based values and guiding principles along with their understanding of the facts of the situation to reach a resolution. Rather than simply accumulating evidence to support preconceived positions, the committed relativist engages in a sophisticated thinking process that takes into account multiple perspectives, situational differences, and relevant values. This complex, principled thinking process leads to intellectually defensible positions.

On occasion, committed thinkers reconsider their own philosophical frames of reference and may revise certain value-based principles in light of emerging knowledge, experience, evidence, and analysis. When such adaptations occur, it is usually because a higher-level principle supersedes one of lower value. For example, a committed thinker might assign greater value to the principles of honor, integrity, human rights, and social justice than to those of personal security and safety. As a result, she might publicly and courageously advocate for the release of women who are incarcerated solely because they left abusive husbands or girls who ran away from adult men whom they had been forced to marry (Human Rights Watch, 2012). She might protest against the use of the death penalty by the state. Based upon the principle that health care is a human right, she might advocate for universal health care. Or, she might "tell the truth" about her agency's fraudulent practices despite threats that she "will lose her job" if she does so.

As you might imagine, when pressured, stressed, or challenged, humans often experience a diminished capacity for complex, deep, or slow thinking. Under pressure, dualistic thinkers tend to become more fervent in their right–wrong views and multiplistic thinkers become more ambivalent and indecisive. When distressed, situational thinkers often lose their ability to process complex ideas, consider diverse perspectives, or adapt to changing circumstances in a rational manner. Committed thinkers, on the other hand, may be more capable of considering various points of view and situational factors, as well as their philosophically based values and principles in reaching rational decisions—despite the feelings of distress associated with challenge, disagreement, and conflict. A coherent sense of identity and a willingness to reconsider positions based upon emerging evidence may enhance their ability to cope with unexpected demands in a thoughtful manner.

Development of critical thinking and scientific inquiry skills requires familiarity with concepts such as claim, argument, assertion, premise, assumption, and conclusion. Whether a friendly neighbor shares a story during a backyard conversation or a scientist publishes an article in a professional journal, humans commonly express information in the form of an argument. In this context, the term **argument** does not mean a disagreement between two or more people. Rather, "to argue is to produce considerations designed to support a conclusion. An argument is either the process of doing this . . . or the product, i.e. the set of propositions adduced (the premises), the pattern of inference and the conclusion reached" (Blackburn, 1996, Argument section, para. 1).

In effect, an argument represents an attempt to establish the truth or validity of an idea through a series of statements. Arguments contain two major parts. One part, the **claim** or **conclusion**, is the proposed idea or position. Other terms for claims and conclusions are *propositions, thesis statements, assertions,* or *central arguments.* In research studies, claims and conclusions are often called hypotheses and conclusions, respectively.

The second part of an argument is the premise. **Premises** are the grounds or foundations that support claims and conclusions. Alternate terms for premises are *data, support, findings,* or *evidence.* Solid data (for example, facts, results from scientific studies, empirical findings) represent strong evidence to support a claim or conclusion. If the data are weak, they may, in effect, merely represent another claim rather than serve as genuine support for the original claim. An unsubstantiated claim supported by another unsubstantiated claim is not much of an argument.

Recognizing Logical Fallacies

Social workers' abilities to examine an argument, assess the legitimacy and relevance of claims and conclusions, and evaluate the credibility of evidence are becoming increasingly significant because we are in the midst of an extraordinary and continuously expanding information explosion. Information of all kinds and quality is widely disseminated through the popular media, and especially via the Internet. Much of this information is of dubious value. Most of us realize that opinions are not facts, beliefs are not truths, and all information is not knowledge. Many statements—even those expressed by professionals, professors, and other authorities—reflect flawed logic or faulty reasoning and contain readily identifiable logical fallacies. Moore and Parker suggest that a "fallacy is mistake in reasoning" (2012, p. 110). Pine (1996) suggests that a **logical fallacy** "is an argument that is usually psychologically persuasive but logically weak." Logical fallacies commonly appear in the "everyday exchanges of ideas, . . . newspaper editorials, letters to the editor, political speeches, advertisements, disagreements between people, and so on" (pp. 113–114).

If you are alert for them, you can find logical fallacies in journal articles, textbooks, formal talks, papers, and presentations. We can recognize them in our own thoughts and in the words we speak or write. Indeed, logical fallacies appear in every facet of life and from every imaginable source. Although advertisers, politicians, and sales representatives are widely recognized as purveyors of false information through persuasive but logically fallacious arguments, helping professionals also engage in such practices—sometimes intentionally but often unwittingly. Indeed, we suspect that a majority of human beings may be considered **unreflective thinkers** who typically do not recognize logical fallacies in their own or others' arguments. Indeed, humans seem to be quite susceptible to quackery of all kinds (Barrett & Jarvis, 1993), and we commonly accept various superstitious beliefs as "true" (Fiske, 1978; Holbach, Meslier, & Voltaire, 1972; Pandey, 2009; Park, 2008; Rhodes, 2012; Shermer, 1997; Vyse, 1997). Shermer (1997) uses the term **pseudoscience** to reflect aspects of these phenomena. Social work professors and students are certainly not exempt.

Scholars in the field of logic and communication have identified hundreds of informal logical fallacies. In the paragraphs that follow, please find a few of the more common. Notice the two-letter "codes." You may use them to annotate fallacies that appear in various written and oral statements. By regularly using the codes, you can strengthen the ability to assess the credibility of your own and others' claims, assertions, and arguments.

Perhaps the two most common logical fallacies are **confirmation bias (CB)** and **attribution bias (AB).** In confirmation bias, someone seeks, finds, or perceives only those reasons or evidence to support a currently held belief; and fails to look for, notice, comprehend, or integrate reasons and evidence that challenge the validity of that belief. Indeed, confirmation bias is commonly reflected in many college papers as students conduct literature reviews limited to books and articles that support their theses while ignoring resources that refute them. Manifestations of confirmation bias are apparent throughout contemporary society and, perhaps especially, in the political, economic, and religious arenas where simplistic ideology dominates public discussion.

Despite our advanced education, professional people are not immune to the insidious temptations of confirmation bias. For example, a social worker who serves in a psychiatric facility and specializes in the psychological treatment of individual patients tends to "discover" that the "causes" of most clients' troubles are psychiatric or psychological in origin, and that the solutions involve either psychotropic medications or some form of psychotherapy. Conversely, the social worker who helps vulnerable communities organize themselves to seek and petition for greater and fairer police protection, improved schools, and increased employment opportunities tends to recognize causes and solutions that are political, legal, sociocultural, or economic in nature. The psychologically oriented social worker is less likely to search for or discover social, environmental, economic, or political causes and solutions just as the community-oriented social worker is less likely to find psychological or psychiatric factors.

"*Attribution* refers to the way in which people explain their own behavior and that of others. An *attribution bias* occurs when someone systematically over- or underuses the available information when explaining behavior" (Turner & Hewstone, 2009, p. 42). Social workers, obviously, regularly seek to explain the causes of troubling human behavior and various social issues such as poverty, inequality, discrimination, oppression, and genocide. We also attempt to formulate hypotheses about how best to help people resolve problems and address issues. Although social workers encourage clients and others to participate in generating explanations and creating hypotheses, we bring scientific knowledge and research findings into the process. In so doing, we remain aware of our human tendencies to confirm our biases and to attribute causality based on those biases.

Attribution bias primarily involves judgments about the locus of causation (or responsibility) for a particular behavior or phenomenon. In Chapter 2, we mentioned the "fundamental attribution error" which involves the tendency to explain human behavior (especially others' misbehavior) in terms of personal, internal, or psychological causes rather than social, situational, or interactional terms. Indeed, in our attempts to understand or explain some behavior, many of us tend to think in dichotomous terms. That is, we pinpoint either internal factors (personal qualities) or external factors (the situation, context or environment) as "the cause" of the problem. It will not surprise you that we humans tend to view our own negative behavior ("I" and "us") as the result of external factors beyond *our* control; and the negative behavior of others ("you" and "them") as the result of internal factors within *their* control. Conversely, we often explain *our* positive behaviors as the result of internal or personal factors (such as "intelligence," "grit," "work ethic") and *their* positive behaviors as the result of external factors, random chance, or luck in a fashion similar to that presented in Table 3.2.

Some attribution biases are associated with sexism, racism, classism, and other oppressive phenomena. We reflect the **ultimate attribution error** when we blame "undesirable" people for the miserable conditions in which they exist and victims for the crimes committed against them. We might, for example, assert that "she was raped because she wore a short skirt and walked in a provocative manner" or even "Yeah, she said 'no' but she really wanted it." Rather than holding the rapist responsible for his behavior or explaining the violence in terms of social and cultural factors, we blame the victim for the violation that occurred to her. Similarly, we might claim that some people are "poor and unemployed because they are lazy." Rather than recognize the lack of employment opportunities, endemic discrimination of various forms, the enduring effects of historical oppression, and other social, economic, and environmental factors, we hold poor people responsible for their poverty, and claim that unemployed people cause their own unemployment.

Conversely, we might claim that rich people are fully responsible for their own wealth because "they are so talented" or "they work so hard." As a consequence, we might attribute the accumulation

TABLE 3.2 Attribution Biases		
	Internal Cause and Responsibility (Personal Factors)	**External Cause and Responsibility (Situational/Environmental Factors)**
Socially Acceptable (Positive) Behavior	Us "I did it all by myself." "I have special talent" "We deserve credit."	Them "He was lucky to be in the right place at the right time." "The stars lined up." "They get special treatment."
Socially Unacceptable (Negative) Behavior	Them "You made your bed, now lie in it." "It's your own fault." "They're to blame for their own misfortune."	Us "It's not my fault." "I was unfortunate to be in the wrong place at the wrong time." "The system is rigged against us."

of enormous wealth primarily to personal traits and individual behavior. In so doing, we could easily neglect the factors of privilege and other historical and contextual factors—including the fact that invested wealth (such as stocks) almost universally grows at a much faster rate than do wages from labor (Piketty, 2014).

As social workers, we seek to transcend the dangers of confirmation and attribution bias—including the fundamental and ultimate attribution errors—by recognizing our human tendencies toward simplistic, dichotomous, and moralistic thinking. We try to maintain our person-in-environment perspective and avoid adopting causal and explanatory hypotheses that are exclusively individual or personal in nature. We pay attention to both the person and the situation in our efforts to understand.

Although confirmation and attribution biases represent especially problematic fallacies, there many others. Here are a few: *ad hominem* (AH), *anecdotal evidence* (AE), *appeal to pity* (AP), *begging the question* (BQ), *biased sample* (BS), *burden of proof* (BP), *false dilemma* (FD), *personal experience* (PE), *popular belief* (PB), *popular practice* (PP), *post hoc* (PH), *red herring* (RH), *same cause* (SC), *slippery slope* (SS), *straw man* (SM), and *wishful thinking* (WT).

There are hundreds of logical fallacies and thousands of variations (Bennett, 2012; Damer, 2013; Ward, Edwards, & Ward, 2012; Whyte, 2005).[3] As social workers, we must think critically about all aspects of our professional work—including the sources used and the thinking processes adopted to guide our judgments, decisions, and actions. Logical fallacies and faulty reasoning represent genuine threats to the quality and validity of our conclusions. If we recognize our fallacious thinking, then we may take steps to control, manage, or counteract it in order to improve the quality of our decisions and behavior. In this regard, social work professionals are similar to scientists in that every research project involves numerous threats to validity. Scientists, therefore, must be alert both to flaws in their own logic and reasoning and also to the risks and threats associated with the design, phases, and procedures of their research endeavors. Researchers recognize the various threats to the validity of their studies and seek to control or manage those threats to increase the likelihood of credible results. In so doing, however, scientifically minded researchers recognize that even the very best studies seldom yield definitive findings. Rather, they think in terms of probabilities. That is, they recognize that their findings—even when threats to validity are controlled—reflect a certain probability of being true or false. Indeed, when researchers publish the results of their studies, they commonly report the statistical probability that their findings might be due to unknown factors or to "chance." Researchers understand that determining that a claim or hypothesis reflects a high probability of validity (or a low probability of error) is usually the best result possible. Absolute certainty is rare.

Scientific Inquiry

In pursuit of valid conclusions, scientific researchers attempt to control for or manage the numerous threats to internal and external validity and reduce the probability of false positives and false negatives while increasing the likelihood of true positives and true negatives. As Table 3.3 shows, when someone holds a belief, asserts a claim, or proposes a hypothesis that something is true, and it actually is true or valid, we call that a **true positive**. When someone believes, claims, or hypothesizes that something is false or invalid, and it actually is false or invalid, we call that a **true negative**. A **false positive** occurs when someone asserts that something is true or valid, but it actually is false

---

[3] In addition to excellent books on the topic, several webpages provide guidance about informal logical fallacies. For example, "The Fallacy Files" website at **http://www.fallacyfiles.org/index.html** contains an extended list of fallacies (Curtis, 2001–2014). Also see the "You Are Not So Smart" website at **http://youarenotsosmart.com/** (McRaney, 2015) and the "Your Logical Fallacy Is" site at **https://yourlogicalfallacyis.com/** (Richardson, 2015). Finally, find the "An Illustrated Book of Bad Arguments" at **https://bookofbadarguments.com/** (Almossawi, 2013).

TABLE 3.3 True and False Positives and Negatives		
	The Claim, Conclusion, Assessment, or Hypothesis Is Actually True	The Claim, Conclusion, Assessment, or Hypothesis Is Actually False
Belief That the Claim, Conclusion, Assessment, or Hypothesis Is True	True Positive (Valid)	False Positive (Invalid)
Belief That the Claim, Conclusion, Assessment, or Hypothesis Is False	False Negative (Invalid)	True Negative (Valid)

or invalid. A **false negative** results when someone suggests that something is false or invalid, but it actually is true or valid.

These terms are often used in reference to medical laboratory tests. When we provide some blood or urine for testing, laboratory personnel analyze the sample and submit a report containing the results. We might learn, for instance, that a test shows signs of elevated cholesterol levels in our blood. If accurate, the results would represent a true positive. That is, the test indicates that we have high cholesterol and we actually do. If the test shows that we do not have high levels of blood cholesterol when we in fact do not, then the results would represent a true negative. Occasionally, however, the results of medical lab tests are inaccurate. That is, a test might indicate we have high cholesterol when we actually do not. This would be a false positive. A false negative would occur when a test fails to show we have high cholesterol when we actually do.

These same processes occur in social work. For example, suppose a social worker, her supervisor, and a parent all believe that Susie, a 14-year-old, uses marijuana and amphetamines. They base their beliefs (that is, their claims or conclusions) on changes in Susie's behavior, her performance in school, and her social network. However, Susie insists that she is not using those or any other drugs. After several random blood and urine samples are taken and tested by a reliable laboratory, the results confirm that she is telling the truth. The adults' beliefs represent a false positive. They believed that their conclusions were accurate when they were actually false. Susie's statement represents a true negative. She denied that she was taking drugs and indeed she really was not using them.

Another example of a false positive includes a child-protection worker's conclusion that a child's parents are abusive and neglectful when they are actually engaged, caring, and protective. Of course, such invalid claims and conclusions can have devastating effects. Parents wrongfully accused of child abuse—especially sexual abuse—can experience a lifetime of pain and suffering because of the aftereffects of false allegations. Like false positives, however, false negatives can also have disastrous and sometimes life-ending consequences. Suppose, for example, a social worker concludes that her depressed client Jesse is not suicidal when he actually is. When Jesse commits suicide a few days later, the social worker realizes that her conclusion was mistaken. Had the social worker reached a different conclusion, she might have taken assertive action to protect Jesse from his own suicidal motives and plans.

Additional instances of false negatives include claims or conclusions that a person is not homicidal when he actually is, that a man did not rape a woman when he did, that a spouse was not violent toward her partner when she was, that a social service program is ineffective in helping its clients when it actually is effective, or that human activity does not contribute to global climate change when it truly does. Others include claims that human slavery no longer exists when it does, or that the genocide of approximately 6 million Jewish people and another 5 million disabled persons, gays and lesbians, the Romani, and other ethnic minorities during the Holocaust did not occur when it actually did.

In our efforts to increase the likelihood of true positives and true negatives and reduce the likelihood of false positives and false negatives, we must think critically and scientifically about our hypotheses, judgments, and actions. Indeed, social workers engage in scientific inquiry to (1) reduce the likelihood of harm to clients and others affected by our ideas and actions; (2) increase the probability of positive outcomes for people—especially those affected by our services; (3) improve the ongoing quality of policies, programs, and practices in general; and (4) increase the effectiveness of programs and practices that affect our own current clients.

The Council on Social Work Education (2015) expects graduates of accredited programs to "use practice experience and theory to inform scientific inquiry and research; apply critical thinking to engage in analysis of quantitative and qualitative research methods and research findings; and use and translate research findings to inform and improve practice, policy, and service delivery" (p. 8).

Although a single approach to scientific investigation probably does not exist, various **scientific methods** do tend to follow a similar several-stage process with a clear purpose in mind (see Figure 3.1). As Robert Persig (1974) wrote in *Zen and the Art of Motorcycle Maintenance*, "The real purpose of scientific method is to make sure Nature hasn't misled you into thinking you know something you don't actually know" (p. 108).

Most scientific endeavors include the following steps:

1. Recognize a problem or phenomenon for investigation.
2. Review the relevant research literature to learn what others have discovered and to determine if someone else has already investigated the phenomenon or solved the problem.

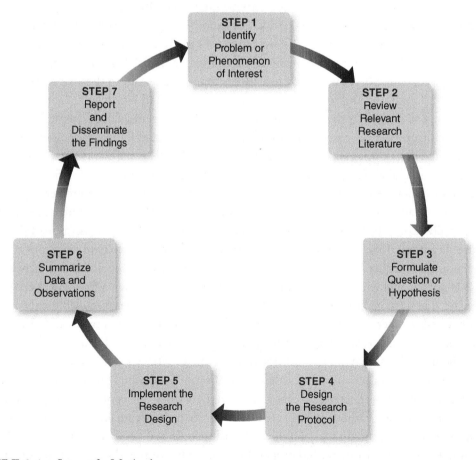

FIGURE 3.1 Scientific Method

3. Formulate a specific research question or hypothesis that captures what you hope to test or investigate. Typically, the question is phrased in an "if A, will B?" or an "if C, then D" fashion. For example, as social workers we hope to resolve social problems such as hunger, poverty, unemployment, oppression, discrimination, or exploitation. We might, therefore, formulate a question such as, "If a government implements a proposed social policy intended to reduce the incidence of a particular social problem, will the incidence among the population actually decrease?" Or, we might prepare a hypothesis such as, "If we provide people affected by the social problem a particular kind of social work service, they will experience a reduction in the frequency, intensity or severity, extent, or duration of that social problem." We could also phrase a research question in the form of a **null hypothesis**. That is, we could anticipate that we will find "no difference" in average outcome among members of a group that receive a service or experience a particular phenomenon and members of a group that experience something else. For example, we might prepare a null hypothesis such as, "There will be no (statistically significant) difference between the average severity and duration of the social problem among members of a group who receive professional social work services and the average severity and duration of the social problem among group members who receive peer support."

4. Design a research protocol to answer the question or test the hypothesis. Identify relevant independent variables and determine the dependent variable or variables that will be used to measure the incidence, frequency, severity, or duration of the problem or phenomenon. Control for or manage threats to internal and external validity.

5. Implement the research design, make and record observations, take measurements, and collect data.

6. Summarize the observations, measurements, and data. Conduct statistical or other analyses.

7. Disseminate findings and conclusions in the form of a report or research paper. Provide descriptive information about the problem, the population or sample, the variables, and the research design so that other researchers may replicate the investigation.

Contemporary scientists and researchers fully recognize that there has never been a single "scientific method." There are several. Indeed, the National Science Teachers Association board of directors endorsed a position statement about the nature of science. The board suggests that all credible scientific approaches reflect certain common premises and processes (2000, July):

> Among these are a demand for naturalistic explanations supported by empirical evidence that are, at least in principle, testable against the natural world. Other shared elements include observations, rational argument, inference, skepticism, peer review and replicability of work. (para. 3)

Although some social workers conduct large-scale scientific research studies on a full-time basis, most of us regularly use skills of scientific inquiry for two main purposes: (1) to search for and locate practice-related research studies, analyze them for their quality and relevance, and translate credible findings for use in our professional activities; and (2) to evaluate the effectiveness of our service to clients. We may refer to these two forms of scientific inquiry as nomothetic and ideographic research, respectively (Cournoyer, 2004; Cournoyer & Powers, 2002). When combined and integrated, they constitute the essential elements of **evidence-based social work**.

Evidence-based social work involves the mindful and systematic identification, analysis, and synthesis of nomothetic and ideographic evidence of practice effectiveness as a primary part of

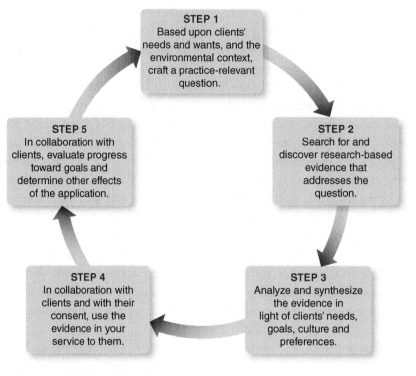

FIGURE 3.2 Steps in Evidence-Based Practice

an integrative and collaborative process concerning the selection, application, and evaluation of service to members of target client groups. The evidence-based decision-making process includes consideration of professional ethics and experience as well as the cultural values and personal judgments of consumers. (Cournoyer, 2004, p. 4).

Evidence-based practice involves several steps[4] (see Figure 3.2). The first involves the identification or creation of a question that propels the process. The **practice-relevant question** should be formulated in a precise manner so that it includes (1) a social problem, issue, or goal; (2) a client or other target population; (3) at least one practice or policy approach or intervention, or an assessment tool or instrument; and (4) an effect or outcome.

The **search** involves (1) identification of keywords and their synonyms derived from the question; (2) preparation of a specific, keyword-based plan about where and how to conduct the search; (3) formulation of guidelines for analyzing and criteria for including and excluding materials located through the search; (4) implementation of the search plan; and (5) discovery and storage of located resources.

The **analysis** involves (1) careful review of the discovered resources to determine their relative credibility; (2) exclusion of resources that fail to meet guidelines and inclusion criteria, and selection of those that do; (3) organization, synthesis, and translation of the selected resources into meaningful practice or policy principles and guidelines; and (4) consultation with prospective clients or others potentially affected by the implementation of a policy or plan.

The **application**[5] involves (1) collaborative decision making with clients or affected others about the goodness-of-fit between the evidence-based practice or policy and their personal and

---

[4] For a more comprehensive review of these processes, see Cournoyer (2004).

[5] See the contracting as well as the working and evaluating skills in later chapters.

cultural values, traditions, capacities, and preferences; (2) adaptations based upon the professional's practice experience and the unique characteristics of the individual, family, group, organization, or community; and (3) implementation of the agreed-upon plans.

The **evaluation**[6] involves (1) collaborative measurement or assessment of the outcomes and effects of the practice or policy (for example, progress toward problem resolution or goal achievement as well as client satisfaction); (2) incorporation of findings to adapt, revise, or change the practice or policy to improve the quality of the process and the effectiveness of the outcomes; and (3) application of the new or revised plans and continued evaluation of outcomes and effects (Cournoyer, 2004).

As social workers search for research-based evidence of policy, program, or practice effectiveness, we typically use keywords derived from well-crafted, practice-relevant questions to guide our investigation. We also identify sources likely to contain descriptive reports of relevant research studies. In contemporary practice, many social workers can readily access online bibliographic databases of journal articles, books, reports, and dissertations. Of course, colleges and universities, and many health and social agencies purchase access to fee-based, commercial databases where the full text of research articles and entire books may be viewed. In addition, many public libraries now include such access for their subscribers.

Suppose, for example, you were about to begin work in a family services program that has the mission of eliminating (that is, substantially reducing) domestic violence in your community. You might first prepare a clearly stated *practice-relevant research question* to guide your search for knowledge about the chosen topic and ways to reduce its incidence or impact. You might formulate a question such as, "What does the research evidence suggest about the effectiveness of family-oriented social services in reducing or eliminating domestic violence among intimate adult partners?" You could then create a table of synonyms and keywords (see Table 3.4)[7] to create subject terms, phrases, or keywords that capture the central components of your research question.

You would then use these keywords to conduct a search of the research literature, including databases such as PubMed, PsycArticles, PsychInfo, SocIndex, Sociological Abstracts, and Social Work Abstracts. Your initial search may lead you to identify the names and organizations of leading researchers as well as the leading academic journals in the field. You can add those names, organizations, and journal titles as keywords for subsequent searches. Once you have collected an array of research articles, you then select those that meet your inclusion criteria. For example, for well-researched topics, you might include only those studies that contain a large sample of participants; include control or comparison groups; adopt random assignment; clearly describe the intervention regimen; use credible dependent measures; explain how attrition was addressed; and conduct analyses that involve the use of relevant statistical procedures.

Fortunately for helping professionals, many researchers and several organizations conduct systematic reviews of the research literature that pertain to topics of interest to social workers. For example, the **Cochrane Collaboration** (2012) conducts rigorous analyses of the research literature in health and medicine, including some on psychosocial and psychiatric topics. The **Campbell Collaboration** (2012) conducts systematic reviews of the pertinent research literature in the areas of education, social welfare, and criminal justice. The Department for International Development (2012) prepares systematic reviews on topics related to international development. The Collaboration for Environmental Evidence (2012) hosts a library of systematic reviews that pertain to environmental issues. The International Initiative for Impact Evaluation (2012) sponsors a database of systematic reviews related to the impact of social and economic development activities.

[6] See the working and evaluating skills in a later chapter.
[7] Adapted from Table 2.2 of Cournoyer (2004, p. 34).

TABLE 3.4	Sample Table of Synonyms and Keywords Related to Intimate Partner Violence

"What does the research evidence suggest about the effectiveness of family-oriented social services in reducing or eliminating domestic violence among intimate adult partners?"

	Population	Social Problem	Social Service	Research-Based Evidence of Effectiveness
1	Adult(s)	Batter, battering	Approach	Best practice
2	Couple	Domestic violence	Counseling	Consensus statement
3	Domestic partner	Intimate partner violence	Family	Effects, effective, effectiveness
4	Intimate partner(s)	Partner violence	Guideline	Efficacy
5	Marriage, marital	Relationship conflict	Intervention	Empirical
6	Partner(s)	Spouse abuse	Manual	Evaluation
7	Spouse, spousal		Model	Evidence
8			Policy	Meta-analysis
9			Program	Outcome
10			Protocol	Promising
11			Psychotherapy	Research
12			Social work	Standard
13			Strategy	Study
14			Technique	Trial
15			Therapy	
16			Treatment	

The **Evidence for Policy and Practice Information and Coordinating Centre (EPPI)** offers guidance, training, and support to researchers and research consumers; conducts systematic reviews; refines methodologies for undertaking research syntheses; and studies "the use/non-use of research evidence in personal, practice and political decision-making, supporting those who wish to find and use research to help solve problems" (EPPI-Centre, 2012, Welcome to the EPPI-Centre, para. 2).

Organizations such as EPPI, the Cochrane Collaboration, and the Campbell Collaboration carefully "filter" research studies that meet or exceed certain selection criteria. Then, they synthesize their findings for use by helping professionals and policy makers.

In our efforts to appraise the quality of relevant research studies, we first consider the question of their likely credibility or validity. There are several kinds of validity. For example, **construct validity** involves the strength of the relationship between the way the phenomenon under investigation is conceptualized and measured and the actual phenomenon itself. **Conclusion validity** refers to the strength of a relationship of some kind—causal or correlational—between the activity under investigation and the outcome.

Two other types of validity are especially relevant for social work. These are *internal* and *external validity*. We use the term **internal validity** to refer to a research design's capacity to determine that an independent variable caused change in a dependent variable. For example, in the helping professions, researchers and practitioners are interested in whether or not a particular policy, program, practice approach, or intervention strategy actually works—that is, accomplishes the goal of helping the people it is designed to help. **External validity** refers to the research design's capacity to permit findings to be generalized, or externalized, to a larger population. In other words, can we reasonably extend the findings beyond the relatively small sample of participants to the population from which they were drawn (Roth & Fonagy, 1996)?

A research study seeking to determine the effectiveness of a teenage violence prevention program in Indianapolis, Indiana, would reflect internal validity if it could accurately determine whether or not (and, ideally, to what degree) the program caused a reduction in teenage violence in that city. The study would reflect external validity if the findings could be generalized beyond Indianapolis to other cities and towns in the United States or throughout the world.

Researchers generally attempt to avoid or minimize threats to validity. Just as critical thinkers seek to avoid logical fallacies, scientific researchers try to control or manage threats to internal and external validity.

Recognizing Threats to Internal and External Validity

Earlier, we discussed a few especially troublesome logical fallacies and identified several others. We now do the same for the various threats to internal and external validity in the conduct of scientific research (Campbell, Cook, & Cook, 1979; Campbell & Stanley, 1966; Cook & Campbell, 1979; Grinnell, 2011; Grinnell, Gabor, Unrau, & Gabor, 2010; Isaac & Michael, 1971; Rubin & Babbie, 2007; Yegidis & Weinbach, 2002). Indeed, you may see overlap between some logical fallacies and a few threats to validity in research studies. For example, a major threat to validity involves our old nemesis **confirmation bias** (sometimes called researcher bias). Even sophisticated researchers are not exempt from our general human tendency to confirm our own biases, expectations, and hypotheses. Researchers also tend to find what they expect to find and, usually inadvertently and unconsciously, they may subtly encourage or reward participants in the intervention group to change in the expected direction and, thereby, confirm their hypotheses. This threat to internal validity may become an external threat if researchers know which participants are in an intervention group and which are in a comparison group. Researchers' actions to confirm their biases may cause changes among participants in such a way that they lose their status as a representative sample of the larger population.

A second major threat to validity, involves the **selection of participants** and the method by which they are assigned to control or intervention groups. Participants in research studies understandably vary from one another in certain respects. Some may be taller, heavier, darker, or older than others. Some may have less education or less income; some may be introverted, whereas others may be extroverted in social relations. These and other variations could potentially affect the outcomes of the study. For this reason, experimental (for example, intervention or treatment) groups are usually paired with control or comparison groups. When the selection and assignment from the population to the experimental and control groups are random, there is a good chance that the average characteristics of each group will be about the same. When randomization is not feasible, sometimes pertinent characteristics of participants are "matched" so that each group reflects a similar composition. However, when the average characteristics of the groups differ from one another, the researchers cannot determine if the intervention actually caused the effects. The differing characteristics of the groups, rather than the intervention, could have led to the results.

A third threat involves **attrition**. During the course of a research study, some participants may discontinue. They may drop out for various reasons—some for individual (internal) reasons and some for situational (external) reasons. Some participants may become ill or die; others may move to a new location because of a change in employment or life circumstances. Some participants choose to leave the study because they have benefited in some way or perhaps because they lose interest, and some leave because they experience the procedures as aversive, offensive, or harmful.

Attrition threatens the validity of the study because the people who drop out may differ from those who remain. As a result, the groups (for example, intervention and control or comparison) may become dissimilar and nonequivalent or "mismatched." Furthermore, the resulting "sample" may become unrepresentative of the population from which it is drawn.

There are many other threats to internal and external validity in research studies. The validity of research studies may be affected by *history*, *maturation*, *reactivity*, *instrumentation effects*, *repeated testing effects*, *statistical regression toward the mean*, *pretest intervention interaction*, *selection intervention interaction*, and even *causal ambiguity*—where we cannot be sure whether the independent variable (an intervention) caused change in the dependent variable or vice versa (Campbell & Stanley, 1966; Grinnell, 2011; Royse, 1995; Rubin & Babbie, 2007; Yegidis & Weinbach, 2002).

Understanding Research Designs

Awareness and understanding of the threats to internal and external validity aid us in our review and analysis of research studies. Knowledge of various research designs and their comparative strengths and weaknesses helps as well. Many excellent studies are qualitative or nonexperimental in nature. They often contribute extraordinarily useful information about particular problems and specific population groups, and especially how people are affected by various circumstances. They are, however, usually less useful for determining cause-and-effect relationships (for example, establishing that a practice intervention contributes to achievement of clients' goals). Experimental, quasi-experimental, and single-system research designs are usually better for that purpose.

In our search for evidence of policy, program, or practice effectiveness, social workers generally prefer to use findings from research studies that manage threats to internal and external validity, and can reasonably establish a causal relationship between intervention and outcome. Indeed, some proponents of evidence-based practice have proposed hierarchies of preferred research approaches. For example, Nathan and Gorman (2007) rank research studies into six general types ranging from the scientifically most rigorous *Type I Studies* that "involve a randomized, prospective clinical trial. Such studies also must involve comparison groups with random assignment, blinded assessments, clear presentation of exclusion and inclusion criteria, state-of-the-art diagnostic methods, adequate sample size to offer statistical power, and clearly described statistical methods" (p. xii) to *Type 6 Studies* "that have marginal value, such as case studies, essays, and opinion papers" (p. xiii).

In recognition of the increasingly sophisticated nature of contemporary systematic reviews and meta-analyses of the research literature, and their special value in regard to evaluating practice effectiveness, Guyatt, Sackett, and Sinclair (1995) propose a somewhat different classification approach:

- Level 1: High-Quality Systematic Reviews and Meta-Analyses
- Level 2: Randomized Controlled Studies with Clear Results
- Level 3: Randomized Controlled Studies with Unclear Results
- Level 4: Cohort Studies
- Level 5: Case Controlled Studies
- Level 6: Cross-Sectional Surveys
- Level 7: Case Reports (Greenhalgh, 1997)

Contemporary social workers must be proficient in accessing and assessing current research studies related to social problems they address, the clients they serve, and the services they provide. Typically, this means that we must locate, carefully read, and analyze recent research studies in our fields of practice. Technological advances over the course of the last few decades now enable researchers to conduct sophisticated systematic reviews and meta-analyses of relevant research studies (Akobeng, 2005; Bronson & Davis, 2012; Pai et al., 2004). Especially popular as a tool for determining evidence-based and best practices in medicine, systematic reviews and meta-analyses are becoming more common among other helping professions and disciplines as well (Hunt, 1997).

Unlike modern systematic reviews and meta-analyses, traditional literature reviews can easily be influenced by researchers' intentional or unintentional confirmation biases and may not be truly systematic, objective, comprehensive, or rigorous. Influenced by their preconceived beliefs and predictions, traditional reviewers expect to find and often do indeed locate studies and sources that support their own ideas. Resources that challenge, contradict, or refute their views somehow remain undiscovered, ignored, or dismissed. As a "study of studies," truly systematic reviews and meta-analyses of the research literature better manage such threats to validity and, because the methodology is clearly described, other researchers may replicate the review and meta-analysis to determine if equivalent findings result.

One limitation in both the Nathan and Gorman (2007) and the Guyatt et al. (1995) schemas may be the relatively low-level placement of **single-system design research**. The external validity limitations of single-system research are obvious. Social workers recognize that we cannot generalize to larger populations the results of single-system evaluations of our work with individuals, families, groups, organizations, and communities. Random selection from larger populations and random assignment to experimental or control groups are generally impossible in the context of day-to-day social work practice. Therefore, the particular clients that we serve may not be representative of one or more larger populations. Nonetheless, single-system evaluation is enormously meaningful to service recipients and others affected by the work we do. Perhaps more importantly, single-system evaluation can readily be incorporated as a regular, routine aspect of all of our professional activities, and its use can directly enhance the quality and effectiveness of our services. Indeed, several research studies suggest that helping professionals' incorporation of regular systematic evaluative feedback processes in service to others significantly contributes to positive outcomes (Anker et al., 2009; Crits-Christoph et al., 2012; Duncan, 2012). When combined with systematic examination of the research-based practice literature, professional experience, collaboration with clients, and critical thinking, single-system evaluation completes the notion of evidence-based social work.[8]

Intellectual Virtues

In our examination of practice-relevant research, social workers attempt to maintain a truly professional and scientific perspective. We recognize threats to validity, identify logical fallacies in our own and others' claims and conclusions, engage in sophisticated analysis, and adopt rigorous standards of scholarship. Paul and Elder (2012) propose an array of **intellectual virtues** or **intellectual standards** that may guide social workers and other scholars as we engage in critical thinking, scientific inquiry, and lifelong learning. We can consider them in the form of virtuous traits[9] and their polar opposites (see Paul & Elder, 2012, pp. 4–5):

1. Intellectual Confidence in Reason versus Intellectual Distrust of Reason
2. Intellectual Fair-mindedness versus Intellectual Unfairness
3. Intellectual Integrity versus Intellectual Hypocrisy

---

[8] See Chapter 12 for more information about single-system evaluation.

[9] For more information see the "Valuable Intellectual Traits" (Foundation for Critical Thinking, 2014, Sept.) and the "Universal Intellectual Standards" (Paul & Elder, 2010, Oct.) webpages on The Critical Thinking Community website at **www .criticalthinking.org**.

4. Intellectual Sense of Justice versus Intellectual Disregard for Justice
5. Intellectual Humility versus Intellectual Arrogance
6. Intellectual Empathy versus Intellectual Self-Centeredness
7. Intellectual Autonomy versus Intellectual Conformity
8. Intellectual Courage versus Intellectual Cowardice
9. Intellectual Perseverance versus Intellectual Laziness

The intellectual virtues apply to the way we think and learn, and speak and write about practice, policy, professional issues, and perhaps even the way we live our lives. Most importantly for us as social workers, they affect the people we serve. If we recognize that the essential common element of both critical thinking and scientific inquiry is *learning*, then these principles apply to formal learning (for example, academic courses, seminars, workshops, conferences, training institutes) as well as informal learning (for example, self-directed reading of research studies and systematic reviews of the literature; consultation and conversations with colleagues and community members; and work and evaluation with our individual, family, group, organization, and community clients). If we apply both the social work code of ethics and the intellectual virtues to our professional activities and especially to our lifelong learning, our clients and colleagues and the members of our community will almost certainly benefit.

As you consider these universal intellectual virtues in conjunction with the logical fallacies and the threats to internal and external validity, you probably recognize numerous similarities and areas of commonality (see Figure 3.3). Without scientific evidence, logic alone can lead us to reasonable—but false—conclusions based on invalid premises. Without critical thought, scientific evidence alone can lead to unwarranted implications and generalizations, and inappropriate applications. Without intellectual virtues or standards, we can easily lose perspective and, perhaps most important of all, neglect the primacy of the people we serve.

Reviewing Research Studies

When social workers become familiar with the numerous forms of logical fallacies, the fundamentals of scientific inquiry, the basics of research designs, various threats to internal and external validity, and the intellectual virtues, we can usually quickly recognize credible from incredible arguments. When we hear commercials and infomercials or read advertisements about magical pills for weight loss or increased sexual prowess, and magnets or special crystals to reduce pain or cure disease, we

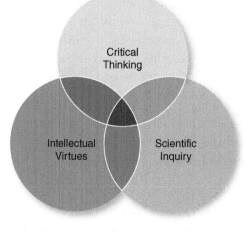

FIGURE 3.3 Critical Thinking, Scientific Inquiry, and the Intellectual Virtues

view them with great skepticism. When we read Web-based materials that lack authors' names or affiliations and provide facts and statistical findings without citing original sources or providing references, we dismiss them as unsubstantiated claims. When we receive an e-mail message from an unknown "legal representative" who announces that a million dollars in our name has been discovered in the bank of a distant country, we do not reply to the message. Rather, we immediately deposit the message in our spam folder. When we hear spokespeople from one political campaign berate an opposing candidate, we remain properly skeptical of the assertions. Claims such as these are easy to appraise—and easy to dismiss.

On the other hand, assessing the credibility of articles that appear in professional journals can be quite difficult. Many articles are theoretical in nature while others reflect the opinions of their authors. Some contain summaries or discussions of studies conducted by other researchers. We might refer to these as **authority-based** (Gambrill, 1999, 2001) as opposed to **research-based**. Authority-based articles reflect the thoughts and suggestions of people who have some status vis-à-vis the topic. For example, a senior social worker who, for 25 years, has served adult men who have molested children may be ascribed some degree of expert status. If he publishes an article that contains his experience-based opinions about how best to help this particular client population, we would consider it authority-based. Similarly, when a client who recovered from years of childhood sexual abuse writes an article about the best and worst psychosocial services she received, she does so as an authority. She experienced the events and is an expert about her own life. Authority-based articles are often extremely helpful to social workers—providing us with perspective, ideas to consider, and often useful anecdotal material. However, they do not carry the same degree of scientific credibility as research-based articles.

Research-based articles are generally even more challenging to understand and evaluate than authority-based, opinion pieces. Authors of research articles often use arcane terminology and commonly apply statistics in describing the significance of their findings. Members of the general public are typically ill-equipped to comprehend the various facets of research studies and appraise the credibility of results. As professional social workers, however, we need to review and evaluate research studies that relate to the profession's mission as well as our own particular service roles and functions, the social problems we address, and the clients we serve. Certainly, many vulnerable populations, groups, and communities might benefit if more social workers actually conducted research studies—especially those about the outcomes of social policies and intervention practices. However, we must, at a minimum, be able to read, understand, and appraise research articles. Because social work endorses a person-in-environment perspective, we must be able to read research articles that appear in medical, sociological, psychological, economics, anthropological, policy and political, administration, cultural, and epidemiological journals as well as those that emanate from our own profession.

Genuine research articles can be distinguished from others by the clear specification of research questions or hypotheses; definition of core terms and concepts; detailed description of the research design, methods, and measures; systematic analysis of the data; presentation of findings that logically derive from the analysis; and discussion of those findings. A central feature of credible research is its potential for replication. If a study cannot be repeated by other researchers, its findings must be viewed with caution. When studies are replicated and similar results obtained, the conclusions achieve increased credibility.

Most research articles reflect an organizational structure that includes some or all of the sections outlined below. These sections are not mutually exclusive. Some researchers merge two or more, or use additional sections to increase clarity and ease of reading.

- Abstract
- Introduction

- Method
- Analysis
- Findings/Results
- Discussion
- References

Before you begin to review a research article, first ask yourself why you intend to read it. Is it about a topic that interests you personally or professionally? Has it been assigned to you by a professor? What is your level of motivation to read and understand the contents? At this point in time, are you able to focus your attention, concentrate, and critically consider the material? If your purpose is unclear and your interest level, motivation, and concentration levels are low, take steps to "get your head together." Sometimes, you can dramatically alter your mental state by taking a few moments to relax your body, perhaps through a short meditation exercise or several deep breaths, and clear the clutter from your mind. In particular, replace any preconceived conceptions, assumptions, or biases with genuine open-mindedness. Remember the logical fallacies and the intellectual virtues. Social workers need mental discipline in many aspects of our professional lives—before meeting with a client, a supervisor, a group of potential funders, or perhaps a legislative committee. By comparison, preparing to review a research article—even a complicated one—should be quite manageable.

When you are ready to begin, realize that understanding and evaluating research articles takes time and patience (Greenhalgh, 2001). Many studies require several readings to comprehend the contents and recognize their strengths and weaknesses. Keshav (2007) recommends a three-pass approach. However, as busy social work students and practicing professionals, two readings may be all we can manage.

First Reading

First, read the title, abstract, and information about the author. Make note of the author's discipline, organizational affiliation, and contact information. Notice if any conflicts of interest are mentioned. For example, a researcher may be funded by a company, foundation, or governmental agency; or may be employed by or receive funds from a source that could be affected by the results of the study. In addition to financial and status conflicts, all of us also have implicit conflicts of interest. For example, a medical researcher benefits when a new diagnostic entity—for which a prescription drug or a clinical procedure may be applied—is "discovered." Similarly, social workers benefit when a social problem—for which social services may be needed—is publicized. In both instances, demand increases and "markets" for their respective professional services tend to expand, providing opportunities for themselves and their colleagues.

Abstracts involve brief summaries of the research. They are sometimes prepared quickly and may not have been as carefully or as precisely crafted as the contents of the article itself. Recognizing that abstracts may not be fully accurate, we generally refrain from paraphrasing or quoting passages from them and refer to the actual text of articles instead.

Next read the introduction to identify the focus of the article and clarify the research questions or hypotheses. The purpose of the study should be clearly specified so that readers can determine if the questions are addressed and answered, and the objectives achieved. The introductory section should also contain some mention of the type of research study. Determine if the research study is qualitative, quantitative, or perhaps of a mixed nature containing both aspects. Identify the context for the study. Are earlier research studies in the field mentioned—perhaps in a literature review? Is there discussion of some theoretical basis for the goals and questions pursued through the study? Does the study represent a continuation and extension of previous research? Is it a replication study? Does the study make a genuine contribution to the knowledge base in this particular area?

Are key terms or concepts defined and assumptions explicitly stated? What is the quality of the writing?

After reading the introduction, scan the remaining section and subsection headings to gain a sense of the organizational structure. Then, read the section that contains a summary of the findings and a discussion of their possible meaning and implications. This section may be titled "discussion" or perhaps "conclusions."

Determine if the conclusions section fulfills the stated purpose of the study and answers each of the research questions. There should be a logical and coherent flow from the introduction, through the section headings, and on to the conclusions. If the structure is disorganized, lacks coherence, or if the conclusions fail to address the identified purpose of the study, become a bit skeptical. Prepare yourself for some critical thinking.

Finally, examine the references section. Notice the names of the cited authors, the sources, and the kinds of publications. Do the references come from credible (for example, refereed published journals) or more questionable sources (for example, popular magazines, newspapers, or websites)? What is the proportion of research-based to authority-based references? Do the authors cite the work of other researchers in addition to their own publications?

Second Reading

Now that you are familiar with the purpose, research questions, and conclusions of the study, read the article more carefully. Refer to Nathan and Gorman's (2007) six general types or Guyatt et al.'s (1995) seven categories (outlined earlier in this chapter) to classify the research approach. Research studies may occur in many forms and may involve experiments, surveys, interviews, or several other forms of data collection. Once classified, decide if the research design described in the article could reasonably yield valid, reliable, and relevant answers to the stated research questions. Also, identify any potential threats to internal and external validity inherent in the research method and determine if the author addresses those threats. If the design does not fit the stated purpose (for example, a descriptive case study cannot determine that a policy, program, or intervention caused a positive outcome) or if the design and its implementation contain several uncontrolled threats to internal or external validity, become more skeptical.

Many research studies incorporate control or comparison groups, often randomly assigned, as a means to manage various validity threats. Control groups serve valuable functions and may help to identify powerful **placebo**[10] effects. Many participants make substantial progress toward problem resolution, symptom reduction, or goal achievement when provided a placebo treatment (for example, a sugar pill or friendly listening). Therefore, before a program or practice can be considered effective, experimental group participants must, at a minimum, reflect considerably better outcomes than control group participants who receive a placebo (Brody & Brody, 2000; Specter, 2011, Dec. 12; Womack, Potthoff, & Udell, 2001). When the sample size is large, significant differences at the $p < 0.01$ and especially at the $p < 0.05$ level are fairly easy to obtain. A drug that is only modestly better than a sugar pill may not actually be especially effective. If participants in a social program or service progress only slightly more than people in a waitlisted control group who receive periodic phone calls from a concerned volunteer, we might raise serious questions about its impact—even if the differences reflect significance at, say, a $p = 0.05$ level.

Control groups that involve an established, proven intervention, rather than a placebo, represent a more rigorous comparison. Their use results in a fairer competition. As social workers, we look

---

[10] *Placebo* refers to a positive effect that follows provision of an inert or neutral intervention. On the other hand, *nocebo* refers to a negative effect following such a provision.

for psychosocial programs, practices, and policies that are both superior to placebo and, whenever possible, better than at least one strong alternative intervention.

Although they lack control group comparisons, single-system ($N = 1$, single-case, or single-subject) studies are extremely useful for individual social workers who genuinely want evaluative feedback from and about the clients they serve. Clients are more likely to improve when professional helpers formally and systematically seek such feedback (Anker et al., 2009; Crits-Christoph et al., 2012; Lambert & Shimokawa, 2011). When a social worker aggregates the results of several of her own $N = 1$ studies, she may be able to distinguish the characteristics of those clients who reflect favorable outcomes and service satisfaction from those whose goals are not achieved and are less satisfied with the quality of service. Recognize, however, that the findings from your $N = 1$ studies, even when aggregated, cannot reasonably be generalized to larger populations of either clients or social workers. Clients are not usually randomly assigned to particular social workers offering discrete services; and, social workers who conduct such single-system studies are probably not representative of "average" social workers. As such, $N = 1$ studies are not generalizable, despite their utility to our clients and to ourselves. Their external validity must be questioned.

As you continue to read the article, consider the study's participants: Who are they? How were they selected? Where did they come from? What are they like? Are they truly representative of a particular population so that we might reasonably extrapolate findings to that larger group? For example, some studies involve only male adults who have been assigned a particular classification or diagnosis. Whatever findings emerge from such studies cannot legitimately be applied to children, to women, or to other men that have not been so classified. Also, recognize that the identification and selection of participants may be based upon invalid or unreliable criteria. For example, many psychiatric diagnoses are of questionable validity. Furthermore, the process by which people are diagnosed may be unreliable. In addition, participants classified according to a particular psychiatric diagnosis may vary widely in terms of the symptoms experienced, their severity, or their duration. As a result, generalization from the study sample to the larger population of people assigned the same diagnosis may be unwarranted.

As you proceed to review the article, examine the embedded charts, tables, figures, and diagrams. Compare them to the narratives contained in the analysis, results, or findings sections. Identify any discrepancies between the graphic and narrative materials. Check the arithmetic. Mathematical errors are not uncommon, and tables and charts sometimes contain obvious errors.

Look carefully to determine how participants who drop out or otherwise fail to complete the study are addressed. Some researchers fail to incorporate noncompleters in their analyses. A few, occasionally and fraudulently, encourage certain participants—those who are not scoring in a desired direction—to discontinue. If such discontinued participants are excluded from the analysis, a study's results can appear much more positive than is actually warranted. For example, suppose a researcher is studying the effectiveness of a particular practice or program in helping clients address intimate relationship problems. Let's say 100 couples are included in the study. Fifty are randomly assigned to a program specifically designed to help couples improve the quality of their relationship by enhancing their communication and problem-solving skills. The other 50 are assigned to meet with a person who listens carefully and empathically but does not identify a focus or purpose for the meetings, does not offer any advice, and does not teach any communication or problem-solving skills. In other words, these couples receive a placebo in the form of friendly and supportive listening. All couples have the same number of 1-hour meetings, at the same 1-week intervals, and over the same 6-week period. They also complete the same before and after measures of relationship satisfaction, and communications and problem-solving ability. The researcher concludes that the "after" scores on all measures indicate that the couples provided with communications and problem-solving skills services made significantly greater gains in terms of relationship satisfaction and communications and problem-solving ability than did the couples who were provided with a good listener. However, as you examine a table containing the before and after scores of the two groups of couples, you notice that fewer than 100 couples are included. You also observe that 45 of the original 50 couples who received "good listening" but only 34 of the original 50 couples who received skills training had both before and after scores. What happened to the 21 missing couples? Did they drop out before completing the 6-week study? If so, why did they discontinue? Did they return to complete the "after" measures? Could it be that a larger proportion of the skills group discontinued because they were dissatisfied with the nature or quality of the service? What are the implications of the greater number and proportion of missing data from the experimental group participants? How does the researcher address the absence of data from 21 percent of the couples? Does the researcher compare only the scores of completers from the two groups? If so, is it possible that the finding of significant improvement of the skills-focused couples over the listening-only couples represents a distortion of the evidence? Could it be that some of those who discontinued early were not benefiting from the service? Might some have experienced relationship deterioration and dropped out to forestall more problems? What if the noncompleters were included in the data analysis? Would the results be essentially the same or might they differ from the published findings? Is it conceivable that the good-listening service might have been as effective as the skills-focused service, and may have been more satisfying to participants?

Authors of credible research articles explicitly discuss the strengths and weaknesses of all aspects of the study, and highlight the limitations of the findings. They describe how they deal with incomplete data and take steps to ensure that the analysis and the findings are indeed based upon all the evidence. As you read research articles that include favorable but exclude unfavorable data, question their legitimacy and credibility. Identify logical fallacies that appear in the narrative and graphic contents of research articles. You may use the two-letter, logical fallacy codes that we discussed earlier in this chapter to note relevant passages. Also, apply the universal intellectual virtues to the material. Some articles—even a few that appear in professional journals—reflect lapses in humility, fairness, integrity, precision, logic, or other intellectual standards. Indeed, a few are, quite simply, irrelevant to the field of study or fail to contribute to the knowledge base.

Annotating

As you complete your second reading, prepare a summary annotation of each research article in word-processed form for entry into a reference management database[11] or spreadsheet. If you enter summary notations into a database, you may easily search for, find, and refer to them later as needed. Suppose, for example, you decide to submit a proposal to your state legislature. You think the state should develop and implement a program intended to facilitate foster children's access to college or technical education. In addition to anecdotal and local demographic information, you would also need research-based evidence to support your written proposal and, perhaps later, your oral testimony to a legislative committee.

In preparing annotated summaries, write concisely and avoid duplication. You may use the following section headings to organize relevant information for your annotated reference database of research articles:

1. Bibliographic Information:
   a. Author(s)
   b. Date of Publication

---

[11] You may create a bibliographic database or spreadsheet with an open source office suite such as those available at **www.openoffice .org** or **www.libreoffice.org**, or commercial products such as Microsoft Office. Specific reference management software products are commercially available. A few of the more recognizable are Citavi, EndNote, ProCite, and Reference Manager.

       c. Article Title

       d. Journal Name

       e. Volume Number

       f. Issue Number

       g. Page Numbers

2. Date of (Your) Access and Review:

3. Author's Abstract:

4. Your Notes about the Research Study:

       a. Type of Research Study (see Nathan and Gorman [2007] or Guyatt et al. [1995]):

       b. Key Terms and Concepts:

       c. Characteristics and Number of Participants in the Study:

       d. Participants Selection Process:

       e. Research Questions or Hypotheses:

       f. Measures Used:

       g. Threats to Internal and External Validity:

       h. Results (Brief Narrative Summary):

       i. Statistical Findings:

       j. Strengths and Weaknesses of Study:

       k. Quoted Passages and Page Numbers:

A database containing annotated entries of relevant research articles may be searched, sorted, and cross-referenced for use in preparing program proposals, formatting in-text citations, and finalizing references or bibliography sections. Of course, such a database is extremely helpful for numerous professional social work functions such as creating grant and research proposals, annual reports, position papers, and, obviously, writing papers for a university assignment.

About the "New" Statistics

Researchers usually present findings in statistical as well as narrative and graphical form. Some social workers, often unnecessarily but perhaps understandably, hesitate to examine statistics contained in research articles because they involve numbers and strange symbols. Although you should refer to research and statistics textbooks for more detailed information, be aware that the probable accuracy of a statistical finding is affected by the *power* associated with its application. **Statistical power** may be described as the probability that a particular statistical procedure will correctly detect a difference in a sample when such a difference actually exists in the larger population. For example, in the context of social work–related research, low power increases the likelihood of discovering and reporting false negative and sometimes false positive findings (see Table 3.3 earlier in this chapter). In other words, if the size of a sample is small, a statistical procedure may indicate a greater difference than actually exists or, more commonly, fail to identify a significant difference despite the fact that there is one. For instance, a researcher may compare the outcomes of two types of social work interventions designed to help unemployed people obtain employment. Within 3 months of the conclusion of the study, it appears that an almost identical proportion of participants in each group have become gainfully employed. The researchers conclude that the interventions were essentially equivalent in terms of effectiveness—because they detected no significant difference between average employment outcomes of the two groups of participants. Unfortunately, the size of the sample was small and the statistical power low. A later study involving a much larger number of participants subsequently determined that one intervention produced much better employment gains than the other. Social workers who rely on the results of the earlier, low-power study might wrongly conclude that both interventions might legitimately be considered for use with unemployed clients. Those who read the high-power, larger study recognize that one approach clearly represents a superior option.

In order to decrease the chances of false findings, researchers often conduct power analyses as part of the planning process to determine an optimum sample size. If we neglect such analyses, we run the risk of finding and reporting erroneous results because a sample size is too small or, sometimes, too large. Just as low-power studies can fail to detect a substantial difference between groups, high-power studies can sometimes exaggerate the significance of a trivial difference. Given a large enough sample, you can usually find something that appears statistically significant—if you run enough statistical procedures on different aspects of the data. Remember, at the $p = 0.05$ and $p = 0.10$ levels, about 5 and 10 times out of 100, respectively, we may expect to obtain significance as a result of random chance alone.

Furthermore, some peer reviewers may not be sufficiently knowledgeable about statistical power to recognize the dangers. As a result, articles are sometimes published in refereed journals despite the presence of false negative and false positive findings. If social workers are unaware of these issues, we may overestimate the credibility of some research articles.

In addition, certain statistical procedures are designed for use with particular types of data, others for application to small or large sample sizes but not both, and some are only appropriate for particular research designs. In other words, statistical procedures may occasionally be used in an improper manner so that any findings can reasonably be questioned. For example, various t-tests can legitimately be used with continuous data but not with dichotomous or categorical data. Similarly, the Chi Square, Fisher's Exact, and McNemar tests may be applied to categorical but not continuous or interval level data.

Most of us have heard the frequently quoted phrase, "Lies ... damned lies ... and statistics." Indeed, discovery of a significant difference between groups or variables does not necessarily suggest that the difference is truly meaningful. As Albert Einstein reputedly said, "not everything that can be counted counts; and not everything that counts can be counted." Furthermore, perhaps inadvertently as a result of naiveté or unconscious bias, some researchers may use statistics inappropriately to produce favorable results. Greenhalgh (2001) identifies the following "10 Ways to Cheat on Statistical Tests When Writing Up Results":

1. Throw all your data into a computer and report as significant any relation where $p < 0.05$.
2. If baseline differences between the groups favour the intervention group, remember not to adjust for them.
3. Do not test your data to see if they are normally distributed. If you do, you might get stuck with non-parametric tests, which aren't as much fun.
4. Ignore all withdrawals (dropouts) and non-responders, so the analysis only concerns subjects who fully complied with treatment.
5. Always assume that you can plot one set of data against another and calculate an "r value" (Pearson correlation coefficient), and that a "significant" r value proves causation.
6. If outliers (points that lie a long way from the others on your graph) are messing up your calculations, just rub them out. But if outliers are helping your case, even if they seem to be spurious results, leave them in.
7. If the confidence intervals of your result overlap zero difference between the groups, leave them out of your report. Better still, mention them briefly in the text but don't draw them in on the graph and ignore them when drawing your conclusions.
8. If the difference between two groups becomes significant four and a half months into a six month trial, stop the trial and start writing up. Alternatively, if at six months the results are "nearly significant," extend the trial for another three weeks.

9. If your results prove uninteresting, ask the computer to go back and see if any particular subgroups behaved differently. You might find that your intervention worked after all . . . (in a small subset of the sample).

10. If analysing your data the way you plan to does not give the result you wanted, run the figures through a selection of other tests. (Greenhalgh, 2001, p. 77)

In addition, some differences may be statistically significant but may not represent a practical difference. For example, let's consider a hypothetical study of men who were violent toward their intimate partners. Suppose that researchers discover a significant, favorable difference between the average rates of violence of a small number of men who completed a 30-day jail diversion program when compared to an equivalent number of men who spent 30 days in jail. They also report that the probability that the observed difference results from chance alone is less than 5 percent ($p = 0.048$). The findings seem to indicate that the diversion program yields a substantially better outcome, in terms of reduced domestic violence, than a month in jail. However, before we fully endorse the diversion program, let's consider the meaning of the p-statistic. The $p = 0.048$ finding indicates that an average difference in domestic violence level between the participants in the diversion and jail experiences would be incorrectly detected (when there actually is no difference) almost 5 times out of every 100. In terms of significance testing, lower p-values are better than higher ones: $p = 0.01$ reflects a lower risk of a false finding than $p = 0.05$ which, in turn, reflects less risk than $p = 0.10$, and so on. However, because the null hypothesis serves as the basis for most statistical procedures (that is, we seek to find that there is "no difference" between two groups or two variables), discovering a difference at a given p-value may not mean much at all.

The hypothetical study mentioned above reveals a significant difference at the $p = 0.048$ level in the average rate of partner abuse when men who completed a jail diversion program are compared to those who served 30-day jail terms. Suppose that the majority of men in both groups discontinued violence altogether. However, two of the men who completed the jail diversion program continued a pattern of intimate partner violence at an average of once per week and two of the men who fulfilled their 30-day sentence in jail engaged in violence at a twice-weekly average rate. As a result, the average rate of violence appears considerably lower for participants in the diversion program. Does that mean that the jail diversion program is clearly superior to a 30-day jail sentence in reducing subsequent partner violence? Perhaps not; the same number and percentage of men from each group continued to engage in weekly violence.

Although research and statistical procedures can sometimes lead to questionable results, the proper use of statistics in the right context with appropriate data tends to increase precision and illuminate findings. Indeed, statistics generally serve to moderate threats to validity and increase the likelihood of obtaining accurate findings. However, significance testing alone does not directly indicate the size of the difference between groups or variables. Therefore, editors of professional journals such as those sponsored by the American Psychological Association (2009b) now require researchers to complement significance testing and the resulting p-values with effect size (ES) statistics.[12] The ES statistics reveal the amount of difference and the direction of that difference between two groups, or the magnitude of relationship between two variables (for example, before and after, or baseline and intervention phase scores). In other words, they reveal the size of the effect. **Effect size statistics** are especially useful when attempting to determine the efficacy of an intentional intervention such as a psychosocial program or practice, or a drug or medical procedure. Therefore, social

---

[12] We anticipate that additional professional journals will begin to require researchers to publish confidence intervals (CIs) to complement effect sizes and significance levels. As an estimate of both the precision and the stability of numerical finding, confidence intervals indicate the probability (usually 95%) that an outcome obtained in a sample-based study also occurs within a given range in the larger population (for example, plus or minus 3 points).

workers and others in the helping disciplines find them more meaningful, informative, and practical than statistical significance tests alone. Effect size statistics can, for example, indicate how much better or worse are the outcomes for participants in one program compared to those in another. They reveal the size and direction of the difference. Extremely useful for outcome evaluation, they can be applied to studies of the effectiveness of policies, practice approaches, and many other factors associated with change-related efforts. Importantly, they may also be used in single-case studies ($N = 1$) of direct service to individuals, dyads, families, groups, organizations, and communities. You may recall that the use of formal, systematic evaluative feedback as routine part of service is associated with markedly improved outcomes (Hawkins et al., 2004; Lambert, 2010a, 2010b; Lambert & Shimokawa, 2011; Slade et al., 2008).

Effect size may be calculated in several different ways depending, in part, upon the nature of the research question, the type of data, and the chosen statistical test.[13] They may be derived from score averages on a standardized measurement, percentages (for example, the percentage of clients who achieve their goals), or correlations. Calculations differ for ANOVAs, *t*-tests, correlations, and regressions. To illustrate, let's assume that we want to determine the size of the difference between a group of people participating in an 8-week Type-2 diabetes prevention program (experimental group) and a group of people who are waiting to start the program (waitlisted control group). All participants are pre-diabetic and at high risk of developing diabetes in the near future. Blood sugar levels serve as the effectiveness measure (dependent variable). In other words, we seek to determine if the prevention program is more effective at lowering blood sugar levels than being waitlisted. To calculate an effect size (*ES*), you could subtract the mean (average) blood level of the waitlisted *control group* ($CG\overline{x}$) from the average level of the *experimental group* ($EG\overline{x}$) at the end of the 8-week program and then divide the result by the *standard deviation of the control group* (*CGSD*). That formula is:

$$ES = \frac{EG\overline{x} - CG\overline{x}}{CGSD}$$

You may also calculate an effect size for each client system you serve if you use before and after (pre-, post-, or follow-up) measures that relate to the agreed-upon problem or goal. For example, suppose a new client comes to you and says, "I'm too judgmental about others. I immediately think critical and negative thoughts about the people I'm with—no matter who they are." After some exploration with you, she decides that she is even more judgmental about herself. She adds that dimension as a problem for work. Together, you hypothesize that if she can first become more self-compassionate, she might then find it easier to respond more empathically and more generously toward others. She agrees to collect data about her daily level of self-compassion on the basis of a 10-point subjective rating scale where *1 = Little or No Daily Self-Compassion* and *10 = Maximum Daily Self-Compassion*. Together, you decide that the self-compassion ratings for the 7 days following the first meeting will serve as the baseline. Following that 7-day period, you will meet again and begin the intervention phase. She agrees to continue to record daily self-compassion ratings throughout the course of your work together and will share them during your weekly meetings (see Table 3.5).

These daily self-compassion ratings may also be displayed in graphic form. Clients seem to understand and value visual presentations of numerical data such as depicted in Figure 3.4.

You may obtain a no assumption effect size (NAES) for $N = 1$ data such as those related to daily self-compassion presented above by applying the formula displayed below. You simply calculate the

---

[13] A Web-based effect size calculator (Wilson, 2012) may be found on The Campbell Collaboration website at **http://www .campbellcollaboration.org/resources/effect_size_input.php**.

TABLE 3.5	Example of a Daily Subjective Rating Record
Date	**Daily Self-Compassion Rating (1–10 Scale)**
Baseline	
2-Apr	4
3-Apr	3.5
4-Apr	4
5-Apr	4.5
6-Apr	3.5
7-Apr	4.5
8-Apr	4
Intervention: Week 1	
9-Apr	6
10-Apr	7
11-Apr	7.5
12-Apr	7
13-Apr	8
14-Apr	8
15-Apr	7
16-Apr	7.5
Intervention: Week 2	
17-Apr	8
18-Apr	8.5
19-Apr	8
20-Apr	8.5
21-Apr	9
22-Apr	8.5
23-Apr	9
Follow-Up	
4-Jun	6.5
5-Jun	7
6-Jun	7.5
7-Jun	7
8-Jun	8
9-Jun	7.5
10-Jun	7

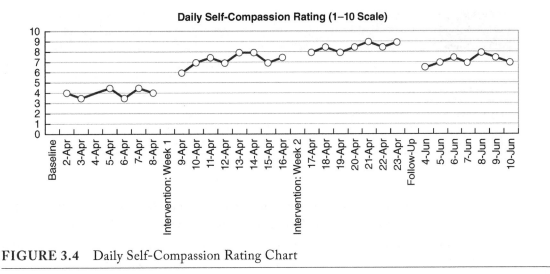

FIGURE 3.4 Daily Self-Compassion Rating Chart

average (mean) of the *baseline* ratings ($B\overline{x}$); subtract the mean of either the *intervention* phase or the follow-up phase ($I\overline{x}$), and divide by the *standard deviation (BSD)* of the *baseline* ratings.

$$NAES = \frac{I\overline{x} - B\overline{x}}{BSD}$$

Let's apply the formula to the self-compassion example described above. During the baseline phase, the client's average daily self-compassion rating was 4.0; her average during the 2-week intervention phase was 7.96; and the follow-up average was 7.21. The standard deviation of the baseline data was 0.41. We enter the average daily self-compassion rating for the intervention and baseline phases, and the baseline SD into the formula as follows:[14]

$$NAES = \frac{7.96 - 4.0}{0.41}$$

$$NAES = 9.66$$

When the average intervention phase rating is compared to the average baseline rating, the result is a "no assumptions effect size" (NAES) of 9.66.[15] We could also consider the follow-up phase average daily self-compassion rating of 7.21 in relation to the baseline average to obtain an NAES of 7.83. Note that the follow-up ratings were, on average, somewhat lower than the intervention phase ratings but remained higher than the baseline ratings. Nonetheless, the effect sizes obtained when baseline data are compared to both intervention and follow-up data reflect extraordinarily large changes in the positive direction. The fact that none of the intervention or follow-up phase ratings overlap with any of the baseline ratings indicates an unusually strong effect.

There are several different ES statistics. A simple and straightforward approach is to report the size of the effect in percentage terms. Suppose, for example, you serve as a social worker in an inner-city high school. Fewer than half of the students graduate. You plan and implement a pilot

---

[14] A Web-based tool for managing and displaying $N = 1$ outcome data, and for calculating no assumption effect sizes is available at **http://www.interventioncentral.org/tools/chart_dog_graph_maker**.

[15] This unusually high effect size is the result of the small number of data points, the small range and limited variation in ratings, and especially the small standard deviation in the baseline phase. In general, you may expect effect sizes to fall in the 0 to 3.0 range.

TABLE 3.6	Illustrative Example of Effect Size in Percentage Term (Simulated Data)
	Graduates
Innovative Program	19 (76%)
Usual Services	8 (32%)
Effect Size	44%

study intervention to increase the graduation rates of at-risk students. You identify 50 of the most at-risk students and randomly assign half to an innovative program while the other half receives the usual services.[16] As illustrated in Table 3.6, 19 of the 25 students (76 percent) in the experimental program graduate while 8 of the others (32 percent) do. We can conclude that the experimental program reflects a 44 percent effect size (76 percent minus 32 percent). In other words, the experimental program yielded a 44 percent higher graduation rate than did the usual services afforded to at-risk students—a substantial effect indeed!

The most widely used ES statistics do not directly involve percentages. Cohen's *d*, Hedges *g*, and Glass's Δ derive from averages and standard deviations. A Cohen's *d* of 0.0 suggests that there is no difference. Cohen cautions that the meaning of *d* should be viewed in relation to the particular context of a study and argues against rigid interpretative rules. Nonetheless, he offers these general guidelines for effect sizes based upon mean differences: *d* = 0.2 suggests a small effect equivalent to a difference of about one-fifth of one standard deviation; *d* = 0.5 indicates a moderate effect equivalent to a difference in the range of one-half a SD; and *d* = 0.8 represents a large effect equivalent to a difference of about four-fifths of a SD (Cohen, 1988).

Suppose, for example, we conduct a study comparing the outcomes of clients served by social workers who adopt a strengths-based practice model (the experimental condition) with those served by social workers who adopt a problem-focused model (the comparison condition). Let's assume that we apply Cohen's effect size procedure to these hypothetical outcome data and obtain an effect size of *d* = 2.0. If the study is credible, we would have to conclude that the former approach is considerably more effective than the latter (at least for clients in the study). Indeed, *d* = 2.0 indicates that the average outcome score of the strengths-based group is two standard deviations above that of the problem-focused group. If valid, that would indeed represent a very large difference!

Several other effect size–related statistics are beginning to appear in journals that publish research articles about the impact or effectiveness of various events, conditions, or interventions. These include the *number needed to treat* (NNT), *relative risk* (RR), and *odds ratio* (OR). Effect size, number needed to treat, relative risk, and odds ratio all reflect, in somewhat different ways, the size and direction of difference. Such statistical estimates are extremely useful for the purposes of informing us and our clients about the likelihood of a positive outcome from a particular treatment or service. In addition, they can help decision makers distinguish more effective from less effective policies and programs. However, there is also another, extremely important benefit. When incorporated in systematic reviews of the research literature, effect size statistics enable researchers to combine the statistical findings of multiple studies through meta-analyses (Glass, 1976).

When researchers conduct a genuine systematic review, they collate all empirical evidence that fits pre-specified eligibility criteria in order to answer a specific research question. They adopt

---

[16] In intervention research, "usual services" may be termed "treatment as usual" or TAU.

explicit, systematic methods that are selected with a view to minimizing bias, thus providing more reliable findings from which conclusions can be drawn and decisions made (Antman, Lau, Kupelnick, Mosteller, & Chalmers, 1992; Oxman & Guyatt, 1993). The key characteristics of a **systematic review** are:

- A clearly stated set of objectives with pre-defined eligibility criteria for studies.
- An explicit, reproducible methodology.
- A systematic search that attempts to identify all studies that would meet the eligibility criteria.
- An assessment of the validity of the findings of the included studies, for example through the assessment of risk of bias.
- A systematic presentation, and synthesis, of the characteristics and findings of the included studies. (Higgins & Green, 2011, Section 1.2.2 What is a systematic review?)

Once all the research studies that meet the quality criteria are included in the systematic review of the literature, statistical methods are used to combine and summarize the findings. "**Meta-analysis** is the use of statistical methods to combine results of individual studies. . . . By statistically combining the results of similar studies we can improve the precision of our estimates of treatment effect, and assess whether treatment effects are similar in similar situations" (The Cochrane Collaboration, 2002).

Meta-analyses use the figures and statistics presented in multiple research studies to calculate effect sizes. Suppose, for example, that your systematic review of the research literature yields several high-quality studies that meet your inclusion criteria. If the studies contain group means, d-statistics, means t-scores, Z-scores, F-statistics, r-correlations, or p-values, along with standard deviations and the number of participants in the treatment and control or comparison groups, then those values may be converted to a common statistic for combination and meta-analysis (Hunt, 1997).

Rather than simply assuming that each high-quality study is equivalent in credibility and value, meta-analytic procedures incorporate a weighting process. Larger studies of greater power are weighted proportionately higher than smaller studies to compensate for the error risks associated with low-power research investigations. Additional processes account for variability in the reliability of measures and other factors. The resulting meta-analytic statistical procedures yield weighted mean correlations, weighted standardized means, or other overall effect size estimates.

For example, Cabral and Smith (2011) completed a meta-analytic study of research studies about the matching of clients and professional helpers in terms of race or ethnicity. In particular, they investigated clients' preferences about helpers' race or ethnicity, perceptions about helpers' of their own versus another race or ethnicity, and service outcomes. Fifty-two studies met their inclusion criteria for the meta-analysis about racial preference. Using Cohen's procedure, they found an average effect size of $d = 0.63$. The results suggest that clients, in general, tend to reflect a moderately strong preference for helpers of their own race or ethnicity. Cabral and Smith also included 81 studies of clients' perceptions about their professional helpers. That meta-analysis yielded an average effect size of $d = 0.32$—suggesting a modest tendency of clients, on average, to perceive professional helpers of their own race or ethnicity slightly more positively than others. Interestingly, in terms of service effectiveness, their meta-analysis of 53 studies of client outcomes produced an average effect size of $d = 0.09$. This suggests that, in general, the mental health outcomes of clients who received services from professional helpers of their own race or ethnicity were not noticeably superior to those who received services from helpers of a different race or ethnicity. In addition, the researchers observed that the consequences of matching clients and professional helpers on racial or ethnic dimensions were highly variable. For instance, the average effect sizes for all three dimensions (client preference for race or ethnicity of helper, client perception of helper, and mental health services outcomes) among those studies involving African Americans were considerably higher than those studies involving participants from other racial and ethnic groups. These findings highlight the importance of context in understanding human behavior. We can readily understand how some African Americans might, at least initially, be somewhat suspicious about the motives of white professionals.

Lifelong Learning

Knowledge is expanding and changing at a speed never before known in human history. Some of what we considered true 10 years ago we now know to be false. Other "accepted truths" rapidly become obsolete as researchers continue their studies and advance the professional knowledge base. Given the pace of growth in research-based knowledge, social workers are pressed to stay abreast of the most recent studies. At the same time, we yearn for additional knowledge to help us better serve others. In our efforts to contribute, most social workers recognize that personally and collectively, we always need to know a great deal more than we currently do—despite the ever-expanding knowledge explosion.

Much of the world and most of North American society are well into the "third wave" (Toffler, 1983), when knowledge and learning attain extraordinary value. As a form of wealth and power, access to high-quality, relevant knowledge is distributed unevenly among societies and populations. Constituting another kind of inequality, "haves" can be distinguished from "have nots" by the ease and extent to which they can access current, relevant, and accurate knowledge, and the facility with which they can adapt and improve based on it. To paraphrase Herbert Gerjuoy's suggestion, "Tomorrow's illiterate will not be . . . (those) . . . who can't read; . . . (they will be those who have) . . . not learned how to learn" (quoted in Toffler, 1971, p. 414).

Davis and Botkin (1994) suggest that the total knowledge in the world, on average, doubles about every 7 years. In some fields, the doubling of knowledge occurs even more rapidly. As many social workers realize from the rapid obsolescence of their personal computers and cell phones, the rate of change in the technological sciences is simply astonishing. However, the information explosion is hardly limited to high technology (Gleick, 2011). It affects the helping professions as well. As a social worker, you might wonder how much of what you now believe to be true is actually false. You might ask how much of what you learned 1 or 2 years ago is now obsolete. We may reasonably anticipate that more and more of what you now "know" will become less and less relevant, valid, and applicable with each passing year.

Unless social workers continuously and aggressively pursue additional learning, and think critically about the information we access, we will inexorably fall further and further behind the knowledge curve. If we do not continue to learn throughout our social work careers, clients could suffer because of our ignorance. We simply must find ways and means to keep current during this never-ending, always expanding knowledge explosion. If we are to serve our clients effectively, up-to-date, valid, and reliable knowledge is vital. We must become "critically thinking, learning people" within the context of "learning organizations," "learning communities," and "learning societies" (Cantle, 2000; Gould & Baldwin, 2004; Senge, 1992). One way to emphasize and track our growth and development is through the preparation and maintenance of a learning portfolio for use throughout our professional careers (Cournoyer & Stanley, 2002). As Hoffer (1973) suggests, "In a time of drastic change, it is the *learners* who inherit the future. The *learned* usually find themselves equipped to live in a world that no longer exists" (p. 22).

In addition to the many personal benefits that result from lifelong learning and the use of a professional learning portfolio, social workers are ethically obligated to improve their knowledge and skills throughout their careers. Indeed, the Code of Ethics of the National Association of Social Workers (2008) includes several ethical principles that reference this responsibility. Consider these excerpts:

- Social workers should provide services and represent themselves as competent only within the boundaries of their education, training, license, certification, consultation received, supervised experience, or other relevant professional experience (Section 1.04.a).
- Social workers should provide services in substantive areas or use intervention techniques or approaches that are new to them only after engaging in appropriate study, training, consultation, and supervision from people who are competent in those interventions or techniques (Section 1.04.b).
- When generally recognized standards do not exist with respect to an emerging area of practice, social workers should exercise careful judgment and take responsible steps (including appropriate education, research, training, consultation, and supervision) to ensure the competence of their work and to protect clients from harm (Section 1.04.c).
- Social workers should accept responsibility or employment only on the basis of existing competence or the intention to acquire the necessary competence (Section 4.01.a).
- Social workers should strive to become and remain proficient in professional practice and the performance of professional functions. Social workers should critically examine and keep current with emerging knowledge relevant to social work. Social workers should routinely review the professional literature and participate in continuing education relevant to social work practice and social work ethics (Section 4.01.b).
- Social workers should base practice on recognized knowledge, including empirically based knowledge, relevant to social work and social work ethics (Section 4.01.c).

The ongoing knowledge explosion and the related changes in information and technology are dramatically affecting social workers, our clients, and communities and societies throughout the world. Combined with scientific inquiry and critical thinking, lifelong learning helps us to grow continuously, develop, and improve so that we may respond effectively and serve clients competently throughout our professional careers. The most effective social workers engage in an ongoing search for valid and relevant knowledge to inform and guide our helping efforts. In effect, we dedicate ourselves to continuous, lifelong learning in formal and informal, professional and nonprofessional, and planned and unplanned contexts.

Preparing and Implementing Learning Goals and Plans

Following graduation and licensure, social workers routinely participate in continuing professional development and related educational activities. Indeed, our social work ethics obligate us to engage in ongoing professional development to maintain or enhance our knowledge and skills. In many locales, social workers must participate in regular continuing professional education to maintain their license to practice.

Much lifelong learning can occur through professional workshops, conferences, institutes, and seminars. Some social workers take relevant college or university courses to enhance their professional development and, of course, many engage in active, independent learning based on their own goals and plans.

Specifying your own **learning goal** represents the first step in a three-step process which also involves developing and then implementing a learning plan, and evaluating and documenting progress toward goal achievement. Suppose, for example, that you have completed your formal social work education and now serve as a professional social worker in some part of the world. You have recently taken a new position that requires you to work with members of a specific ethnic minority

TABLE 3.7	Learning Goal and Plans for Learning and Evaluation
Learning Goal	
Learning Plan	
Evaluation and Documentation Plan	

group about which you know almost nothing and with whom you have no experience. You might first use a word-processing program to create a table similar to that shown in Table 3.7, then use that table to record a specific learning goal that relates to the identified ethnic minority group, outline your plan to pursue that goal, and identify a tangible means to evaluate and document progress toward the achievement of your learning goal.

We identify learning goals based upon an assessment of our learning wants and needs. A common impetus involves the professional roles and functions we aspire to fulfill in our service as social workers. For example, a social worker might be assigned to supervise four or five other professionals. Inexperienced in supervision, she might establish a goal to learn about contemporary supervision theories and practices. Another typical motivation for learning involves our practice experiences. For example, based upon measures of both outcome and client satisfaction, a social worker might recognize that he is quite ineffective in his efforts to help a certain category of clients (for example, members of a particular age, racial, or ethnic group or those affected by a particular problem). Wanting to better help clients, he decides to learn about evidence-based practices for service to that particular group of clients.

Careful preparation of learning goals according to certain educational standards tends to improve the quality of our plans as well as increase the likelihood of goal accomplishment. When we write learning goals that are descriptive and contain within them a clear action verb and a tangible outcome indicator, we increase the probability of both pursuing and achieving those goals. Furthermore, we become better able to demonstrate or "prove" that we have indeed accomplished them—as documented by our outcome indicators and incorporated in our professional learning portfolios.

For instance, suppose I say, "I want to learn about human trafficking" and establish that as my learning goal. It is a very timely and important topic indeed. Even a brief review of the research literature yields shocking information about the buying and selling of human beings throughout the world. Yes, slavery continues here in the 21st century.

Once I identify the topic, I might search for relevant materials and do some reading about human trafficking. However, I might do so in a casual way that raises questions about the nature and credibility of the resources I find. My efforts might not produce tangible evidence of learning or I might gradually lose interest in my learning goal.

On the other hand, suppose I establish this as my learning goal:

Within 30 days from today's date, I will complete a systematic search of the professional journals for credible research articles about the characteristics, needs, problems, and issues faced by trafficked humans from at least one region of the world; review, analyze, and synthesize the high-quality, relevant research literature; and prepare and distribute a 10-page summary report of my learning.

This version of an individualized learning goal is more specific and descriptive, and contains precise action verbs such as *search, review, analyze, synthesize, prepare,* and *distribute.* It also contains both a time frame and a tangible outcome indicator in the form of the 10-page report. The report documents the nature, extent, and quality of the learning. We can refer to the document in the future to refresh our memories or, importantly, to serve as a basis for additional learning, and

TABLE 3.8	Brief Descriptions of Bloom's Taxonomy of Cognitive Learning Objectives

1. **Recollection.** The ability to recall is the basic level of learning and refers simply to the ability to remember material such as facts and basic theoretical terms and concepts.

2. **Comprehension.** The ability to comprehend refers to an understanding of the material. This is often demonstrated by providing an explanation, summary, or interpretation of the material. Comprehension implies recognition or recollection. Therefore, when we pursue comprehension-level learning, we presume that recollection-level learning either is a part of that process or has previously occurred.

3. **Application.** The ability to apply knowledge refers to use of the material in a particular situation. In social work, this might be demonstrated through the use of rules, methods, and principles in applying a skill in service to or for a client. Application implies comprehension (and recollection). Therefore, when we pursue application-level learning, we presume that comprehension-level learning either is a part of the process or has previously occurred. In other words, we cannot apply something that we cannot recollect and do not understand.

4. **Analysis.** The ability to analyze involves the careful identification and examination of the various elements of the material. Relationships among and between components are carefully considered in terms of organizational structure and internal coherence. Although we might argue that application sometimes involves deep thought, analysis represents the first substantive critical thinking dimension contained within Bloom's taxonomy. Like application, analysis cannot occur without recollection and understanding. That is, we cannot analyze something that we do not remember and do not understand. In addition, analysis often requires understanding of how knowledge has been applied. For example, we might analyze how a policy, program, service, or practice has been implemented with an individual, family, group, organization, or community.

5. **Synthesis.** The ability to synthesize includes pulling together elements in a new way to form an innovative structure. The creation of a new conceptual model could be a form of synthesis. Synthesis represents the second critical thinking dimension contained within Bloom's taxonomy. Synthesis typically involves analysis. In the cognitive sense, synthesis could not proceed until or unless an analysis was complete. Therefore, when we aspire to synthesis-level learning, we presume that analysis-level learning is part of the process or has previously occurred. For example, we could not reasonably propose changes (a form of synthesis) to a current policy, program, service, or practice without a careful, systematic analysis.

6. **Evaluation.** The ability to evaluate involves the determination of the relative value of knowledge for a defined purpose. Typically, this would include the creation, adoption, or adaptation of evaluative criteria as an application tool followed by its use in measuring or evaluating phenomena. Evaluation represents the third critical thinking dimension contained within Bloom's taxonomy. Evaluation, then, involves analysis and synthesis. In the cognitive sense, evaluation could not proceed until or unless an analysis was complete. A new or adapted evaluation tool could not be created without synthesis. Therefore, when we pursue evaluation-level learning, we presume that analysis and synthesis have or will occur. It is difficult to imagine a situation where a valid, reliable, and relevant evaluation process could proceed before or without careful analysis and synthesis.

for inclusion in our professional portfolios. For instance, based upon accomplishment of this initial learning goal, I might subsequently want to learn how best to provide culturally sensitive and effective social work services to trafficked humans; or to learn about policy and program initiatives that reflect evidence of effectiveness in reducing the extent of human trafficking.

Careful preparation of learning objectives that contain precise, descriptive action verbs tend to promote learning and advance its evaluation. In academic settings, Bloom's Taxonomy of Cognitive Learning Objectives (see Table 3.8) is widely used as a guide for the formulation of learning objectives (Bloom & Krathwohl, 1956).[17] If you examine the learning objectives contained in the required course syllabi of most accredited BSW or MSW curriculums, you would probably observe

---

[17] Anderson and Krathwohl (2001) offer a revised version of the taxonomy that clarifies the original in the following fashion: (1) *Remembering*, (2) *Understanding*, (3) *Applying*, (4) *Analyzing*, (5) *Evaluating*, and (6) *Creating*. Marzano (2001) proposes

a progression toward higher levels of Bloom's Taxonomy over time. Early courses (for example, first semester or year) often place greater emphasis on *recollection, comprehension,* and some *application* whereas later courses tend to emphasize *application* and the critical thinking dimensions of *analysis, synthesis,* and *evaluation.*

In addition, the test items contained in the nationally standardized social work licensing exams sponsored by the Association of Social Work Boards (ASWB) are prepared according to **Bloom's taxonomy**. Because of its nature as a high-stakes examination, most of the items correspond to the application, analysis, synthesis, or evaluation levels of cognitive learning. Few items require applicants to recall or comprehend relevant knowledge without also applying, analyzing, synthesizing, or evaluating it for social work practice.

Although commonly used for academic or test-development purposes, we can also use Bloom's taxonomy to help us formulate our own, individualized personal and professional learning goals. You might phrase your learning goals to include a clear action verb that corresponds to a desired level of Bloom's taxonomy, a time frame, and a product that documents your learning. Table 3.9[18] contains a list of several action verbs that you might consider.

Planning for goal achievement becomes quite straightforward if we formulate our learning goals precisely so that they include an action verb, a time frame, and a tangible product or performance that can be used for evaluation of and evidence for goal accomplishment. An early step involves identifying and scheduling tasks associated with acquiring information needed to learn what you seek to learn and produce what you have specified as your outcome indicator.

Once you have all the needed resources in hand, proceed to read, review, analyze, and synthesize the information so that you may fully understand and apply it to your goal. Incidentally, if you analyze and synthesize what you read and review, and write about it in your own words (and perhaps incorporate it into a database), you dramatically increase the likelihood of retaining that information in long-term memory. If one of your learning goals involves application—that is, the development of skill or competence in a practice-relevant behavior—then you should probably schedule regular practice sessions. In both learning about and learning to do, incorporate self-evaluation and, if possible, obtain feedback from others. For example, after you have written a draft version of a document related to your learning goal, ask a couple of competent and trusted colleagues to review it and provide feedback about its quality vis-à-vis the universal intellectual standards. Ask them to identify any logical fallacies and highlight areas that are difficult to understand. Also, be sure to ask them to identify the strengths of the paper and provide you with social support. If you are learning a skill or refining a practice behavior, ask a colleague to observe you demonstrating it. When possible videotape your practice sessions to make it easier for you to self-evaluate and for others to provide constructive feedback. Request that your reviewers highlight areas of strength as well as weakness, and welcome their positive social support for your efforts.

Consider your colleagues' feedback and, if it seems reasonably accurate and useful, make changes in your written product or in the way you are practicing the skill or practice behavior. After making the revisions, conduct another self-evaluation before completing the final version of the document or implementing the skill or practice behavior in your professional work.

Documenting Learning

When you have implemented your plans and made progress toward your learning goals, store relevant materials and especially your final products or outcomes in a Lifelong Learning

---

a version that proceeds as follows: (1) *Knowledge Retrieval,* (2) *Comprehension,* (3) *Analysis,* and (4) *Knowledge Utilization* (Heer, 2012).

[18] Adapted from Cournoyer and Stanley (2002).

TABLE 3.9	Selected Action Verbs Corresponding to Bloom's Taxonomy				
Recollection	**Comprehension**	**Application**	**Analysis**	**Synthesis**	**Evaluation**
Duplicate	Classify	Adapt	**Analyze**	Arrange	Appraise
Highlight	**Comprehend**	Adopt	Appraise	Assemble	Arbitrate
Indicate	Construe	**Apply**	Audit	Build	Argue
Identify	Define	Choose	Break down	Collect	Assay
Label	Describe	Conduct	Calculate	Combine	Assess
List	Discuss	Demonstrate	Categorize	Compile	Criticize
Locate	Explain	Dramatize	Chart	Compose	Defend
Match	Express	Employ	Compare	Constitute	Determine
Memorize	Interpret	Exercise	Contrast	Construct	Estimate
Name	Report	Exploit	Criticize	Create	**Evaluate**
Order	Restate	Illustrate	Diagram	Design	Grade
Point out	State	Implement	Differentiate	Develop	Judge
Recall	Translate	Operate	Discriminate	Formulate	Rank
Recognize		Practice	Dissect	Generate	Rate
Recollect		Schedule	Distinguish	Hypothesize	Support
Remember		Select	Examine	Organize	Value
Repeat		Sketch	Experiment	Originate	
Reproduce		Solve	Inventory	Plan	
Underline		Use	Question	Predict	
			Study	Prepare	
			Test	Propose	
				Synthesize	

Portfolio—similar to the Social Work Skills Learning Portfolio that you create as you complete this book. In today's world, an electronic portfolio is usually superior to a paper version in that you may include a range of products that result from your lifelong learning projects. For instance, you may include digitized photos and drawings, or audio or video-recording demonstrations of your practice competencies.

When electronic versions of your learning outcomes are not available or cannot be digitized, you may simply store them in folders or boxes in a file cabinet. Whether in paper or digital form, however, such documentation serves many purposes. For example, you may (1) review material to refresh your memory about something you have learned before, (2) use a document as a foundation for more advanced learning in the same or a similar area, (3) distribute documents to colleagues or policy makers to advance their learning and raise their consciousness, or (4) share selected items in interviews for employment. Indeed, some employers now request samples of professional writing as a part of the application process. If you have ready access to a few examples of your best work, you can easily respond to such requests. If you have a video-recording of your competent demonstration of various practice skills, you may offer to provide that as well.

In lifelong learning, social workers seek to remain scientifically minded, logical in our critical thinking, and faithful to our code of ethics and the universal intellectual standards. When we reflect these principles in our own efforts to learn, we increase the likelihood that the individuals, families, groups, organizations, and communities we serve will also subsequently benefit from our learning as they receive higher-quality care. Failure to keep abreast of findings from emerging research studies and reluctance to engage in relevant professional development activities may constitute a breach of ethics or a violation of social work licensing regulations, and may contribute to allegations of malpractice. Indeed, continuous lifelong learning has become an essential aspect of contemporary professionalism. Clients and the community at large have every right to expect that social workers are up-to-date. In addition, most of us accrue great personal, as well as professional, satisfaction when we routinely think critically, engage in scholarly inquiries, and pursue opportunities to learn and grow throughout our lives.

SUMMARY

Critical thinking, scientific inquiry, and lifelong learning have become especially important for social workers during the 21st century. The popular media and the ever-expanding Internet regularly and increasingly disseminate misleading, superstitious, pseudoscientific, and false information—much of it in the form of advertising and propaganda. We may anticipate that many people are susceptible to unsubstantiated claims and statements of all kinds. In the United States alone, millions of dollars are spent each year on ineffective diet pills and plans, longevity potions and supposed cancer cures, male and female sexual enhancement products, and a host of other "quick cures" promoted by "doctors" and "experts" of one kind or another. "Get rich quick" schemes are also prevalent. Many cite pseudoscientific research studies and anecdotal endorsements, and virtually all contain obvious logical fallacies in their advertisements and marketing materials.

Although the general public may easily be duped by incredible claims, anecdotal stories, and pseudoscientific articles that appear in the mass media and on the Web, as professionals we must remain scientifically minded, critically thoughtful, logical, and alert to unsubstantiated and poorly supported assertions. We need to rely upon findings from credible research studies—rather than widely available but highly questionable popular material. In addition, where and when appropriate, we help our clients and members of our communities become more sophisticated thinkers and active learners in their own right. Otherwise, they can remain susceptible to the powerful misleading and manipulative propaganda and the pseudoscientific messages that are increasing exponentially throughout the world.

CHAPTER 3   Summary Exercises

Reflective Exercises

1. Reflect on and integrate the results of this chapter's content and the learning exercises through a brief discussion of the implications of critical thinking and scientific inquiry and lifelong learning as aspects of professionalism in social work practice. Prepare your discussion in the form of a two- to three-page word-processed report (500–750 words) titled "Critical Thinking, Scientific Inquiry, and Lifelong Learning in Social Work." When you finish your

report, save the document file as "CritThink_in_SWK" and deposit it in your Social Work Skills Learning Portfolio.

Write-Now Exercises

Use the space below each of the following write-now exercises to record your responses.

1. Go to Appendix 4 and Appendix 5 and complete the Critical Thinking Questionnaire (CTQ) and the Lifelong Learning Questionnaire (LLQ). These instruments will help you assess selected aspects of critical thinking and lifelong learning. They are not graded tests. You cannot pass or fail. Furthermore, the validity and reliability of the instruments remain unestablished. They are not precise tools. Therefore, please view the instruments and your results as catalysts for you to consider how you conceptualize and approach critical thinking and lifelong learning.

   When you have completed the questionnaires and calculated the results, record your scores. Consider the implications of your responses to the items by writing brief answers to the following questions: (a) What do your responses suggest about your approach to critical thinking and lifelong learning? (b) Why might critical thinking and lifelong learning be especially important for social workers during the 21st century? (c) What steps might you take to become a more proficient critical thinker and lifelong learner?

2. Conduct a scholarly search to locate a copy of a genuine systematic review that contains a meta-analysis. You might use the keywords "systematic review" or "meta-analysis" along with a term that reflects a major contemporary social problem of your choice. You might use any of the scientific bibliographic database services available through your college or university, or through your public library. You could also access **www.pubmed.gov**[19] to find a citation and then secure the article from another source as needed. If you need help, consult your research librarian. If you are authentic, empathic, and respectful, librarians can be absolutely incredible resources! Once you find an article that meets your criteria, read it carefully to become familiar with an example of a systematic review and meta-analysis. It should be distinctly different from more general reviews of the literature with which you are probably quite familiar. Record the citation in APA style format. Then, prepare a brief one-paragraph critique of the paper.

3. Conduct an Internet search to find Michael Shermer's discussion of 10 science-minded questions to consider in evaluating the credibility of claims. Originally presented as "Baloney Detection: How to draw boundaries between science and pseudoscience, Part I" and "More Baloney Detection: How to draw boundaries between science and pseudoscience, Part II" in the November and December issues, respectively, of the journal *Scientific American* (Shermer, 2001, Dec., 2001, Nov.), you may also use the keywords "Shermer baloney detection" to locate his YouTube video on the topic (2009). The questions are based, in part, on Carl Sagan's famous "baloney detection kit" as contained in *The Demon Haunted World* (1995). Use the space below to record the 10 "Baloney Detection" questions.

---

[19] Although the PubMed resource includes links to some full-text articles, most citations contain only bibliographic details and an abstract. Once you locate the citation, you may have to go to your library, another online source, or request the article through interlibrary loan.

CHAPTER 3 Self-Appraisal

As you finish this chapter, please reflect on your learning by using the following space to identify any ideas, terms, or concepts addressed in Chapter 3 that remain confusing or unclear to you:

Next, respond to the following items by carefully reading each statement. Please use a 1-to-10-point rating scale (where *1 = strongly disagree* and *10 = strongly agree*) to indicate the degree to which you agree or disagree with each statement. Place a check mark at the point that best reflects your view at this particular point in time. If you're truly *undecided*, place your check at the midpoint (5.5) mark.

1. I can discuss the processes of critical thinking, scientific inquiry, and lifelong learning.

    |___|___|___|___|___|___|___|___|___|___|
    1   2   3   4   5   6   7   8   9   10

2. I can use critical thinking skills to assess the credibility of a claim, conclusion, or argument, and to evaluate the quality of a research study.

    |___|___|___|___|___|___|___|___|___|___|
    1   2   3   4   5   6   7   8   9   10

3. I can recognize logical fallacies in my own and in others' written and verbal communications.

    |___|___|___|___|___|___|___|___|___|___|
    1   2   3   4   5   6   7   8   9   10

4. I can use scientific inquiry skills to formulate a precise question and search for, discover, and analyze research studies related to a practice or policy-relevant topic.

    |___|___|___|___|___|___|___|___|___|___|
    1   2   3   4   5   6   7   8   9   10

5. I can incorporate the universal intellectual virtues in my scholarly and professional activities.

    |___|___|___|___|___|___|___|___|___|___|
    1   2   3   4   5   6   7   8   9   10

6. I can assess my lifelong learning needs, establish learning goals, prepare learning plans, and document learning progress.

    |___|___|___|___|___|___|___|___|___|___|
    1   2   3   4   5   6   7   8   9   10

Diversity and Difference; Human Rights; Social, Economic, and Environmental Justice; and Policy–Practice

A s social workers, we serve an incredibly wide and varied array of individuals, families, groups, organizations, communities, and sometimes entire societies. We constantly engage diversity and difference; and often recognize extraordinary acts of courage, determination, resilience, generosity, sacrifice, and heroism. Unfortunately, we also frequently observe profound assaults on human dignity, flagrant disregard for basic human rights, and pervasive and

(Continued)

Core Competencies

The content addressed in this chapter supports the following core EPAS competencies:

- Competency 2: Engage Diversity and Difference in Practice

- Competency 3: Advance Human Rights and Social, Economic, and Environmental Justice

- Competency 4: Engage in Practice-Informed Research and Research-Informed Practice

- Competency 5: Engage in Policy–Practice

- Competency 6: Engage with Individuals, Families, Groups, Organizations, and Communities

- Competency 7: Assess Individuals, Families, Groups, Organizations, and Communities

- Competency 8: Intervene with Individuals, Families, Groups, Organizations, and Communities

- Competency 9: Evaluate Practice with Individuals, Families, Groups, Organizations, and Communities

Chapter Goals

Following completion of this chapter, you should be able to reflect upon and discuss:

- Diversity and difference in human relations.

- Intersectionality.

- Accepting others and respecting autonomy.

- Human rights.

- Social, economic, and environmental justice.

- Policy-practice.

insidious forms of social, economic, and environmental injustice. As social workers act to secure and ensure human rights and dignity, advance justice, and promote social well-being, we rely upon our capacities to engage, respect, accept, and advocate for others who often differ, at least in some ways, from ourselves.

Diversity and difference, human rights, social justice, economic justice, and environmental justice are complex and often quite controversial concepts. Nonetheless, along with social well-being, they represent major focal points for social work practice in general and for policy–practice in particular (see Figure 4.1).

Diversity and Difference

In *The Social Work Dictionary*, the term **diversity** is defined as "variety, or the opposite of homogeneity. In social organizations the term usually refers to the range of personnel who more accurately represent minority populations and people from varied backgrounds, cultures, ethnicities, and viewpoints" (Barker, 2014, p. 124). The Council on Social Work Education (2015) indicates that the "dimensions of diversity are understood as the intersectionality of multiple factors including but not limited to age, class, color, culture, disability and ability, ethnicity, gender, gender identity and expression, immigration status, marital status, political ideology, race, religion/spirituality, sex, sexual orientation, and tribal sovereign status" (2015, p. 7).

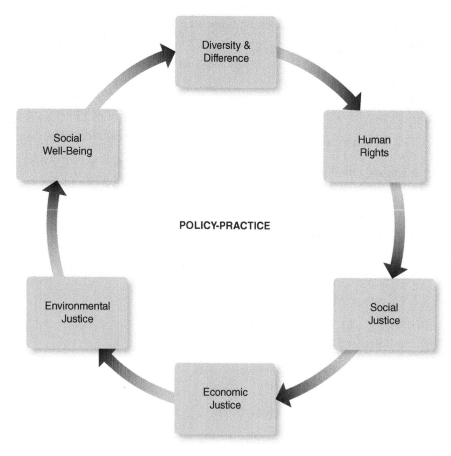

FIGURE 4.1 Focal Points for Policy–Practice

Intersectionality

The notion of **intersectionality** adds sophistication to the topic of diversity. Rather than approaching it as a unidimensional phenomenon, diversity is viewed in terms of multiple, interacting factors, identities, or perceived characteristics (Jaramillo, 2010). Intersectionality incorporates "and" instead of "or." Rather than age or race or sex, it becomes age-and-race-and-sex-and-economic status-and-occupation-and-religion-and-sexual orientation-and-political views. Such a multidimensional perspective recognizes that people often view themselves in different and more nuanced ways than others perceive them.[1] If we consider only the dimensions included in the 2015 EPAS (and, of course, there are many more), the complexity becomes apparent (see Table 4.1). For example, a young person could self-identify on any one or more of these dimensions and numerous others, and do so in various ways at different times and in different contexts (Mehrotra, 2010). In addition, other people might assign quite different diversity dimensions to her than she identifies for herself. They too might emphasize certain dimensions at various times and circumstances. Furthermore, she might be subject to discrimination due to some form of **interlocking oppression** (Hulko, 2009). Interlocking oppression is a form of subjugation that is based upon multiple, interacting factors (for example, a female child of minority racial and minority religious status may be subject to discrimination and abuse in school and playground settings). Of course, in some contexts, she might experience privilege due to another constellation of factors (for example, youth and physical beauty).

Intersectionality[2]:

> starts from the premise that **people live multiple, layered identities** derived from social relations, history and the operation of structures of power. People are members of more than one community at the same time, and can simultaneously experience oppression and privilege (e.g. a woman may be a respected medical professional yet suffer domestic violence in her home). **Intersectional analysis aims to reveal multiple identities, exposing the different types of discrimination and disadvantage that occur as a consequence of the combination of identities.** (Association for Women's Rights in Development, 2004, Aug., p. 2)

Let's consider, for example, the aspect of gender. Many of the equality gaps and *ceilings* that appear when men are compared with women are well known. For example, you probably know that in the United States in 2013, full-time working women received 22 percent less than full-time working men. You may not realize that the gap was least in Washington, DC, at 8 percent less and highest in Louisiana at 44 percent less (American Association of University Women, 2014). The differences reflect an effect of intersectionality: gender and location of employment. We can also add additional dimensions, such as gender, age, race, educational level, physical attractiveness, ableness, and others to appreciate how the combination of factors affect wage gaps. You might

---

[1] We wonder if adoption of intersectional perspectives in our relationships just might diminish hatred and possibly violence toward others. Hate-filled speech is typically unidimensional rather than multidimensional in form. For example, we might hear something like, "God hates gays," or "You &%^@?#! socialist," or "Godless Atheist!" We're unlikely to hear something like, "God hates attractive, well-educated, altruistic, gay people who are military veterans and contribute 50% of their income to charities, volunteer 15 hours each week in food pantries, sing in church choirs, rescue abused and abandoned cats, and love their mothers."

[2] The Consortium on Race, Gender and Ethnicity (CRGE) at the University of Maryland sponsors an Intersectional Research Database, publishes *Intersections & Inequality*, and offers resources through the Consortium's website at **www .crge.umd.edu**.

TABLE 4.1	Intersectionality: 16 Diversity Dimensions	Age	Class	Color	Culture	Disability and Ability	Ethnicity	Gender	Gender Identity and Expression	Immigration Status	Marital Status	Political Ideology	Race	Religion/Spirituality	Sex	Sexual Orientation	Tribal Sovereign Status
Age																	
Class																	
Color																	
Culture																	
Disability and Ability																	
Ethnicity																	
Gender																	
Gender Identity and Expression																	
Immigration Status																	
Marital Status																	
Political Ideology																	
Race																	
Religion/Spirituality																	
Sex																	
Sexual Orientation																	
Tribal Sovereign Status																	

Note: This table is based upon dimensions identified in the 2015 EPAS. Of course, many more dimensions could be included.

speculate about the differences in Louisiana in the wages of black women compared to white women, or compare the incomes of college-educated black women with those of white men who did not complete high school.

Gender is an extraordinarily powerful factor in explaining difference—especially when combined with other dimensions. Even when considered as a single variable, however, it remains enormously influential. You probably know that throughout most of human history, men and women existed in nearly equal proportions, that is, about 50 percent male and 50 percent female.[3] In 2013, about 107 boys were born for every 100 girls (Central Intelligence Agency, 2014). Over a lifetime, the male–female proportion tends to balance out due to higher mortality rates and shorter life spans for boys and men. Indeed, the female population slightly exceeds 50 percent in more than half of all nations. For example, in 2013, the United States was 50.8 percent female (56.5 percent for those 65 and older), South Africa 51.5 percent, El Salvador 52.6 percent, Hong Kong SAR 53.2 percent, and Estonia 53.6 percent (World Bank, 2014a).

In an example of how human values, policies, and practices dramatically affect nature, however, several nations have much smaller female populations. For instance, Bahrain reflects a female population of 37.8 percent, Kuwait 40.2 percent, Oman 36.4 percent, the United Arab Emirates 29.9 percent, and Qatar 23.5 percent (World Bank, 2014a).[4] The female population percentage in China and India, at 48.2 percent and 48.3 percent, respectively, may not appear especially disparate. Their populations are so large, however, that the consequences are staggering. There are 50 million more men than women in China and 43 million more in India. In contrast to the world average ratio of 1.07 male to every one female birth, in China and India, the ratio is 1.11 and 1.12 males to one female, respectively. The net result is that, worldwide, there are almost 60 million more men than women (Bauer, 2015, Jan. 31).[5]

What explains this discrepancy? Might it be that some societies and cultures clearly and explicitly, or subtly and implicitly, tend to (1) value men more highly than women; (2) view women in a unidimensional rather than multidimensional or intersectional manner; and (3) reflect myriad and insidious forms of sex discrimination and subjugation that endanger female embryos, infants, girls, and women?[6] Could it be that females are less valued than their male counterparts in cultures where infanticide of girl babies is more common than for boys? Might we anticipate that in cultures where men are considered superior, women would tend to experience higher rates and more intense forms of social and economic injustice? In such contexts, we might, for example, expect to find cultural practices such as lesser pay for women than for men engaged in the same work; subordination and servitude of women in marriage; cultural acceptance of physical punishment and verbal abuse of daughters and wives by husbands, fathers, and brothers; social exclusion of girls and women from family and community decision making—including decisions about the use of family planning; obstacles and prohibitions against women holding political or religious office; travel restrictions for women; limitations on women's free speech; barriers to the pursuit of education or employment by girls and women; female genital cutting (typically involving the excision of at least the clitoral glans and hood); and forced marriage of females—including young girls (child brides). Finally, let's hypothesize that in male-privileged communities, we can expect double standards in the nature and application of religious and secular policies and laws, in social mores, and in the attribution of blame.

Girls and women experience assault, insult, and oppression in so many contexts, so often, and in so many ways that estimating the degree or extent of gender inequality in a society represents a

---

[3] This 1-to-1 ratio has survival value for the human species. See Carvalho, Sampaio, Varandas, and Klaczko (1998) for an evolutionary explanation of what's called Fisher's Principle.

[4] Some of the population imbalance in Arabian Peninsula nations is due to large numbers of male immigrant workers who are prohibited from bringing wives and daughters with them.

[5] Imagine the long-term implications of a substantial gender imbalance for the human species.

[6] Despite these barriers, surviving women tend to live longer than men. The longevity gap, however, is relatively small in highly developed countries.

major challenge.[7] No single measurement tool can adequately capture its complexity or the enormity of its impact. Despite the complications, the UNDP uses two primary measures to assess aspects of *gender inequality*: the **Gender-related Development Index (GDI)** and the Gender Inequality Index (GII). The GDI reflects "disparity in human development achievements between women and men in three dimensions: health, education, and living standards" (2013, Nov. 15, para. 1). The GDI is presented in the form of a female-to-male ratio. Ratios of 0.975 and above are classified as reflecting "very high human development." Those below 0.834 reflect "low human development"[8] (2013, Nov. 15).

The UNDP uses the **Gender Inequality Index (GII)** to complement the GDI. The GII seeks to assess:

> women's disadvantage in three dimensions—reproductive health, empowerment and the labour market—for as many countries as data of reasonable quality allow. The index shows the loss in human development due to inequality between female and male achievements in these dimensions. It ranges from 0, which indicates that women and men fare equally, to 1, which indicates that women fare as poorly as possible in all measured dimensions. The health dimension is measured by two indicators: maternal mortality ratio and the adolescent fertility rate. The empowerment dimension is also measured by two indicators: the share of parliamentary seats held by each sex and by secondary and higher education attainment levels. The labour dimension is measured by women's participation in the work force. The Gender Inequality Index is designed to reveal the extent to which national achievements in these aspects of human development are eroded by gender inequality, and to provide empirical foundations for policy analysis and advocacy efforts. (United Nations Human Development Programme, 2011)

In 2013, the five nations reflecting the lowest GII ratios (lesser gender inequality) were Slovenia, Switzerland, Germany, Sweden, and Denmark. The five highest GII countries (greater gender inequality) were Yemen, Niger, Chad, Afghanistan, and Mali. At that time, the United States ranked 47th[9] among the 152 surveyed nations. Neighbors Canada and Mexico ranked 23th and 73th, respectively (United Nations Human Development Programme, 2011).

Clearly, gender is a powerful variable in understanding diversity and difference. But it is only one of numerous facets that people might apply to themselves or to others. Consider the examples of Sue and Hussein, who reflect numerous intersectional dimensions:

In her private life, Sue Kim views herself as a young, lesbian woman of Korean ancestry, and a member of the Unitarian faith. In her work life, she sees herself as a lawyer. Others, of course,

---

[7] The insidious nature of sexism is apparent well into the 21st century. As reflected in the incidence of sexual assault on the campuses of comparatively safe U.S. colleges and universities (Anderson, 2014, July 1), and in the armed forces (including the military service academies), women remain at risk. Indeed, many institutions continue to disguise, cover up, or underreport the nature and extent of sexual assaults on their students, staff, and service members (Department of Defense, 2015, May 1; Smith & Freyd, 2014; Yung, 2015). In addition, some victims experience social and administrative retaliation for reporting sexual assaults (Winkle, Rock, Coffey, & Hurley). See the films *The Hunting Ground* (Dick, 2015) and *The Invisible War* (Dick, 2012) for documentary illustrations of the situation on college campuses and in the military, respectively.

[8] You may access current world human development information, including gender development and gender inequality as well as multidimensional poverty indices at the UNDP website. Go to the Public Data Explorer at **http://hdr.undp.org/en /data-explorer**.

[9] One of the factors that contributes to a lower Gender Inequality Index is the proportion of women in the parliament (or Congress). In 2013, about 18.2% of congressional seats in the United States were held by women—despite the fact that women outnumber men in the nation's population. Several other countries do better: 55% of the parliamentary seats in Chile, 54.4% in Argentina, 44.7% in Sweden, and 42.5% in Finland are occupied by women (United Nations Development Programme, 2015).

emphasize different dimensions as they observe or interact with her. Indeed, Sue has been subject to various forms of prejudice, discrimination, and oppression because of others' perception of her as "different." Nonetheless, she maintains a strong and coherent sense of identity and self-respect. Generous toward and accepting of others, she also feels a great deal of self-compassion (Neff, 2011).

Hussein Ali is a 50-year-old individual who has unambiguous male physical characteristics. He views himself as masculine, male, and heterosexual. Originally from the country of Uganda, he legally immigrated more than 25 years ago and is now a naturalized citizen. He has dark brown skin color and believes in Allah, the God of the prophet Mohammed. He speaks five languages. Although some people consider him disabled, Hussein does not—despite the fact that at age 8, his left leg was amputated after he stepped on a landmine. He wears a state-of-the-art artificial leg that enables him to walk, run, ride bicycles, and snow ski. He regularly plays tennis and golf. He is a graduate of Harvard University with a PhD in economics. He works as an investment banker and earns an annual income of approximately $575,000. His net worth is more than $12 million. He is a father, husband, and grandfather. In political terms, he views himself as socially progressive and fiscally conservative. And, that represents only a few of the hundreds of ways Dr. Ali is "unique," "different" or "diverse." The multidimensional aspects and the complexity associated with this one person are staggering. Imagine the extent of diversity within groups and communities when we recognize that people tend to view themselves and others in various ways at different times and in different circumstances.

When a number of individuals are grouped in some way (for example, into a community, an organization, a household, or an interest group), they differ according to multiple intersectional dimensions of diversity (for example, skin color, height, weight, age, gender, political views, religious affiliation, language, physical or mental ability, status of some kind, appearance, or attractiveness). When their individual characteristics reflect heterogeneity, we may call that group "diverse." The wider the range and type of differences among the members of the group, the greater is the degree or extent of diversity. Substantial diversity is highly valued in some contexts and strongly devalued in others.

Bankers such as Dr. Ali, stockbrokers, and other financial experts recognize the value of diversity in investments. Indeed, the term *diversified stock portfolio* is commonly used to suggest that someone has invested in a wide range of different kinds of companies or industries so that if one suffers a downturn, others remain to compensate. Diversified investments provide much greater financial security than, say, investment in a single business or even several companies in the same industry (for example, auto corporations such as General Motors, Ford, and Chrysler).

Mayors of cities and towns also prefer to have a diversified base of businesses, industries, and other employment opportunities for their constituents. Similarly, employers prefer to have access to a diversified population who can meet the staffing and production needs of their companies and organizations. A diversified workforce and a wide range of employment opportunities tend to maintain social and economic stability—even when circumstances are uncertain and challenging. Contrast that with a "one-company town" where most people work for a single employer. If that company fails or relocates to a different state or nation, the consequences for the community and its people can be disastrous.

Over the long term, open, diverse and heterogeneous human social systems are more healthy, vibrant, and resilient than those reflecting extreme homogeneity. Recognizing that greater diversity generally tends to benefit humankind, social workers tend to celebrate individual and cultural differences as valuable forms of **social capital** (Coleman, 1988; Lin, 2001). Even when human diversity is highly regarded, however, engaging those who differ from ourselves requires considerable sensitivity and especially acceptance. In subsequent chapters, we explore skills associated with culturally sensitive communication for engaging diversity and difference. At this point, we focus on acceptance of others as a vital element of both valuing and engaging diversity and difference in social work practice.

Accepting Others and Respecting Autonomy

Acceptance of others involves processes of self-awareness, cultural understanding, and valuing and joining with people regardless of their degree of similarity or difference. As social workers providing needed services to often highly vulnerable people and to widely diverse communities, we hope to transcend the powerful psychological and social forces that maintain patterns of prejudice, privilege, ethnocentrism, xenophobia, rankism (Fuller, 2002), and discrimination. Social workers require a capacity to accept all people—those who differ from as well as those who resemble ourselves in appearance, background, attitudes, abilities, and behavior (Armstrong, 2010; Berlin, 2005). Human beings deserve social workers' genuine understanding and acceptance. Such acceptance involves respect for the dignity and autonomy of those we encounter—a form of respect that is often easier to apply to "people of similarity" than it is to "people of difference." We humans seem primed to view those most like ourselves as fully equal, capable, and entitled to make their own decisions; and to see those who differ as less equal, less able, and less entitled to respect and self-determination.

In the context of diversity and acceptance of others, the term **reverence** seems especially meaningful (Woodruff, 2001). Reverence involves an attitude of deep respect or awe and humility in the presence of another. Although reflecting a religious or spiritual connotation, the concept of reverence aptly captures the special attitude social workers reflect as we express cultural sensitivity and acceptance of others. In our service to people, reverence is crucial (Berlin, 2005).

In highly competitive, pluralistic, and violent societies, however, it is exceedingly difficult to develop genuine reverence for others. Our prejudices and privileges may limit our capacity to do so. **Prejudice** is "an opinion about an individual, group, or phenomenon that is developed without proof or systematic evidence. This prejudgment may be favorable but is more often unfavorable and may become institutionalized in the form of a society's laws or customs" (Barker, 2014, p. 332). **Privilege** is "a special right, advantage, or immunity granted or available only to a particular person or group of people" ("privilege," 2010). Such advantages include extraordinary access, opportunities, benefits, and resources that are usually unavailable to non-privileged others; and, exemptions from certain obligations, duties, or liabilities to which the unprivileged are commonly subject.

Some privileges are obvious. For example, corporate executives who donate large sums of money to support the campaigns of political candidates are virtually guaranteed face-to-face access to those politicians after they are elected. Similarly, in the context of admissions to prestigious colleges and universities, legacy students (children of alumni) are commonly viewed more favorably than equally well-qualified, non-legacy applicants.

Many privileges, however, go unnoticed by most privileged and some non-privileged peoples alike. They are, in effect, "invisible privileges." For example, common myths such as "anything is possible if you are talented and willing to work hard" may interfere with our ability to notice our own or others' privileged status (Stiglitz, 2013, Feb. 16). Widespread acceptance of such myths leave us more susceptible to both "blaming victims" and accepting extreme levels of economic inequality and social injustice (Markman, 2012, July 27; Savani & Rattan, 2012; Savani et al., 2011; Valor-Segura et al., 2011; Van Prooijen & Van den Bos, 2009).

Privilege is the often:

> invisible advantage and resultant unearned benefits afforded to dominant groups of people because of a variety of sociodemographic traits. Privilege provides economic and social boosts to dominant groups while supporting the structural barriers to other groups imposed by prejudice. (Franks & Riedel, 2008, para. 1)

The concept of invisible privilege is often difficult to grasp. Indeed, high status, powerful people and groups receive so many special advantages and entitlements that they can appear as natural, expected, and "deserved."

Wealth, of course, conveys enormous privilege. Many rich people feel entitled to talk directly and regularly with elected representatives and appointed officials at the local, state, and federal levels; to receive extremely low or "no-interest" bank loans; to invest surplus money with stockbrokers and hedge fund managers; and to employ several attorneys—including at least one who works exclusively to minimize tax obligations. Many wealthy people believe that they truly deserve 500, 1,000, or 10,000 times the income of minimum-wage workers. Some think that it is perfectly normal and legitimate to avoid taxes altogether or to be taxed at much lower rates than working people. Interestingly, despite their extraordinary advantages, perks, and privileges many of the richest and most privileged families in the United States consider themselves "average" and "middle-class" (Baker, 2014; Chetty, Hendren, Kline, et al., 2014; Chetty et al., 2014; Frank, 2015; Madland, 2015; Primack, 2011; Schutz, 2011; Wise, 2008).

Certain occupational positions are accompanied by a range of privileges. Members of the U.S. Congress, for example, receive benefits and perquisites far beyond those available to average citizens. Many congressional entitlements result from legally instituted policies and practices, some from the position's status and influence, and some from associations with rich and powerful donors. For instance, members of the U.S. Congress are exempted from some legal requirements that apply to most American citizens.[10] The Constitution contains a "Privilege from Arrest" passage that protects members of Congress from civil arrest during or when traveling to or from sessions. They cannot be sued for slander for any comments made during speech or debate on the floor of Congress; and, through the "Franking Privilege" members may send mail to constituents at no cost. Travel usually occurs at taxpayer expense—including visits to various parts of the world on "fact-finding" trips.

Among the most significant congressional privileges, however, involves the opportunity to vote on legislative proposals—including those for which they have a real or apparent conflict of interest. Members of Congress remain free to buy or sell stocks, or maintain ownership in companies while holding office. They may have financial investments in businesses and corporations that they investigate, oversee, or regulate as well as those who might benefit from the passage or rejection of tax and regulatory policies or other legislative initiatives. Added to these privileges are ready opportunities for highly paid employment after they complete their terms.

Despite relatively modest average salaries, certain other occupations also convey special privilege—some of which are the product of policies and many others which result from tradition or custom. Many police officers, for example, have the use of department vehicles

---

[10] The STOCK Act was enacted into law in 2012. The Act reversed the long-standing privilege accorded to members and staff of the U.S. Congress to engage "legally" in insider trading (a crime for the rest of us). However, in 2014, when the Securities and Exchange Commission (SEC) began to investigate a congressional staffer for the alleged crime of insider trading, the Congress denied the SEC's right to investigate. In effect, the privilege to commit insider trading crimes without fear of legal consequence remains intact (Office of the General Counsel U.S. House of Representatives, 2014, July 4). If we cannot investigate, we cannot prosecute.

for personal, off-duty use as well as when they are on the job. Some officers accept restaurants' offers of free drinks and meals, many appear able to violate traffic laws that other citizens must obey, and some avoid prosecution for felonious crimes because of their position and associations.

White people in the United States also accrue privileges that remain unavailable to most persons of color. Whites generally have more opportunities for and access to high-quality schools, colleges and universities, and to well-paying jobs than do people of color. Conversely, African Americans and Hispanic Americans have fewer opportunities for or access to quality educational experiences and to well-paying jobs than do white Americans. Whites are less likely than people of color to be arrested and convicted—even when they have actually committed crimes; and, if they are convicted, they tend to receive more lenient sentences. Many people, including most social workers, are well aware that whites generally occupy a privileged status in North American society. Nonetheless, despite the fact that whites are more likely than people of color to receive benefits from private and public welfare services, some white people sincerely believe, albeit inaccurately, that racial and ethnic minority populations receive "entitlements" that whites cannot obtain. Indeed, ordinary discussions about **white privilege** or **white supremacy** can become extremely tense—perhaps because they threaten long-held beliefs and traditional positions of status and power. As Robin DiAngelo (2011) suggests, **white fragility** "is a state in which even a minimum amount of racial stress becomes intolerable, triggering a range of defensive moves. These moves include outward display of emotions such as anger, fear and guilt, and behaviors such as argumentation, silence and leaving the stress-inducing situation. These behaviors, in turn, function to reinstate white racial equilibrium" (p. 54).

Most social workers also recognize that many men possess privileges unavailable to most women. Indeed, assumptions of **male superiority** are so ingrained that in interactions with some women, many men appear arrogant, self-centered, insensitive, and rude. Many women wonder, "Why do so few men 'get it?'" Others ask, "Why do so many women 'accept it?'" In our service to clients and in our advocacy work, social workers frequently struggle with these same questions. Humans are usually quite reluctant to give away power, status, and other advantages. We can quite easily postulate that **male privilege** continues partly because of custom, tradition, and often deeply held cultural beliefs but more importantly because of the extraordinary benefits that result. The question about why so many women today continue to defer to and accept subordination, subjugation, and control by men as if they were lords and masters from some bygone era is more difficult to explain—unless, that is, we adopt a person-in-environment perspective. When we examine the social and physical environment, and consider parallel processes, we quickly realize that women are socialized, indoctrinated, and periodically rewarded (albeit modestly) for accepting inferior positions in relationships and in society; for tolerating the status quo; and especially for "knowing their place." The same processes apply for other non-privileged groups. In addition to the socialization, indoctrination, and occasional modest "gifts," the threat of violence undergirds systems of privilege. Whether it involves individual men emotionally or physically abusing, assaulting, or raping women; police forces brutalizing or killing "uppity" African Americans who appear disrespectful and disobedient; or vigilante groups attacking immigrants, gay men or lesbian women, or transgender persons, the potential for violence and the resulting fear remains constant in the minds and hearts of many non-privileged peoples. As of early August 2015, at least 14 transgendered persons had been fatally beaten, stabbed, or shot since the beginning of the year (Human Rights Campaign & Trans People of Color Coalition (TPOCC), 2015, Aug. 14).

Despite extraordinary advantages, privilege involves corresponding vulnerabilities. Status and power, and the benefits that accompany them can be lost—sometimes within a shockingly short time frame. Consider, for example, the phenomenon of **heterosexual privilege** within the United States and most of Europe. Tragically, prejudice, discrimination, and violence against members of LGBTQIA communities continue. Nonetheless, the extent of anti-gay bias by the general population—first in Europe and then in the United States—has dropped dramatically in a matter of several decades. The popular outrage against unequal treatment of gay and lesbian couples forced many states to legislate more flexible marriage laws; and, the U.S. Supreme Court decided that states could not legally deny marital rights to same-sex couples. Clearly, the degree and extent of heterosexual privilege has diminished considerably within a remarkably few years. Yes, full equality remains a distant vision. Nonetheless, we can now imagine a future when a person's sexual orientation is simply accepted without judgment, hate, disgust, aversion, or violence. Many social workers find inspiration and hope in both the activist processes by which changes were encouraged and the emerging, more fair and egalitarian outcomes.

Although much privilege remains invisible, some is all too obvious. We easily recognize it when human traffickers view the women and children they enslave as chattel; when husbands consider the women they marry and the children they produce as possessions; and when militia leaders kidnap and coercively recruit "child soldiers." In the United States, some aspects of **white privilege** and **male privilege** are extremely visible. Clean shaven, white men wearing business suits are rarely "stopped and frisked" or arrested; black and brown people often are. White men and white women are rarely brutalized or killed by police; black and brown people frequently are.

Most of us also recognize that "beautiful people"—male or female—are more likely to receive employment offers, higher grades in school, invitations to social events, proposals of various kinds, job promotions, and, of course, much more personal attention than those of us who are not so good-looking. Interestingly, few of us publicly acknowledge the existence of a **beauty bias** or **beauty privilege**, although we know it operates in multiple and pervasive ways (Berry, 2007; Rhode, 2010).

Indeed, outward physical characteristics and appearance remain powerful factors in perception and judgment. Most humans are attracted to youth and beauty. Many of us from Euro-centric cultures equate beauty and "lightness" with goodness and innocence or purity, and associate unattractiveness and "darkness" with evil and guilt or sin. We can readily observe these themes in common mythologies: The good prince—who is light-skinned—wears white clothes and silver armor, dons a white hat, and rides a white stead. The evil prince—who is dark-skinned—wears black clothes and armor, dons a black hat, and rides a black horse.

Most social workers recognize the ridiculousness of judging humans by the color of their skin, hat, or horse, or by the symmetry and proportionality of their face and body. Nonetheless, as obvious as it is, the beauty privilege remains invisible to some who possess it and many who do not.

Consider this scenario: A robbery has just been committed by a male wearing a mask and gloves. The police observe two people walking nearby. One has an oval, symmetrical face; his teeth are even, clean, and bright. He is lean, fit, and looks like he could model jeans or tee shirts in a television commercial. The other has a round, asymmetrical facial structure. His eyes, nose, mouth, and ears are disproportionate to one another; and many of his teeth are discolored or missing. He is obese, his hair is unkempt, and his head appears too small for his body. Do you have any doubt about which of the two would be the prime suspect?

Obviously, prejudice and privilege are closely related to each other and to overt discrimination. **Discrimination** involves the "treatment of people based on identifiable characteristics such as race, gender, religion, or ethnicity" (Barker, 2014, p. 121). Like prejudice, discrimination may be positive or negative (for example, favoring members of a particular group so that they are privileged or disfavoring members of a group so that they are oppressed or disenfranchised). Predictably, people in historical or contemporary positions of power and privilege are especially likely to engage in both forms of discrimination, and to do so without realizing it. Indeed, privileged peoples may lack conscious awareness of and fail to recognize the discriminatory nature of their own words and actions (Benjamin, 2009; Halley, Eshleman, & Vijaya, 2011; Kivel, 2002; Potapchuk, Leiderman, Bivens, & Major, 2005; Rothenberg, 2002; Saucier, Miller, & Doucet, 2005). The privileged often attribute their success and status to their own efforts while ignoring contributing situational and contextual factors. As social workers, however, we seek to transcend the powerful psychological and social forces that maintain privileged and prejudicial attitudes, and discriminatory behavior. We try to recognize our own privileged perspectives, embrace the value of diversity, and genuinely revere those who differ from us in appearance, background, beliefs, abilities, and behavior; and to accept others on their own terms. Such a profound level of **acceptance** involves recognition and respect for others' power and autonomy—something that can be difficult when we intentionally or unintentionally dominate the helping relationship with our status and expertise. Berlin (2005) recognizes this dimension by suggesting that "acceptance of another combines a recognition and endorsement of the other's autonomy (his or her own separate views, goals, feelings, experiences, and capacity to act) with a feeling of affiliation with or connection to him or her" (p. 484).

Acceptance and **respect for autonomy** do not come easily in a heterogeneous society in which people vary widely in power, status, economic resources, race and ethnicity, religion, culture, education, opportunity, and ideology. If you are similar to most North Americans who aspire to become professional social workers, you have observed prejudicial attitudes and both covert and overt forms of discrimination. In all likelihood, you have also experienced prejudicial thoughts and have personally discriminated against others. Indeed, you may have been quite unaware of your implicit attitudes and unconscious reactions that tend to preference some and diminish others.[11] Of course, you have also probably been affected by others' prejudicial attitudes and discriminatory behaviors toward you; and have had experiences where others have attempted to limit or deny your right to make your own decisions and determine your own life course. You have probably also done the same to others—perhaps out of a sense of kindness, concern, and a desire to protect them from risk and danger—or unconsciously as the result of implicit attitudes. As policy makers, program leaders, and social workers in practice quickly come to realize, we may unwittingly manipulate, overprotect, and control others in our efforts to help. As we do so, others' autonomy and sense of personal power may be lost or diminished. Recognizing such well-intentioned tendencies, as well as the likely presence of implicit preferential attitudes, social workers take extra care to encourage, facilitate, and celebrate clients' autonomy—including the right to make independent decisions about matters affecting themselves and their lives.

Occasionally, some members of "out" groups, especially those who have experienced prolonged oppression, judge themselves negatively and critically on the basis of a perceived majority standard. Some may feel ashamed of being who they are, limiting their personal power and self-expression. In contrast, some members of "in" groups reflect attitudes of privilege. They may consider themselves deserving or entitled simply because of their group's traditional status and power. Some may be unable to conceive of limits to their freedom and autonomy. This "tendency to consider one's own group, usually national or ethnic, superior to other groups using one's own group or groups

---

[11] Might we assume that many beliefs and practices embedded in our ancestors' cultures would also become our own? If so, wouldn't we be expected to hold implicit and explicit beliefs, attitudes, reactions, and behaviors associated with the genocidal treatment of Native American populations, the enslavement of persons of African birth or heritage, the oppressive treatment of "newer" immigrants, the subjugation of women and children, and the harassment and persecution of persons in the LGBTQIA community?

as the frame of reference against which other groups are judged" (Wolman, 1973, p. 129) is called **ethnocentrism**.

The forms and manifestations of privilege, prejudice, and discrimination are myriad and insidious. We humans absorb and internalize the values and attitudes, and discriminatory reactions common in our cultures. Indeed, many of us view ourselves as special or entitled to preferential treatment—at least at some times or in certain contexts. As social workers, however, we try to manage these implicit attitudes and explicit cultural traditions in order to better accept, respect, and revere those human beings who differ from ourselves.

In our acceptance and reverence for others, however, social workers do not shut down our brains. We maintain our scientific perspective and continue to think critically about the institutions, ideologies, and other aspects of the contexts in which people live and function. In revering others, we are not obligated to accept the unacceptable or tolerate the intolerable. We need not approve of violence as we accept a man who murdered his wife, a mother who abused her son, a policeman who killed an unarmed child, men who fire-bombed African American churches, a religious leader who encouraged followers to kill abortion doctors, or political leaders who started unnecessary wars. Indeed, our unconditional acceptance of and reverence for individual human beings do not require that we endorse beliefs, institutions, or cultural practices that threaten others or harm the environment that supports life on planet earth.

Human Rights and Social, Economic, and Environmental Justice

The concepts of human rights and social and economic justice are at least as complex as the topics of diversity and difference. Our perspective, position, status, roles, and responsibilities powerfully influence our views of human rights and justice. For example, a mother whose daughter was raped and murdered might be less concerned with the human rights of the perpetrator than with ensuring that he is caught and punished. Similarly, military and security officials might be more concerned with protecting their nation from a terrorist attack than with the human rights of potential attackers. Soldiers in battle are less concerned with the human rights of enemy combatants firing bullets and missiles at them than they would be with eliminating the immediate threat to their own survival. A parent and home owner confronted by an armed burglar is probably more concerned with the protection of her family and home than with the human rights of the trespasser.

On the other hand, the mother of someone accused of a major crime might be highly concerned with the human rights of the accused. So might the mother of a teenage girl stoned by a group of men because she kissed a boy, or the parent of a political prisoner. A civil rights lawyer might well focus on the violation of individual human rights in the case of an abused and tortured inmate, an enslaved girl of 12 forced into prostitution, a starving child, an intellectually challenged adolescent convicted of murder and sentenced to death by execution, or families denied an opportunity to rent apartments because they "are" homosexual, racially mixed, old and disabled, or because they worship the "wrong god."

Human Rights

Social workers are properly concerned with human rights of various kinds: the rights of children to adequate food, nutrition, and safety; the rights of women to equal protection under the law and to opportunities in society; and the rights of disabled people to equal access to education and other public services. We are also concerned about human rights in regard to the protection of children, women, and other vulnerable persons from abuse, exploitation, and oppression. However, our clients include people viewed as "perpetrators" as well as those considered "victims." Furthermore, through our person-in-environment perspective, we emphasize the rights and well-being of both individuals and the communities and societies in which people live. Such a multidimensional view may lead to various intellectual dilemmas. We may be forced to address questions such as, "On this occasion, should we focus more on the rights and wants of the individual, or on the needs and well-being of the family, group, organization, or community?" Indeed, the tension between **private interest** and **public good**, inevitable in many contexts, seems especially pertinent as we consider human rights. And, this tension becomes more pronounced when we consider that some cultures emphasize one aspect more than the other (for example, private interest more than public good; or, vice versa). Furthermore, some cultures place considerable value on respect for and obedience to authority whereas others value individual, independent thought and action. For instance, people in many Western cultures—including the United States—often hold individual rights and responsibilities in high regard but view established authority with considerable suspicion. In some other cultures, people tend to value strongly the well-being of the group, the community, and society; and generally view authority with considerable respect and deference. Finally, people in some regions of the world engage in a continuous struggle to survive because of inadequate food and water supplies, long-term drought, few economic opportunities, or violent conflict and war. Under such conditions, consideration of the general welfare may seem less urgent than finding a source of clean water, a loaf of bread, or a refuge from gunfire, grenades, and landmines. Yes, the topic of **human rights** is extremely complex indeed!

Edmundson (2004) suggests that "Human rights recognize *extraordinarily* special, basic interests, and this sets them apart from rights, even moral rights, generally" (p. 191). We can trace aspects of the concept of human rights from the Babylonian Code of Hammurabi in about 1754 BCE (Wright, 2009) to England's *Magna Carta Libertatum* in 1215, and on to Thomas Spence's *The Real Rights of Man* (1775), Thomas Paine's *The Rights of Man* (1791), the Bill of Rights in the United States, and the Declaration of the Rights of Man and of the Citizen in France in 1789. After World War II, however, widespread dissemination of information about the Holocaust, and the formation of the United Nations led the newly created General Assembly of the United Nations to approve the Universal Declaration of Human Rights (UDHR) in 1948.

The UDHR contains an array of 30 universal human rights (General Assembly of the United Nations, 1948). Some of them require governments to restrain their power vis-à-vis individuals' human rights. For example, the UDHR states that governments may not infringe upon individuals' rights to freedom of opinion, expression, and movement; freedom of thought, conscience, and religion; freedom from torture; freedom from slavery; and the right to a fair trial. Others require governments to take positive action to provide individuals with access to particular opportunities and resources. Under the UDHR, for example, individuals have rights to education, to work and equitable compensation, to rest and leisure from work, and to an adequate standard of living, including food, clothing, housing, and medical care. In addition to the rights of individual humans, the UDHR also refers to the rights of families, groups, and communities of people. For example, families have a right to privacy and are entitled to protection from unnecessary state intrusion. Furthermore, people, collectively as well as individually, have a right to engage in cultural activities and share knowledge gained from scientific enterprise.

The rights (see Box 4.1 for an easy read version) are "intended to be universal and indivisible—that is, all humans have the right to them regardless of culture, political system, ethnicity, or any other characteristic (universal), and a country cannot select which rights it should grant; all humans should have all rights (indivisible)" (Mapp, 2008, p. 17).

Box 4.1 UNIVERSAL HUMAN RIGHTS: PLAIN LANGUAGE VERSION

Article 1: When children are born, they are free and each should be treated in the same way. They have reason and conscience and should act towards one another in a friendly manner.

Article 2: Everyone can claim the following rights, despite a different sex, different skin color, speaking a different language, thinking different things, believing in another religion, owning more or less, being born in another social group, (or) coming from another country. It also makes no difference whether the country you live in is independent or not.

Article 3: You have the right to live, and to live in freedom and safety.

Article 4: Nobody has the right to treat you as his or her slave and you should not make anyone your slave.

Article 5: Nobody has the right to torture you.

Article 6: You should be legally protected in the same way everywhere, and like everyone else.

Article 7: The law is the same for everyone; it should be applied in the same way to all.

Article 8: You should be able to ask for legal help when the rights your country grants you are not respected.

Article 9: Nobody has the right to put you in prison, to keep you there, or to send you away from your country unjustly, or without a good reason.

Article 10: If you must go on trial this should be done in public. The people who try you should not let themselves be influenced by others.

Article 11: You should be considered innocent until it can be proved that you are guilty. If you are accused of a crime, you should always have the right to defend yourself. Nobody has the right to condemn you and punish you for something you have not done.

Article 12: You have the right to ask to be protected if someone tries to harm your good name, enter your house, open your letters, or bother you or your family without a good reason.

Article 13: You have the right to come and go as you wish within your country. You have the right to leave your country to go to another one; and you should be able to return to your country if you want.

Article 14: If someone hurts you, you have the right to go to another country and ask it to protect you. You lose this right if you have killed someone and if you yourself do not respect what is written here.

Article 15: You have the right to belong to a country and nobody can prevent you, without a good reason, from belonging to another country if you wish.

Article 16: As soon as a person is legally entitled, he or she has the right to marry and have a family. Neither the color of your skin, nor the country you come from nor your religion should be impediments to doing this. Men and women have the same rights when they are married and also when they are separated. Nobody should force a person to marry. The Government of your country should protect your family and its members.

Article 17: You have the right to own things and nobody has the right to take these from you without a good reason.

Article 18: You have the right to profess your religion freely, to change it, and to practice it either on your own or with other people.

Article 19: You have the right to think what you want, and to say what you like, and nobody should forbid you from doing so. You should be able to share your ideas—also with people from any other country.

Article 20: You have the right to organize peaceful meetings or to take part in meetings in a peaceful way. It is wrong to force someone to belong to a group.

(Continued)

Article 21: You have the right to take part in your country's political affairs either by belonging to the Government yourself of by choosing politicians who have the same ideas as you. Governments should be voted for regularly and voting should be secret. You should get a vote and all votes should be equal. You also have the same right to join the public service as anyone else.

Article 22: The society in which you live should help you to develop and to make the most of all the advantages (culture, work, social welfare) that are offered to you and to all the men and women in your country.

Article 23: You have the right to work, to be free to choose your work, and to get a salary that allows you to live and support your family. If a man and a woman do the same work, they should get the same pay. All people who work have the right to join together to defend their interests.

Article 24: Each work day should not be too long, since everyone has the right to rest and should be able to take regular paid holidays.

Article 25: You have the right to have whatever you need so that you and your family: do not fall ill; do not go hungry; have clothes and a house; and are helped if you are out of work, if you are ill, if you are old, if your wife or husband is dead, or if you do not earn a living for any other reason you cannot help. Both a mother who is going to have a baby and her baby should get special help. All children have the same rights, whether or not the mother is married.

Article 26: You have the right to go to school and everyone should go to school. Primary schooling should be free. You should be able to learn a profession or continue your studies as far as you wish. At school, you should be able to develop all your talents and you should be taught to get on with others, whatever their race, their religion or the country they come from. Your parents have the right to choose how and what you will be taught at school.

Article 27: You have the right to share in your community's arts and sciences, and in any good they do. Your works as an artist, a writer or a scientist should be protected, and you should be able to benefit from them.

Article 28: To make sure that your rights will be respected, there must be an "order" that can protect them. This "order" should be local and worldwide.

Article 29: You have duties towards the community within which your personality can fully develop. The law should guarantee human rights. It should allow everyone to respect others and to be respected.

Article 30: No society and no human being in any part of the world should act in such a way as to destroy the rights that you have just been reading about. (United Nations, 2004, Annex 1)

Note: Permission to reprint granted by the Office of the United Nations High Commissioner for Human Rights.

Since 1948, several other human rights–related documents have been endorsed by much of the international community. Together with the UDHR, the International Covenant on Civil and Political Rights (General Assembly of the United Nations, 1966a) and the International Covenant on Economic, Social, and Cultural Rights (General Assembly of the United Nations, 1966b) along with their optional protocols are considered the "International Bill of Human Rights" (United Nations Office of the High Commissioner for Human Rights, 1996). We might add to these central documents, the Convention on the Elimination of All Forms of Discrimination against Women

(United Nations, 1979), the Convention on the Rights of the Child (General Assembly of the United Nations, 1990, Sept. 2) and its protocols, and the Convention on the Rights of Persons with Disabilities (United Nations, 2006, Dec. 13). Collectively, they help us comprehend the nature and meaning of "human rights." As Amnesty International (1997) states:

> **Human rights** can be defined as those basic standards without which people cannot live in dignity as human beings. Human rights are the foundation of freedom, justice and peace. Their respect allows the individual and the community to fully develop. . . . They are proclaimed in the Universal Declaration of Human Rights. Also, documents such as the International Covenants on Human Rights set out what governments must do and also what they must not do to respect the rights of their citizens. (paras. 1–3)

Human rights reflect certain characteristics: They are **innate** or **inherent**. Each person is born with them. They do not have to be granted by anyone else. Human rights are also **universal**. They apply to all humans—no exceptions. Each and every one of us have human rights; and we always have them. They are **inalienable**. They cannot be taken away. Human rights are **indivisible**. All humans inherently possess all human rights all the time. We cannot be denied any of them— regardless of status or circumstance.

Integral to our rights, however, is our responsibility to respect the human rights of others. Not surprisingly, our rights sometimes conflict with our responsibilities. Article 1 of the UDHR suggests that we adopt "a spirit of brotherhood" in our interactions with one another. This includes the manner in which we address the inevitable tensions among "my rights," "your rights," and "our rights." Sometimes, we recognize that full exercise of our own rights so profoundly violates those of others that we defer; and do so as brothers and sisters within the human family. At other times, however, individuals, groups, or states assert their rights so absolutely that their actions place people in danger.

Let's consider a brief example. Suppose Greg and Sarah belong to a religion that relies on faith, prayer, and spiritual healing to cure physical illness. They avoid medical doctors and refuse interventions such as surgery or medication. Their 3-year-old child Eddie becomes feverish, vomits, and cannot evacuate his bowels. From a medical perspective, it appears that he has an obstructed bowel. If provided quickly, medical intervention is almost always successful. Treatment may include placement of a tube through the nose into the gastric system and the provision of fluids and electrolytes along with pain and antiemetic medications. If medical treatment is delayed and the blockage does not clear, surgery may be required. Unfortunately, unresolved and untreated bowel obstruction is often fatal.

Greg and Sarah love Eddie and they suffer along with him. They pray constantly and engage in spiritual healing. Church elders attend the boy, pray for him, and anoint him with oils. However, the bowel blockage continues, Eddie's health deteriorates, and within a few days, he dies.

In caring for Eddie, Greg and Sarah assert several of their human rights. These include the right to "freedom of thought, conscience, and religion" and the right "to manifest (their) religion or belief in teaching, practice, worship and observance" (Article 18); and their right to protection from "arbitrary interference with (their) privacy, family, (and) home" (Article 12) (General Assembly of the United Nations, 1948).

Only 3 years of age and Sarah and Greg's child, Eddie nonetheless has a right to be recognized "everywhere as a person before the law" (Article 6); a right "to medical care" (Article 25) and, most importantly, "the right to life" (Article 3). Furthermore, "childhood (is) entitled to special care and assistance . . . [and] . . . all children shall enjoy the same social protection" (Article 25) (General Assembly of the United Nations, 1948).

The Convention on the Rights of the Child reinforces the special protections afforded to all children including the principle that "the best interests of the child shall be a primary consideration" in decision making (Article 3). States[12] are expected to "ensure the child such protection and care as is necessary for his or her well-being" (Article 3); "recognize that every child has the inherent right to life ... (and) ... ensure to the maximum extent possible the survival and development of the child" (Article 6); "recognize the right of the child to the enjoyment of the highest attainable standard of health and to facilities for the treatment of illness and rehabilitation of health ... (and) ... ensure that no child is deprived of his or her right of access to such health care services ... (and) ... take all effective and appropriate measures with a view to abolishing traditional practices prejudicial to the health of children" (Article 24) (General Assembly of the United Nations, 1990, Sept. 2).[13]

As we consider these various human rights, the conflict becomes clear. Sarah and Greg have the right to their religious beliefs and practices, and a right to the protection of their family from arbitrary state interference. These are considered "first generation" rights in that they focus on individual liberties. In this case, their first-generation rights conflict with Eddie's special rights as a child: his right to health care, to treatment that is in his best interest and, most importantly, his right to life. Based on their protected religious beliefs, Greg and Sarah attempt to care for Eddie through their traditional methods of spiritual healing and refuse to allow medical intervention. In so doing, however, they neglect Eddie's rights to health care and to life. In such circumstances, others in society have an obligation to ensure them on his behalf. Eddie's right to health care and other security-oriented rights (such as rights to food, shelter, employment, education, and a reasonable standard of living) are called second-generation rights. They are typically sponsored or endorsed by the state.

In essence, the human rights community at large recognizes that faith—even religious faith—does not supersede scientific knowledge when the faith-based practices jeopardize the health and life of the child. In such circumstances, the security and safety rights of children take precedence over the liberty rights of their parents. This, however, is not a universal view. Some states and cultures consider parents' rights to practice their religion and to raise their children as they see fit as more important than their children's rights to health and life.

Indeed, states address conflicts between liberty and security rights in different ways.[14] Consider, for example, the "right to life" and the "right to safety." Use of the death penalty clearly involves a violation of the right to life. However, people also have a right to safety from others' violent behavior. Some countries seek to protect their general population from such violence through torture-free incarceration—respecting both the safety rights of people in the community as well as the rights of violent offenders to life. Others impose the death penalty for some violent offenses. In so doing, they convey respect for community safety rights but violate the right of offenders to their lives. By 2013, some 140 nations had discontinued the practice of capital punishment—a substantial change from the 17 countries which had done so by 1977. However, the United States, North Korea, Iran, Iraq, China, Syria, Saudi Arabia, and some 51 more countries retain the death penalty (Amnesty International, 2013). In addition, many more, including the United States, permit the

---

[12] In this discussion, the term *states* is used broadly to include nations, tribes, and communities; and the governing bodies that enact and enforce policies.

[13] Each year, dozens of children and adults in the United States die due to refused medical care on religious grounds. In recent years, several children from a single church in Oregon died as faith healings were adopted instead of medical treatment. Two died from burst appendices, two more due to diabetes, another from a urinary tract infection, a 9-day-old from pneumonia, and a 15-month-old who only needed an antibiotic to deal with an infection (Tilkin, 2013, Nov. 7). A few years ago, Oregon changed its law to better protect minor children. However, based on the principle of religious freedom, some states still permit faith healing in lieu of medical treatment—even for life-threatening conditions.

[14] Drone strikes against suspected terrorists in other countries reflects how the United States currently (2015) addresses the conflict between the security rights of the nation's population and the liberty rights of those targeted. "Extraordinary rendition" of suspects represents another resolution of the tension between "our" and "their" rights.

use of solitary confinement in prison although coerced isolation may represent a form of torture and violate Article 5 of the UDHR.

Despite the freedoms of thought and religion contained in Articles 18 and 19, about one-quarter of all countries maintain anti-blasphemy laws. Some 21 nations do not permit **apostasy**—that is, the right to reject one's religion or change to another (Pew Research Center, 2014, May 28). Indeed, the penal codes of numerous countries prohibit **blasphemy**, apostasy, and atheism. Some can impose the death penalty for "cursing God." Several countries can punish alleged adulterous women and rape victims through public stoning, whiplashing, imprisonment, or beheading. In an extreme form of victim-blaming, rape victims are considered in some cultures to have "caused" the crime of rape by, for example, walking alone on a public street. Throughout much of the world, women remain subordinate to men, earn less than men for the same work, and have fewer rights than men. Millions of young girls—some as young as 8 years old—continue to be forced into marriage to adult men; and female circumcision remains widely practiced. Several religions explicitly assign women a lower status than men and refer to sacred texts to support blatant sex discrimination. Many such religious and cultural practices become legislated and serve both as God's law and the law of the land. In such contexts, the idea of full human rights for women and girls remains inconceivable.

The rights of gay and lesbian peoples also remain largely unrecognized and unprotected in many parts of our world. Although considerable progress is evident in Europe and some parts of the United States, a large number of nations and many religions continue to discriminate against and oppress members of **LGBTQIA** (lesbian, gay, bisexual, transgender, queer, questioning, intersexed, allies, and/or asexual) communities. Some religions prohibit gay people from membership, and at least one endorses their execution. Many countries (and some U.S. states) retain laws that criminalize homosexual behavior. And, as we social workers know, in many parts of the world, gay people are denied the right to marry, adopt children, and work in certain occupations. The political and cultural obstacles are enormous. As is the case for women and girls, gay people are unlikely to achieve full human rights throughout the world anytime in the near future.

In a modest signal of potential change, however, the United Nations Human Rights Council (UNHRC) in 2011 voted 23 to 19 to pass a resolution *"Expressing grave concern* at acts of violence and discrimination, in all regions of the world, committed against individuals because of their sexual orientation and gender identity" (2011, June 15, p. 1). Included among those voting for the resolution were Europe, many Latin American nations, and the United States. Opponents included Nigeria, Pakistan, Russia, and Saudi Arabia. China and two other nations abstained. In 2014, the UNHRC continued this initiative by "*Welcoming* positive developments at the international, regional and national levels in the fight against violence and discrimination based on sexual orientation and gender identity" (2014, Sept. 22, p. 2).

A formal UN declaration of human rights for LGBTQIA peoples remains unlikely as many religiously dominated nations maintain anti-homosexual legislation. In 2014, some 78 countries had laws against homosexual activity. Between 5 and 11 of these nations can impose the death penalty for homosexual behavior (Itaborahy & Zhu, 2014). Although Europe is entirely free of such legislation and in 2003, the U.S. Supreme Court determined that anti-sodomy laws were unconstitutional (*"Lawrence v. Texas,"* 2003), some 13 U.S. state legislatures have yet to repeal those statutes so that LGBT people remain vulnerable to arrest in those locales (Mogul, Ritchie, & Whitlock, 2011). Shortly after federal courts struck down state laws that limited marriage to heterosexual couples ("one man and one woman"), several states responded by proposing Religious Freedom Restoration Acts (RFRA) that appear similar to the federal RFRA passed into law in 1993. Unlike the federal act, however, these more recent state versions extend religious freedom rights to businesses, corporations, and other commercial entities. For example, suppose a pizza restaurant owner determined that homosexual behavior constitutes a "sin and an abomination" according to his religious beliefs. Based upon his beliefs, he could prohibit his employees from selling pizzas to people who appeared gay, lesbian, or transgendered. Similarly, a bakery could refuse to sell wedding cakes intended for consumption at same-sex marriage celebrations. It remains conceivable that some medical doctors and clinics could deny health care to people they consider "sinful" in some way.

Such "religious freedoms" seem to conflict with federal laws and regulations that protect individuals against discrimination on the basis, for example, of race, skin color, sex, age, ethnic heritage, religion (or no religion), national origin, political beliefs, or disability (U.S. Department of Labor, 2015); and, on the basis of Executive Order 13672, gender identity and sexual orientation (Department of Labor Office of Federal Contract Compliance Programs, 2014). Indeed, some aspects of recent state-sponsored RFRA initiatives appear to establish a "right to discriminate"—perhaps especially against members of the LGBTQIA community—as long as such discrimination is based on religious grounds.

Although 113 nations legally protect the right of consenting adults to engage in private homosexual behavior, marriage of same-sex couples remains limited to 14 countries (Itaborahy & Zhu, 2014, p. 9). Throughout much of the world, employers, landlords, religious organizations, and businesses maintain a legal right to discriminate against people on the basis of sexual orientation and gender identity.

Social, Economic, and Environmental Justice

Although many social workers worldwide readily concur with the principles contained in the International Bill of Human Rights, several nations have signed but not ratified all of the covenants and conventions. Nonetheless, social workers benefit from familiarity with these internationally supported human rights because they represent a vital dimension in our consideration of social, economic, and environmental justice.

Social Justice

Like human rights, social justice involves many forms and dimensions. As Van Soest and Garcia (2003) observe, "The term 'social justice' is widely used in social work without a clearly articulated and shared definition or understanding of it" (p. 44). They encourage us to ask these questions: "What is justice? What is fairness? Is life fair or just? What kind of justice can be expected?" (p. 44).

As a starting point, we can view **social justice** as a condition in which human rights are cherished as inviolate and indivisible. In other words, human rights—perhaps as envisioned in the International Bill of Rights—serve as a touchstone by which social justice can be considered. Without some consensus about human rights, we could not determine what is just or unjust. In a just world, human rights are respected by people and social systems wherever we live, work, or play. Furthermore, human rights education would be widespread.[15]

Social justice, of course, involves different aspects. **Distributive justice**, for instance, involves the allocation of opportunities, costs, and benefits within social systems. Distributive justice is commonly associated with economic justice—how resources and wealth are distributed within and among groups, communities, and societies—and with society's responsibility for and accountability to

---

[15] You might ask yourself how much you were introduced to principles of human rights or civil rights in your own educational experiences in lower, middle, and high school years. A secondary question might be, "During my formal education, how much emphasis was placed on 'students' rights' so that I knew the nature and extent of my rights and responsibilities as well as how to file a grievance when one or more of my rights were abridged?" Finally, as you pursue higher education in social work, you might ask how much you are learning about the rights of prospective, current, and former clients so that you can better respect them and offer advice when their rights are violated.

individuals for ensuring their fundamental human rights. **Procedural justice** refers to the ways and means of interaction and decision making between individuals or within a group, organization, community, or society. Procedural justice involves the fairness of processes involved in, for instance, negotiations of agreements or contracts, selection of authorities (for example, governing officials, judges), and the development and implementation of laws, policies, and programs. **Retributive justice** refers to punishment, rehabilitation, compensation, or restitution for harm done by or to one or more members of the social group. **Restorative justice** involves attempts to repair damage done to those negatively affected by offenses. Whereas retribution tends to be associated with revenge upon and punishment of offenders, restoration is associated with efforts, as far as humanly possible, to repair or recompense those negatively affected by damaging offenses. Offenders' restorative efforts sometimes result in transformative experiences for themselves as well as their victims.

Intergenerational justice involves the opportunities, resources, and burdens one generation leaves to others. When previous generations, for example, capture, transport, and enslave millions of human beings, amass an enormous public debt, or create a toxic global ecology, questions of intergenerational justice arise. Subsequent generations are affected by the actions and inactions of earlier generations. **Environmental justice** refers to the distribution of risks and benefits associated with environmental conditions. When, for instance, one group of people is routinely exposed to toxins in the earth, water, or air whereas another group has ready and plentiful access to fresh water, clean air, and rich soil, we may reasonably raise questions about environmental justice.

Over the centuries, many philosophers and social scientists have explored the topic of justice. To determine whether a society is just, Sandel (2009) suggests that we "ask how it distributes the things we prize—income and wealth, duties and rights, powers and opportunities, offices and honors. A just society distributes these goods in the right way; it gives each person his or her due. The hard questions begin when we ask what people are due, and why" (p. 19).

Sandel (2009) identifies three major aspects of justice: "welfare, freedom, and virtue" (p. 19). As depicted in Figure 4.2, these elements sometimes complement each other (or overlap) and sometimes conflict (or separate). Promotion of the general welfare may conflict with some features of individual freedom or virtue. For instance, a society may engage in the torture or murder of suspected terrorists in an attempt to safeguard its residents from violent attack. The maltreatment or killing constitutes nonvirtuous behavior that violates the freedom and human rights of suspects

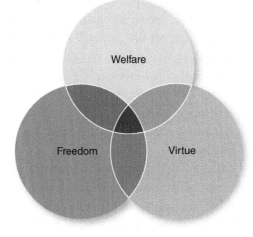

FIGURE 4.2   Sandel's Three Aspects of Justice
Adapted from Sandel's (2009) conceptualization.

despite the fact that it is undertaken in an attempt to protect the society's population (that is, to maintain the general welfare).

A society may prize the opportunity for individuals and families to accumulate enormous personal wealth (freedom) despite the promotion of corruption and economic inequality. Excessive selfishness and greed may conflict with views about virtue, and severe economic inequality tends to impact the general welfare. On the other hand, efforts to distribute wealth more evenly or to promote universal access to education, employment, or health care (despite their virtuous intent and the benefit to a large proportion of a population) would usually be unsuccessful in a society where individual freedom is valued more highly than virtue and the general welfare.

The late John Rawls has been an influential figure in the intellectual exploration of the topic of social justice. Author of *A Theory of Justice* (1971, 1999) and *Justice as Fairness* (1958; Rawls & Kelly, 2001), Rawls' ideas can be controversial. Indeed, some have been criticized (Sandel, 1982). Nonetheless, his works serve as a useful introduction to the topic of social justice. His approach involves several key concepts and principles.

The idea of the **original position** (Rawls, 1971) involves the assumption of a hypothetical **veil of ignorance**. In other words, participants to a negotiation or discussion agree to operate as if they are unaware of their own and others' sex, age, class, race, and status or place in the social structure. Through this hypothetical veil of ignorance, participants transcend narrow, individual self-interest to devise and agree upon contracts or policies that benefit all participants and nonparticipants alike. Based upon reason rather than self-interest or prejudice, decisions reached when stakeholders adopt the original position tend to lead to fair and reasonable distribution of the costs, risks, and benefits associated with an endeavor.

Once we assume the original position, we can more easily understand concepts of justice and fairness, and envision the consequences of laws and principles that discriminate against certain people in terms of opportunity or outcome. If we abandon the original position, self-interest takes over. For instance, if I am male and own a farm or a business and a slave, and consider my wife and children as forms of quasi-property, then I might well propose a process of decision making (for example, voting processes) that includes only male property owners and excludes women, children, and slaves from participation. However, if I adopt the original position, I might well ask questions such as, "What might be the implications of such a decision-making process on me—if I were ignorant about my status now or in the future? I might or might not own property. I might or might not be a man, a woman, a child, or a slave? What would I consider fair and just if I did not know in advance what status I might hold and therefore could not determine how a policy or procedure would personally affect me?"

In some ways, Rawls' original position represents a form of "golden-rule" thinking through which we anticipate the effects of our actions on anybody and everybody affected by those actions. The "golden rule" suggests, in effect, that we "do to others what we would have them do to us." In Confucian philosophy, the concept of *Jen* involves virtues of goodness and benevolence (for example, interest, concern, and care for others—regardless of their station or circumstances). Confucius captures the essence of Jen through the passage "Do not do to others what you would not like them to do to you." This is sometimes referred to as the "silver rule," which naturally serves to complement and complete the "golden rule."

By adopting Rawls' original position, we become more able to consider the implications of our own or others' actions on people who differ from ourselves and to be more fair to others in our words and deeds. We might even become less egocentric, less ethnocentric, less xenophobic, and perhaps even less anthropocentric in our thoughts and actions. Rawls suggests that when we adopt the original position we become more likely to propose reasonable ideas and to think carefully about the ideas of others. If we were to do so, we would engage in discussions until everyone—each adopting the original position—reached a decision that everyone considers fair and just.

Compare such a perspective and approach with those common in today's financial, political, and industrial circles. In contemporary life, status, privilege, wealth, and power—including access to power—tend to dominate the processes of decision making.[16] This raises the question of procedural justice. Unless organized into groups, less powerful people, members of minority communities, immigrants, refugees, current and former prisoners, unemployed individuals and families, persons assigned a severe psychiatric diagnosis, less educated or less able people, and homeless people rarely have genuine input into decision-making processes—even though they are often significantly impacted by the results.

Rawls suggests that, in essence, justice is **fairness**. If people were, somehow, able to adopt the original position in their consensual pursuit of fairness and social justice, they would likely agree on two fundamental principles. The first principle holds that all people have an absolute, inviolate right to certain fundamental liberties—including the right to free speech and participation in decision-making processes that affect us, others, and the community or society as a whole.[17] The second principle suggests that we, collectively, as a community or society of equals—each of us possessing these fundamental liberties—might agree that in certain areas, under certain circumstances, and at certain times, some degree of inequality (in terms of distribution of wealth, power, or opportunity) serves to benefit the community or society as a whole substantially more than equal distribution under the same conditions. However, we might also decide that the collective benefits of such defined and limited unequal distribution must clearly outweigh its negative effects. Finally, in order to ensure justice as fairness, we would likely adopt the **difference principle**. That principle holds that we might decide to accept some forms of inequality if, but only if, that inequality is directed toward and benefits the least powerful and least advantaged among us. If we adopt the original position, most of us would consider forms of distribution that benefit the powerful and advantaged at the expense of the powerless and disadvantaged to be unfair and unjust.

Along with immigrants, current and former prisoners are among the least powerful and least advantaged people in the contemporary United States. Indeed, when certain groups of people are disproportionately incarcerated in jails and prisons, we may appropriately raise questions about the fairness of the *retributive justice* system (Western, 2006). In 1980, about 500,000 people were imprisoned in the United States; by the end of 2013, the number of incarcerated adults had grown to 2,227,500—the highest number of prisoners and the highest incarceration rate (910 per 100,000 adults) in the world. If we add the number of adults who remain in probation or parole to the number of those incarcerated in the United States the total comes to 6,906,200 adults (1 of every 35) who were under the supervision of correctional systems at the end of 2013 (Glaze & Kaeble, 2014, Dec. 19). Millions more have completed their prison sentences and the terms of their paroles but continue to be denied certain basic rights. For example, ex-felons interested in higher education are typically ineligible for federally sponsored student loans, public housing, and many social

---

[16] In the famous or infamous 5-to-4 decision ("*Citizens United v. Federal Election Commission*," 2010), the U.S. Supreme Court endorsed the right of large organizations—including corporations—to make unlimited contributions to influence elections through political campaign advertising. The ruling had the effect of granting human rights to corporations (corporate personhood) and, in effect, permitting the "purchase of elections."

[17] Voter participation in the United States has declined dramatically in recent decades. Lower voter rates are probably due, in part, to increased obstacles to voting. In addition, however, there appears to be growing belief that the system is "rigged" (through gerrymandering, the "legal" buying of elections, and the dominance of mostly rich, white males in legislative bodies). Indeed, the notion that the views of average people are essentially ignored is supported by research findings "that economic elites and organized groups representing business interests have substantial independent impacts on U.S. government policy, while average citizens and mass-based interest groups have little or no independent influence" (Gilens & Page, 2014, p. 564). In terms of electoral integrity in 2013, the United States was ranked 25th of 86 nations overall and especially low in both campaign finance and voting district boundary-making. The common practice of changing boundary lines (gerrymandering) to favor a particular political party compromised electoral integrity in the United States (Norris, Frank, & Martínez i Coma, 2014a, 2014b).

programs. In many states, former offenders are denied the right to vote,[18] run for public office, or serve on juries. Many remain ineligible for licensure in professions such as social work and various other occupations. A large number of parents cannot regain custody of their children after their release from prison. Many are denied bank loans, employment, and private housing. Punishment continues long after they completed their sentences and "done the time." It is not unreasonable to suggest that many people—once incarcerated—are effectively assigned a "life sentence."

By way of comparison, in mid-to-late 2013, Japan incarcerated about 54 people per 100,000; Denmark about 73 per 100,000; and France about 98 per 100,000 (Walmsley, 2013, Nov. 21). Furthermore, incarceration rates vary within nations. For example, in 2013, the U.S. states of Arkansas, Arizona, Texas, Georgia, Alabama, Mississippi, Oklahoma, and Louisiana reported incarceration rates of 1,010 to 1,420 per 100,000 in adult population. Conversely, the rates of Maine, Minnesota, Massachusetts, Rhode Island, and Vermont ranged between 350 and 400 per 100,000 in adult population (Glaze & Kaeble, 2014, Dec. 19).

The high overall rate of incarceration in the United States and the disproportionate imprisonment rates for African Americans has been referred to as **mass incarceration**, a "new form of slavery," and "The New Jim Crow" (Alexander, 2010). Several factors contribute to this phenomenon. These include, for example, the imprisonment of children (some as young as 8 years old and many sentenced to life without parole); rigid sentencing laws that prevent judges from considering circumstantial and environmental factors; long-term prison sentences for drug users and sellers; and the privatization of prisons. If more prisoners lead to greater profits, we can expect for-profit penal institutions to encourage higher rates of imprisonment (Pelaez, 2014, Mar. 31).

The costs associated with mass incarceration are stunning. In 2012, the average annual cost per prisoner across the United States was $31,286 and varied by state. For example, the cost in New York was about four times the cost in Kentucky: $60,076 and $14,603, respectively (Henrichson & Delaney, 2012, Jan.).[19]

At the end of 2013, the total number of adult African American (black) males incarcerated in U.S. federal or state prisons exceeded that of white males by more than 70,000. In 2010, about 12.6 percent of the nation's population identified themselves as black or African American, 72.4 percent described themselves as white, and 16.3 percent as Hispanic or Latino (U.S. Census Bureau, 2012). However, slightly more than 37 percent (see Table 4.2) of the male prison population was black, about 32 percent was white; and slightly more than 22 percent was Hispanic or Latino (Carson, 2014, Sept. 30; Glaze & Kaeble, 2014, Dec. 19; Humes, Jones, & Ramirez, 2011, Mar.).

The incarceration rates for African American and Hispanic or Latino populations are disproportionately higher than their percentage of the population would predict. Both groups are severely overrepresented in prisons, African Americans dramatically so. Conversely, white males are substantially underrepresented. About 1 percent of men of Hispanic or Latino origin and nearly "3% of black male U.S. residents of all ages were imprisoned on December 31, 2013, compared to 0.5% of white males" (Carson, 2014, Sept. 30, p. 2). At that time, 18- to 19-year-old African American women "were almost 5 times more likely to be imprisoned than white females" in the same age range (Carson, 2014, Sept. 30, p. 8).

The number and rates of "stop and frisk" encounters, arrests, and convictions of persons of color are as disproportionate as those for incarceration rates. Police abuse also falls more upon African American and Hispanic people. Indeed, "driving while black" (Meeks, 2000) and, more recently, "walking, standing, running, bicycling, making eye contact, or sitting while black" have

---

[18] Denial of voting rights after people fulfill all the terms of a prison sentence represents another form of "voter suppression" as young men and women of low-income and minority status are disproportionately arrested, convicted, and imprisoned.

[19] By way of comparison, Utah spends an average of about $6,206; Kentucky $9,391; and New York $19,552 per year to educate each public school child.

TABLE 4.2	Percentage of U.S. Population by White, Black, and Hispanic Ethnic Origin and by Percentage of Inmates in State and Federal Prisons in 2013				
White (not Hispanic or Latino)		Black or African American		Hispanic or Latino	
Percentage of U.S. Population	Percentage of U.S. Prison Population	Percentage of U.S. Population	Percentage of U.S. Prison Population	Percentage of U.S. Population	Percentage of U.S. Prison Population
62.6%	33.33%	13.2%	36.20%	17.1%	21.90%

Note: Includes inmates 18 years of age and older with greater than 1-year sentences assigned to state and federal adult prisons. Numbers are rounded (Glaze & Kaeble, 2014, Dec. 19). Population data from U.S. Census Bureau (2013, July 1)

become memes that reflect some of what Michelle Alexander captures in *The New Jim Crow: Mass Incarceration in the Age of Colorblindness* (2010).

In 2014–2015, several African American men and boys were killed by police in various cities and towns throughout the United States. This led to community protests about institutionalized racism and the dehumanization of minority populations by police departments and governmental officials. Slogans began to appear on signs, bumper stickers, and tee shirts: "Black Lives Matter," "Don't Shoot," and "I Can't Breathe!" On April 12, 2015, Mr. Freddie Carlos Gray, Jr., a young African American in Baltimore, was injured while in police custody. Subsequently hospitalized, he died on April 19th. The reason for his arrest: a Baltimore police lieutenant "made eye contact" with Mr. Gray who "subsequently ran away" from police. A pursuit ensued before Mr. Gray surrendered to police officers without resistance. He was then placed into a Baltimore Police Department van where "Mr. Gray suffered a severe and critical neck injury as a result of being handcuffed, shackled by his feet and unrestrained inside of the BPD wagon. . . ." (Mosby, 2015, May 1).

Many deaths in police custody do not receive impartial investigations or subsequent prosecution. During the 2005–2015 time frame, only "54 officers nationwide . . . (were) . . . criminally charged after they shot and killed someone in the line of duty" (Cholakov, Kelly, Kindy, & Schaul, 2015, Apr. 11, para. 1) In the case of Mr. Freddie Gray, however, Maryland State Attorney Marilyn Mosby brought charges against six Baltimore police officers. The alleged offenses included second-degree depraved murder, manslaughter, assault, false imprisonment, and misconduct in office (Mosby, 2015, May 1). She noted that police officers "failed to establish probable cause for Mr. Gray's arrest as no crime had been committed by Mr. Gray. Accordingly . . . (the officers) . . . illegally arrested Mr. Gray" (Mosby, 2015, May 1)—an arrest that led directly to his death.

Unfortunately, homicides by police are not uncommon. During the 2003 through 2009 time frame, at least 2,931 people were killed by police during arrest-related activities (Bureau of Justice Statistics, 2011, Nov.). During the 7-year period ending in 2012, about 400 people were killed by police each year. Close to two each week involved a black person and at least one white police officer. About 18 percent of black deaths by police each year were children or youth under the age of 21. Only 8.7 percent of white deaths by police fell into that age range (Johnson et al., 2014, May 8). In 2014, "at least 304 black people were killed by police in the United States" (Mapping Police Violence, 2015). More than 100 of the 304 were unarmed.

In the month of March 2015 alone, "36 black people were killed by police. . . . (That's about) one black person every 21 hours" (Mapping Police Violence, 2015).[20] Between January 1 and June 11, 2015,

---

[20] Based in part on the limitations associated with official U.S. statistics on police violence, in May 2015, *The Washington Post* published analyses of police shootings during the previous decade (Kindy, 2015, May 30; Kindy & Kelly, 2015, Apr. 11). At about that time, *The Guardian* newspapers began to publish an interactive database entitled "The Counted: People Killed by Police in the U.S." Find it at **http://www.theguardian.com/us-news/series/counted-us-police-killings**.

at least 506 people were killed by police in the United States. Some 249 were white, 144 were black, 79 were Hispanic/Latino, 10 were Asian or Pacific Islander, 5 were Native American, and 19 were of unknown or other ethnicity (*The Guardian*, 2015, June). Many of those killed by police demonstrated behaviors typical of easily recognized mental health problems (Bouchard, 2012, Dec. 9).

Obviously, poor judgment, impulse control problems, and racist attitudes of individual police officers play significant roles in police brutality. Individual characteristics are important and officers bear personal responsibility for their actions. However, a much larger factor in police misconduct involves the systemic and institutionalized racism, sexism, ableism, and other forms of prejudice and discrimination that pervade our institutions and our cultures. Individuals mirror the society at large; our beliefs, behaviors and processes parallel those of the larger systems in which we function.[21] As social workers seeking to understand and to help, let's recognize **parallel processes** throughout our micro, mezzo, and macro systems; and always maintain our focus on the person-in-environment as the fundamental unit of attention. If we ignore the environment and attend only to the person, our understanding will be incomplete and inaccurate.

Just as a mere handful of soldiers were charged and convicted of crimes related to the torture and inhumane treatment of Iraqi prisoners in the Abu Ghraib detention facility during the 2003 to 2006 time period (CNN, 2013, Oct. 30), police officers are only rarely charged with crimes for the death or injury of detainees. High-level officials of the organizational systems and cultures that perpetuate racial violence usually escape criticism or censure. A typical explanation involves the "few bad apples" justification. Our systems and processes, and our environments remain unexamined and unindicted. In other words, the individual alone—the "bad apple"—is deemed fully responsible and guilty; while our leaders, our culture, our history, and, of course, the rest of us are viewed as blameless and "innocent."

As social workers, we question the utility and the validity of such one-dimensional explanations. As does Philip Zimbardo in regard to the Abu Ghraib crimes (Zimbardo, 2007), social workers tend to think in person-in-environment terms. Rather than viewing individuals as completely autonomous free agents, we seek to understand people, problems, and issues from a multidimensional perspective. In so doing, we often find sources of individual behavior in the larger political, economic, religious, and cultural systems where people live, work, and recreate.[22] This includes our view of individual police officers who misbehave. They too tend to be creatures of their cultures, their circumstances, and the primary peer groups with which they affiliate.

As reflected by civil lawsuit settlements, police brutality and other forms of misconduct are not only common, they are widely recognized and anticipated by police departments and by city and other governmental officials. Many of the larger cities in the United States pay out millions of dollars each year to settle civil suits against their police departments. It's so common that cities incorporate large budgetary line items for settlements as an anticipated "cost of doing business." The figures are enormous. During the 5-year period from 2009 to 2014, New York City paid some $428,000,000 to settle claims which included the police department as a defendant (Brown, 2014, Oct. 10). Other cities also spend millions in settlement costs. Philadelphia "paid out more than $40,000,000 in damages and settlements as a result of nearly 600 misconduct lawsuits brought against the police department since 2009" (Feathers, 2014, Oct. 20, para. 1). "Brutality-related lawsuits have cost Chicago taxpayers $521 million over the last decade" (Shaw, 2014, Apr. 14, para. 3). During

---

[21] The insidious nature and extent of racism in the United States today is dramatically captured in the streaming video *Racism Is Real* distributed by Brave New Films (Marcano, 2015). See it at **www.bravenewfilms.org** or on YouTube and elsewhere. Also see the video *A Matter of Place* sponsored by The Fair Housing Justice Center. See it at **http://www.fairhousingjustice .org**, YouTube, Vimeo, and elsewhere.

[22] See the subsection entitled "Parallel Process" later in this chapter.

the 2011 to 2014 time period, the city of Baltimore "paid about $5.7 million . . . (plus an additional $5.8 million in legal fees) . . . over lawsuits claiming that police officers brazenly beat up alleged suspects" (Puente, 2014, Sept. 28, para. 1).

Funded largely through the U.S. 1033 program, local police departments and personnel receive military weapons designed to wage war on enemy combatants (Balko, 2013). The military equipment is free. In addition to Armored Personnel Carriers (APCs) and Mine Resistant Ambush Protected (MRAP) vehicles, many local police forces possess military-grade body armor, assault weapons, flashbang grenades, smoke bombs, bomb suits, night vision goggles, and battering rams—the same equipment used by soldiers in Iraq and Afghanistan (Musgrave, 2014, Oct. 14).

> Pentagon donations to the police reached $532 million in 2012 and $449 million in 2013. The figure has already topped $750 million in 2014. Why? The accelerating pace of the withdrawal from Afghanistan. . . . With more and more hardware set to become available over the coming 12 months, Americans are going to have to get used to their police officers resembling a well-equipped special-forces unit. This is despite the fact that violent crime reached an all-time low in the United States in 2010. (McCarthy, 2014, Aug. 15)

Equipped and trained as they are, police personnel often look and behave more like soldiers in a war zone than fellow citizens whose purpose is "to protect and to serve."[23] The **militarization of policing** "encourages officers to adopt a 'warrior' mentality and think of the people they are supposed to serve as enemies" (American Civil Liberties Union, 2014, p. 3).

A study of SWAT team activities by 20 local law enforcement agencies found that SWAT teams were deployed some 800 times during 2011 and 2012. Some 79 percent of SWAT missions were to execute search warrants—usually related to drug activity. Indeed, 62 percent of the time, teams were sent out to conduct a search for drugs, 28 percent of the time for other reasons, and 9 percent for unknown reasons. "Only a small handful of deployments (7 percent) were for hostage, barricade, or active shooter scenarios" (American Civil Liberties Union, 2014, p. 5).

> SWAT was created to deal with emergency situations such as hostage, barricade and active shooter scenarios. Over time, however, law enforcement agencies have moved away from this original purpose and are increasingly using these paramilitary squads to search people's homes for drugs. (American Civil Liberties Union, 2014, p. 2)

By virtue of their roles and responsibilities, police officers are often placed in physical danger. A substantial number die in the line of duty—most as a result of automobile or motorcycle accidents—but many are killed by suspects. During the decade ending at the conclusion of 2013, an average of about 57 police officers were shot, stabbed, or beaten to death each year in the United States (National Law Enforcement Officers Memorial Fund, 2014, Dec. 30). Regardless of who kills or beats whom, however, it is clear that violence represents a significant social problem in the United States. Obvious disparities in the racial and ethnic composition of our prisons and in suspects detained, arrested, brutalized, or killed by police raise serious concerns about the role of racism throughout the criminal justice system. "Racial minorities are more likely than white Americans to be arrested; once arrested, they are more likely to be convicted; and once convicted, they are more likely to face stiff sentences" (The Sentencing Project, 2013, Aug., p. 1). One of every three black men and one of every six Latino men end up in prison at some point during their lives—compared to 1 of 17 white men (The Sentencing Project, 2013, Aug.). "More African

---

[23] This motto was first adopted in 1955 by the Los Angeles Police Academy and subsequently in 1963 by the entire Los Angeles Police Department (LAPD).

Americans are under correctional control today—in prison or jail, on probation or parole—than were enslaved in 1850" (Alexander, 2010, p. 175).[24]

Slavery was officially outlawed in the United States when the 13th Amendment to the U.S. Constitution was ratified on December 18, 1865. The 14th Amendment, in July 1868, guaranteed all Americans—including black Americans—equal protection under the law; and, the 15th Amendment granted African American men, but not women (of any race or ethnicity), the right to vote.[25] The conclusion of the Civil War and the ratification of the 14th, 15th, and 16th Amendments were, obviously, celebrated by black Americans who had endured nearly 250 years of slavery. Reconstruction generated further optimism as many African Americans ran for and were elected to public office. Unfortunately, hopes for genuine freedom and equality were short-lived. The sharecropping system, instituted following the end of the war—was a modest improvement at best. Whites owned the land and black Americans did the back-breaking work. In return, they received a small share of profits. When federal troops left the southern states in 1878, most gains were quickly reversed as **Jim Crow** legislation proliferated throughout the former Confederate states. In the post-Reconstruction era, laws were enacted that segregated blacks from whites in nearly all areas of life. Other laws made it extremely difficult and often impossible for African Americans to vote; seek political office; attend "white" schools, colleges, and universities; or secure high status, high-paying employment. The Ku Klux Klan (KKK) and other white supremacist groups continued to terrorize black communities by burning crosses in front of homes, setting fire to churches, raping women and girls, and lynching people who challenged whites, asserted their human rights, or simply existed. Under Jim Crow, most African Americans were only marginally better off than they had been under slavery.

Considerable progress occurred during the 1950s and the 1960s when black power and civil rights movements led to legal challenges of Jim Crow laws. The *Brown v. Board of Education* decision of 1954 effectively overturned the "separate but equal" approach permitted under the 1896 *Plessy v. Ferguson* decision. The Court concluded that separate educational facilities were "inherently unequal." The **Voting Rights Act of 1965** essentially required states to uphold the terms of the 14th and 15th Amendments. In the *Loving v. Virginia* case of 1967, the Court determined that state laws prohibiting interracial marriage were unconstitutional.

Unfortunately, the popular optimism of the civil rights era has faded—just at it had during Jim Crow. During the first decade and one-half of the 21st century, so many African Americans have lost or been denied well-paying jobs; so many have been obstructed from voting in public elections; so many have been stopped by police, arrested, charged, convicted, and imprisoned; and so many have been beaten, brutalized, and killed—many by police—that social workers may reasonably ask if we are experiencing another age of repression. As Michelle Alexander suggests (2010), the nation appears to be in the midst of a new Jim Crow era that approximates the original. Indeed, the parallels between the two periods are striking. We probably should not be surprised. Our nation has a long tradition of black enslavement, abuse, exploitation, and dehumanization that began nearly 400 years ago. Today's racially oppressive structures and processes parallel those that began when federal troops left the former Confederate states in 1878.

Parallel Processes: The term **parallel process** was originally used to reference the often remarkable similarities between the relationship of patients and their psychoanalysts, and the relationship of those analysts and their clinical supervisors. Phenomena in one context were so much like those

---

[24] About 3.5 million black adults were in the correctional system (in prison or on parole or probation) at the end of 2007 (The Pew Center on the States, 2009, Mar. 2). Approximately 3.2 million black people were enslaved in 1850 (The New York Times, 1860, July 31).

[25] Women were not granted the right to vote until the 19th Amendment was ratified in 1920.

occurring in the other that it almost seemed that they were physically connected in some way. The relationship processes appeared to function in parallel fashion.

Over the decades, the concept of **parallel process** has expanded considerably to refer to the similarities among structures, beliefs, patterns, and processes at various levels or at different times within a society or culture.

> When two or more systems—whether these consist of individuals, groups, or organizations—have significant relationships with one another, they tend to develop similar affects, cognition, and behaviors, which are defined as *parallel processes*. (Smith, Simmons, & Thames, 1989, p. 13)

The "individual" racism apparent when a white man burns an African American church or brutalizes a black man is reflected in the "systemic" racism apparent in segregated housing policies of the past and practices of the present; in the lynchings of the past and the mass incarceration and police killings of the present; and in the denial of human and voting rights in the past and the voting suppression of the present. Apparent at the individual, group, organization, community, and societal levels in the past, the parallel processes of racial oppression continue into the present.

The African slave trade in the Americas began in 1501 when the first African slaves were shipped to Santa Domingo in the Caribbean. Once started, the buying and selling of black human beings flourished throughout the "New World" for more than three centuries.

In 1619, 20 Africans were delivered as "cargo" to Jamestown, Virginia. During the nearly 250 years that followed, at least another 500,000 were imported to what would become the United States. Millions more were transported from Africa to the Caribbean and to Central and South America. They were bought and sold as property. Considered members of a "subhuman" species, African slaves were denied the basic rights afforded indentured servants, other residents, and, of course, property-owning white men. In agricultural areas, slaves were commonly viewed and treated as a form of livestock whose function was to work the fields and breed additional slaves. Just as a calf born to a steer automatically became the property of the owner, so did the children of slaves. Ownership of human slaves was legal in the colonies and, through omission, remained so under the Articles of Confederation of 1777[26] and later under the U.S. Constitution.

In 1780, Pennsylvania passed the Gradual Abolition Act which emancipated all children born to slaves after that date.[27] In Massachusetts and its districts of Vermont and Maine, slavery was effectively abolished in 1783 when the superior court under Chief Justice William Cushing ruled that slavery was inconsistent with the Commonwealth's new constitution which stated that, "All men are born free and equal, and have certain natural, essential, and unalienable rights; among which may be reckoned the right of enjoying and defending their lives and liberties; that of acquiring, possessing, and protecting property; in fine, that of seeking and obtaining their safety and happiness" (Massachusetts Constitutional Convention of 1779, 1780, June 15). Through that court decision, "the right of Christians to hold Africans in perpetual servitude, and sell and treat them as we do our horses and cattle" (Cushing, 1783, p. 8) was deemed unconstitutional—at least in Massachusetts.

Elsewhere, however, slavery continued to thrive throughout the emerging country. According to the 1790 census, 700,000 or 18 percent of the 3.8 million population were slaves. "In South Carolina, 43 percent of the population was slave. In Maryland 32 percent, and in North Carolina 26 percent. Virginia, with the largest slave population of almost 300,000, had 39 percent of its

---

[26] The Articles of Confederation do not mention slaves nor the institution of slavery. However, slavery had been lawful under British rule and in 1777 had been widely practiced throughout the Colonies for more than 150 years.

[27] If born after 1780, the children of slaves in Pennsylvania were technically free at the time of their birth. However, the Act held that they must remain in servitude until the age of 28. At that point, they obtained their actual freedom.

population made up of slaves" (Mount, 2010, May 20, The Founding Fathers and the Constitution Section, para. 1). In 1787, the Constitutional Convention met in an attempt to improve upon the Articles of Confederation and create a system of government for the United States. Issues related to slavery were central to the negotiations. Although several delegates held abolitionist sentiments, most recognized that a new constitution could not be ratified unless slavery was permitted; and, indeed, it was. Interestingly, the term *slave* or *slavery* does not appear in the U.S. Constitution although a few passages pertain to the issue.

The question of how to count slaves arose in regard to taxation and representation. Delegates from large slave-holding states wanted slaves counted as whole persons for the purposes of deciding the number of state representatives in Congress, but not counted for determining the amount of taxes states paid to the federal government. As it appears in Article 1, Section 2 of the original U.S. Constitution, a compromise was reached in which "other Persons" (that is, slaves) were counted as three-fifths of a "free Person" for the purposes of both taxation and representation. In other words, under the nation's constitution, each slave, although prohibited from actually voting in elections, was valued at 60 percent of a person for purposes that benefited states, the federal government, or both.

Another passage in the original U.S. Constitution pertains to "fugitive" slaves. According to Article IV, Section 2 "No Person held to Service or Labour in one State, under the Laws thereof, escaping into another, shall, in Consequence of any Law or Regulation therein, be discharged from such Service or Labour, But shall be delivered up on Claim of the Party to whom such Service or Labour may be due." In other words, African slaves who escaped or ran away from their "owners" to another state—even to abolitionist states such as Massachusetts—had to be returned to their owners by that state.

Without mentioning it explicitly, one passage within the Constitution addresses the African slave trade. Article I, Section 9 states that, "The Migration or Importation of such Persons as any of the States now existing shall think proper to admit, shall not be prohibited by the Congress prior to the Year one thousand eight hundred and eight, but a tax or duty may be imposed on such Importation, not exceeding ten dollars for each Person." In other words, states could continue to import African slaves for at least another 20 years. In 1808, Congress could decide to enact legislation to prohibit, or to continue, such importation.[28]

The Preamble to the U.S. Constitution of 1789 states that, "We the People of the United States, in Order to form a more perfect Union, establish Justice, insure domestic Tranquility, provide for the common defence, promote the general Welfare, and secure the Blessings of Liberty to ourselves and our Posterity, do ordain and establish this Constitution for the United States of America." African slaves, however, were not included among "we the people" and most of the delegates to the Constitutional Convention never intended them to be. Indeed, "we the people" also did not include women or children, and people who were not "land owners" were extremely suspect.

More than two and one-quarter centuries after approval of the U.S. Constitution, the country has yet to confront the insidious and corrupting consequences of our long history of human slavery and discrimination. Indeed, many contemporary black Americans are mistreated in ways that are shockingly reminiscent of the abuse inflicted upon African slaves before and freed slaves after the Civil War. In other words, the processes parallel each other and will probably continue to do so until the nation reaches a deeper level of compassionate understanding. Public airing and acknowledgement of past and present acts of inhumanity—perhaps through some kind of truth and

---

[28] On March 25, 1807, Congress passed "An Act for the Abolition of the Slave Trade" which prohibited the importation of slaves into the United States.

reconciliation process—might represent a small step (Hayner, 2002; Meierhenrich, 2008; Scott, 2014). It would not be unprecedented.

The United States Commission on Wartime Relocation and Internment of Civilians (1983), for example, publicly acknowledged, apologized, and awarded more than one billion dollars in damages for the mistreatment and dehumanization of Japanese Americans and Alaskan Aleuts who were forcibly relocated into internment camps during World War II. In 1993, the U.S. Congress passed and President Clinton signed into law an acknowledgement and apology for the 1893 overthrow of the Kingdom of Hawaii (United States, 1994; United States Senate Committee on Indian Affairs, 1993) and in 2009, the U.S. Congress passed and President Obama quietly signed into law the Native American Apology Resolution (King, 2011, Dec. 3; McCollum, 2010, Jan. 6). These latter apologies, however, did not provide for damages or reparations, and included disclaimers to limit their use as evidence in civil lawsuits.

In regard to the treatment of people of African heritage, legislation has been introduced in the U.S. Congress and different bills have passed each house. However, a joint resolution was never adopted as disagreements on the issue of reparations could not be resolved. As a result, official U.S. acknowledgement and apology for the 250 years of African slavery and the subsequent racial oppression of African Americans remains unexpressed (Johnson III, 2014, June 17; Scott, 2014).

Based upon the notion of parallel process, we predict that patterns, structures, and processes—such as racial oppression—evident in larger or stronger social systems would appear in smaller or less powerful systems as well. If violence is embraced and widely practiced at the macro-system level by, for example, the national military and federal police; then we can also expect it by local police forces at the mezzo-system level. If police-sponsored violence is acceptable, it would also be common among armed community groups—some of which are called "gangs," "criminals," "thugs," "vigilantes," or "terrorists" while others are known as "private security firms," "neighborhood watch groups," or perhaps even "citizen-militias." If violence is pervasive at the macro and mezzo levels, we can also expect to see it at the micro-system level as well. Likely parallels would include physical punishment and cruelty toward children, women, disabled persons, frail elderly, and nonhuman animals. We would also expect regular outbreaks of individual violence within families, on neighborhood streets, and in public establishments such as schools, places of religious worship, stadiums, clinics, college campuses, shopping malls, or performance halls (Blair & Schweit, 2014; Waller, 2002).

If widespread fraud and corruption is evident in political, governmental, financial, criminal justice, religious and educational systems, we have every reason to expect it to occur among individuals, families, and small groups. If self-centered and narcissistic attitudes and behaviors are prevalent among the rich and powerful, they would occur among those less well off as well.

Fortunately, however, parallel processes are not limited to dysfunctional phenomena. Prosocial patterns can also occur. If, for example, integrity is widely endorsed and practiced, and readily apparent in larger systems, we can expect to find it in smaller systems as well. Similarly, if respect for human and civil rights and tolerance for diversity and difference are highly valued and easily recognized in larger systems, we would also find them within individuals, families, groups, organizations, and communities.

The power of political, economic, and cultural forces at the macro-system levels are almost impossible to overestimate. Occasionally, however, individuals at the micro-system level—especially those who organize themselves into communities of interest—can change their own perspectives and behaviors in such a way that it spreads to larger systems. Such a "bottom-up" approach is certainly less common than the more usual "top-down" paradigm. Nonetheless, every once in a while, we see processes that emerge at the micro level appear in parallel form at the macro levels as well. Captured in the popular phrase, "Be the change you wish to see in the world," a single person can influence a few others who, in turn, can influence a few more who, in turn can. . . .

Economic Justice

Questions about economic justice arise when there are major differences in the amount and extent of wealth and poverty in different areas or populations within a region or nation or differences between regions and nations (Edelman, 2012; Smiley & West, 2012). As you know, the *distributive* aspect of economic justice generally refers to the allocation of economic opportunities and resources among a population. In order to assess the fairness of an economy and its distributive systems, processes, and especially outcomes, we need principles and guidelines such as those suggested by the UDHR. They serve as benchmarks. Once we have them, we can create tools to measure the discrepancy between the ideal and the actual.

Among the most common ways to view a nation's economy is through its **gross domestic product (GDP)**. GDP refers to the total value of all goods and services produced within that country during a specific period of time—typically a year. In formal terms, GDP can be calculated through a formula where C = personal <u>consumption</u> expenditures, I = business <u>investments</u>, G = <u>government</u> spending, X = <u>exports</u>, and M = <u>imports</u>:

$$GDP = C + I + G + (X - M)$$

Once a nation's annual GDP is determined, we can divide it by the size of the population to estimate the average yearly per capita income. For example, the annual GDP for the United States in 2014 was approximately 17.6 trillion dollars (Bureau of Economic Analysis, 2014, Dec. 23). At the end of that year, the U.S. population was 320,087,963. Through simple division of those two figures, we can determine that the average annual per capita GDP in 2014 was $54,985.

GDP, however, fails to account for other factors that affect economic well-being (Stiglitz, Sen, & Fitoussi, 2010; Whitby, Seaford, Berry, & BRAINPOoL Consortium Partners, 2014, Mar. 31). For example, the cost of living varies in different parts of the world. A dollar in one nation may purchase a great deal more, or less, than in another. Therefore, a more realistic way to estimate annual income for the purposes of comparison is to adjust for cost of living variations. The result of such an adjustment is called **purchasing power parity (PPP)**.

In 2013, both the United States and China reflected annual GDPs greater than 16 trillion dollars in PPP terms. If the 28 member states of the European Union were considered a "nation," it too would reflect a GDP in that range (World Bank, 2013a). When annual per capita GDPs were calculated for specific nations in PPP terms, Qatar reflected the highest amount at $136,727 per person. Other high per capita GDP's included Luxembourg at $90,410; Kuwait at about $90,000; Singapore at $78,763; Brunei Darussalam at $71,777; Norway at $65,461; Switzerland at $56,565; Saudi Arabia at $53,644; and the United States at $53,042. Macao, a special administration region (SAR) in China reflected an extraordinarily high per capita GDP of $142,599. At the other end of the spectrum, however, the average annual per capita GDP in the Central African Republic was $604. Malawi's was $780; the Democratic Republic of Congo $809; Liberia $878; and Niger $916 (World Bank, 2014b). Can you imagine attempting to live on $1.50 to $2.00 per day? Millions of people do.

The differences between rich and poor nations are enormous. Disparities, however, exist within nations as well. Indeed, one of the problems with per capita GDP, whether PPP adjusted or not, is its presentation in the form of an "average." Means (or averages) can be quite misleading. For example, the 2013 per capita GDP of $53,042 in the United States indicates absolutely nothing about how the $17.42 trillion in GDP is distributed among its population.

Given the limitations of basic indicators such as means and medians, how do we measure inequality? Perhaps the most widely known measure of income inequality is the **Gini index**. Also known as the Gini ratio or Gini coefficient, the index is based upon a relatively simple and straightforward assumption. That is, an equal distribution of income or wealth is one in which each participant has an equal and proportionate share of the whole (Gini, 1921). Deviation from that equal distribution reflects some degree of inequality. For example, a nation in which every person (or, every household) enjoyed an equal share of that nation's income (or wealth) would reflect a Gini index of zero (0). In other words, no person (or household) would reflect any more or any less than anyone else. On the other hand, a Gini index of 100 (or 1.0) would indicate that the entire nation's income or wealth was possessed by one person or household while the remainder of the population earned or possessed nothing at all. A higher Gini[29] reflects greater inequality.

For example, the Organisation for Economic Co-operation and Development (OECD) (2013) reported that in 2012 Australia had a pre-tax and transfer income Gini index of 46.0 and an after-tax and transfer income Gini of 32.4; Finland had a pre-tax income Gini of 48.6 and an after-tax of 26.1; Korea a before of 33.8 and an after of 30.7; and the United States a pre-tax income Gini of 50.8 and an after-tax Gini of 39.9 (2013). As of 2010, the United States reflected greater after tax and transfer income inequality than all but 3 of 34 industrialized countries[30] (Organisation for Economic Co-operation and Development, 2011). The World Bank reported 2013-year after-tax income Gini indices of 25.0 for Sweden, 25.8 for Norway, and 28.3 for Germany. Such indices reflect less inequality than the United States and, for example, Turkey at 40.0, Argentina at 44.5, Mexico at 47.2, Chile at 52.1, or South Africa at 63.1 (World Bank, 2013b).

Progression toward more income equality or regression toward greater inequality can be reflected by changes in the Gini index over time. For example, the pre-tax Gini for the United States rose from 39.1 in 1969 to 47.6 in 2013 (DeNavas-Walt & Proctor, 2014, Sept.). The trend toward greater and greater economic inequality throughout the United States and much of the world (Johnson, 2011, Sept. 15) has, in effect, become "the new normal" (Osberg, 2014, Feb. 10). In 2013, 92 individuals owned as much wealth as the bottom 50 percent (about 3.5 billion) of the world's population (Oxfam, 2015, Jan. 19). We can anticipate that unbalanced growth, where the real income at the very top grows disproportionately higher than the bottom 99 percent, will continue for the foreseeable future.

In the United States, for example, many people recognize that wealth is unevenly distributed. However, most of us remain largely ignorant of the magnitude of that disparity. Suppose we reside in a little nation of 10 people. As a whole, the 10 of us have amassed wealth valued at $1,000,000. For our purposes, let's consider wealth to be equal to the total of owned assets (stocks, property, bank accounts) minus liabilities (debt due to loans and other obligations). The average wealth for each of us is $100,000 ($1 million divided by 10). However, that average could be obtained as a result of one person possessing wealth of $1 million, while the other nine have nothing at all (extremely unequal distribution); or through all 10 people having $100 thousand each (perfectly equal distribution). However, let's imagine that the wealth of our little nation is distributed as follows: Two people possess $160,000 each in net wealth, two more have $110,000 each, two have $105,000 each, two have $70,000 each, and the remaining two have $55,000 each in total wealth. Such a distribution—where those in the top quintile have about 2.9 times the wealth of people in the bottom quintile—reflects considerable wealth inequality; but nowhere close to the levels of inequality present in today's United States and throughout the world.[31]

---

[29] A Gini index of 66.7, for example, may alternatively be reported as 0.667. The 66.7 represents two-thirds of 100; the 0.667 represents two-thirds of 1.

[30] This data set included information from 34 OECD nations.

[31] In our "little nation" of 10 people, the top quintile (2 people) owns 32%, the next 20% (2 people) owns 22%, the middle quintile (2 people) owns 21%, the next to the bottom quintile (2 people) owns 14%, and the bottom 20% (2 people) own 11% of our total aggregate wealth. According to Norton and Ariely (2011), this is the wealth distribution Americans would ideally prefer.

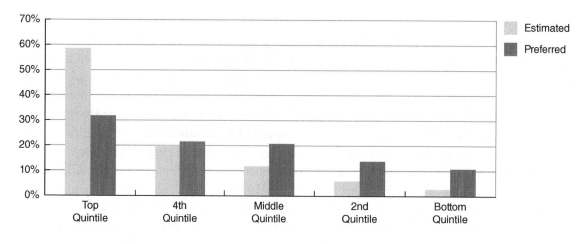

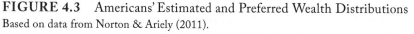

FIGURE 4.3 Americans' Estimated and Preferred Wealth Distributions
Based on data from Norton & Ariely (2011).

In a now famous study, Norton and Ariely (2011) asked a representative sample of about 5,500 Americans to "indicate what percentage of wealth they thought was owned by each of the five quintiles in the United States, in order starting with the top 20% and ending with the bottom 20%" (2011, p. 10). Respondents estimated that the top quintile owned about 59 percent of the total wealth of the nation; the second quintile about 20 percent; the third about 12 percent; the fourth about 6 percent; and the bottom 20 percent about 3 percent. When asked to propose an "ideal" distribution of wealth, based on the assumption that people would randomly be assigned to quintiles, respondents suggested that the top quintile should possess about 32 percent of the nation's wealth; the second quintile about 22 percent; the middle about 21 percent; the fourth about 14 percent; and the bottom quintile about 11 percent (2011).[32] The contrast between Americans' estimates about wealth distribution and our preferred ideal distribution is glaring (see Figure 4.3).

The true distribution of wealth in the United States, however, is far more unequal than most Americans estimate and even more than we would prefer. In 2013, the top 3 percent of American family households actually owned 54 percent of the nation's total wealth and the next 7 percent owned another 21 percent. In other words, the top 10 percent (that is, the upper half of the top quintile) of the 122,952,000 American households owned 75 percent of the nation's wealth (Figure 4.4). The remaining 90 percent owned 25 percent (Bricker et al., 2014, Sept.; DeNavas-Walt & Proctor, 2014, Sept.).

This figure stands in stark contrast to most Americans' perceptions, and their preferences, about wealth distribution. Most of us would like to see a much more equal country (Norton & Ariely, 2011).

Both wealth and household income are influenced by race and ethnic origin. The annual median income (that is, incoming money from any and all sources during a 12-month period) for American households in 2013 was nearly $52,000 (DeNavas-Walt & Proctor, 2014, Sept.). Recall that the median indicates that 50 percent of the population reflect a higher and 50 percent reflect a lower number. The median of a population sometimes differs markedly from the average. Indeed, the average household annual income for the approximately 123 million households in 2013 was about $72,641 (Bureau of Labor Statistics and the Census Bureau, 2014). However, the average

---

[32] These are precisely the percentages used earlier for our "little nation" of 10 people.

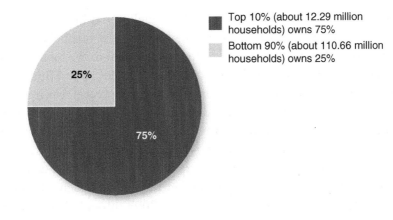

FIGURE 4.4 Percentage of Nation's Wealth: 2013

Data from DeNavas-Walt and Proctor (2014, Sep.)

for the bottom 20 percent of households was $11,651; the average for the top 20 percent was $185,206. The top 5 percent of households earned an average of $322,343 in 2013.

The total aggregate annual income for U.S. households was $8.93 trillion in 2013. However, like wealth distribution, income distribution varies considerably according to population characteristics. For example, in 2013 (see Figure 4.5), Hispanic households' median annual income was more than $17,300 less than that of white households, and black households reflected a median annual income that was $23,672 less (Bureau of Labor Statistics and the Census Bureau, 2014).

In 2013, married-couple family households reflected a median annual income of $76,509. Family households headed "by men with no wife present" had a median annual income of $50,625 while those headed "by women with no husband present" was $35,154—a gap of more than $15,000 per year. A gender gap is also apparent in 2013 incomes for men and women. Full-time employed men earned $50,033 in median annual income while full-time employed women earned $39,157; or, about 78 percent of what men earned (DeNavas-Walt & Proctor, 2014, Sept.). This represents some progress from the 77.4 percent in 2010—but nowhere close to gender equality in annual income (DeNavas-Walt, Proctor, & Smith, 2011).

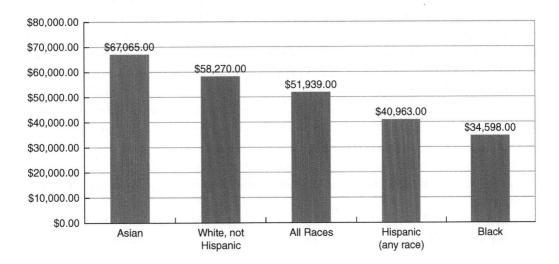

FIGURE 4.5 Median Annual Household Income by Race and Hispanic Origin in 2013

Data from Bureau of Labor Statistics and the Census Bureau (2014).

In 2012, the top 10 percent accrued 51 percent of the total pre-tax income generated within the United States. This is some 2 to 3 percent higher than in 1928—the year before the Great Depression began.[33] At that time, the top 10 percent had about 48 percent of the total U.S. annual income. Their share of income dropped considerably in the years preceding and during World War II. After the war, the share of income accrued by the top 10 percent each year remained within the 32.5 to 34.5 percent range for more than three decades. In 1982, however, that lengthy period of stability began to change. At that time, the top 10 percent had incomes valued at close to 36 percent of the U.S. total. By 1992, their share grew to 42 percent and by 2012 and 2013, to 51 percent (Saez, 2014, Oct.; Saez & Zucman, 2014, July). More than half of all U.S. income in those 2 years was accrued by the top 10 percent of the population which, not coincidentally, own 75 percent of the nation's total wealth (see Figure 4.4). Indeed, "from 2009 through 2012, while the economy was recovering from one of the biggest economic downturns in recent memory, *116 percent* of the income growth went to the top 10 percent (with the top 1 percent alone taking home 95 percent of the income gains); this extreme result is possible because the bottom 90 percent actually saw their incomes fall, on average, during this growth period" (Tcherneva, 2014, Oct. 6, para. 2).

This increasingly unequal distribution of income and wealth is also reflected in savings rates. From 1917 until 2000, the bottom 90 percent had been able, on average, to place at least some of their incomes each year into savings. During the 2000 to 2010 period, however, that changed. The bottom 90 percent, on average, used up their savings; many went into debt; and, of course, the overall value of homeowners' dwellings decreased dramatically when the housing bubble burst in 2007–2008. By 2012, the bottom 90 percent began to save a bit again—at an average of about 1 percent of their incomes.

By way of contrast, in 2012, the top 1 percent saved about 39 percent of their incomes. The next 9 percent of the population (the top 10 percent minus the top 1 percent) has also saved. Between 1940 and 2000, they saved, on average, between 20 percent and 30 percent of their incomes each year. However, their annual savings rate began to decline sharply in the early 1980s, falling to an average of about 8 percent during the recession that began at the end of 2007 and continued through the middle of 2009. By 2012, their savings rate increased to about 12 percent (Saez & Zucman, 2014, July).

Compared to the rest of the top 10 percent, however, the top 1 percent and especially the top 0.01 percent have accrued enormous incomes and wealth since 1980; and the rate of growth in their share of the economic pie is increasing. In 1978, the top 1 percent possessed about 24 percent of the nation's wealth. In 2013, their share was about 39 percent. During that same period, however, the share of wealth owned by the top 0.01 percent grew from about 7 percent to about 22 percent (almost as much as the top 1 percent together had owned in 1978). In other words, the magnitude of the dramatic increase in wealth inequality in the United States is almost entirely due to the surge in wealth by the top 0.01 percent (Saez, 2014, Oct.; Saez & Zucman, 2014, July).

You have probably noticed that the degree of economic inequality varies according to the measure used: wealth or income. The severity of inequality is most apparent when we consider wealth. In the United States, the vast majority of residents have some income, and some income may be supplemented by tax benefits and social programs. However, relatively few possess wealth. Unless families generate more income than is needed for a basic lifestyle, they cannot save, invest, or accumulate wealth.

As noted above, in 2013, the bottom 90 percent owned about 25 percent of the nation's wealth while the top 10 percent possessed 75 percent. However, the top 0.01 percent alone possessed some

[33] In the summer of 1929, the economy slowed. However, the prices of stocks continued its unjustified rise. On October 24, 1929, panic set in and the stock market began its crash; the Great Depression followed.

TABLE 4.3	Poverty Rate in the United States by Gender, Race, and Hispanic Origin: 2013				
	White (not Hispanic)	Black	Hispanic (any race)	Asian	Total Population
Percent in Poverty	9.6%	27.2%	23.5%	10.5%	14.5%

Data from U.S. Census Bureau (U.S. Census Bureau, 2013c).

22 percent of the nation's total wealth. To put that into perspective, in 2013, one-one-hundredth of American households (that's about 12,295 families) owned between one-fifth and one-quarter of the aggregate wealth of the United States. In 2014, the wealthiest 400 Americans identified on that year's Forbes 400 list together owned about $2.29 trillion in net wealth—an increase of $270 billion from the year before. To make the list, a net worth of at least $1.55 billion was required. The average wealth per person on the Forbes 400 was about $5.7 billion, and more than 100 billionaires failed to make the cut (Dolan & Kroll, 2014, Sept. 29).

Contrasted with the Forbes 400 and the top 0.01 percent, most Americans possess little or no wealth, and have modest incomes. Indeed, the **poverty rate** in the United States in 2013 was 14.5 percent (0.5 percent less than in 2012 but 2 percent higher than in 2007). Based upon federal thresholds[34] for that year, more than 45.3 million lived in poverty during 2013 (U.S. Census Bureau, 2013b). These millions included, for example, single people (under the age of 65) with annual incomes under $12,119 or those older than 65 with incomes less than $11,173; single parent and two children households with incomes under $18,769; and two parent and two children households with incomes less than $23,624 (U.S. Census Bureau, 2013d).

As shown in Table 4.3, rates of poverty in 2013 varied greatly according to race and ethnicity. In terms of gender, 13.1 percent of males and 15.8 percent of females were in poverty, as were 19.9 percent of children and youth under the age of 18. Despite social security programs, 9.5 percent of Americans 65 and older (6.8 percent for men and 11.6 percent for women) were in poverty as were some 28.8 percent of people with a disability. In 2013, 11.2 percent of all American families were in poverty. Different types of families reflected different poverty rates. For example, 5.8 percent of married-couple families; 15.9 percent of male householders (with no wife present); and 30.6 percent of female householders (with no husband present) fell beneath the poverty thresholds (U.S. Census Bureau, 2013a).

In 2013, approximately 14.7 million children (19.9 percent) were in poverty in the United States (Kids Count Data Center, 2013a), and more than half of all students in public schools were from low-income families who met eligibility requirements for federally sponsored subsidized meals (Suitts, 2015, Jan.). As social workers would expect, children's poverty rates varied substantially by race and ethnicity (Table 4.4). The percentage of black, Hispanic, and American Indian children in poverty continued to occur at much higher rates (32.8 percent to 39.1 percent) than white and Asian children (13.5 percent to 13.6 percent) (Kids Count Data Center, 2013a).

In addition, some states reflect substantially higher poverty rates than the national average. In 2013, at between 20 percent and 24 percent, Arkansas, Louisiana, New Mexico, and Mississippi experienced higher than average poverty rates, and substantially more so than, for example, Alaska and New Hampshire at 9 percent or Maryland at 10 percent. The U.S. territory of Puerto Rico reflected a 45 percent poverty rate in 2013 (Kids Count Data Center, 2013b).

---

[34] Poverty thresholds differ slightly from federal poverty guidelines. Thresholds are used for statistical purposes—including counting the number of people and families in poverty. Poverty guidelines are used to determine eligibility for benefits and programs.

TABLE 4.4 Children's Poverty in the United States by Race and Ethnicity: 2013	White (not Hispanic)	Black	Hispanic (all races)	Asian and Pacific Islander	American Indian
Number of Children in Poverty	5,108,000	4,008,000	5,717,000	473,000	254,000
Percent of Children in Poverty	13.5%	39.1%	32.8%	13.6%	37.3%

Data from Kids Count Data Center at **http://datacenter.kidscount.org/**.

As you might imagine in a capitalist nation, substantial differences in poverty, incomes, and wealth are evident throughout the population. Such variations are hardly new. What is new, however, is the rapidly decreasing size of the "middle-class" and the increasingly large economic gap between the "rich" and the "poor." We have not seen such extreme income and especially wealth inequality since the "Gilded Age" (Bartels, 2008; Krugman, 2014, May 8; Piketty, 2014). Particularly since the "Great Recession" that began in 2008, income inequality has become a topic of considerable popular discussion (Galbraith, 2012; Pizzigati, 2012; Stiglitz, 2012, 2013, Feb. 16). Indeed, terms such as the "New Gilded Age" (Bartels, 2008; Krugman, 2014, May 8), the "New Robber Barons" (Bartels, 2008; S. Fraser & Moyers, 2014, Dec. 19; Krugman, 2014, May 8), and the "American Plutocracy" (Brenner, 2013, Apr. 1) have emerged to capture the dramatic trend toward increasing economic inequality since 1980.

The emergence of the "Occupy Wall Street" movement was motivated in large part by the disparity between the economic status of ordinary people and the extraordinary salaries, bonuses, and overall wealth of bankers, fund managers, brokers, and financiers. Especially in light of the pervasive fraud and corruption, greed, and failure in the financial markets along with subsequent tax-supported "bailouts," some people of modest means began to protest the unfairness and injustice inherent in severe income and wealth inequality. They argued that massive accumulation of wealth by a few (the top "one percent" and especially the top 0.01 percent) negatively affects the many (the "99 percent" or 99.99 percent) and diminishes the general welfare. Many asserted that a **living wage** is a human right, and that greater economic equality benefits everyone (Byrne & Wells, 2012).

In opposition to the "occupy" movements, other people and groups suggested that individual autonomy and freedom from governmental regulations are, in effect, more important than other values—including the general welfare. They claimed that any individual person or family should be free to accumulate as much personal wealth as possible, and that such economic freedom represents a fundamental human right. They also indicated that high incomes, great wealth, and considerable inequality serve as necessary incentives for effort and innovation, and helps everyone by helping the overall economy (Van Gelder, 2011).

Although the increasing level and extent of **economic inequality** has generated some interest in political contexts and the mainstream media, public discussions about poverty, childhood poverty, or differential rates of poverty by sex, race, family composition, or geographical location are virtually absent. Many social workers view the **invisibility of the poor** as a major obstacle to our mission of ending poverty and promoting social and economic justice. Some engage in education and consciousness-raising efforts designed to bring public attention to issues of poverty and to challenge widespread misinformation and misattributions about poor people and their circumstances. However, ideological thinking and its inherent confirmation bias tends to characterize most discussions about the "why" and "what to do" aspects of poverty. Strongly held, dogmatic, opinionated beliefs often prevail as facts are minimized and rational analysis diminished. Nonetheless, many social workers continue in efforts to raise consciousness and influence changes in economic policies and practices. In so doing, however, we avoid simplistic views and solutions and we embrace a scientific and critical thinking perspective that includes the active participation of people actually affected by poverty and by social and economic injustice.

The concept of **relative poverty** incorporates the dimension of social context—so important to social workers who adopt a person-in-environment perspective. A common way to determine relative poverty involves calculating how far away a family's annual income is from a nation's (or state's or city's) median annual income. If 60 percent of the median annual household income is selected as the relative poverty line in a country (or city or state), then any family household that earns or receives less than that amount would be considered poor—within the context of that locale. Let's use the 2013 median household income in the United States to illustrate (DeNavas-Walt & Proctor, 2014, Sept.). Sixty percent of nearly $52,000 is about $31,200. Households earning that amount or less would be considered poor—in relative terms. Of course, adjustments can be made for family or household size and geographic location.

Economic mobility is another dimension to consider within the context of poverty and inequality. In general terms, mobility refers to the number or proportion of people in a lower economic category that move to a higher category during a specified period of time. Although people move back and forth from higher to lower and from lower to higher categories, social workers are primarily interested in upward mobility—especially for those at the lowest levels. That is, we are concerned about people in poverty increasing their annual income and overall security so that they have more to live on and become less vulnerable to changing socioeconomic circumstances. This aspect of security represents a vital element in social well-being. People who live, literally, check to check, lack the resources necessary to respond to emergencies and sudden changes in social or economic circumstances. Those who have substantial investments, savings accounts, retirement funds, property, and other forms of wealth are in a much better position to survive the inevitable ups and downs of life.

Social workers also focus on **intergenerational income mobility**—that is, the number and proportion of children born to parents in poverty rising to a higher economic status in adulthood. We might ask, "What percentage of children born in poverty escape that poverty?" Although "pulling oneself up by one's bootstraps" or "movin' on up" represents a central motif of the American Dream, the United States reflects less intergenerational mobility than several other developed countries such as Canada, Norway, Finland, and Denmark (Chetty, Hendren, Kline, & Saez, 2014, June). The intergenerational mobility or "opportunity" rates in the United States have remained stable for the past several decades. Between 42 percent (Jäntti et al., 2006, Jan.) and 50 percent of "children born to low income parents become low income adults" (Corak, 2006, p. 1). Approximately 8 of 100 children from the bottom quintile rise to the top quintile at some point during their lifetimes (DeParle, 2012, Jan. 4); and, the chances of doing so vary considerably depending on several factors—including geography. The percentage of children from Charlotte, Milwaukee, Atlanta, Dayton, or Indianapolis who move from the bottom to the top quintile (4.4 to 4.9 percent) is less than half what it is for children from San Jose, San Francisco, Washington DC, Seattle, or Salt Lake City (10.8 to 12.9 percent) (Chetty et al., 2014, June).[35] In contrast to those from the bottom rung, "affluent children often remain so: one of every three 30-year-olds who grew up in the top 1 percent of the income distribution was already making at least $100,000 in family income. . . .

---

[35] For more information about income mobility and geographical factors, see The Equality of Opportunity Project at **http://www.equality-of-opportunity.org/**.

Among adults who grew up in the bottom half of the income distribution, only one out of 25 had family income of at least $100,000 by age 30" (Leonhardt, 2013, July 22, para. 23).

Changing demographics can also affect income distribution. From 2014 to 2060, the number of people 65 years of age and older is projected to grow from 46,255,000 to 98,164,000—an increase of almost 52 million (or 112.2 percent). Meanwhile, the size of the "working age" population (18–64 years) should increase from 198,903,000 to 236,323,000—a growth of about some 37.4 million (or 18.8 percent). The size of the under 18 years of age group is expected to grow from 73,591,000 in 2014 to 82,309,000 in 2060—an increase of about 11.8 percent or 8.7 million (Colby & Ortman, 2015, Mar.). These shifts have obvious implications for intergenerational economic justice in terms of "who supports whom."

Dependency ratios "are an indicator of the potential burden of the dependent population, approximated by those under 18 years and those 65 and older, on those in the working age populations. The ratios are calculated by dividing the number of people in the dependent age groups by the number in the working ages and then multiplying by 100" (Colby & Ortman, 2015, Mar., p. 7). In 2014 there were almost 199 million working age people (18 to 64) for nearly 120 million non-working age (under 18 and 65 and over). By 2060, the numbers should be about 236.3 million working age and 180.5 million non-working age. By 2060, the overall dependency ratio of 60.25 in 2014 will increase to 76.37. At that time, there will be approximately 76 people in the non-working ages (under 18 and 65 and over) for every 100 people in the 18 to 64 working-age range (Colby & Ortman, 2015, Mar.).

Age groupings such as these obviously represent only rough indices of employment and dependency. Some working-age people are unemployed or underemployed while many under 18-year-olds work and pay taxes. Furthermore, an increasing number of 65 and older persons remain employed well into their 70s.

A single statistic or dimension can never capture the complexity of a large data set or a complex issue such as poverty or inequality. Dependency ratios, the Gini index, and relative poverty and mobility indicators are far from perfect measures of income or wealth inequality. Nonetheless, they represent useful attempts to gauge the extent of and, perhaps, progress toward the elimination of poverty and the advancement of some aspects of social and economic justice.

Within the United States, poverty guidelines are used to determine eligibility for various social programs such as Head Start, school breakfast and school lunch programs, legal services, and for securing federal community block grants. For example, the federally sponsored Supplemental Nutrition Assistance Program (SNAP), commonly known as food stamps, uses **federal poverty guidelines** to determine eligibility. In 2015, eligibility was limited to households that did not have "countable resources" in excess of $2,250 (or $3,250 when an elderly or disabled person is a part of the household) and have a net income no greater than 100 percent of the poverty guideline. Depending upon various other factors, a single-parent with one child who has a net income of about $1,311 per month might have been eligible to receive some food assistance. The maximum possible allocation for the parent and child was $357 per month in food stamps (U.S. Department of Agriculture Food and Nutrition Services, 2014, Oct. 1).

Poverty, poverty guidelines, and income inequality are also related to the "minimum wage." As it had since 2009, the federal **minimum wage** for 2015 remained at $7.25 per hour. In theory, this minimum applies to most workers. However, some employers avoid paying the minimum through creative employment contracts or the use of volunteers or interns. There are also several exceptions to the law. For example, full-time students, student-learners, workers with disabilities, and tipped-employees may legally receive less than the minimum.[36]

---

[36] For more information, use terms such as minimum wage and the Fair Labor Standards Act (FLSA) to search the U.S. Department of Labor website at **www.dol.gov**.

TABLE 4.5	2015 U.S. Poverty Guidelines for the 48 Contiguous States and the District of Columbia
Number of Persons in Family or Household	Poverty Guideline
1	$11,770.00
2	$15,930.00
3	$20,090.00
4	$24,250.00
5	$28,410.00
6	$32,570.00
7	$36,730.00
8	$40,890.00

Notes: For families/households with more than 8 persons, add $4,160 for each additional person.

Dollar amounts are slightly higher for Hawaii and Alaska. The Census Bureau does not use these poverty guidelines to calculate the number of poor people. The Census Bureau uses "poverty thresholds" for that purpose.

Data from U.S. Department of Health and Human Services (2015a).

In 2015, a person who worked 40 hours per week at the federal minimum wage of $7.25 per hour earned a total of $15,080 in pre-tax income over the course of 52 weeks (that is, 2,080 work hours). That's $3,310 more than that year's poverty guideline (Table 4.5) for a single-person household, $850 less than the guideline for a two-person household, and $9,170 less than the poverty guideline for a family of four.

If a single female parent with one child worked full-time at minimum wage for 12 months, she would earn pre-tax income of $15,080. That is $850 less than the $15,930 U.S. Department of Health and Human Services (HHS) poverty guideline for a two-person family (2015a). Without counting the FICA deduction, state, federal, and local taxes; and any sales taxes due on purchases; she and her child would have $1,256.67 each month (or $290.00 each week) to provide for herself and her child. If she did not have savings of more than $2,250, she and her child might also be eligible for SNAP benefits (food stamps).

Families with minimum wage (or less) incomes are likely to remain in poverty even when working full-time, 52 weeks per year. Budgeting for housing, child care, utilities, food, clothing, transportation, costs associated with medical and dental care, and unanticipated expenses on a poverty-level income is incredibly challenging (Ehrenreich, 2001). Under such circumstances, saving for an emergency fund, college, or retirement and investing in stocks or bonds are virtually impossible. Daily expected and especially unexpected expenses take up all available resources for millions of poor families. Nothing extra is left over. Sometimes, the economic dilemmas are excruciating. "Do we pay to fix the car (again) because we need it to get to work or do we pay for auto insurance? We can't pay both." "Should we pay the water bill or the gas bill?"

Furthermore, "poverty costs a lot" (Blow, 2015, Jan. 18). In the United States for example, many low-income people do not have bank accounts. They are the **unbanked**.

Unbanked consumers spend approximately 2.5 to 3 percent of a government benefits check and between 4 percent and 5 percent of a payroll check just to cash them. Additional dollars are spent to purchase money orders to pay routine monthly expenses. When you consider the cost for cashing a bi-weekly payroll check and buying about six money orders each month, a household with a net income of $20,000 may pay as much as $1,200 annually for alternative service fees—substantially more than the expense of a monthly checking account fee. (Beard, 2010, p. 6)

In addition, low-income families pay a substantially higher percentage of their income for state and local taxes than do those of greater income. According to the Institute on Taxation and Economic Policy:

- *Virtually every state tax system is fundamentally unfair*, taking a much greater share of income from low- and middle-income families than from wealthy families. The absence of a graduated personal income tax and overreliance on consumption taxes exacerbate this problem.

- *The lower one's income, the higher one's overall effective state and local tax rate.* Combining all state and local income, property, sales and excise taxes that Americans pay, the nationwide average effective state and local tax rates by income group are 10.9 percent for the poorest 20 percent of individuals and families, 9.4 percent for the middle 20 percent and 5.4 percent for the top 1 percent. (Davis et al., 2015, Jan., p. 1)

As Barbara Ehrenreich, author of *Nickel and Dimed* (2001) and *Bait and Switch* (2005), Charles Blow (2015, Jan. 18), and others have observed "it costs a lot to be poor" (Baer, 2015, May 4; Ehrenreich, 2014, Jan. 13). Because of limited resources, low-income families often become subject to disproportionately high fees and penalties from banks, credit card companies, landlords, utilities, loan services, and collection agencies. Despite the nearly 200-year-old injunction against "debtors' prisons" in the United States, people at the lowest economic strata are, in fact, sometimes incarcerated simply because they lack sufficient funds to pay fees, costs, or debt payments (Shapiro, 2014, May 21).[37] Lacking funds for bail or bonds, many low-income people remain in jail for months or years while awaiting trial for minor legal infractions.[38]

The **privatization** of jails and prisons, probation programs, some child welfare services, roads, parking meters, and other systems motivate commercial companies to charge high late fees and penalties, and often excessive prices for low-cost services. For example, phone calls to and from many jails and prisons are now privately managed by a few companies. As the *New York Times* reported, a 15-minute telephone call to anywhere but a jail or prison in Pennsylvania costs about 60 cents (about 4 cents per minute). However, if the call is to a prison inmate, the charge for the same 15-minute call jumps to about 20 cents per minute or $12.95 (Williams, 2015, Mar. 30). The reason: Private corporations have been granted exclusive contracts. Lacking competition or regulation, the companies can—as monopolies usually do—charge the highest rates possible. Since alternate means of telephone correspondence are prohibited, family members have no choice but to use the private system.

Another added cost to workers is **wage theft**. In what would seem to be criminal conduct, some employers literally steal a portion of their employees' labor or wages through a variety of methods (Bobo, 2009). Forms of theft include (National Consumers League, 2011, July):

- Paying less than the legal minimum wage for labor requiring minimum wage pay; or, not paying employees at all. This applies especially to immigrant workers.

---

[37] See Brittany Washington's short film *To Prison for Poverty* (2014) available at **http://www.bravenewfilms.org /toprisonforpoverty** and the May 21, 2014, National Public Radio Morning Edition broadcast entitled *Supreme Court Ruling Not Enough to Prevent Debtors Prisons.*

[38] At the age of 16, Kalief Browder was accused of the theft of a backpack. He was arrested and incarcerated in Rikers Island prison while awaiting trial. Offered a reduced sentence if he pled guilty, he refused—proclaiming his innocence. During his more than 1,000-day period of imprisonment, Kalief was assaulted and beaten by at least one corrections officer and several inmates, and was held in solitary confinement for about two-thirds of his stay. After some 3 years, the charges against him were dismissed and he was released. The ordeal, however, left its mark. At the age of 22, he took his own life (Gonnerman, 2015, June 7).

- Demanding that employees work extra-time or overtime without commensurate pay. Called "off the clock work," workers may have to work through lunch and coffee breaks, and come in early or stay beyond the end of the work shift to perform additional labor without additional pay; or without legally required overtime pay.
- Confiscating tips from service staff who receive less than minimum wage pay "because" (or so it is claimed) they are overcompensated by tips.
- Stealing from workers' pension or Federal Insurance Contributions Act (FICA) funds or illegally using them for inappropriate purposes.
- Deducting additional fees—beyond those legally required by federal, state, or local law—without providing commensurate benefits for those fees. The deductions effectively lower employees' wages, sometimes beneath the legal minimum.
- Paying workers with fee-based "debit" or "payroll" cards instead of no-fee checks.

Although few federal, state, or local resources are allocated or expended in either the investigation or prosecution of wage theft, the problem is widespread and the cost to workers enormous. Indeed, most Americans remain ignorant of the facts.

> Wage theft is a far bigger problem than bank robberies, convenience store robberies, street and highway robberies, and gas station robberies combined. Employers steal billions of dollars from their employees each year by working them off the clock, by failing to pay the minimum wage, or by cheating them of overtime pay they have a right to receive. Survey research shows that well over two-thirds of low-wage workers have been the victims of wage theft, but the governmental resources to help them recover their lost wages are scant and largely ineffective. (Eisenbrey, 2014, Apr. 2, para. 1)

Despite the fact that the overall monetary losses due to wage theft, fraud, and forms of "white collar" financial crimes are many times greater than losses from "street" robberies and burglaries, most police funds are targeted for the latter category of criminal behavior; along with, of course, drug sales and use. Few business owners, banking or credit card company executives, or hedge fund operators are ever investigated and fewer still prosecuted for the, literally, billions of dollars stolen each year from their employees and customers (Eisenbrey, 2015, Feb. 13).

Although hundreds of executives were prosecuted and convicted of finance-related crimes during the savings and loan crisis of the 1980s, as of May 2014, only one top banker has been incarcerated for his part in the widespread fraud and financial misconduct that led to the Great Recession of 2008 (Eisinger, 2014, Apr. 30b). It is conceivable that socioeconomic class or status and economic influence with state and federal officials and legislators may affect the differential levels of enthusiasm with which policing agencies pursue financial fraud, wage theft, and other "white collar" crimes. Despite assertions to the contrary, class distinctions are evident throughout the criminal justice, political, and economic dimensions of American society (Massey, 2007). In discussing the "very rich," F. Scott Fitzgerald famously wrote "They are different from you and me" (1926, Jan. & Feb., para. 3).

One of the clearest distinctions between those at the highest levels of the economic pyramid and those at the bottom involves the two fundamental sources of income: labor income and capital income. **Labor income** involves pay for work. **Capital income** derives from the return on wealth (that is, returns from invested savings and inheritance). The most well-to-do families generate substantial capital income from their accumulated wealth. That is, their "money works for them" by making more money. Indeed, over the course of more than 80 years (1928–2014), investments in the Standard and Poor's 500 stock market reflected an average rates of return of about 11.53 percent. If your ancestors had invested $100 in 1928 and did absolutely nothing but automatically reinvest dividends, their one hundred dollars would have grown to $289,995.13 in 2014 (Damodaran, 2015, Jan. 5). Compare that to the growth in wages and salaries based on labor. During the period from 1964 to 2014, the average hourly wage grew from $2.50 to $20.67. Unfortunately, that growth was almost entirely due to inflation. When adjusted for inflation, and using constant dollars, the average hourly wage grew less than one-fifth of 1 percent per year during the past 50 years. "In real terms the average wage peaked more than 40 years ago: The $4.03-an-hour rate recorded in January 1973 has the same purchasing power as $22.41 would today" (DeSilver, 2014, Oct. 9, para. 5). In other words, for the past 40 years average inflation-adjusted hourly wages have either stagnated or declined. "What gains have been made, have gone to the upper income brackets. Since 2000, usual weekly wages have fallen 3.7% (in real terms) among workers in the lowest tenth of the earnings distribution, and 3% among the lowest quarter. But among people near the top of the distribution, real wages have risen 9.7%" (DeSilver, 2014, Oct. 9, para. 7).

Invested wealth and incomes derived from wealth tend to rise over time, and generally do so at a much higher rate than inflation. Except for top executives of major companies, financial managers, elite athletes and performers, however, income from labor—especially physical and service labor—grows very little or not at all from decade to decade. Globalization, technological innovation, and steep declines in union membership have effectively reduced the value of most labor.[39] Consequently, the bottom 50 percent of U.S. households have accumulated little, if any, wealth during the past 50 years. Indeed, 90 percent of U.S. households saw their real net wealth decrease by 25 percent during the period between 2000 and 2012 (Brenner, 2013, Apr. 1). These differential growth rates—that for returns on investment and the incomes of "elite workers" versus that for labor in general—help to explain the phenomena of growing inequality.

In the United States, the idea of distributing wealth through governmental action such as minimum wages or a guaranteed basic family income has traditionally received only modest legislative support. A **maximum wage** (Pizzigati, 1992) or some other limit to the size of individual or family income or wealth has never been seriously considered. In the last several decades, proposals to tax the top income groups at higher rates have garnered limited support from members of Congress—most of whom receive the bulk of their campaign finances from rich individuals and corporate groups.

It comes as no surprise to most social workers that income from investments is taxed at considerably lower rates than income earned through individual labor. In addition, sophisticated but usually legal means to defer or avoid taxes have been available to those with sufficient resources to employ tax consultants and influence tax legislation. For instance, the "carried interest loophole allows hedge fund and private equity managers, two of the highest-paid job categories in America, to pay a tax rate of only 20 percent instead of the 39 percent income tax rate they would otherwise pay. They justify this lower rate by claiming their earnings are related to investment gains, not the time they spend managing other peoples' money" (Klinger, 2015, May 21, para. 2). Thousands of these fund managers take advantage of this **hedge fund loophole** to pay 19 percent less income tax than laborers.

---

[39] If life on earth continues in its current form, we can predict that at some point in the future, technology advances will nearly eliminate the need for human labor. Intelligent machines will produce and distribute needed goods and services without much routine human guidance. In effect, human labor will not be essential for the production of wealth or the sustainment of human life. Under such conditions, our traditional notion that "we work to earn" will be severely challenged—since only a small percentage of humans will generate income through labor. At that point, humans will have to ask, "If not on the basis of labor, how can and how should we distribute wealth that is actually generated by machines?" Of course, if we were wise, we might begin to ask those questions now.

Despite the fact that most Americans do not inherit money and only a small percentage inherit more than $100,000 (Gokhale & Kotlikoff, 2000, Oct. 1), the amount of wealth that may be passed on tax-free to heirs continues to increase. In 2014 up to $5,340,000 of an estate were not subject to federal inheritance tax, and in 2015 it rose to $5,430,000. Exemption of more than $5 million from the **death tax,** as inheritance or estate taxes are commonly called, represents a major benefit to the top 1 or 2 percent of U.S. households but has little or no relevance to the vast majority of families who have only modest wealth, if any, to pass on to their heirs.[40] In 2015, the six heirs to the Walmart fortune held combined assets in the range of $175 billion. We might wonder what might happen to the size of the public treasury if all inherited wealth and income from investments were taxed at the same rate as income based on labor. How many more resources would become available, at least potentially, to reduce inequality, shrink the public debt, or fund initiatives for the common good?

In April 2015, the U.S. House of Representatives voted to repeal the estate tax in its entirety. If approved by the Senate and signed by the President, an unlimited amount could be transferred tax free after death to one's heirs. Toward the end of 2014, more than 500 individuals in the United States each possessed more than one billion dollars (Dolan & Kroll, 2014, Sept. 29) and in early 2015, some 142,000 households each held assets (not counting the value of their primary residence) greater than $25 million. If inherited wealth were completely tax-free or only minimally taxed, the comparative power and influence of the richest individuals and families would surge in comparison to people whose income is based upon wages from labor. Wages are taxed as ordinary income and, as such, are taxed at substantially higher rates that investment dividends, capital gains, and inherited estates.

Several of the nation's founders were deeply concerned about recreating the aristocratic and plutocratic systems prevalent in Europe by endorsing the accumulation and concentration of huge wealth in the hands of a few families. Under a death-tax free system, all wealth would remain in the hands of heirs and grow at least as fast as investments typically do. Indeed, the U.S. "tax code strongly favors income from capital gains—increases in the value of assets, such as stocks—over income from wages and salaries. These preferences are economically inefficient.... They are also highly regressive, since capital gains are heavily concentrated at the top of the income scale" (Marr & Huang, 2015, Jan. 18, para. 1).

In considering questions of economic justice, social workers might reconsider Franklin Delano Roosevelt's proposed "Economic Bill of Rights." In his January 11, 1944, State of the Union message to Congress during World War II, he said:

> It is our duty now to begin to lay the plans and determine the strategy for the winning of a lasting peace and the establishment of an American standard of living higher than ever before known. We cannot be content, no matter how high that general standard of living may be, if some fraction of our people—whether it be one-third or one-fifth or one-tenth is ill-fed, ill-clothed, ill housed, and insecure.
>
> This Republic had its beginning, and grew to its present strength, under the protection of certain inalienable political rights—among them the right of free speech, free press, free worship, trial by jury, freedom from unreasonable searches and seizures. They were our rights to life and liberty.
>
> As our Nation has grown in size and stature, however—as our industrial economy expanded—these political rights proved inadequate to assure us equality in the pursuit of happiness.

---

[40] In 2013, millionaires made up a majority of the U.S. Congress (almost 51%). At that time, the median net worth of our national legislators was $1,029,505—some 18 times the average household's median net worth of $56,355 (Choma, 2015, Jan. 12).

We have come to a clear realization of the fact that true individual freedom cannot exist without economic security and independence. "Necessitous men are not free men." People who are hungry and out of a job are the stuff of which dictatorships are made.

In our day these economic truths have become accepted as self-evident. We have accepted, so to speak, a second Bill of Rights under which a new basis of security and prosperity can be established for all regardless of station, race, or creed.

Among these are:

- The right to a useful and remunerative job in the industries or shops or farms or mines of the Nation;
- The right to earn enough to provide adequate food and clothing and recreation;
- The right of every farmer to raise and sell his products at a return which will give him and his family a decent living;
- The right of every businessman, large and small, to trade in an atmosphere of freedom from unfair competition and domination by monopolies at home or abroad;
- The right of every family to a decent home;
- The right to adequate medical care and the opportunity to achieve and enjoy good health;
- The right to adequate protection from the economic fears of old age, sickness, accident, and unemployment;
- The right to a good education.

All of these rights spell security. And after this war is won we must be prepared to move forward, in the implementation of these rights, to new goals of human happiness and well-being.

America's own rightful place in the world depends in large part upon how fully these and similar rights have been carried into practice for our citizens. For unless there is security here at home there cannot be lasting peace in the world. (Roosevelt, 1944, Jan.11)

Environmental Justice

Along with cultural and developmental rights, **environmental rights** are included among the "third generation rights." These involve "the rights to live in an environment that is clean and protected from destruction" (Amnesty International, 1997, Categories of Rights, para. 3). Under this principle, humans have rights to clean air, pure and plentiful water supplies, uncontaminated soil, and a climate that can sustain life—now and in the future. People, however, also have a right to economic development—to generate income and wealth to enhance their lives. This is especially true for developing nations and those in poverty. The concept of **sustainable development** addresses these sometimes competing aspirations.

Sustainable development seeks to meet the needs and aspirations of the present without compromising the ability to meet those of the future. Far from requiring the cessation of economic growth, it recognizes that the problems of poverty and underdevelopment cannot be solved unless we have a new era of growth in which developing countries play a large role and reap large benefits. (United Nations World Commission on Environment and Development, 1987, Apr., Ch. 1, para. 49)

As is the case in economics, where diversified portfolios, workforces, and markets are highly valued, the scientific disciplines of biology and ecology also view diversity as a hallmark of health. In general, ecosystems that contain a large and wide variety of plant and animal life at different ages or stages of development tend to be healthier and better able to withstand challenges and threats than those which reflect fewer varieties. In effect, greater diversity enhances security and sustainability.

Recognition of the importance of **biodiversity** for the planet earth and the future of humanity led to a United Nations–sponsored international treaty at the Rio de Janeiro Earth Summit in June 1992. The Convention on Biological Diversity treaty has three main goals: (1) to conserve biological diversity, (2) to use biological diversity in a sustainable fashion, and (3) to share the benefits of biological diversity fairly and equitably (United Nations Conference on Environment and Development, 1992). The idea of sustainable development incorporates recognition of the importance of both biodiversity and environmental health.

Biodiversity is integrally related to the issue of economic development. Urban, technological, and industrial growth can diminish biodiversity and challenge the earth's capacity for sustainability. Concern about the slow pace and direction of international agreements regarding the health of the earth led to a global gathering of about 30,000 individuals, activists, and representatives of both governmental and nongovernmental organizations (NGOs) in Cochabamba, Bolivia, on April 22, 2010. The conference led to the approval of two documents that question the motivation and capacity of current national governments and the United Nations to address environmental issues and climate change. The documents are (1) The Universal Declaration of the Rights of Mother Earth and (2) People's Agreement (World People's Conference on Climate Change and the Rights of Mother Earth, 2010a, 2010b).

In 2011, the United Nations Environment Program issued a major report entitled "Towards a Green Economy: Pathways to Sustainable Development and Poverty Eradication" (2011), and in 2012, some 20 years after the first Rio summit, a second UN-sponsored conference (Rio+20) was held. The United Nations Conference on Sustainable Development resulted in a number of voluntary commitments and a report titled "The Future We Want" (United Nations, 2012a, 2012b). As did earlier reports, this document acknowledged that poverty reduction requires sustainable development through the "greening" of various dimensions of the economy. The human population is growing at a rapid pace. If we continue at or near our current pace, the February 2015 population of about 7.3 billion will grow to between 9 and 11 billion by 2050 (Afrin, 2014). If a human population that large is to thrive on a planet with finite resources, then our approach to agriculture, meat and fish management, water processing, forest management, energy production, manufacturing, waste processing, building construction, transportation, tourism, and urban development require massive change from "business as usual" (United Nations Environment Programme, 2011).

Efforts to restore and protect the environment so that future generations may flourish involves dilemmas of numerous kinds as first, second, and third generation human rights conflict. In particular, the people and governments of developing nations where incomes often range from $1 to $2 per day desperately want to grow their economies, build an industrial and manufacturing base, increase agricultural production, provide employment, and convert their natural resources into usable wealth. Unless undertaken in a green or sustainable manner, however, economic growth in developing countries negatively affects the environment—just as it does, and has done, in developed nations since the Industrial Revolution.

Does human activity affect the environment? Let's conduct a brief thought experiment. Visualize the earth as it would be today had humans never existed and compare it, in before and after fashion, with how it is today. Imagine the forests, prairies, wetlands, and the oceans unaffected by the presence of humans. Then picture our cities, highways, dams, bridges, tunnels, buildings, trucks, trains, planes, boats, sewage systems, garbage cans, and even the litter that often collects on river banks and roadsides. Humans' impact is obvious. Less apparent, however, are our effects on other forms of life—other animal and plant species; and the water, soil, and the layers of gases that surround the earth. Held in place by gravity, the atmosphere protects our world from the sun's heat and radiation, and from most meteors. Without the 78 percent nitrogen, 21 percent oxygen, and 1 percent water vapor that envelop the earth, humans and many other life forms could not exist.

In this context, the social work notion of person-in-environment is especially apt. Humans exist in a bubble of gases (an atmospheric environment) that allows us to live, but the way we live affects that bubble. As a result of our activity, the earth's atmosphere is changing and so are the oceans, forests, other animals, and the climate. If humans continue to disregard the earth and its atmosphere, our species will not thrive and may not survive.

> Most projections of climate change presume that future changes—greenhouse gas emissions, temperature increases, and effects such as sea level rise—will happen incrementally. A given amount of emission will lead to a given amount of temperature increase that will lead to a given amount of smooth incremental sea level rise. However, the geological record for the climate reflects instances where a relatively small change in one element of climate led to abrupt changes in the system as a whole. In other words, pushing global temperatures past certain thresholds could trigger abrupt, unpredictable, and potentially irreversible changes that have massively disruptive and large-scale impacts. At that point, even if we do not add any additional CO_2 to the atmosphere, potentially unstoppable processes are set in motion. We can think of this as sudden climate brake and steering failure, where the problem and its consequences are no longer something we can control. In climate terms, abrupt change means change occurring over periods as short as decades or even years. (Molina et al., 2014, p. 6)

The world's climate is changing. Most people recognize that. According to a January 2015 New York Times–Stanford University poll, 81 percent of Americans "said that climate change was caused at least in part by human activities" (Davenport & Connelly, 2015, Jan. 30, para. 14) and "83 percent of Americans, including 61 percent of Republicans and 86 percent of independents, say that if nothing is done to reduce emissions, global warming will be a very or somewhat serious problem in the future" (Davenport & Connelly, 2015, Jan. 30, para. 9). Most Americans may be influenced by the scientific evidence. Some "97% of climate scientists have concluded that human-caused climate change is happening" (Molina et al., 2014, p. 1). The consensus among scientists is nearly unanimous. However, a surprisingly high percentage of members of the U.S. Congress either deny that climate change exists or challenge the legitimacy of the scientific evidence. Some may be influenced by other factors, including, perhaps, the campaign contributions of corporate donors.

Here are a few facts: (1) the levels of greenhouse gases in the earth's atmosphere are increasing;[41] (2) over the course of the past century, the average global temperature has become about 1.4°F warmer;[42] (3) ice sheets and snow packs are melting, and sea levels are rising; (4) as CO_2 levels increase, the earth's oceans are becoming more acidic ("the other CO_2 problem");[43] (5) the size of the world's forests are decreasing (Lindquist et al., 2012);[44] (6) the arrival of the spring season is

---

[41] "After remaining relatively stable at around 280 parts per million (ppm) for millennia, carbon dioxide (CO_2) began to rise in the nineteenth century as people burned fossil fuels in ever-increasing amounts. This upward trend continues today with concentrations breaking the 400 ppm mark just last year. The rate of increase during the past 100 to 150 years has been much more rapid than in other periods of the Earth's history" (Molina et al., 2014, p. 3).

[42] "The projected rate of temperature change for this century is greater than that of any extended global warming period over the past 65 million years" (Molina et al., 2014, p. 3).

[43] Oceans absorb a great deal of the world's CO_2 emissions leading to greater acidity—indicated by decreasing pH scale scores. As a consequence, shellfish (such as crab, crayfish, lobster, mussels, oyster, and shrimp) and corals have already become less able to create shells and coral skeletons (which cluster into coral reefs), respectively. As the oceans become increasingly acidic they become more like vinegar, then like lemon juice, and eventually like battery acid.

[44] Between 2000 and 2005, the global rate of net forest loss was 6.3 million hectares (more than 15,567,639 acres) per year (Lindquist et al., 2012). Plants and algae process CO_2 during photosynthesis and produce oxygen as waste. Humans and other organisms require that waste (oxygen) to live.

occurring earlier in the year and we can soon expect the fall season to arrive later; and (7) extreme weather events are happening more often (Molina et al., 2014).

The heat waves, droughts, severe storms, floods, and other natural disasters that occur more frequently due to climate change represent immediate dangers for current populations. The risks associated with continued or accelerating rates of climate change for future generations, however, are even greater.[45]

Despite international agreements and initiatives such as the 1992 United Nations Framework Convention on Climate Change and the 1997 Kyoto Protocol—which the United States did not endorse—average global temperatures continue to rise. In 2009, some 114 nations supported the Copenhagen Accord. Recognizing that average global temperature had already risen by about 0.8° Celsius (1.4° Fahrenheit) since 1880, signatories targeted 2°C (3.6°F) as the maximum limit for global warming over pre-industrial levels (United Nations Framework Convention on Climate Change, 2009, Dec. 18). In other words, participants agreed that the earth could tolerate no more than another 1.2°C (2.2°F) increase in average global temperature levels.

However, the safety of the 2°C maximum increase figure has been questioned. Scientists such as James Hansen suggest that the greater atmospheric CO_2 from fossil fuel emissions associated with global warming of 2°C:

> would spur 'slow' feedbacks and eventual warming of 3–4°C with disastrous consequences. Rapid emissions reduction is required to restore Earth's energy balance and avoid ocean heat uptake that would practically guarantee irreversible effects. Continuation of high fossil fuel emissions, given current knowledge of the consequences, would be an act of extraordinary witting intergenerational injustice. (Hansen, Kharecha, Sato, Masson-Delmotte, & Ackerman, 2013, Abstract, para. 1)

Others, such as Lumumba Di-Aping from the Sudan observed that Africa would be disproportionately affected by an average increase in global warming of 2°C because the African continent "would heat up by substantially more. . . . (It) would turn Africa into a furnace" (Montagne, Harris, Oppenheimer, & Di-Aping, 2009, Dec. 10, para. 6).

The environmental effects of climate change are not limited to humans. Bird migration routes are changing and several animal species are relocating to cooler climates. In addition, the human manufacture and use of herbicides and insecticides, and the disposal of toxic chemicals into the environment affect many forms of life. Their presence throughout the environment and in our food products may be related to the rise in cancer rates among humans (McCormick, 2009). Other animals are affected as well.

By 2014, approximately 90 percent of the 1 billion monarch butterflies that lived in the United States in 1996 had vanished—due in large part to the use of herbicides designed to eradicate the milkweed plant (U.S. Fish and Wildlife Service, 2015, Feb. 9). We have also seen a dramatic decrease in honey bee populations in many parts of the world (Goulson, 2010). In North America alone, colony collapse disorder (CCD) has left the continent "with fewer managed pollinators than at any time during the last 50 years. In this region, honey bees pollinate nearly 75 kinds of fruits such as almonds, avocados, cranberries and apples, as well as crops like soybeans" (United Nations Environment Program, 2010, p. 4). In a news release, the Executive Director of the United Nations Environment Program (UNEP) Achim Steiner said, "Human beings have fabricated the illusion that in the 21st century they have the technological prowess to be independent of nature. Bees underline the reality that we are more, not less dependent on nature's services" (United Nations Environment Program, 2011, Mar. 10, para. 13).

---

[45] See Naomi Klein's *This Changes Everything* (2014) for a powerful message about the urgent need for change.

Awareness of the dangers of insecticides, pesticides, and herbicides is not a new phenomenon. In the early 1960s, the extraordinary Rachel Carson called attention to the issue of environmental contamination in *Silent Spring* (1962, 2002):

> Along with the possibility of the extinction of mankind by nuclear war, the central problem of our age has therefore become the contamination of man's total environment with such substances of incredible potential for harm—substances that accumulate in the tissues of plants and animals and even penetrate the germ cells to shatter or alter the very material of heredity upon which the shape of the future depends. (p. 8)

In addition to agricultural poisons, other human-made products affect the environment and endanger plants and animals. The inhalation of asbestos fibers, for example, often results in mesothelioma among humans (and probably among other mammals as well). Environmental contaminants can affect numerous biological processes including hormone production and function; and cardiovascular, respiratory, and digestive systems. Pollutants may damage human DNA, cause the suppression or overexpression of genes, and may lead to epigenetic change and epigenetic inheritance. As a consequence, "gene products that suppress tumor growth may not be produced, allowing individual tumor cells in the body to grow out of control, leading to cancer . . . [and some epigenetic changes] . . . may be passed on to future generations" (Reuben & The President's Cancer Panel, 2009, p. 3).

Several nations have placed restrictions on the production and use of asbestos products. Fewer governments have done so for plastics. Plastic products are notoriously difficult to recycle. Most is processed as trash and it remains unclear where all the plastic waste goes (Thompson et al., 2004). In the period 2007–2013, researchers documented more than 5 trillion pieces of plastic floating in the world's oceans (Eriksen et al., 2014). The floating debris weighed an estimated 250 tons—far less than the several millions of tons produced each year (Eriksen et al., 2014). Where does the rest go?

Fish and other ocean animals are often caught in larger pieces of plastic while smaller particles are ingested. For example, when the millions of small lantern fish rise to the ocean surface to eat zooplankton, they also swallow plastic particles. Because lantern fish are a main food supply for large fish such as tuna, salmon, and mahi-mahi, many of us consume plastic when we enjoy our favorite seafood dishes (Boyle, 2011, Jan. 6).

Certainly, much plastic waste ends up in or on our soil—some intentionally so in landfills—but much of it on shores, in or alongside streets, highways, railroads; and in pastures, forests, and farmland. We might reasonably hypothesize that land animals such as cattle, swine, and fowl also ingest plastic particles in some quantity. When humans, in turn, eat steak, bacon, or chicken, we consume the microplastics or microbeads, invisible to the eye, that were part of the animals' food supply. We also absorb plastic-related chemicals when we drink or eat from plastic containers, ingest food that has been packaged or microwaved in plastic, or prepared in overheated nonstick cookware (Vos, 2014, Oct. 2).

The environmental risks to life on earth are becoming more and more obvious. Nonetheless, many politicians and religious leaders continue to deny its reality. For example, in 2011 the governor of Florida prohibited state employees, independent contractors, and volunteers involved with the Florida Department of Environmental Protection from using the terms *climate change, global warming, sea-level rise,* and *sustainability* in any verbal, written, or electronic communications. Rising ocean levels represents an immediate threat to the flat state of Florida. Nonetheless, state workers were instructed to use the term *nuisance flooding* instead of *rising sea levels* (Scott & Korten, 2015, Mar. 8). Aware of the First Amendment of the U.S. Constitution, many Americans assume that the federal, state, and local governments "shall make no law . . . abridging the freedom of speech." Employers, however, remain privileged in their remarkable ability to limit their employees' freedom of expression (Barry, 2007).

Despite a strong **anti-science movement** (Boudry, Blancke, & Pigliucci, 2014; Lilienfeld, Lynn, & Lohr, 2015; Otto, 2012, Oct. 16; Park, 2008; Thyer & Pignotti, 2015) in the United States, some "climate change deniers" have changed their minds (Lomborg, 2010). In addition, concern for the environment has grown dramatically among the general public. In fact, a large majority of Americans consider global warming to be a "serious" problem, support legislation to curtail greenhouse gas emissions, and express their willingness to use tax contributions for that purpose (MacInnis, 2013). Despite the widespread popular support, most federal legislation to address climate change has not made its way through Congress.

Rising apprehension about climate change and environmental damage has led to the development of various environmental indices. One of the best known is sponsored by the Yale (University) Center for Environmental Law and Policy and the Center for International Earth Science Information Network at Columbia University. The **Environmental Performance Index (EPI)** is calculated on the basis of 22 snapshot and trend indicators within and across policy categories such as environmental burden of disease, water and water resources, air pollution, biodiversity and habitat, forestry, fisheries, agriculture, and climate change. "These policy categories track performance and progress on two broad policy objectives: Environmental Health and Ecosystem Vitality" (Yale Center for Environmental Law and Policy, 2012, p. 1).

In 2014, Switzerland, Luxembourg, Australia, and Singapore reflected the most environmentally friendly EPI scores whereas Afghanistan, Lesotho, Haiti, Mali, and Somalia reflect the least. At that time, the United States ranked 33rd[46] of the 178 nations. Neighbors Canada and Mexico reflected ranks of 24 and 65, respectively, in terms of environmental performance (Yale Center for Environmental Law and Policy, 2014).

Progress in environmental performance is a result of several factors including, among others, increasing use of cleaner and more efficient renewable energy sources; growth in construction of green buildings; expansion of land reserves and reforestation efforts; improvement in waste management; increased use of recycled materials; and decrease in carbon emissions. Several nations and regions are making headway. In 2014, Germany was ranked the most energy-efficient of the 16 nations with the largest economies. The United States was ranked 13th. Only Russia, Brazil, and Mexico received lower ranks (Young et al., 2014, July).

Some countries are gradually abandoning the use of coal or other fossil fuels to generate electricity. Denmark, for example, has established a national goal of becoming fossil fuel free by the year 2050 (Franck & Møller, 2014, Sept. 1). By comparison, the United States has made limited progress, leading the American Council for an Energy-Efficient Economy (ACEEE) to report:

> The inefficiency in the U.S. economy means a tremendous waste of energy resources and money. . . . In the past decade the United States has made limited progress toward greater efficiency at the national level. . . . (Several other) countries may have an economic advantage over the United States because using less energy to produce and distribute the same economic output costs them less. Their efforts to improve efficiency likely make their economies more nimble and resilient. This raises a critical question: looking forward, how can the United States compete in a global economy if it continues to waste money and energy that other industrialized nations save and can reinvest? (Young et al., 2014, July, p. xi)

In the United States, we expend enormous amounts of energy, release tons of greenhouse gases, manufacture millions of nearly unrecyclable plastic products, and directly or indirectly spread pesticides, herbicides, and various other toxic chemicals into the air, ground, and water. As the world's largest economy, we have a disproportionately greater negative impact on the world's environment

---

[46] A rank of 1 reflects the most environmentally friendly nation; 178 reflects the least.

than warranted by the size of our population. This, of course, leads humans in North America and elsewhere to raise questions of environmental justice for themselves and for future generations. Indeed, in an illustration of intergenerational and environmental justice advocacy, the young people's group *iMatter: Kids vs Global Warming* initiated a campaign called "Live As If Our Future Matters." The *iMatter* youngsters attempt to educate legislators, conduct demonstrations and marches, and take legal action (iMatter: Kids vs. Global Warming, 2015). Unfortunately, in December 2104, the U.S. Supreme Court decided not to hear the iMatter cases. The justices' decision leaves lower court rulings intact, leading Alec Loorz, one of the then high school students who filed lawsuits against state and federal governments, to say:

> Climate change is the most urgent issue of inter-generational justice that perhaps our species has ever faced. I do not understand how our courts continue to absolve the federal government from responsibility to care for the only planet which we call home.... We will continue bringing claims to the courthouse steps until our voices are heard and action is being taken to protect our future. I do believe that one day we will find a judge who has the courage to issue the necessary orders and secure the rights of my generation to a healthy and stable climate system. (iMatter: Kids vs. Global Warming, 2014, Dec. 8)[47]

Concern about humans' impact upon the earth is not limited to young people. On June 18, 2015, Pope Francis issued a formal letter on the topic of the environment to all Roman Catholics. In his Encyclical Letter, *Laudato Si' On Care for Our Common Home*, he called upon "every person living on this planet" to correct the "global environmental deterioration" we have caused and become better stewards of "our Sister, Mother Earth . . . (who) . . . 'groans in travail' . . . because of the harm we have inflicted on her by our irresponsible use and abuse." "We have come to see ourselves as her lords and masters, entitled to plunder her at will." "We have forgotten that we ourselves are dust of the earth; our very bodies are made up of her elements, we breathe her air and we receive life and refreshment from her waters" (Bergoglio, 2015, June 18).

■ Policy–Practice

Valuing diversity and difference, and accepting others, are basic to helping others address problems in living as well as taking action to advance human rights, eliminate poverty, and promote social, economic, and environmental justice. In our everyday work with individuals, families, groups, organizations, and communities, social workers routinely advocate for the rights of clients, collaboratively pursue social and economic justice for and with them, and seek to promote their social well-being. The social work skills associated with these activities appear in subsequent chapters. However, social workers also recognize that the personal problems, issues, and challenges that individuals and family clients face frequently relate to unjust policies present in the larger society. Policies and practices represent a central element of our person-in-environment perspective. Indeed, they often cause more problems than they solve.

Imagine, for example, a city of about 21,000 people. More than two-thirds of its citizens are African American. The 54-person police force has 51 white and three black officers. The police chief is white. The city manager is white. The municipal judge is white. Five of the six-member

---

[47] No matter how credible, facts about injustice simply do not stimulate the emotional intensity that pictures often do. The Foundation for Deep Ecology recently published a book entitled *Overdevelopment, Overpopulation, Overshoot* (Butler, 2015). Containing powerful pictures of our world, it may help to make the effects of "progress" and "growth" more real. Please review the free online version at **https://populationspeakout.org/the-book/** and, if it inspires you to take action to protect mother earth, please do so.

city council are white; one is African American. The mayor—who may break any tied votes in city-council decisions—is white and a former member of the police department.[48]

As a social worker in such a city, you might wonder if some of the personal and family problems experienced by African American clients you serve could be related to unjust policies and practices of a police department, city government, and municipal court system that are overwhelmingly white. If you examine the situation, you might find evidence of nepotism as well as hiring practices that favor white applicants; racial profiling and undue violence in police arrests of African Americans; disproportionate stops and arrests of African Americans; excessive court-imposed penalties and fines assigned to African Americans; and direct and indirect suppression of voting opportunities for African Americans. You might even wonder if the city government and the police department are more concerned about generating revenue through the issuance of traffic tickets, fines, fees, and penalties than they are with fairness, justice, or public safety (United States Department of Justice Civil Rights Division, 2015, Mar. 4). Based on such an understanding, you might determine that many of the problems your clients face can be traced more to the social, political, and legal environment and an entrenched power structure than to the individuals and families you serve. As a result, you might decide to participate with members of the community in social, political, and perhaps legal action to address pervasive social and racial injustice.

At one time or another, almost all social workers engage in the analysis, development, and promotion of policies and programs. We might, for example, help to create an agency policy, establish a new program to address a community need, or collaborate with others in preparing a legislative proposal. Sometimes we recognize an injustice that warrants social action—perhaps in the form of a public demonstration or protest, or even a lawsuit. Such macro-system-focused activities are integral to social work and represent a central part of our professional mission. Indeed, Iatridis (2008) states that all social workers "should understand and analyze the effects of social policy decisions on clients. Consequently, they should participate in the formulation and modification of social policy, being active at multiple social policy levels, including the personal, the organizational, the community, and the legislative" (para. 2). We refer to this aspect of social work as *policy–practice*.

Although the term *policy–practice* has been described in various ways, virtually all go beyond dispassionate analysis to incorporate the notion of political or community action intended to change the policies or practices of some system. For example, Rocha (2007) defines **policy–practice** "as a change approach that uses advocacy and community practice techniques to change programs and policies at multiple systems levels, targeted communities, local, state, and federal governments, agencies, bureaucracies, and the courts" (p. 1). In the context of the social work skills, we view policy–practice as a natural extension of the **advocacy** efforts we undertake with and on behalf of individuals, families, groups, and communities. Schneider and Lester (2001) suggest that "social work advocacy is the exclusive and mutual representation of a client(s) or a cause in a forum, attempting to systematically influence decision-making in an unjust or unresponsive system(s)" (p. 64).

Advocacy can involve work on behalf of a particular client (for example, individual, family, group, organization, or community). This is sometimes called **case advocacy**. In addition, we may advocate with or on behalf of a group of people or a community confronting a similar issue. For example, members of an ethnic minority group may observe that a state or federal program or policy, or local programmatic practice appears discriminatory. This is sometimes called **class advocacy**, community action, or political or legislative advocacy—depending upon the focus and target of the effort.

---

[48] You might review articles about Ferguson, Missouri, in the context of the August 9, 2014, police killing of Michael Brown. Also consider the "race gap" in police departments across the United States (Ashkenas & Park, 2015, Apr. 8; Badger, Keating, & Elliott, 2014, Aug. 14) and whether police officers do or should live in the communities they serve (Silver, 2014, Aug. 20).

Finally, we might advocate in pursuit of a particular cause or purpose. For example, we might act to eliminate discrimination, promote equal access and opportunity, confront injustice, advance human rights and social justice, encourage social development, or enhance social well-being. This form of advocacy may involve aspects of case and class advocacy as well as social and collective action, judicial advocacy, and occasionally civil disobedience; and all are elements of policy–practice.

As you might expect, several aspects of professionalism and most of the skills and competencies needed in general social work practice are needed in policy–practice and social action as well. As in all social work practice, we must reflect integrity, knowledge and expertise, self-understanding, and self-control in our policy–practice and advocacy efforts. And, because the demands are so challenging, we need considerable social support and personal well-being to carry on.

Critical thinking and scientific inquiry, and lifelong learning are especially significant in policy–practice because data collection, aggregation, and analysis are essential, as are review and synthesis of relevant research literature. We often engage groups, organizations, and communities in collaborative advocacy efforts, or encourage them to engage in self-advocacy. Periodically, we analyze current or proposed social policies and programs, develop program plans, or draft policies for possible legislative action. In addition, we often provide expert testimony to legislative committees or in courtroom proceedings.

All of these functions require that we use sophisticated and culturally sensitive talking and listening skills as well as the skills associated with preparing, beginning, exploring, assessing, contracting, working and evaluating, and ending. In policy–practice, we often use these skills in work with both clients as well as other individuals, groups, organizations, communities, and with various decision makers (for example, legislators, executives, boards of directors). In addition, we frequently focus as much on policy- and program-relevant documents as we do on the human beings affected by them.

Indeed, the focus on policies involves a double edge. A national or local policy or program may affect hundreds, thousands, or millions of people. If carefully prepared, the benefits may be far-reaching indeed. On the other hand, policies and programs can also produce unintended and unexpected consequences that can be positive for some people and negative for others. Furthermore, unless a policy is determined by direct, universal vote, each individual person in the population affected by that policy is likely to have little or no say in its design or implementation.

Suppose, for example, a vocal segment of a community advocates for the enactment of legislation to require all convicted felons, upon completion of their criminal sentence and release from prison and parole, to wear electronic monitoring devices for the remainder of their lives. In certain areas, such legislation could easily become law—over the objections of the former prisoners, their families, and others concerned about the fairness of continuous, lifelong punishment for those who have already completed the terms of their criminal sentence.[49] Members of the general public who are afraid and concerned about their personal safety and those who prefer more severe and lengthy punishment for offenders would probably support its passage. So would people, businesses, and corporations that would benefit economically from such legislation. Companies that manufacture the devices and individuals who would be employed to monitor their electronic activity would certainly lobby for its passage. Indeed, many might well contribute to the reelection campaigns of pro-passage legislators.

Consider another example. Suppose a number of large, well-financed companies in either the U.S. health insurance or the banking industry sought to maintain their large share of the economic market, prevent the introduction of additional competition, and continue to minimize regulatory

[49] Such laws might subsequently be overturned by the U.S. Supreme Court on the basis of the "cruel and unusual punishment" provision of the Eighth Amendment to the U.S. Constitution.

oversight. Those companies might form associations and employ lobbyists to influence legislators. The associations might prepare and distribute position papers and proposed pieces of legislation. They might advertise widely in the popular media. They might fund academics and researchers to prepare scholarly papers. Employees of the companies might make large donations to legislators' reelection campaigns. Some companies might offer to open branch offices in legislators' districts—if the legislators support the companies' positions. Given their financial resources, their easy access to decision makers, and the effectiveness of their lobbyists, it is quite likely that the health insurance companies or the banks would secure legislative policies they want regardless of the consequences to millions of individuals and families affected by those laws and regulations.

Advocates for social and economic justice engage in some of the same activities as do political lobbyists. Indeed, lobbying and advocating share many common activities—although social work advocates typically have access to fewer funds and resources, and profit motives usually play a smaller part. Assume, for example, that you are a social worker who works with émigrés seeking asylum and refuge in North America. Many are trying to escape the violence and deprivation so common in several parts of the world. The refugees vary in terms of language, religion, ethnic community, culture, dress, and customs. However, they share needs for housing, employment, education, health and mental health care, legal assistance with immigration processes and procedures, and help with the complexities of making the transition to a different nation and culture. If they are undocumented, they may be incarcerated in facilities such as the T. Don Hutto Detention Center in Taylor, Texas.[50] In addition to individual adults, some detention centers hold families—including mothers with young children—for months or years at a time while they await review of their immigration cases. Many of the detention facilities are operated by private, for-profit prison-management companies.[51]

Over the course of more than 10 years, you have assisted and advocated for immigrants and refugees, usually on a case-by-case basis. You regularly visit immigrants in detention centers and coordinate volunteers to do the same. At this time, you hope to expand your small program by securing additional funding through private and public sources. You would also like to see changes in state, local, and federal policies and practices to reduce obstacles and facilitate immigration and resettlement of asylum-seeking refugees. In effect, you plan to engage in class advocacy and policy-practice with and on behalf of current and future refugees.

In pursuing these goals, you might prepare a **policy–practice plan**[52] that includes the following steps:

1. Based upon your experience with asylum-seeking immigrants and refugees, prepare a clear statement of (a) refugees' basic needs and the obstacles they face; and (b) the problems with existing policies. Include information about the human impact of current practices as well as their implications for human rights, social justice, and social well-being. As you draft a problem statement, seek input about issues and concerns from refugees as well as other service providers.

2. As you continue to refine your problem statement, conduct a scholarly and systematic review of the research literature related to (a) the nature, origin, development,

---

[50] The T. Don Hutto Detention Center was made famous in the documentary film *The Least of These: Family Detention in America* (Lyda & Lyda, 2009). Information about the film is available at **http://theleastofthese-film.com/**.

[51] On July 24, 2015 U.S. District Judge Dolly Gee ruled that the policy and practice of incarcerating immigrant mothers with their children in detention centers is unlawful because it violates a 1997 court settlement.

[52] Advocacy with and for refugees and immigrants requires extraordinary legal expertise. The relevant laws and regulations have become intricate and complex—especially since the onset of the "war on terror" and the adoption of associated legislation such as the Patriot Act. Social workers engaged in refugee casework and advocacy would necessarily work closely with attorneys who specialize in immigration law.

incidence, and extent of the problems refugees confront, (b) the past, present, and potential policies intended to address those problems, and (c) the positive and negative impact of existing policies. Also examine the legislative record associated with the introduction, debate, and passage of current policies. Finally, review state or federal judicial actions and decisions that relate to the problem and the policies.

3. If feasible, complement your review of the research literature and the legislative and judicial records through surveys, focus groups, and other data collection efforts with refugees affected by current policies. Also correspond directly with researchers, policy makers, and policy analysts in the field.

4. Based upon the knowledge gained from the earlier processes, finalize your statement of the problem and generate an array of plausible and, if possible, evidence-based approaches to problem resolution. Typically, this involves preparation of a range of potential changes to current policies, programs, or practices. Sometimes, however, new and innovative proposals are included. Once you generate a list of plausible solutions, seek feedback about the list from refugees, other service providers, and, if possible, researchers and policy makers.

5. In collaboration with refugees and other stakeholders, review the list of proposals. Consider their likely positive and negative effects and implications, anticipate costs and benefits, and estimate potential risks and rewards for both asylum-seeking refugees as well as those likely to be affected by proposed solutions. Identify potential sources of support and opposition. Rank each proposal in terms of (a) likely effectiveness, (b) relative advantages and disadvantages, and (c) probability of adoption and implementation. Choose the optimum proposal.

6. In consultation with refugees and other stakeholders, prepare a specific strategy and plan to secure adoption of the chosen proposal for change (for example, revisions in current policies, programs, or practices; or something entirely innovative). Be sure to identify ways to include and involve constituents throughout the process. Identify needed resources and relevant stakeholders, formulate short- and long-term goals and associated action steps, establish time frames, and choose means and measures to assess progress and evaluate outcomes.

7. In collaboration with people affected by the problem and other stakeholders, recruit and mobilize supporters, and implement the plans. Anticipate the actions and reactions of opponents and develop plans to counter them. Use contemporary communication technology to coordinate activities and maintain and accelerate momentum. Evaluate progress and make adjustments to the plans based upon assessment data. Continue efforts until your proposal is approved and implemented.

8. Once implemented, evaluate the outcomes of the new or revised policy, program, or practice. Collect and analyze data related to negative as well positive outcomes, and remain alert for unintended favorable and unfavorable consequences. Based upon ongoing assessment and evaluation data, and feedback from consumers and other stakeholders, prepare recommendations for improvements to the now current policy, program, or practice. Develop plans to secure approval of these suggestions.

As you review these eight steps, you may be reminded of other processes that we have explored. Notice the similarities between these steps and the seven stages of practice, the processes included in scientific methodology, the steps in evidence-based practice, and the activities associated with life-long learning. Consider how many aspects of professionalism are involved in these processes. Integrity, knowledge and self-efficacy, critical thinking and scientific inquiry, and lifelong learning are all essential elements of advocacy and policy–practice. Recognize the significance of diversity and difference as well as the importance of human rights and social, economic, and environmental justice for the promotion of personal and social well-being. Finally, remember that your advocacy work takes time and energy. You, personally, need substantial social and emotional support to maintain your motivation and continue your professional efforts as an advocate for those with little power and limited resources in a social and economic environment that is always challenging and often hostile.

Indeed, initial efforts to ensure human rights, eliminate poverty, and secure justice are commonly met with extraordinary resistance by those who have a stake in the status quo. In the United States, for example, privileged whites often adopt indirect methods to maintain power and restrict African Americans, Hispanic Americans, Native Americans, and members of other minority groups from access to jobs, housing, education, political office, and even opportunities to vote in elections. Remarkably, a substantial segment of non-privileged whites also endorse these sentiments. Many are influenced by their own socialization or seduced by racist myths and divisive rhetoric that frame issues in an "us" against "them" (or, "white" versus "black" and "brown") fashion.[53] **Dog whistle politics** is a term used to refer to coded appeals that engage racist motives, fears, and hatred. For example, instead of using the "N-word" to refer to black people, political, religious, or special interest spokespeople merely use the terms *those on welfare, food stamp recipients, beneficiaries of affirmative action*, or *thugs* to convey the idea that ethnic minorities in general; and brown and black people in particular constitute the root cause of social and economic problems (Haney-López, 2014). Like dogs that have been trained to engage in specific behaviors at the sound of a whistle, some humans respond to code words and symbols with predictably racist beliefs, words, and sometimes deeds.[54]

As irrational as it seems to be, some people place blame for their own personal difficulties and for public troubles on the descendants of people who were kidnapped, transported across an ocean, and forced to labor throughout their lives as slaves; on those who experienced discrimination and disenfranchisement under the original Jim Crow policies; on those who currently struggle under "newer" versions of those same insidious practices (Alexander, 2010); and on all those who continue to suffer from systemic, institutionalized racism. The term *blaming the victim* could not be more apt (Ryan, 1971, 1976).

Victim-blaming is so powerful a phenomenon that many non-privileged whites publicly oppose policies and programs that are clearly in their own best personal and family interest. Apparently based on a false assumption that helping low-income families supplement their diets with a little extra food encourages laziness and government dependency, a substantial number of white people—including many who have personally received benefits—adamantly oppose the Supplemental Nutrition Assistance Program (SNAP). Of course, most food stamp recipients are children, elderly, or disabled; most do not receive additional cash welfare benefits; most work—although in low-paying jobs; and most are white (United States Department of Agriculture, 2014, Dec.). Nonetheless, for many, the term *food stamp recipient* serves as a code for "black person on welfare." Facts matter little when the dog whistle is blown.

---

[53] See, for example, books and articles about "the southern strategy" in American politics of the 1960s and 1970s (Aistrup, 1996).

[54] On the evening of June 17, 2015, a self-proclaimed, white supremacist shot and killed nine African Americans engaged in religious study at the historic Emanuel African Methodist Episcopal Church in Charleston, South Carolina. Tragically, racially motivated killings are not uncommon in the United States. They have occurred regularly since the first groups of Africans were kidnapped, brought to Virginia, and sold into slavery. Many murders were specifically intended to instill fear and terror, and keep black people "in their place." The practice of "terror lynching" was especially pernicious. In 12 Southern states alone, 3,959 black people were lynched during the period from 1877 to 1950 (Equal Justice Initiative, 2015). This number does not include racially inspired murders of other kinds; nor does it include killings that occurred in other states (Pfeifer, 2013) or in the years before 1877 and after 1950.

In a genuinely democratic, open society informed by reason and evidence, the major forms of policy–practice would be scholarly and evidence-based in nature. Social workers and others would engage in scientific inquiry and critical thinking to develop and then propose policies for the amelioration of social problems, achievement of social goals, and promotion of the public good. Decision makers would review the evidence-informed proposals and, through peaceful, civil, thoughtful dialogue and discussion, determine which initiatives reflect the highest probability of successful outcomes. Policies would be implemented and their effects evaluated. Based on the evidence, changes would be made to improve processes and outcomes.

Unfortunately, policy decisions are rarely based on credible evidence and rational discourse. In the contemporary United States, policy proposals are often written and endorsed by vested interests who make major contributions to the campaigns of legislators, offer free perks, and employ lobbyists to promote and facilitate the legislative process. Known as the **revolving door**, many legislators leave public office to become lobbyists for industries and other special interests (Public Citizen's Congress Watch, 2005, July). Former members of the House of Representatives may begin to lobby their former colleagues as early as 1 year and ex-Senators 2 years after leaving office. Intimately acquainted with the inner operations of the legislative process, they wield substantial influence with their former colleagues, and receive enormous salaries. Not surprisingly, the door also revolves in reverse. Many former lobbyists, sometimes referred to as "hired guns," accept positions on the staffs of legislative office holders and their committees (Bryner, 2011, July 12). Furthermore, the revolving door is not limited to the legislative branches of government. The executive branch reflects a parallel process. Employees of several Wall Street banks receive financial incentives to accept government jobs. Goldman Sachs, for example, offers a lump sum cash bonus and a guarantee of re-employment following their term in public service (Dayen, 2015, Feb. 4). The number of Goldman Sachs executives who take positions with the government is so large that the company is sometimes called "Government Sachs" (Baram, 2011, May 25).

Reflecting dual allegiances, the "revolvers" and "reverse revolvers" in both the executive and legislative branches of government ensure that the interests of their former and future employers are protected and promoted. The extent and degree of special interests' influence on policy decisions is difficult to overstate. The dollar amount is staggering. In Washington, DC, much more money is spent on lobbying than it costs to pay for the salaries and benefits of all members of Congress and their staff employees combined. In 2014, 11,781 people were officially registered to lobby the 535 members of the House and Senate (Bump, 2015, Apr. 21). A total of $3.24 billion were spent on lobbying in that year alone (Center for Responsive Politics, 2015). Political Action Committees (PACs), candidates, and political parties receive billions more—most from a small number of contributors. During the 2014 election cycle, only 0.23 percent of the U.S. population made political contributions of $200 or more. However, their contributions accounted for two-thirds of the more than $3.67 billion spent that year. "In the 2014 elections, 31,976 donors—equal to roughly one percent of one percent of the total population of the United States—accounted for an astounding $1.18 billion in disclosed political contributions at the federal level" (Olsen-Phillips, Choma, Bryner, & Weber, 2015, Apr. 30, para. 1).

Compared to major campaign contributors and lobbyists, the vast majority of moderate and low-income people have little or no effect upon public policy in the United States—except, that is, when we organize, mobilize, and take social action. Popular social movements, protests, boycotts, marches, and demonstrations reflect the primary means by which non-privileged people can influence public policies and practices.

If social workers intend to make good on our commitment to "promote social justice and social change with and on behalf of clients . . . (and) . . . strive to end discrimination, oppression, poverty, and other forms of social injustice" (National Association of Social Workers, 2008), then we must supplement our rational, evidence-based policy analyses and proposals with energetic social action. Social workers cannot, indeed should not, do it alone. We must collaborate with people whose human rights are violated and those directly affected by social, economic, and environmental injustice. Social workers routinely partner with clients and others in our service to individuals, families, and groups. Let's also do so on a larger scale by actively participating with organizations and communities dedicated to the promotion of human rights and justice through social, political, and economic action.

SUMMARY

In this chapter, we explored (1) diversity and difference; (2) human rights; (3) social, economic, and environmental justice, and (4) policy–practice. This knowledge complements dimensions of professionalism addressed in earlier chapters: integrity, knowledge and self-efficacy, self-understanding and self-control, social support and well-being, critical thinking, scientific inquiry, and lifelong learning. We require such knowledge and abilities when we engage in direct service with others. However, they are just as crucial for policy–practice and other forms of class advocacy. Indeed, our professionalism must be especially rigorous when we engage in macro-level activities. Although policy and cultural changes have the potential to help large numbers of people, they can also cause damage to just as many or more. All social work activities involve the risk of harm associated with unintended consequences. If, as professionals, we engage in scientific inquiry and think critically before we engage in policy–practice and advocacy, we reduce the chances of negative and increase the chances of positive effects.

CHAPTER 4   Summary Exercises

Reflective Exercises

1. Go to the Implicit Association Test (IAT) website at **https://implicit.harvard.edu/implicit**. Once there, go to the Project Implicit Social Attitudes box. You may choose to register with your e-mail or proceed as a guest. Once inside, select the Race ("Black–White") IAT as a first test of your implicit attitudes. Later, you might decide to complete the Skin-Tone ("Light Skin–Dark Skin") IAT, the Weapons ("Weapons–Harmless Objects") IAT, the Sexuality ("Gay–Straight") IAT, or perhaps another of the IATs available on the site.

   Please recognize that the scores obtained may produce interpretative results that you do not expect and would not prefer. Implicit bias should not be mistaken for conscious bias. Many people have worked hard to change their conscious prejudices and have made enormous progress in overcoming pervasive cultural bias. Nonetheless, it should come as no great surprise, for example, that most white people throughout the United States reflect implicit bias against black people. The IAT results are presented as a "*d* score" effect size. A *d* score of 0 to .14 suggests little or no implicit preference for whites (or, little or no implicit bias against blacks). Scores from .15 to .34 suggest a *slight* implicit preference for whites; from .35 to .64 indicate a *moderate* preference; and .65 and higher indicate a *strong* implicit preference for whites along with a corresponding bias against blacks.

   Record or save a copy of your IAT results. Then use an Internet search engine to locate copies of Chris Mooney's *Mother Jones* piece entitled "The Science of Why Cops Shoot Young

Black Men" (2014, Dec. 1) and his *Washington Post* piece entitled "Across America, whites are biased and they don't even know it" (2014, Dec. 8). Read the two short articles. Using them as context, reflect on the meaning of your own implicit association scores and those of white people in the United States to prepare a discussion of implicit attitudes and quick judgments in the form of a one- to two-page word-processed report (250–500 words). Title the report "Implicit Attitudes and Quick Judgment in Social Work." When you finish, save the file as "IAT_in_SWK" and include it in your Social Work Skills Learning Portfolio.

2. Reflect on this chapter's content about diversity and difference, intersectionality, accepting others, and respecting autonomy. Use your word-processing program to prepare a one- to two-page (250–500 words) report entitled "Valuing Diversity and Difference." As part of the paper, explore how and why so many people tolerate, justify, and sometimes even celebrate hatred of other humans based on characteristics such as skin color, religious or nonreligious beliefs, physical appearance, clothing, gender, sexual orientation, language, occupation, immigration status, or economic class. Also discuss what you and other social workers might do to both strengthen your own ability to value diversity and difference, to accept others, and to encourage others to do so as well. When you finish, save the document file as "Val_Div_and_Dif" and include the report in your Social Work Skills Learning Portfolio.

3. Reflect upon the information about rates of incarceration, human poverty, income and wealth distribution, gender inequality, environmental performance, and social well-being discussed in this chapter. Use your word-processing program to prepare a one- to two-page (250–500 words) report in which you identify those facts that most surprise, shock, or disturb you. Specify those that most challenge your own views about human rights and social, economic, and environmental justice; and briefly explain why you're challenged. Next, discuss how and why many people remain passive in the face of flagrant violations of human rights and widespread disregard for basic principles of social justice. Finally, identify how social workers could become more active and effective in raising public awareness; preventing human rights violations; and ensuring social, economic, and environmental justice. Title the report "What Social Workers Can Do about Injustice." Save the report as "Soc_Action_in_SWK" and include it in your Social Work Skills Learning Portfolio.

Write-Now Exercises

Use the space below each of the following write-now exercises to record your responses.

1. Access the Internet and use a search engine to locate and download the complete descriptions of the 30 human rights included within the United Nations Universal Declaration of Human Rights.[55] Reflect upon these rights and the values that undergird them. Now use an informal 0–10 rating scale (say from "not at all important" to "extremely important") to identify the relative importance of human rights education during your childhood. In other words, in your school, family, and culture, how much were you (a) taught about human rights, (b) encouraged to use them as guidelines for considering "right" and "wrong," and (c) positively recognized for exercising your own human rights and defending the rights of others—especially "unpopular others"? Next, use the scale to rate your current views about the importance of human rights today—to you personally and to your family, groups, organizations, and communities; and to your nation and society. When you've recorded your ratings below, reflect upon the following questions: Why are my ratings similar or different? Then, ask yourself, How much

---

[55] The list presented earlier in Box 4.1 is a "plain English" version of the UDHR.

do I and other members of my primary social groups (a) know about human rights; (b) use them as guidelines for considering "right" and "wrong"; and (c) support people who exercise their own human rights or act to protect the rights of others?

2. What do you think would happen to recidivism rates in the United States if prisoners were treated with dignity and respect, allowed to learn skills needed within the contemporary job market, and permitted full human rights (including the right to vote) upon completion of their sentences? What do you think would happen to the rate of violent crime if the sale, possession, and use of drugs were decriminalized? What do you predict would happen to the rate of nonviolent, non-drug-related crime, if nonviolent offenders served alternate sentences instead of incarceration? What might happen to the rates of incarceration if for-profit prisons and privatized probation and parole services were converted back into state or nonprofit facilities?

3. What do you predict will happen to human society if the average global temperature rises more than 2°C (3.6°F) above pre-industrial levels, the amount of CO_2 in the earth's atmosphere approaches 1 million parts per million, and the oceans become more and more like vinegar? What do you think you and other social workers *should* do about the climate crisis? What do you think you and other social workers *will* do?

4. Imagine a world where technology has advanced so far that less than half of the adult human population has to "work" to satisfy the wants and needs of the entire population. Most "work" would be completed by computers, robots, and other "intelligent machines." Under such circumstances, how would you like to see income and wealth distributed to adults who do not have income-producing "jobs"? What opportunities or programs would you propose to foster social well-being among large populations of people for whom "work" as we know it is unavailable?

CHAPTER 4   Self-Appraisal

As you finish this chapter, please reflect on your learning by using the following space to identify any ideas, terms, or concepts addressed in Chapter 4 that remain confusing or unclear to you:

Next, respond to the following items by carefully reading each statement. Please use a 1-to-10-point rating scale (where *1 = strongly disagree* and *10 = strongly agree*) to indicate the degree to which you agree or disagree with each statement. Place a check mark at the point that best reflects your view at this particular point in time. If you're truly *undecided*, place your check at the midpoint (5.5) mark.

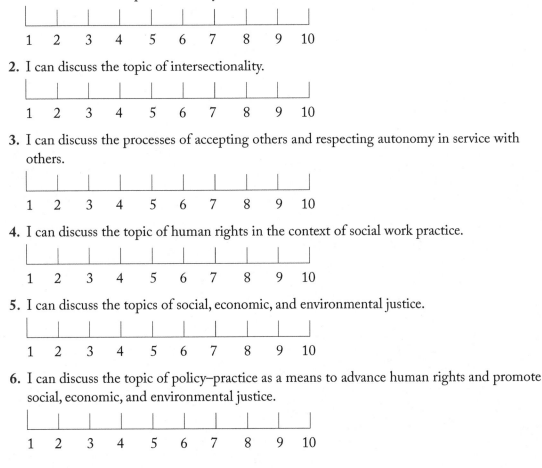

1. I can discuss the topic of diversity and difference in human relations.

   1   2   3   4   5   6   7   8   9   10

2. I can discuss the topic of intersectionality.

   1   2   3   4   5   6   7   8   9   10

3. I can discuss the processes of accepting others and respecting autonomy in service with others.

   1   2   3   4   5   6   7   8   9   10

4. I can discuss the topic of human rights in the context of social work practice.

   1   2   3   4   5   6   7   8   9   10

5. I can discuss the topics of social, economic, and environmental justice.

   1   2   3   4   5   6   7   8   9   10

6. I can discuss the topic of policy–practice as a means to advance human rights and promote social, economic, and environmental justice.

   1   2   3   4   5   6   7   8   9   10

Social Work Values and Ethical Decision Making

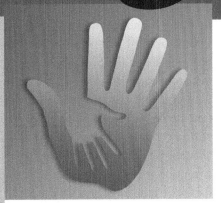

In this chapter, we conclude the exploration of professionalism with the topics of social work values and ethical decision making. Our professional social work values, attitudes, and ethics pervade all aspects of our working lives. Each decision we make and every action we take involve ethical, frequently legal, and sometimes moral considerations. As a result, ethical decision making is a crucial aspect of professionalism in social work practice.

We confront intricate ethical dilemmas daily as we attempt to serve others, advance human rights, and promote social, economic, and environmental justice. Moral issues arise when we challenge unjust laws, policies, and practices. To address these challenging issues, we need a thorough understanding of social work values and ethics (Reamer, 2013b) and those legal obligations that affect and inform our work. Such understanding involves a great deal more than familiarity with legal statutes, case law, and ethical codes. We require a solid grasp of the underlying values.

Chapter Goals

Following completion of this chapter, you should be able to:

- Identify and discuss the legal duties that apply to helping professionals.

- Access laws that affect the practice of social work in your locale.

- Discuss the fundamental values of the social work profession.

- Discuss the moral values that guide professional helping activities.

- Discuss the ethical principles and standards that inform social work practice.

- Identify the relevant values, legal duties, and ethical principles that apply in various professional contexts and situations.

- Determine the relative priority of competing legal and ethical obligations when ethical dilemmas arise in specific circumstances.

- Use critical thinking and scientific inquiry skills to reach ethical decisions and plan appropriate action.

Core Competencies

The content addressed in this chapter supports the following core EPAS competencies:

- Competency 1: Demonstrate Ethical and Professional Behavior

- Competency 4: Engage in Practice-Informed Research and Research-Informed Practice

- Competency 6: Engage with Individuals, Families, Groups, Organizations, and Communities

You should know your social work code of ethics and be able to identify the legal and ethical principles that apply to specific situations. When principles conflict, you need the capacity to address and resolve the dilemma. Specifically, you must think critically to determine which ethical principles or legal obligations should take precedence over others in situations where several competing responsibilities apply.[1]

In our service to clients, social workers use information from a variety of sources: theoretical knowledge, knowledge from research studies, wisdom gained from life experience and service to clients, the expertise of colleagues and supervisors, and agency policies and procedures. One source of information, however, serves as a screen for all others. The values, ethics, and obligations of the profession are preeminent. We must consider every aspect of practice, every decision, every assessment, every intervention, and virtually every action we undertake as social workers from the perspective of our professional ethics and obligations. Ethical responsibilities take precedence over theoretical knowledge, research findings, practice wisdom, agency policies, and, of course, our own personal values, preferences, and beliefs. This dimension supersedes all others—including our religious views and, sometimes, the law of the land. As a central component of professionalism, ethical decision making requires special attention. This chapter focuses exclusively on this theme by providing you with opportunities to develop proficiency in the ethical decision-making skills.

Ethical decision making involves consideration of several dimensions and, of course, a great deal of careful thought. As a basic foundation, social workers must recognize those legal duties that apply to all professional helpers; understand the state, local, and federal laws and regulations that affect the profession and practice of social work; thoroughly comprehend the core social work and relevant moral values; and have ready access to a copy of the social work code of ethics.

When confronted with ethical issues, you first use your foundational knowledge to identify those values, legal duties, and ethical principles that pertain to the specific concerns, people, and circumstances. Be sure to adopt a fair and coherent approach to data collection. If several competing obligations apply, you then determine which take precedence over others. Adopt a decision-making process that includes reference to values, laws, regulations, and ethics; and maintain professional-quality records about your ethical decision-making processes. In your records, include a description of and a rationale for your decision. On occasion, you may decide to take action and, sometimes, you conclude that the most ethical course is to take no action. Finally, monitor and evaluate the effects and outcomes of your decision and the actions you take. Include the results in your records and, if necessary, revise your action plans and take additional steps as needed.

Understanding Our Legal Obligations

Along with counselors, nurses, psychiatrists, and psychologists, social workers are members of the professional helping community. As such, you are subject to certain legally determined obligations or duties. These derive from common law, legislation, regulations, and various court decisions.

---

[1] You may access the National Association of Social Workers (NASW) Code of Ethics at **www.socialworkers.org**; and the "Ethics in Social Work, Statement of Principles" of the International Federation of Social Workers (IFSW) and the social work ethical codes of several other nations via **www.ifsw.org**.

Some legal obligations coincide with the responsibilities suggested by social work values and the code of ethics; others do not. You are responsible for understanding both the legal duties that apply to all professional helpers as well as those specific to social work and social workers. In particular, you need information about the laws and regulations that govern the profession and practice of social work in your locale. Obtain a copy of the licensing law and accompanying regulations that apply to you. Many are available through the Internet.[2]

The Association of Social Work Boards (2015a) website provides links to statutes and regulations throughout the United States and to the Canadian provinces of Alberta, British Columbia, Manitoba, New Brunswick, Newfoundland and Labrador, Nova Scotia, Ontario, Québec, Prince Edward Island, and Saskatchewan. In addition, the ASWB site includes a database that you might use, for example, to compare the social work laws and regulations in two or more states or provinces (2015b).

Despite a plethora of laws and regulations, the legal duties of professional helpers are not always clear. They are certainly not permanent. Various professional and governmental bodies regularly promulgate new policies and modify or rescind old ones. Courts process thousands of cases each year. Many are precedent setting and lead to regulatory changes. As new laws and policies emerge, they influence the legal duties of professional helpers, including social workers. Obviously, you are subject to these evolving legal responsibilities.[3]

Consider, for example, the topic of malpractice. *Malpractice* "is a form of negligence that occurs when a practitioner acts in a manner inconsistent with the profession's standard of care—the way an ordinary, reasonable, and prudent professional would act under the same or similar circumstances" (Reamer, 2015, p. 4). **Malpractice** is:

> willful or negligent behavior by a professional person that violates the relevant code of ethics and professional standards of care and that proves harmful to the client. Among a social worker's actions most likely to result in malpractice are inappropriately divulging confidential information, unnecessarily prolonged services, improper termination of needed services, misrepresentation of one's knowledge or skills, the provision of social work treatment as a replacement for needed medical treatment, the provision of information to others that is libelous or that results in improper incarceration, financial exploitation of the client, sexual activity with a client, and physical injury to the client that may occur in the course of certain treatments (such as group encounters). (Barker, 2014, p. 257)

In legal terms, malpractice, or *mal praxis*, by professional social workers is a form of tort; that is a "civil wrong." A tort involves wrongdoing for which damages may be sought through legal action. A person or group may file a lawsuit in civil court because of injury or suffering resulting from the "wrongful actions or inactions" (Saltzman & Proch, 1990, p. 412) of the professional person. The plaintiff, often a client or a member of a client's family, typically seeks monetary damages to

---

[2] In the United States, all 50 states, the District of Columbia, Puerto Rico, and the U.S. Virgin Islands have enacted laws regulating social work. For example, Title 25 Article 23.6 of the Indiana State Code governs the licensure and practice of social work in the state (IN.gov, 2015, Jan.). You may find that article of law by searching the state of Indiana government website.

[3] Complicating matters is the fact that some enacted laws clearly violate basic principles of human rights and civil liberties. In the United States, it may take some time before sufficient popular discontent pressures legislators to correct an unjust local, state, or federal law; or before it can be challenged and reversed by the courts. Sometimes, of course, unjust laws remain in effect, leading justice advocates to participate in large-scale social movements or engage in purposeful civil disobedience.

compensate for injuries or suffering. Occasionally, courts impose additional damages to punish the professional person guilty of malpractice.

Malpractice involves poor or substandard professional service that results in harm. Failure to meet an accepted standard of care and harm done to a client are the two usual criteria on which malpractice cases are determined. There are three common forms of malpractice: (1) **malfeasance**—where the professional intentionally engages in a practice known to be harmful, (2) **misfeasance**—where the professional makes a mistake in the application of an acceptable practice, and (3) **nonfeasance**—where the professional fails to apply a standard, acceptable practice when the circumstances warrant such practice. The first form of malpractice involves intent to harm, or malice, and may constitute criminal behavior, whereas the other two entail negligence or carelessness. The first two forms of malpractice consist of acts of commission and the third involves acts of omission (Kitchener, 2000; Reamer, 1995b, 2015).

Malpractice lawsuits may be filed against helping professionals for a wide range of behaviors. For example, in California, following treatment by a psychiatrist and a family therapist, a woman accused her father of childhood sexual abuse. Based on his daughter's allegations that he had molested her when she was a child, the man was fired from his job and his wife divorced him. Since the time of the allegations, both his daughter and former spouse refused to have contact with him (Ewing & McCann, 2006; Johnston, 1997).

The man initiated a malpractice lawsuit against the helping professionals. The court concluded that they had acted improperly by suggesting that the client's emerging recollections of previously "repressed memories" were necessarily true and valid. In this case, the court did not assert that the daughter's memories were false—only that the validity of the retrieved memories could not be determined because the helping professionals' words and actions were leading and suggestive. The client, in this case, did not originally remember experiences of childhood abuse. Rather, the memories emerged following the words and actions of the professionals who, in effect, suggested to the client that she had probably been the victim of sexual abuse during childhood. The court awarded the accused father several hundred thousand dollars as compensation for the damage caused by the helping professionals' malpractice (Ewing & McCann, 2006; Johnston, 1997).

During the 1990s, a large number of malpractice lawsuits were filed against practitioners who facilitated "recovery of repressed memories" (Wakefield & Underwager, 1992). Indeed, the topic of repressed, recovered, and false memories has become extraordinarily controversial in recent years—both in and out of courtrooms. Research studies suggest that human memories are quite unlike audio or video recordings. Rather, "memories are records of people's experiences of events and are not a record of the events themselves" (British Psychological Society, 2008, p. 2). The poor reliability of eyewitness testimony in criminal justice proceedings highlights this phenomenon. Indeed, as initially reported by Borchard (1932) and confirmed by numerous studies since then, "the most common cause of wrongful convictions is eyewitness misidentification" (Gross, Jacoby, Matheson, Montgomery, & Patil, 2004, p. 18). In their study of the U.S. criminal justice system, Gross et al. (2004) found that 64 percent of those wrongfully convicted but subsequently exonerated involved mistaken eyewitness identification of the defendant.

Helping professionals can reduce their role in promoting and reinforcing inaccurate recollections by avoiding leading questions, suggestive comments, and speculative interpretations about past events. Be wary of concepts such as "repression." As Mercer points out, "it's inappropriate to conclude that a lack of memory for an event means that the event must have happened and been repressed" (2013, p. 251). Remain skeptical of psychological concepts and constructs that lack empirical support. We can also seek guidance from our professional associations. Indeed, the associations of social work, psychology, and psychiatry have all published cautionary statements about professionals' approach to the recovery of childhood memories (Alpert et al., 1996; American Psychiatric Association, 2000b; British Psychological Society, 2008; National Association of Social Workers, 1996, June). The associations hope these guidelines will protect clients from unnecessary pain and suffering, and reduce the risk of legal action against their professional membership.

The precise number of lawsuits filed against social workers is difficult to determine. However, the rate of grievances against social workers has increased over the years and undoubtedly will continue to grow in the future. Of course, if a lawsuit is filed against you, it certainly does not necessarily mean that you actually engaged in wrongdoing. Some lawsuits are unwarranted, harassing, and even frivolous. You could be the best social worker in the country and still be sued. Nothing you do can guarantee immunity from legal action. However, if someone does sue you, the best defense is undoubtedly ethical, competent, and well-documented service solidly grounded in current practice-related research (Bogie & Coleman, 2002).

This is an area where critical thinking, scientific inquiry, and lifelong learning are especially relevant. Consider, for example, the technique of "holding time." A procedure associated with certain attachment-based therapies, **holding time** may involve coercive restraint. That is, practitioners or parents firmly "hold" a child within their grasp despite the child's efforts to escape. Practitioners have used the technique with infants, children, adolescents, and occasionally with adults. According to the underlying assumptions, holding time may rectify poor attachments with parents or others, sometimes through reliving the experience of birth ("rebirthing"). **Coercive restraint therapies (CRT)** incorporate practices that:

> involve the use of restraint as a tool of treatment rather than simply as a safety device. While restraining the child, CRT practitioners may also exert physical pressure in the form of tickling or intense prodding of the torso, grab the child's face, and command the child to kick the legs rhythmically. Some CRT practitioners lie prone with their body weight on the child, a practice they call compression therapy. Most practitioners restrain the child in a supine position, but some place the child in prone when using restraint for calming purposes. (Mercer, 2005, Introduction, para. 2)

Tragically, this form of unconventional "treatment" has been implicated in the deaths of several children. For example, the adoptive father of a 3-year-old girl received a prison sentence of 5 years for using compression therapy and a form of visceral manipulation (that is, pushing his fist deep into the child's abdomen for several minutes) that led to the girl's death. A 10-year-old girl died during a "rebirthing experience" in which she was swaddled in a flannel sheet and physically compressed by two practitioners. The practitioners repeatedly told her to try to escape from the fabric "womb." However, each time she tried, the practitioners physically prevented her from doing so—apparently in an effort to simulate the difficulty associated with actual birth. Despite the girl's calls for help, cries that she could not breathe, and emission of vomitus, the practitioners ignored her pleas and continued to sit on her and hold her down. Several minutes after she stopped making sounds or movements, the practitioners let up. When finally released from the fabric restraint, the girl was dead. The practitioners received multi-year sentences in prison. The case led to enactment of a Colorado law that prohibits the use of birthing reenactments that involve the risk of physical injury or death (Mercer, 2005, 2014; Mercer, Sarner, & Rosa, 2003).

We might think that helping professionals would never take actions that have the potential to injure or kill people, especially children. Such is not the case. Let's hypothesize that somewhere, sometime, someone will use an obviously dangerous or inhumane therapeutic procedure if:

1. A difficult problem exists (such as unrelenting disobedience and aggressive behavior by a child—especially a foster or adopted child).
2. An "expert authority" educates practitioners in the use of a procedure—with or without cautions.
3. The procedure is described in a book, article, or distributed electronically through television or the Internet.
4. The procedure has a conceptual "ring of truth" and appears to "make sense" in the form of a logically fallacious argument. An "authority" might, for example, claim that a problem of current disobedience by the child is the result of failed bonding with the biological mother at the time of birth; the child's body (if not the conscious brain) remembers the trauma; other procedures are ineffective; and the child's body must relive the experience of birth to resolve the problem.
5. The professional culture permits or implicitly encourages passive acceptance of authority-based information and simplistic, dualistic, or uncritical thinking.
6. The professional culture allows or indirectly endorses the use of scientifically untested or pseudoscientific practices.
7. Use of the procedure produces financial, social, or emotional rewards for the practitioner or the employing organization.

When these conditions exist, some practitioners will invariably teach or adopt risky procedures. Injury or death will eventually result—even when good intentions motivate practitioners. Indeed, most sincerely want to help. Following a death, however, various participants tend to blame one another. A practitioner might denounce the expert. The expert, in turn, faults the practitioner for administering the procedure in an improper or "unauthorized" manner. Of course, civil or criminal proceedings follow. The courts determine the responsibility of various parties, assign punishments to guilty practitioners, and sometimes award financial compensation to the victim or the victim's family. Interestingly, the agencies that employed the practitioners; the professions to which they belonged; the insurance companies that reimbursed them for risky and scientifically untested procedures; and the academic institutions that educated them rarely receive criticism. As is often the case in misconduct of all kinds, the surrounding cultures, larger systems, and high-level leaders that tolerate or encourage misconduct often escape scrutiny or responsibility.[4]

Although some social workers engage in unprofessional, unsafe, or even illegal conduct, most of us do not. Warranted or unwarranted, however, clients and their families sometimes sue social workers. Indeed, the increasing frequency of litigation against helping professionals should cause us concern even though the probability of a lawsuit, especially for social workers, remains quite low. Social work is a personally and professionally satisfying career. The litigious nature of contemporary life, however, underscores the importance of understanding the current legal milieu as well as those duties that apply to all social workers and other helping professionals.

---

[4] See Zimbardo's *The Lucifer Effect* (2007), Mitchell's *Democracy's Blameless Leaders* (2012), Taibbi's *Griftopia* (2011), and Eisinger's *New York Times Magazine* article "Why Only One Top Banker Went to Jail for the Financial Crisis" (2014, Apr. 30a) for examples of these phenomena.

Several categorical themes emerge from reviews of grievances and lawsuits filed against social workers over the past few decades (Reamer, 2013a, 2013b, 2015). The risk of complaints or litigation increases when professionals engage in misbehavior such as:

- *Treatment without consent.* A client may allege that professional treatment procedures occurred without informed consent; the parents of a minor child may assert that their child received treatment without their awareness or consent.

- *Professional incompetence, incorrect treatment, or failure to treat.* A client may assert that a social worker did not provide competent professional services, as indicated by the use of inappropriate, inadequate, or unconventional assessment procedures or interventions, or by the failure to provide service when needed.

- *Failure to maintain currency with advances in the knowledge base.* A client may claim that a social worker did not keep abreast with contemporary research findings that pertain to the client, the problem, or the situation. Evidence for knowledge deficiency may involve inadequate continuing professional education or inability to respond to questions about current practices.

- *Failure to diagnose, or flawed assessment, or incorrect diagnosis.* A client may assert that a social worker failed to undertake an appropriate biopsychosocial interview or recognize signs of a problem or disorder; formulated an erroneous assessment; or assigned an incorrect diagnosis.

- *Failure to report suspected abuse or neglect.* A client, a client's family, or a state agency may allege that a social worker had information of possible child endangerment yet failed to report suspicions to relevant authorities.

- *Reporting suspected abuse or neglect.* A client or a client's family may assert that a social worker who reported to state authorities suspicions that a child was being abused or neglected did so without adequate evidence and, as a result, caused severe and irreparable damage to the affected parties.

- *Failure to consult or refer to other professionals or specialists.* A client or client's family may allege that a social worker should have consulted a medical doctor when it became apparent that the problems and symptoms revealed by the client suggested the real possibility of a medical condition.

- *Failure to prevent a client's suicide.* The family of a client who committed suicide may assert that a social worker knew or should have known that the client was suicidal yet failed to take action necessary to protect the client from his or her own suicidal impulses.

- *Causing a client's suicide.* The family of a client who committed suicide may allege that a social worker's words or actions provoked the client to take his or her own life.

- *Failure to warn or protect third parties.* A person injured by a client may assert that a social worker knew or should have known that the client was potentially dangerous and intended to harm the person in question yet failed to take action to notify the targeted individual or relevant authorities and protect her or him from the client's violent actions.

- *Inappropriate release of a client.* A client or a client's family may allege that the social worker and other professionals were negligent in permitting a client to leave their care and supervision while the client was in a state of acute distress or incapacity.

- *False imprisonment or arrest.* A client may claim that his or her commitment to a facility, such as a psychiatric institution or drug treatment center, or police arrest constituted wrongful detention or incarceration, and violated his or her civil rights.

- *Failure to provide adequate care or supervision for a client in residential settings.* A client or a client's family may assert that the neglectful and inadequate care provided by a social worker or staff members under the social worker's supervision caused injury or death.
- *Assault or battery.* A client may allege that a social worker made threatening remarks or gestures, or engaged in improper or inappropriate physical contact.
- *Intentional infliction of emotional distress.* A client may claim that a social worker's actions, such as use of a counseling procedure or perhaps the removal of a child from the home of a biological parent, so traumatized the client as to cause significant mental or emotional distress.
- *Sexual impropriety.* A client may allege that a social worker used professional authority and expertise for the purposes of sexual seduction and exploitation.
- *Breach of confidentiality.* A client may allege that a social worker intentionally or unintentionally communicated confidential information to an unauthorized party.
- *Breach of contract, poor results, or failure to cure.* A client may believe that a social worker promised (or guaranteed) that a certain outcome would occur as a result of the social worker's service. When the anticipated outcome did not occur, the client may allege that the social worker failed to fulfill the terms of the contract. Because the marriage ended in divorce, the client may assert that the social worker did not fulfill the terms of the agreement.
- *Invasion of privacy.* A client may assert that a child abuse investigation or other form of exploration and assessment was overreaching or harassing in nature.
- *Defamation of character, libel, or slander.* A client may believe that a social worker, orally or in writing, made an untrue and derogatory statement that harmed the client's reputation.
- *Violation of a client's civil rights.* Clients may allege that a social worker or employees under the social worker's supervision violated their civil rights, perhaps, for example, by confiscating personal property or embezzling funds.
- *Failure to be available when needed.* A client may assert that a social worker was inaccessible or unavailable when he or she was in urgent need of service.
- *Inappropriate termination of treatment or abandonment.* A client may allege that a social worker concluded treatment abruptly or unprofessionally.
- *Malicious prosecution or abuse of process.* A client may claim that a legal action initiated by a social worker, for instance in a child-protection case, was undertaken with full knowledge that the case would be dismissed by the court and therefore was maliciously intended.
- *Inappropriate bill collection methods.* A client may assert that the social worker used invasive and improper means in an attempt to collect on bills that were outstanding.
- *Statutory violations.* A client, employing organization, or other stakeholders (persons with "legal standing") may file a lawsuit against a social worker for violating requirements of the state law under which social workers are legally certified or licensed.
- *Inadequately protecting a child.* A client, the client's family, or a state agency may assert that injury to a child resulted from neglectful and inadequate care provided by a social worker.

- *Violating parental rights.* The parents of a child may assert that a social worker violated their rights by, for example, providing professional services to their child without their informed consent or for withholding information from them.
- *Inadequate foster care services.* A client, the biological parents of a child, or a state agency may assert that a social worker placed a child in a foster-care setting that provided inadequate or injurious care.

Certain settings and some forms of practice are associated with a greater risk for litigation. For example, because child welfare work often involves the provision of involuntary services, there is a greater likelihood of both civil and criminal legal action against social workers employed in such settings. As alluded to earlier, practices that involve the exploration or "recovery" of "repressed memories" have led to numerous malpractice lawsuits. Some of these resulted in multimillion-dollar judgments against the helping professionals involved. In June 1996, the National Association of Social Workers issued a Practice Update urging that "social workers who practice in the area of recovered memories should be mindful that this is a high-risk area of practice in an environment of intense controversy" (Summary section, para.1).

Although most malpractice litigation occurs in civil court, social workers may occasionally be subject to criminal action related to the nature and extent of their professional services.

> In Colorado, for example, a caseworker and her supervisor were criminally prosecuted when a child with whom the caseworker was working was killed by her parents. The parents had been reported to the worker as abusive but the worker had chosen to keep the child in the home. The worker and her supervisor were convicted. (Saltzman & Proch, 1990, p. 428)

In this Colorado case, an appellate court later overturned the criminal convictions on technical grounds. Nonetheless, the case illustrates the enormous responsibilities associated with professional social work practice, as well as the litigious nature of contemporary society.

Carefully review the laws and regulations that affect the practice of social work in your locale and those that may relate to your service areas. Laws related to child abuse and neglect, elder abuse, domestic violence, civil rights, sexual harassment, psychological testing, psychotherapy and counseling, child custody, marriage and divorce, and adoption probably pertain in some way to most social workers. Social workers in the United States should be familiar with the Americans with Disabilities Act (ADA) of 1990; the Keeping Children and Families Safe Act of 2003 and the Child Abuse Prevention and Treatment Act (CAPTA); the Health Insurance Portability and Accountability Act of 1996 (HIPAA); the Patient Safety and Quality Improvement Act of 2005 (PSQIA); the standards for privacy of individually identifiable health information (the "privacy rule"); the HITECH Act; the federal confidentiality regulations regarding the privacy rights of people receiving alcohol or drug abuse (substance abuse) treatment services; the Family Educational Rights and Privacy Act (FERPA) of 1974; and other laws and regulations that directly affect social workers and their clientele. Undoubtedly, as time passes, there will be changes in the nature and extent of the legal responsibilities that apply to social workers, but the general legal duties or obligations presented in Figure 5.1 and discussed below are likely to remain in effect for many years to come (Everstine & Everstine, 1983, pp. 227–251).

Legal duties tend to parallel those human rights and obligations that are highly valued by a society. In the United States, many fundamental rights are evident in the Bill of Rights of the Constitution, other amendments, and decisions of the federal courts. As we explored in Chapter 4,

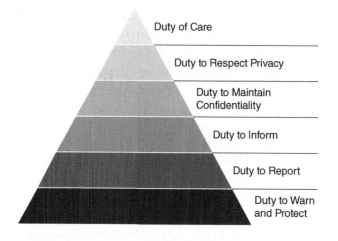

FIGURE 5.1   Legal Obligations of Helping Professionals

the Universal Declaration of Human Rights (General Assembly of the United Nations, 1948) describes the protections afforded, in theory at least, to all people in all countries throughout the world. Article 1 of the declaration begins with the phrase, "All human beings are born free and equal in dignity and rights." Most legal duties that pertain to helping professionals' obligations involve aspects of one or more fundamental human rights.

Duty of Care

As a professional social worker, you are legally obligated to provide a reasonable standard of care in delivering social work services. Clients have a right to expect that you will discharge your professional responsibilities in a competent manner. There is an implied contract to that effect. Services provided should meet at least an adequate standard of care—as determined in part by the social work profession and in part by common expectations of helping professionals. Social workers provide services to a diverse clientele in a wide range of settings. Therefore, social workers must reflect competence not only in the fundamentals of social work practice but also in helping clients address specific problems and goals. Indeed, all social workers must be able to access, critically review, and incorporate into our service those results from scientific research that relate to the people we serve, the issues they face, and the environments in which they live. In addition, we also must engage our clients in the systematic evaluation of progress toward goals.

Social workers who work with families addressing child abuse and neglect issues must be competent in both social work and child welfare practice, and engage in routine evaluation of both client safety and progress toward goal attainment. Those who serve diverse population groups must reflect cultural sensitivity as well. Social workers attempting to help Buddhist immigrants from Laos must know a good deal about Laotian culture, Buddhist beliefs, and, of course, the problems and processes associated with transitions into a new society. Social workers who engage in policy–practice and advocacy must know a great deal about political processes and legislative decision making; about policy and program design, development, and implementation; and about organizing social action. In such macro-level practice, we should be cognizant of the outcomes or likely outcomes of current or proposed policies and programs; the social issues or problems for which the policies and programs refer; and, of course, the people affected or potentially affected by those current or proposed policies and programs. Obviously, as professionals, social workers must know a great deal about a lot of things, and we must be able to learn a great deal more in rapid fashion.

In terms of duty of care expectations, the NASW publishes standards of social work practice in, for example, child welfare; school social work services; work with military service members, veterans, and their families; family caregivers of older adults; and clients with substance use problems (National Association of Social Workers, 2015c). The Association also provides practice tools that can be extremely useful. Here are a few examples: "An Overview of 2015 Medicare Updates for Clinical Social Workers," "Domestic Violence, the National Association of Social Workers Comprehensive Overview," "A Consumer's Guide to the 2014 Affordable Care Act Changes," and "Caught in the Middle: Supporting Families Involved with Immigration and Child Welfare Systems" (National Association of Social Workers, 2015d). In addition, NASW may issue special reports such as "Ebola: A Social Work Guide" (National Association of Social Workers, 2015a) or policy statements to guide social workers in their professional service activities (National Association of Social Workers, 2015e).

Spurred on by demands for increased accountability and heightened expectations for quality service and better outcomes, social work educators have begun to publish textbooks that emphasize a scientific evidence base for practice (see, for example, Bronson & Davis, 2012; Drisko & Grady, 2012; Glisson, Dulmus, & Sowers, 2012; Guo & Bielefeld, 2014; Palinkas & Soydan, 2012; Royse, Thyer, & Padgett, 2016; Thyer, Dulmus, & Sowers, 2013; Thyer & Pignotti, 2015). Recognizing that an evidence-based perspective includes systematic evaluative feedback from clients as well as findings from high-quality research studies, contemporary social workers are familiar with assessments, services, and interventions that reflect strong theoretical and empirical support.

Professional, governmental, and nongovernmental organizations have begun to publish practice guidelines based on comprehensive reviews and systematic analyses of the relevant research literature. For example, the National Guideline Clearinghouse is a public resource for evidence-based clinical practice guidelines (U.S. Department of Health and Human Services, 2015b). Although focused primarily on health and mental health care, some guidelines relate to topics of direct interest to social workers in other settings. For example, a quick search using keywords such as "abuse," "homeless," "gay," or "suicide" returns a number of potentially relevant guidelines. The Substance Abuse and Mental Health Services Administration (SAMHSA) also provides open access to a wealth of information of use to both professionals and service consumers. In addition to publications about patient rights, cultural competence, ethics and values, health disparities, prejudice and discrimination, program evaluation, protection and advocacy, and service coordination among many others, SAMHSA also publishes numerous practice guidelines and related resources (Substance Abuse and Mental Health Services Administration, 2015b). The National Registry of Evidence-based Programs and Practices (NREPP), also sponsored by SAMHSA, includes 350 or more interventions that reflect scientific evidence of practice or program effectiveness (Substance Abuse and Mental Health Services Administration, 2015a). We hope the social work profession follows suit by approving and publishing social work practice guidelines based on systematic reviews and comprehensive analyses of research-based evidence.

If your social work activities are congruent with generally accepted theories, findings from high-quality research studies, and current professional practice guidelines, you probably meet the reasonable standard of care expectation. The use of unusual interventions, activities, or procedures that do not have a sound professional rationale and credible evidence to support their safety and effectiveness could place you at increased risk of liability. Social workers who reflect genuine competency in their professional work, maintain records that document their activities, and measure and report progress toward goal attainment typically exceed the criteria for a reasonable standard of care.

Several additional responsibilities may be included under the general **duty of care**. For example, as a professional social worker, you must be available and accessible to the clients you serve. Clients should be informed about whom to contact and what to do in case of an emergency. Similarly, before taking a vacation, a medical leave, or a sabbatical, you should inform clients well in advance and arrange for equivalent, substitute professional coverage. You must also take action to ensure the physical protection of clients you determine to be (1) imminently dangerous to other persons, (2) imminently dangerous to themselves, or (3) so gravely disabled as to be unable to provide minimal self-care (Everstine & Everstine, 1983, p. 232). You might have to arrange for careful supervision or perhaps hospitalization of such clients.

Professional record keeping also relates to the duty of care obligation. Complete, accurate, timely documentation of the nature, scope, provision, cost, progress, and outcomes of your service serves as evidence of reasonable professional behavior. At a minimum, you should include information concerning the identity of the people you serve, relevant consent forms, dates and kinds of services, assessments and plans, reports of meetings and service-related activities, evaluation of progress toward goals, and closing summaries. Of course, records are primarily for the client in that they help you, the social worker, remember relevant information and maintain your focus on agreed-upon goals for work. If you were to become ill or injured, or die unexpectedly, your records could aid in maintaining service continuity (Kagle & Kopels, 2008).

Record keeping suggests at least a modicum of professionalism. They may also support the quality of your professional service. Accurate, complete, descriptive records are your single most important defense in the event of an ethical misconduct claim or a malpractice lawsuit. Professional records that are absent, notations that are sparse, and those that appear altered after the fact can serve as evidence of inadequate care or perhaps even fraudulent behavior.

Duty to Respect Privacy

As a professional social worker, you have a **duty to respect the privacy** of people you serve. Under most circumstances, you are not entitled to intrude on the privacy of prospective or current clients. Privacy includes an individual's body and physical space (home or residence, locker, automobile, wallet or purse, or clothing), and those aspects of personal life that constitute a symbolic region of privacy (Everstine et al., 1980). Consider, for example, the case of a penniless traveler who seeks your professional help in obtaining transportation to her home in a neighboring state. If you were to ask her for information about her sexual history—a topic clearly unrelated to the issue of concern—you would probably violate her right to privacy.

Similarly, suppose you hold strong religious beliefs. Your personal faith provides much needed spiritual support and comfort in your daily life. However, you serve as a social worker in a public child and family welfare agency. If you were to proselytize your religious beliefs with clients, you would violate their privacy. In a sense, this would be similar to a telemarketer who calls your home or a door-to-door salesperson who, uninvited, tries to sell you a product. You have not requested the information but you get it anyway. Social workers must have a sound professional reason for entry into these private physical or symbolic regions.

Although a right to privacy is more implicit than explicit in the U.S. Constitution, it has grown in significance both inside and outside the helping professions (Etzioni, 1999; McWhirter & Bible, 1992). The Universal Declaration of Human Rights is more definitive. Article 12 states that: "no one shall be subjected to arbitrary interference with his privacy, family, home or correspondence, nor to attacks upon his honor and reputation. Everyone has the right to the protection of the law against such interference or attacks" (General Assembly of the United Nations, 1948). As rights to privacy have evolved, so have the threats to them. Technological advances increasingly endanger privacy. Risks to privacy are inherent in all forms of video and audio communications recording equipment; computer and cell phone hardware and software; and in wireless technology and the Global Positioning Systems (GPS) housed within devices. The Internet and its "clouds" contain virtually limitless electronic storage capacity—enabling large-scale "data-mining" for various purposes. On a more earthly plane, advancements in sensing and imaging technology (in hospitals or clinics, airports, or other venues); and increased speed and sophistication of DNA, urine, and blood testing—especially when results are electronically stored—may endanger privacy. Growing along with advances in technology is the expansion of governmental, industrial, and personal electronic surveillance. Indeed, some social service agencies and academic institutions engage in routine monitoring and electronic recording of employees' computer activity, e-mail messages, videoconferences, and cell phone usage. In addition, professionals sometimes engage in consultation activities or provide direct services via telephone or through videoconferencing technology. These transmissions may be recorded—overtly or covertly—and subsequently disseminated. The risk to the privacy of electronic correspondents is obvious (Reamer, 2013a).

Respect for privacy rights is not universal—even among helping professionals and consumers—and the risks are not limited to electronic or digital activity. Personnel in some school systems routinely search students' school lockers—often without students' or their parents' consent. Drug testing via blood or urine may be required as a condition for employment, or for the receipt of service in some social welfare programs. Students, clients, and travelers may be subject to virtual or actual body searches. Police may stop people on the street and search them for weapons ("stop and frisk") or demand that they display identification papers. Dogs may "sniff" out drugs or explosive materials. When government, industry, and powerful people devalue privacy rights, the ethos tends to spread throughout the larger society and into our cultures—including our professions and organizations. Clients' rights to privacy could easily become another casualty (Akrivopoulou & Garipidis, 2012; Klosek, 2007).

Duty to Maintain Confidentiality

Professional social workers have a **duty to maintain the confidentiality** of information clients convey to them. Derived from the right to privacy, this obligation applies, in general, to all helping professionals. The laws that certify or license social workers require that information shared by clients remain confidential. Indeed, some laws use the term **privileged communication** in describing this legal obligation. "Confidentiality refers to the professional norm that information shared by or pertaining to clients will not be shared with third parties. Privilege refers to the disclosure of confidential information in court proceedings" (Reamer, 1994, p. 47). When laws specify that clients' communications are privileged, you must meet an even higher standard of confidentiality. Under the protection of privilege, it becomes much more formidable, even for a judge, to force you to reveal confidential information without your clients' consent.

In 1996, the U.S. Supreme Court in *Jaffee v. Redmond* specifically upheld a U.S. Court of Appeals decision extending privilege for confidential client communications to licensed social workers during the course of psychotherapy. Redmond, a police officer, received psychotherapeutic counseling from a licensed social worker. Following an on-duty shooting death, the plaintiffs' lawyers attempted to subpoena the social worker's case records. The social worker and Redmond, the client, refused to provide the requested information. Based partly on that refusal, the court awarded damages to the plaintiffs. The Court of Appeals overturned that decision and the U.S. Supreme Court upheld the reversal. This decision is notable. It reinforces the doctrine of privilege for psychotherapy clients and specifically includes licensed social workers along with psychiatrists and psychologists as professionals who might provide such services in a privileged context (Lens, 2000).

The advent of computerized record keeping, organizational networks, management information systems, agency, governmental, and insurance company databases, the Internet, and managed care systems has seriously complicated the confidentiality issue. Advances in computer and communications technology may have contributed to increased productivity and efficiency, and perhaps even to improvements in the quality of social services. However, as information about clients becomes increasingly easy to access, use, and share, it becomes more difficult to safeguard their confidential records. Despite these complicated challenges, the basic duty remains intact. Indeed, in some areas the responsibilities of professionals to protect client privacy and confidentiality have increased.

The U.S. **Health Insurance Portability and Accountability Act** (**HIPAA**) and the associated Standards for Privacy of Individually Identifiable Health Information (the **Privacy Rule**) reflect federal efforts to protect the confidentiality of personal health information.

> A major goal of the Privacy Rule is to assure that individuals' health information is properly protected while allowing the flow of health information needed to provide and promote high quality health care and to protect the public's health and well-being. The Rule strikes a balance that permits important uses of information, while protecting the privacy of people who seek care and healing. (Office for Civil Rights, 2003, p. 1)

All health information that could identify individual people is protected under the Privacy Rule. Organizations and practitioners must safeguard names and addresses, telephone numbers, Social Security numbers, dates of birth or death, diagnoses, treatments, bank information, and any other personal data. We must protect the privacy of information, including demographic data, which relate to:

> the past, present, or future physical or mental health or condition of an individual; the provision of health care to an individual; or the past, present, or future payment for the provision of health care to an individual; and (i) That identifies the individual; or (ii) With respect to which there is a reasonable basis to believe the information can be used to identify the individual. (Office for Civil Rights, 2013, p. 15)

In general, information shared by clients is their property. It is not yours or that of your employing organization or agency, even though you incorporate that information in a case record or computerized database. Under most circumstances, clients must give genuinely informed consent before you may share information with another person or organization. Even when clients provide consent, however, you should carefully consider the nature, form, and extent of information to provide. Suppose, for example, a client has relocated to another state across the country and requests that you forward a copy of her records to another social worker who will provide continuing services. If the case record contains information that is no longer accurate, comments about third parties, or other irrelevant information, you might inform the client that you would like to exclude such references from the records before sending them. Although it might represent more work for you, a summary of services rather than a duplicate set of the case records may provide more protection for the client and could actually be more useful to the new social worker.

Duty to Inform

As a professional social worker, you are obligated to educate clients and prospective clients concerning the nature and extent of the services you and your agency offer. Under HIPAA, you must also inform clients about privacy policies. In addition, helping professionals should address matters such as cost, length of treatment, risks, probability of success, and alternate services that may be appropriate. This is where you apply your knowledge of evidence-based practices, practice guidelines, and community resources. You should also provide information concerning relevant policies and laws that could affect clients during the provision of social services. For example, early in the process, you should notify clients about your legal obligation to report indications of possible child abuse and neglect and certain other crimes (for instance, elder abuse or, in some locations, spousal abuse). You should also inform clients that, should a person's life be at risk, you intend to take action to protect that person, even if it means violating some aspects of their confidentiality.

The **duty to inform** clients about these limitations and conditions represent a fundamental part of fair and due process. At times, it may also relate to individuals' rights regarding self-incrimination. If you recall from the Fifth Amendment to the U.S. Constitution, people cannot be compelled to testify against themselves. This provision derives from the common law principle, *Nemo tenetur seipsum accusare* ("no one is obligated to accuse him or herself"). The requirement that police officers must provide *Miranda* warnings to suspects ("*Miranda v. Arizona*," 1966) reflects this principle.[5] Certainly, meetings with social workers are usually not equivalent to police arrests and interrogations, or to courtroom proceedings. Nonetheless, clients have a right to know that, under some circumstances, you might disclose information that could potentially become incriminating evidence in some subsequent civil or criminal litigation.

Typically, you should also give clients information regarding your qualifications, fields of expertise, and, when relevant, areas about which you have limited knowledge or experience. Similarly, you should inform clients about any actions you might take that pertain to their care—such as consultation with colleagues and supervisors, or provision of information to insurance companies. Of course, you should inform clients well in advance before you discontinue services or transfer them to another helping professional.

Several fundamental civil rights—including due process, equal protection, privacy, and dignity—pertain to the duty to inform. Such an informed understanding is an essential part of the agreement in which a client, in effect, employs a social worker to provide professional services within the context of a **fiduciary relationship** (Kutchins, 1991, 1998). "Fiduciary relationships emanate from the trust that clients must place in professionals. . . . The professional's obligations are far greater than those of a commercial vendor" (Kutchins, 1991, p. 106). Indeed, within the context of these special relationships, clients have a right to provide informed consent (O'Neill, 1998).

Informed consent involves the following dimensions:

1. *Disclosure.* Relevant information must be fully and clearly provided to the client by the helping professional.

---

[5] Interestingly, although suspects are expected to tell the truth during interrogations, police officers are not required to do so. They may lie to suspects and are often trained to do so. For example, officers may legally say that they have concrete evidence of a suspect's guilt when they do not; fabricate evidence to confuse a suspect during an interrogation; use fake polygraph equipment; or deceptively play one suspect against another to elicit a confession (Leo, 2008; Young, 1996).

2. *Capacity.* The client must be competent or capable of understanding, rationally evaluating, and anticipating implications and potential consequences of decisions and actions.
3. *Voluntariness.* The client must have genuinely free choice to accept or reject proposed activities—direct or indirect coercion or intimidation confounds such freedom.

If one or more of these aspects are absent, then clients cannot truly provide fully informed consent (Koocher & Keith-Spiegel, 1990; Meyer & Weaver, 2006; Reamer, 1987).

When you purchase services from an automobile mechanic or a house painter, you have certain rights. For example, you have a right to honest answers to questions you ask. In general, however, it is your responsibility to learn as much as you can before you purchase such services. *Caveat emptor*—let the buyer beware—is a major principle. The mechanic or painter is not required to provide additional information or consider what might be in your best interest. Helping professionals, however, assume added responsibilities because of clients' vulnerability and the potential for exploitation. Therefore, social workers have an "affirmative obligation to disclose more information than is requested" (Kutchins, 1991, p. 106) to ensure that clients are fully aware of aspects of the services that they might not have asked about or even considered.

Duty to Report

Professional social workers have a legal **duty to report** to designated governmental authorities indications of certain "outrages against humanity." Although the specific procedures for reporting may vary somewhat from place to place, as a social worker you must report suspicion of certain criminal behavior, including "child abuse, child neglect, child molestation, and incest" (Everstine & Everstine, 1983, p. 240; Meyer & Weaver, 2006). Over the course of the past several decades, governmental bodies have enacted laws that expand the kinds of behavior subject to obligatory reporting. In some locales, social workers must also report indications of abuse, neglect, and exploitation of persons who are elderly, physically or mentally challenged, or developmentally disabled.

The duty to report relates to several fundamental human rights. Article 1 of the Universal Declaration of Human Rights holds that "all human beings are born free and equal in dignity and rights"; and Article 3 indicates that "everyone has the right to life, liberty and security of person." Article 4 states that "no one shall be held in slavery or servitude"; and Article 5 specifies that "no one shall be subjected to torture or to cruel, inhuman or degrading treatment or punishment" (General Assembly of the United Nations, 1948).

The duty to report is perhaps most obvious in the case of child abuse and neglect. Within the United States, all states require that helping professionals report instances of suspected child abuse or neglect to governmental authorities. Along with medical doctors, psychologists, nurses, and teachers, social workers are typically included among the group of "mandated reporters" specifically mentioned in legislation. Mandated reporters who fail to notify authorities of suspected abuse may be subject to severe legal penalties.

Duty to Warn and Protect

Social workers also bear some responsibility to notify potential victims and take action to safeguard people a client might harm. This **duty to warn and protect**, derived from the same human rights that warrant reporting crimes against humanity, means that helping professionals sometimes take action to protect the lives of others who are or could be in danger. Of course, accurate prediction of future dangerousness is hardly a science. Despite the risk of false positives—concluding that people are dangerous when they actually are not—the safety of others sometimes outweighs the rights of clients to privacy and confidentiality (VandeCreek & Knapp, 2001; Woody, 1997).

The famous *Tarasoff v. Regents of the University of California* decision established that helping professionals are sometimes obligated to take action to protect the lives of third parties (Kagle & Kopels, 1994). Suppose, for example, that during an interview, a client with a history of violence toward others reveals a specific intention to kill a former lover. You ask additional questions and you conclude that the client indeed poses a clear and present danger to that person. Under such circumstances, you would (1) try to arrange for protective supervision of the client—perhaps, for example, through temporary hospitalization, (2) warn the intended victim of the threat, and (3) notify legal authorities of the danger. Of course, because such actions violate some aspects of the client's right to confidentiality and perhaps to privacy, you should clearly document why you have taken this course of action. In such instances, you would be wise to quote the client's words, cite gestures, and provide related evidence to support your conclusion that the client is potentially dangerous to another person. Also, document when and how you notified the relevant parties and whom you contacted.

The duty to warn or the duty to protect others is similar but not equivalent to the duty to report. For example, legal statutes require social workers to report suspicions of child abuse. Indications of present or past child abuse are sufficient to warrant a report—which usually involves the identification of an alleged victim and alleged perpetrator, if known. The social worker does not need to know that child abuse actually occurred to submit a report. Suspicion alone is sufficient, and social workers who report in good faith are typically immune from liability. In the case of potential violence toward other adults, however, suspicion alone is insufficient ("*United States v. Hayes,*" 2000). The social worker must have reasonable evidence to conclude that the client poses a real and significant threat of violence toward another (Recent cases, 2001). In such cases, social workers are not immune from liability, as is typical in cases involving reports of suspected child abuse. Therefore, we must exercise due professional care in reaching decisions about clients' dangerousness and in carrying out our obligation to warn and protect.

Understanding the Fundamental Values and Ethics of Social Work

In addition to the legal obligations that apply to all helping professionals, social workers must also conform to the fundamental values and ethics of the social work profession. Social workers and social work educators have energetically discussed the topic of social work values since the emergence of the profession during the late 19th century. The discussion will undoubtedly continue throughout the 21st century, especially as the world becomes increasingly interconnected and interdependent through globalization, internationalization, and digitalization.

In discussing values, the International Federation of Social Workers (2012, Feb. 23) states:

> Social work grew out of humanitarian and democratic ideals, and its values are based on respect for the equality, worth, and dignity of all people. Since its beginnings over a century ago, social work practice has focused on meeting human needs and developing human potential. Human rights and social justice serve as the motivation and justification for social work action. In solidarity with those who are disadvantaged, the profession strives to alleviate poverty and to liberate vulnerable and oppressed people in order to promote social inclusion. Social work values are embodied in the profession's national and international codes of ethics. (Values, para. 1)

Although there is some divergence of opinion regarding the application of fundamental social work values, there is considerable consensus about the values themselves. For example, the National

Association of Social Workers (2008) identifies the core values for social work in the Preamble to its Code of Ethics:

> The mission of the social work profession is rooted in a set of core values. These core values, embraced by social workers throughout the profession's history, are the foundation of social work's unique purpose and perspective:

> - Service
> - Social Justice
> - Dignity and Worth of the Person
> - Importance of Human Relationships
> - Integrity
> - Competence

> This constellation of core values reflects what is unique to the social work profession. Core values, and the principles that flow from them, must be balanced within the context and complexity of the human experience. (Preamble, paras. 3-4)

The Council on Social Work Education (2015) endorses the six core values identified in the NASW Code of Ethics and adds two more:

- Human Rights; and
- Scientific Inquiry (see Figure 5.2).

These eight **fundamental social work values** serve as an extremely useful foundation for thinking critically about practice issues and ethical dilemmas. They are invaluable in helping social

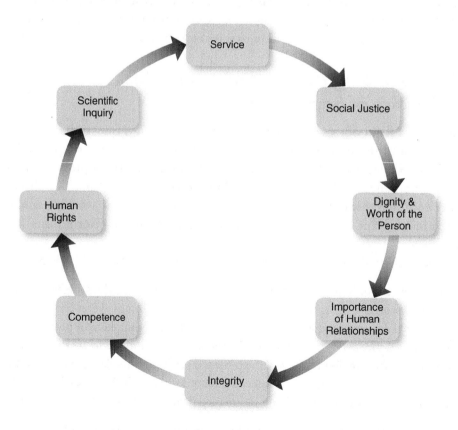

FIGURE 5.2 Fundamental Social Work Values

workers define a professional identity and establish a social work frame of reference. As abstract concepts, however, values are not usually specific enough to guide ethical decision making. Codes of ethics serve that function. Ethical principles and standards derive from the fundamental social work values, but appear in more concrete and prescriptive form. Reference to a code of ethics helps social workers make practice decisions that are congruent with fundamental social work values.

To practice ethically, you need a thorough understanding of both the fundamental social work values and the principles and standards that guide ethical decision making. As suggested earlier, the Code of Ethics of the National Association of Social Workers (2008) serves as the primary reference throughout the United States. The preamble of the NASW code suggests that:

> The primary mission of the social work profession is to enhance human well-being and help meet the basic human needs of all people, with particular attention to the needs and empowerment of people who are vulnerable, oppressed, and living in poverty. A historic and defining feature of social work is the profession's focus on individual well-being in a social context and the well-being of society. Fundamental to social work is attention to the environmental forces that create, contribute to, and address problems in living.
>
> Social workers promote social justice and social change with and on behalf of clients. "Clients" is used inclusively to refer to individuals, families, groups, organizations, and communities. Social workers are sensitive to cultural and ethnic diversity and strive to end discrimination, oppression, poverty, and other forms of social injustice. These activities may be in the form of direct practice, community organizing, supervision, consultation, administration, advocacy, social and political action, policy development and implementation, education, and research and evaluation. Social workers seek to enhance the capacity of people to address their own needs. Social workers also seek to promote the responsiveness of organizations, communities, and other social institutions to individuals' needs and social problems. (2008, Preamble, paras. 1–2)

Carry a copy of the Social Work Code of Ethics with you during your professional activities. You will frequently need to refer to it throughout the course of your service with and for clients.

Violations of the code may serve as grounds for malpractice lawsuits or grievances filed with social work licensing boards or professional associations. The *NASW Procedures for Professional Review* (2012) contains detailed descriptions concerning the procedures and processes by which complaints are submitted and adjudicated.

As you would expect, claims of ethical misconduct against social workers fall into most of the same categories as do malpractice lawsuits. Although a majority of claims are filed by clients or family members of clients, a substantial number are submitted by employees, subordinates, or supervisees and coworkers or colleagues. In addition, employers or supervisors sometimes file professional grievances against social workers in their employ or under their supervision.

The most common ethical violations include the following: sexual activity with clients; dual relationships with clients; other boundary violations with clients; failure to seek supervision or consultation; failure to use accepted practice skills; failure to keep up with advances in relevant knowledge; fraudulent behavior; premature or improper termination; inadequate provision for case transfer or referral; failure to maintain adequate records or reports; and failure to discuss policies as part of informed consent (Strom-Gottfried, 1999, 2000a, 2000b, 2003).

Addressing Ethical Dilemmas

Several authors have suggested sequential steps for the process of ethical decision making (Dolgoff, Loewenberg, & Harrington, 2012; Mattison, 2000; Reamer, 1995a; Rhodes, 1986, 1998) or ethical problem solving (Reamer & Conrad, 1995). Congress (1999, 2000), for example, encourages social workers to adopt the **ETHIC Model of Decision Making** and proceed through the following steps or processes:

> **E**—Examine relevant personal, societal, agency, client, and professional values.
> **T**—Think about what ethical standard of the NASW code of ethics applies, as well as relevant laws and case decisions.
> **H**—Hypothesize about possible consequences of different decisions.
> **I**—Identify who will benefit and who will be harmed in view of social work's commitment to the most vulnerable.
> **C**—Consult with supervisor and colleagues about the most ethical choice. (Congress, 2000, p. 10)

Reamer (2000) suggests a seven-step process for ethical problem solving:

1. Identify the ethical issues, including the social work values and duties that conflict.
2. Identify the individuals, groups, and organizations that are likely to be affected by the ethical decision.
3. Tentatively identify all possible courses of action and the participants involved in each, along with possible benefits and risks for each.
4. Thoroughly examine the reasons in favor of and opposed to each possible course of action, considering the relevant ethical theories, principles, and guidelines; codes of ethics and legal principles; social work practice theory and principles; personal values (including religious, cultural, and ethnic values and political ideology), particularly those that conflict with one's own.
5. Consult with colleagues and appropriate experts (such as agency staff, supervisors, agency administrators, attorneys, ethics scholars).
6. Make the decision and document the decision-making process.
7. Monitor, evaluate, and document the decision. (p. 361)

The National Association of Social Workers outlines an ethical decision-making framework called **DECISIONS**:

- Determine the facts.
- Ethical considerations? If so, what ethical standards apply?
- Consider the impact of values. Determine the personal and moral values involved.
- Impact of Self (how is the person of the social worker influencing this dilemma?)
- Stakeholders, who are they?
- Incorporate professional literature review.
- Other considerations: standards of practice, agency policies, regulatory and/or legal considerations, consultation.
- Narration of your decision: be prepared to articulate your decision. Do some critical thinking and be confident.
- Secure and support your decision through excellent documentation and evaluation of the outcome of the decision. (National Association of Social Workers, 2015b)

The sequential steps identified by social work scholars such as Congress (1999, 2000), Dolgoff et al. (2012), Reamer (2013b), and the NASW (2015b) reflect well-reasoned, logical processes—especially when you can adhere to all of the applicable ethical principles. Unfortunately, this is often impossible. When numerous principles and legal duties apply and some conflict with each other, you are faced with an ethical dilemma. In other words, conforming to one standard (for example, duty to report) necessarily requires that you violate another (for example, duty to maintain client confidentiality). When ethical and legal obligations conflict, which do you ignore? Which do you respect? How do you decide?

How to address and resolve moral and ethical dilemmas has been the subject of philosophical discussion for centuries (Holmes, 2003). In contemporary times, many social workers have questions about whether to base ethical decisions on certain fixed values and principles through a deductive, deontological, absolutist process, or through the analysis of individual cases via inductive, teleological, consequentialist, utilitarian, or relativistic reasoning. A social worker adopting a utilitarian perspective would consider the relative good versus harm of the probable consequences of the ethical decision and accompanying action in the particular case. A social worker adopting a deontological view would apply the chosen principle, rule, or law regardless of the potential consequences (Mattison, 2000).

Professional codes of ethics tend to reflect a strong deontological emphasis. Such rules are written and codified so that they may be precisely followed. Formal sanctions may be imposed when ethical guidelines are violated. On the other hand, social work also emphasizes a person-in-environment perspective—suggesting that circumstances play a part in all processes, including those involving ethical dilemmas. Indeed, the NASW Code of Ethics explicitly suggests that social workers adopt advanced and sophisticated critical thinking processes to address ethical issues in a professional manner. Note these passages:

> Specific applications of the Code must take into account the context in which it is being considered and the possibility of conflicts among the Code's values, principles, and standards.
>
> Further, the NASW Code of Ethics does not specify which values, principles, and standards are most important and ought to outweigh others in instances when they conflict. Reasonable differences of opinion can and do exist among social workers with respect to the ways in which values, ethical principles, and ethical standards should be rank ordered when they conflict. (2008, Purpose of the NASW Code of Ethics, paras. 3–4)

The NASW Code of Ethics does not assign a particular value, weight, or rank to each ethic. Therefore, you may and indeed should consider the array of applicable ethical principles, as well as the particulars of the situation, circumstances, and potential consequences of ethical decisions and actions. Of course, this complicates the decision-making process. The sheer number of factors inherent in each unique case situation is often daunting. A clear ranking of the principles or an ethics hierarchy or algorithm would certainly make it easier to apply the principles—from a deontological perspective. However, fixed application of ranked principles reduces our capacity to consider unique situational aspects.

Certainly, there are risks associated with both the deontological and the teleological approaches—especially when taken to the extreme. Case-by-case, inductive reasoning may lead social workers to, in effect, justify or rationalize any decision on the basis of the exigencies of the situation (Jonsen & Toulmin, 1988). Conversely, strict deductive application of prioritized ethical principles can contribute to petty, bureaucratic-like thinking—a kind of *tyranny of principles*—that fails to appreciate the need to sometimes make exceptions to the "rules" (Toulmin, 1981). Furthermore, some rules and regulations—often in the form of state laws or local ordinances—are manifestly unjust, contributing to racism, sexism, ageism, heterosexism, ableism, and other forms of social, economic, and environmental injustice. If social workers blindly adhere to unjust laws we, in effect, become collaborators in institutionalized oppression rather than advocates for justice and liberation. Sophisticated, committed relativistic thinking may be required to negotiate these intellectual complexities (Perry, 1970, 1981, 1982).

Considering Motives and Morals

In considering the contextual or situational aspects of moral and ethical issues, you might consider the dimensions of **motives, means, ends, and effects (MMEE)** (Fletcher, 1966). Explore your own motives, examine the means by which you plan to address the issues and implement the decision, assess the impact of the ends you envision, and identify the probable effects of your proposed actions. These considerations reflect age-old intellectually challenging questions such as, "Who should participate in the decision-making process?" "Who should make the final choice?" "Do the ends justify the means?" "Are my motives pure?" "Have I considered the potential impact of my actions upon others?" "Is this fair?"

These lead to issues specific to social work: "Is a social worker ever justified in using 'bad means' to pursue a 'good end'?" "Should a social worker steadfastly adhere to 'good means' even when the outcome is likely to be 'bad'?" "Should a social worker ever make a decision that affects another without that person's knowledge and participation?" "Should a social worker ever place an ethical obligation above a legal duty or, conversely, a legal duty above an ethical standard?" And, "Should social workers ever place our personal beliefs or preferences above our professional values and ethics?"

One of the hallmarks of professional social work status is continuous and ongoing consideration of value and ethical issues in service to others. Because you have the potential to harm as well as help, to exploit as well as empower, and to suppress as well as liberate, you must consciously, deliberately, and reflectively examine your thoughts, feelings, and actions in both moral and ethical terms (Goldstein, 1987; Schon, 1990).

Motives

In exploring **motives**, consider your primary and secondary purposes as both a person and a social worker. In accord with your status as a privileged professional, you assume weighty moral, ethical, and legal responsibilities for others and for society. Ideally, your primary motives and those that influence your decisions and action are consistent with our professional values and ethics (for example, service, social justice, respect for people, integrity, scientific inquiry, and competence). However, you also reflect personal motives (for example, fear of legal action, desire to assert your own agenda or will, sympathy, pity, or spite). In carrying out your social work functions, you may and indeed should acknowledge your personal aims as you shift focus and emphasize your professional motives. Once we consciously recognize our personal motivations, we can then gently put them aside in order to do our best professional work. If we deny or ignore them, they may "leak" into our helping activities and sabotage our professionalism.

As part of the process, ask yourself questions such as, "If I was a client and my social worker acted on these motives, what would I think of that social worker and how would I feel?" "What would happen if social workers everywhere took action based upon these motives?"

Means

In exploring **means**, consider the various "hows" and "ways" you might proceed. Determine who should be involved in decision making and decide how you and other participants might implement the action plans. Means include the processes of data gathering and decision making as well as those for planning and acting. Ask yourself, "Are the means consistent with my professional values and ethics?" "Are the means likely to produce the desired end or outcome?" "How will people and situations likely be affected by my use of these means?" If the means are not consonant with social work principles or the associated effects appear potentially harmful, ask yourself, "Have I genuinely considered all other means to these ends that would enable me to adhere to my professional values and ethics and ensure that the effects are beneficial?" If acceptable means are indeed unavailable, ask yourself, "Do the desired ends justify these undesirable means and the potential associated effects?"

Finally, you might ask yourself, "If I were a client and my social worker adopted these means, what would be my reaction?" "What would happen if social workers everywhere adopted these means?"

Ends

Consider the nature of the envisioned goals or **ends** and determine if they are personal or professional. Ask yourself, "How were these goals determined?" "Who participated in their identification and definition?" "Toward whom or what are these goals targeted?" "Are the people affected by the pursuit and accomplishment of these goals aware of their existence and involved in their selection?" "Would I be professionally proud to accomplish these goals?" "Are these goals consistent with our understanding of the issues, the mission of the agency or program, and the purpose of the social work profession?"

You could also ask yourself, "If I were a client in similar circumstances, how would I respond to these goals?" "What would happen if all social workers and their clients pursued these goals?"

Effects

In exploring **effects**, consider the additional consequences that could result from adoption of the identified means and accomplishment of the envisioned ends. Beyond the direct impact on the targeted people-in-environment, your decisions and actions may affect you, other clients, other persons, and related social systems. These "side effects" may be positive or negative, and energy enhancing or energy depleting depending on their nature, intensity, duration, and a host of other factors. Sometimes, the side effects are potentially so damaging that they outweigh even the most desirable ends. For example, suppose that a social worker learned about a survey instrument that successfully identifies adult males who abuse children. However, the rate of "false positives" is extremely high. In fact, there is at least one inaccurate identification for every accurate one. The ends are certainly desirable: to protect children from abuse and identify adult male offenders who need service. However, the side effects are so onerous (false identification of innocent people) that the means could not reasonably be used without several additional safeguards.

Consider another example: Suppose an intervention (means) designed to reduce or prevent drug abuse among urban adolescents successfully enables 42 percent of participants who previously abused drugs to discontinue drug usage altogether. What great news! However, 33 percent of participants who had not previously used drugs begin to do so—perhaps because of the information and connections established through involvement with other participants. If these figures are accurate, the severity of the side effects or the "collateral damage" would warrant suspension or alteration of the service—perhaps, for example, by limiting the program to those youth who are currently misusing substances.

Finally, you might ask yourself, "If I were subject to these effects, how would I react?" "Would I personally be willing to accept the side effects to achieve the intended goal?" "What would happen if these side effects were experienced widely throughout the world?"

Social workers, of course, consider motives, means, ends, and effects (MMEE) in an integrative fashion. We explore them in relation to each other and within the context of scientific knowledge, laws and policies, and professional values and ethics. For example, let's consider a social worker who hopes to protect a small child from physical harm (a desirable motive). She elects to lie to the allegedly abusive parent (undesirable means) in an effort to prevent injury to the child (a desirable end). In reaching the decision and taking the action, the social worker, in effect, decides that the undesirable means are justified by the desirable ends. In so doing, she willingly accepts responsibility for any adverse consequences that might subsequently happen to her or others because of the deception. For example, if the lie is discovered, she would acknowledge it in a fashion such as, "Yes, I lied; and I take full responsibility for what happened because of that lie."

This approach reflects contextual thinking based on an estimation of the likely consequences of the action; in this case, the lie. A major danger in such analysis is that the means may or may not yield the intended ends. That is, the lie may not protect the child from harm. You cannot accurately predict nor can you guarantee the future. The lie may achieve the anticipated ends, may have no effect whatsoever, or may exacerbate the problem through unanticipated or adverse effects. Whatever happens, the social worker may conclude, "My intentions were good. I wanted to protect the child from injury, so I lied."

Another social worker in a similar situation may adopt a deontological approach and conclude that lying is always wrong—regardless of the circumstances. The social worker may think, "I cannot lie" (desirable means) to the allegedly abusive parent, even if I anticipate an adverse response that increases the likelihood of physical injury to the child (an undesirable end). I cannot predict future events or guarantee outcomes. Therefore I should be honest." Whatever happens, the social worker may conclude, "At least I did not lie." However, the act of not lying may have been followed by physical harm to the child. The means may have been good but the ends extremely unfortunate.

Relying solely on relevant ethical or legal standards, or exclusively on the characteristics of the situation, does not necessarily lead to a clear decision or plan of action. Both teleological and deontological approaches reflect strengths as well as weaknesses, and risks as well as benefits.

Despite the challenges associated with efforts to rank moral or ethical values, some scholars have developed hierarchies to help social workers address ethical dilemmas in which one ethic conflicts with another. For example, Dolgoff et al. (2012) propose a seven-level hierarchical **Ethical Principles Screen**. In describing the screen, they suggest that the protection of human life is the paramount moral and ethical obligation. Ranked first or highest, this principle takes precedence over all other moral values or ethical principles. Therefore, social workers who learn that a client intends to kill a former lover would take action to protect the potential victim, even if they abridged other ethical principles in the process.

Dolgoff et al. (2012) place social justice in the second position. This complex principle involves basic fairness by suggesting that, "all persons in the same circumstances should be treated in the same way—that is, persons in equivalent situations have the right to be treated equally. At the same time, persons in different situations have the right to be treated differently if the inequality is relevant to the issue in question. Unequal treatment can be justified when other considerations such as beneficence (the duty to do good and not harm others) outweigh the social justice principle or on the grounds that such unequal treatment will promote greater social justice" (p. 81). Conceptually, this idea is similar to the **difference principle** that emerged in our exploration of social justice in Chapter 4.

Let's elaborate with an example. Competent adults of equivalent status usually have the right to engage in consensual sex. However, an adult does not have the right to engage in sexual activities with a child, even with the child's apparent consent, because their comparative status and power are obviously unequal. Similarly, because of the power associated with professional status and function, a social worker may not have sex with a client, even when the client is an adult and takes the initiative or provides full consent. This leads to a double standard where there is one rule for adults and another more favorable standard for less powerful and more vulnerable children, and one rule for professionals and another less restrictive expectation for their clients. We justify such double standards on the basis of the unequal power among the participants. In such circumstances, we accept double standards that favor more vulnerable or less powerful persons if, but only if, they benefit the less advantaged (Rawls, 1999; Rawls & Kelly, 2001). Most social workers abhor the more common double standards—that of favoring the advantaged or privileged at the expense of the disadvantaged.

Consistent with social work's emphasis on individual rights and self-determination, and respect for diversity and difference, autonomy and freedom occupy the third position. This principle encourages social workers to "make practice decisions that *foster a person's autonomy, independence, and freedom*" (Dolgoff et al., 2012, p. 81). Of course, a client's right to independent action is not limitless. A person does not have an autonomous right to kill others, abuse or exploit a child, batter a spouse, or falsely scream "fire" in a crowded theater.

Consonant with the duty of care, the **principle of least harm** is ranked fourth, indicating that "when faced with dilemmas that have the potential for causing harm, a social worker should attempt to avoid or prevent such harm. When harm is unavoidable, a social worker should always choose the option that will cause the least harm, the least permanent harm, and/or the most easily reversible harm. If harm has been done, the social worker should attempt where possible to repair the harm done" (Dolgoff et al., 2012, p. 82).

Consistent with our professional obligation to advance human rights and social justice, and promote social well-being, the fifth principle holds that a "social worker should choose the option that promotes a better *quality of life* for all people, for the individual as well as for the community" (Dolgoff et al., 2012, p. 82).

In line with our legal duties as professional helpers, the sixth principle involves privacy and confidentiality. Dolgoff and colleagues suggest that a "social worker should make practice decisions that strengthen every person's *right to privacy and confidentiality*. Keeping confidential information inviolate is a direct derivative of this obligation" (2012, p. 82).

Truthfulness and full disclosure occupies the seventh position. Consistent with our sense of professional integrity, this principle holds that social workers should be honest and "speak the truth and to *fully disclose all relevant information*" to clients and others with whom we interact. "Social and professional relationships require trust in order to function well, and trust, in turn, is based on honest dealing that minimizes surprises so that mutual expectations are generally fulfilled" (Dolgoff et al., 2012, p. 82).

Dolgoff et al. (2012) offer the Ethical Principles Screen to social workers as an aid for organizing and ranking aspects of ethical dilemmas when two or more ethical obligations conflict. Facing such an ethical dilemma, a social worker would first classify the aspects of the situation according to the seven fundamental ethical principles. Once categorized, the social worker then applies the Ethical Principles Screen to determine which aspect should take precedence over others. In most cases, elements of the ethical dilemma classified according to the first ethical principle are superior to those associated with the second through seventh principles. Those aspects of the situation that relate to the second ethical principle are superior to those associated with the third through seventh principles, and so on. Of course, if you can conform to all dimensions of the code of ethics, you do not need the Ethical Principles Screen. You would simply respond in the ethical manner. Ethical dilemmas arise when conflicts exist among various legal obligations and ethical standards. In such circumstances, you must make a decision about which duty should take precedence.

Dolgoff et al.'s (2012) hierarchical screen helps us think about specific dilemmas within the context of abstract principles. Indeed, philosophers have long argued that certain fundamental moral principles exist and that they can and should guide decision making in all aspects of life. Some helping professions, notably medicine, have promoted certain basic moral values for medical service to others (Beauchamp & Childress, 1983; Koocher & Keith-Spiegel, 1990). These include the following.

Beneficence

The principle of **beneficence** suggests that helping, protecting, and promoting the well-being and welfare of clients and others is a primary moral value. In other words, professionals engage in "good deeds" through "good means" and must sometimes accept personal risk or sacrifice to carry out our responsibilities. Beneficence incorporates Dolgoff et al.'s (2012) first principle by including the protection of human lives. Beneficence is reflected in the legal duty of care and the duties to inform, report, and warn and protect.

Nonmaleficence

The principle of **nonmaleficence** suggests that the professional should do everything possible to avoid harming clients or others in our efforts to serve. We may capture this value through the admonition, "First, do no harm!" It is reflected in ethical and legal codes concerning the quality of care so that clients and others do not suffer unnecessary harm as a result of services they receive. This moral value incorporates Dolgoff et al.'s (2012) fourth principle, that of least harm, and involves thinking in terms of "utility" or usefulness. The professional carefully considers the nature and extent of potential harm in attempts to implement "good acts." Our duty of care requires us to promote the greatest good with the least possible harm. For example, if efforts to help one person resulted in injury to a dozen others, we might ask, "Is it useful to cause that much harm to gain that degree of benefit?" Similarly, a client and worker might decide that standing up for oneself by becoming more assertive is a desirable goal. However, if standing up to an employer leads the client to lose a desperately needed job, then the damage done might well outweigh the good. "Although the goal is worthy, it's not useful to lose my job to achieve it." Indeed, the worker and client might reasonably decide to first pursue the goal of assertiveness in a safer context.

Justice

The principle of **justice** suggests that people have a right to equal treatment unless a disparity of power or capacity warrants differential treatment. Equal access and equal opportunity are components of justice, as is consideration of extenuating or mitigating factors and environmental circumstances. Helping professionals are thus obligated to provide fair and equitable treatment to all. In social work, the value of justice applies to individuals, groups, organizations, communities, and societies. This moral value includes Dolgoff et al.'s (2012) second principle, that of social justice and their fifth principle, that of quality of life. We may also implicitly consider social justice as an aspect of the legal duty of care. Indeed, unjust practices may well fail to meet expectations of a reasonable standard of care.

Suppose, for example, that after a year or so of employment, you come to realize that your public, nonprofit social service agency "cherry picks" clients. In other words, intake workers and receptionists are trained to screen in those prospective clients who have insurance coverage or are able to pay full fees while "diplomatically" screening out those who are uninsured or lack financial resources. The motivations of agency administration might be understandable: greater revenue for the same amount of (or perhaps even less) staff effort. However, the process is unjust, and reflects the usual unjust double standard: those with more resources are privileged while those with fewer resources are disenfranchised.

Autonomy

The principle of **autonomy** suggests that people generally have a fundamental right to liberty, freedom, and self-determination. They have a right to govern their own affairs and make decisions about actions that affect them or their well-being. This value reflects Dolgoff et al.'s (2012) third principle, that of autonomy and freedom, and is implicit in the legal duty to respect privacy.

Respect for autonomy is challenging for most people, including social workers who endorse the principle. The difficulty may come from cultural legacies where obedience and subordination to authorities (lords, masters, commanders, bosses, religious leaders, political leaders, teachers, and parents) are highly valued and expected. In our positions of status and power vis-à-vis many clients, social workers may expect that our ideas, suggestions, and advice should be embraced and followed. Some clients and some people, however, have different ideas, and maintain them despite what we think would be in their own best interest. Unless others would be at risk of harm due to our clients' decisions and actions, we social workers transcend our tendency to control or subordinate others and instead celebrate their freedom and autonomy. Few people actually think for themselves—what social workers would call "critical thinking." Most of us remain stuck within the "boxes" of the ethnic, religious, political, and cultural paradigms in which we were socialized. When clients and others escape those boxes to engage in independent thought and autonomous action, we may rejoice in their freedom.

Privacy

The principle of **privacy** derives partly from the right to self-determination. In the context of privacy, people have a right to control the nature and extent of intrusion into their bodies or into their personal lives and private spaces. Even the publication of clients' names threatens privacy. We might ask, for example, if a social worker calls out the full name of a client in a waiting area so that other clients and visitors may overhear, has that social worker abridged that client's right to privacy and violated his or her own legal duty to respect it?

Confidentiality

The principle of **confidentiality** is associated with those of autonomy and privacy. In essence, clients retain ownership of information shared with helping professionals. Therefore social workers may not share clients' information without their expressed permission. To do so would violate the legal duty and our ethical obligation to maintain confidentiality. As illustrated in Dolgoff et al.'s (2012) sixth principle, clients maintain fundamental rights to privacy and confidentiality. Neither the assumption of the role of client nor the receipt of service diminishes these rights.

Fidelity

The principle of **fidelity** or "good faith" suggests that clients and others may expect helping professionals to be honest and to keep their commitments. This moral value incorporates Dolgoff et al.'s (2012) seventh principle, that of honesty and full disclosure, and is inherent in the legal duty of care. Fidelity involves honesty, veracity, and integrity. We expect helping professionals to tell the truth, to refrain from any forms of dishonesty, fraud, and deception, and to honor commitments made to clients and others.

The values reflected in the Ethical Principles Screen (Dolgoff et al., 2012), the core social work values, the seven moral values, and the legal duties of helping professionals reflect similar but not completely identical themes. The values contained in the Ethical Principles Screen are rank-ordered; the other values and duties are not.

Application of a predetermined, fixed hierarchical system of values or principles that could apply to all ethical dilemmas regardless of the circumstances might help social workers reach quick decisions. Unfortunately, we cannot indiscriminately apply such algorithms. The people, issues, circumstances, and other pertinent factors vary much too widely for such an approach. However, once you understand the facts of a situation and identify the applicable duties and obligations, you may wisely consider the more abstract moral values and principles as you conduct ethical analyses. For example, in one instance, a social worker—in conjunction with a client—may determine that autonomy and self-determination are more important than human life or quality of life (beneficence).[6] In another situation, the risk of harm (nonmaleficence) may outweigh the potential good (beneficence). Although a universal hierarchical scheme is appealing, let's maintain our person-in-environment perspective and recall the advantages of committed relativism. Intellectual flexibility and integrity are consistent with the characteristics of professionalism and, obviously, critical thought and careful judgment are essential for ethical decision making.

Identifying Ethical and Legal Implications

In addition to understanding them, social workers must determine which values, legal duties, and ethical principles pertain to a particular practice situation. This requires careful thinking as you consider both the facts and the obligations.

To illustrate, let's use the "What about Bob?" case situation.[7]

CASE SITUATION: WHAT ABOUT BOB?

Shortly after graduating with your social work degree, you began to work at a social service agency that offers counseling to people experiencing personal or family troubles. You have now served there for nearly 1 year. You and other social workers often help women and couples who are dealing with relationship problems. Bob supervises your work. He is married with two teenage children and has more than 20 years of postgraduate practice experience. In turn, Jane supervises Bob's work. She also has many years of experience—although not quite so many as Bob. However, she has earned a doctoral degree in social work and serves as the agency's director of social services. She is responsible for overseeing all direct service programs and activities. Jane has one 10-year-old daughter from a previous relationship. She has been single for several years but seems quite happy and content. Despite the stresses associated with her professional responsibilities, she always seems to be in good spirits. She is open, available, friendly, and invariably helpful to staff members.

One morning, Jane asks you to step into her office. She looks pale, sad, and quite upset. She says, "Bob had a heart attack early this morning. He is in the Intensive Care Unit at the local hospital. A nurse notified his family and they are now with him at the hospital. At this point, there is a 50–50 chance that he will survive. If he makes it through the next 8 hours, his chances will improve. Whatever happens though, we must reassign his clients to other staff. I would like you to assume responsibility for five of his clients. Here are the case records. During Bob's absence, I will serve as your immediate supervisor. Any questions?"

Jane's eyes are wet and red. She looks so dismayed that you quickly say "no" and promptly leave her office. You also feel bad—for Bob, his spouse and children, for his clients who will miss him, and for Jane—who must have had a close friendship with Bob over these many years.

---

[6] See, for example, books and articles about Terri Schiavo, a woman in a persistent vegetative state who was kept alive for years through force-feeding before finally being allowed to die. The Florida legislature and Governor Jeb Bush, and then the U.S. Congress and President G. W. Bush intervened to maintain her life support despite evidence that she would have chosen death in such circumstances. Like many others, this case raised the question of, "Whose life is it?" or "Whose body is it?" and "Who gets to decide about me?" The values of personal autonomy and quality of life are pitted against the value or sanctity of human life as perceived by others.

[7] Special thanks to Professor Heather McCabe, JD, MSW, of the Indiana University School of Social Work for reviewing this case.

You return to your office and look over the case records. Since you have 30 minutes available in your morning schedule, you telephone the five newly assigned clients. Reaching four of them, you inform them that Bob is ill and you will be taking over for him during his absence. You were unable to make phone contact with Julie, the fifth client. However, you notice that she has an appointment scheduled with Bob for later this afternoon. Fortunately, your calendar is open at that time. You plan to meet with Julie and talk with her face-to-face about the situation.

Before the meeting, you review the case record. You learn that Julie is 28 years old and had met with Bob once each week for the past 6 months. The identified problem is grief. Julie's boyfriend of nearly 6 years suddenly ended their relationship when offered a better job in another state. Up until that point, Julie thought that she and her boyfriend would soon marry and have children together. Stunned by his abrupt departure, Julie felt stupid for trusting in him and bitter about wasting all those years. According to the case record, Julie hoped to overcome the feelings of grief, loss, and resentment, and move forward in her life. In the record, Bob had made a note that Julie also hoped to find a new and better relationship within the next year. The records indicated that Julie was progressing steadily and had nearly recovered from the breakup. In a notation from a meeting about 1 month ago, Bob wrote that "Julie reports that she has found someone new—someone much more thoughtful, mature, and loving than she had ever known before." At that time, he also noted that Julie would probably resolve the original problems and achieve her service goals within another 2 months.

Upon Julie's arrival at the agency, you greet her and ask her to join you in your office. When you inform her about Bob's illness, her face turns ashen and she bursts into tears saying, "But he was fine when he left me last night."

You are surprised and confused by her remark. After a short pause, you follow up with a few questions. Julie readily responds in detail by saying that Bob and she had become lovers about 6 weeks earlier, and that he had been visiting her at her place every night after work. She said that they would have fabulous sex and then talk for several hours before Bob went home to his own family to spend the rest of the night.

Julie went on to say that Bob plans to divorce his wife as soon as his teenage children leave home. She says, "Once that happens, we'll move out of town and get married. Bob even wants to have a child with me. Of course, he still cares for his wife and wants to spare her as much pain as possible. She doesn't know about me yet and he doesn't want to tell her until the kids are gone."

At that point, Julie breaks into tears again. Sobbing, she says, "He just has to survive. I'm so happy with him and he's so happy with me."

You then ask if Bob had talked with her about the ethical problems of social workers becoming romantically involved with their clients. She says, "Yes. We discussed that. He said he knows that it is wrong but he loves me so much that he simply cannot resist. He said we couldn't say anything to anyone until after he gets the divorce and finds a new job."

When Julie pauses, you ask, "Now that you've told me about the relationship with Bob, what do you think will happen?" She quickly turns to me, glares, and says, "This conversation is entirely confidential. My words are privileged. If you mention one word about this to anybody, my lawyer will sue you for every penny you have. Do you understand? You do not have my permission to share what I have told you with anyone else."

Julie then stands up to leave. As she departs, she says, "I know that there is no charge for today's meeting and that you will not record anything about our conversation in my case files. Good-bye." ∎

As Julie leaves the meeting, you feel several emotions and considerable distress. Indeed, you might react to her statement about a romantic relationship with her social worker with thoughts such as, "How could Bob do that? That's so wrong!" You might feel disappointment, sorrow, anger, or even disgust. You could judge Bob harshly and view him as a sinner, a criminal, a pitiful creature, or even a "pig."

Of course, judgmental thoughts and feelings can be useful to human beings in general and to social workers in particular—at least for a brief time. They help us to recognize boundary lines that separate acceptable from unacceptable behavior in our personal and professional cultures. However, social workers cannot remain long in such emotionally reactive or judgmental states. If we did, we might act improperly to relieve our own discomfort rather than take appropriate steps to address an issue or correct an injustice.

Upon hearing Julie's comments about Bob, you could feel confused, anxious, and uncertain about how to respond or what to do. You might even wish that you had never met her and never heard what she said. You could even hope that the problem would "just disappear."

In such a state, you might be tempted to "forget" that Julie mentioned anything about a relationship with Bob or, as Julie requested, neglect to record that information in the case record. Such avoidance might provide some temporary relief. However, you actually did hear and you truly do remember what she said, and you are a social worker in a service organization with professional legal and ethical obligations. To ignore the reality and fail to pursue the potential implications of Julie's statements would place you in another kind of ethical jeopardy. True, the act of "intentional forgetting" would protect Julie's current right to confidentiality; however, you would neglect your ethical responsibilities to your colleagues, the agency, our profession, and conceivably other current and previous clients that Bob has served. Furthermore, Julie might later change her mind about Bob's behavior and decide that he had, after all, taken advantage of her. At that point, your "lapse in memory" and lack of timely and accurate documentation would become apparent, and your omission might constitute malpractice of the nonfeasance kind.

After some thought, you realize that you must, of course, keep a timely, accurate record of your meeting with Julie, and that you must take some kind of action. If you remain distressed, you might immediately run to your new supervisor and dump everything in her lap. That too would provide some relief. However, as an emotional reaction rather than a purposeful action based on thoughtful reflection, it too involves risks. Let's calm ourselves first (self-regulate), and then shift into a cognitive frame of mind. In dealing with complex ethical or practice issues, we need critical thinking much more than personal judgment and emotional upset. We separate our personal views and assumptions from our professional values and ethics, and then maintain our focus on our duties and responsibilities. In other words, we make a shift from a personal into a professional perspective and address the dilemma accordingly.

Examining motives, means, ends, and effects can help us move in the direction of professionalism. You briefly ask yourself questions such as, "What are my personal motives here?" "Do I primarily hope to reduce the unpleasant feelings and subjective discomfort that I feel?" "Would I prefer to sidestep this hassle and 'not get involved'?" "Do I want to avoid being sued by Julie for breaking her confidence?" "Am I motivated to punish Bob for his apparent bad behavior or perhaps even to reprimand Julie to some extent? After all, she must have known that Bob is married with children. And, she threatened me with legal action!" "Might I identify with Bob and hope to protect him from the consequences of his actions?"

You then shift to a professional perspective by asking, "What are (or what should be) my professional motives in this situation?" "Am I primarily interested in ensuring the rights and well-being of our client?" "Do I hope to protect other clients from potential harm?" "Am I motivated to respect Bob's rights and consider his well-being during this time?"

After considering motives, you think about possible means and ends. You might address the issue of ends first. "What do I see as the most desirable ends (goals) in this situation?" "Who should be involved in establishing them?" "Would the ends address or resolve the identified problem—that is, the possibility that Bob has engaged in ethical misconduct that could result in harm?" "Are the goals clearly professional rather than personal in nature?" "Do they clearly address Julie's needs and those of other clients as well as those of the organization and the profession?" In terms of means, you might ask, "Would our planned action likely lead to the desired outcome?" "Who are the stakeholders here and who should be involved in the process?" That is, who should be involved in collecting data, assessing, goal setting, and action taking? "What would represent fair and just procedures in this situation?" "Would the means reflect 'due process' for those involved and remain consistent with our moral and professional values, agency guidelines, and our ethical principles?"

When you consider the possible effects, you begin to realize the gravity of the situation and the seriousness of the possible consequences. Bob's reputation, his professional license and career, his job and income, his marriage and family, and perhaps even his life could be affected by the suspicion of wrongdoing, the means by which it is investigated and its accuracy determined, and the actions taken following any decisions. If Bob did have sexual contact with Julie, she could recognize harm at some point in the future. She might not feel injured at the moment but that could easily change as the days and weeks pass. In addition, Julie's rights could be abridged and her well-being affected by the processes undertaken to pursue the question of Bob's alleged misbehavior. Indeed, Julie could begin to feel that her dignity has been assaulted twice—first as a result of Bob's misconduct and second through the investigation. If you reveal her identity or disclose her confidential information without her informed consent, Julie might file a lawsuit against you and the agency for violating her privacy rights and causing her serious emotional distress.

As Bob's supervisor, Jane's status and career are also at risk. If the suspicion about Bob's misconduct is true, Julie, the agency's administration, or the social work licensing board could claim that Jane failed to supervise Bob in a conscientious, competent, and professional manner. She could become the subject of an ethics review and perhaps a legal proceeding. Whether or not her supervision was satisfactory, Jane could experience substantial distress. It is conceivable that she could lose her job and perhaps her career. If the agency lacks a structure, policies, and procedures for addressing staff misconduct or fails to follow them, it too could be subject to ethical censure and perhaps legal action. Its reputation as well as that of social workers and social service agencies in general could suffer as others make generalizations based upon the incident. "If one social worker does it, many do too." Or, "That's what happens in all of those agencies."

A brief MMEE review can help you to recover from the shock of the encounter with Julie. Putting your judgmental thoughts and emotional reactions aside, you access a calm, peaceful, centered, and professional state of mind; and review the facts as you currently know them. Based on your brief meeting with Julie, you know that she said that she has been romantically involved with Bob for the past 6 weeks or so. She also demanded that you maintain the privacy of her privileged communications; stated that you do not have her permission to reveal her identity or anything about her relationship with Bob to anyone; and said that if you did, she would sue you for breach of confidentiality.

Let's consider the credibility of Julie's claims. Can you reasonably presume that Julie's remarks about Bob are true? Might she lie? Deception does not seem likely in the circumstances. She apparently first learned about Bob's life-threatening health status and hospitalization from you.

Her comments appeared to be part of an immediate, spontaneous response to that information. She seemed sincere and her words seemed credible.

Although unlikely, it nonetheless remains conceivable that Julie might experience episodes of delusional thinking—perhaps especially at times of extreme distress. If so, she might sincerely believe that she has a relationship with Bob when she actually does not.[8] Again, this is improbable and you currently have no evidence for either delusion or deception on her part. However, its consideration helps to maintain a sense of some uncertainty and much humility—if only to avoid confirmation bias. Instead of "guilty as charged," your view of Bob becomes something like "probably guilty" or even "innocent until proven guilty." Conversely, your perception of Julie's claims become "probably true" rather than "absolutely true." Furthermore, by thinking in terms of probabilities rather than certainties, you become a better and more sophisticated analyst. Your inquiry becomes more rational and scientific in nature, and the quality of your thinking improves.

You are certain that Bob's sexual contact with Julie, if true, would not only be wrong; it could jeopardize his client's well-being. Imagine the scenario: a client seeks help to recover from the effects of a lover's rejection only to have her social worker engage her in a sexual relationship. His actions not only prevent her from resolving the presenting problem in an adaptive manner but also lead, almost inevitably, to another rejection—this time by the very social worker responsible for helping her. If, in fact, Bob has become sexually involved with Julie, he could inflict the same kind of damage that caused her to seek help in the first place.

As the professional social worker who heard Julie's statements, you are primarily responsible for making early judgments about process. You realize, however, that you cannot and should not handle this alone. You need consultation.

Under most circumstances, you would contact your long-time supervisor Bob—who had served as Julie's social worker. He knows the most about her and her situation. However, Julie's comments raise questions about possible unethical conduct on his part. Furthermore, Bob is currently hospitalized with a life-threatening cardiovascular condition. You cannot and should not contact him, certainly not at this point. You then wonder if you can discuss the situation with your new supervisor Jane or perhaps other professionals in the agency (Dolgoff et al., 2012).[9]

Can you ethically and legally share Julie's identity or the information she disclosed with anyone else inside or outside your organization? Could you, for example, discuss the situation with a colleague who might help you think through the issues? Could you talk with the state social work licensing board or the National Association of Social Workers' ethics office;[10] the risk management services associated with your professional liability insurance company; the agency's legal advisor; or perhaps a personal attorney of your own? And, if you decide that you can ethically share information with and seek consultation from others, should any of them be involved in the process of deciding what to do?

You might even wonder if Julie should be invited to participate. After all, she is the client and you have a primary responsibility for her well-being. And, what about Bob? Can you divulge the information to him: a professional colleague, your previous supervisor, and the subject of Julie's remarks—if and when he recovers from his current life-threatening condition? You might recall that the 6th Amendment to the U.S. Constitution refers to a right to know the nature of the charges, the identity of accusers, and the right to confront those accusers—at least in a court of law. Would failure

---

[8] Within the mental health field, a delusional belief that one has a special relationship with another person—often a celebrity of some kind or perhaps a person of some status or authority—is sometimes called "erotomania."

[9] Seeking legal advice is, of course, permissible and frequently warranted. When you are represented by legal counsel, your words are protected by attorney–client privilege.

[10] Members of the National Association of Social Workers may contact the Office of Ethics and Professional Review (OEPR) at 800-742-4089 on Mondays and Wednesdays from 1:00 P.M. to 4:00 P.M. ET and Tuesdays and Thursdays from 10:00 A.M. to 1:00 P.M. Go to **https://www.socialworkers.org/nasw/ethics/consultation.asp** for current information.

to inform Bob about Julie's statement that she has a sexual relationship with him represent a violation of fair or due process in regard to his rights? Can or should he participate in the process in some way?

Despite these questions, you would normally first contact your current immediate supervisor; share the information you have; discuss the factors you've identified; and request that she collaborate with you in the decision-making process. The primary exception to this would be if your supervisor has a conflict of interest or a dual relationship with an interested party: in this case, Bob or Julie. For example, a conflict would exist if Jane had previously been romantically involved with Bob or if they have a dual relationship, such as owning a business together. She might also have a conflict of some sort with Julie. If Jane does have a dual relationship with Bob or Julie, or some other conflict of interest in this situation, she would be ethically obligated to say so and then recuse herself from the process.

Agency consent and HIPAA forms typically describe clients' rights to privacy and confidentiality as well as common exceptions to those rights. Clients' rights commonly extend to agency personnel who contribute to the delivery and improvement of services. Supervisors and auditors may review case records, and administrative staff file and store them. Of course, clients' right to confidentiality extends to these other agency personnel. They too are obligated to protect clients' private information.

Assuming that Julie has previously provided consent to this common form of agency-wide, extended confidentiality, discussion with your current supervisor would not violate her rights. Typically, social workers may discuss our work with our supervisors and sometimes with professional colleagues in staff meetings. Some agencies permit the use of client names in staffing sessions; others do not. In the "What about Bob?" case, you would not discuss the situation in a staffing session or with other colleagues—because of its sensitive nature and the risk of confidentiality violations. Other staff members might be so tempted to gossip—inappropriately and unethically though it might be—that both Julie's and Bob's rights might be jeopardized. However, talking with your supervisor is not only permitted, it is imperative. Indeed, you are ethically required to "take responsible steps (including . . . supervision) to ensure the competence" of your services and "protect clients from harm" (1.04c). In addition, social agencies are ethically obligated to provide supervisory resources (3.07c).

As your current supervisor and a more experienced professional, Jane might assume leadership and say, "I'll take over from here." At that point, you might say "whew!" and conclude that you have properly fulfilled your ethical obligations. However, some supervisors become overwhelmed and immobilized by such heavy responsibilities. In our situation, for example, Jane might become concerned about her own professional liability as Bob's supervisor. She might wonder if she could have somehow prevented Bob's misbehavior if she had provided better supervision or been more observant. Jane might become so distressed about her own potential legal or ethical vulnerability that her ability to function declines. Many supervisors are mature, competent, and motivated to do the right thing. Some, however, are not. If your supervisor fails to follow through, you might have to, perhaps by contacting the human resources officer or the chief executive of the agency.

For our purposes, let's assume that Jane is free from any conflict of interest and quite prepared to take responsibility for the quality of her supervision with Bob and all other subordinates. When you inform her about the situation, she says she will assume the leadership role. However, she asks for your assistance in the processes of data collection and ethical decision making. She might view this as a learning opportunity for you as a fairly new social worker. Or, she might prefer a collegial "witness" to steps taken to address the issue. As a participant in the process, you could fulfill that function.

Jane then asks you to do some background work and present her with a preliminary analysis of the ethics involved in this situation. You reflect for a few moments and then suggest that you would first like to review the ethical code, state laws, and the HIPAA regulations to identify relevant ethical and legal principles and rules. You also want to consult with lawyers who possess expertise in such matters; carefully review the agency's policies and procedures manual; and conduct a search for published material about "sexual misconduct with clients." Following that, you hope to synthesize that information and complete an ethical analysis of the current situation. Your analysis should help you, Jane, and an agency executive or attorney to formulate an action plan. Jane endorses your suggestions and you leave to locate and review relevant resources.

You retrieve your copy of the NASW Code of Ethics and begin to consider the six major social work values and their associated ethical principles. It appears that the following apply in this situation: *service* ("Social workers elevate service to others above self-interest"); *social justice* ("Social workers strive to ensure access to needed information, services, and resources; . . . and meaningful participation in decision making"); *dignity and worth of the person* ("Social workers respect the inherent dignity and worth of the person . . . (and) . . . treat each person in a caring and respectful fashion . . . (and) . . . are cognizant of their dual responsibility to clients and to the broader society. They seek to resolve conflicts between clients' interests and the broader society's interests in a socially responsible manner consistent with the values, ethical principles, and ethical standards of the profession . . . (and) . . . enhance clients' capacity and opportunity to change and to address their own needs"); *importance of human relationships* ("Social workers recognize the central importance of human relationships"); *integrity* ("Social workers behave in a trustworthy manner . . . [and] . . . are continually aware of the profession's mission, values, ethical principles, and ethical standards and practice in a manner consistent with them . . . [and] . . . act honestly and responsibly and promote ethical practices on the part of the organizations with which they are affiliated"); and *competence* ("Social workers continually strive to increase their professional knowledge and skills and to apply them in practice") (National Association of Social Workers, 2008).

Next you refer to the Council on Social Work Education's EPAS (2015) for two additional key values: *human rights* ("advocate for human rights at the individual and system levels"); and *scientific inquiry* ("apply critical thinking to engage in analysis of quantitative and qualitative research methods and research findings; and use and translate research evidence to inform and improve practice, policy, and service delivery") (2015, pp. 7–8).

At this point, you recall that some textbooks identify several overarching moral values as well as certain legal duties that apply generally to helping professionals. You conclude that the moral values of *beneficence, nonmaleficence, justice, autonomy, privacy, confidentiality,* and *fidelity* all apply in some way to this situation. In addition, you recognize that you have a legal *duty of care,* a *duty of confidentiality,* and a *duty to respect the privacy* of the client. You also have a *duty to inform* the client and provide full disclosure about matters affecting her, her rights, and her well-being. It is also conceivable that you might have a *duty to report* or a *duty to warn and protect* persons whose lives are in danger.

The HIPAA regulations appear to emphasize clients' rights to privacy and confidentiality, recognizing that the safety of the client or others may sometimes supersede those protections. You can find nothing in them to provide guidance about possible ethical misconduct by a professional colleague. However, it appears that "de-identified" information may be disclosed in some circumstances. "De-identified health information neither identifies nor provides a reasonable basis to identify an individual . . . (or) . . . the individual's relatives, household members, and employers" (U.S. Department of Health and Human Services, 2003, May, p. 4).

You then proceed to examine the laws governing the practice of social work in your state. If you live and work in Indiana, you might find that Title 839, Article 1, Rule 3, Sections 4(b) and 4(b)(6–8) of the Indiana Administrative Code[11] contain the following passages:

(b) The competent practice of social work and clinical social work includes acting within generally accepted ethical principles and guidelines of the profession and maintaining an awareness

[11] Please refer to the legal codes and regulations in your state or province. The state of Indiana's are used for illustrative purposes only.

of personal and professional limitations. These ethical principles include, but are not limited to, the following:

(6) Relationships with clients shall not be exploited by the social worker or clinical social worker for personal gain. A social worker or clinical social worker shall not violate such positions of trust and dependency by committing any act detrimental to a client.

(7) A social worker or clinical social worker shall not abandon or neglect a client in need of immediate professional services without making reasonable arrangements for the provision or the continuation of services.

(8) The social worker or clinical social worker shall under no circumstances engage in sexual activities with clients. (IN.gov, 2015, Jan.)

As part of the duty to inform, the Commonwealth of Virginia along with several other states legally require that helping professionals "upon learning of evidence that indicates a reasonable probability that another mental health provider is or may be guilty of a violation of standards of conduct as defined in statute or regulation, *advise his patient of his right to report* such misconduct to the Department of Health Professions" (The Center for Ethical Practice, 2010, Aug. 15).

You also learn how consumers may file complaints about a licensed social worker with social work licensing boards or perhaps states' offices of the attorney general. In Indiana, the "Attorney General investigates complaints filed by consumers and decides whether to seek disciplinary action against the license holder before the appropriate board or commission" (IN.gov, 2015).

You then examine the agency's policies and procedures manual to look for guidance about responding to a colleague's possible misconduct. The manual contains a section about how clients may submit complaints but nothing about how staff members should address concerns about a colleague's impairment or misbehavior. The manual does not contain any reference to an ethics committee or a process by which ethics issues may be discussed and addressed. You make note of those omissions. At a later point, you might advocate for changes to the policies and procedures manual, and the agency's organizational structure.

You wonder if a search of the professional literature might yield pertinent information and perhaps guidance. A quick review of the NASW website reveals a page entitled "How to Properly File a Request for a Professional Review (RPR)" and the "NASW Procedures for Professional Review Manual" in downloadable format (National Association of Social Workers, 2012). Another document entitled "Criminalization of Psychotherapist Sexual Misconduct" identifies some 23 states that "criminalize sexual contact between psychotherapists and clients and nearly all of these states classify the violations as felony offenses" (Morgan, 2013, May, para. 2).

The *Encyclopedia of Social Work* contains several pertinent chapters including, for example, "Ethics and Values" (Reamer, 2008a), "Professional Liability and Malpractice" (Chase, 2008), "Confidentiality and Privileged Communication" (Polowy, Morgan, Bailey, & Gorenberg, 2008), "Professional Conduct" (Abbott, 2008), "Professional Impairment" (Peebles-Wilkins, 2008), "Sexual Harassment" (Fogel, 2008), "Consumer Rights" (Linhorst, 2008), and "Recording" (Kagle, 2008).

A search for relevant books produces titles such as *Sexual Involvement with Therapists* (Pope, 1994), *The Wages of Seeking Help: Sexual Exploitation by Professionals* (Bohmer, 2000), *Sexual Exploitation in Professional Relationships* (Gabbard, 1989), and *Clinical Social Worker Misconduct* (Bullis, 1995). Several chapters in books also address the sexual misconduct issue (see, for example, Pope & Vasquez, 2011; Reamer, 2013b, 2015) as do numerous journal articles (see, for example, Barnett, 2014; Ben-Ari & Somer, 2004; Disch & Avery, 2001; McNulty, Ogden, & Warren, 2013; Moggi, Brodbeck, & Hirsbrunner, 2000; Pope, 1988; Pope, Keith-Spiegel, & Tabachnick, 1986; Sonne & Jochai, 2014). As you review the literature, you discover that sex between helping professionals and their clients or patients is not uncommon, occurring in the range of 1 to 12 percent of all therapeutic relationships. You also learn that the vast majority of incidents involve male therapists and female clients, followed by male therapists and male clients, then female therapists with male clients, and finally female therapists with female clients (Garrett & Davis, 1998; G. M. Miller & Larrabee, 1995; Moggi et al., 2000; Parsons & Wincze, 1995; Pope, 1990, 1994, 2001). You read that the rates of therapeutic sexual misconduct may be diminishing—perhaps because of the severe professional and legal consequences, including its criminalization in many states (Morgan, 2013, May) and the large monetary awards granted to plaintiffs in civil suits (Reamer, 2015). You also note that many clients and patients sexually exploited by their helping professionals subsequently suffer considerable psychosocial distress (Ben-Ari & Somer, 2004; Bernsen, Tabachnick, & Pope, 1994; Celenza, 1991; Disch & Avery, 2001; Folman, 1991; Gabbard, 1989; Gechtman, 1989; McNulty et al., 2013; Mittendorf & Schroeder, 2004; Moggi et al., 2000; Pope, 1988, 1990, 2001; Pope & Vetter, 1991; Rutter, 1989; Sonne & Jochai, 2014).

You could create a table (see Table 5.1) to record your ethical obligations and responsibilities as the current social worker, Jane's as the supervising social worker for Bob and now for you, and Bob's as the previous, now implicated social worker. You might include the agency's responsibilities as well.

At this point you return to your well-used copy of the NASW Code of Ethics (2008) to determine which general and which specific ethical principles might apply in the current situation. You review the section headings and conclude that principles from at least five of the six sections are involved (see Table 5.2): social workers' ethical responsibilities (1) to clients; (2) to colleagues; (3) in practice settings; (4) as professionals; and (5) to the social work profession. You might wonder if you have responsibility to (6) the broader society as well.

TABLE 5.1 Multidimensional Ethical Matrix				
Sections of the NASW Ethical Code	You: The Current Social Worker	Jane: The Supervising Social Worker	Bob: The Previous Social Worker	The Social Service Agency
Social workers' ethical responsibilities	What were and what now are your ethical obligations and responsibilities as the current social worker in this case situation?	What were and what now are Jane's ethical obligations and responsibilities as Bob's supervisor in this case situation?	What were and what now are Bob's ethical obligations and responsibilities as the previous social worker in this case situation?	What were and what now are the agency's ethical obligations and responsibilities as the employing organization in this situation?
1. to clients				
2. to colleagues				
3. in practice settings				
4. as professionals				
5. to the social work profession				
6. to the broader society				

TABLE 5.2	NASW Ethical Principles That Apply to the "What about Bob?" Case
1.01 Commitment to Clients	3.01 Supervision and Consultation
1.02 Self-Determination	3.04 Client Records
1.03 Informed Consent	3.06 Client Transfer
1.06 Conflicts of Interest	3.07 Administration
1.07 Privacy and Confidentiality	3.09 Commitments to Employers
1.09 Sexual Relationships	
1.11 Sexual Harassment	4.03 Private Conduct
1.15 Interruption of Services	4.04 Dishonesty, Fraud, and Deception
1.16 Termination of Services	
	5.01 Integrity of the Profession
2.01 Respect (for colleagues)	
2.05 Consultation	
2.06 Referral for Services	
2.11 Unethical Conduct of Colleagues	

In regard to specific NASW ethical principles, you notice that social workers have a primary commitment to clients (1.01). This corresponds to the values of beneficence and nonmaleficence as well as the legal duty of care. You, Bob, Jane, and the agency are obligated to respect Julie's interests and promote her well-being. Consistent with values of autonomy, fidelity, privacy, and confidentiality as well as the legal duties of care, privacy, and confidentiality, all previous, current, and future social workers must "respect and promote" Julie's right to self-determination (1.02). Social workers must also provide services based on full, complete informed consent (1.03), and protect Julie's rights to privacy and the confidentiality (1.07) of "all information obtained in the course of professional service" (1.07c).

Corresponding to the duty of care and the values of beneficence and nonmaleficence, social workers must avoid conflicts of interest and dual relationships (1.06). Social workers must never make sexual advances or engage in sexual harassment (1.11); "under no circumstances engage in sexual activities or sexual contact" with clients (1.09a); and never "participate in, condone, or be associated with dishonesty, fraud, or deception" (4.04). Social workers should "seek the advice and counsel of colleagues whenever such consultation is in the best interests of clients" (2.05a), and "disclose the least amount of information necessary to achieve the purposes" of consultation (2.05c). In addition, social workers must maintain sufficient, timely, and accurate records about the services (3.04a); ensure continuity of care to minimize the unavoidable interruption of services (1.15) or unexpected transfer (3.06); and avoid abandoning clients or terminating services abruptly when they still need them (1.16). Indeed, as a social worker your primary commitment to the client, the duty of care, and the values of beneficence and nonmaleficence suggest agency professionals continue to offer social services to Julie or refer her to a helping professional unaffiliated with your agency (2.06).

Social workers have ethical responsibilities to our colleagues as well as to our clients. In discussions about Bob or interactions with him, you should be respectful and "avoid unwarranted negative criticism" (2.01). However, since you have reason to wonder if Bob acted unethically you should take action to "discourage, prevent, expose, and correct" that misconduct (2.11a); "seek resolution by discussing" your concern with Bob if it "is likely to be productive (2.11c); and if "necessary . . . take action through appropriate formal channels" (2.11d). Finally, if it turns out that the allegations of misconduct are unwarranted, you have a responsibility to "defend and assist" Bob should he need your help (2.11e).

We are also ethically responsible to our employers, our profession, and the broader society. Social workers must educate employers about the code of ethics and its implications (3.09a); and never let the "organization's policies, procedures, regulations, or administrative orders" impede ethical practice (3.09d). Furthermore, we should use organizational funds and resources wisely and for their intended purposes (3.09g). As professionals, we "should work toward the maintenance and promotion of high standards of practice" (5.01) and never let our private conduct negatively affect our ability to provide effective services in an ethical manner (4.03). Social work administrators, in turn, are responsible for providing "appropriate staff supervision" (3.07c), and for ensuring that "the working environment for which they are responsible is consistent with and encourages compliance with the *NASW Code of Ethics*." In fact, "social work administrators should take reasonable steps to eliminate any conditions in their organizations that violate, interfere with, or discourage compliance with the *Code*" (3.07d).

Now let's review the available information and then ask a few questions that build upon the identification of values, legal duties, and ethical principles that apply in this situation. We know that Julie said she is sexually involved with her social worker. If accurate, Bob has almost definitely violated the ethical prohibitions against sexual contact with a client. He may also have entered incomplete or inaccurate information into the client's case records. He might have billed Julie for the provision of professional services that he did not actually provide. If true, Bob's intimate behavior with Julie could indicate a pattern of inappropriate and potentially damaging relationships with clients. At this point, however, Julie apparently does not feel harmed. She has not filed a complaint against Bob. In fact, she demands that you fully respect her rights to privacy and confidentiality, and implicitly her rights to autonomy and self-determination.[12]

Faced with such complexity, you might question how you could possibly fulfill your ethical responsibilities to the profession and the agency while simultaneously meeting your duties to provide the best possible care to Julie, ensure her autonomy, protect her privacy and her confidentiality, and inform her clearly and fully about her rights and privileges. Then there is the troublesome "What about Bob?" question. How do you meet your ethical responsibilities to him as a colleague and at the same time meet your obligations to his past, current, and perhaps future clients; the agency that employs you; and the profession to which you both belong?

The client's legal and human rights and several of your ethical responsibilities appear to conflict with other ethical principles and perhaps even some legal duties. It places you in an ethical dilemma—one of thousands to come during the course of your career. Because they are so common, social workers must be prepared to adopt and to document fair, just, and defensible processes for deciding what to do whenever such quandaries emerge. In other words, we need ethical decision-making skills.

Ethical Decision Making

Based on your initial review of this case situation, you conclude that the major elements of the dilemma involve conflicts between your ethical responsibilities to (1) the identified client; (2) the implicated social worker; (3) other current, former, and potential future clients; (4) the agency; and (5) the profession. If you reveal the name or identity of the client without her consent as you undertake an investigation of the implicated social worker's conduct, you violate her right to autonomy, privacy, and confidentiality. If you protect the client's privacy and confidentiality rights as you probe the possibility of unethical behavior, you might weaken the data collection process.

---

[12] Julie may not maintain her current view over the long term. Indeed, at some point in the future, Julie may conclude that Bob indeed violated her rights and his ethics. A complaint or lawsuit could then follow.

Bob could more easily deflect or deny general questions than those containing names, dates and times, places, and detailed descriptions. Similarly, anonymous claims of professional misconduct submitted to a professional ethics committee or a state licensing board may also be dismissed on the grounds of hearsay or insufficient evidence. In addition, if you publicly reveal the name or identity of the implicated social worker and it turns out that the allegations are false, you violate your responsibility to a professional colleague and place yourself in considerable ethical and legal danger as well.

The value of beneficence, the duty of care, and our commitment to service involve the promotion of personal and social well-being and the protection of human life. You ask yourself, "Could Julie's life or that of anyone else be at risk now or later?"

At this point, Julie does not appear to represent a current danger to herself or others. However, if she actually did have an intimate relationship with Bob, a psychosocial crisis might ensue if Bob were to die due to cardiovascular illness or to reject her following his recovery. You do not know if Julie has ever been seriously depressed or suicidal in the past, but the unexpected loss of a significant relationship might trigger emotional upset in anyone. In her case, it could be a second major loss in less than 1 year. If her belief about a relationship with Bob is delusional or deceptive, then a sudden collapse of that delusion or the recognition by others that she dissembled could also prompt a crisis. You recognize that Julie's well-being must be addressed—now and for some time to come.

Bob's life and well-being appear to be at considerable risk because of the heart condition. If Julie's revelations are valid and Bob survives, he too could experience a severe psychosocial crisis at the point he learns that others suspect him of ethical misconduct. Julie could be so motivated to make amends to Bob for her "slip of the tongue" that she might notify him of her lapse. Becoming aware that he is under suspicion of ethical misconduct might stimulate enough distress to trigger another cardiovascular episode. Although you are unaware of any history of self-harm, you know that other professionals in similar situations have hurt themselves and a few have assaulted witnesses. It is conceivable that Bob could become a risk to himself or others later on in this process. In addition, Bob's illness currently leaves him quite vulnerable. Even if Julie's statements are untrue, an investigation about possible sexual relationships with clients would cause distress that, due to his fragile health, could become life-threatening. You propose to consider Bob's health status and his risk of mortality as you make plans to address the issue.

Let's next consider the value of justice. As a social worker, you are concerned about the imbalance of power in this situation (the "difference principle"). As Bob's client, Julie has much less status, power, and influence than he does. As the more powerful person in the relationship, he has a special ethical responsibility to ensure her safety and well-being, and to avoid exploiting his position for personal satisfaction or benefit. Despite the fact that she is an adult, her status as Bob's client leaves her vulnerable to his greater power. Indeed the very nature of her presenting concern—that of grieving the loss of an intimate relationship—could leave her susceptible to anyone who responds to her with kindness, understanding, and compassion. In popular language, she is especially susceptible to a "rebound relationship." If, in fact, Bob did engage in a sexual relationship with Julie, you and others in the agency are obligated to provide her with full and accurate information about the pertinent ethical guidelines, her rights and privileges in the situation, and to provide or arrange for services to help resolve the original issue as well as facilitate her recovery from any damage caused by Bob's misconduct.

These same obligations apply to other clients with whom Bob may have misbehaved. You anticipate that Jane will initiate an inquiry into Bob's work with his current and former clients, perhaps focusing especially on female clients. If he engaged in other instances of sexual misconduct, your agency becomes obligated to those people as well. If sufficient evidence emerges,

Jane, the agency, and those clients who decide to do so may file complaints with the state's social work licensing board and the professional association for further investigation and review. If Bob's misconduct is confirmed, your agency and the profession or state become responsible for imposing sanctions so that current and future clients are protected from the risk that he might misbehave again.

You next consider the related values of autonomy and self-determination, privacy and confidentiality, and nonmaleficence (do no harm; the least possible harm; or the most reversible harm). Julie has the right to freedom from undue influence and control. As an apparently competent adult, she is free to make decisions for herself and to exercise control over her body and her property. Indeed, social workers typically encourage autonomous, independent functioning. In this situation, however, you, Jane, and other agency personnel involved in deciding what to do may challenge her right to autonomy. Although Julie currently wants you to keep everything she said completely confidential, you want to discover the truth about Bob's behavior. If you, Jane, or an agency executive or attorney proceed to investigate the issue, you could effectively override her right to autonomy and self-determination. Julie has not engaged in unethical behavior. The code of ethics does not apply to her. Although Bob cannot ethically have a sexual relationship with Julie, she does not bear that same burden. She is free to have relationships with whomever she wants; and, at this point in time, she demands that her remarks about Bob remain absolutely confidential. Can you disregard her autonomy rights because of Bob's possible misbehavior?

You then examine the agency's informed consent policies and procedures as well as HIPAA regulations to determine how clients' privacy and confidentiality rights are explicated. Many agencies provide clients with copies of policies that specify circumstances when their right to confidentiality may not be preserved. Such exclusions typically involve suspicions of child abuse or indications that someone's life may be in danger. Fewer agencies specify that client confidentiality rights may be breached if a service provider engages in professional misconduct. You review the case record and discover that the consent form that Julie signed lacks such a provision. Therefore, she can reasonably conclude that her rights to privacy and confidentiality cannot be violated due to suspicions that her social worker engaged in misconduct.

The Code indicates that "Social workers may limit clients' right to self-determination when, in the social workers' professional judgment, clients' actions or potential actions pose a serious, foreseeable, and imminent risk to themselves or others" (1.02). "The general expectation that social workers will keep information confidential does not apply when disclosure is necessary to prevent serious, foreseeable, and imminent harm to a client or other identifiable person" (1.07c). You wonder if respecting Julie's rights to confidentiality, autonomy, and self-determination might somehow result in such severe harm that violating her rights could be justified?

You then consider the value of fidelity. Obviously, honesty is a key aspect of fidelity. Our clients expect us to tell them the truth and to eschew both lies of commission as well as deception through omission. The value of fidelity, however, goes beyond sincere truth telling. Social workers must proactively share information that pertains to our clients or their situation, or might affect their well-being. The duty to inform reflects this value. Julie's disclosure about her intimate relationship with Bob triggers an obligation to provide her with pertinent information about the ethical and legal prohibitions against sex with clients, dual relationships with clients, and boundary violations, as well as the reasons for those rules. In addition, concern for her well-being, the value of beneficence, and the duty of care suggest that you offer to provide or arrange for continuing supportive services.

The duty to warn and protect does not seem to apply in this situation. Currently, the risk that Julie might become violent toward self or others appears low. The duty to report would also not generally apply in this situation as it usually involves suspicion of child abuse, elder abuse, or the abuse of especially vulnerable adults. However, the laws in your locale may include a requirement to report professional misconduct. In submitting a complaint, most states would not permit disclosure of affected clients' names or identifying information without their expressed, informed consent. The duties to respect privacy and to maintain confidentiality take precedence. Of course, most complaints of professional misconduct are filed by clients or their family members, and include both identifying information as well as details of alleged ethical violations. However, when clients remain too fragile to tolerate the stress associated with the process or decline to permit release of information, other professionals or agency administrators may file grievances without the name or identifying characteristics of affected clients. Obviously, such "de-identified" grievances carry considerably less weight than those that include names, dates, details, and supporting evidence of misconduct.

Given the importance granted to clients' autonomy, privacy, and confidentiality rights, and the very few exceptions to them, Julie could understandably feel severely disrespected if you or the agency use your superior status and authority to disclose her identity and her privileged information. She might even conclude that your betrayal of her privacy is just as bad as Bob's betrayal of his ethics.

Based on your analysis of the competing obligations, you plan to respect Julie's right to autonomy, privacy, and confidentiality to the maximum extent possible—until or unless she provides informed consent to release that information. You hope to do her no harm, or at least no more harm. As you proceed through the ethical decision-making process, you intend to keep Julie's well-being clearly in mind. Indeed, you and your agency maintain special obligations regarding Julie's welfare during this time. You recognize that the situation is likely to become more, rather than less, chaotic and stressful in the near future.

Plans and Action Steps

In preparing a plan to address the ethical issues and complications, you decide to undertake the following steps:

Step 1: Arrange for an information-sharing meeting with Julie.

When you first met with Julie, she did not view Bob's behavior as a violation of her rights or dignity, nor as misconduct on his part. She also demanded that you protect her rights to privacy and confidentiality. Your own analysis as well as the recommendations of your supervisor, staff at NASW's Office of Ethics and Professional Review, and the agency's legal consultant converge in the opinion that the obligations to protect her identity and confidence are paramount. Those duties take precedence at this time. However, all of you also agree that you must provide the affected client with (1) a copy of the code of ethics and relevant information about social workers' legal and ethical obligations—especially those that pertain to dual relationships and sexual contact with clients; (2) a full explanation of the reasons for the establishment of ethical standards and laws prohibiting sexual relations with clients; (3) forms and guidance about how and where to submit formal complaints of professional misconduct should she subsequently decide to file a grievance; (4) a clear, genuine, and open-ended offer for continuing counseling or other supportive services; and (5) assurance that her rights to privacy and confidentiality will be honored until or unless she provides informed consent to disclose her identity and her privileged communications.

Step 2: Conduct a thorough review of Bob's case records.

The review and examination of Bob's case records falls within Jane's responsibility and authority as Bob's supervisor. She and perhaps another designated ethics auditor plan to review Bob's case files, paying special attention to the records of clients that reflect demographic characteristics similar to Julie's. They intend to look for progress notes that resemble the content and language contained in Julie's files. If any such records are identified, they will be stored in a separate and secure place. They might be needed later.

Step 3: Arrange for an information-sharing and data-gathering meeting with Bob.

If and when Bob's health improves enough for him to be interviewed, Jane plans to arrange for a meeting. Another professional should accompany her. The human services officer, the chair of the agency's ethics committee, the chief executive, or perhaps the agency's attorney would be logical choices. In the meeting with Bob, they intend to introduce the issue of sexual involvement with clients in general terms. They will not mention Julie's name nor disclose identifying information or confidential communications without Julie's fully informed consent. Jane plans to begin in a fashion such as the following: "Bob, I have to ask you some sensitive questions about possible ethical misconduct. I'm here as your supervisor and will make notes about our discussion. Do you understand? Yes? Okay. Let's begin. 'Are you aware of the legal and ethical prohibitions about sexual relations with clients?' (Jane displays the code of ethics and relevant state laws or regulations.) Yes? Okay. 'During the course of your employment with our agency, have you ever made sexual advances toward or become sexually involved with any current or former client?'"

If Bob denies that he engaged in any such behavior, she might summarize his statement in a fashion such as, "Thank you Bob. I am making a note that you categorically deny having sexual contact with any current or former client during your employment as a social worker with this agency. Is that accurate? Yes. Okay."

If Bob declines to respond or does so in an ambiguous manner, Jane could rephrase and repeat the question until Bob responds with a definitive answer. If he continues to avoid the question, she could say, "Thank you Bob. I am making a note that you neither deny nor affirm that you have engaged in sexual contact with any current or former clients during your employment as a social worker with this agency. Is that accurate? Yes? Okay."

If Bob admits to the misconduct, perhaps by saying, "Julie told me that she let it slip that we are involved," Jane would record his words and thank him for his honesty. She should neither confirm nor deny that Julie is the source of your information—unless Julie has previously provided consent. Jane might then follow up with a question about involvement with other clients. She could say, "Well Bob, we both know that a sexual relationship with a client represents an ethical violation. You've mentioned one client. Have you had sexual contact with any other current or former clients?" Jane would record his response to this question as well. She would again thank him and then provide him with forms and guidance about how he can "self-report" his own misconduct to the state licensing board and professional association.

Finally, Jane would inform Bob that she will convey the substance of this meeting to the agency's administrative group which will consider the facts and make decisions about his status. She indicates that he will receive information about his rights and obligations throughout the process.

Step 4: Arrange for a decision-making meeting and take action based on the decision-making group's decisions.

At Jane's suggestion, key people in your agency (such as the CEO, Chair of the Board of Directors, the Human Resources Officer, the Ethics Committee Chair, and the agency's attorney) meet to review the question of Bob's alleged misconduct. If Bob has acknowledged the ethical lapse, the agency imposes sanctions. The usual consequence for sexual misconduct is termination of employment for "cause." In addition, the agency submits a claim of professional misconduct to the state licensing board and the professional social work association, describing the self-acknowledged misconduct. Do not include Julie's name or identifying characteristics unless she provides consent to release that information.

If Julie reconsiders the situation and waives her right to privacy and confidentiality in order to submit a claim of ethical misconduct against Bob, agency staff can help her complete the process. Or, if she would prefer, the agency may submit the claim to the professional or state authority on her behalf as well as the agency's. If Bob denies the allegation or declines to respond to the question of sexual contact with clients, and sufficient evidence exists to support Julie's allegation of an extra-therapeutic relationship with Bob (in the form, for example, of letters from Bob to Julie, text or e-mail messages, photographs, or video clips), the agency imposes sanctions, terminates his employment, and submits an ethical misconduct claim to the state authority and the professional association.

If Bob declines to respond to questions about ethical misconduct or if he categorically denies making sexual advances or having sexual contact with any clients, and Julie continues to expect privacy and confidentiality, the agency suspends Bob from practice while conducting further investigations. The agency determines which, if any, of Bob's former clients may safely be contacted for general follow-up about the nature, quality, and effectiveness of the services received by the agency. If some can safely be contacted, ask what they liked and what they disliked about the way they were treated by their social worker. Request that they share those concerns or questions they have about the social worker's personal or professional behavior. Explore any identified concerns in greater depth. If any suggest that unethical conduct may have occurred, request specific details. If it appears that any clients may have been subject to Bob's (or any other professional's) sexual advances, arrange for an information-sharing meeting such as the one you had earlier with Julie (see Step 1 above). Thank each of the former clients and prepare written summaries of their responses and remarks.

If additional evidence of ethical misconduct does not emerge and Julie does not change her mind about releasing her identity and confidential information, reinstate Bob and provide close supervision. The passage of time may prove informative. If suggestions of Bob's misconduct are true, he might leave his family "for Julie." Alternately, he might reject Julie "for his family." In the former case, the now public relationship with Julie confirms the allegation of unethical behavior. In the latter case, Julie could respond to his rejection with understandable anger. She might then decide to waive her rights to privacy and confidentiality and choose to submit an ethical misconduct claim. She could also file a lawsuit against Bob. Regardless of its source, if credible evidence subsequently emerges to support a claim of ethical misconduct, the agency can then impose sanctions and submit an ethical misconduct complaint to the state licensing authority and the professional association (see Table 5.3 for summary of possible actions).

TABLE 5.3 Summary of Agency's Possible Actions		
	Julie Provides Informed Consent to Release Her Name and Her Statements Concerning a Sexual Relationship with Bob	Julie Does Not Provide Informed Consent to Release Her Name and Her Statements Concerning a Sexual Relationship with Bob
Bob Acknowledges Sexual Misconduct with One or More Clients	*Agency imposes sanctions and submits an ethical misconduct complaint to state licensing bureau and professional association.*	*Agency imposes sanctions and submits an ethical misconduct complaint to state licensing bureau and professional association.*
Bob Declines to Respond to Questions or Categorically Denies Sexual Misconduct with Any Clients	*Agency suspends Bob while gathering additional information. Agency formally requests Bob's attendance at a meeting to respond to Julie's statement. If he declines to respond to questions or denies any sexual conduct, and fails to provide evidence to refute Julie's allegations, the agency imposes sanctions and submits an ethical misconduct complaint to the state licensing bureau and professional association.*	*Agency suspends Bob while gathering additional information. If additional evidence of ethical misconduct does not emerge and Julie does not change her mind about releasing her identity and confidential information, the agency reinstates Bob and provides close supervision for a substantial period of time.* *If evidence subsequently emerges to support a claim of ethical misconduct, the agency imposes sanctions and submits an ethical misconduct complaint to state licensing bureau and professional association.*

SUMMARY

The values, ethics, and legal obligations that guide social workers pertain to every aspect of professional practice. Indeed, you should consider ethical principles more important than theoretical knowledge, research findings, agency policies, and, of course, your own personal views.

To make sound ethical decisions in social work practice, you should be familiar with the fundamental human rights of all people and the basic moral values involved in ethical decision making. You also need to know and understand the values of the profession, the principles reflected in the social work code of ethics, and the legal obligations affecting your practice. In addition, you need to identify the ethical principles, standards, and legal duties that may apply to particular situations. Finally, when different values, ethical principles, or legal obligations conflict, you must be able to determine which ones take precedence over others.

The skill of ethical decision making is fundamental to social work practice. Without such skill, you cannot legitimately claim professional status. Indeed, attempting to provide social work services without regard for ethical principles would be unconscionable.

CHAPTER 5   Summary Exercises

Reflective Exercises

1. Assume that you have been providing social work services to a married couple that has indicated a desire to improve the quality of their relationship. You and the clients have agreed that direct, open, and honest communication is a relationship goal. Each has also expressed that sexual fidelity is an important dimension of their marriage.

   Between the fifth and sixth meetings, you receive a telephone call from one of the partners who says, "I think it would help you to know that I am romantically involved with another person. My spouse does not know and I know that you will not reveal this information because of your legal obligation to maintain confidentiality. I want you to know about this other relationship because I think it will help you to help us. I have come to respect your expertise. You are doing a wonderful job. Thank you."

Use a word-processing program to (a) list the specific ethical principles from the NASW Code of Ethics and identify those legal duties that you believe apply to the case; (b) if a conflict between two or more legal or ethical obligations exists, conduct an ethical analysis and prepare a plan to resolve the ethical dilemma; (c) describe the actions you would probably take as a social worker in this situation; and (d) provide a brief rationale to support those actions. Title the document "Confidentiality and the Couple." Save the document file as "Couple_Confidentiality" and deposit it in your Social Work Skills Learning Portfolio.

Write-Now Exercises

Use the space below each of the following write-now exercises to record your responses.

1. Imagine that you serve as a supervisor in a nonsectarian social services agency that provides social and counseling services to families and children of all kinds and compositions. One of the professionals you supervise is a relatively young social worker who has worked in the agency for just a few weeks. During one of your early supervisory meetings, you begin to discuss a case that you plan to assign to her. The case involves a lesbian couple who recently migrated to your community. They want professional help to accomplish two goals: First, they want to get married. They want to know if gay marriage is legal in this state and, if it is not, how and where they can go to become a legally married couple. Second, they hope to have a child—preferably through artificial insemination or, if that fails, through adoption. They would like help in discussing these issues and making plans to accomplish these goals. As you describe the case, the young social worker says, "I'm sorry, I am a religious person who believes that homosexuality is a sin and gay marriage is simply wrong."

   As the young social worker's supervisor, what would you identify as the ethical issues in this situation? What would you advise her to consider? What would you suggest that she do?

CHAPTER 5   Self-Appraisal

As you finish this chapter, please reflect on your learning by using the following space to identify any ideas, terms, or concepts addressed in Chapter 5 that remain confusing or unclear to you:

Next, respond to the following items by carefully reading each statement. Please use a 1-to-10-point rating scale (where *1 = strongly disagree* and *10 = strongly agree*) to indicate the degree to which you agree or disagree with each statement. Place a check mark at the point that best reflects your view at this particular point in time. If you're truly *undecided*, place your check at the midpoint (5.5) mark.

1. I can identify and discuss the legal duties that apply to helping professionals.

    1   2   3   4   5   6   7   8   9   10

2. I can access laws that affect the practice of social work in my locale.

    1   2   3   4   5   6   7   8   9   10

3. I can discuss the fundamental values of the social work profession.

    1   2   3   4   5   6   7   8   9   10

4. I can discuss the moral values that guide professional helping activities.

    1   2   3   4   5   6   7   8   9   10

5. I can discuss the ethical principles and standards that inform social work practice.

    1   2   3   4   5   6   7   8   9   10

6. I can identify the relevant values, legal duties, and ethical principles that apply in various professional contexts and situations.

    1   2   3   4   5   6   7   8   9   10

7. I can determine the relative priority of competing legal and ethical obligations when ethical dilemmas arise in specific circumstances.

    1   2   3   4   5   6   7   8   9   10

8. I can use critical thinking and scientific inquiry skills to reach ethical decisions and plan appropriate action.

1	2	3	4	5	6	7	8	9	10

Chapter 5 concludes the professionalism part of *The Social Work Skills Workbook*. Of all the issues that pertain to professionalism, none is more important than the issue of the "goodness of fit" between one's personal beliefs, characteristics, motivations, and ambitions and the requirements of social work practice. At some point, you must honestly address the following questions: "Am I personally suited for this profession? Are my beliefs, motives, attributes, and characteristics compatible with those needed by social workers? Am I capable of putting aside my own personal beliefs when they conflict with the values and ethics of the profession, and my service obligations as a social worker? Am I ready for the challenges and sacrifices that social work entails?" These questions are fundamental to the consideration of personal and professional integrity. As a way to address them, please complete the following summary exercise. It will help you explore your motives for selecting this profession and evaluate your overall readiness to pursue social work as a profession.

1. Reflect upon and integrate the results of the exercises you completed in Part 1 (Chapters 1–5) of the skills book by preparing a summary analysis and assessment of your overall readiness for professional social work. Prepare your assessment in the form of a four- to five-page, double-spaced, word-processed report (1,000–1,250 words) titled "Summary Assessment of My Motivation, Readiness, and Suitability for the Profession of Social Work." When you finish, save the document file as "My_Readiness_for_SWK" and include it in your Social Work Skills Learning Portfolio. In your report, be sure to address the following dimensions.

   a. *Career plans.* Look ahead to the professional social work career to which you aspire after graduation. Describe the setting, the nature of the issues, and the kinds of people with whom you would most prefer to work. Identify and describe the personal qualities and attributes that you think will be required of you to practice social work ethically and effectively in such a context.

   b. *Client and setting preference.* Identify those settings, issues, and people with whom you would least prefer to work. Discuss the reasons for these preferences. What are the implications of those reasons for your personal and professional development? Would you be able to manage and put aside your personal preferences, if and when needed, in order to provide professional services in such a situation?

   c. *Critical events.* Identify one or two major factors or incidents in your personal, familial, or situational experience that contributed to your choice of social work as a career. Discuss how they affect your current readiness and motivation for professional social work practice.

   d. *Satisfying and challenging aspects.* What do you anticipate will be the single most rewarding or satisfying part of being a professional social worker? What will be the single most difficult, challenging, or unsatisfying part?

   e. *Outstanding questions.* Based upon your reflection and responses, identify two or three questions that you would want to ask an outstanding, highly experienced social worker.

   f. *Readiness for social work.* Reflect upon your reactions and reflections to the content and exercises related to integrity, self-understanding and self-control, knowledge, expertise, and self-efficacy; social support and social well-being; critical thinking and scientific inquiry; lifelong learning; diversity and difference; human rights and social, economic, and environmental justice; policy–practice; and social work values and ethical decision making. Then, ask yourself:

- "Do I possess or can I develop the personal capacities necessary to function effectively as a professional social worker?"
- "Am I ready to accept the challenges and sacrifices that social work entails?"
- "Am I willing to regulate my personal judgments and manage my personal beliefs and behavior to adhere to the core values and ethical principles of the social work profession?"
- "All things considered, am I really suited for this profession?"

If your answers include a negative response, check out your conclusions by meeting with an adviser, a social work professor, or a vocational counselor. If your conclusions are confirmed through discussions with others, proceed to identify other careers for which you may be better suited. If your answers are all affirmative, make note of personal areas that require further exploration and identify those capacities you need to strengthen. Outline a plan to do so.

PART 2

Social Work Skills

Talking and Listening: The Basic Interpersonal Skills

I n this chapter, we explore the basic interpersonal skills of talking and listening. These include the processes social workers adopt to access a place of peace, engage diversity and difference with cultural sensitivity, observe and listen accurately and compassionately, and exchange information with others. They apply in our professional activities and, of course, in our personal lives as well. For convenience, we use the term *talking* to refer to the processes involved in sending and *listening* to refer to those used in receiving messages—regardless of the

(Continued)

Chapter Goals

Following completion of this chapter, you should be able to:

- Access a place of peace.
- Engage diversity and difference with cultural sensitivity.
- Discuss the talking and listening skills.
- Communicate nonverbally in social work contexts.
- Communicate verbally and in writing for social work purposes.
- Listen (hear, observe, encourage, and remember) in social work practice.
- Listen actively in professional contexts.

Core Competencies

The content addressed in this chapter supports the following core EPAS competencies:

- Competency 1: Demonstrate Ethical and Professional Behavior
- Competency 2: Engage Diversity and Difference in Practice
- Competency 3: Advance Human Rights and Social, Economic, and Environmental Justice
- Competency 6: Engage with Individuals, Families, Groups, Organizations, and Communities
- Competency 7: Assess Individuals, Families, Groups, Organizations, and Communities
- Competency 8: Intervene with Individuals, Families, Groups, Organizations, and Communities
- Competency 9: Evaluate Practice with Individuals, Families, Groups, Organizations, and Communities

means of transmission.[1] When combined with nonjudgmental observation, these skills are especially significant for engaging diversity and difference. Unless social workers can both understand and be understood by the people we hope to serve, our knowledge and expertise are of limited value.

Social workers need well-developed communication skills in all phases and aspects of practice. Inadequate skills in sending and receiving messages can impede development of a productive professional relationship and prevent a successful outcome. Such deficiencies are especially problematic in intercultural and multicultural contexts with people who differ from ourselves. Proficient talking and listening skills contribute to clear expression and accurate understanding during exchanges with individuals, families, groups, organizations, and communities of diverse backgrounds and views. Indeed, highly developed competence in talking and listening is essential for engaging diversity and difference.

Accessing a Place of Peace

In social workers' efforts to help people affected by social problems, eliminate poverty, and promote social, economic, and environmental justice, we seek to establish places of safety and peace where people can communicate freely and expressively without fear of harm. We usually arrange meetings with clients and prospective clients in physical spaces that, of course, protect their rights to privacy and confidentiality and also convey a sense of personal safety. Certainly, when social workers help soldiers or refugees in areas of armed conflict, in regions that have suffered natural or human-made disasters, or in communities where violence is prevalent, the actual degree of safety may be limited. Even there, however, we seek to create an atmosphere of peace within the spaces and places we meet with others. Importantly, we also **access a place of peace** within ourselves.

Many social workers actively seek to reduce violence and promote peace through their community development and community organization work with urban gangs, neighborhood residents, recreational organizations, police departments, school systems, and sometimes military units. Others work with international groups such as the United Nations Educational, Scientific and Cultural Organization (UNESCO), Amnesty International, Doctors Without Borders, and Human Rights Watch to reduce conflict and further understanding between competing ethnic or religious groups. Some social workers engage in social action intended to promote peace by, for example, protesting war, torture, and brutality; seeking to eliminate human trafficking; or by opposing death penalty laws—and, they do so through peaceful, nonviolent means. Indeed, much of this kind of peace-focused work involves the use of the principles and skills of nonviolent or compassionate communication (Rosenberg, 1995, 1999, 2003b, 2012).

Peace and violence each have aspects that are sometimes overlooked. Peace, for example, is often viewed primarily as the absence of war and violent conflict. When the shooting, bombing, and killing subside, we call it peace. Let's refer to that state as **negative peace**, that is, the absence of overt violence. **Positive peace**, on the other hand, goes beyond negative peace to include

---

[1] People vary widely in their physical ability to speak, hear, see, read, or write. In this book, we use the terms *talking* and *listening* to refer to the transmission and reception of communication messages—regardless of the medium. Many superbly effective social workers communicate through alternate means (for example, sign language, mime, and through interpreters, speech synthesizers, TDD, voice recognition systems, and other forms of communication).

constructive human communication, understanding, inclusion, cooperation, participation, connectedness, and ultimately human integration (Galtung, 1964).

In a similar fashion, violence is commonly regarded as primarily physical in nature. We recognize violence when humans hit, strike, beat, poison, stone, bludgeon, rape, molest, stab, cut, shoot, bomb, and otherwise directly injure or kill other humans. The violence may involve two or more individuals, groups, tribes, communities, or nations. Let's view that physical aggression as direct violence. **Direct violence** can take place in schools and playgrounds, and in homes or streets as well as in war zones and conflict areas.[2]

Rather than overt physical aggression, **indirect violence** involves insult, ridicule, shame, discrimination, domination, oppression, slavery, involuntary servitude, apartheid, exclusion, bullying, and other forms of personal social, economic, and environmental injustice. Indirect violence includes unjust structures, systems, customs, beliefs, mores, practices, and processes that deny basic human rights, limit opportunities, and increase the risk of disease, injury, death, or destruction to individuals, groups, communities, or cultures. It often appears in subtle and insidious ways (Galtung, 1990). Like direct violence, the indirect forms also occur in myriad places and contexts. These include families, homes, schools, organizations, neighborhoods, communities, and nations—sometimes with the sponsorship and encouragement of powerful political, economic, and ideological interest groups.

These dimensions of peace and violence are represented in Table 6.1. Recognize that negative peace (that is, the absence of direct violence) does not necessarily lead to the achievement of positive peace. Putting a stop to assaults and killings is necessary but insufficient. The various forms of indirect violence must also be addressed. Positive peace building is needed before, during, and after physical conflicts. As social workers, we seek to eliminate both direct and indirect forms of violence and to foster positive as well as negative peace. It seems quite apparent that violent means hardly ever result in peaceful ends, and even more rarely achieve positive, durable peace. As Gandhi observes, "I object to violence because when it appears to do good, the good is only temporary; the evil it does is permanent" (Dalton, 1996, p. 43).

Nonviolent social action and nonviolent communications represent peaceful means to pursue peaceful aspirations. However, we live in a world and an era where *cultures of violence*

TABLE 6.1	Violence and Peace: Direct and Indirect	
	Violence	**Peace**
Indirect	*Indirect Violence* (Presence of Exclusionary, Oppressive, and Unjust Structures, Systems, and Processes)	*Negative Peace* (Absence of Direct Physical Violence)
Direct	*Direct Violence* (Presence of Physical Violence)	*Positive Peace* (Presence of Inclusive, Just, and Integrative Structures, Systems, and Processes)

[2] It is theoretically possible to conceptualize two extremes of direct physical violence. *Offensive violence* involves an assault or attack that is not precipitated by an assault, attack, or intrusion. In other words, the violent act is offensive rather than defensive in nature. *Defensive violence* involves physical aggression intended to protect against offensive violence. Of course, after a period of violent exchanges, it becomes quite difficult to distinguish offensive from defensive violence. "Who started it?" becomes a thorny question.

are ubiquitous. Language represents a central aspect of culture; it reflects our values and beliefs, and frames the way we perceive events in the world. In many human cultures, we learn at an early age to think and communicate in a language of violence. Rosenberg (1995) refers to this as the **Jackal language** or, the **language of the head**.[3] When we speak Jackal, we label, classify, or categorize people; and we diagnose behavior and infer motives in a manner that involves moralistic evaluation and judgment. Ultimately, certain people are classified as "worthy" or fully "human" while others are determined to be "unworthy" or "subhuman." Some degree of right and wrong or good and bad is expressed or implied so that we feel justified in blaming, shaming, shunning, censoring, confining, punishing, torturing, or killing certain others.

In response to violent speech, listeners are typically expected to accept or at least tolerate the judgment and comply with implicit or explicit demands. Such communications constitute indirect violence—even when the moralistic judgment represents an attempt to help or educate, or is communicated with the best of intentions. As is the case with all forms of violence, some people submit to the aggression, diminishing themselves in the process; some react in a passive-aggressive manner through covert violence or sabotage; and others respond in kind—in a violence for violence fashion.

Few humans are able to transcend Jackal socialization to accept aggressors' humanity and seek to understand their feelings and their needs. That requires a quite different language—a **language of peace** or a language of a "compassionate heart" rather than one of the "head." Rosenberg (1995) calls this the **Giraffe language**. When we speak Giraffe, we access our compassion and empathy, and draw upon our kinship with other members of the human family. We seek to understand rather than to classify, label, or judge. Instead of blaming others for our feelings and actions, we take responsibility for them—but do so in Giraffe as well. That is, we remain compassionate and loving toward ourselves just as we do with others. When we think in the language of peace, we can gently take responsibility for our mistakes and our sins or crimes without blasting ourselves with violent messages of blame, shame, guilt, and fear. Indeed, we must do so if we hope to engage others in a similarly compassionate and nonviolent manner.

A language of peace, Giraffe nonetheless reflects remarkable strength and power. Emerging as it does from our feelings of love and kinship rather than from the feelings of shame and fear that characterize the language of violence, Giraffe speakers are secure, not weak. They can tolerate ambiguity and uncertainty; appreciate differences of perspective and opinion; and even change their minds when presented with rational argument and evidence. Jackal speakers, on the other hand, often appear dominant and powerful on the outside but feel insecure and afraid on the inside. They tend to be controlling rather than in control. In violent cultures, ambiguity and uncertainty cause confusion and anxiety, differences of perspective and opinion are unwanted and unappreciated, and rational arguments and evidence do not influence beliefs. Indeed, the egregious acts of rage and hate that sometimes appear in the rhetoric and actions of religious and political extremists may actually emerge from deep and profound fears. Imagine the psychological danger and the emotional threat to those whose privileged positions are based on violence: "If everyone is treated fairly and equitably, then we (people like me) could lose our status and power; and perhaps even our identity."

---

[3] For information about nonviolent communications—sometimes called compassionate communications—please refer to books, articles, and videos by Marshall B. Rosenberg (2003a, 2003b, 2004, 2005a, 2005b, 2005c, 2012).

In Giraffe cultures, people are unafraid of change and routinely make observations, rather than judgments, intended to facilitate understanding. Observations are factual descriptions of things heard or seen. Nothing is inferred about motives—whether "good" or "bad." Written and verbal descriptions remain free of "right" or "wrong" evaluations. Jackal is a language of "I'm right and you're wrong; agree with me or else!" Whereas Jackal always contains explicit or implicit demands, Giraffe involves requests. "I prefer . . ." (or) "I'd really like . . ." (or) "I request. . . ." The requests may be assertive but they are never aggressive or passive-aggressive. Forms of indirect violence are avoided. Giraffe messages do not convey blame, shame, or ridicule; and they do not contain labels. Indeed, they are free from words of classification, judgment, or evaluation (Rosenberg, 1992; Strumska-Cylwik, 2012).

If, for example, I say, "Your wages are too low," "You are beautiful," "He's a pedophile," or "I am so stupid," then I am thinking and speaking Jackal. I'm making judgments. Notice that evaluations can be favorable as well as unfavorable. Even when favorable, however, they can be problematic. The person I call beautiful may wonder if I judge other aspects of his or her appearance or behavior—perhaps on a 1-to-10 scale, as in "she or he is a 10!" Messages that include words such as "low," "high," "beautiful," "ugly," "smart," or "stupid" contain inferences or speculations. So do diagnostic terms such as "narcissistic," "borderline," "depressed," "sociopathic," or "schizophrenic." They are interpretations or speculations rather than factual descriptions of something observed; and they suggest some degree of "goodness" or "badness," "rightness" or "wrongness," "sickness" or "health," and a certain level of human worthiness or unworthiness.

Observing without evaluating, however, is difficult to do. Most of us have been socialized in cultures where Jackal is the primary language for thought and speech. As a result, we automatically judge events and people. The question "How are you?" is almost always answered in some sort of evaluative way: "Good," "Not bad,' "OK," or "Terrible!" A question such as "What do you think of him?" may elicit a slew of judgments, including, "He's a hunk!" or "He's trouble," or "He's bright but lacks common sense." Indeed, whenever we apply words to a thing, a person, or an event, we usually engage in some kind of judgment, classification, or evaluation. We almost immediately apply evaluative words to people or phenomena. The words arise so quickly that we sometimes forget that an observation—based upon our sensory apparatus (eyes, ears, nose, skin, tongue)—occurs first and our thoughts and words about those sensations follow, albeit only milliseconds later. We can gain a semblance of this by blindfolding our eyes and pinching our noses, and then tasting different foods to observe the experience. Even then, it's difficult to avoid judgment. As Krishnamurti suggests (1980, May 10), "when you observe a tree, that thing, the very observation is through words, the moment you see it you call it a tree." He urges us "to look at that thing without the word . . . without analysis, without judging, without evaluating, just to observe" (para. 9). Try that. Look at a tree, a plant, or perhaps a blade of grass without "thinking" thoughts or words. Just observe and experience; then, notice what happens to you. The experience may help you take a step away from the indirect violence of our dominant cultures and a step toward a place of peace within yourself. It may even represent a subtle step toward positive peace throughout the human family that so many of us desire.

Indeed, if social workers hope to promote peace, we must be peaceful people who speak a peaceful language. When we avoid judgment and remain kind and compassionate with ourselves and with those we might otherwise classify as "them" instead of "us," we stand a chance at a peaceful connection. As the 13th-century Persian poet Rumi writes, "Out beyond ideas of wrongdoing and rightdoing, there is a field. I'll meet you there" (Rumi & Barks, 1995, p. 36). Let's do our best to meet our clients, and each other, in such a place of peace.

EXERCISE 6-1 Accessing a Place of Peace

1. By virtue of our mission, social workers frequently encounter unpleasant and sometimes repulsive circumstances. Occasionally, we meet and sometimes provide help to people who have engaged in repugnant acts of cruelty—acts that provoke distaste, aversion, and perhaps hatred. Obviously, social workers must somehow overcome such thoughts, feelings, and sensations if we are to provide professional quality service—regardless of others' actions or characteristics. This exercise is intended to help social workers learn to transcend feelings of disgust and revulsion by first provoking them and then accessing a place of peace where such feelings do not exist.

   Recognize that this exercise—involving your imagination only—may, and probably should, result in some personal discomfort. Prepare yourself accordingly.

   First, clear your mind of thoughts and images. Next, think of a person engaged in a behavior that you find nauseating, disgusting, abhorrent, and absolutely wrong, bad, or evil. It could be an act that is based on a universal taboo such as incest, child sex abuse, or the torture of a baby. The act might be something that is patently offensive to members of your culture or religion. Or, it could be an act that you, personally, find repugnant. For example, you might find it disgusting to imagine an attractive 12-year-old eating fresh, uncooked, and extremely bloody animal flesh.

   Review various scenarios until you find one that involves a person doing something that provokes extreme disgust, distaste, and aversion in you. Once you identify the scene, do the following:

   a. Visualize the person engaged in the offensive behavior with as much detail and clarity as possible. Try to imagine the sounds, the smells, and perhaps the tastes as well as the sight. As the image becomes clearer and clearer, notice your bodily sensations, your feelings and emotions, and the words or ideas that enter your mind. Become aware of any urges or impulses to take action of some kind. Then stop! Remove the offensive scene from your memory and clear your mind once again.

      Use the space below to make a brief list of the bodily sensations, the feelings, the words or ideas, and the urges to act that you experienced while you envisioned the scene. Become especially aware of the words of judgment, censure, contempt, scorn, and disapproval that came to mind.

   b. Now, imagine that you are actually present and extremely close (within a few feet) as the person engages in the repulsive behavior. Use the space below to describe what you think you would probably say and do. Be as honest with yourself as possible.

c. Next, revisit the original "disgusting" scene that you imagined. This time envision it clearly and in detail but do so entirely without words, without thoughts, without explanations, without hypotheses about causes, and without any intention to do anything. Instead, just focus on the imaginary scene. Stay with the mental picture for a while. Gently deflect any words and thoughts that enter your mind, and refocus on the scene. Continue to do so until all that remains is your awareness of the imaginary scene—without applying any words to it. You may begin to experience something. You might feel a sensation in your body or perhaps an emotion. If you do, shift your focus to that experience for a while, again without words or judgment—just experience it. As you focus, notice any changes that occur to your bodily sensations or your emotions. You may notice that the process of observing and experiencing—without words and judgment, and without any immediate intent to act—can result in internal change. Many people become more accepting of themselves; more connected to and more compassionate with other humans; and in a better state to consider the question about whether or not to take action; and, if so, what and how to do so. The process of observing and experience without evaluation may take us to a place of peace—a place where we can do our best work engaging people of all kinds, and helping them meet their needs and pursue their dreams.

If you are able to access a place of peace within yourself, continue to focus inwardly without judgment until you feel fully accepting of yourself, the world, and people around you. Let that feeling move to your face—including your eyes and mouth. Focus especially on the sensations in your lips. There are so many nerve endings in our lips that many humans can experience quite varied sensations there by simply imagining different things, by focusing on different parts of the body, or by configuring our lips into slightly different positions. If we can connect, for example, a physical sensation in our lips with the internal state of peace and compassion, we can sometimes return to that state with just a tiny movement to our mouth and lips.[4]

Use the space below to describe and then reflect on the experience of trying to observe without evaluating, to see without words. After that, identify at least one other way that you personally might be able to achieve a state of peacefulness when your mind and body are expressing strong messages of judgment and violence.

---

[4] I call this process "Looking Inward for Peace and Serenity" (LIPS). This little technique helps me move into a place of peace and compassion when I wish to do so. I often do a "lip adjustment" in advance of and sometimes during encounters with other people. Subjectively, it feels as if I have just the beginnings of a smile. When I do that, my lips and mouth become warm and my body relaxes. My interest in others increases, and I experience a slight urge to move toward whomever I'm with. I become a whole lot more patient with both myself and others. I've used the LIPS technique for more than 35 years and share it with you to use as you please. I hope you find it helpful too.

Engaging Diversity and Difference with Cultural Sensitivity

Culture "is a learned worldview or paradigm shared by a population or group and transmitted socially that influences values, beliefs, customs, and behaviors, and is reflected in the language, dress, food, materials, and social institutions of a group" (Burchum, 2002, p. 7). In a sense, the culture of a group, organization, or community is similar to an individual's personality. **Cultural sensitivity** refers to "the ability to recognize, understand, and react appropriately to behaviors of persons who belong to a cultural or ethnic group that differs substantially from one's own" ("cultural sensitivity", 2007). **Competence** refers to the ability to complete a task or activity, or to fulfill a responsibility correctly, effectively, or proficiently. In the context of professional social work practice, then, **cultural competence** is the awareness, knowledge, understanding, sensitivity, and skill needed to conduct and complete professional activities effectively with people of diverse cultural backgrounds and ethnic affiliations. However, the notion of cultural competence should not be misinterpreted to mean that we ever become fully or completely culturally competent—even in regard to people within our own cultures (Dean, 2001). Rather, cultural competence is an ongoing developmental process that is "never ending and ever expanding" (Burchum, 2002, p. 14).

In its Standards of Cultural Competence, the National Association of Social Workers (2001) indicates that:

> Cultural competence refers to the process by which individuals and systems respond respectfully and effectively to people of all cultures, languages, classes, races, ethnic backgrounds, religions, and other diversity factors in a manner that recognizes, affirms, and values the worth of individuals, families, and communities and protects and preserves the dignity of each. (p. 11)

In addition, the National Association of Social Workers (2008) emphasizes the importance of cultural competence by including in its Code of Ethics a discrete section titled Ethical Responsibilities to Clients: Cultural Competence and Social Diversity. That section includes the following passages:

1. Social workers should understand culture and its function in human behavior and society, recognizing the strengths that exist in all cultures. (Section 1.05.a)
2. Social workers should have a knowledge base of their clients' cultures and be able to demonstrate competence in the provision of services that are sensitive to clients' cultures and to differences among people and cultural groups. (Section 1.05.b)
3. Social workers should obtain education about and seek to understand the nature of social diversity and oppression with respect to race, ethnicity, national origin, color, sex, sexual orientation, age, marital status, political belief, religion, and mental or physical disability. (Section 1.05.c)

Ngo-Metzger and colleagues (2006) take a multidimensional perspective in proposing a culturally competent framework for quality services in health care. They identify three general categories of factors. These include (1) consumer factors, (2) provider factors, and (3) system factors. Included among the *consumer factors* are race or ethnicity, age, gender, socioeconomic status including income and education, health literacy, insurance status, utilization aspects including availability of time and transportation, English proficiency, expectations, religion or spirituality, beliefs and values, and explanatory models. Among the *provider factors* are race or ethnicity, age, gender, training or specialty, experience with diverse populations, language competency, communication style, religion or spirituality, beliefs and values, and explanatory models. The *system factors* include access including ease

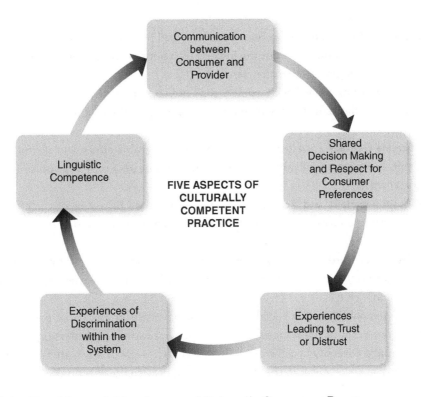

FIGURE 6.1 Ngo-Metzger's Five Aspects of Culturally Competent Practice
Adapted from Ngo-Metzger's conceptualization

of appointment scheduling, short wait list, and adequate time during visits; convenient location of the care facilities; diverse workforce that represents the consumer population; coordination of care between different providers and health care settings; and quality improvement environment with continued patient feedback. These factors interact throughout the service experience. In addition, Ngo-Metzger et al. (2006) identify five interactional aspects that affect the quality of culturally competent care: (1) Communication between Consumer and Provider, (2) Shared Decision Making and Respect for Consumer Preferences, (3) Experiences Leading to Trust or Distrust, (4) Experiences of Discrimination with the System, and (5) Linguistic Competence (see Figure 6.1).

More than a decade ago, the board of directors of the National Association of Social Workers (2001) approved standards for cultural competence in social work practice (see Box 6.1). A few years later, the NASW (2007) endorsed a set of indicators for assessing the level of achievement of the NASW standards for cultural competence in social work practice. These indicators, associated with the 10 standards, provide specific guidance concerning the knowledge, attitudes, and abilities that culturally competent social workers can demonstrate.

Box 6.1 NASW Standards for Cultural Competence in Social Work Practice

Standard 1. Ethics and Values Social workers shall function in accordance with the values, ethics, and standards of the profession, recognizing how personal and professional values may conflict with or accommodate the needs of diverse clients.

Standard 2. Self-Awareness Social workers shall seek to develop an understanding of their own personal, cultural values and beliefs as one way of appreciating the importance of multicultural identities in the lives of people.

(Continued)

Standard 3. Cross-Cultural Knowledge Social workers shall have and continue to develop specialized knowledge and understanding about the history, traditions, values, family systems, and artistic expressions of major client groups that they serve.

Standard 4. Cross-Cultural Skills Social workers shall use appropriate methodological approaches, skills, and techniques that reflect the workers' understanding of the role of culture in the helping process.

Standard 5. Service Delivery Social workers shall be knowledgeable about and skillful in the use of services available in the community and broader society and be able to make appropriate referrals for their diverse clients.

Standard 6. Empowerment and Advocacy Social workers shall be aware of the effect of social policies and programs on diverse client populations, advocating for and with clients whenever appropriate.

Standard 7. Diverse Workforce Social workers shall support and advocate for recruitment, admissions and hiring, and retention efforts in social work programs and agencies that ensure diversity within the profession.

Standard 8. Professional Education Social workers shall advocate for and participate in educational and training programs that help advance cultural competence within the profession.

Standard 9. Language Diversity Social workers shall seek to provide or advocate for the provision of information, referrals, and services in the language appropriate to the client, which may include use of interpreters.

Standard 10. Cross-Cultural Leadership Social workers shall be able to communicate information about diverse client groups to other professionals. (National Association of Social Workers, 2001, pp. 4–5)

Development of cultural sensitivity tends to occur over time. Cross, Bazron, Dennis, and Issacs (1989) propose a cultural competency continuum that proceeds in the fashion suggested in Figure 6.2.

In Stage 1 of the cultural competency continuum, individuals, families, groups, organizations, and communities actively disrespect, deny, or diminish the culture of diverse others through their beliefs, attitudes, policies, practices, words, and behaviors. In Stage 2, diverse cultures are indirectly disrespected or diminished through forms of bias and discrimination that are routine, established, and institutionalized. In Stage 3, policies and practices are applied "blindly" without regard to the unique characteristics, needs, beliefs, and preferences of diverse others with the result that diverse minority or less-powerful cultures are disadvantaged. In a diverse and multicultural world where power and influence are disproportionately distributed, more dominant or powerful individuals and groups tend to apply their own cultural standards as if those standards were necessarily free from bias and fundamentally true, right, and universal.

Stage 4 involves recognition of and familiarity with diverse cultures and their beliefs, practices, needs, and preferences. Stage 5 applies knowledge reflected in Stage 4 to action. That is, individuals, families, groups, organizations, and communities actively respect, affirm, and value the culture of diverse others through their beliefs, attitudes, policies, practices, words, and behaviors. In Stage 6, the knowledge and action reflected in Stages 4 and 5 are refined and enhanced so that cultural diversity becomes highly valued and celebrated as a focus for further growth, learning, and human and social development (Cross et al., 1989; National Center for Cultural Competence, 2004).

Social workers are also aware of how our implicit biases often lead to subtle, and sometimes blatant, **microaggressions** that simultaneously insult, assault, or demean others while conveying a

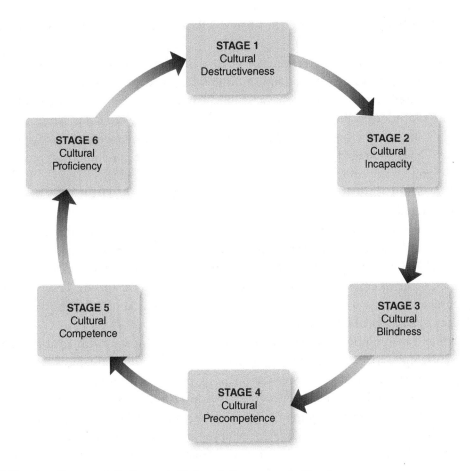

FIGURE 6.2 Cross and Colleague's Cultural Competence Continuum
Adapted from Cross, Bazron, and Dennis' conceptualization

sense of our own superiority, entitlement, and privilege. "Simply stated, microaggressions are brief, everyday exchanges that send denigrating messages to certain individuals because of their group membership" (Sue, 2010a, p. xvi). Rowe (1990) refers to **microinequities** as "tiny, damaging characteristics of an environment, as these characteristics affect a person not indigenous to that environment. They are distinguished by the fact that for all practical purposes one cannot do anything about them; one cannot take them to court or file a grievance" (p. e4). They include "apparently small events which are often ephemeral and hard-to-prove, events which are covert, often unintentional, frequently unrecognized by the perpetrator, which occur wherever people are perceived to be 'different'" (Rowe, 2008, p. 45).

Implicit biases, microaggressions, and microinequities are easy to spot—if you are a regular target (Brogaard; Owen et al., 2014; Sue, 2010a, 2010b). Do you recognize any of these: "That's so gay!" "You're so articulate" (to a black man). "I didn't expect you to be so smart" (to a Latina woman). "So, what are you?" (to a biracial person). "So, how does your new plumbing work?" (to a transgendered person who has undergone gender affirmation surgery). "You have such a pretty face" (to an obese woman). "Do you speak English" or "You speak English so well" (to a third-generation American-born teenager of Iranian ancestry). "Where are you from?" (to almost any person of color). "You're so different from other African Americans" (or Jews or Muslims or members of any commonly stereotyped group). "You're so beautiful for a lesbian." "Have a great Christmas Holiday!" (to a Muslim, Hindu, Jewish, or atheist person). "Bring your girlfriend" (to a gay man). "So, can you have sex?" or "How to you do it, you know, have sex?" (to a person with a physical disability). "Do you work here?" (to a black or Latina woman shopping in a department store).[5]

The impact of a single microaggression may be modest. However, when they occur repeatedly from different people, at different times and in different contexts, the cumulative effects can be debilitating. Commonly targeted for microaggression, people of difference may attempt to become less visible, more withdrawn, and less expressive while feeling more suspicious, alone, unwelcome, and excluded. Some become assertive and rationally confront people when microassaults occur. Others are fed-up and outraged at the pervasiveness of both macro- and microaggressions. They may lash out angrily at inequities—large or small (Nadal, 2013; Nadal et al., 2011; Nadal, Skolnik, & Wong, 2012; Owen et al., 2014; Platt & Lenzen, 2013; Rabow et al., 2014; Woodford, Howell, Silverschanz, & Yu, 2012).

Fortunately, in addition to microaggressions, humans may also express affirmations in little ways. According to Rowe (2008) **microaffirmations** are those "apparently small acts, which are often ephemeral and hard-to-see, events that are public and private, often unconscious but very effective, which occur wherever people wish to help others to succeed" (p. 46). These include welcoming gestures and similar acts of inclusion, listening attentively, acknowledging others' contributions, and offering support when another is distressed.

Language and communication may be among the most important dimensions of culture. Language, for example, affects our thoughts, feelings, and behavior and influences those of others. Language permits communication between and among people and profoundly affects both the processes and outcomes of interpersonal encounters. Within a few years, most social workers in the United States will require proficiency in at least one other language besides English. Schools and departments of social work might encourage or require their students to learn a second language. The growth of the Hispanic population suggests that many social workers should know Spanish as well as English, but competency in other languages is also needed to serve diverse populations, including the large numbers of first- and second-generation immigrants and refugees who come to North America.

Inclusive Cultural Empathy

Understanding the meaning of words is, of course, only one aspect of the numerous challenges and opportunities associated with intercultural communication. Recognizing our common humanity is another. Indeed, the objective of effective intercultural communication is much more than basic understanding. Rather, it is more akin to the notion of **inclusive cultural empathy** (Pedersen, Crethar, & Carlson, 2008)—a state that involves the processes depicted in Figure 6.3.

In seeking to incorporate *inclusive cultural empathy* within ourselves, we (1) accept and value those who belong to different cultural groups, (2) learn something about others' cultures, and (3) engage others in ways that convey respect for their cultural affiliations. Pedersen et al. (2008) also adopt a broad and expansive view of culture. Much like the concept of **intersectionality** that we discussed earlier, they recognize that each of us is a member of many communities and several cultures. In this sense, each of us is "multicultural." Social workers, therefore, require an inclusive conception of culture and an open, curious, and humble approach to diverse others. Though we may not share all the communities and cultures of other people, we certainly share some. Furthermore, as members of the same human species, we share many more similarities than we do differences.

[5] See the Microaggressions Project website (Lu & Zhou, 2015) at **www.microaggressions.com** or on Facebook for hundreds of examples as submitted by contributors throughout the world.

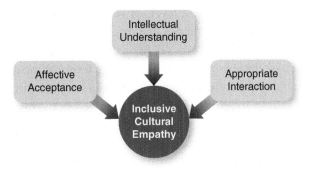

FIGURE 6.3 Pedersen and Colleagues' Processes of Inclusive Cultural Empathy

Pedersen, P. B., Crethar, H., & Carlson J. (2008). Inclusive cultural empathy: Making relationships central in counseling and psychotherapy. Washington, DC: American Psychological Association

Indeed, DNA studies confirm that distinct, identifiable subspecies or "races" do not appear among modern human beings.

While different genes for physical traits such as skin and hair color can be identified among individuals, no consistent patterns of genes across the human genome exist to distinguish one race from another. There also is no genetic basis for divisions of human ethnicity. People who have lived in the same geographic region for many generations may have some alleles in common, but no allele will be found in all members of one population and in no members of any other. Indeed, it has been proven that there is more genetic variation within races than exists between them. As we engage diversity and difference, let's appreciate our commonalities as well as value our distinctions. "DNA studies indicate that all modern humans share a common female ancestor who lived in Africa about 140,000 years ago" (Human Genome Project Information, 2008, Will genetic anthropology establish scientific criteria for race or ethnicity?, para. 1).

Bill Nye, the "Science Guy," observes that "Tribalism exists in the animal kingdom, and this is what I think is at the base of (racism). It started because you've got these tribes and you've got different skin color as a result of ultraviolet light. We're all the same, from a scientific standpoint. There's no such thing as race—but there is such a thing as tribalism" (Nye, 2015, May 4).

Bill Nye's reference to ultraviolet light as a factor in the determination of skin color, reflects his understanding of the role of the environment and natural selection in the amount of melanin pigmentation in human skin. Humans require modest but regular exposure to ultraviolet light from the sun to stimulate production of vitamin D in our bodies. Vitamin D serves many necessary physiological functions such as defending against several cancers as well as infections from viruses, bacteria, and fungi. Insufficient vitamin D is also associated with rickets and osteoporosis. On the other hand, too much ultraviolet light (radiation) is associated with skin cancer as well as damage to our bodies' folate supplies. Insufficient folate is associated with anemia, diminished sperm cell production, and increased risk of miscarriage and certain infant deformities. To address the benefits and risks associated with too much and too little sunlight (and the respective levels of vitamin D), human skin contains the pigment melanin. Associated with skin color, melanin functions as a protective screen against ultraviolet radiation. In the tropical regions of our planet—especially where forests are sparse and access to shade difficult—more melanin and darker skin protects against cancer while letting in enough ultraviolet light to produce vitamin D.

In environments high in ultraviolet radiation, melanin-rich, dark skin has genuine survival value. However, in extreme latitudes—especially far to the north where ultraviolet radiation is low for much of the year, dark, melanin-rich skin protects so well that only minimal amounts of ultraviolet light are absorbed and insufficient levels of vitamin D produced (Del Bino & Bernerd, 2012; Jablonski, 2004, 2006, 2012; Jablonski & Chaplin, 2000, 2010, 2013). It is hardly surprising, then, that as early humans migrated from central Africa to other parts of the globe, natural selection processes tended to favor those with the most adaptive levels of melanin for the amount and intensity of sun and ultraviolet radiation in particular regions. As a result, members of the human species vary considerably in skin coloration from "very dark brown . . . to a near yellowish pink. . . . There are no people who actually have true black, white, red, or yellow skin. These are commonly used color terms that do not reflect biological reality" (O'Neil, 2013, para. 1).

In sum, we are a single human species. Our differences in skin color are the result of our evolutionary adaptation in different geographical regions to life under the sun. The only "races" that exist are those that reside in the individual minds and belief systems of human beings throughout the world. Unfortunately, those beliefs are deeply ingrained and cause no end of trouble. Nonetheless, we remain "brothers and sisters" in an extremely intelligent family. Of all the animal species, we humans should be able to overcome our ancestors' beliefs and develop the following three major characteristics of **inclusive cultural empathy**:

Affective acceptance involves recognition, awareness, and acknowledgment "of culturally learned assumptions and a network of comemberships across cultural boundaries that include both cultural patterns of similarity and difference" (Pedersen, Crethar, & Carlson, 2008, p. 54). Such emotional acceptance involves awareness of our own culturally based patterns, expectations, and perceptions as well of those of other cultures, and an appreciation of how cultures influence communication. We also accept the limitations of our self-awareness and knowledge about other cultural traditions. Indeed, humility helps us maintain a sense of genuine curiosity about cultures and a sincere interest in others.

Intellectual understanding involves factual knowledge of cultural similarities and differences among those involved in an exchange. Often this involves social workers and clients, but it may also include community members, representatives from other groups, organizations, or nations. Such cognitive understanding usually evolves from knowledge gained from the professional and scientific literature; conversations and experiences with people and groups from other cultures; findings from research about various communities and studies of intercultural communication; and outcomes of policies, programs, and practices that incorporate cultural components. We should also recognize the current state of our knowledge and its limitations (Goode, Dunne, & Bronheim, 2006). Each cultural group contains great diversity. Sometimes, the "within group" differences are even greater than the "between groups" differences. Let's remember that some individuals within any cultural group differ markedly from the average characteristics of the group as a whole. We can never assume that a member of any cultural group is necessarily like others in that group. This is especially true when we incorporate the notions of inclusiveness and intersectionality.

Appropriate interaction includes those interpersonal "skills and abilities to incorporate both similarities and differences in a plan for working together by reframing the culturally learned assumptions and information to bring about constructive change" (Pedersen, Crethar, & Carlson, 2008, p. 54). Inclusive cultural empathic skills enable us to communicate effectively and serve people with whom we share cultural similarities as well as cultural differences.

In our desire to help, social workers need interpersonal competencies as well as attitudes of cultural acceptance, awareness of self and others, and relevant knowledge. We could be highly accepting and very knowledgeable; however, without communications skills we would be unable to engage others in meaningful and productive ways. Social workers must be able to communicate verbally and nonverbally with people from diverse communities and cultures and, when necessary, use interpreters in appropriate and effective ways (U.S. Department of Health and Human Services Office of Minority Health, 2009a).

The teaching and learning of intercultural communication skills for helping professionals has gained credibility and momentum in recent years. For example, the Office of Minority Health offers free online cultural competency education programs (2009b). Numerous scholarly publications also serve as resources. The sheer quantity of academic work related to intercultural communication in counseling and social work is impressive indeed (Balgopal et al., 2008; Brammer, 2004; Deardorff, 2009; Fong, 2003; Fontes, 2008; Gudykunst & Kim, 2003; Hofstede & Hofstede, 2005; Hogan, 2012; Ivey, Ivey, & Zalaquett, 2010; Ivey, Ivey, Zalaquett, & Quirk, 2012; Lie & Lowery, 2003; Lum, 2003, 2008; Neuliep, 2012; Pedersen, Crethar, & Carlson, 2008; Pedersen, Draguns, Lonner, & Trimble, 2008; Roysircar, 2003; Roysircar, Sandhu, & Bibbins, 2003; Sorrells, 2013; Sue, 2006; Sue & Sue, 2008).

Whenever possible, search out scholarly materials about those diverse groups and communities you serve in your field practicum or expect to serve in your professional roles following graduation. Learn about the core assumptions, beliefs, and common practices of various religious and philosophical perspectives (Hinnells, 2010; Monahan, Mirola, & Emerson, 2011; Renard, 2002). Recognize the ways religious and cultural attitudes may divide or unite us (Haidt, 2012; Putnam & Campbell, 2010) and explore the relationships between religion and human rights (Witte & Green, 2012), social and economic justice, and social well-being. Try to gain some personal experience with various communities as well. Visit neighborhoods, attend religious services, view movies, and talk with community leaders and community members to gain a depth of understanding that you cannot get through scholarly materials alone. Approach others with humility and sincere curiosity. Most will be more than happy to help you learn about their communities and cultures.

Awareness and knowledge go hand in hand. Your initial thoughts, feelings, and attitudes about other cultures and your social behavior with them are very likely to change as you gain knowledge about their norms, values, history, religious beliefs, ceremonies, apparel, and social customs, and especially as you spend time with diverse others. Suppose, for example, that you experience negative judgmental thoughts about a culture that reflects a formally organized, patriarchal family structure where women and children assume lesser overt status and power. Your view might change if you learned that historically such a family structure served survival needs in a society where death was a common punishment for social deviance.[6] You might also discover that within that culture's religious traditions, the father is viewed as the primary connecting link between women or children and God or heaven. Without such knowledge, you might be judgmental or dismissive; with it, you might be more understanding and better able to communicate with respect and inclusive cultural empathy. Lacking appreciation of their culture, you might begin an initial meeting with a family or community group by talking first with children or adolescents, rather than the fathers and elders. As a result, you might unwittingly express disrespect for their culture and alienate the family or the community. Your ignorance could lead them to withdraw from helpful services and perhaps reject needed resources.[7]

---

[6] As used here, "deviance" refers to a "difference from the norm." In other words, deviant behavior is unusual or infrequent in a statistical sense. Despite the fact that severe punishment may result, deviant behavior is not necessarily "bad," "sinful," or "criminal."

[7] Being sensitive to culture does not mean that social workers *approve* of every culture's customs and practices, nor does it suggest that we necessarily *agree* with the assumptions, premises, and beliefs contained within various cultural worldviews. Certainly, we remain sensitive to individual and cultural differences, and show respect for the dignity and humanity of the people themselves. However, respect for people does not require us, for example, to endorse the ideas or the practices reflected in the male oppression of women and children; the killing of homosexual or atheist people; or the racist white supremacy that leads to brutal beatings and murders of humans of darker skin color. Indeed, in some social work roles, our primary mission involves raising consciousness, confronting, challenging, and changing the beliefs and behaviors associated with these and other forms of injustice; and doing so while respecting the humanity of the people who hold those beliefs and engage in those behaviors that offend our notions of social, economic, and environmental justice.

Cultural insensitivity and communication deficits may lead members of some groups and communities to avoid human and social service organizations altogether. Does it surprise you that certain population groups seek psychological and social services at lower rates than do others? Are you aware that early dropout rates are much higher for some racial and ethnic groups than for others? Culturally insensitive communications may be part of the explanation.

As you proceed on the never-ending path toward enhanced cultural sensitivity, first learn about various facets of culture that directly relate to the services you provide. Regardless of your practice setting, you can probably readily identify a number of current or prospective clients from a cultural tradition that differs from your own and about which you know little. Once identified, you might seek to learn about the following:

> (1) [the group's] religious or spiritual orientations and views of metaphysical harmony, (2) cultural views of children, (3) cultural style of communication—whether information is transmitted primarily through spoken words or through the context of the situation, the relationship, and physical cues, (4) culturally prescribed and proscribed behaviors in formal and informal relationships, (5) family structures and roles; child-rearing practices including nurturing, meeting physical and psychosocial needs, methods of discipline (including use of corporal punishment), (6) norms of interdependency, mutuality, and obligation within families and kinship networks, (7) health and healing practices, and (8) views of change and intervention. (Samantrai, 2004, p. 34)

Of course, many other factors affect communication with diverse others. For example, in one culture, the concept of time as measured by "the clock" may be highly valued. Being "on time" may be associated with responsibility, reliability, courtesy, commitment, and perhaps wealth. In such a culture, the phrase "time is money" may be used. However, in another culture, clock time may hold much less value. The natural rhythms of the movement of the sun and moon, the changing of the seasons, and the ebbs and flows in human relationships may assume greater importance. There, the concept "when the time is right" may be evident in social relations and interpersonal communications.

Other culturally relevant dimensions of communication include preferences about proximity or the degree of space between people, the expression of emotion, the nature and extent of eye contact, the acceptability of touch, the degree of hand or other physical movements, and the ease with which intimate or personal topics are discussed. History is often a remarkably significant aspect of culture that may be overlooked in our efforts to deal with current issues. For instance, suppose one cultural group experienced severe oppression by another for several generations. Their ancestors may have been enslaved or perhaps subject to "ethnic cleansing" or genocide. What might happen if your name or appearance reminds clients of people who oppressed, tortured, and decimated their ancestors? In such circumstances, the cultural history may emerge as a powerful part of the immediate present.

Indeed, powerfulness and powerlessness tend to remain significant phenomena for individuals and groups who have experienced either or both. Being a "somebody" or a "nobody" profoundly affects people and the way we communicate with others. The poet Emily Dickinson (Johnson, 1955) understood this when she wrote: "I'm nobody! Who are you? Are you a nobody too?" (p. 206)

In discussing the attitudes and actions of "somebodies" toward "nobodies," Fuller (2002) uses the term **rankism** to refer to the uses and abuses of power by those of higher rank in relation to those of lower rank. The feelings of shame, humiliation, indignity, or inferiority felt by a "nobody" when abused, oppressed, enslaved, imprisoned, or exploited, or even when addressed with superiority, arrogance, or condescension by a "somebody" are pretty much the same whether it appears as racism, sexism, ageism, ableism, lookism, heterosexism, or other insidious "isms." When a professor demeans a student, a colonel ridicules a private, an employer humiliates an employee, a parent shames a child, a senator ignores a citizen, a social worker belittles a client, or the people of one culture denigrate those of another, the resulting dehumanization frequently has long-lasting effects.

Social workers' expression of cultural sensitivity involves awareness and management of rankism in all its myriad manifestations. The role of social worker involves a position of status and rank relative to clients. Of course, the difference in status is not, in itself, necessarily a negative. Indeed, as we discussed in earlier chapters, the prestige and competence implicit in professional status are significant factors contributing to effective service outcomes. However, when we professionals begin to view ourselves as "somebodies" and clients as "nobodies," the beneficial aspects of the differential status can easily turn into the deleterious effects of rankism.

In communications about others, prominent signs of rankism involve the judgmental use of the terms "I" and "you," "us" and "them," and the application of labels or classifications. Terms such as "ally" and "enemy," "doctor" and "patient," or even "social worker" and "client" can reflect obvious or subtle forms of rankism. In our efforts to understand and support clients, social workers may unwittingly adopt moralistic evaluations, comparisons, and metaphors that actually hinder our professional efforts.

Perhaps the best-known depiction of a common moralistic metaphor is the "dramatic triangle." Apparent in the Greek tragedies and many novels, plays, movies, TV soap operas, and common gossip, the triangle reflects tension or conflict among three parties, forces, themes, or perspectives. A typical form includes a hero or heroine who confronts a villain or overcomes an obstacle to rescue a worthy or desirable victim.

Karpman (1968, 1971) refers to a **dramatic triangle** (see Figure 6.4) in families, groups, and organizations that includes the roles or positions of persecutor, victim, and rescuer. Of course, these terms have judgmental connotations and also reflect rankism. The persecutor demeans and subordinates the victim, and the rescuer—sometimes from a position of moral superiority—attempts to liberate and safeguard the vulnerable person or group. Occasionally, a rescue may occur without the implicit or explicit consent of the rescued and, of course, the rescuer may need to combat, defeat, control, or subordinate the persecutor in the process.

The dramatic triangle is readily apparent in cultural mythologies (Campbell, 1972; Campbell & Moyers, 1988) and political philosophies (Morone, 2003). During wartime or times of struggle, leaders tend to emphasize moralistic metaphors and dramatic triangles where one country, ethnic community, people, or coalition is viewed as "good," another as "bad," and a third as "victimized."

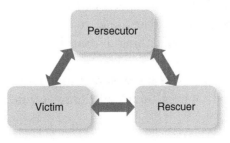

FIGURE 6.4 Dramatic Triangle

The European theater of World War II provides a clear example of a dramatic triangle—at least from a North American perspective: Great Britain, the United States, and their allies represent the "good" coalition, whereas Hitler and the Nazis represent the "bad." At first, the innocent victims included the nations of Poland, Belgium, France, and other countries invaded by Hitler's forces. Tragically, it was only very much later that Jews, disabled persons, the Romani, gay and lesbian people, and other cultural groups imprisoned and murdered during the Holocaust were identified and recognized as victims.

In his January 2002 State of the Union address, President George W. Bush referred to North Korea, Iran, and Iraq when he said: "States like these and their terrorist allies constitute an axis of evil, arming to threaten the peace of the world" (Bush, 2002, para. 20). In so doing, he used a moral metaphor and established a triangle. In effect, he identified those three national governments (the axis) as evil sponsors of terror, the residents of the United States and their allies (and perhaps the general populations of the three countries in question) as potential victims, and the United States and its allies as heroic protectors and perhaps rescuers. "Us-and-them" thinking is evident. As is common in such triangles, however, the roles often shift—sometimes quite rapidly. From a victim's perspective, a hero can quickly change to that of persecutor or oppressor. Indeed, a victim can sometimes feel quite victimized by a hero soon after a purported rescue. We might wonder how many Iraqis and Afghanis who initially viewed American soldiers as liberators (that is, heroes) later viewed them as occupiers (that is, persecutors). Similarly, we might ask how many U.S. soldiers have changed their view of themselves from that of heroic rescuers to that of unappreciated victims.

As opposed to moralistic triangles, however, some triangular relationships can contribute to motivation, cooperation, energy, productivity, love, and perhaps even peace in various contexts—including those that involve cross-cultural exchange. Whereas the dramatic triangle depicted in Figure 6.4 tends to reflect "I-and-you" or "us-and-them" orientations where "either/or" patterns emerge, other triangles may reflect a "we" perspective where "both/and" messages are common.

In "either/or" interactions, each person or group assumes a single role or position at a time (for example, rescuer, victim, or persecutor) and "I" and "you" or "us" and "them" are highly distinct; and labels are commonly assigned. Such interactions tend to involve some distrust and suggest a potential for conflict or competition (Whitfield, Whitfield, Park, & Prevatt, 2006). Sentences often contain "Yes, but . . ." or "No . . ." phrases that challenge the value of another's message.[8] Common themes might include: "It's either you or me." "It's us or them." "You're wrong; I'm right." "I win; you lose."

In "we" triangles, all parties tend to be inviting, trusting, and cooperative. Labels and classifications are used minimally and nonjudgmentally, or avoided altogether. All parties assume roles of nurturer and motivator, and nurtured and motivated, and do so at or near the same time. Sentences often contain "Yes, and . . ." phrases that support and elaborate upon another's words. For example: "Yes, that's a really good point and to that I'd like to add. . . ." Messages that involve "we" and "us" are also common: "All of us have something to contribute and we can all benefit." "You have an excellent idea *and* here's another one."

Especially when social workers know something about others' core beliefs and values, their wants and needs, and their cultural traditions, we can promote "we" relationships that

---

[8] To capture the risk of escalating tension and conflict, helping professionals sometimes use the phrase, "Never put your *but* in front of an angry person."

de-emphasize both "I" and "you," and "us" and "them" perspectives. Indeed, learning about other peoples and their cultures, becoming aware of the many forms of rankism, and considering the nature and implications of various metaphors and conceptualizations are usually extraordinarily enriching endeavors—both personally and professionally. However, let's remain aware of the dangers of stereotypes and overgeneralizations. The power of mass media, public education, and mainstream society is such that minority cultures are sometimes assimilated by majority cultures. The often dramatic differences between first and third generations of immigrant families typify the speed with which humans adapt to new social environments. Similarly, the amount of wealth, extent of formal education, age, and degree of isolation from other groups all influence the rate and extent to which adaptation occurs. Members of cultural groups vary greatly from one another. Some welcome acculturation and assimilation whereas others resist them.

Let's balance our growing knowledge of diverse cultures with the reminder that extraordinary diversity exists within each cultural group. You might, for example, serve in an agency where interviewers routinely assign clients to a racial or ethnic category based on their physical characteristics. When completing an intake form, some workers might "check a box" to signify a racial or ethnic category because "he looks Hispanic" or, on the telephone, "she sounds African American." Such practices involve considerable risk. The person labeled Hispanic may think of himself as Puerto Rican or perhaps Latino. A woman classified as Asian might view herself as Thai, or that "white boy" might proudly consider himself Cherokee.

Acknowledge our strong human tendencies toward ethnocentrism, overgeneralization, rankism, and that extremely tempting process of "assumption making." The most respectful approach is to ask prospective clients for their input. If racial or ethnic classifications are truly useful for agency purposes, we might simply ask, "In terms of race or ethnicity, what do you consider yourself?" If the answer does not fit the list of categories, you might add a new one. Also, recognize that many people self-identify as multiracial, mixed, or interracial whereas others may include one or more racial identities and an ethnic identity as well (for example, white and Hispanic). You might also provide clients an opportunity to "decline to identify" themselves according to a racial or ethnic group. Furthermore, you might ask yourself and other agency personnel questions such as "Why is this information needed and how might it be used?" "What are the risks and benefits associated with the collection and use of such information?" "How will clients who provide information benefit from its collection and use?" "Do the benefits outweigh the risks?"

Changing Demographics

Despite the fact that "everyone communicates," effective interpersonal communications are among the most difficult activities human beings undertake. The challenges facing workers and clients in their professional encounters are often even more extreme. People tend to ascribe various and sometimes unexpected meanings to the verbal and nonverbal, conscious and unconscious messages they express and receive. Culture plays such a large part in the process of effective communication that highly developed sensitivity is essential.

Furthermore, the importance of culturally sensitive communications with diverse groups and communities increases with each passing decade. According to population projections of the U.S. Census Bureau (2015), the estimated population of approximately 322 million in 2015 will grow to about 417 million by the year 2060. The implications of a population that approaches half a billion are staggering—even in a country as resource-rich as the United States. Growth in overall size, however, reflects only part of the picture. The nation's racial and ethnic composition will change dramatically as well.

During 2010–2011 the number of white births was outnumbered by newborns from other racial groups: 49.6 to 50.4 percent of all births, respectively (Morello & Mellnik, 2012, May 17). When combined, minorities currently constitute the majority in several states (for example, Hawaii, Texas, California, New Mexico) and in 13 major cities. By 2060, ethnic minorities will constitute a substantial majority. In that year, only 44 percent of the population will be non-Hispanic, single-race whites. The crossover is expected to happen in 2044. At that time, the United States will become a "majority-minority" nation. During the 2030s and 2040s the non-Hispanic white population is projected to decline from some 66.2 percent of the total population in 2014 to 43.6 percent in 2060. From 2014 to 2060, the Hispanic population is expected to grow from 17.4 percent to about 28.6 percent of the U.S. population whereas the black population should grow from 13.2 percent to about 14.3 percent. The Asian population will grow from 5.4 percent to 9.3 percent of the U.S. population by 2060. In addition, the percentage of people who self-identify as belonging to two or more racial groups is estimated to grow from 2.5 percent in 2014 to 6.2 percent in 2060 (Colby & Ortman, 2015, Mar.).

In earlier chapters, we considered various aspects of professionalism—including our attention to diversity and difference; human rights and social, economic, and environmental justice; and social well-being. Obviously, culturally sensitive communication skills are vital in regard to these dimensions. When we engage diversity and difference in our interactions with others, we recognize that each person has culturally based views about all sorts of things, including roles related to the seeking, giving, and receiving of help; and expectations about beginning and ending social and professional encounters.

EXERCISE 6-2 Engaging Diversity and Difference with Cultural Sensitivity

1. Access the Internet and use a search engine to first locate a list of ethnic groups in the world and then a list of racial and ethnic groups in the United States. Alternately, you could go to your university or library to locate books or other print material containing such lists (see, for example, Levinson, 1998). Recognize that various sources may use different definitions of *ethnic group* or *ethnolinguistic group*. For example, if you search the online version of *The World Factbook of the U.S. Central Intelligence Agency* using the keywords "field listing ethnic groups," you should find a tabular list of ethnic groups by percentage of population in the world's nations (Central Intelligence Agency, 2015). If you use the keywords "lists of contemporary ethnic groups" in a search engine such as Google, Yahoo, or Bing, you would probably locate a relevant Wikipedia entry (2015). If you access the "Community Facts" page of the American Fact Finder website at **http://factfinder.census .gov/**, you can search for demographic data related to a particular population group in the country as a whole, by state, or by city or town.[9] You might notice that the list of racial, ethnic, and ancestry groups used by the U.S. Census Bureau differs somewhat from those used by other organizations.

Once you gain a sense of the hundreds of ethnic groups throughout the world and the country, select one that interests you and about which you know little or nothing. For example, you might decide to learn about the Hmong or perhaps the Navajo, the Amish, or the

[9] The U.S. Census Bureau provides the *American FactFinder Deep Linking Guide* to help learners search the FactFinder website. See **http://factfinder.census.gov/files/AFF_deep_linking_guide.pdf**.

Druze, Persian, Armenian, Kurdish, Sikh, Haitian, or Bantu ethnic groups. Once you have made your choice, conduct a library, bibliographic, or Internet search to identify three or four cultural "do's and taboos" in verbal or written communication style or approach with members of that ethnic group. Be sure to include at least one "do" that conveys respect and at least one "taboo" that suggests disrespect (Axtell, 1998, 2007). Use the space below to list the "do's" and "taboos" and to cite the source of the information. Remember that members of a particular racial, ethnic, linguistic, cultural, or national group or tribe are not "all alike." Indeed, variations within groups might sometimes be greater than those between groups.

Finally, use your knowledge of the cultural "do's" and "taboos" to write a short message to a member of your chosen ethnic group.[10] Prepare it in English, and be sure to clearly demonstrate respect for the cultural traditions of your correspondent.

Talking and Listening

Effective communication requires skills in both **talking** and **listening**. That is, we must be able to transmit understandable messages as well as receive and comprehend messages transmitted by others. We also need skills in active listening. Active listening is a form of communication through which we clearly demonstrate that we are seriously attempting to understand what others express.

Most people find it extremely challenging to communicate fully and accurately with others. Social workers are no exception. Despite our value system and our education, many of us listen, think, talk, write, and express ourselves nonverbally more in the language of the head (Jackal) than we do in the language of the compassionate heart (Giraffe). Here are some of the common errors we sometimes make in talking and listening:

- Interacting in a patronizing or condescending manner.
- Interrogating (rather than interviewing) by asking questions in rapid, staccato-like fashion.
- Focusing on ourselves (for example, formulating questions before understanding the other's message, self-consciously monitoring our internal experiences, evaluating our own performance).
- Attending predominantly to a single dimension of a person's experience (for example, just thoughts or just feelings; only the personal or only the situational; just the negative or just the positive).
- Interrupting frequently with a comment or question.
- Failing to listen or remember.
- Selectively listening with an "agenda" or "theory" so that we interpret others' messages to match our own beliefs and opinions, and confirm our own biases.

---

[10] If you communicate primarily through sign language, computer-mediated speech, or another means, please approximate this exercise in the message-sending mode you use with clients.

- Neglecting to use a person's name, mispronouncing or changing it (for example, referring to "Catherine" as "Cathy" or "Josef" as "Joe"), or assuming a degree of formality or informality that does not match that of the client's (for example, "Mr. Jones" when he would prefer "Bill," or "Jane" when she prefers "Mrs. Smith").
- Neglecting to consider the cultural meaning of the interview for a particular person or family.
- Failing to demonstrate understanding through active listening.
- Using terms that stereotype people or groups.
- Offering suggestions or proposing solutions too early in the process (on the basis of incomplete or inaccurate understanding of the person-issue-situation).
- Making statements in absolutist terms (through, for example, words such as "always," "never," "all," or "none").
- Prematurely disclosing personal feelings, opinions, or life experiences.
- Confronting or challenging a person before establishing a solid relationship and a genuine base of accurate understanding.
- Speculating about causes of issues before adequately exploring the problem and situation, or before learning about the person.
- Prematurely pushing for action or progress from a person who has not indicated a readiness for action.
- Using clichés and jargon, or using a single phrase over and over so that it seems insincere.
- Making critical or judgmental comments, including pejorative remarks about other people or groups (for example, other professionals, agencies, and organizations).
- Displaying inappropriate or disproportionate emotions (for example, acting extraordinarily happy to meet a new client or weeping excessively when a person expresses painful feelings).

Communicating Nonverbally

A great deal of human communication is nonverbal. As social workers, we should be keenly aware of the significance of body language. Factors such as posture, spatial distance, facial expression, eye contact, gait, and body positioning represent important forms of communication (Ivey et al., 2012; Kadushin & Kadushin, 1997; Kostić & Chadee, 2015; Poyatos, 2002a, 2002b).[11] In professional encounters with others, our body language should be congruent with our verbal language. Clients often notice discrepancies and inconsistencies between what we say verbally and what we express nonverbally. When we present ourselves in an incongruent fashion, others may be confused about us and our message. When we express ourselves congruently, people are more likely to understand our communications and to experience us as genuine and sincere.

In addition to verbal and nonverbal congruence, social workers typically hope that our body language communicates attention to and interest in the other person, as well as caring, concern, respect, and authenticity. On some occasions, social workers need to express messages in an assertive manner that conveys authority. To emphasize one element or another, changes in body language may be necessary.

In beginning interviews with prospective clients, you should typically adopt an open or accessible body position—the nonverbal language of the Giraffe (Egan, 2010; Evans, Hearn, Uhlemann, &

---

[11] If you are visually or hearing challenged, or move about with assistance (for example, with the support of walking aids or perhaps a service dog), please reflect on the potential nonverbal communication effects on clients and colleagues. Also, consider how you might best address the nonverbal dimension of communication in your service to others.

Ivey, 2008; Ivey et al., 2012). If standing, you may hold your arms and hands loosely along your sides. If seated, you can place your hands on your lap. Arms held across the chest, behind the head, or draped over an adjoining chair may reflect inattention or unreceptiveness. Tightly clasped hands, swinging legs or feet, pacing, looking at a watch or clock, or drumming one's fingers tend to communicate nervousness or impatience. Slouching in a chair may suggest fatigue or disinterest. Sometimes, however, you may need to assume an informal body position to increase the comfort and decrease the threat experienced by another person. For example, in working with children, you might sit on the floor and talk while playing a game. With teenage clients, significant encounters may occur while sharing a soft drink, shooting pool, or leaning against a fence or wall. Important exchanges may take place while you transport a client to a doctor's office or a food pantry, while you help carry groceries, or when you enjoy a snack together.

The frequency and intensity of eye contact varies according to the people involved, the purpose of the meeting, the topic under discussion, and a host of other factors. In general, you should adopt seating or standing arrangements that allow for but do not force eye contact between the participants. Although it is common for social workers to attempt rather frequent eye contact, especially when clients are talking, the degree and intensity should vary according to the individual and cultural characteristics of the person, the issues of concern, and the context of the meeting. People from many cultures experience regular eye contact as positive and rewarding, but those from several other cultures do not. "Some cultural groups (for instance, certain Native American, Eskimo, or aboriginal Australian groups) generally avoid eye contact, especially when talking about serious subjects" (Ivey, 1988, p. 27).

In certain cultures, dropping one's eyes to avoid direct eye contact conveys respect, whereas steady, direct eye contact signifies disapproval. For some groups, eye contact is more likely when talking than when listening, but the exact opposite is true in other cultures. In all cases, however, you should not stare. Staring can constitute a violation of the other's space and may be experienced as a challenge or threat. Associated with dominance and patriarchy among several species (Smuts, 1995), staring often reflects a power differential—a nonverbal form of the Jackal language. Many people of majority status and those affiliated with favored groups feel entitled to peruse, appraise, and glare at people of minority or less favored status. For example, many men believe it quite acceptable to stare or leer at women. In North America, many whites commonly watch and observe people of color in a different way than they do other whites. There are numerous other examples. However, as a social worker interested in relationships characterized by equality, mutual respect, and joint participation, your eye contact should never be so intense or continuous that it becomes an intrusion, a privacy violation, or a form of intimidation or superior rank.

Attending (Carkhuff & Anthony, 1979; Evans et al., 2008; Ivey et al., 2012) or "physically tuning-in" (Egan, 2010) are terms frequently used to describe the process of nonverbally communicating to others that you are open, nonjudgmental, accepting of them as people, and interested in what they say. A general purpose of attending is, in fact, to encourage others to express themselves as fully and as freely as possible. During the beginning phase especially, your nonverbal presentation is at least as important as any other factor in influencing clients' responses to you.

There is substantial literature regarding the skill of attending. For example, Carkhuff and Anthony (1979) suggest that counselors face their clients squarely, at a distance of 3 to 4 feet, without tables or other potential obstacles between the participants. They further recommend regular eye contact, facial expressions showing interest and concern, and a slight lean or incline toward the other person. Using the acronym **SOLER**, Egan (2010) also suggests that we *squarely* face the person, assume an *open* body position, sometimes *lean* slightly toward him or her, maintain *eye* contact, and do so in a *relaxed* manner.

Many of these guidelines are useful, but they tend to reflect nonverbal characteristics common among adult, majority-member, middle- and upper-class North Americans. Many children, members of ethnic-minority groups, and people of lower socioeconomic status commonly demonstrate quite different nonverbal characteristics in their social interactions. Facing some people too directly, too squarely, and too closely may infringe on personal territory and privacy. For others, a distance of 4 feet would be much too far for an intimate conversation. Therefore please be flexible in your attending and physical positioning. Closely observe the nonverbal expressions of the other person and respect them. Also, within these general guidelines, assume a comfortable body position. Trying to understand another person requires energy and concentration. Physical discomfort could distract you and you might become less attentive. However, do not assume such a comfortable position that you lose interest. Dozing off during an interview does not convey attention and concern!

When seated positions are desirable and available (for example, when interviewing an adult in an office setting), place the chairs so that they create an angle of between 90 and 135 degrees. This allows other people to direct their eyes and bodies toward or away from you as desired, and it affords you the same opportunity. Matching, movable chairs are preferred. They provide flexibility and suggest that you and your clients are "on the same level." Physically leaning toward clients at points when they are sharing emotionally charged material usually demonstrates concern and compassion. However, carefully observe their reactions. Some clients may find the added closeness too intimate or even intrusive, especially during the early stages of the working relationship.

Of course, many times you have limited control over the placement of chairs or even the location of the interview setting. Often an exchange occurs during a walk or an automobile drive, in a kitchen during mealtime, while the client is caring for children, and sometimes even while others are watching television. As a relationship develops and you begin to understand the meaning of various gestures to the client, it may become possible to ask to move a chair closer or lower the volume on the television. Such requests may be quite meaningful to clients, as they realize that you actually do want to hear what they say!

In the contemporary world, electronic communications represent a primary mode of correspondence between people. We may not fully recognize the significance of the nonverbal aspects of our telephone conversations; text messages; tweets; e-mails; Facebook postings, "likes," or "shares;" or even our Instagram photos. The use of ALL CAPS can be received as a scream, failure to use the recipient's name to begin a message may seem abrupt, and the use of various emoticons and avatars may easily be misunderstood or interpreted. Even in "old technology" such as the telephone, the manner in which we begin and end conversations, the length or brevity of our messages, the tone of our voice, and actions such as placing someone on hold my be received in unexpected ways. Photographic images that are embedded, and those that intentionally or unintentionally accompany our messages and postings can also stimulate various responses from others, and especially from clients who may be especially sensitive to social workers' correspondence. In principle, this is similar to the way we decorate our offices and ourselves. Imagine that you're about to begin an interview with a woman who has just experienced a late-term miscarriage. She is devastated and is convinced she cannot ever carry a baby to term, and she wants a baby more than anything. On your desk is a framed picture of you with your baby daughter in your arms. The impact on the client may be positive or negative, and the reaction may or may not prove helpful or unhelpful in the long run. Nonetheless, your personal pictures—just as those that appear in your electronic messages and postings—are often viewed as part of your identity.

The same occurs with other symbols we display. Suppose, for example, you are dedicated to your Christian religion. You wear a visible cross around your neck and you have a copy of the King James Version (KJV) of the bible prominently displayed in your bookshelf. Your first client of the day happens to be of a different religion or no religion at all. He or she might be Jewish, Muslim, or Hindu; or perhaps agnostic or atheist. Although we cannot predict the nature of the client's reception to your "nonverbal" religious messages, we can be certain that some reaction will result. It may be covert or overt, and it may be productive or counterproductive. We do not know for sure. We do know that, as professionals, social workers are responsible for what we communicate and how we express it, and that includes the nonverbal aspects as well as the verbal aspects of our interaction with others.

EXERCISE 6-3   Communicating Nonverbally

1. Recruit a friend or colleague to join you in a few nonverbal experiments.[12] After you have completed them, use a word-processing program to summarize both your responses and your partner's to each of the questions. Also, include your respective observations and discoveries as well as any questions that might arise in a document entitled "Reflections on a Nonverbal Exercise." Save the file as "Nonverb_Ex" and deposit it within your Social Work Skills Learning Portfolio.

   a. Position yourself face-to-face with your partner at a distance of approximately 4 feet. Look directly into his or her eyes until you become uncomfortable. When that occurs, simply avert your eyes. Now, move to 3 feet, then to 2 feet, each time looking directly into your partner's eyes until you experience discomfort. Then turn away. Share your reactions with each other. Now, experiment with different kinds and degrees of eye contact within a 2- to 4-foot range. For example, try looking at your partner's cheekbone or mouth instead of directly into her or his eyes. Share your reactions. Experiment further by looking into your partner's eyes for several seconds and then slightly change your focus so that you look at a cheekbone for a few seconds; then return your gaze to the eyes. Follow that by looking at your partner's mouth for a few seconds, and then return to the eyes. What are your partner's reactions to these eye contact experiments? What are your own?

   b. Place two chairs squarely facing one another (front to front) approximately 2 feet apart. Be seated. Share your thoughts and feelings as you sit face-to-face and nearly knee-to-knee. Is it comfortable for both of you, for only one, for neither? If it is uncomfortable, alter the distance until it becomes comfortable. Ask your partner to do the same. Finally, compromising if necessary, move the chairs until you arrive at a mutually comfortable distance. Change the placement of the chairs so that instead of directly facing one another, they now are side by side in parallel position, approximately 6 inches apart. As you and your partner take your seats, share your respective thoughts and feelings. Now increase the angle so that the chairs form a 90-degree angle. Share with one another your reactions to this arrangement. Now increase the angle an additional 45 degrees. Share your reactions to this position. Which of the various arrangements does your partner prefer? Which do you?

   c. Based on the results of your experimentation, place the chairs in the position and at the angle that is reasonably comfortable for both you and your partner. Some compromise may be necessary. Now, maintaining a more or less neutral facial expression and without saying a word, try

---

[12] If you are visually or physically challenged in some way, please adapt these exercises accordingly. Be sure to incorporate the implications of your challenges in your discussions.

to show through your body language, but without changing your facial expression, that you care about your partner and are interested in his or her thoughts and feelings. Continue to experiment with three or four different body positions, attempting to demonstrate concern and interest, for approximately a minute each. Following each position, seek feedback from your partner concerning her or his reactions. What is your reaction? What did you learn from the exercise?

d. Assume a body position that your partner indicates reflects caring and interest. Now begin to experiment with different facial expressions. First, let your face become relaxed in its more or less usual state. Retain this facial expression for about 30 seconds while your partner observes and experiences the effect. After a half-minute, seek feedback from your partner about his or her observations and reactions. Then experiment with other facial expressions through which you hope to express silently (1) interest and curiosity, (2) compassion, (3) affection, (4) joy, (5) sadness, (6) disappointment, (7) disapproval, (8) anxiety, and (9) anger. Hold each facial expression for a minute or so while your partner tries to determine the feeling you are trying to express. Share your experience, observations, and discoveries with one another, and summarize them in your report.

Communicating Verbally and in Writing: Talking

The words you choose, the sound and pitch of your voice, the rate and delivery of your speech, and your use of language may suggest a great deal to clients and others with whom you interact.[13] During a typical first contact—whether face-to-face, via telephone, or by letter, fax, or e-mail—use easily understandable words and phrases. Keep it simple. Save arcane and esoteric language for professors! Avoid evaluative terms that are so common in Jackal-speech. Even words such as *good*, *okay*, or *right*—through which you intend to convey support and encouragement—may suggest to a client that you are making evaluative judgments about people. A client may have thoughts such as: "If you judge me or my actions positively without knowing much about me, can you really be objective?" "At this point, you approve of me. I'd better not say anything that might lead you to disapprove. I guess I'll keep the real issues to myself." The same result can occur if we express premature judgments about other people, groups, organizations, or institutions. Clients might wonder, "If you so quickly judge others, will you also do the same to me?"

Especially during the early stages of work, be careful about sharing opinions or hypotheses. Use of diagnostic, medical, legal, or psychological terminology, or social work jargon may suggest to clients that you might judge, label, or classify them before fully understanding all the intricacies of their circumstances. Labels of all kinds, even positive ones, can significantly affect the tenor of your relationships with clients and the course of your work together. Variations of the verb *to be* often result in a labeling effect. Suppose, for example, that you were to say, "He is a child abuser." Because the word "is" suggests an equivalence between "he" and "child abuser" (that is, "he" equals "child abuser"), we would tend to view that human being through the conceptual screen of "child abuser." Rather than a human being who has abused a child, he becomes a child abuser who might possibly have some human qualities.

Of course, we should not tolerate the abuse or exploitation of children or other vulnerable people. Perhaps especially among social workers, such offenses tend to elicit strong emotional reactions. However, even terms that are not so emotionally laden can have deleterious labeling effects. When you think or say, "She is young," "They were foolish," "He was manipulative," "She is seductive,"

---

[13] If you use assisted communication systems or other forms of "talking" (for example, sign language) that do not involve voice and speech, please consider their potential effects on communication with others. Just as "tone of voice" may have meaning in a conversation between hearing people, a signed message may convey "tone" as well.

"He is aggressive," "They are poor," "He is white," "He is disabled," or "She is unmarried," you reflect conclusions that are primarily derived from your own rather than from others' experience of themselves.

The human being convicted of the crime of child abuse may experience himself as a weak, impulsive person guilty of a terrible sin. The person who appears to you to be young may experience herself as old beyond her years. Indeed, she may even question her own sexual identity and wonder whether she is truly female. The behavior that you consider foolish may have resulted from an excruciating examination of various possibilities. The manipulation that you infer may represent an attempt to maintain a sense of personal control or perhaps salvage some dignity by a person who feels humiliated. What you perceive as seductive may be naturally warm and friendly interpersonal expressions that are entirely consistent with that person's familial and cultural traditions. What you consider aggressive may constitute an effort to counter powerful feelings of fear and anxiety. What you view as poverty, someone else may consider as freedom from the petty pursuit of money and material goods. The person you regard as a white male might view himself as Hispanic and may have adopted an androgynous philosophy in which the concepts of masculine and feminine have little relevance. The man you think is disabled may regularly play wheelchair basketball and tennis and possess computer skills beyond any you can imagine. The person you consider unmarried may have long ago determined for herself that the institution of marriage was anathema to a liberated perspective.

Inferences, speculation, and labels about people are risky at all times and especially so during the early phases of a relationship. As you interact with others, adopt the Giraffe language in thought and speech and try to embrace the frame of reference of the person who is communicating. Be especially careful when you use forms of the verb *to be*. In general, use words that are descriptive rather than inferential and simple rather than complex.

We social workers seek to learn about sociological theories and research findings that pertain to different groups, especially cultural groups common in our communities, and populations at risk of oppression, exploitation, and discrimination. For example, in talking and listening with clients, you might benefit from research findings suggesting that men and women tend to adopt different conversational styles (Basow & Rubenfeld, 2003; Mulac et al., 1998; Tannen, 1990, 1994, 2001), that some Native American clients may find personal questions about their "individual identity" intrusive or foreign (Blount, Thyer, & Frye, 1992; Gilbert & Franklin, 2001; Good Tracks, 1973; Lewis & Ho, 1975; Weaver, 2004; Weaver & Bearse, 2008), and that some Hispanic or Latino clients may prefer an extended, informal beginning (Castex, 1996; Delgado, 2007; Longres, 1995; Wodarski, 1992; Zuniga, 2001, 2003). As a result of sociocultural knowledge, you may be tempted to generalize about people, perhaps because of their perceived membership in a certain class or group (for example, poor, rich, black, transgendered, disabled, diabetic, or Democrat). When tempted, however, be alert to the danger of stereotypes and our human tendency to engage in confirmation bias.

Although many men use conversational styles quite different from those of many women, some men adopt conversational styles that are quite similar to those of many women. Some Native Americans experience personal questions from a social worker as an expression of interest and concern, and some Latino clients prefer a direct, businesslike approach as they begin with a social worker. All women are not the same; nor are all men, all people of color, all children, all gay or lesbian people, all social workers, or even all professors. Be sensitive to and carefully consider factors of gender, class, ethnicity, ableness, sexual orientation, gender identity, religious or nonreligious affiliation, and cultural associations. However, also recognize that, despite our nearly identical DNA, each individual person is unique. Each person differs, at least to some extent, from common characteristics of the "average" member of his or her class or group.

As an interview proceeds, you may attempt to match the client's language mode. Some people favor words associated with hearing; others prefer those identified with seeing; still others like words that indicate sensing or touching. For example, if you use words such as "hear," "sound," "noise," "loud," or "soft" with people who favor an auditory language mode, you enhance the likelihood of mutual understanding. Your potential value may also increase. A similarly favorable reaction is likely if you were to use "see," "view," and "perceive" with people who prefer a visual language mode, or "feel," "sense," and "touch" with those who favor tactile language (Bandler & Grinder, 1979).

In general, try to adopt a speaking style that is moderate in tone and speed of delivery. Through your speech, convey that you are truly interested in what the client has to say (Ivey, 1988, p. 22). Sometimes, however, you may deliberately increase or decrease your rate of speech to match the pace of the client. On other occasions, you may purposely slow your pace to lead a fast-talking client into a slower speaking mode. In some circumstances (for example, when working with a client with some loss of hearing), you may lower the pitch of your voice to be more audible. Generally, when you speak or write, active voice is preferable to passive voice, and each unit of speech should not be so long or complex as to impede understanding. Short messages are easier to comprehend, as are single questions. Multipart and multiple-choice questions can confuse others.

In written communications, adopt a professional attitude consistent with the qualities and characteristics discussed in earlier chapters. Badly written, poorly formatted documents that contain spelling mistakes, grammatical errors, logical fallacies, and fail to reflect critical thought, a scholarly perspective, or the universal intellectual standards are likely to be dismissed by recipients.

In general, write in relatively short sentences. Use active voice, get to the point, provide a rationale for or evidence to support your position and, when needed to strengthen a position, include one or more illustrative examples. Gear your language to your audience. If you are communicating with other helping professionals you may use relevant jargon to capture complex phenomena that are best described through sophisticated terminology. In other contexts and for other audiences, avoid jargon altogether. Use succinct, descriptive, and businesslike language. Unless your purpose requires an evaluation or professional judgment, avoid speculative language. Distinguish opinions and conclusions from observations and facts.

Organize your document in an orderly fashion. You may use actual section headings or simply conceptualize each paragraph or two as a section so that the heading is implied. Obviously, there are many various documents that social workers prepare. These include notations made as part of case records (written or, increasingly, electronic), agendas and minutes of meetings, formal position papers ("white papers"), grant applications, business plans and, of course, a seemingly endless number of e-mail messages.

In addition to case records, the most commonly prepared documents are probably letters, memorandums, and e-mails. Professional letters are organized in "business letter" fashion. If you prepare letters as part of your role with an organization, use the agency's letterhead paper. However, if you are not writing as a representative of your agency but rather from your perspective as a professional social worker, use your personal letterhead paper—or include your name followed by earned credentials (for example, Sue Wong, MSW, LSW indicates that Ms. Wong has earned a Master of Social Work degree and is currently a Licensed Social Worker). Along with your name, place your address, center-justified, at the top of the first page.

As you prepare a professional letter, keep its purpose in mind. Ask yourself, "What do I hope to accomplish through this letter?" Once answered, outline the steps needed to accomplish it. Typically, the first paragraph contains a succinct summary of your purpose and, when needed, a brief introduction of yourself. The remaining paragraphs may be used to elaborate upon that purpose by, for example, summarizing factual information about the nature and extent of a problem or issue along with an illustrative example or two to provide a "human face" (without risking privacy or violating confidentiality); providing a rationale as to why action is needed; identifying a few reasonable approaches and then discussing the advantages and disadvantages as well as potential risks and potential benefits of each; and then recommending the approach you prefer. A concluding summary often helps to reinforce the message.

As in all professional documents, carefully edit and reedit the letter; be sure to credit sources, avoid plagiarism, and double check for spelling, grammatical, and logical errors. Avoid unusual fonts. Instead use a traditional font—such as Times New Roman—in 12-point size. Left justify all text (with the exception of your name and address which is centered at the top). Most professional letters reflect a structure similar to that illustrated in Box 6.2.

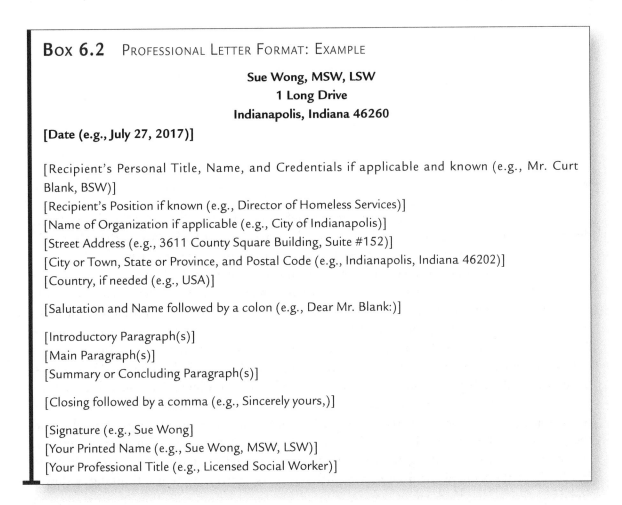

Box 6.2 PROFESSIONAL LETTER FORMAT: EXAMPLE

Sue Wong, MSW, LSW
1 Long Drive
Indianapolis, Indiana 46260
[Date (e.g., July 27, 2017)]

[Recipient's Personal Title, Name, and Credentials if applicable and known (e.g., Mr. Curt Blank, BSW)]
[Recipient's Position if known (e.g., Director of Homeless Services)]
[Name of Organization if applicable (e.g., City of Indianapolis)]
[Street Address (e.g., 3611 County Square Building, Suite #152)]
[City or Town, State or Province, and Postal Code (e.g., Indianapolis, Indiana 46202)]
[Country, if needed (e.g., USA)]

[Salutation and Name followed by a colon (e.g., Dear Mr. Blank:)]

[Introductory Paragraph(s)]
[Main Paragraph(s)]
[Summary or Concluding Paragraph(s)]

[Closing followed by a comma (e.g., Sincerely yours,)]

[Signature (e.g., Sue Wong)]
[Your Printed Name (e.g., Sue Wong, MSW, LSW)]
[Your Professional Title (e.g., Licensed Social Worker)]

Memorandums are intra-agency or interdepartmental communications. For example, a social worker might send a memorandum to the executive director of her agency. She might forward copies to her supervisor and colleagues within the agency who might find the information relevant to their roles and responsibilities. Similarly, a social work student might send a memo to a professor, an adviser, the dean or director of the program, or perhaps to colleagues in a class or to fellow members of a student association or organization.

Approach the preparation of memos with the same level of professional care that you do with letters. Keep the purpose and audience in mind, and remember that your professional reputation is often reflected in the nature and quality of the documents you prepare. Most memos reflect a structure similar to that illustrated in Box 6.3.

Box 6.3   MEMORANDUM FORMAT

MEMO

To:
CC:
From:
Date:
Subject:

[text here]

E-mail communication represents an increasingly popular means for professional correspondence. There are, however, major risks associated with e-mail and, of course, other electronic forms of communication such as texting, tweeting, and posting through various social media forums. A primary danger involves the often short time span between a thought, feeling, or sensation and its electronic expression and transmission. A major advantage of letters, memos, position papers, and other reports is that we can prepare drafts, put them away for an hour or a day while we reflect upon them, and then return to revise and edit—perhaps two or three times—before distributing them. Such a time-lapse allows for both System 1 ("fast") and System 2 ("slow") thinking (Stanovich, 1999; Stanovich & Toplak, 2012). As Kahneman (2011) suggests, **System 1 thinking** "operates automatically and quickly" (p. 21) whereas **System 2 thinking** involves concentrated, complex intellectual processing. Both thinking systems are incredibly important and needed by social workers. System 1 includes our automatic, intuitive thoughts and the immediate, often unconscious, application of various heuristics or algorithms or, sometimes, stereotypes. System 1 thinking also tends to engage our reactive emotions so that we become less likely to think deeply or from new or different perspectives. System 2 thinking is slower and deeper in nature; tends to involve conscious, logical processing, reflection and analysis; and can include hypothetical reasoning. System 2 thinking is hard work—requiring the use of "a lot of little grey cells" as Agatha Christie's Hercule Poirot might say. Although the process may be slower than we might prefer, deep thinking may lead to alternate, creative, and innovative perspectives or approaches. Whereas System 1 thinking is readily apparent among many other animals, System 2 thinking may be unique to human beings. Even for humans, however, the exclusive application of one thinking system without the other would not benefit members of our species, and certainly not social workers and our clients.

E-mail and other forms of electronic communication are especially amenable to fast thinking—which, in professional contexts, can have deleterious effects upon social workers, their agencies and colleagues, the profession and, unfortunately, sometimes clients and other people. To counter the temptation to "think fast, type fast, and press the send button," consider the following practices:

- Do not use your organization's e-mail or cell phone service to send private messages or to send professional messages that are not associated with your agency roles and functions (that is, when you are not serving as a representative of the agency). Create a personal e-mail account through a free service provider (for example, **www.hotmail .com**, **www.gmail.com**, and numerous others) and use your own phone for personal and for nonagency-related professional correspondence.

- Do not send messages to clients via e-mail—unless a client clearly and fully understands the numerous risks associated with electronic transmission of sensitive material, and provides informed consent for such communication. Simply put, e-mails are not and cannot be considered secure. Their confidentiality and privacy cannot be safeguarded.

- When sending e-mails to colleagues within and outside your agency, ensure that clients' identities and confidential materials are excluded. Also, remember that e-mails are retained somewhere in electronic storage and can be hacked or retrieved by others. Indeed, some organizations monitor the e-mail and computer activity of their employees. A few do so in a covert manner. Of course, e-mail correspondence may be used in legal proceedings, both criminal and civil, as well as in professional disciplinary reviews. As a result of "unprofessional" e-mail messages, social workers may be demoted or discharged, and their professional reputations tarnished.

- Create professional e-mail messages in a separate word-processing program. Review it carefully at least one time and use the spell-check and grammar-check features before you copy and paste the message into your e-mail system. You might also decide upon the routine use of a time delay—say 10 or 15 minutes—before you transfer your message from the word-processing to the e-mail system. That way, you have at least some time to reflect upon the message and, perhaps, engage your capacity for slow, analytic, System 2 thinking.

EXERCISE 6-4 Talking

1. Imagine that you are serving as a social worker in a community outreach program. The program seeks to locate homeless people in the area and inform them of community resources that might enhance their lives and well-being. Several services for homeless individuals and families are available. These include temporary housing and food provision; medical and dental care; job training and placement; and ongoing counseling. Use a word-processing program to prepare a preliminary "Outreach Script" to help you plan what you might say to homeless people in introducing yourself and describing the services available through the program. Save the document with the filename "Outreach_Script." Reflect upon the text and then revise as needed. Familiarize yourself with the script—but do not memorize it. Now, imagine that you're approaching a homeless person who seems to be camping in a small wooded section near a downtown river. Then, without referring to the script, make a 2- to 3-minute audio recording of what you might say when you first introduce yourself and describe the services your program provides.[14]

   Replay the recording and review your speech, vocal patterns, and language usage. Examine the words you said and consider them from the point of view of a person who has not invited you and probably does not want your company. In fact, anticipate that the person has strong and mixed feelings whenever a stranger approaches or intrudes. Take a moment to reflect upon the thoughts and feelings the person might experience.

---

[14] If you are visually or physically challenged in some way, please adapt these exercises accordingly. Be sure to incorporate the implications of your challenges in your discussions.

After that, use the space provided below to address the following questions: What might your speech and tone of voice suggest about your approach and attitude toward the person? Do your voice and speech convey qualities of interest, respect, kindness, confidence, and hopefulness? If you were that person, how would you like to be approached, addressed, and engaged? Use the space below to identify one or two aspects of your own talking that you would like to strengthen in preparation for your roles and functions as a professional social worker.

2. As you know, the "talking" skills include written as well as verbal forms of communication. Use a word-processing program to prepare two professional-quality documents: (a) a letter and (b) a memorandum. As a topic for both documents, choose a social problem that has recently been the subject of local, national, or international news. Select a problem that reflects social work's mission to eliminate poverty or to address various forms of social, economic, or environmental injustice. Be sure to choose one that truly interests you. For example, you might be concerned about human trafficking, or the illegal procurement and sales of human organs, or perhaps injustices associated with application of the death penalty. You might question the practice of stoning women accused of adultery, the forced marriage of girls to adult men, or the practice of female circumcision. You might be concerned about racism, racial profiling, or police brutality toward people of color. You might be concerned about economic inequality or social immobility; drought, famine, hunger, and starvation; or perhaps the socioeconomic impact of climate change.

As social workers, we are well aware of a seemingly infinite number of major social problems. Choose one that engenders passion and energy. Then, draft a "Letter" to the editor of a newspaper, your legislative representative, or a piece for a blog. You do not have to mail the letter or publish the blog. View the exercise as an opportunity to practice your written communication skills. In the letter, use a paragraph or two to introduce the nature and scope of the problem, and provide an illustrative example. Use the remaining paragraphs to suggest some action—perhaps in the form of a policy or program, legislation, or steps that other concerned people might take. Prepare the document carefully so that it reflects clarity and professionalism. Ensure that it is free of spelling and grammatical errors as well as unsubstantiated assertions and other logical fallacies.

After you edit and finalize the letter, prepare an alternate version in the form of a "Memorandum." To do so, make an electronic copy of the letter that you prepared and then edit it so that it appears in the form of a memorandum. Label the word-processed documents "Draft_Letr_1" and "Draft_Mem_1" and include them in your Social Work Skills Portfolio.

▆▆▆ Listening

Listening involves the use of your sensory capacities to receive and register the messages expressed verbally and nonverbally by others.[15] The listening skills include **hearing** or *receiving* others' words, speech, and language; **observing** their nonverbal gestures and positions (Carkhuff & Anthony,

---

[15] If you are visually or physically challenged in some way, please adapt these exercises accordingly. Be sure to incorporate the implications of your challenges in your discussions.

1979; Ivey et al., 2012); **encouraging** them to express themselves fully (Ivey, 1988; Ivey et al., 2010; Ivey et al., 2012); and **remembering** what they communicate.

Most of us are rather poor listeners, tending to pay more attention to our own thoughts and feelings than to the messages others are trying to convey. Competent listening rarely comes naturally. Yet listening, more than any other skill, is essential for effective social work practice. It requires two actions. First, you minimize attention to your own experiences (for example, thoughts, feelings, and sensations). Then, you energetically concentrate on the client with a determination to understand—rather than evaluate—what the client is experiencing and expressing.

For most of us, one of the genuinely humanizing events in life occurs when we feel truly understood by another person. When you listen attentively with a compassionate heart and a genuine intention to understand and empathize, you convey a special degree of respect. When you listen in the Giraffe language, you demonstrate that you value others and are interested in what they have to say. In a sense, careful listening is a gesture of love. Because of this, empathic listening is a dynamic factor in social work practice. It has several purposes. First, effective listening enables you to gather information that is essential for assessment and planning. Second, it helps clients feel better—often by reducing tension or anxiety, heightening feelings of personal safety and well-being, and encouraging greater hope and optimism. Third, attentive listening encourages clients to express themselves freely and fully. Fourth, effective listening usually enhances your value to clients. Finally, attentive listening often contributes significantly to positive change in clients' self-understanding and self-efficacy as well as their problem-solving and goal-seeking capacities.

To listen effectively, you need to manage your own impulses, tendencies, and predispositions. This is essentially a matter of self-awareness and self-discipline—those professional characteristics we discussed earlier. You hold back from fully experiencing and freely expressing your own reactions, ideas, or opinions. Such self-discipline involves temporarily suspending judgment and action so you can better hear and understand other people. As a social worker, you are probably highly motivated to help resolve problems. In your desire to serve, you may sometimes be tempted to rush to conclusions and solutions. Although life-threatening situations often require immediate intervention, engaging in premature assessment, offering advice early, or proposing action before understanding the issues and the person-in-environment typically interferes with effective, empathic listening. Frequently, it also has unintended adverse consequences. In most circumstances, you would be wise to listen carefully and fully before assessing or intervening. As Shulman (2009) suggests, "Workers who attempt to find simple solutions often discover that if the solutions were indeed that simple, then the client could have found them without the help of the worker" (p. 126).

Self-disciplined listening may involve some use of silence. Social workers "frequently perceive silence as a hindrance and a hazard to the progress of the interview. . . . The professional assumption is that talking is better" (Kadushin, 1983, p. 286). This is certainly not always the case. Periods of silence, pauses in the exchange, are vital elements in effective communication. Sometimes people need time to transition to System 2 thinking and reflect upon phenomena in more complex or deeper ways. Of course, you should not let silence continue so long that it becomes an anxious contest to see who will speak first. Do recognize, however, that with some clients, at certain moments, silence can be a powerfully helpful experience. "Instead of a threat, silence should be seen and utilized as an opportunity" (Kadushin, 1983, p. 294).

Hearing refers to the process of listening (that is, receiving messages), which involves attending to the speech and language of other people. Numerous factors can impede or obstruct hearing. A room might be noisy, or a person might talk softly or mumble. Someone may speak in a foreign language or adopt an unfamiliar dialect. Another person might use words you do not understand or use them in different ways than you do. Effective hearing involves diminishing the obstacles and focusing entirely on the words and sounds of the other person. It also involves reducing the tendency to hear selectively because of our inclination to judge the words and sounds of others, and confirm our own assumptions and preconceptions. In attempting to hear clearly, we hope to take in and remember the messages sent by the speaker. In listening, process is as important as content. Therefore try to hear more than the words themselves. Listen as well to the person's manner of speaking including pace, pauses, and intonations. Connect empathically as you try to hear the meaning and feeling just beyond or just beneath the words actually said.

Another vital element in the listening process is the skill of observation. **Observing** (Carkhuff & Anthony, 1979; Ivey et al., 2012) occurs when you pay attention to the client's physical characteristics, gestures, and other nonverbal behavior. Nonverbal communication is at least as informative as verbal expression and sometimes more so, especially in multicultural contexts. As a social worker, try to observe nonverbal manifestations of energy level, mood, and emotions as well as indirect signs and signals. Quite often, clients do not directly express their feelings through verbal speech. Without staring, try to observe carefully so you notice nonverbal expressions of feeling.

The purpose of observing is to gain a better and more complete understanding of the ways in which the client experiences the world. During interviews, attend to subtle or indirect communications. These may relate to themes of power or authority, ambivalence about seeking or receiving help, difficulties in discussing topics that involve a stigma or taboo, and inhibitions concerning the direct and full expression of powerful feelings (Shulman, 2009). You may pick up more indirect communications from nonverbal rather than verbal expressions, so observe closely. Be careful, however, to avoid the tempting tendency to observe with judgment and reach premature conclusions. That is, avoid thinking in Jackal. Instead, observe from your place of peace, and adopt Giraffe language as your preferred mode of listening. Use descriptive language to capture your observations. Later, you may formulate extremely tentative hypotheses based on the words and the nonverbal gestures someone has expressed. Such tentative hypotheses are not, in any sense, true or valid. They represent, rather, preliminary hunches!

Among the specific aspects to observe are (1) facial expression, (2) eye contact, and (3) body language, position, and movement. In observing, look for predominant facial expressions, head and body positions, physical gestures, and patterns of eye contact during communication exchanges. Consider them in light of cultural affiliations as well as the immediate context. Also, look for the nature and timing of changes in these nonverbal indicators. These may suggest feeling states such as contentment, calmness, acceptance, joy, sadness, fear or anxiety, and anger. Based on these observations, tentatively consider what these expressions, gestures, and behaviors might suggest about how this person experiences herself or himself and feels about the problem or issue of concern. Also, imagine what they indicate about how the person thinks and feels about you, about this meeting, and about the context for the meeting.

Encouraging (Ivey et al., 2012) is a form of listening that involves some talking. You can encourage other people to continue expressing themselves by making very brief responses in the form of single words, short phrases, or sounds and gestures that invite them to continue their expression. Some examples of brief verbal encouragers include: "Please go on." "And?" "Uh huh." "Mmmm." "Yes." "Please continue."

Nonverbally, you may further communicate encouragement by nodding, making attentive eye contact, gesturing slightly with your hands, and leaning or inclining toward the client. Repeating a portion of a phrase or a key word that a client uses may also constitute encouragement. Such brief responses enable you to demonstrate that you want to hear more, but you do so without interrupting with a lengthy statement of your own. However, avoid using the same encouragers over and over. After a while, their repeated use may suggest a lack of sincerity. Also, recognize that the use of minimal encouragers alone is insufficient. Active-listening communications are necessary to demonstrate accurate empathic understanding.

The final dimension of listening involves **remembering** what the client communicates. Hearing and observing are skills without much inherent value unless you can retain the information received. Remembering is the process of temporarily storing information so that you may use it later—for example, to communicate understanding, make thematic connections between messages expressed at different times, prepare a written record, or develop an assessment.

EXERCISE 6-5 Listening

1. Please recruit a friend or colleague to join you in a listening exercise. Indicate that the purpose of this exercise is to help you become a better listener. Ask your partner to identify a topic of genuine personal interest that the two of you might discuss for approximately 10 minutes. As the listener, your tasks are to encourage your partner to discuss the subject; to hear and comprehend what she communicates; and to remember what was said and done. Keep in mind that your partner's perspective is paramount. Withhold your own opinions; refrain from judgments or evaluations in both speech and thought. This is your partner's time. Let the discussion proceed in whatever way and direction your partner wishes. Encourage her to communicate freely and fully, and try not to interfere with the flow of expression. As your partner talks, listen attentively and observe carefully. At the end of the 10-minute period, thank your partner and proceed with the following:

    First, ask your partner to reflect upon her or his experience of the exchange. Then, ask your partner to give you truly honest feedback about how well you listened. Say that you sincerely want to become a better listener so that genuine feedback is needed. You might also say that whatever your partner says, your feelings will not be hurt because this is a practice exercise and you plan to improve.

    As you obtain feedback from your partner, be sure to take notes. Explore nonverbal as well as verbal factors. For instance, ask about eye contact, facial expressions, body positions and movements, physical gestures, tone of voice, rate of speech and its audibility in terms of their relationship to listening. Did your partner feel you were interested in what she had to say; that you understood and remembered her words; and you were nonjudgmental about her and what she said?

    Ask about points at which your partner felt that you listened especially well as well as those when you did not. Finally, ask your partner for suggestions about what you might do to improve upon your listening abilities and become a better listener.

    Thank your partner again and say good-bye.

    Let some time pass and then reflect upon the exercise, your partner's observations, and your own. Then, use your notes as a starting point to word-process a document to (a) summarize your partner's comments and suggestions; (b) identify aspects of your listening skills that you would like to strengthen; and (c) outline brief plans by which to become a better listener. Save the "Reflections on a Listening Exercise" document in a file labeled "Listen_Ex." Save it to your Social Work Skills Learning Portfolio.

▮ Active Listening

Active listening combines talking and listening skills in such a way that others feel both understood and encouraged to share more. It is a form of feedback. You listen carefully and communicate your understanding of a speaker's messages by reflecting or mirroring them back. In essence, you paraphrase the client's message. Ideally, your words should be essentially equivalent to or synonymous with, but not identical to, those of the client. If the client communicates factual content, your active-listening response should convey that factual information. If the client expresses feelings, reflect those feelings in your active-listening response and do so at an equivalent level of intensity. If the client shares conceptual ideas, paraphrase them through active listening so that you accurately capture his or her meaning.

Active listening represents a clear and tangible demonstration that you have understood or at least are trying to understand what a client has expressed. It indicates that you want to comprehend fully and accurately the messages communicated. Active listening shows that you are interested in the client's views, feelings, and experiences. Because it conveys empathy and furthers understanding, there is simply no substitute for active listening. It constitutes a major element of the vital feedback loop between you and your client. If you do not listen actively, you are more likely to miss part of a client's message and thereby misunderstand, distort, or misrepresent it. Furthermore, if you fail to listen actively or if you paraphrase in a consistently inaccurate fashion, you discourage the client from free and full expression. You also significantly diminish your own value in the relationship. Clients look forward to being understood. If you do not accurately communicate understanding, clients may feel unheard, disappointed, and alienated. Experiences of oppression, discrimination, abuse, or exploitation have left many clients feeling profoundly misunderstood throughout their lives. When you, as a professional social worker, communicate sincere and accurate understanding, the impact can be positive indeed. However, if the clients feel that you too, like so many before, also misunderstand, a powerfully adverse effect may result. Experiencing yet another repetition of alienation, such clients may wish they had never sought your services in the first place.

Active listening combines the talking and listening skills into three steps:

- Step 1: **Inviting**. Through your body position, facial expression, speech, and language, indicate that you are prepared to listen. Often, you can invite the other person to express himself or herself by asking a question such as "What happened?" or "How did this all come about?" It is not always necessary, however, to ask a specific question. Many clients begin to talk about themselves and their concerns as soon as you begin to attend to them with your eyes, face, and body.
- Step 2: **Listening**. When a client responds to your invitation to speak and begins to talk, you listen carefully by attempting to hear, observe, encourage, and remember. In this step, you essentially use your ears and brain to receive and retain the messages sent by the other person.
- Step 3: **Reflecting**. Periodically, as the client pauses at the conclusion of a message segment, paraphrase his or her statement. For example, a client might say, "I'm really frustrated with my boss. He says he wants production, production, production! But then he comes down to my shop and spends hours shooting the breeze." In active listening, you could say in response, "You're annoyed with him because he tells you he wants you to work harder and harder but then he interferes when you're trying to do so." Here is another example. Suppose a client says, "Ever since I was 7 years old, I felt fat and ugly." You might say, in active listening, "From the time of your childhood up through the present time, you've thought of yourself as overweight and unattractive." By communicating an equivalent message, you demonstrate empathic understanding.

Active listening is, of course, most useful when you have accurately understood and paraphrased the client's message, but it can be helpful even when you have not. Sometimes you may misunderstand a message or miss part of it as your attention wanders, or the client may misspeak and send an incomplete or confusing message. In such cases, your sincere attempt to understand by active listening almost always elicits further expression from the client.

A client may spontaneously express confirmation when your active listening response accurately reflects his or her message. The client may say something such as "Yeah, that's right." Then the client often simply continues to talk. On those occasions when your response is not entirely accurate but is close enough to demonstrate that you have heard some of the message and are genuinely trying to understand, the client may say, "Well, no. What I meant was . . ." He or she may then try to restate the message so that you can understand. However, when you are extremely inaccurate, perhaps due to your own lack of interest or attention, the client may very well respond with an emphatic "No!" and then become much less expressive. A similar phenomenon can occur when you do not listen actively often enough. If you only talk or only listen but do not actively listen, you may discourage clients from expressing themselves freely and fully.

When we are first developing skill in active listening, social workers tend to make several common errors:

- Using so many of the client's own words that your paraphrased reflections sound like mimicry.
- Repeatedly using the same lead-in phrases (for example, "I hear you saying . . ." "It sounds like . . .").
- Trying to be clever, profound, or interpretive—playing the role of "brilliant analyst" or "clever detective" tends to indicate that you are listening more to your own thoughts and speculations than to the client's message.
- Responding only to facts, thoughts, and ideas or just to feelings and emotions rather than listening actively to all dimensions of the client's expression.
- Interrupting frequently to reflect the client's message.
- Using active listening following every short phrase or statement.

EXERCISE 6-6   Active Listening

In the spaces provided, write the words you might say in active listening to the following statements:

1. CLIENT: My husband thinks I'm an alcoholic. I'm here because he made me come. Sure, I drink. I drink a lot. But he's the reason I drink.

2. CLASSMATE: I've missed the last three classes and don't know what's going on in here. Today is the day of the midterm exam and I know I'm going to flunk. I'm so uptight, I can't think straight.

3. WOMAN WHO LOST HER 12-YEAR-OLD CHILD TO GANG VIOLENCE: I never wanted to live in this cesspool. We just couldn't afford to move to another neighborhood. There are gunshots almost every night and the police rarely come by—that is, until after someone's been killed. Drug dealers and street walkers are everywhere. I feel so guilty that my

lovely daughter had to live and to die here. It's just so unfair. If you don't have much, you have to live where you can and that means somebody, sometime is gonna die.

4. SUPERVISOR: I am disappointed that you did not follow up with the Sanchez family. You know those children are at risk and I expected you to visit them again last week.

5. PROFESSOR: I wonder if the match between your personal values and those of the social work profession is a good one. From your comments in class and the papers you've written, it seems to me that your views differ quite a bit from those of most social workers.

6. SOCIAL WORK COLLEAGUE: I am working with a family that is driving me up the wall. I know I have a problem here. I get so angry at the parents for being so passive. I work so damn hard and they don't do a thing!

7. CHILD: Sometimes my mommy's boyfriend is mean to her. He hits her and she ends up crying a lot. I don't like him at all.

8. COMMUNITY LEADER: I appreciate your offer to help with our community organization and development efforts. However, the social workers we've had before have never worked out.

9. CLIENT WHO SEEMS ANGRY OR FRUSTRATED: I have to tell you that I've been to a counselor before. All she did was repeat my words back to me and then ask me what I'd like to do. Well, I want advice from somebody who really knows something about this problem—not someone who just wants to be my friend. I need an expert who has helped other people resolve the same problem I'm dealing with.

SUMMARY

The basic interpersonal skills of accessing a peaceful place, engaging diversity and difference, and talking and listening (that is, sending and receiving messages) are fundamental to all aspects of human interaction, including the phases and processes of social work practice. To communicate effectively as a social worker, you use all the sensory faculties at your command in sending and receiving messages. In addition, you regularly combine the talking and listening skills in the form of active listening. Active listening conveys empathy by overtly demonstrating that you are making a genuine effort to understand.

Highly developed communications skills contribute to clear expression and accurate understanding during exchanges with individuals, families, groups, organizations, and communities. Integral to cultural sensitivity and the promotion of peace, they are essential for engaging diversity and difference with people of diverse views and traditions.

CHAPTER 6 Summary Exercises

1. With the informed consent of a friend or colleague from a cultural tradition that differs in some substantial way from your own, make a video recording[16] of a 15-minute conversation. Indicate that you are trying to practice your interviewing skills and would like to conduct an interview about her choice of career. Tell your partner that she will not have to answer any questions that evoke discomfort. Be sure to indicate that your professor and perhaps some of your classmates may review the recording to provide feedback about the quality of your talking and listening skills. Ask your colleague for permission to both record the interview and to use it exclusively for the purpose of your learning. In other words, obtain informed consent. You might mention that if your colleague is interested in viewing the recording and perhaps providing additional feedback once you have completed the assignment, you would truly welcome and appreciate that as well.

   During the interview, explore how your colleague came to make the career choice that she did. Conduct the interview from a "place of peace" and with cultural sensitivity. Explore influential and motivational factors. Ask about your partner's hopes and aspirations as well as issues and concerns regarding the chosen career. Use the skills of talking, listening, and active listening to encourage your colleague to share as much as possible about the career decision. At the conclusion of the interview, ask your colleague to reflect upon the experience and then complete a copy of the Talking and Listening Skills Rating Form contained in Appendix 6.

   When your partner has completed the instrument, ask her for immediate reactions to and feedback about the experience—perhaps by elaborating upon responses to items included in the rating form. Ask about cultural sensitivity. At what points were aspects of her culture especially well recognized, appreciated, or respected; when were they not? Also explore the aspect of peacefulness. Ask about those times when your partner felt that you were truly at ease or at peace, and genuinely free from judgments, evaluations, labels, and diagnoses. Also ask about those times when you used terms that suggested some form of judgment—good or bad. Try to identify those words.

   Explore nonverbal factors such as your eye contact, facial expressions, body positions and movements, physical gestures, tone of voice, rate and volume of speech as well as its modulation. Ask if you appeared genuinely interested in what she had to say. Ask how well your partner thinks that you understood and remembered what was said, and if she feels that you fully accepted her. Ask about exchanges when she felt especially heard and understood, and those when she did not. Ask about your attempts to reflect back and paraphrase her words. Which times were you truly on target; when were you off?

   Finally, ask your partner to offer suggestions about how you could become more culturally sensitive and improve upon your talking and listening skills. When your partner finishes, express your gratitude, offer your thanks, and say good-bye.

   Summarize your partner's feedback in a draft document. Later, you'll be able to incorporate it into a self-evaluation report. Next, play the video recording. Prepare a word-processed transcript that accurately reflects what was said and by whom but **do not use your colleague's name**. Use *interviewee* to refer to her words. Save the document to a file entitled "Early_Intvue_Transcript." Identify each of the talking and listening skills that you used during the conversation. For example, identify as talking a statement you made or a question you asked that came from your frame of reference. Identify as active listening your attempts to communicate your understanding of your partner's expressions. Use your word-processing software

---

[16] Since the interview is recorded, maintain the anonymity of your partner as much as humanly possible. Erase or destroy the recording as soon as you complete the requirements for the learning exercises.

TABLE 6.2	Transcription and Skill Identification Format	
	Transcript	**Skill Used**
Interviewer	Record the words you said here.	Identify the talking and listening skill used—if any—here.
Interviewee	Record what your partner said here.	Use this space to make observations or comments to advance your learning.
Interviewer	Record the words you said here.	Identify the talking and listening skill used—if any—here.
Interviewee	Record what your partner said here.	Use this space to make observations or comments to advance your learning.

to organize the transcript according to the format outlined in Table 6.2, but *be sure to disguise the identity of the person you interviewed*.

After you complete the transcript, use it along with the video; your colleague's responses to the Talking and Listening Skills Rating Form and her comments and suggestions; and your own observations to evaluate your cultural sensitivity, your peacefulness, and your proficiency in the talking, listening, and active-listening skills. Word-process a two- to three-page (500–750 words) report titled "An Early Interview: Self-Evaluation Report." In your paper, respond to the dimensions suggested by statements in the Talking and Listening Skills Rating Form by addressing questions such as the following: How did your verbal and nonverbal communications reflect sensitivity and respect for various aspects of your colleague's culture? How did your facial expressions, head movements, tone of voice, body positions, and physical gestures communicate that you were genuinely interested in your partner and everything she said? How clearly and audibly did you speak, and what might your tone of voice and speech modulation suggest about your attitude toward your colleague? Were your words and language familiar to your colleague so that she could easily understand everything you said? How did your verbal communications and nonverbal expressions convey nonjudgmental interest in, attention to, and respect for your partner and everything she expressed? How well did you remember what was communicated during the interview? How did you summarize and reflect back your partner's messages so that she felt truly heard and understood?

Conclude the report by identifying those aspects of the talking and listening skills that you need to improve. Outline the dimensions of your plans to do so.

If you have your interview partner's permission and informed consent, ask your instructor or one or two social work classmates to review the videotape and offer evaluative feedback about your attitude of peace, your cultural sensitivity, and the nature and quality of your talking, listening, and active-listening skills. Consider the feedback. If constructive, revise your word-processed report to accommodate the new information. Once you have edited and finalized your report save it to a document file entitled "Early_Intvue_Self-Eval" and include it along with the interview transcript in your Social Work Skills Learning Portfolio.

2. Reflect on the content and the exercises contained in this chapter, your experience with the recent interview, and the self-evaluation report. Based on your observations and reflections, word-process a succinct one- to two-page letter to yourself. Prepare it as a formal business letter in the best professional quality possible. Address it to yourself. In the letter, describe a plan by which you might become a more culturally sensitive and more empathic listener who can communicate with people in a warm, genuine, peaceful, and respectful manner. Identify how you would know that you had progressed in these areas. When you have finished, save the document file as "Letter_to_Self" and include it in your Social Work Skills Learning Portfolio. Make a note in your calendar to read the letter in one year's time.

CHAPTER 6 Self-Appraisal

As you finish this chapter, please reflect on your learning by using the following space to identify any ideas, terms, or concepts addressed in Chapter 6 that remain confusing or unclear to you:

Next, respond to the following items by carefully reading each statement. Please use a 1-to-10-point rating scale (where *1 = strongly disagree* and *10 = strongly agree*) to indicate the degree to which you agree or disagree with each statement. Place a check mark at the point that best reflects your view at this particular point in time. If you're truly *undecided*, place your check at the midpoint (5.5) mark.

1. I can access a place of peace.

```
1   2   3   4   5   6   7   8   9   10
```

2. I can engage diversity and difference with cultural sensitivity.

```
1   2   3   4   5   6   7   8   9   10
```

3. I can discuss the talking and listening skills.

```
1   2   3   4   5   6   7   8   9   10
```

4. I can communicate nonverbally in social work contexts.

```
1   2   3   4   5   6   7   8   9   10
```

5. I can communicate verbally and in writing for social work purposes.

```
1   2   3   4   5   6   7   8   9   10
```

6. I can listen (hear, observe, encourage, and remember) in social work practice.

```
1   2   3   4   5   6   7   8   9   10
```

7. I can listen actively in professional contexts.

```
1   2   3   4   5   6   7   8   9   10
```

Preparing

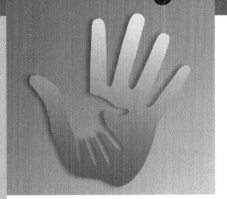

This chapter should help you learn skills used in the **preparing** phase of social work practice. Initial meetings set the tone and influence the general direction of subsequent interactions. In fact, the nature of your first contacts with people often determines if there will be another encounter. Without preparation, we could easily lose our cognitive and emotional equilibrium as we encounter individuals, families, groups, organizations, and communities of diverse cultural traditions struggling with highly complex

(Continued)

Chapter Goals

Following completion of this chapter, you should be able to:

- Discuss the purposes and functions of preparing.

- Engage in preparatory reviewing.

- Engage in preparatory exploring.

- Engage in preparatory consultation.

- Engage in preparatory arranging.

- Engage in preparatory empathy.

- Engage in preparatory self-exploration.

- Center yourself.

- Engage in preliminary planning and recording.

Core Competencies

The content addressed in this chapter supports the following core EPAS competencies:

- Competency 1: Demonstrate Ethical and Professional Behavior

- Competency 2: Engage Diversity and Difference in Practice

- Competency 3: Advance Human Rights and Social, Economic, and Environmental Justice

- Competency 4: Engage in Practice-Informed Research and Research-Informed Practice

- Competency 5: Engage in Policy Practice

- Competency 6: Engage with Individuals, Families, Groups, Organizations, and Communities

- Competency 7: Assess Individuals, Families, Groups, Organizations, and Communities

- Competency 8: Intervene with Individuals, Families, Groups, Organizations, and Communities

- Competency 9: Evaluate Practice with Individuals, Families, Groups, Organizations, and Communities

and challenging issues in often extraordinarily difficult circumstances (Branch Jr. & Gordon, 2004; Burke & Parker, 2007; Gleeson & Philbin, 1996; Hartman, 1978; Hayes, Humphries, & Cohen, 2004; Kovacs & Bronstein, 1999; Sar, 2000). The same holds true when social workers engage in social activism. In the context of a public protest or demonstration, lax or inadequate preparation could turn a nonviolent, peaceful action into a violent encounter. Careful preparation can make the difference between safety and injury or even death.

In a meta-analysis of some 125 research studies, Wierzbicki and Pekarik (1993) found that the average early-dropout rate in outpatient mental health services was approximately 47 percent. Client factors associated with early dropout included limited formal education, lower socioeconomic status, and racial-minority status. "It is not uncommon in a variety of mental health settings for 50 percent of clients to leave treatment without the prior knowledge and agreement of their therapists (Pekarik, 1983; Pekarik & Stephenson, 1988; Phillips, 1985; Viale-Val, Rosenthal, Curtiss, & Marohn, 1984)" (Campbell, Baker, & Bratton, 2000, p. 134). More recent studies—using more precise definitional criteria for premature termination—suggest an early dropout rate of approximately 20 percent. Some diagnostic categories reflect slightly lower and some reflect slightly higher rates, but the overall average of early dropouts remains at about 1 of every 5 clients. This figure also holds relatively constant for different therapeutic approaches. In fact, the "similarity in dropout rates for the majority of the disorder categories suggests that clients' decisions to drop out may depend more on other therapy variables (e.g., common factors, client characteristics, and therapist characteristics) rather than the specific type of treatment that is used" (Swift & Greenberg, 2014, p. 193). Indeed, findings of a meta-analysis of 11 studies "indicate that clients with weaker therapeutic alliance are more likely to drop out of psychotherapy" (Sharf, Primavera, & Diener, 2010, p. 637).

In a study of nearly 14,000 people served in 17 mental health centers, Sue (1977) found that when compared with white clients, a significantly greater percentage of minority applicants did not return following an initial visit. In a more recent study of 44 helping professionals in a university counseling center, racial or ethnic minority clients were more likely than white clients to "no show" and discontinue without notification, that is, through unilateral termination. This study confirmed findings from earlier studies that this particular form of dropout is associated with a poorer quality of therapeutic alliance and unsatisfactory outcome. Indeed, the 44 professionals reflected differential rates of unilateral termination by minority clients. This suggests that professional helpers' individual qualities and their ability to demonstrate respect and express empathy play a substantial role in clients' decision to continue or discontinue services (Owen, Imel, Adelson, & Rodolfa, 2012).

Of course, demographic and contextual factors also contribute to early discontinuation. In a study of children, researchers found that "Drop-out from play therapy is more likely to occur among families headed by a single parent who is young and economically disadvantaged" (Campbell et al., 2000, p. 133). Not surprisingly, when helping professionals expect people who have few economic resources to take off time from work, arrange for and pay for transportation, and then travel considerable distances to attend a treatment in which they are not included and which appears to involve another adult playing games with their children, questions of the value of the treatment arise. However, these factors are not limited to play therapy or children's services. The same considerations apply to early dropout among adults as well (Swift & Greenberg, 2012).

Indeed, differences between the personal and cultural expectations of clients and professional helpers represent a clear, albeit partial, explanation for early dropout or discontinuation of needed services. When professional helpers fail to express accurate understanding of clients' view of the problems (that is, how clients conceptualize the issues), the rate of dropout triples. Indeed, the actual length of service appears to be determined primarily by clients' expectations of anticipated duration (Epperson, Bushway, &

Warman, 1983; Pekarik, 1988, 1991; Pelkonen, Marttunen, Laippala, & Lonnqvist, 2000; Wierzbicki & Pekarik, 1993).

Although several factors are undoubtedly involved with premature discontinuation, insufficient and ineffective preparation for first meetings is certainly part of the problem. Effective preparation and careful planning can make the difference.

Let's try to be personally and professionally ready to perform competently from the first moment of contact. Use the preparing skills before the first meetings with individuals, families, groups, organizations, and communities with whom you interact as part of your professional responsibilities. Then continue to use them in advance of each subsequent encounter.

■ Preparatory Reviewing

Preparatory reviewing involves examining and considering information available to you and your agency before an initial contact with clients or other constituents (Kadushin, 1983). When an individual, family, group, organization, or community has previously received service from your agency, review the relevant case records. When a telephone contact or an intake interview has preceded the first meeting, examine notes concerning the nature and substance of that interaction. For first meetings with other people, such as an agency director, a client's medical doctor, or a new supervisee, thoughtfully review relevant materials concerning the general purpose of the meeting and any topics likely to emerge. When meeting with a family system or subsystem, a group, an organization, or a community, preparatory reviewing becomes, if anything, even more important as you ponder various intra- and intersystem factors and dynamics. Consider the myriad and complicated factors associated with planning activities associated with a social movement–related public action. A protest against injustice or a human rights demonstration involving hundreds of people requires a careful review of facts related to the pertinent issues, close examination of permit requirements and other legal and safety regulations, and, of course, study of the physical space and facilities. The effectiveness of a social action can sometimes depend upon access to bathrooms!

Preparatory reviewing helps you grasp significant facts and circumstances before meetings. This reduces the need for applicants, clients, or other people to repeat information they have previously provided. It allows for more efficient use of time and helps people feel that what they say is valued and remembered.

In some instances, failure to review available materials could constitute professional negligence or malpractice. For example, suppose a teenage boy contacts your agency. He has a history of making serious suicide attempts following conflicts in romantic relationships. Your agency has served him off and on during the past several years, and this pattern of suicidal action is well documented in his case file. He requests an appointment "right away," indicating that he needs help because his girlfriend just "dumped" him. She decided to date another boy. If you fail to review the case record, you may decide to give the teenager an appointment several days later, not realizing the serious, immediate risk of suicidal behavior.

As another example, suppose you are about to interview a family with a history of both spousal and child abuse. Both patterns are well documented in agency files. Imagine the risks associated with failure to review those materials before the meeting.

Groups, organizations, and communities may also have factions or "histories" that pertain to the purpose for the meeting and our preparation. For instance, suppose you are about to meet with a small group of leaders to establish a direction and goals for your work with their community organization. Your agency has previously worked with the organization and the community it represents. Imagine what could happen if you did not know that since your agency's last contact, the organization had split into two because of a conflict over its mission and the misuse of funds by its director. There are now two subgroups—one led by the former director and another by former board members—purporting to serve the same community. Imagine a first meeting in which you were unaware of these current circumstances.

In a similar fashion, suppose you are about to meet with the leaders of two urban street gangs that have engaged in turf wars over the past decade. Hundreds of deaths and injuries have resulted. Imagine the potential harm if you arrive without a deep understanding of each group's internal organizational structure, the history of their origin and development, their current means of income generation, their initiation rituals, and their territorial boundaries. If you have not done your homework and have not thoroughly prepared for the meeting, a genuine disaster could ensue.

There are also numerous practical reasons for reviewing relevant information before a visit. You may learn, for example, that a prospective client is hard of hearing or does not speak any of the languages spoken in your agency, so that an interpreter will be required. You might find out that a person uses a wheelchair and has a canine companion. Such knowledge could enable you to rearrange your office to allow enough open space for the wheelchair and service dog.

In social action that involves intentional civil disobedience, knowledge about demonstrators' prior arrest or conviction histories is vital. Most forms of planned civil disobedience—such as failure to obey a police officer's request that demonstrators move "behind a demarcation line"—lead to misdemeanor arrests and minor fines or punishments in the form of community service. However, even such a minor offense can result in a criminal justice nightmare if demonstrators have previous misdemeanor arrests or other convictions in their records. Social action coordinators should also be aware of participants' personal status and medical condition. Suppose, for example, no one is aware that one of the demonstrators is diabetic and requires insulin injections. If she were arrested without proper medical documentation, some police might be reluctant to permit her access to her medication and her injection kit. Furthermore, it might be 24 or 48 hours before those arrested are processed and released on bond or on their own recognizance. Reviewing participants' needs in advance can help to ensure their safety during such activities.

Although many benefits are associated with the preparatory review of informative materials, there are potential risks as well. Some records and related documents contain hearsay information or opinions written as if they were undisputed facts. You may inadvertently accept at face value information that is essentially false, distorted, biased, or incomplete. Some records contain profiles, assessments, or diagnoses that can lead you to form a stereotypical impression of a person or group before you actually meet. Such profiles may have been inaccurate when initially recorded, or they may have since become so. The person or people, the issue, or the situation may have changed, sometimes dramatically, since the last entry. In preparatory reviewing, recognize that information contained in case records or other forms of written material may be incomplete or erroneous. The same holds true for oral comments. Recollections and interpretations of words, events, and exchanges can vary widely from person to person and, from time to time in the same person. Dedicate yourself to maintaining an open mind during the preparatory reviewing phase.

EXERCISE 7-1   Preparatory Reviewing

1. At 10:13 A.M. on January 12, Ruth Gordon, an agency social worker, received a telephone call from a woman identifying herself as Mrs. Nancy Cannon. The social worker jotted a few notes concerning the call on a telephone contact form (see Box 7.1). Ms. Gordon later gave the notations to you as the social worker assigned to conduct the initial face-to-face interview and, if appropriate, to provide needed professional services.

Demonstrate your use of the preparatory reviewing skill by examining the contents of Box 7.1. Use a pen or pencil to highlight information that you, as the social worker, would want to remember for a first meeting with Mrs. Cannon. Use the space below to outline potential themes or issues.

Box 7.1 TELEPHONE CONTACT

January 12, 10:13 A.M. Mrs. Nancy Cannon telephoned from her place of work (the Capital Insurance Company—phone 234-6213). She sounded concerned. She said that on the previous Saturday night, her 14-year-old daughter Amy had come home after her 9:00 P.M. curfew, smelling of alcohol. She says that she "grounded" her daughter but now wants to talk with a social worker about the situation. Mrs. Cannon requested an appointment for herself alone, indicating that she wanted to sort things out with someone before she dealt further with her daughter.

Mrs. C. reported that this was the first such incident. She said, "I've never had any trouble whatsoever from Amy. She's been a wonderful child." She stated that she had not sought professional help before and that this was her first contact with any social service or mental health agency. She indicated that her husband, Amy's father, had recently filed for divorce and had left the home approximately 6 weeks ago. Mrs. C. wondered whether that might be connected with Amy's misbehavior over the weekend.

Disposition: An appointment was scheduled with an agency social worker for tomorrow at 12:00 noon. Mrs. C. requested a lunch-hour appointment, if at all possible, to reduce the amount of time away from her job.

Ruth Gordon, BSW, LSW
Licensed Social Worker

■ Preparatory Exploring

The skill of **preparatory exploring** involves asking questions and seeking information about a prospective client or others, a problem or issue, and a situation—prior to the meeting. This is an important but often neglected skill. Receptionists, intake workers, or executives from your agency may talk with people before you first meet with them. They often have useful information that can improve the quality of the first contact. Similarly, referral sources from outside your agency may have knowledge that can help. As part of making a referral on behalf of another person or group, family members, physicians, judges, teachers, religious leaders, other helping professionals, and governmental officials often contact social service agencies. They may possess important information concerning the person or group, the presenting issue and situation, and sometimes even the nature of the service needs. As a natural part of the process of talking about the referral to your agency, you may appropriately inquire about the person or group, issue, and situation with the referral source. Usually, you would not have permission to seek information from other sources. For that, you would need the informed consent of the client. However, when someone makes a referral for another person, family, group, organization, or community, you may appropriately seek information from the referring source. Regardless of the source of information, however, realize that what you hear from others reflects their own perspectives. Other people may view things in quite a different way, and you may too.

Preparatory exploring is also applicable for people previously served by colleagues in your own agency. For example, by reviewing agency files, you may learn that another social worker in the agency, Ms. Castillo, had previously served a client you are about to see. Once you learn that, you could ask her for pertinent information about the case.

In advance of a social action, such as a public protest or demonstration, preparatory exploring can help to ensure the safety of participants, bystanders, and police authorities. For example, suppose you're helping to coordinate a protest at the state capitol against legislation intended to privilege (that is, to give extraordinary advantages or exemptions) a particular group of people while simultaneously restricting the civil rights of another category of people. If you engaged in preparatory exploration with the relevant police personnel as well as city and capitol building authorities, you could help to reduce the probability of physical violence. Indeed, you might even be able to meet the capitol police assigned to monitor demonstrations to learn about both formal policies as well as informal practices regarding demonstrators who intentionally engage in civil disobedience.[1]

The use of the preparatory exploring skill can result in a more positive and productive first meeting. However, information gained through the preparatory exploring process should not lead you to stereotype people or form fixed impressions about the nature of an issue and situation. You can resist such temptations by consciously distinguishing fact from opinion and recognizing that the views of one person often differ from those of others.

In preparatory exploring, remain open to information that may help you be a more effective service provider. You may note names and relevant demographic data such as phone numbers, addresses, or special needs and circumstances. You may learn the preferred pronunciation of names. Details concerning the nature, severity, and urgency of the issue are, of course, extremely important, as are indications of the strengths and resources available to the people involved.

EXERCISE 7-2 Preparatory Exploring

1. At 3:15 P.M. on Wednesday, Father Julio Sanchez, a Catholic priest in a largely Mexican parish, telephones you at your agency. He indicates that a family of seven needs help. He says that the parents and older children are migrant workers. He reports that the family had been traveling to a new work site when their automobile broke down. In the space provided, write

---

[1] Public demonstrations, protests, and marches are protected forms of speech under the U.S. Constitution. Let's hope that never changes. As such, they do not constitute acts of "civil disobedience." However, if a demonstrator fails to follow a lawful order by police or, for example, violates a building or fire code, that could represent civil disobedience and might lead to an arrest. Indeed, in contexts where public demonstrations are common, police typically give warnings before proceeding with arrests. Many times, key social activists intentionally disobey those warnings and willingly accept arrest to highlight the importance of the pertinent issue. In effect, they "walk the talk."

the questions you would ask and identify the information you would seek as you use the skill of preparatory exploring with Father Sanchez.

Preparatory Consultation

The skill of **preparatory consultation** may be used in two primary ways. The first involves seeking advice from a social work supervisor or professional colleagues within your agency concerning an upcoming visit with a prospective client or other constituents. The second involves consultation with experts or examination of published material related to a topic that appears relevant to a forthcoming meeting.

When engaging in preparatory consultation with agency-based colleagues, you may usually be fairly open about details that pertain to an upcoming meeting. Your supervisors and other members of your service program or unit are just as responsible for protecting the privacy and confidentiality rights of your clients as you are of theirs. When consulting with outside experts, however, social workers must be more circumspect and seek information in ways that do not compromise clients' rights. For example, suppose you are about to meet with a new client who mentioned during the initial telephone contact that she is an undocumented immigrant and expects to be deported within the next few weeks. However, her children are U.S. citizens and she wants them to remain in this country. She seeks your help in exploring options and locating the best available care of her children during her absence. She anticipates being away for at least 1 year and perhaps many more.

Given this limited information, many social workers would wisely consult experienced immigration attorneys. In addition, we might also access government websites to review up-to-date information about deportation policies and processes, as well as potential resources for children of deported parents. You might contact a governmental representative by phone or through an Internet "live chat" service. In seeking information, however, you would avoid the use of her name, address, or other identifying characteristics—unless you had her expressed informed consent to do so. Otherwise, you could easily violate her rights to confidentiality and privacy.

Clients' privacy rights are usually safer when social workers consult online published works such as professional books, research articles, or legal statutes. However, be a bit careful in your choice of keywords so that your client's anonymity remains intact.

Commonly, social workers would seek consultation from professional colleagues to consider tentative objectives for an interview, seek advice, or discuss other service-related issues. The specific nature of the consultation, however, varies from situation to situation. On one occasion, you might discuss possible locations for the interview. In another, you might inquire about cultural customs of a particular religious or ethnic group about which you have limited knowledge. On occasion, you might seek advice concerning how best to ensure your own safety when you are about to interview someone who has previously been physically violent toward people in positions of authority. In still another, you might focus on the agency policies or legal obligations that could apply in a particular case. In advance of public protests, demonstrations, boycotts, or marches, consultation with veteran civil rights attorneys as well as experienced activists can reduce the risk of violence as well as enhance the impact of the social action. By engaging in preparatory consultation, you can enhance the quality of initial meetings, encounters, and initiatives. The investment of time it takes to consult scholarly works and talk with a colleague, supervisor, or an experienced stakeholder can pay significant dividends in effectiveness.

Similarly, a search for accurate information about legal regulations, governmental policies, and potential resources that might pertain to a policy issue, a social injustice, or a potential client's needs can dramatically accelerate progress toward a successful outcome. So might a search for intervention approaches or practices that reflect strong scientific evidence of effectiveness. For example, imagine that you are about to meet a new client for the first time. During the initial telephone contact, he mentioned that he has a few medical issues and sometimes experiences episodes of syncope when he meets people for the first time. Social workers who do not know the definition of syncope might be wise to conduct a search for the word's meaning, a description of how it occurs, and perhaps what might be done to help people when they have an episode. In the absence of such knowledge, the client would have to spend quite some time providing an explanation to the social worker. And, the social worker who is ignorant about syncope might be ill-prepared to respond helpfully should the client experience an episode during the interview.

Obviously, social workers benefit when we can efficiently access valid, reliable, and relevant information about topics, issues, programs, practices, and resources that pertain to the people we serve. In general, clients benefit when their social workers are more rather than less knowledgeable. However, the ever-expanding electronic Web raises challenging questions about the extent of the privacy rights of prospective and current clients, and other people with whom we interact in our roles and functions as social workers. The line between a legitimate and an illegitimate Internet search is not entirely clear. For example, people with access to a computer could use a person's name or address to conduct a search for information about that person or family. Such a search might yield newspaper stories, links to social media entries, images, references to court appearances or legal documents, and perhaps to facts about economic status, religious or political affiliation, memberships in groups and organizations, and a great deal more. Social workers everywhere are grappling with the moral and ethical implications of such person-focused Internet searches. The issue may be captured in questions such as these: "Should I, as a social worker, conduct an Internet search about a particular client or prospective client without that person's consent?" "Does an Internet search that includes a client's name or other identifying characteristics constitute a violation of that client's right to privacy and confidentiality?" "If I do conduct such a search, should it be considered a professional social work activity and should the results of the search be incorporated in the client's case record? If it is not a legitimate social work activity, do I have the right to use my agency's computer resources and time in my workday to conduct such a search?" "If I conduct an Internet search using a client's name as a keyword and do so as a personal rather than a professional activity, will the information I garner affect the quality of my work and the nature of the working relationship with that client? What if I am under oath during a legal proceeding and I am asked if I had ever conducted an Internet search for information about a client, how should I answer?"

As you gain actual social work practice experience, you may begin to feel less need for preparatory consultation. Please be cautious about such an attitude. Preparatory and ongoing consultation with colleagues and supervisors is often incredibly useful and sometimes necessary to help us maintain emotional balance and equilibrium. Please remember that our basic unit of attention is the person-in-environment. The perspective is not just for clients; it includes social workers as well. If social workers operate in solo fashion—without the wisdom and expertise available in our social environment—we increase the risk of foreseeable and preventable mistakes. Consultation with experts and review of relevant published professional literature can be invaluable and, in some instances, truly lifesaving. Even after years of experience, there are unexpected, unusually complicated circumstances where preparatory and ongoing consultation can make the difference between effective and ineffective meetings, and between positive and tragic outcomes.

EXERCISE 7-3 Preparatory Consultation

1. You work in an agency that serves an elderly population in the community. On Tuesday morning, a woman telephoned the agency and talked with you about her neighbor Mrs. Anderson. According to the caller, Mrs. Anderson is 89 years old and lives by herself in an apartment. The caller reported that Mrs. Anderson has not left her apartment in 3 days and would not answer her door or telephone. The neighbor did say, however, that she could hear someone moving about in the apartment. Immediately following the phone call, you examined agency files and discovered that Mrs. Anderson had not previously received agency services. Use the following space to identify the information you would seek and the issues you would address as you consult with your supervisor before taking action concerning Mrs. Anderson.

2. You work in an agency that serves people who are unemployed. Your major function is to help people obtain jobs or to secure regular incomes through grants or programs of various kinds. As you review a pile of intake forms, you learn that in about 2 hours you will meet with an unemployed man for the first time. According to the form, Mr. Gaines is about 47 years of age and served in Iraq and Afghanistan. He was awarded numerous service-related medals and was honorably discharged from the U.S. Army several years ago. Use the following space to describe how you would search for and consult credible published material as you prepare to meet with Mr. Gaines about unemployment-related issues.

■ Preparatory Arranging

The skill of **preparatory arranging** involves logistical preparation for a meeting. It includes scheduling an appointment, ensuring that there is adequate time and privacy, and organizing the physical environment. You may have to secure an interview room, locate an interpreter, rearrange furniture, or find a whiteboard or drawing tablet. It includes considering the appropriateness of your apparel, appearance, and perhaps even hygiene. Some people are put off by a social worker's noticeable body odors; other people are allergic to perfumes or colognes and react adversely to such scents. Some cultures reflect preferences that we can easily respect—if we know about them and make the necessary accommodations ahead of time. Avoiding cultural *faux pas* is much easier than rectifying them.

Preparatory arranging could involve any number of considerations. For example, in advance of social action, you might arrange for carpools or buses to help transport demonstrators and assemble a group of attorneys who could intervene if or when participants are arrested for acts of civil disobedience. Before meeting with a family, you might provide transportation or secure temporary child care so that you can meet separately with a parent. You might reserve a large room in a school or community building to meet with a group or a neighborhood organization.

In making arrangements, be sure to consider the significance of the environment for clients and other people who may be involved (Kadushin, 1983). For instance, many people assign special meaning to their homes and might feel ill at ease should you arrive before adequate preparations have been made. Food may also have special significance to a family, and family members may reserve certain chairs in a home for specific people. Groups and organizations often reflect similar characteristics. Imagine the potential reaction if you sat in the chair reserved for the leader of a group or the CEO of an organization. Pay close attention to the subtle signals and context so that you may convey respect and sensitivity for the familial, cultural, and systemic meanings associated with each unique encounter.

In agency settings, preparatory arranging includes considering the potential effects of the physical environment. Ensure that clients have a comfortable place to sit and children have a play area when they arrive at the agency. Check to see that interviewing rooms are sufficiently soundproofed so that privacy can be assured. When you have office space assigned to you, arranging involves selecting and displaying pictures, posters, and other items such as college degrees, professional certificates, and your social work license. At times, you may also need to reposition furniture to accommodate the number of people expected to attend a meeting.

The office environment can have a powerful impact on people. Suppose, for example, that you provide social services in an area where firearms are widely prized. You would be unwise to decorate your office wall with a poster that reads, "Ban handguns." The titles of books on your shelves can have a similar effect. You could needlessly alienate many people. Personal, political, or religious books and symbols may interfere with others' ability to experience you as an objective professional who genuinely respects them.

In sum, preparatory arranging should facilitate communication and diminish interference and distraction. Although it requires some time and reflection, ultimately such preparation improves efficiency and increases the probability of a successful engagement.

EXERCISE 7-4 Preparatory Arranging

1. Assume that you are a social worker in a high-security men's prison. You share an office with another worker. The office contains two desks, chairs behind and next to each desk, two bookcases, two telephones, and two file cabinets. In addition, there is a small area containing a sofa,

two comfortable chairs, and a small coffee table. You have a 10:00 A.M. appointment scheduled with Mr. Somes, a prisoner. The topic for conversation is the serious illness of his wife of 23 years. According to a report you have just received from her physician, it appears that Mrs. Somes will die sometime within the next few days.

As the appointment time approaches, you notice that your social work colleague remains at his desk, actively engaged in paperwork. You had expected him to be out of the office, as he usually is at this time of day. Use the following space to discuss how you would use the skill of arranging before the meeting.

◼ Preparatory Empathy

Preparatory empathy involves envisioning the world and the current circumstances from another person or group's perspective and experience. Try to anticipate what others are likely to sense, feel, think, imagine, and do as they meet with you, especially for the first time but for later meetings as well. Even before an initial face-to-face meeting, anticipatory empathy heightens your sensitivity to possible agendas, thoughts, feelings about themselves, feelings about you, the presenting problems and issues, and the circumstances. Through preparatory empathy, you try to anticipate others' subjective experience related to seeking or receiving social service and to this particular meeting with you. Put yourself in others' shoes to gain increased appreciation for their motivations and feelings about the contact, their thoughts and feelings about engaging with an authority figure, and potential issues related to factors such as gender, sexual orientation, stage of life, culture, ethnic background, and socioeconomic status.

Preparatory empathy regarding cultural and ethnic aspects is especially important. Members of some cultural groups may be ambivalent or conflicted about social workers and about social services. Many have adopted negative stereotypes of social workers—which you may need to transcend. Certain people may prefer a slow and informal beginning. Others might find it difficult to share personal information about themselves and their families. Some may be concerned that you might challenge or criticize their culture-based, traditional gender and family roles. In most instances, visiting an agency or meeting with a social worker is hardly a simple request for service. The meaning of such contact can be extraordinarily complicated for many people and especially for members of diverse groups. Be sensitive to the potential cultural implications of upcoming meetings.

Preparatory empathy involves trying to experience what others may be thinking and feeling before an encounter occurs. For instance, in advance of a public demonstration or protest, you would engage in preparatory empathy with people who hold an opposing point of view and certainly with the police charged with responsibility for ensuring public safety. It can be eye-opening to put yourself in the "other's shoes" and potentially extremely helpful if you do so before you meet face to face.

As you engage in preparatory empathy in advance of a meeting or encounter, recognize that your preliminary understanding may be considerably off target. By definition, preparatory empathy is always

Box 7.2 Preparatory Empathy: Example

If I were in Mrs. Cannon's shoes, I might feel anxious for, concerned about, and disappointed in my daughter. I would also love her a great deal. I might feel responsible for her behavior and perhaps even guilty about my own parenting. I might feel uncertain about how to proceed. I could very well feel inadequate and maybe frightened. I would be concerned about what the future might hold for Amy and for me. I am aware that my husband's divorce petition and his recent departure from the home may have adversely affected my daughter, and I might feel angry at him—on both my daughter's behalf as well as my own. If I believed I could have been a better spouse or taken actions to prevent his departure, I might also feel guilty about the separation and upcoming divorce proceedings. I might perceive the divorce as the result of some misbehavior of my own and experience conflicted feelings about what's happening. Regardless of how the separation and divorce process began, I would feel a great deal of stress during this period. I would probably feel confused about the present and fearful about the future. I might be concerned about finances, after-school supervision of Amy, and my ability to guide and discipline Amy under these new circumstances. I might wonder if there is another person in my husband's life and if there is now or ever will be someone else in mine. I might question my capacity to assume the roles of single person and single parent, my ability to deal with my husband around parental issues concerning Amy, and dozens of other issues provoked by my husband's departure and Amy's recent behavior. I would probably feel highly distressed and perhaps overwhelmed by the events of recent weeks. If sadness and grieving have not yet occurred, I might begin to experience them soon. I may even have begun to anticipate that not only has my husband left the household, but eventually Amy will also leave. After all, she is already 14.

Mrs. Cannon seems to be of a different ethnic background than my own and I am at least 10 years younger. I have never been married and do not have children of my own. Mrs. Cannon may ask about my marital and parental status. Because of these cultural and status differences, she may experience me as unable to understand and appreciate her situation. She may even see me as less able to help her, because I have not personally experienced these same difficulties.

based on incomplete information. Therefore, our impressions are always tentative, always preliminary, and always subject to immediate change based on others' actual communications. Even when your preparatory empathy proves to be inaccurate, however, it remains a productive activity because it enhances your readiness to listen carefully and sensitively to people when you finally do meet in person.

Let's return to the upcoming visit with our new client, Mrs. Nancy Cannon. A social worker engaging in preparatory empathy might review the telephone contact notes (see Box 7.1) and then go through a process such as described in Box 7.2.

Engaging in the skill of preparatory empathy helps to sensitize you to what others might experience at the time of first meetings and encounters. By empathizing in advance, you increase the likelihood that you will approach people as unique human beings with all of the complexity that entails. A major challenge in this form of anticipatory empathy, however, is resisting the temptation to narrow your view of people so that it leads to a kind of stereotyping rather than to enhanced openness and sensitivity.

EXERCISE 7-5 Preparatory Empathy

1. Assume that you are a social worker in a general hospital. This morning, a physician contacts you and asks that you accompany her while she informs the mother and father of a 23-year-old man that their son has been infected with the human immunodeficiency virus (HIV). The physician wants you to provide support and social services to the family after she informs them of the

diagnosis and prognosis. Use the following space to discuss how you would engage in the skill of preparatory empathy in advance of a meeting with the parents of the HIV-positive patient.

◼ Preparatory Self-Exploration

In addition to preparatory empathy, social workers also engage briefly in **preparatory self-exploration** before meeting with others. Preparatory self-exploration is a form of self-analysis or introspection through which you, a human being who happens to be a social worker, identify how you might personally be affected by your interaction with this particular person, family, group, organization, or community; the specific issues of concern; and the unique circumstances. In self-exploring, you ask yourself questions such as "How am I likely to feel about this person or these people in this context? How are the cultural and demographic similarities or differences between us likely to affect me? Given what I know about the issues and circumstances what personal reactions might I experience?"

The purpose of this skill is to identify the potential effects of your own personal history, characteristics, needs, biases, emotional tender spots, philosophical or religious views, and behavioral patterns on clients and others you are about to encounter. Self-exploration helps to bring into conscious focus those aspects of your personal self that might affect the nature and quality of your engagement with and service to people.

Preparatory self-exploration also involves identifying other factors that may affect your readiness to provide service. For example, there may be extraneous circumstances unrelated to the people or problems that might influence you. Your readiness to engage could be affected if you have a splitting headache, are grieving the loss of a significant relationship, are trying to figure out how to pay for major repairs to your automobile, have just lost out on an opportunity for promotion, did not sleep last night, or are worried about a family member of your own. Similarly, if you are about to engage in some form of social activism—perhaps to protest proposed legislation to both waive all state and local taxes, and donate a substantial portion of a public park to a for-profit company in an attempt to recruit it to the state while simultaneously limiting child welfare benefits to a total of 1 year during the course of the child's lifetime. You are so furious that you become worried you might lose your composure during the event. You realize that you must determine the unrecognized reasons for your rage. You ask yourself, "Why does this particular proposal trigger so much more rage than other legislative schemes that have been even more unjust than this one?" Identifying the factors and their effects on you constitutes a step toward managing them so that they do not interfere with the provision of high-quality professional services to your clients or with your constructive, nonviolent social activism intended to advance human rights and promote social, economic, and environmental justice.

EXERCISE 7-6 Preparatory Self-Exploration

1. Assume that you are a social worker in an agency that provides psychosocial counseling services to sexually abused children. You have recently begun to work with Cathy, a 7-year-old whose biological father molested her for a period of 4 years. About a month ago, Cathy's father forced

her to perform fellatio. The incident led to his arrest and departure from the family home. Released on a bail bond until his trial begins, you are about to interview Cathy's father for the first time. The general purpose of the meeting is to gather information on which to base a tentative assessment of his potential to benefit from a pretrial counseling program. Use the following space to summarize the results of your self-exploration in anticipation of the meeting.

Centering

Preparatory self-exploration enables you to identify personal factors that might affect your ability to engage people and provide high-quality service. Once identified, you attempt to manage or contain them through **centering**. As part of this centering process, you ask yourself "What can I do to ready myself personally before the meeting or activity begins?" Centering involves organizing your personal thoughts, feelings, and physical sensations so that they do not interfere with your professionalism, performance, and delivery of social services. Much of the time, centering involves "accessing a place of peace" where we are free from evaluative judgment (Rosenberg, 2012) and nondefensiveness (Ellison, 2009). Depending on the time, context, and social work purpose, however, centering might also involve mobilizing our courage to participate in a public demonstration and perhaps even engage in civil disobedience to protest exploitation of workers, subordination of women, and brutal treatment of racial or ethnic minorities or members of the LGBTQIA community. Accessing a place of peace is useful preparation for all encounters and represents a vital aspect of centering. In centering, however, we focus on the particulars of the circumstances and our roles and purposes in order to conduct ourselves in the most professional manner possible.

Suppose, for example, you had once been the victim of date rape. At the time of the violation, you somehow minimized its significance. Now, however, you are aware that you still have strong feelings and some unresolved issues about the event. You have decided to seek out a social worker for help in this matter. As you review the intake form of a new client you will meet later today, you read that 2 weeks earlier a man raped her on their first date.

Through preparatory self-exploration, you might recognize that you remain unsettled about your own experience, even though it happened years earlier. You could also realize that you will probably not serve this client well if your own emotions about rape interact with hers. Therefore, you might access a place of peace and then center yourself by taking a few deep breaths, engaging in a brief relaxation exercise, and compartmentalizing (temporarily putting into an enclosed area of yourself) your personal experience so that you will be able to give your full attention to the client. As part of the process, you say to yourself, "I'm still tender about being raped but I'm able to manage my feelings of rage, shame, and fear so that they don't get in the way of my service to this client. Because it is obvious, however, that I still have unresolved issues, I commit to schedule an appointment with a social worker experienced in service to rape victims. I plan to telephone her agency office at 11 o'clock, when I have a free hour."

In centering, you might engage in brief stress-management exercises to reduce emotional reactivity and promote self-control. Positive self-talk, visualization, muscular relaxation, journal writing, and brief mindful meditation may be useful. However, under no circumstances should you deny or minimize your personal issues and strong feelings. Rather, manage them temporarily and develop specific plans to address them at another time and in a different place.

EXERCISE 7-7 Centering

1. Assume that you have an appointment to meet with a new client in approximately 10 minutes. While finishing a brief coffee break with a colleague, you learn that everyone else in the agency received a pay raise of 7 percent. Despite the fact that you have earned outstanding evaluations and recently received a promotion, you know that you only received a 3 percent raise. In the following space, describe how you would access a place of peace and then center yourself before the meeting.

■ Preliminary Planning and Recording

Social workers engage in **preliminary planning** before meetings, contacts, and interviews with individuals, families, groups, organizations, and communities with whom we interact as part of our professional responsibilities. We plan before social media blitzes, protests, demonstrations, marches, boycotts, and other forms of social activism. Of course, planning is not limited to initial meetings or first encounters. Social workers plan in advance of subsequent meetings and activities as well. Begin the process of formulating preliminary plans by asking and answering questions such as "Why is this meeting, event, or activity occurring? What is its overall purpose? What do we hope to accomplish? What is our tentative agenda? What might be the agenda of other people who will be involved or affected by this encounter? What might they hope to accomplish? What would we consider success? What might success look like to others? What are our functions or roles in this meeting, activity, or event? How do we wish to begin? What things should we say? What questions should we ask? What might others want to ask of us? What kind of interactional process would we like to see? What kind might others want or expect? How do we hope the meeting will conclude? How might others like to see it end?"

The specifics of preliminary planning for meetings vary somewhat according to the purpose for the meeting, activity, or event; the circumstances; how many people are involved; and who they are. In general, the number of considerations increases as size and complexity grow. Let's classify social work encounters into three common categories: (1) *information-gathering*; (2) *information-sharing*; and (3) *change-making*. In **information-gathering** encounters, social workers encourage people to discuss the problems or issues of concern and their circumstances, their aspirations and goals, their views and feelings about themselves, and their preferences and strengths. As they express themselves, they may share facts as well as opinions, thoughts as well as emotions; and they may reveal information verbally, nonverbally, and sometimes through other means as well. By listening well as people share information, social workers gather a great deal of information and gain some understanding of them and their situations. Interestingly, as others talk and we listen, they also "hear themselves." Consequently, many grow in self-understanding and do so primarily because they are encouraged to share by an attentive, interested listener.

In **information-sharing** encounters, social workers provide needed or useful knowledge or professional opinions. You might offer information about a program, policy, or resource in your attempt to respond to a request or address a perceived need. You might educate people about a topic of concern or about possible strategies and methods to address particular problems or pursue selected goals. You might share an appraisal, assessment, or evaluation based upon one or more testing instruments or obtained through one or more information-gathering interviews. And, sometimes, you might offer a professional opinion or suggestion, make a formal recommendation, or submit a proposal.

In the context of social activism, information-sharing may take the form of **consciousness-raising**. Activists may share facts and analyses through social media, films, videos, press releases, flyers, newspaper articles, letters to the editor, public testimony in legislative hearings and sometimes in court proceedings, and through public speeches in the community or during demonstrations.

In **change-making** encounters, you engage others in attempts to modify aspects of the person-in-environment system. The targets of change may range from the personal to the political or from the individual to the society. For example, one client might seek change in an unwanted situation (for example, securing food or obtaining housing, relocating to a safer neighborhood, finding a lover, or separating from a spouse). Another client might want to accept an undesirable but inevitable reality (for example, by adjusting expectations, forgiving another, or becoming more mindful). Some clients hope to change their feelings or emotions (for example, become less anxious, less depressed, more passionate, or more content). Others want to alter their thinking or their thoughts (for example, think more deeply or more optimistically, or experience more gratitude); and some want to change their behavior (for example, speak more clearly, become more assertive or more self-controlled, discontinue consumption of alcohol, or make more frequent gestures of love and affection).

Change may also be directed toward various aspects of small and large social systems (for example, a couple, a mother and child, a family, a formal or informal group, an organization or institution, a community, or a society). Targets for change might include social systems' missions or structures, cultural rules or operating principles and policies, communication or decision-making processes, or perhaps feedback mechanisms. Change targets may also include the built and natural environments. For example, you might advocate for increased lighting in heavy crime areas, more recreational areas, cleaner air or water, reforestation and sustainable energy initiatives, or more efficient and more accessible public transit. Meetings may involve clients and significant others in their world, people who might become clients but have not yet done so, and stakeholders of various kinds. You might, for example, meet with legislators or government leaders, community representatives, business executives, potential funders; and, perhaps most importantly, with non-privileged people potentially affected by various proposed or dedicated action. Change-making encounters may include direct or indirect action and frequently incorporate advocacy and aspects of policy–practice. Social workers realize that changes to policies, programs, and practices can have profound effects upon social systems of all sizes—from the child of a young, unemployed, single mother to a starving population in a drought-stricken region of the world.

Most of the time, social workers can readily identify a tentative, general purpose for an upcoming encounter. Sometimes, of course, a meeting serves more than one purpose. Many involve aspects of information-gathering and information-sharing as well as change-making. Once the purpose or purposes are identified, however, you may sketch out preliminary plans for the encounter.

The primary purpose of many first meetings is information-gathering. In such instances, you might formulate general but flexible plans concerning what data to seek and from whom. For example, in planning for a first meeting with a family, you may have to decide whether to see all family members together or to see some of them separately. If you plan to see members individually or in the form of smaller subsystems (for example, mother–daughter dyad or parental dyad), you determine whom to interview first, second, and so forth. The same questions apply in work with groups, organizations, and communities.

Consider the case of a prospective client who telephoned to request a meeting. She expressed an interest in resolving a family problem. Your tentative plans might look something like those depicted in Box 7.3.

Preliminary planning enables you to begin meetings in a coherent and purposeful fashion. The process yields a flexible structure, which can help you come across as organized, professional, and competent. The **planning record** that results from preparation may take several forms and include various components. Many agencies use a telephone contact form (see Box 7.1) to make relevant notations about the caller, the reason for the call, and the substance of the conversation. A more extensive **intake form** provides space to record identifying characteristics of the people involved (for example, name, gender, age, occupation, family role, address, and phone numbers), the presenting need, problem, or issue (for example, reason for contact, preliminary description of the issue of concern, indication of desired goals or outcomes), and the circumstances. Although you should always view notes

---

BOX 7.3 PRELIMINARY PLANS: EXAMPLE OF A HELP-SEEKING FAMILY

- Engage in introductions.
- Share your ideas about the general purpose and direction for the meeting (that is, information-gathering).
- Establish the ground rules for the process.
- Address any questions or uncertainties concerning the agency, you as the social worker, the purpose, the process, or the ground rules.
- Determine the identities and characteristics of the family or household members.
- Explore the presenting issues that stimulated the phone contact.
- Explore the history and development as well as the consequences of the issues.
- Explore risk and protective factors (that is, those factors likely to increase and decrease the probability of an occurrence of the issues).
- Examine how the family has attempted to address these issues and determine the outcomes of those efforts.
- Explore strengths within the family or household system and identify available resources that might contribute to a resolution of the issues.
- Explore the client's quality of life.
- Establish goals for service.
- Conclude the interview with some sense of what will happen next in the process.

Box 7.4 PRELIMINARY NOTES: MRS. NANCY CANNON

January 13
Mrs. Nancy Cannon—seems to prefer "Mrs."

Presenting concern: 14-year-old daughter Amy alleged to have drunk alcohol and come home after her 9:00 P.M. curfew. First such incident; Mrs. Cannon wonders if her daughter's behavior may be related to Mr. Cannon's (Amy's father) recent departure from the home and subsequent divorce petition. He left the home about 6 weeks ago. I am uncertain about what triggered the separation and divorce process. Mrs. Cannon wants a noontime appointment to avoid time away from work. Could there be financial constraints or concerns about keeping her job?

Rose Hernandez, BSW, LSW
Licensed Social Worker

---

based on telephone conversations as preliminary and tentative, they often provide valuable information when you subsequently engage a person, family, group, or organization in a face-to-face meeting. Many workers also develop, often in brief outline form, a summary of their preliminary plans for the meeting. For example, Rose Hernandez, the social worker scheduled to conduct the initial face-to-face interview with Mrs. Cannon, might make a few notes in advance of her first meeting (see Box 7.4). Notice how useful these brief notes could be in helping her to be prepared from the very first moment of contact.

Ms. Hernandez might also prepare preliminary plans such as that depicted in Box 7.5. She will be ready to engage Mrs. Cannon. Imagine the likely differences in interview quality, efficiency, and effectiveness between their meeting and one with a social worker who does not engage in preliminary planning.

Box 7.5 PRELIMINARY PLANS: MRS. NANCY CANNON

- Introduce myself, my professional affiliation, and my role or function with the agency. Use "Mrs. Cannon" as initial reference to her and ask how she would prefer to be addressed.
- General purpose for the meeting appears to be information-gathering. Collect relevant information related to Mrs. Cannon, her daughter Amy, the issue of concern, and the situation. Explore the separation and divorce issue as well as the nature of Mr. and Mrs. Cannon's relationship as Amy's parents. For example, are they both concerned about the drinking? Are they both interested in addressing Amy's drinking; and are they together in their views about how it should be addressed? In exploring, realize that Amy's drinking behavior may or may not be related to her parent's marital situation. Also, recognize that Mrs. Cannon may also want help in regard to the marital relationship or its dissolution.
- Make sure that Mrs. Cannon understands the limits of confidentiality, including duty to report indications of child abuse or neglect. Describe the mutual nature of this working relationship and invite her active participation.
- Explore the apparent presenting issue (that is, Amy's drinking episode) as well as other aspects of Amy's social world (for example, her school performance, friendships, and social and recreational activities). Track the history and development of Amy's drinking behavior and the Cannons' marital conflict. Attempt to identify risk and protective factors vis-à-vis the drinking.

(Continued)

- Clarify Mrs. Cannon and Amy's current household situation and their quality of life; inquire about Mr. Cannon's circumstances as well. Identify significant others who are involved with the three family members.
- Explore strengths of Mrs. Cannon, Amy, and perhaps Mr. Cannon. Identify available resources that might relate to a resolution.
- Explore in detail how Mrs. Cannon, Amy, and Mr. Cannon have attempted to deal with Amy's drinking or other "misbehavior" and how they are coping with the separation and divorce. Identify approaches that have been helpful and those that have been ineffective.
- Explore what Mrs. Cannon would consider an optimal resolution to the problems of concern.
- Conclude the interview with a specific next step. Consider the possibility of a second appointment, perhaps with Amy and Mrs. Cannon together, Amy alone, Mr. Cannon alone, or possibly Mr. and Mrs. Cannon together.

Rose Hernandez, BSW, LSW
Licensed Social Worker

In promoting human rights and advancing social, economic, and environmental justice through social activism, the processes of planning are similar to those for serving individuals, couples, families, organizations, groups, and communities. The major difference is that you and other activists may not know and may never come to know the identity of every person directly affected by human rights violations and other forms of injustice. Many will remain unaware of your efforts on their behalf. However, you will certainly become familiar with numerous people whose lives have been disrupted or damaged by injustice. Indeed, many of the most affected regularly participate in social actions intended to seek justice for themselves, their loved ones, and to others who have also been unjustly treated.

The planning records for social activism are generally fairly similar to those for other social work meetings or activities. Coordinators document the purpose and goals, outline an agenda, describe the arrangements, and identify desired outcomes. In most cases, social workers engaged in activism do not have a "client" per se. As such, records and documents of all kinds remain unprotected by laws and regulations that safeguard those of formal clients. Therefore, your documents could become public. Keep that in mind as you make and record plans for social action events and activities.

EXERCISE 7-8 Preliminary Planning and Recording

1. At this point, you are about to become acquainted with five case situations that we will use throughout the remaining chapters. The five include Mr. K, Loretta, the S family, Mrs. F, and a social service organization that we affectionately call "the troubled agency." As a way to learn something about each of them, use any or all of the preparing skills (preparatory reviewing, preparatory exploring, preparatory consultation, preparatory arranging, preparatory empathy, preparatory self-exploration, and centering) that would help you prepare written preliminary plans for an initial meeting with each of the five clients. Use word-processing software to create plans according to a format such as that shown in Box 7.3 earlier in this chapter. When finished, record the five plans in separate sections of a document entitled "Preliminary Plans for Five Clients." Label the document file "Plans_for_5_Clients." Save it in an electronic folder entitled "Five Clients" and include the folder in your Social Work Skills Learning Portfolio.

a. As a social worker in a multipurpose social service agency, you frequently serve individuals, couples, and families experiencing various life problems. You know that you are soon scheduled to meet Mr. K for an initial interview. At this point, you know that he is 55 years of age and seems to be struggling socially, emotionally, and psychologically with the aftereffects of a divorce from his wife of many years. It appears that his former spouse initiated the divorce and she currently remains unwilling to consider any kind of reunification.

b. As a city-employed social worker for homeless and "street" people, you notice a woman standing alongside the intersection of a highway. As cars stop, she displays a cardboard sign that reads, "Homeless and Hungry—Will Work for Food." One of your functions is to reach out to people in such situations, educate them about available resources, and, if they agree, arrange for them to obtain food and shelter, and access a fairly wide range of social and medical services. You are about to initiate contact with the woman.

c. You about to meet for the first time with the blended S family. You understand that the family contains seven members: Mr. and Mrs. S and five children. Some of the children are "hers" from a previous relationship and some are "his" from a former marriage. You know only that the family seeks professional help for problems of family tension and conflict.

d. You will soon begin an initial interview with Mrs. F. You have learned that she is concerned about the safety and well-being of her two preteen daughters. Mrs. F indicated that she is of Latina background and fluently speaks both Spanish and English.

e. You serve as a social worker and organizational consultant. The board of directors of a local social service agency has contracted with you to help staff and other stakeholders address several serious problems. In 1 week, you are scheduled to meet with a group of people associated with the agency. You anticipate that the group will be fairly large and include several members from the agency's board of directors, the director of the agency, three program coordinators, four social workers, two administrative staff members, and two consumers (that is, two current or former clients).

SUMMARY

The preparing skills enable you to provide professional social work services efficiently and effectively from the first moment of contact. They are used extensively before initial meetings, events, and activities, and, in advance of subsequent encounters as well.

CHAPTER 7   Summary Exercises

1. Use word-processing software to describe your use of the preparing skills in advance of first meetings in the following four case scenarios. In other words, demonstrate how you would apply the relevant preparing skills (preparatory reviewing, preparatory exploring, preparatory consultation, preparatory arranging, preparatory empathy, preparatory self-exploration, centering, and preliminary planning and recording) in these particular situations. Please *label* each of the preparing skills you use in each case situation. When finished, combine your work into a single "Preparing for Four Meetings" document with a section for each of the four cases. Save the document to a file labeled "Prep_for_4_Mtgs" and deposit it in your Social Work Skills Learning Portfolio.

a. You serve as a community organizer in a low-income, high-crime area of town. A large percentage of the community is unemployed; neighborhood gangs patrol the area; drug sales and drug use are widespread; and teenagers and adults engaged in prostitution operate openly on the streets. You want to help members of the community organize themselves to address these concerns and improve their neighborhoods. You hope to recruit a team of community members to provide leadership. Toward that end, you invited a number of residents along with representatives from various groups and organizations. You reached out to several concerned parents, two ministers, a priest, a rabbi, an imam, and a representative from the local secular humanist association. You also invited a school principal, three teachers, two other social workers, two social service agency directors, a community relations police officer, one local state legislator, two members of the city council, and a neighborhood specialist with the mayor's office. Almost all have agreed to come to an organizational meeting on the following Wednesday evening. You have arranged for the use of a meeting room at a neighborhood church. Use word-processing software to demonstrate how you would use relevant preparing skills in advance of the first group meeting.

b. You serve as a social worker in a mental health center. Earlier in the day, a woman telephoned your agency and said she wanted to talk with someone about a recent incident. She said that about a week earlier, she met a man in a bar. He drove her home and then raped her. At first, she thought she could manage the aftereffects of the crime on her own. However, she now realizes that she needs professional help to cope. During the telephone conversation, she said, "I'm falling apart." You have an appointment with her in a few hours but have some time now to prepare. Use word-processing software to demonstrate how you would use relevant preparing skills in advance of the first meeting with this new client.

c. A police officer called your social services agency to say that she is bringing in a family of six (two parents and four children who range in age from less than 1 to 7 years). They had been sleeping in their dilapidated Chevy in a rest area on the highway. The officer said that they appear hungry, thirsty, and exhausted. Use word-processing software to demonstrate how you would use relevant preparing skills in advance of the first meeting with the family.

d. You are a social worker who specializes in work with both victims and perpetrators of child sex abuse. In 2 hours, you are scheduled to meet with Mr. T for the first time. He has been charged with the crime of molesting the 13-year-old daughter of a woman friend. Out of jail on a bail bond, Mr. T's lawyer advised him to contact a helping professional right away and begin to receive counseling. Use word-processing software to demonstrate how you would use relevant preparing skills in advance of the first meeting with Mr. T.

Chapter 7   Experiential Interviewing Exercise

At this point you have gained beginning familiarity with the characteristics of professionalism, accessing a place of peace, and culturally sensitive communications. You have practiced the basic skills of talking and listening, and experimented with the preparing skills. It is now time to prepare for an experiential interviewing exercise. The multiweek learning activity is intended to help you gain proficiency in the social work skills within a safe and fairly realistic context. For this experience, you will assume the role of social worker while another person assumes the role of "practice client." The exercise occurs over the course of several weeks. If your professor or field instructor does not assign a classmate or provide a "standard client"[2] to serve that function, you can recruit someone to serve as your "practice client." You also must gain the consent of a social work instructor or another professional social worker to serve in the dual roles of your supervisor and the client's advocate. If you are completing *The Social Work Skills Workbook* as part of a course, your professor is an obvious choice for this role. In accepting the role of supervisor, she should formally agree to be available to consult with you, respond to questions, and provide suggestions and advice as you function as a student social worker during the process. In serving as client advocate—the other role—she should also formally agree to be available to the practice client who may have questions, concerns, problems, or complaints during the multiweek exercise. If you are in a practicum experience, your field instructor might fulfill these functions. Regardless of the setting, however, do not undertake this learning exercise until you secure a professional social worker to serve in these essential roles.

If a practice client is not assigned to you, consider asking a classmate or another student[3] who is completing or has already completed *The Social Work Skills Workbook* to assume the role. However, do not ask peers who are in a fragile state—perhaps due to a major loss or conflict, a serious medical condition, a significant life change, or a personal or family crisis. After all, you are practicing skills here, not actually providing social work services. Your colleague should realize that she is helping you to learn. Practice clients may or may not derive some personal benefit from the exercise. The purpose is educational in nature. It is not intended to help people dealing with serious concerns, and we certainly do not want to add additional stress or pressure to people who are currently quite vulnerable.

Before you attempt to recruit someone for the practice client role, prepare and make plans for the meeting—as you would for any other. Fully understand the guidelines for the experiential interviewing exercise, including the nature and scope of your responsibilities, and the expectations of the practice client (see Appendix 7). You also need copies of information material to provide to potential practice clients. These include a summary description of the exercise, a description of the practice client role, contact information for the supervising social worker/client advocate, and a "Practice Client Consent Form" (also available in Appendix 7).

As you review the requirements for the exercise, first highlight those aspects that are especially significant and make notations about anything that is unclear. Identify any questions that you might have for your instructor or classmates. In other words, think critically about the exercise and identify any practical or ethical issues that might warrant additional consideration. Second, use the skills of preparatory exploring and preparatory consultation, as needed, with your instructor and classmates. Third, make necessary arrangements for the recruitment contact and schedule a time and place. Although you will not make an audio or video recording[4] of recruitment contacts, you will require

---

[2] Some programs employ people to serve as "standard clients" or "standardized simulated clients" for students. When provided scripts and training, many people can portray clients in a profoundly realistic manner. They can all operate from a prescribed role description and identify the same problems, personal characteristics, and environmental circumstances for each social work student. Also, they are usually unknown to social work students, which adds a sense of realism to the interview series. Many medical schools employ simulated patients for this purpose and often require students to complete interviews several times throughout the course of their education. Social work programs would be wise to invest the resources to do the same.

[3] It is usually better to recruit a classmate or colleague whom you know only slightly if at all. Avoid close friends and acquaintances as the temptation to lose "role integrity" is greater when they serve as practice clients. With unfamiliar practice clients, such temptations are usually fairly weak and the experience quite realistic as you learn about people and explore topics for the very first time.

[4] Video recordings are especially valuable for learning purposes because they contain so much information. Nonverbal communications such as facial expressions as well as physical movements and gestures of both social worker and client are sometimes more informative than the stated words. However, video recordings also involve considerable risk to the privacy and confidentiality rights of the parties involved—and especially to those of the practice client. Obviously, if a practice client appears on video, she or he can be recognized—even though a fictitious name is used. Therefore, if you video record the meetings, you must be extraordinarily protective of the recording; ensure that no copies are made; and destroy the recording when you have completed the exercise.

copies of the exercise guidelines and the consent form if your colleague accepts your invitation to participate in the exercise.[5] Fourth, engage in self-exploration and then in preparatory empathy to heighten your sensitivity to both your own as well as your colleague's possible thoughts, feelings, sensations, and behaviors about the recruitment contact and the possibility of undertaking the experiential learning exercise. Fifth, identify or develop and then practice some means to access a place of peace and center yourself in advance of a recruitment meeting.

Finally, prepare a brief hand or typewritten outline of your plans for the recruitment contact. Be sure to understand the educational nature and primary purpose for the exercise, as well as your role as the student social worker and the role of the practice client (see Appendix 7). Remember that the five meetings will be audio- or video-recorded and be clear about the confidentiality requirements. Finally understand the functions of the professional social worker serving in the dual roles of your supervisor and the client's advocate.

CHAPTER 7   Self-Appraisal

As you finish this chapter, please reflect on your learning by using the following space to identify any ideas, terms, or concepts addressed in Chapter 7 that remain confusing or unclear to you:

Next, respond to the following items by carefully reading each statement. Please use a 1-to-10-point rating scale (where *1 = strongly disagree* and *10 = strongly agree*) to indicate the degree to which you agree or disagree with each statement. Place a check mark at the point that best reflects your view at this particular point in time. If you're truly *undecided*, place your check at the midpoint (5.5) mark.

1. I can discuss the purposes and functions of preparing.

   | 1 2 3 4 5 6 7 8 9 10 |

2. I can engage in preparatory reviewing.

   | 1 2 3 4 5 6 7 8 9 10 |

3. I can engage in preparatory exploring.

   | 1 2 3 4 5 6 7 8 9 10 |

---

[5] Later, if your colleague agrees to serve in the role of practice client, you will need time for the meetings, a quiet and private meeting location with chairs, audio or video recording equipment, and perhaps pencils, notepads, drawing paper, or other materials.

4. I can engage in preparatory consultation.

```
| | | | | | | | | | |
1   2   3   4   5   6   7   8   9   10
```

5. I can engage in preparatory arranging.

```
| | | | | | | | | | |
1   2   3   4   5   6   7   8   9   10
```

6. I can engage in preparatory empathy.

```
| | | | | | | | | | |
1   2   3   4   5   6   7   8   9   10
```

7. I can engage in preparatory self-exploration.

```
| | | | | | | | | | |
1   2   3   4   5   6   7   8   9   10
```

8. I can center myself.

```
| | | | | | | | | | |
1   2   3   4   5   6   7   8   9   10
```

9. I can engage in preliminary planning and recording.

```
| | | | | | | | | | |
1   2   3   4   5   6   7   8   9   10
```

Beginning

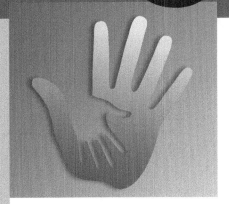

This chapter should help you learn skills needed during the beginning phase of social work practice. This phase formally begins when you, in your role as a social worker, and another person or people first encounter each other. Because first impressions are so important, the initial contact often affects future encounters. Similarly, the beginning portion of each subsequent contact tends to influence the course of those interactions as well.

The beginning skills are commonly used quite extensively during the first few meetings. Whether the encounters involve clients or other people, be clear about purposes and expectations. Such clarity and transparency facilitate engagement and communication with referral sources, colleagues from your own or other agencies, government officials, parents, community representatives, fellow social activists, and others with whom you interact as part of your professional responsibilities. Typically, you also use several beginning skills during the early portions of subsequent encounters.

Competent use of the beginning skills helps ensure that meetings are purposeful and productive,

(*Continued*)

Chapter Goals

Following completion of this chapter, you should be able to:

- Discuss the purposes and functions of beginning.
- Introduce yourself.
- Seek introductions from others.
- Describe an initial purpose for meetings and interviews.
- Orient others to the process.
- Discuss policy and ethical factors.
- Seek feedback.

Core Competencies

The content addressed in this chapter supports the following core EPAS competencies:

- Competency 2: Engage Diversity and Difference in Practice
- Competency 6: Engage with Individuals, Families, Groups, Organizations, and Communities

and that relationships are positive. An effective beginning results when you and a prospective client or other people accomplish the purpose for which you first meet (for example, information-gathering, information-sharing, or change-making) and reach a mutual agreement concerning a next step in the process (for example, conclude your relationship, continue to work together, or arrange for service from another professional or agency).

Typically, social workers make contact with people in one of these ways:

- Individuals, families, groups, organizations, and communities may reach out to a social worker or agency for help with a problem they have identified as being beyond their means of solution.
- A social worker may reach out to offer services to people who are not initially seeking help.
- Someone else may conclude that an individual, family, group, organization, or community is affected by a serious problem that threatens their own or others' welfare and requests that a social worker or agency intervene to provide services. (Compton, Galaway, & Cournoyer, 2005, pp. 165–166)

Contact may occur, for example, when a supervisor or agency executive assigns you responsibility for organizing and leading a task force or committee. A judge may order a defendant or someone convicted of a crime or misdemeanor to receive services from you and your agency. A community group might seek your help in developing a program, preparing a funding proposal, or advocating for a change in a governmental policy. People panhandling on the street may ask you for money—providing you with an opportunity to educate them about various social service programs and perhaps help to arrange a first meeting.

Social workers also initiate or join social action movements to address systemic and structural injustices in society. Indeed, our awareness of such larger systemic problems may increase through our service to individuals, couples, and families. In other words, we recognize that many personal and family problems are directly and inextricably tied to cultural, social, and political policies and practices. Social workers are so aware of this bond that we adopt a person-in-environment perspective. We never focus on the individual person alone. We always seek to understand the contextual and systemic factors that help to explain personal problems. In fact, social workers observe so many personal problems that result from social, economic, and political injustices that we could just as easily adopt an *environment-in-person* perspective. In other words, the injustices of the society appear within the personal lives of the individuals, families, and communities we serve. As we discussed earlier, they reflect parallel processes.

More than a half-century ago, the sociologist C. Wright Mills recognized and popularized the idea of a direct relationship between **personal problems and public issues** (1956, 1959, 1963). Another sociologist, Howard S. Becker (1994) summarizes this notion as follows:

> Mills' famous dictum holds that personal troubles are public problems. What seem to be the private troubles of a single person are the result, at the individual level, of the working out of the problems of the society that person lives in. Being without a job is a terrible personal trouble, but it is neither the result nor the fault of anything the unemployed have done. Rather, it is the working out, for them, of society's inability or unwillingness to provide full employment. (p. 175)

Because of social work's person-in-environment perspective and our recognition that personal problems reflect public issues—often in the form of parallel processes—many social workers join or organize social action movements dedicated to addressing those public issues that affect so many people in the United States and the rest of the world. Of course, the nature of initial contacts may vary somewhat according to the number of people involved and their relationships with one another. First contacts with individuals differ somewhat from those with couples and families, which in turn vary from those with small groups, organizations, communities, and social action movements. Similarly, initial encounters via telephone, e-mail, instant message, text, webcams, or assorted Web-based social networks differ from those that involve face-to-face interaction in the same physical space. Nonetheless, regardless of the particular mode of communication, during the early part of most first meetings with systems of all sizes, we hope to facilitate an exchange of introductions, establish a tentative direction or purpose for the meeting, outline the usual expectations of clients or involved others, describe the relevant agency or organizational policies, pertinent laws, and information about ethical principles that might apply during this and any subsequent encounters. We seek to ensure that prospective clients and others understand the parameters or boundaries of our work together. This is a crucial part of the beginning process because it addresses our legal and ethical obligations with respect to informed consent. Throughout the beginning phase, we also regularly seek feedback concerning information discussed. Prospective clients and others sometimes need additional clarification about complex or confusing policies and principles.

Introducing Yourself

At the beginning of any first meeting, be sure to identify yourself by full name and profession, and by agency or departmental affiliation. For example, at the beginning of a meeting in the agency where he works, a social worker might say in greeting, "Hello Mr. and Mrs. Adabu. My name is Dan Majors. I'm a social worker here at the family service agency. I specialize in helping people who are dealing with family issues of one kind or another."

At the start of a visit to the home of a prospective client, another social worker might say, "Hello Mrs. Perez (offers hand to shake),[1] I'm Joanna Kapoor. I'm a social worker with the local school system. I work with families in our school district. Please call me Joanna." In meeting a bilingual Mexican American family for the first time, an English-speaking social worker might nonetheless say a few words of greeting in Spanish along with a brief statement of regret that she is not fluent in that beautiful language. At first contact with some Asian clients, a respectful lowering of the head to approximate a modest bow may augment the introductory ritual.

At the start of a community group meeting, a social worker might say, "Welcome everyone! My name is Leslie Nguyen. I'm a social worker with the city. I work with people in neighborhoods interested in developing a sense of community and increasing both safety and well-being throughout the area. Please call me Leslie."

In most circumstances, a friendly facial expression and a warm handshake often serve as helpful beginning gestures. Generally speaking, people prefer it when professionals take an active rather than passive approach in initial contacts. When culturally appropriate, handshakes increase others' satisfaction with the social interaction. Interestingly, handshakes are associated with increased neurological activity in the nucleus accumbens (NAcc)—which "is a central component of the reward pathways . . . and of preference related signals (Haber & Knutson, 2010; Knutson, Rick, Wimmer, Prelec, & Loewenstein, 2007; O'Doherty, Buchanan, Seymour, & Dolan, 2006) that motivate approach of potentially rewarding cues in the environment (Knutson, Adams, Fong, & Hommer, 2001), as well as to experiencing positive emotions such as excitement (Bjork et al., 2004)" (Dolcos, Sung, Argo, Flor-Henry, & Dolcos, 2012, p. 2303). However, when you are uncertain whether physical touch is culturally appropriate, simply present a copy of your business card at the time of first contact. That way you

---

[1] Please be acutely aware that handshakes or other forms of "touch" between people may constitute a taboo in some cultures and contexts. For example, a handshake between a male and a female might be viewed as immodest by members of some Jewish and Muslim sects. In this instance, the social worker made an educated guess that a handshake would be welcomed by Mrs. Perez. Many social workers recognize that some cultural customs also reflect aspects of male privilege and sexism.

can avoid the awkwardness of offering your hand only to have other people decline it or reluctantly accept it—despite their religious traditions. If you are sensitive to the cultural signals, you can easily avoid feelings of tension, discomfort, guilt, or anger that result from unwanted touch.

In fact, providing others with your business card represents a useful supplement to identifying yourself by name, profession, and agency affiliation. For example, as part of her introduction to families, Joanna Kapoor routinely gives out her business card.

> **Joanna Kapoor, BSW, MSW, LSW**
> Licensed Social Worker
> Center Township School District
> 902 W. New York Street
> Indianapolis, IN 46202-5156
> Telephone 317-274-6705

A few informal comments about everyday topics (for example, the weather, transportation) may also help people feel more at ease, but do not overdo it. Spending too much time with chitchat may frustrate clients who are grappling with serious concerns and urgently wish to discuss them. Always consider your introduction and informal remarks in light of the context and purpose. Be especially sensitive to cultural factors. People that you meet for the first time fully realize that you do not yet truly know them as individuals. Too much informality or excessive enthusiasm may be premature and, in some cultures, quite rude. In many contexts, you would use your surname rather than your given name. For example, "Mrs. Grandbois" may seem less culturally intrusive than "Judy."

In office settings, a display of your university degrees, social work license, and professional certificates can contribute to the introductory process. Clients may notice where you earned your college degree and that you have a license to practice social work in your locale. Indeed, some licensing laws specifically require the public display of your social work license. Along with pertinent agency materials, you might offer clients a brief printed biographical summary of your professional background, training, and your areas of expertise.

EXERCISE 8-1 Introducing Yourself

Refer to your preliminary plans (see Exercise 7-8) as you begin your initial meetings with Mr. K, Loretta, the S family, Mrs. F, and the "troubled agency."

1. It is now time for your first meeting with Mr. K—the divorced 55-year-old. Use the space below to write the words you would say and describe the actions you would take in introducing yourself to Mr. K. Please place quotation marks around the words you expect to use.

2. You have parked your car and are about to open the door and walk over to the woman standing alongside the intersection of a highway. She's holding a sign that reads, "Homeless and Hungry—Will Work for Food." Use the space below to write the words you would say and describe the actions you would take in introducing yourself to the woman. Please place quotation marks around the words you expect to use.

3. You are about to meet for the first time with the blended S family that seems to be in considerable interpersonal distress. Use the space below to write the words you would say and describe the actions you would take in introducing yourself to the family. Please place quotation marks around the words you expect to use.

4. You will soon begin an initial interview with Mrs. F—the Latina mother who is concerned about the safety of her two preteen daughters. Use the space below to write the words you would say and describe the actions you would take in introducing yourself to Mrs. F. Please place quotation marks around the words you expect to use.

5. A week has passed and you are about to begin a meeting with a good size group of people associated with a local social service agency. In your roles as social worker and organizational consultant, you hope to help the agency resolve several serious problems within the group. Use the space below to write the words you would say and describe the actions you would take in introducing yourself to the group. Please place quotation marks around the words you expect to use.

▮ Seeking Introductions

People's names tend to hold special significance. Early in first meetings, encourage people to say their names, and then try to pronounce them correctly. Thereafter, periodically throughout the interview, refer to them by name. For example, after introducing yourself, you might say, "And your name is . . . ?" If you already know the person's name, you might ask, "And you're Mr. Benoit?[2] Is that right? Am I pronouncing your name correctly?" Then ask how the person prefers to be addressed (Miss, Ms., Mrs., Mr., Reverend, first name, or nickname). People from cultural groups that have experienced oppression may be especially sensitive to premature informality. In the United States, for example, white slave owners commonly addressed adult slaves by first name or by calling them "boy" or "girl" or by a racial epithet. Over time, the slave owners' surnames replaced the slaves' original African names. In a form of racial rankism and ridicule, some European Americans called Native Americans "chief" or "squaw" or by the demeaning terms "injun" or "redskin." Although most social workers would never intentionally insult another person, sometimes ignorance and insensitivity lead to just such a result.

Frequently, clients may share additional forms of identification during the exchange of introductions. Suppose, for example, a new client introduces herself by saying, "I'm Mrs. Jones. I'm the mother of this mob." From her words, you might infer that she prefers to be called "Mrs. Jones" and that the role of parent represents a significant part of her personal and social identity. In some organizational contexts, a person's title or role may be preferred. For instance, if you testify in a court or in a legislative committee meeting, you would be wise to refer to the judge as "your honor" or "Judge Sanchez" and to the legislative representatives as "Madam Chairperson," "Senator Yung," or "Representative Jabbar."

In family and group contexts, you may ask members to introduce themselves through a "go around." In a group context, the introductions can actually proceed in clockwise or counterclockwise fashion. In family contexts, however, especially in many cultures, it is often more respectful to seek introductions in order of age or status. For example, you might begin with the parents and then move to the children in order of age from old to young. Because initial family and group meetings often provoke anxiety, you could incorporate a stress-reducing, ice-breaking dimension to the introduction process. For example, you might ask family members or group participants to introduce themselves and share a few of the thoughts they had as they anticipated

---

[2] You might experiment with different ways that the Benoit surname could be pronounced.

coming to this first meeting. In formal group or organizational contexts, however, it is often wise to move right on to the purpose for the meeting. For example, when meeting with a board of directors, a legislative committee, or a community association, you might begin with the leadership and then proceed in "go around" fashion. Frequently, in such settings, you may simply request that the formal leader or your contact person introduce the other members. Like other groups and organizations, social action movements vary in their leadership structures and philosophy. Many are openly democratic; others have a hierarchical structure. As a formal or informal leader, you would vary the introduction-seeking processes accordingly.

EXERCISE 8-2   Seeking Introductions

Refer to your earlier responses (see Exercises 7-8 and 8-1) as you continue to use beginning skills in your initial meetings with Mr. K, Loretta, the S family, Mrs. F, and the "troubled agency."

1. You have begun your first meeting with the 55-year-old Mr. K by introducing yourself. Now, use the space below to write the words you would say and describe the actions you would take in seeking introductions from him. Please place quotation marks around the words you expect to use. Then, identify anything else you might say. Finally, offer a brief rationale for the words you chose and the actions you took.

2. You have approached the woman standing alongside the intersection of a highway. While she held a sign that reads, "Homeless and Hungry—Will Work for Food." You also introduced yourself to her. Now, use the space below to write the words you would say and describe the actions you would take in seeking introductions from her. Please place quotation marks around the words you expect to use. Then, identify anything else you might say. Finally, offer a brief rationale for the words you chose and the actions you took.

3. You have begun the first meeting by introducing yourself to the S family. You know that it is a blended family and that not all of the children have the same last name. However, you do not actually know which children are from which relationships. Use the space below to write the words you would say and describe the actions you would take in seeking introductions from them. Please place quotation marks around the words you expect to use. Then, identify anything else you might say. Finally, offer a brief rationale for the words you chose and the actions you took.

4. You have begun the initial meeting with Mrs. F by introducing yourself. Now, use the space below to write the words you would say and describe the actions you would take in seeking introductions from her. Please place quotation marks around the words you expect to use. Then, identify anything else you might say. Finally, offer a brief rationale for the words you chose and the actions you took.

5. You have begun a meeting with a fairly large group of stakeholders in a local social service agency by introducing yourself. Now, use the space below to write the words you would say and describe the actions you would take in seeking introductions from them. Please place quotation marks around the words you expect to use. Then, identify anything else you might say. Finally, offer a brief rationale for the words you chose and the actions you took.

Describing Initial Purpose

As part of the preparation process (see Chapter 7), social workers anticipate a tentative general purpose for a meeting. Then, when you actually begin, you can suggest an initial purpose as a possible focus for the meeting. Especially in initial meetings, prospective and actual clients typically tend to look to you for leadership. After all, you are the professional person in a position of authority. The same holds true if you are convening a group of community members, chairing a committee meeting, or leading a task force or advocacy group. Therefore, clearly but succinctly discuss your view of the purpose for the meeting. Without some beginning guidance from you, people are likely to feel quite uncertain about a process that is usually quite stress provoking. By tentatively **describing an initial purpose,** other participants usually feel a sense of relief as they conclude that you possess some competence and might, indeed, know what you are doing.

Building on the work of Vinter (1963) and Hansenfeld (1985), Garvin (1997) identified the following overarching purposes for most social work agencies, programs, and services:

Socialization "involves helping persons viewed as 'normal' and who are progressing from one status to another. Examples of this are assisting adolescents to assume adult responsibilities, middle-aged persons to plan for retirement, and school children to make better use of their learning environments" (p. 40). **Identity development** is an aspect of a socialization service in which social workers help people clarify their own goals and roles. Supporting adolescents as they explore social identity issues or consider career goals, facilitating a women's consciousness-raising group, or helping gay, lesbian, or bisexual people decide whether or not to come out are examples of identity development purposes. **Skill development** involves helping people develop the abilities needed to achieve the goals they establish. Educational counseling, training or "coaching" activities (for example, assertiveness training, social and communication skills, parenting skills, budgeting skills, time-management skills, study skills), and transition facilitation activities (for example, retirement preparation, divorce adjustment for both adults and children, helping adults entering or returning to college) contribute to skill development. Such socialization activities help people to acquire the knowledge and skills associated with the roles and goals to which they aspire.

Resocialization involves "helping people viewed as not experiencing 'normal' phases of development or role transitions. Such people are often labeled 'deviant,' and therefore experience conflict with others" (p. 40). **Social control** activities may occur in agencies that have a relationship with one or more aspects of the criminal and juvenile justice, child and adult protection, educational, and some medical systems. Typically, the "targets" of social control activities have not yet decided to accept a nondeviant, socially acceptable role. Although many social workers are reluctant to consider themselves agents of social control, the purpose of such activities and the goals of their employing agencies (or those of funding sources) sometimes involve the control and management of unwanted behaviors, and, obviously, the people who exhibit them. Activities offered in prisons, training schools, alcohol and drug treatment centers, many residential organizations, certain mental health agencies, and some hospitals are often solely or primarily social control in nature. People associated with crime and delinquency, sexual offenses, violence, substance abuse, and deviance often receive services intended to serve the purpose of social control. Indeed, in many educational, mental health, and social service agencies, social control is frequently an unspoken but strong element of a, supposedly hidden but often quite public, agenda. As you might imagine, in many contexts the purpose of social control interacts with an intent to punish—perhaps accompanied by the idea that infliction of pain or discomfort is "for their own good."

Rehabilitation services and activities may occur in agencies and institutions such as psychiatric facilities, mental health centers, social service agencies, and the treatment programs of correctional settings. Typically, people who voluntarily seek rehabilitation services identify certain behavior patterns as problematic (for example, as deviant, maladaptive, dysfunctional, or sick) and choose to pursue a more functional, healthful, or socially acceptable path. Rehabilitation services help the members develop the knowledge, skills, and attitudes necessary to fulfill functional, accepted, and socially desirable roles. Many social, psychiatric, educational, and substance abuse services fall into this category, as do many self-help programs where members openly acknowledge their faults, failures, or addictions (for example, sex, relationship, drugs, alcohol, and so on) and undertake personal efforts to overcome them. In traditional Alcoholics Anonymous (AA) meetings, people usually begin to speak with a phrase such as, "Hello, I'm Paul. I am an alcoholic." Such introductions reflect personal ownership of a problem, illness, personal flaw, or moral failing from which the person hopes to recover.

In addition to information-gathering, information-sharing, and change-making, these four overarching social work purposes may provide further context for the general reasons for initial meetings with clients. For example, when it is clear from a preliminary contact that a main issue requires rehabilitation or recovery services, you might identify that your purpose involves helping people develop new ways of thinking, feeling, and behaving so that they can recover from current problems and prevent them from recurring in the future.

Promoting human rights and advancing social, economic, and environmental justice through policy–practice initiatives and social action movements reflect aspects of the socialization and, of course, change-making purposes. Consciousness raising, identity development, and skill-building trainings may help policy advocates and social activists both increase the effectiveness of their efforts and, perhaps, increase their personal safety as well. The primary targets for change, however, are not social workers and other policy advocates and social activists. Rather, we direct our change efforts toward those economic, political, and social systems that maintain the ideologies, systems, structures, and processes which limit human rights and perpetuate the varied and insidious forms of dehumanization and injustice throughout the world.

In some instances, the general purpose for first meetings is clear, and so are the roles that support that purpose. When such a strong degree of clarity exists, you may appropriately describe one or more of the professional social work roles that you expect to assume during the course of your work together (Schwartz, 1971; Shulman, 1992).

Among the more common social work roles are *case advocate, broker, case manager, counselor, educator, evaluator, facilitator, investigator, or mediator*. In serving as a **case advocate**, you represent, defend, or champion the rights of clients and others who might be in need or at risk. As a **broker**, you help to locate community resources and link people with them. As a **case manager**, you coordinate delivery of several different services provided by personnel from one or more agencies or programs. As a **counselor**, you offer support and guidance to people in their efforts to address and resolve problems and accomplish goals. As an **educator**, you provide information, teach, train, coach, or socialize people in the development of knowledge, attitudes, or abilities to enhance their psychosocial functioning. As an **evaluator**, you make judgments and recommendations based on careful, fair, and systematic collection and analysis of pertinent information (for example, recommending child custody arrangements, determining the effectiveness of a social service program, or assessing an applicant's eligibility for services). As a **facilitator**, you help bring people together, enhance their interaction and communication, and encourage them to cooperate in their efforts and actions. As an **investigator** (for example, child- or adult-protective services worker), you carefully and systematically search to uncover hidden or secret information pertaining to the safety and well-being of potentially vulnerable people. As a **mediator**, you serve as a go-between to help various parties address differences or conflicts and to interact more productively.

We also serve other roles. For example, many social workers serve as **administrators, program managers, supervisors,** and **consultants.** Others work as **policy-analysts** and some, albeit far too few, toil as **community organizers, class advocates,** and **social activists.** These last four roles are commonly included within the category of **policy–practice.**

In beginning with involuntary, nonvoluntary, and other ambivalent or reluctant clients or constituents, both the purpose for the meeting and your roles warrant more complete and lengthy description. This is also the case in situations where clients seek a specific service offered through your agency. For example, your agency may sponsor an educationally oriented 6-week group experience for teenagers considering marriage. Because such structured, socialization groups tend to follow a predictable agenda, your social work roles are clear. You will serve as an educator and facilitator within the context of an information-gathering, information-sharing, and change-making group designed to help young people become more aware, more knowledgeable, and perhaps more able to function within the "normal" opportunities and constraints of marriage. Therefore you may appropriately describe to prospective members both an initial purpose and the professional roles that you expect to fulfill during the group experience.

Frequently, however, the exact nature of your professional role is unclear at the time of the first meeting. This often occurs with voluntary clients who seek service from organizations that have several programs and serve a variety of functions, or when social workers are asked to serve as consultants to agencies or community groups. When the professional roles you might assume remain uncertain, the tentative description of general purposes should suffice.

In the following examples, a social worker tentatively describes an initial purpose for a first meeting.

EXAMPLE | ## Describing Initial Purpose

Case Situation: The client is a 30-year-old woman who called the agency a few days earlier to ask for help with a troubled marriage. The worker and client have already exchanged introductions. The worker begins to describe a tentative general purpose for this initial meeting.

Worker: When you phoned the agency the other day, you said that your marriage is on the brink of collapse. You also mentioned that you and your spouse argue all the time. Is that correct? Yes? During our meeting today, I'd like to explore in detail with you what's going on in your relationship and how it how it got to this point. As we gain a better understanding of the circumstances, we can decide together what to do next.

Case Situation: The divorcing parents of a 9-year-old boy are involved in child custody proceedings. The juvenile court hires a social worker to make recommendations to the judge about the placement of the child. At an initial meeting with the boy's father, the worker exchanges introductions and describes a purpose and role.

Worker: Judge Bloom asked me to meet with you, your spouse, and your son Kevin about the issue of custody arrangements. My job will be to gather information from all parties and make recommendations to the judge about the best possible arrangements for Kevin. I'll be meeting with Mrs. Brown [spouse] this afternoon and with Kevin [son] tomorrow morning. After these three meetings,

(Continued)

I should have a basic understanding of the situation. At that time, I'll let you know if any additional meetings will be needed.

I certainly recognize that this is a difficult time for you and for everybody involved. You may feel a bit like you're on trial here. It may seem that way. I'll try my best to make it as reasonable a process as possible. You should know, however, that your son Kevin will be fully considered in these processes. His well-being is our primary focus. I will gear my efforts toward determining what is best for him and his development. I'm sure that you are also concerned about the consequences of the divorce and the upcoming court proceedings for Kevin too. I'd like to approach this interview with Kevin in mind as we try to determine the best custody arrangements.

Case Situation: This is the first meeting of an educational group for people arrested for driving under the influence (DUI) of alcohol. The participants range in age from 16 to 62 and cross gender, ethnic, and socioeconomic-class lines. The group experience involves 12 weekly meetings of approximately 2 hours each. Members participate to decrease the chance of a jail sentence. If they complete the program successfully, their jail sentence is deferred. The worker and group members have exchanged introductions and engaged in some small talk. The worker now proceeds to describe an initial purpose and role.

Worker: The county prosecutor asked me to lead this educational group for the next 12 weeks. I understand that each of you was arrested for driving under the influence of alcohol and that you have chosen to participate in the group in order to reduce the chances of a term in the county jail. I imagine that you all have other places that you would rather be at this time. Some of you may be grateful for this opportunity to avoid a jail sentence. Others may be annoyed that you have to attend these meetings. If I were in your shoes, I'd probably have mixed feelings too. Whatever you feel, I hope the series of group meetings will help you learn a great deal about alcohol use and its consequences. Most importantly, however, I hope the experience will lead you to never again drive a car while under the influence of intoxicating substances. I also hope that you will become passionate advocates who do what's possible to stop your family members and friends from the deadly practice of impaired driving.

Case Situation: The interview setting is the front doorstep of the Frankel residence. It is a large home in an upper-middle-class neighborhood. The social worker knocks on the door. A woman who appears to live there opens the door. Employed by the Child-Protection Service (CPS) Division of the Department of Human Services, the worker is visiting the home unannounced because the agency received a complaint that Mrs. Frankel had severely beaten her 4-year-old son. At the door, the worker exchanged introductions, learned that the woman is indeed Mrs. Frankel, and gave her a business card along with a brochure about CPS.

Worker: Child-Protection Services is responsible for investigating all allegations of abuse or neglect of minor children in this county. We have received a complaint concerning the treatment of your 4-year-old son. I'd like to discuss this situation with you and meet your son. May I come in?

EXERCISE 8-3 Describing Initial Purpose

Refer to your earlier responses (see Exercises 7-8, 8-1, and 8-2) as you continue to use beginning skills in your initial meetings with Mr. K, Loretta, the S family, Mrs. F, and the "troubled agency."

1. You have begun your first meeting with the 55-year-old Mr. K by introducing yourself and seeking introductions from him. Now, use the space below to write the words you would say and describe the actions you would take in describing an initial purpose for the meeting. If you think your social work roles would be clear in this situation, identify them as well. Please place quotation marks around the words you expect to use. Then, identify anything else you might say. Finally, offer a brief rationale for the words you chose and the actions you took.

2. You have made initial contact with a woman standing alongside the intersection of a highway. You have introduced yourself and learned that her name is "Loretta." Now, use the space below to write the words you would say and describe the actions you would take in describing an initial purpose for this contact with her. If you think your social work roles would be clear in this situation, identify them as well. Please place quotation marks around the words you expect to use. Then, identify anything else you might say. Finally, offer a brief rationale for the words you chose and the actions you took.

3. You have begun the first meeting by introducing yourself and seeking introductions from members of the S family. Now, use the space below to write the words you would say and describe the actions you would take in describing an initial purpose for the meeting. If you think your social work roles would be clear in this situation, identify them as well. Please place quotation marks around the words you expect to use. Then, identify anything else you might say. Finally, offer a brief rationale for the words you chose and the actions you took.

4. You have begun the initial meeting with Mrs. F by introducing yourself and seeking introductions from her. Now, use the space below to write the words you would say and describe the actions you would take in describing an initial purpose for this meeting. If you think your social work roles would be clear in this situation, identify them as well. Please place quotation marks around the words you expect to use. Then, identify anything else you might say. Finally, offer a brief rationale for the words you chose and the actions you took.

5. You have begun a meeting with a fairly large group of stakeholders in a local social service agency by introducing yourself and seeking introductions from them. Now, use the space below to write the words you would say and describe the actions you would take in describing an initial purpose for this meeting. If you think your social work or organizational consultant roles would be clear in this situation, identify them as well. Please place quotation marks around the words you expect to use. Then, identify anything else you might say. Finally, offer a brief rationale for the words you chose and the actions you took.

▮ Orienting

During the beginning phase of the working relationship, many clients are quite unclear about what to expect. Certain aspects of the anxiety and ambiguity may be the result of cultural factors, but others may be associated with anticipated vulnerability or simple ignorance. Prospective clients are certainly concerned about the issues that led to the contact, but many are also worried that they may not be able to do what is needed to address those issues (Garvin & Seabury, 1997). In particular, prospective clients may be confused about how they can best help you help them. Ambiguity about what they are "supposed to do" is probably associated with the relatively high premature dropout rates for clients generally, and especially for members of minority status, racial, ethnic, cultural, religious, or linguistic groups; and for those of lower socioeconomic status (Claus & Kindleberger, 2002; Kubetin, 2003; Pelkonen et al., 2000; Sue, 1977; Swift & Greenberg, 2012; Swift, Greenberg, Whipple, & Kominiak, 2012; Wierzbicki & Pekarik, 1993).

Although mass media have contributed to popular familiarity with some facets of social services through television series and motion pictures, and, of course, various talk radio and television

---

BOX 8.1 ORIENTING CLIENTS (GROUP MEMBERS)

We all have problems at some point in our lives. It's part of being human. We've found that talking with other people who are in similar situations often helps resolve those problems. We've planned this group so you can share with each other your issues and concerns as well as your hopes and dreams. Although you are not required to say anything that you wish to keep to yourself, we hope that you will talk openly with one another, listen carefully to what others say, and share your thoughts and feelings about the issues we discuss. We expect all group members to follow the rule of confidentiality. That means that whatever any of you say in the group setting stays here. Things we talk about in the group should not be discussed outside this room.

"therapists" such as *Dr. Phil*, the actual history of formal "for hire" helping relationships with professionals is relatively short indeed. Throughout the centuries, family members, friends, community leaders, elders, and shamans or other religious leaders have helped people deal with various psychosocial issues. Traditionally, family and community members addressed problems of all kinds. Except for visiting religious leaders and indigenous healers, outsiders provided service only on rare occasions.

Although social norms and mores have changed dramatically during the last several decades, most people still find it anxiety-provoking to seek and receive help for psychological and social issues from paid strangers. Such interactions are sometimes associated with a sense of shame and perhaps stigma. You may help clarify the situation by describing how clients can join you as active, collaborative participants in the helping process (Garvin, 1987, 1997). Indeed, **orienting** clients to the process and preparing them for likely activities may lower the early dropout rate and improve service outcomes (Atkins & Patenaude, 1987; Kovacs & Bronstein, 1999; Lambert & Lambert, 1984; Sar, 2000; Shuman & Shapiro, 2002; Swift et al., 2012; Yalom, Houts, Newell, & Rand, 1967).

For example, in the first meeting of a group for adolescents having school problems, you might orient group members in a manner such as illustrated in Box 8.1. You might attempt to orient an individual client in the manner depicted in Box 8.2.

In orienting clients, recognize that expectations necessarily vary according to the reasons clients seek or receive social work services. They also differ in relation to agency setting, its mission and programs, and the composition of the client system—its size and the ages, capabilities, and motivations of its members. As you can imagine, the expectations for an adult client about to begin an intensive 3-month educational and therapeutic group experience for men who batter women would be quite different from those for an 8-year-old child who witnessed her father shoot and kill her mother.

BOX 8.2 ORIENTING CLIENTS (INDIVIDUAL)

You can best help in this process by sharing your thoughts and feelings as freely and as fully as you possibly can. Please ask questions when you do not understand, offer suggestions about what might work better, and give feedback about what helps and what does not. Finally, you can be helpful in this process by trying as hard as you can to take the steps that we plan together. If we work together, there is a good chance we will be able to resolve the issues that led to this visit.

When serving as convener or chairperson of committees, task forces, boards, or community groups or as leader of organizations, we engage in a similar process of orienting fellow members to the roles and expectations associated with participation. After introductions and a description of initial purpose, we help others explore how they may work together toward their desired outcomes.

EXERCISE 8-4 Orienting

Refer to your earlier responses (see Exercises 7-8, 8-1 to 8-3) as you continue to use beginning skills in your initial meetings with Mr. K, Loretta, the S family, Mrs. F, and the "troubled agency."

1. You have completed the introductions and suggested an initial purpose for this first meeting with Mr. K. He said, "OK." Now, use the space below to write the words you would say and describe the actions you would take in orienting him to the process. Please place quotation marks around the words you expect to use. Then, identify anything else you might say. Describe how you think he might respond. Finally, offer a brief rationale for the words you chose and the actions you took.

2. You have made initial contact with an apparently hungry and homeless woman standing alongside the intersection of a highway. You have introduced yourself and learned that her name is Loretta. When you shared your idea of a purpose for the contact along with the roles and functions you might serve, she seemed interested—but cautious. Now, use the space below to write the words you would say and describe the actions you would take in orienting her to the process. Please place quotation marks around the words you expect to use. Then, identify anything else you might say. Describe how you think she might respond. Finally, offer a brief rationale for the words you chose and the actions you took.

3. You have introduced yourself and learned the names of each member of the S family. You suggested a tentative purpose for the meeting and shared the roles you could assume in providing service to them. Mr. and Mrs. S acknowledge your remarks with affirmative nods of the head. The children, however, appear largely disinterested. Now, use the space below to write the words you would say and describe the actions you would take in orienting the family to the process. Please place quotation marks around the words you expect to use. Then, identify anything else

you might say. Describe how you think the family members might respond. Finally, offer a brief rationale for the words you chose and the actions you took.

4. In this first meeting, you have introduced yourself and learned that she prefers to be addressed as Mrs. F. You suggested a tentative purpose for the meeting and shared the roles you could assume in providing service to her and her children. She seemed satisfied. Now, use the space below to write the words you would say and describe the actions you would take in orienting her to the process. Please place quotation marks around the words you expect to use. Then, identify anything else you might say. Describe how you think the family members might respond. Finally, offer a brief rationale for the words you chose and the actions you took.

5. You have begun a meeting with a fairly large group of stakeholders in a local social service agency by introducing yourself and seeking introductions from them. You learned the names and roles or positions of each participant. You suggested a tentative purpose for the meeting and shared the roles you could assume in providing service to them. Several of the members appeared modestly satisfied with your remarks while others had their arms crossed and seemed closed to the possibility that you could actually be of any help. A few, however, responded with clear approval. They appeared cautiously hopeful that things could improve. Now, use the space below to write the words you would say and describe the actions you would take in orienting the participants to the process. Please place quotation marks around the words you expect to use. Then, identify anything else you might say. Describe how you think the group members might respond. Finally, offer a brief rationale for the words you chose and the actions you took.

Discussing Policy and Ethical Factors

An extremely important beginning skill involves **discussing policy and ethical factors**. Mutual understanding of the ground rules is critical for the development of an authentic, honest, and trusting relationship. Describing and discussing these factors constitutes part of the **informed consent** process and represents an essential element of professional service to clients. Failure to explore these factors with clients may seriously damage the working relationship and may sometimes constitute grounds for disciplinary action or even a malpractice suit.

Meetings with constituents, stakeholders, and other nonclients may not require detailed description of the legal and ethical factors associated with client status. However, agency policies and usual operating practices along with common expectations warrant discussion. In general, when meeting with people, social workers describe the parameters and ground rules that do or might apply. It helps make things more transparent and less mysterious, and conveys respect to participants in the process. In a sense, such disclosure relates to the honesty, integrity, and fairness aspects of professionalism.

For example, suppose as part of a social action movement you are helping to coordinate a protest against the execution of a 14-year-old boy who was tried as an adult and convicted for murder. Medical examinations subsequently revealed that the boy has severe brain damage in the frontal lobe—perhaps as the result of abuse during early childhood. You and other participants hope to persuade the governor to cancel the scheduled killing of the boy, and bring public awareness to the injustices associated with capital punishment in this and other instances. You plan to gather on the sidewalk in front of the governor's mansion. Several days prior to the demonstration, you e-mail information to participants about their legal rights and obligations, expected behavior, chances of arrest, what to do if arrested, and additional guidance. As other activists arrive, you distribute flyers containing the same information.

As a social worker, you are guided by certain policies and procedures in the performance of your duties. Some of these originate with the organization with which you are affiliated (for example, agency policies and procedures), others are promulgated by the social work profession in the form of ethical codes and standards, and still others are formulated by governmental bodies and courts through laws, regulations, and legal precedents. People have a right to information about the policies and ethical principles that may apply to them during the course of your work together. Many agencies wisely provide prospective clients with brochures and other publications describing relevant policies. Box 8.3 shows a sample document that a social worker in an agency might provide to prospective clients and use to complement discussion of policy and ethical issues. However, some clients do not or cannot truly understand the full meaning of such written material. You should therefore discuss key policies with most or all prospective clients.

Suppose, for example, an adult male client assumes that everything he says to you will remain confidential. During a counseling session, he tells you that he sometimes uses a wire coat hanger to "spank" his 2-year-old child. Operating on an assumption of "absolute confidentiality," he would probably feel profoundly betrayed when you inform him that you are legally required to report to local child-protection authorities what he told you about the "spankings."

Social workers are very concerned about protecting children from abuse and may sometimes wonder if discussion of policy and ethical factors may inhibit people from revealing pertinent information. Although such discussions probably have little adverse effect on communications, some social workers believe that they do and consequently skim over policies that might provoke discomfort. A few may even avoid them altogether. These are risky practices that not only endanger

Box 8.3 Agency Policies

As a general guideline, whatever clients say during sessions remains confidential among agency personnel. There are, however, a few exceptions. If a client wants the agency to provide information to another person or agency (for example, to a medical doctor), he or she may sign a *Release of Information* form that specifies which information to transfer and to whom. Also, as required by law, indications of possible child abuse or neglect will be reported to child-protection authorities. Similarly, we will not keep confidential information that a person represents a danger to himself or herself or to others. In such cases, we will take action to protect the lives of the people involved. In potentially life-threatening circumstances, the value of human life takes precedence over that of confidentiality.

The agency operates on a *sliding fee* basis. This means that the cost of each individual or family session varies according to clients' ability to pay: the higher the family income, the higher the cost—to a maximum of $55 per session. Group sessions are lower. Reimbursement from insurance companies, where applicable, is the responsibility of the client. However, agency staff members can help clients complete the necessary claim forms.

If you must cancel or reschedule a meeting, please notify the agency at least 1 day before the appointment.

In this agency, we regularly seek feedback from clients about the nature and benefit of meetings with agency professionals. At the beginning and end of most meetings, we ask clients to provide evaluative feedback in our efforts to maintain and improve the quality of our services. In addition, we have a procedure for expressing concerns about the services clients receive or any of the agency policies or practices. If, for any reason whatsoever, you are uncertain about or dissatisfied with the service you receive, please discuss it with your service provider. If you do not receive an adequate explanation, if the service remains unsatisfactory, or if you feel uncomfortable talking directly about the issue with your helping professional, please contact our agency's client representative, Ms. Sheila Cordula, in Room 21 (telephone 789-5432). She will talk with you about your concerns and attempt to address them.

the basic rights of clients, but also place social workers at risk of disciplinary action. In general, failure to discuss policy and ethical factors may actually reduce the likelihood of learning about reportable activities such as child abuse. If consumers conclude that social workers cannot be trusted to tell the whole truth, they may well shun professional services altogether.

In discussing relevant policy and ethical factors, however, social workers consider several aspects of the person-in-environment, including the relative urgency of the issue or problem and the context of the meeting. Suppose, for example, you serve as a social worker in the emergency room of a hospital. An ambulance delivers a severely injured young child who has been in an automobile accident. When the visibly distraught parents arrive, you decide to defer discussion of policy and ethical factors while you inform them about their child's status and try to offer comfort, compassion, and social support. In such instances, a social worker might reasonably decide that the parents' immediate needs take precedence over our obligation to discuss policies. Actually, we should consider all social work skills within the context of the person-in-environment. Such considerations are not limited to discussing policy and ethical factors. Frequently, a skill that is perfectly applicable in one circumstance is completely inappropriate in another. Because social work practice is a professional rather than a technical or bureaucratic endeavor, we must continually make judgments about when and how to best use our social work knowledge and skills.

EXERCISE 8-5   Discussing Policy and Ethical Factors

Refer to your earlier responses (see Exercises 7-8, 8-1 to 8-4) as you continue to use beginning skills in your initial meetings with Mr. K, Loretta, the S family, Mrs. F, and the "troubled agency."

1. So far in this first meeting with Mr. K, things have proceeded fairly quickly. You've completed the introductions and you proposed a tentative purpose for the meeting. You shared how you might participate in the process and outlined how he might as well. At this point, you are ready to discuss policy and ethical factors that might apply in the course of your work together. Use the space below to write the words you would say and describe the actions you would take in discussing relevant policy and ethical factors with Mr. K. Please place quotation marks around the words you expect to use. Then, identify anything else you might say. Describe how you think he might respond. Finally, offer a brief rationale for the words you chose and the actions you took.

2. Your initial contact with Loretta has moved along pretty well. She now appears a little bit less suspicious of you and your motives. She now knows your name and has used it a couple of times. She's aware of what you have to offer and how you might help. She also seems to understand how she might participate in the process. At this point, you are ready to discuss policy and ethical factors that might apply in the course of your work together. Use the space below to write the words you would say and describe the actions you would take in discussing relevant policy and ethical factors with Loretta. Please place quotation marks around the words you expect to use. Then, identify anything else you might say. Describe how you think she might respond. Finally, offer a brief rationale for the words you chose and the actions you took.

3. The first meeting with the S family is proceeding as you anticipated. The parents are involved but the children are fidgety. The parents, however, agree with your proposed purpose for the meeting, understand how you might help, and seem to be ready to participate actively in the process. At this point, you are ready to discuss policy and ethical factors that might apply in the course of your work together. Use the space below to write the words you would say and describe the actions you would take in discussing relevant policy and ethical factors with the S family. Please place quotation marks around the words you expect to use. Then, identify anything else you

might say. Describe how you think they might respond. Finally, offer a brief rationale for the words you chose and the actions you took.

4. As the first meeting with Mrs. F continues, it appears that she is somewhat ambivalent. She seems to like the direction you've outlined and understands how you might help. However, it's not clear that she is ready to participate actively in the process. You wonder if she has doubts that anything could be done by anybody—including you—to have a positive impact on the situation. You register the ambivalence and proceed to the topic of policy and ethical factors that might apply in the course of your work together. Use the space below to write the words you would say and describe the actions you would take in discussing relevant policy and ethical factors with Mrs. F. Please place quotation marks around the words you expect to use. Then, identify anything else you might say. Describe how you think she might respond. Finally, offer a brief rationale for the words you chose and the actions you took.

5. At this point in the initial meeting of a large group of people associated with the local social service agency, you're aware of the presence of different factions or subgroups. It's clear that not everyone approves of your involvement as an organizational consultant. Nonetheless, you have introduced a tentative purpose for the meeting and shared the roles you could assume in providing service to them. You've also outlined how they could participate in the process. The response to those suggestions was mixed. You recognize that you need to explore the subject of policy and ethical factors that might apply to you and to them during the course of your work together. Use the space below to write the words you would say and describe the actions you would take in discussing relevant policy and ethical factors with the members of the "troubled agency." Please place quotation marks around the words you expect to use. Then, identify anything else you might say. Describe how you think members of the group might respond. Finally, offer a brief rationale for the words you chose and the actions you took.

Seeking Feedback

In using the skill of **seeking feedback** (Schwartz, 1976; Shulman, 1992), social workers encourage clients to comment about the proposed purpose for the meeting and our roles, their roles, policy or ethical factors, or any other aspects of our remarks. An important part of effective communications involves checking to see if others have understood your messages and you have understood theirs. Seeking feedback serves this function. As social workers, we routinely seek feedback throughout the entire course of our work with people and do so formally[3] as well as informally. By asking for feedback about your initial description of purpose and roles, and your discussion of policy and ethical factors during the beginning phase, you continue the process of informed consent. You also further promote the idea that this is a collaborative, reciprocal kind of relationship that genuinely involves the active participation of both client and social worker. You invite clients to identify areas that are unclear, share thoughts that have occurred to them, introduce new topics, express disagreement with your comments, and evaluate the process. By seeking feedback, you effectively send a message that workers and clients are cooperative partners who are working toward a common purpose. You convey that you are genuinely interested in what they have to say about what you have said or done, and that you hope they will actively contribute their thoughts, reactions, and suggestions throughout the process.

Typically, social workers seek feedback about purpose, roles, and policy factors through questions such as "How does that sound to you? What do you think about what we've talked about so far? What questions or comments do you have?" Often, people respond to requests for feedback by asking for clarification. This gives you an opportunity to elaborate about purpose, roles, or policy and ethical factors. In general, people who clearly understand these ground rules and believe that you sincerely want their feedback are likely to feel both informed and respected.

EXERCISE 8-6   Seeking Feedback

Refer to your earlier responses (see Exercises 7-8, 8-1 to 8-5) as you continue to use beginning skills in your initial meetings with Mr. K, Loretta, the S family, Mrs. F, and the "troubled agency."

1. You have already covered quite a bit of ground in your first meeting with Mr. K. You have completed introductions, proposed a tentative purpose for the meeting, shared how you might help, described how he could actively participate in the process, and discussed relevant policy and ethical factors that might apply in the course of your work together. Now, use the space below to write the words you would say and describe the actions you would take in seeking feedback from Mr. K concerning anything that you've said or done thus far. Please place quotation marks around the words you would use. Then, identify anything else you might say. Describe how you think he might respond. Finally, offer a brief rationale for the words you chose and the actions you took.

[3] In a later chapter, when we explore the processes and skills associated with evaluating, we consider formal, systematic means of eliciting, gathering, and analyzing evaluative feedback about the quality of the relationship and process, and progress toward goals and outcomes.

2. In your brief time with Loretta, you have already completed introductions, proposed a tentative purpose for the meeting, shared how you might help, described how she could participate, and discussed relevant policy and ethical factors that might apply during the course of your work together. Now, use the space below to write the words you would say and describe the actions you would take in seeking feedback from Loretta concerning anything that you've said or done thus far. Please place quotation marks around the words you would use. Then, identify anything else you might say. Describe how you think she might respond. Finally, offer a brief rationale for the words you chose and the actions you took.

3. In your first meeting with the S family, you have secured introductions, suggested a tentative purpose for the meeting, discussed the roles you might assume in helping, outlined how they could participate in the process, and explored the relevant policy and ethical factors that might apply during the course of your work together. Now, use the space below to write the words you would say and describe the actions you would take in seeking feedback from the family concerning anything that you've said or done thus far. Please place quotation marks around the words you would use. Then, identify anything else you might say. Describe how you think they might respond. Finally, offer a brief rationale for the words you chose and the actions you took.

4. Thus far in your first meeting with Mrs. F, you have exchanged introductions, proposed a possible purpose for the meeting, discussed the roles you might assume in helping, suggested how she could participate in the process, and explored the relevant policy and ethical factors that might apply during the course of your work together. Now, use the space below to write the words you would say and describe the actions you would take in seeking feedback from Mrs. F concerning anything that you've said or done thus far. Please place quotation marks around the words you would use. Then, identify anything else you might say. Describe how you think she might respond. Finally, offer a brief rationale for the words you chose and the actions you took.

5. In your first meeting with the "troubled" social service agency, you have secured introductions, suggested a tentative purpose for the meeting, discussed the roles you might assume in helping, outlined how they could participate in the process, and explored the relevant policy and ethical factors that might apply during the course of your work together. Now, use the space below to write the words you would say and describe the actions you would take in seeking feedback from the group concerning anything that you've said or done thus far. Please place quotation marks around the words you would use. Then, identify anything else you might say. Describe how you think they might respond. Finally, offer a brief rationale for the words you chose and the actions you took.

SUMMARY

During the beginning phase of social work service, you introduce and identify yourself and seek introductions from prospective clients and involved others. Following the exchange of introductions, you describe a tentative initial purpose for the meeting, possibly identify one or more professional roles that you might undertake, orient participants to the process, and identify relevant policy and ethical factors that might apply. Throughout this beginning process, you regularly seek feedback concerning others' understanding of and reactions to your introductory comments. By using the beginning skills, you help to clarify the nature and boundaries or ground rules of the helping process, lessen the initial ambivalence people often experience, and establish a tentative direction for work.

CHAPTER 8   Summary Exercises

1. Building upon your earlier preparation (see Chapter 7 Summary Exercises), use word-processing software to *write the words* you would say and discuss the actions you would take as you meet for the first time with each of the four clients described below. In other words, build upon your previous preparation to demonstrate how you would apply the relevant beginning skills (introducing yourself, seeking introductions, describing an initial purpose and your social work roles, orienting, discussing policy and ethical factors, and seeking feedback) in these particular situations. Please *label* each of the beginning skills that you use and place quotation marks around the words you would say. When finished, combine your work into a single "Four Beginnings" document with a section for each of the four cases. Save the document to a file labeled "4_Beginnings" and include it in your Social Work Skills Portfolio.

   a. In your role as a social worker and organizer, you're about to begin a first meeting with a group of community members (see Summary Exercise 7-1a). They've come together at your invitation to explore what might be done to address the social problems evident within the community. The participants have taken seats around a large table and are ready for you to begin. Please do so.

b. You're about to begin a first meeting with a woman who telephoned the agency earlier in the day to request an appointment right away (see Summary Exercise 7-1b). She said she was raped about 1 week earlier and has now begun to "fall apart." She arrived on time and was shown to your office. You encourage her to sit in a comfortable chair. She does so and then waits for you to begin. You may do so now.

c. You're about to begin a first meeting with a family of six (see Summary Exercise 7-1c). Instead of arresting them for vagrancy or some other charge, a police offer brought them to your agency. She thought they needed help right away. You have escorted the parents and the four children into a spacious meeting room. Everyone has found a seat and is ready for you to begin. Please do.

d. Mr. T arrived on time for the first meeting (see Summary Exercise 7-1d). Now seated in your office, he looks ready for you to begin. Please proceed.

CHAPTER 8 Experiential Interviewing Exercise

Now that you have prepared, attempt to recruit a client.[4] Before doing so, ensure that you have gained a firm commitment from a professional social worker to serve in the dual roles of your supervisor and the practice client's advocate.

When you make initial contact with a prospective practice client, use the beginning skills of introducing yourself and seeking introductions. Identify yourself as a social work student. Inform your colleague that you are learning a large number of social work skills and wonder if she might be willing to be interviewed one time per week over the course of the next several weeks so that you can practice. Tell your colleague that you will assume the role of a social worker and, if she accepts, she would serve in the role of client. Orient your prospective partner to the process by indicating that she would behave as if voluntarily seeking help about one or two personal issues. Provide her with a copy of the "Guidelines for the Practice Client" and the "Practice Client Consent Form" (available in Appendix 7). Other relevant materials contained in that appendix may be useful as well. Indicate that you will meet together five times. Your colleague should understand that you may not be of any actual help with the identified concerns except to the extent that talking about them might be beneficial. The primary purpose is to help you practice skills needed in social work practice.

Discuss policy and ethical factors by informing your colleague that you plan to audio- or video-record the meetings and that you will prepare a written recording based on the interviews. Indicate that you plan to discuss the interviews with your supervising social worker as a way to improve the quality of your work. Mention that, as the practice client, she may—if she wants—read your written case records when they are completed. Assure her that to ensure privacy you will refer to her by a fictitious name (pseudonym) during interviews and in your written notes. Confirm that you will not reveal her actual name to anyone except the supervising social worker without her knowledge and consent.

Explain that she will not have to discuss any aspect of her personal life that she would prefer to keep private. Mention that if you happen to address a topic that she does not want to explore, she may simply say, "I prefer not to talk about that." Remind your colleague that this exercise is entirely voluntary. It is perfectly all right to decline this invitation. Finally, advise her that you are

---

[4] If your instructor has assigned a "standard client" for this multiweek exercise, you may not actually need to complete a "recruitment contact." The "standard client" undoubtedly understands the roles and responsibilities. However, if you have been assigned a classmate or a colleague, please complete the recruitment interview to gain some practice experience and familiarize your "practice client" and yourself with the expectations.

still learning about social work and have not perfected the skills. You will almost definitely make mistakes. Indeed, the primary purpose of the exercise is for you to practice the social work skills. It is certainly not to provide actual social work services.

Be certain to remind your prospective practice client that a professional social worker has formally agreed to serve as your supervisor and will provide guidance as needed. Identify that person by name. Mention that your supervisor will also serve as her advocate so that she may have a professional resource if there are questions, issues, complications, conflicts, or complaints at any point during the learning exercise.

Inform your colleague that if she agrees to participate as a practice client, she should come to each meeting prepared to discuss one or two actual issues that she might conceivably talk about with a close, trusted friend or perhaps even a social worker. However, the issues should be modest and manageable. Ask her to avoid issues that have the potential to overwhelm her natural coping mechanisms. If the issues involve other people (for example, parents, siblings, spouses, children, classmates, professors), request that she either create pseudonyms or refer to them in general terms such as "my sister" or my "housemate."

Inform your colleague that, with the exception of the post-interview evaluation discussions, you will assume the role of social worker from the beginning to the end of each and every meeting. Ask her to do the same in the role of practice client. Agree upon a fictitious name or pseudonym that she plans to use. Keep actual contact information about your colleague (telephone numbers or e-mail addresses) in a private place—perhaps in your personal calendar or address book.

The first 30 minutes of each meeting are reserved for the formal social work interview. When that ends, you and your partner then step out of your respective roles of social worker and practice client to become collaborators in learning. During the remaining 15 minutes or so, discuss the interview with each other. She can share thoughts and feelings about the experience and provide you with evaluative feedback. The post-interview processing can substantially enhance learning. Be sure to take notes during those exchanges.

If your colleague understands what is expected and provides formal consent to participate, schedule a time and place to meet privately during the next week for the first of five meetings. Save 45 minutes to an hour to ensure that you have enough time for the actual interview. Exchange contact information in case a meeting must be rescheduled or information shared during intervals between meetings, and be sure that the practice client has contact information for her client advocate.

At this point you have secured the commitment of a professor, field instructor, or other professional social worker to serve as your supervisor and as advocate for the practice client. You have been assigned or successfully recruited a colleague to assume the role of practice client and have secured her written consent to participate in the several-session experiential interviewing exercise. You have also become familiar with and gained some experience with the exploring skills. In many respects, the preparing, beginning, and exploring skills are elaborations of the basic talking and listening skills. They complement the characteristics of professionalism that you learned about earlier.

You will soon engage your practice client in the first meeting. First, however, use the preparing skills to increase the probability that the crucial initial interview is positive and constructive. You might start by recognizing that your function is to help the client resolve issues and achieve goals. Although this is an educational experience and the practice client is a colleague, she is a real human being with genuine feelings and emotions. During this series of interviews, your words and actions could affect her—for better or for worse. Although relatively modest in nature, the issues she shares with you are true. Therefore, you should adopt the characteristics of professionalism through all aspects and phases of the exercise.

In advance of the meeting, employ the preparing skills that apply in this situation. Some or all of the following skills might be relevant: preparatory reviewing, preparatory exploring, preparatory consultation, preparatory arranging, preparatory empathy, preparatory self-exploration, centering, and preliminary planning and recording. You might also anticipate using the beginning skills and several of the exploring skills during the first meeting with the practice client. As you recall, the beginning skills include introducing yourself, seeking introductions, describing initial purpose and roles, orienting, discussing policy and ethical factors, and seeking feedback. The exploring skills (see Chapter 9) include asking questions, seeking clarification, reflecting content, reflecting feelings, reflecting feelings and meaning, partializing, going beyond, reflecting issues, and reflecting hypotheses.

By the time of the first formal interview with your practice client, be extremely familiar with the parameters of the several-week exercise. If needed, consult with your supervising social worker about the upcoming interviews. Make arrangements for a private place to meet and secure the necessary recording equipment. Obtain pencils, notebooks, and perhaps drawing paper that may be of use. Definitely take the time before the meeting to engage in preparatory empathy and imagine what it could be like for someone to take the risks associated with sharing personal thoughts, observations, and feelings about actual issues with a student social worker. Consider the possible implications and complications inherent in the client role. It makes relatively little difference if the practice client is a colleague or classmate. Sharing personal information can be a challenging and often frightening experience—perhaps especially when it is audio- or video-recorded. Through preparatory empathy, you should be better prepared to be culturally sensitive, to respect the personhood and the potential vulnerabilities of the practice client, and to recognize the risks involved in this process. Also engage in self-exploration and discover means to find a place of peace and center yourself in advance of encounters with your practice client. Finally, use word-processing software to prepare written "Plans for the First Interview." Save the word-processed document with the label "Intvue_1_ Plans" and deposit it in an "Experiential Interviewing Exercise" folder or section of your Social Work Skills Learning Portfolio.

CHAPTER 8 Self-Appraisal

As you finish this chapter, please reflect on your learning by using the following space to identify any ideas, terms, or concepts addressed in Chapter 8 that remain confusing or unclear to you:

Next, respond to the following items by carefully reading each statement. Please use a 1-to-10-point rating scale (where *1 = strongly disagree* and *10 = strongly agree*) to indicate the degree to which you agree or disagree with each statement. Place a check mark at the point that best reflects your view at this particular point in time. If you're truly *undecided*, place your check at the midpoint (5.5) mark.

1. I can discuss the purposes and functions of beginning.

    | | | | | | | | | | |
    1   2   3   4   5   6   7   8   9   10

2. I can introduce myself.

    | | | | | | | | | | |
    1   2   3   4   5   6   7   8   9   10

3. I can seek introductions from others.

    | | | | | | | | | | |
    1   2   3   4   5   6   7   8   9   10

4. I can describe an initial purpose for meetings and interviews.

    | | | | | | | | | | |
    1   2   3   4   5   6   7   8   9   10

5. I can orient others to the process.

    | | | | | | | | | | |
    1   2   3   4   5   6   7   8   9   10

6. I can discuss policy and ethical factors.

    | | | | | | | | | | |
    1   2   3   4   5   6   7   8   9   10

7. I can seek feedback from others.

    | | | | | | | | | | |
    1   2   3   4   5   6   7   8   9   10

Exploring

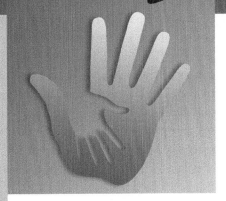

As the beginning phase ends, social workers start to engage clients and others in a mutual process of exploration. This chapter should help you develop proficiency in the **exploring skills**, through which you encourage people to share information, thoughts, and feelings about themselves; the needs, problems, issues, or other concerns that led to the contact; and the social and environmental context in which they function. Through this collaborative process of exploration, you usually learn a great deal, and so do others. Clients and other constituents often gain a more complete and realistic understanding of the issues of concern as well as their impact upon them and their circumstances. In addition, they often enhance their own self-understanding. Indeed, greater self-awareness is a common result because talking openly with other people also involves listening to oneself. As people share their thoughts, ideas, and feelings, they not only perceive your reactions to them and to what they say, but also more fully experience their own thoughts, feelings, and sensations. In group contexts, the effects are enhanced as people experience the reactions of others as well as

(Continued)

Core Competencies

The content addressed in this chapter supports the following core EPAS competencies:

- Competency 2: Engage Diversity and Difference in Practice

- Competency 6: Engage with Individuals, Families, Groups, Organizations, and Communities

- Competency 7: Assess Individuals, Families, Groups, Organizations, and Communities

Chapter Goals

Following completion of this chapter, you should be able to:

- Discuss the purposes and functions of exploring.

- Explore relevant aspects of the person-issue-situation and look for strengths and assets in the person-in-environment.

- Ask questions.

- Seek clarification.

- Reflect content.

- Reflect feelings.

- Reflect feelings and meaning.

- Partialize.

- Go beyond what is said.

- Reflect issues.

- Reflect hypotheses.

their own. Through this process, you collaboratively consider information regarding clients, involved others, needs or problems, and circumstances. You review risk and protective factors. This helps you both identify elements associated with the origin, development, and maintenance of the problems as well as those strengths, attributes, assets and resources that may be useful in working toward resolution. Such information, in conjunction with your own professional knowledge and, of course, the full participation of your clients and others, contributes to the subsequent development of an assessment, service contract, and plans for your work together.

In undertaking the exploration process, we enlist clients or others in a collaborative examination of the current state of the presenting issues as well as an overview of their origin and history. We also review previous attempts to address or overcome them along with the outcomes of those efforts. In addition to needs and problems, we also engage clients in collaborative consideration of wants, aspirations, and goals. In terms of goals, we seek clients' ideas about two kinds: (1) goals that, if achieved, would naturally result in the elimination, reduction, or management of the presenting needs, problems, or issues; and (2) goals that, if achieved, would contribute to a better quality of life and an enhanced sense of well-being. Let's conceptualize these two kinds of goals as **harm reduction** (or problem resolution) and **enhanced well-being,** respectively.

As social workers, we view each client as a unique and significant individual, family, group, organization, or community that functions within the context of a social and physical environment. The characteristics and attributes of the client and those of the environment bear upon the presenting problems and goals. Therefore, we embrace our **person-in-environment perspective**[1] (see Figure 9.1) during the exploration process and attempt to learn about the client and the situation as well as the issues of concern. We look for strengths and assets as well as challenges and obstacles that emerge within biopsychosocial life spheres and the physical environment (see Figure 9.2).

Issues[2] and the goals that relate to them may be viewed as partly or wholly personal or as partly or wholly environmental, or partly or wholly interactional (that is, interactions within

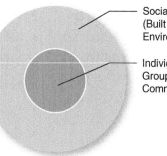

Social & Physical (Built & Natural) Environment

Individual, Dyad, Family, Group Organization, Community, or Society

FIGURE 9.1   Person-in-Environment Perspective

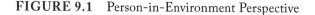

[1] In the context of a person-in-environment perspective, a person is a client. In social work, a client can be an individual, family, group, organization, community, or perhaps an entire society. However, the PIE perspective suggests that all people—clients and others alike—can truly be understood only within the context of their social and physical environment. This becomes especially apparent when social workers engage in policy–practice and social action.

[2] The term *issue* is intended to encompass needs, problems, or concerns identified by people or apparent to others. Issues include problems in living as well as various forms of social, economic, or environmental injustice—including infringements upon and denial of human rights.

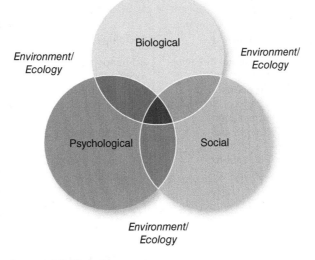

FIGURE 9.2   Biopsychosocial Life Spheres

or between the person and environmental systems). Similarly, clients and social workers may conceptualize personal problems and goals as partially or completely sociological,[3] psychological, or biological. Social issues or social problems may be viewed as the result of widespread individual failings or character flaws; as a consequence of social, economic, or environmental injustices; or as some combination of personal and ecological factors. Understandably, the particular biopsychosocial aspects or dimensions of the issues and goals, and the life spheres or domains within the environmental context, vary from client to client and from social issue to social issue. Social workers, however, maintain a person-in-environment perspective and recognize that personal and environmental factors interact in an interdependent manner. We do so even when exploring **biological dimensions** such as heredity (for example, genetic factors), health and wellness, illness, injury, physiological sensations, and ingested or absorbed chemical substances (for example, medicines, substances such as alcohol and street drugs, environmental chemicals such as lead, pesticides, air and water pollutants that reside within a person's body); **psychological dimensions** such as perceptions, cognitive beliefs, attitudes, expectations (for example, thoughts about self and others, cultural views, religious and spiritual beliefs; ideas about problems and problem solving), images, and individual behavior; and **social dimensions** such as interpersonal encounters, relationships, and patterns of communicating and relating that occur within the context of primary and secondary social systems (for example, families, households, various groups, organizations, neighborhoods, communities, cultures, and societies) as well as practices and traditions common within the client's social environment (for example, the economic, political, educational, religious, and justice systems). Of course, problems and goals within both the built and natural **physical environments** (for example, climate and weather conditions, access to water and fertile soil, housing, air and water quality, noise levels, access to food and clothing, energy resources, transportation, personal privacy, and physical safety) as well as the **social environment** are common. Indeed, as social

---

[3] In this context, the term *sociological* is used in its broadest sense to include economic, political, cultural, and other social systems and the structures and processes associated with them.

TABLE 9.1	Outline of Selected Biopsychosocial and Environmental Dimensions		
Biological	Psychological	Sociological	Natural and Built Environment
• Hereditary Predispositions • Health and Physical Ability • Illness, Disease, Injury • Ingested or Absorbed Chemical Substances	• Individual Behavior • Feelings and Emotions • Cognitive Beliefs and Expectations • Images and Visualizations • Perceptions • Sensations	• Friendship Systems • Family Systems • Employment Systems • Neighborhood Systems • Cultural Systems • Educational Systems • Religious or Spiritual Systems • Health Care Systems • Organizational Systems • Community Systems • Legal Systems • Societal Systems	• Safety/Danger • Air • Water • Food • Shelter/Housing • Clothing • Privacy • Noise/Quiet • Transportation • Energy • Biodiversity • Stimulation: Intellectual, Emotional, Social, Physical

workers, we consider the physical as well as the social context and recognize that social policies, customs, and practices may affect, for better or worse, the biological, psychological, social, and environmental aspects of people's lives.

As you and your clients explore issues and goals from a person-in-environment perspective, you might consider biopsychosocial and environmental dimensions such as those outlined in Table 9.1. As an alternative or supplement to a table, you could also create a concept map (Mueller, Polansky, Foltin, Polivaev, & Other Contributers, 2010) to illustrate potentially relevant biopsychosocial and environmental dimensions.[4]

Concept maps are graphic illustrations that capture significant and relevant ideas or information. You might use them to organize thoughts and observations about various phenomena related to aspects of the person-issue-situation (for example, problems, goals, hypotheses, action steps, evaluation processes). Concept maps are especially useful in the exploration phase and later in the assessment and contracting phases as you and your clients develop case formulations. Figure 9.3 contains selected dimensions of a concept map that social workers and clients might use to guide the process of identifying and exploring key biopsychosocial and environmental dimensions of issues and goals from a person-in-environment perspective.

When social workers prepare individualized concept maps, we replace the categorical dimensions with client-specific information. Figure 9.4 depicts a partially completed concept map of a homeless man who lives just outside the city center under a bridge by a small river. He has declined to identify himself by name, so we refer to him as the "homeless pacer" because he constantly moves—walking, pacing, or, if seated, rocking back and forth—and he lives in Indianapolis, home of the Pacers basketball team.

---

[4] Many word processors allow you to create conceptual maps and graphic illustrations of various kinds. You could also use a dedicated mind-mapping software program such as FreeMind (available at **http://freemind.sourceforge.net**).

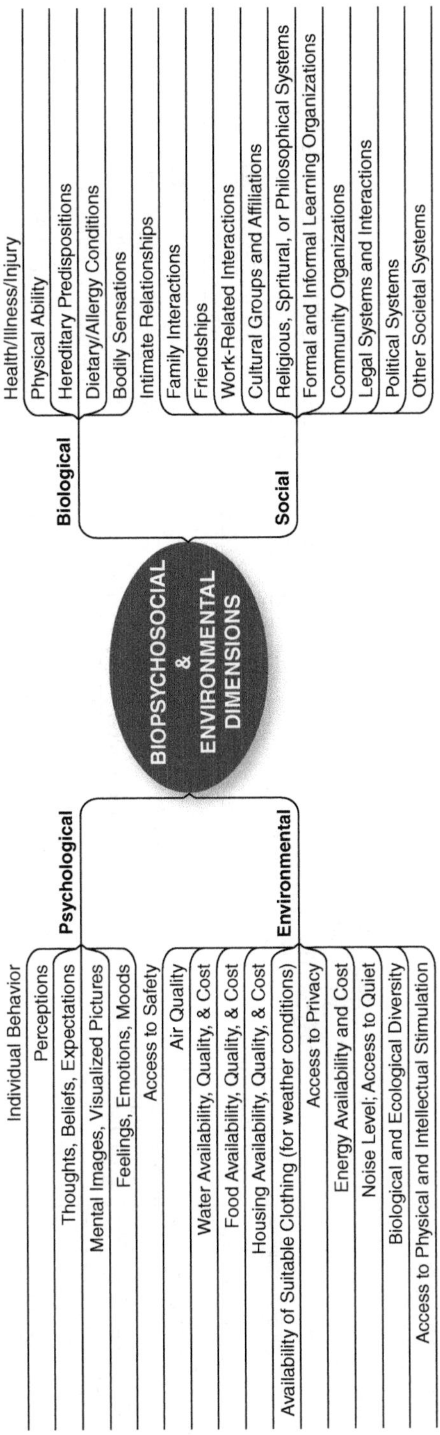

The concept map "Biopsychosocial & Environmental Dimensions" branches into four main dimensions, each with subtopics:

Biological
- Health/Illness/Injury
- Physical Ability
- Hereditary Predispositions
- Dietary/Allergy Conditions
- Bodily Sensations

Social
- Intimate Relationships
- Family Interactions
- Friendships
- Work-Related Interactions
- Cultural Groups and Affiliations
- Religious, Spritural, or Philosophical Systems
- Formal and Informal Learning Organizations
- Community Organizations
- Legal Systems and Interactions
- Political Systems
- Other Societal Systems

Psychological
- Individual Behavior
- Perceptions
- Thoughts, Beliefs, Expectations
- Mental Images, Visualized Pictures
- Feelings, Emotions, Moods

Environmental
- Access to Safety
- Air Quality
- Water Availability, Quality, & Cost
- Food Availability, Quality, & Cost
- Housing Availability, Quality, & Cost
- Availability of Suitable Clothing (for weather conditions)
- Access to Privacy
- Energy Availability and Cost
- Noise Level; Access to Quiet
- Biological and Ecological Diversity
- Access to Physical and Intellectual Stimulation

FIGURE 9.3 Concept Map: Selected Biopsychosocial and Environmental Dimensions

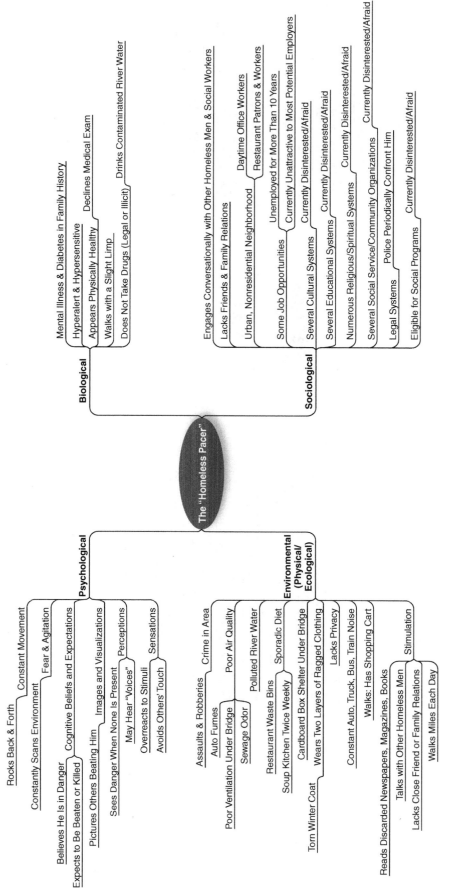

FIGURE 9.4 Concept Map: The "Homeless Pacer"

TABLE 9.2	Exploration Matrix			
		Present	**Past**	**Future**
Issue		1	2	7
Person/Client/People (Biopsychosocial)		3	4	8
Situation (Social and Physical Environment)		5	6	9

Following the introductions and other beginning phase processes, people often feel a strong motivation to discuss the most pressing issues[5] of concern. As the matrix shown in Table 9.2 suggests, you often begin by exploring an issue as currently experienced (cell 1). You might then trace its emergence, history, and development (cell 2).

Exploring the issue involves examining the present status of the concern—its intensity, frequency, and duration—and the context in which it tends to happen (see Table 9.3). As social workers, we hope to discover what happens before, during, and after an occurrence or episode of the issue. In addition, you commonly explore the issue as it has been in the past. Trace or track its development from the time of its initial occurrence to the present. In your exploration, include a careful examination of clients' attempts to resolve, cope with, or avoid the issue (see the later discussion on looking for strengths and assets). Discuss efforts that have been successful, those that were partially successful, and those that were unsuccessful. Identify strengths and assets that clients used in earlier attempts at resolution. As part of this exploration, encourage people to share thoughts, feelings, and behaviors associated with the issue of concern. Of course, as you encourage people to describe the issues that concern them, many naturally begin to discuss aspects of themselves personally as well as dimensions of the situation.

As needed, you may next explore their present view of themselves (Table 9.2, cell 3), followed by a review of past experiences (cell 4). Then, to the degree that further information is needed, you can return to the present situation, including the social context and physical environment

TABLE 9.3	Exploration of the Issue
Onset	Explore the origin of the issue and the circumstances under which it first occurred.
Evolution	Explore the development and course of the issue; when and how it was better or worse; and when and how the client or others addressed or coped with the issue.
Frequency	Explore how often episodes of the issue occur.
Situational Context	Explore when, where, and how episodes of the issue emerge.
Intensity/Severity	Explore the severity or intensity of the issue.
Duration	Explore how long each episode of the issue lasts, and determine how long the issue has existed.

[5] We use the term *issue* to refer to a topic of concern or interest to the client, the social worker, or other interested parties. In this context, an issue may be a need, problem, dilemma, symptom, or aspiration of relevance to participants in the professional relationship. The term *social issue* refers to *social problems* that affect large numbers of people and involve economic, political, and social structures, systems, and processes.

(cell 5), before exploring the situation as it has been in the past (cell 6). Finally, you may encourage people to envision what the future might be like if they, the issue, and the situation remained as it is; and how the future might be if things were to change for the better; or for the worse (cells 7, 8, and 9).

Exploring the person involves encouraging clients to explore aspects of themselves as individual human beings and, when relevant, as members of a family, group, organization, or community. Of course, we do so within the context of the problems and issues of concern. In this dimension, we are especially interested in the *thinking, feeling,* and *doing* aspects of clients' experiences. Seek information about strengths and assets, as well as weaknesses and deficiencies. Explore both the substance of clients' thoughts—whether they occur as beliefs (the words people say to themselves) or as images (the mental pictures people have); and the thought processes (the cognitive steps people take as they move from one idea to another). Within the dimension of feeling, consider clients' emotions (for example, anger, fear, or sadness) as well as physical sensations (for example, energy, fatigue, muscular tension, nausea, or light-headedness). Within the dimension of doing, explore overt behavior (for example, walking, speaking, hitting, or looking) as well as deficits in behavior (for example, behaviors such as assertive statements that clients might adopt but fail to do so).

Sometimes the nature of a problem warrants exploration of personal style or personality characteristics. Clients may discuss traits or attributes that contribute to understanding. For instance, a middle-aged woman may describe herself as being "extraordinarily sensitive to criticism" or remark that "my feelings are easily hurt." An older man might report that he is "emotionally shut down" or perhaps that he has "lost the ability to feel." An appreciation of these characteristics may help in understanding the person-issue-situation and in developing plans to pursue goals.

In addition, the biological or medical history and condition of clients may be pertinent to the exploration process. For instance, diabetes, epilepsy, cardiac problems, and chemical addictions are among the health-related factors that often contribute to an understanding of the person-issue-situation. Similarly, a deeper understanding of the issue may require exploration of clients' spiritual or religious beliefs. Indeed, some religions prohibit the application of certain medical procedures. Others may sometimes consider misfortunes to be the result of sinful behavior. Core beliefs about life's meaning and how to live a good and proper life often influence clients' understanding of themselves and others, their circumstances, and the issues they face.

Because most if not all issues have social aspects, social workers usually encourage clients to share information about their significant relationships and their typical ways of relating to others. For example, clients may describe their preferred relational styles (for example, direct or assertive, passive or indirect, slow or quick to speak or act) and how they react socially during encounters involving conflict or intense emotion (for example, confrontation, immobilization, withdrawal).

Clients' preferred coping processes and their problem-solving strategies are often relevant. Questions such as "How do you cope with stress, disappointment, or frustration?" may lead to deeper understanding and reveal potential directions for work or perhaps avenues for resolution. Similarly, queries such as "When you face problems such as this one, how do you usually go about trying to solve them?" may contribute to an understanding of problem-solving patterns and strategies.

Exploring the situation involves examining current and, when applicable, past circumstances. Collect pertinent information about social and cultural factors, as well as economic, political, and legal aspects of situations that may relate to the issue of concern, or to those assets or resources that might be useful for resolution. Gather information about significant other people, family systems, communities, ethnic affiliations, religious involvement, education, employment, and finances. Be sure to explore the physical environment as well. Housing conditions, air and water quality, and noise levels may be factors. Insect or rodent infestations can be present, and toxins may be present in buildings or in the soil that support or surround them.

Just as individuals think, feel, and behave in habitual ways, families and other social systems also reflect preferred cultural beliefs, emotions, and customary practices. Systems establish ways of communicating and relating, addressing problems, and making decisions. They reflect organizational structures as well. Many are hierarchical, others are more or less egalitarian, and some appear chaotic—lacking structure altogether.

Exploring the future involves examining the issue, the person, and the situation as they may emerge in the future. Explore a continuum of possible future scenarios. For example, you might first explore with the client how the problem and situation would probably be at some point in the future if everything continued along as it is now. What would the client be thinking, feeling, and doing in such a future. Then, you might examine how they might be in a "worst possible case" scenario, where things seriously deteriorate. Finally, you could explore a "best possible case," where the issues are completely resolved. The latter process is often quite enlightening, as it helps you and your clients clarify possible directions for work as well as revealing implicit strengths, assets, resources, and protective factors. Exploring the future also frequently yields an array of potential indicators or benchmarks of a successful outcome.

These nine dimensions overlap. As you explore one area, people often share relevant biopsychosocial and environmental factors that conceptually fit better within another cell or cells. As they share information about themselves, their situation, and circumstances, aspects of needs, problems, and issues often emerge; and sometimes references to goals and aspirations arise as well. While exploring the present, people may reveal material from the past or hopes and fears about the future. You do not need to interrupt to maintain a particular order or sequence. Generally, you may simply encourage people to share relevant information in their own way. Resist the temptation to view the exploration matrix as a fixed interview schedule. Instead, see it as a flexible guide to help you organize the exploration of relevant aspects of the person, problem, and situation over time.

Events and experiences in both the past and the present may affect human beings in profound and often unexpected ways. Expectations concerning the future also influence our current thoughts, feelings, and actions. One way to organize information in the temporal dimension is through timelines. A **timeline** is a simple table that reflects, in shorthand fashion, important events or experiences in chronological order during a designated period. At least two kinds of timelines may be especially useful. A "Critical Events Timeline" provides an opportunity to outline significant or meaningful experiences in a person's life. A "Problem Timeline" provides a means to trace the origin and development of a particular issue or problem. Other timelines may be helpful as well. For example, a "Relationship Timeline" can provide a graphic temporal representation of key moments in a personal, family, or professional relationship. A "Successes Timeline" can facilitate the process of looking for strengths by recording dates of accomplishments, achievements, and other successful experiences. All sorts of timelines are conceivable. You can even extend timelines into the future by imagining or forecasting significant events, moments, or experiences that might occur and could have an impact later on in life.

Creating your own timelines tends to produce considerable self-understanding—because you must actively reflect on important lifetime events. Clients may also benefit from the experience of constructing their own timelines. At times, however, someone else may need to help. For example, a parent might generate a timeline for a child, or a social worker might create a timeline to record critical events in the life of a support group.

The guidelines for creating timelines are quite simple and highly flexible. Feel free to be creative. The basic components are (1) a fairly long, continuous, horizontal or vertical line representing a period of time, (2) several perpendicular, intersecting, or angled lines of shorter length to indicate the dates of selected events, and (3) short descriptions of the events or experiences adjacent to the shorter lines. You may use additional codes or symbols for other purposes as well. For example,

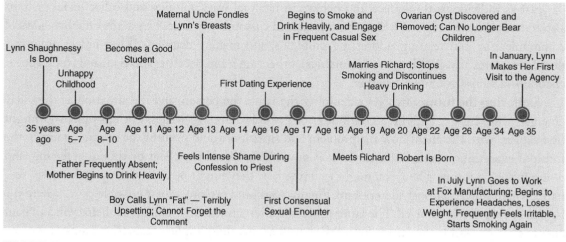

FIGURE 9.5 Critical Events Timeline: Lynn S. Chase

events of a positive nature may be indicated with a plus sign (+), whereas those of a negative nature could be accompanied by a minus (−) sign. You could serve the same purpose by placing positive events above a horizontal timeline (or to the left of a vertical timeline) and those of a negative nature below (or to the right of) the timeline.

Figure 9.5 contains Lynn Chase's "Critical Events Timeline." In this instance, the social worker prepared a preliminary timeline based on information provided by Mrs. Chase. Later, she gave the working draft to Mrs. Chase, who edited the timeline and returned a copy of the updated version.

As you notice, the Critical Events Timeline yields a temporal outline of important experiences in Mrs. Chase's life. When used in the context of serving clients, timelines give both parties ready access to significant information. Both Mrs. Chase and her social worker may use the timeline for easy reference throughout the course of their work together.

Timelines can also be used for policy–practice, public education, consciousness-raising, and social action purposes as well. For instance, social workers may trace the levels of economic equality in the United States over time through the "When Income Grows, Who Gains" timeline available at the "State of Working America" website at **www.stateofworkingamerica.org** (Economic Policy Institute, 2008). Another example, "America's Civil Rights Timeline" can be found on the website of the International Civil Rights Center and Museum (ICRCM) at **www.sitinmovement.org**. The ICRCM is located in Greensboro, North Carolina, where in February 1960, several young African Americans initiated a "sit-in" at the "whites-only" counter in the downtown F.W. Woolworth store.

Timelines can be used to capture the temporal dimensions of phenomena of all kinds from, for example, the history of a particular family to the history of the universe as presented on the Public Broadcasting System (PBS) site at **http://www.pbs.org/deepspace/timeline**. To supplement family timelines, social workers may also help family members prepare intergenerational genograms.

Genograms[6] are graphic representations of family trees or pedigrees[7] (Wattendorf & Hadley, 2005). They provide a picture of the parties involved and a chronology of significant events or themes.

---

[6] Go to **http://www.interpersonaluniverse.net/genogram.html** to view an example of a genogram created with the program Relativity™.

[7] Medical physicians and geneticists often use the term *family pedigree* to describe a graphic representation of illnesses and diseases that occur within three or more generations of a family.

They also help to increase awareness and understanding of how families[8] influence their members. In addition, genograms may be used as "a subjective interpretive tool" (McGoldrick & Gerson, 1985, p. 2) to develop hypotheses about a person's psychosocial characteristics or a family's interactional patterns.

We commonly use certain symbols to prepare family genograms (McGoldrick, Gerson, & Shellenberger, 1999). For instance, we usually use squares to represent males and circles to identify females. Bracket lines represent spousal relationships. A solid bracket line (|___|) reflects a committed couple (for example, marriage or its equivalent). A dashed bracket line (|_ _ _|) indicates a relationship of somewhat lesser commitment. A dotted bracket line (| . . . . |) suggests a relatively uncommitted relationship (for example, a short-term affair). A line extended downward from a relationship bracket line indicates a pregnancy, biological child, or adopted child from that relationship. Separations and breakups or divorces are indicated by one and two slash marks (/ and //) respectively, cutting across the relationship bracket line. We place pregnancies and children from each relationship in order from the earliest to latest, proceeding from left to right. We indicate deaths by an X symbol placed within the pertinent circle or square. If known, we provide names of people and dates of birth, adoption, marriage, separation, divorce, and death alongside the symbols. For example, we might note just above or beneath a bracket line indicating a marriage relationship "mar. 3/18/1997." This indicates that the couple married on March 18, 1997. If this relationship leads to a birth or adoption, such events might be recorded by "dob. 4/21/1999" or "adop. 4/21/1999." If the couple later separates, we could indicate that event by "sep. 4/23/2004." A subsequent divorce could be shown by "div. 5/7/2005."

You may add descriptions of individual people and relationships with brief notations. For example, one family member may have served in the military during a war, and perhaps another suffered from obesity and diabetes. Indeed, some circumstances may warrant a genetic family history (Bernhardt & Rauch, 1993) to trace biological and physiological phenomena across generations. We may also record significant events such as major accidents, injuries, crimes, and changes of residence or occupation. Additional symbols or notations may be used to characterize the nature of selected relationships (McGoldrick & Gerson, 1985; McGoldrick et al., 1999). Very close relationships, those that are emotionally cool, those that are strained, and those that involve conflict may be identified. You may place the sources of information at the bottom of the genogram along with the date and name of the person who prepared the genogram.

Family genograms may be as brief or as extensive as the people gathering information want them to be. Some people pursue their creation with great zeal, spending hours interviewing parents, aunts and uncles, and grandparents. They may even contact distant relatives and former neighbors. Others base their genograms solely on information they personally recall. Usually, the intended purpose for the genogram affects the amount of energy expended in data collection and preparation. Genograms may be prepared in the present—the family as it is now—or the past tense—how it existed at some earlier point. It is even possible to prepare a genogram based on predictions of the future—how a family may appear 5 or 10 years hence. Many people find it useful to take "genogrammatic" snapshots of the family as they remember it at significant points in their development (for example, beginning grammar school, graduating from high school, leaving home, entering military service or college, marrying, or giving birth to or adopting children).

As an illustrative example, consider the Chase family genogram as shown in Figure 9.6. Susan Holder, the social worker who prepared the genogram from Mrs. Chase's perspective, pulled

[8] Not all people have biological or adopted families of origin. Many children grow up in foster-care settings, children's institutions, or hospitals. In such circumstances, some adaptation of the genogram may be necessary to identify significant persons in the individual's life. Sometimes, creation of an eco-map (see the next section) may be more applicable than a genogram.

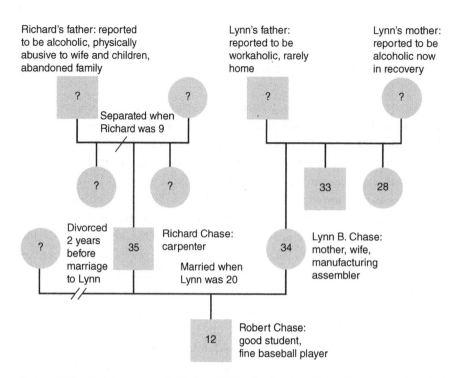

Richard's father: reported to be alcoholic, physically abusive to wife and children, abandoned family

Lynn's father: reported to be workaholic, rarely home

Lynn's mother: reported to be alcoholic now in recovery

Separated when Richard was 9

Divorced 2 years before marriage to Lynn

Richard Chase: carpenter

Married when Lynn was 20

Lynn B. Chase: mother, wife, manufacturing assembler

Robert Chase: good student, fine baseball player

Notes: *Richard's father is reported to have left the family when Richard was approximately 9 years old. Lynn says that Richard, his siblings, and his mother were physically and emotionally abused by his father, who apparently was also an alcoholic.*

Lynn was the eldest child in a family where she remembers that her father was rarely at home and generally uninvolved in family matters. Her mother is reported to have been an alcoholic and was often intoxicated during Lynn's childhood years. Lynn apparently assumed many adult responsibilities at an early age. As a result, she may exhibit some of the characteristics of a "parental child" of an alcoholic family system.

There are noticeable family themes of alcoholism and possibly workaholism. Richard may have been physically and emotionally abused as a child. Both Lynn and Richard may tend to assume great amounts of personal responsibility.

Robert is a good student and a fine baseball player.

Prepared by_____
Susan Holder, MSW
Social Worker

From the perspective of: Lynn B. Chase
Date: January 13

FIGURE 9.6 Chase Family Genogram

together a considerable amount of information in readily accessible form. There are concise notes regarding some major intergenerational family themes and patterns. This genogram could be an important reference in Susan's service to Mrs. Chase.

Although the family genogram is the most common, there are other forms as well. For example, you may sometimes find it useful to collaborate with clients in the preparation of a cultural genogram (Congress, 1994; Hardy & Laszloffy, 1995; Keiley et al., 2002) or perhaps a spiritual genogram (Frame, 2000). In child welfare services, household or placement genograms may be especially helpful (Altshuler, 1999; McMillen & Groze, 1994; McMillen & Rideout, 1996).

As social workers consider aspects of the person-in-environment beyond the intergenerational family system, we may find it useful to prepare an eco-map (Hartman, 1978; Hartman & Laird, 1983). **Eco-maps** complement genograms through diagrammatic representations of the social contexts in which people live (Mattaini, 1990). They readily highlight the energy-enhancing and energy-depleting relationships between members of a primary social system (for example, a family or household) and the outside world (Mattaini, 1990, 1993a, 1993b, 1995). The graphic nature of the eco-map helps to highlight social strengths and deficiencies, and to identify areas of conflict and compatibility. Eco-maps may serve multiple purposes. For example, they may reveal areas where resources may be accessed or changes could occur (Fieldhouse & Bunkowsky, 2002).

As in genograms, squares or circles are used to represent members of the primary social system (for example, the household). We draw these in the middle of a sheet of paper and place them within a large circle. Other significant social systems with which the person, family, or household members interact are also identified and encircled. Lines characterize the interactions and relationships among the identified social systems. A solid line (————) reflects a strong and generally positive relationship; a dotted line (⋯⋯) reflects a tenuous relationship; and a hatched line (////////) reflects a stressful or conflicted relationship. Arrows (→) may indicate the direction of the flow of energy or resources between systems and subsystems. These relationship lines may characterize the exchange of energy among family members. Plus (+), minus (−), and plus-minus (±) signs may be placed adjacent to relationship lines as supplements, indicating that a relationship is energy enhancing, energy depleting, or evenly balanced in terms of energy investment and return.

As an illustrative example, Figure 9.7 contains an eco-map of the Chase family. Using information provided by Mrs. Chase, the social worker depicted important social systems with which the Chase family members interact, illustrating and characterizing the relationships among the systems. When used in the context of providing social work services, the eco-map gives both the worker and client a great deal of information in graphic form. As you can easily observe, Mrs. Chase appears to expend much more energy than she receives from most interactions with other people and social systems.

In addition to dimensions of the presenting issue, critical incidents, historical and interactional patterns, and other relevant dimensions, the exploration process also typically involves identification and review of those risk and protective factors that appear to increase or decrease the probability that a particular phenomenon will occur. In developing a conceptual scheme for viewing risky behavior among adolescents, Jessor and colleagues (1991; Jessor, Bos, Vanderyn, & Turbin, 1995) suggest that there is "a relationship between risk and protective factors in five domains (biology/genetics, social environment, perceived environment, personality, and behavior)" (Astatke, Black, & Serpell, 2000, p. 66).

We can define **risk factors** "as individual or environmental markers that are related to the increased likelihood that a negative outcome will occur" (Small, 2000, para. 2). The concept of risk factors has been common in epidemiological and public health research related to disease, injuries, and risky behaviors (for example, unprotected sex, inadequate diets, limited physical or mental exercise, poverty, violence). Indeed, the Centers for Disease Control and Prevention (CDC) sponsor a Behavioral Risk Factor Surveillance System (BRFSS) to identify and monitor risk factors (Centers for Disease Control and Prevention, 2012).

In addition to risk factors, we may also identify protective—sometimes called "resilience"—factors. **Protective factors** or resilience factors are:

individual or environmental safeguards that enhance a person's ability to resist stressful life events, risks or hazards and promote adaptation and competence. An important but often overlooked aspect of protective processes is that they only operate when a risk factor is present.

Risk and protective factors can exist both within individuals and across various levels of the environment in which they live. Diverse problems can share common risk factors.

Risk factors often co-occur, and when they do, they appear to carry additive and sometimes exponential risks. It is often the accumulation of multiple risks rather than the presence of any single risk factor that leads to negative outcomes. (Small, 2000, paras. 3–5)

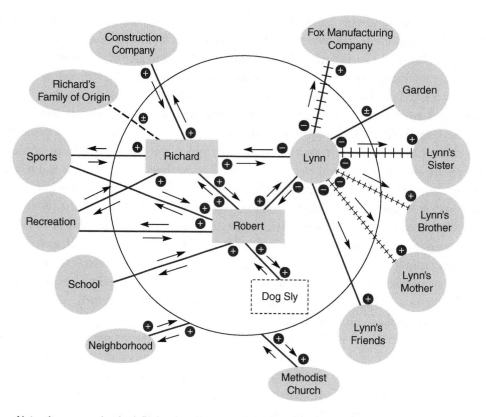

Note: *It appears that both Richard and Robert have reasonable equilibrium in terms of the amount of energy invested and returned. Lynn, however, appears to expend much more energy than she receives. She seems to have a large number of relationships in which she invests but relatively few from which she gains energy.*

Prepared by————————————
Susan Holder, MSW
Social Worker

From the perspective of: Lynn B. Chase

FIGURE 9.7 Chase Family Eco-map

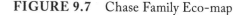

Research involving risk and protective factors associated with various social problems has been quite extensive over the course of the past several decades. Factors associated with the development of psychopathology received early interest (Garmezy, 1985, 1986; Rutter, 1979, 1985, 1987; Werner, 1986, 1989). Those associated with contraction of HIV/AIDS have garnered more recent research attention (Amaro, Raj, Vega, Mangione, & Perez, 2001; Langer, Warheit, & McDonald, 2001; Mullen, Ramirez, Strouse, Hedges, & Sogolow, 2002; Ramirez-Valles, 2002), and substance abuse has a similarly rich research base (Catalano, Hawkins, Berglund, Pollard, & Arthur, 2002; Center for Substance Abuse Prevention, 2001; Epstein & Botvin, 2002; Hawkins, Catalano, & Miller, 1992; Petraitis, Flay, Miller, Torpy, & Greiner, 1998; Wright, 2004). As you can readily imagine, the concepts of strengths, assets, competencies, resilience, and quality of life relate to the notion of protective factors. As you explore issues with clients, you may organize risk and protective factors in tabular format such as depicted in Table 9.4 (Centers for Disease Control and Prevention, 2012). Indeed, many clients can readily identify relevant factors in their own circumstances.

In addition to exploring risks and protective factors directly with clients, scholarly social workers may also review relevant epidemiological research studies. Consider, for example, the risk and

TABLE 9.4	Selected Risk and Protective/Resilience Factors Table for HIV/AIDS	
Risk Factors	**Protective/Resilience Factors**
Unprotected sex (for example, oral, anal, vaginal)	Sexual abstinence
	Sex with a single partner who is HIV-negative and monogamous
	Protected sex (for example, sex with condom)
Sharing needles, syringes, drug equipment or "works," or other objects that could retain blood or bodily fluids	Single use of needles and syringes (including those used to inject medicine, steroids, or vitamins; body piercing; and tattooing)
	Exclusive use of drug equipment or "works," or other objects that could retain blood or bodily fluids
Blood transfusions from HIV-positive blood supply	Tested, safe blood supply

Note: Adapted from the Behavioral Risk Factor Surveillance System (Centers for Disease Control and Prevention, 2012).

protective factors (see Table 9.5) associated with Sudden Unexpected Infant Death (SUID).[9] There seem to be three types of SUIDs: Sudden Infant Death Syndrome (SIDS), Accidental Suffocation and Strangulation in Bed, and Unknown Cause. SIDS is the leading cause of death for infants between the age of one-month and one-year. Almost 3,500 infants in the United States "die suddenly and unexpectedly each year" (Centers for Disease Control and Prevention, 2015, May 26, para. 1).

TABLE 9.5	Selected Risk and Protective/Resilience Factors Table for SUID	
Risk Factors	**Protective/Resilience Factors**
Infant is born preterm	Infant is born at term
Infant is less than 3 months of age	Infant is older than 3 months of age
Exposure to mother's smoking	Mother does not smoke
Infant is not breast-fed	Infant is breast-fed
Infant is not given pacifier (dummy or binky)	Infant uses pacifier after 3 to 4 weeks of breast feeding
Infant is placed in prone position (face down) to sleep	Infant is placed in supine position (face up) to sleep
Parent(s) share bed or sofa with infant (greater risk (greater risk if parents smoke, use drugs, or consume alcohol before sleep; sofa-sharing is even more risky than the already risky practice of bed-sharing)	Baby sleeps in a separate bed in same room and in close proximity to parents
Loose, soft bedding or toys in infant's bed	Toys are absent from infant's bed and blanket placed (or a baby sleeping bag is used) so the infant's head and face cannot be covered
Infant is not immunized	Infant is immunized

Note: Adapted from "Sudden infant death syndrome and advice for safe sleeping" (Horne, Hauck, & Moon, 2015)

---

[9] For additional information, go to the SUIDs section of the Centers for Disease Control and Prevention website at **http://www.cdc.gov/sids/index.htm.**

Social workers may also consider risk and protective factors in relation to social phenomena such as war and peace or civil uprisings. For example, the Institute for Economics and Peace (IEP) observes a significant, one-way relationship between corruption and peace. Their research data suggest that as the level of corruption in a nation grows and expands, it eventually reaches a "tipping point" when, thereafter, even "small increases in corruption are associated with large decreases in peace" (2015b, p. 16). If social workers are aware of these data, we could include "level of corruption" in the preparation of a risk and protective factors table for "peace." In fact, the IEP has developed an empirically based set of 8 Pillars of Peace, which can be used to craft a preliminary risk and protective factors table (see Table 9.6).

Clients, of course, can often reflect upon their own experience to identify risk and protective factors. However, as you explore the person-issue-situation together, you may recognize an imbalance in the degree of attention to problems, troubles, or risk factors versus strengths, resources, and protective factors. Occasionally, clients deny or minimize problems and stridently assert that everything is "just fine." Involuntary and nonvoluntary clients sometimes exhibit just such a "rosy" view—at least at first. Other clients, however, seem to focus primarily on problems, dilemmas, and distressing events. This is quite understandable. Many clients are so distraught that they focus almost exclusively on things that cause them the greatest distress. Helping professionals are frequently educated to do much the same, that is, to attend primarily to symptoms, problems, illnesses, pain, or disorders. Several factors contribute to this "tilt toward troubles." As a social worker, however, ensure that you and your clients adequately explore strengths and resources—as well as problems and needs. Otherwise, you and your clients could conclude the exploration process with an incomplete understanding of both the factors associated with the development and continuation of the problems, as well as the potential resources that might be used to address them.

By **looking for strengths**, you gently—without denying or minimizing the client's reality—explore the strengths, capacities, assets, and competencies within the person-in-environment. Looking for strengths overlaps with the process of identifying protective or resilience factors (Fraser, Richman, & Galinsky, 1999; Gilgun, 1998, 2004a, 2004b; Smokowski, Mann, Reynolds, & Fraser, 2004). You may look for strengths by asking questions, seeking responses to "incomplete" or "fill-in-the-blank" sentences, or through active listening. As they cope with challenging problems and circumstances, clients often reflect extraordinary strength and resilience. Indeed, the term *heroic* applies to many clients.

TABLE 9.6	Risk and Protective/Resilience Factors Table for Peace (Based on IEP's 8 Pillars of Peace)
Risk Factors	**Protective/Resilience Factors**
Dysfunctional government	Well-functioning government
Inequitable distribution of resources (inequality)	Equitable distribution of resources (equality)
Unsound business environment	Sound business environment
Low level of human capital	High level of human capital
Nonacceptance of the rights of others (intolerance)	Acceptance of the rights of others (tolerance)
High levels of corruption	Low levels of corruption
Poor relations with neighbors	Good relations with neighbors

Note: Adapted from "Pillars of Peace" (Institute for Economics and Peace, 2011)

Of course, there are downsides associated with a strengths perspective—just as there are with other conceptual models. A major danger arises when social workers prematurely force clients to look for positive attributes before they have explored the problems and circumstances of greatest concern. You may recall a brief reference in Chapter 5 to dramatically increased dropout rates when helping professionals do not communicate an accurate understanding of clients' views about and experiences of the presenting problem or issue (Epperson et al., 1983; Pekarik, 1988, 1991; Wierzbicki & Pekarik, 1993). Determined searches for strengths that prevent or impede clients' ability to describe and discuss issues of concern in their own way can leave them feeling unheard, misunderstood, and extremely frustrated. Many may not return following an initial visit. Paradoxically, a premature search for strengths may leave clients feeling diminished rather than supported. The effects can be similar to those experienced by a child who has just scraped her knee. It hurts and she is just about to cry. Suppose an adult (for example, a parent or teacher) were to say, "You're so grown-up! You just skinned your knee and I'm sure it hurts a lot. But you're such a big girl you're able to keep yourself from crying!"

That statement might motivate the girl to control her tears and, as a result, she might feel more grown-up. However, she would probably not feel understood. Indeed, the position "I know what you think and feel better than you do" is anathema to empathic understanding. The girl would almost certainly inhibit full and accurate expression of what she really experiences in order to avoid the censure of the adult or perhaps to maintain the image of herself as a "big girl."

Imagine how this pattern might play out between a social worker and a client of any age. Minimizing or denying the other's feelings and experiences—even in an effort to identify strengths—can negatively affect clients' willingness to share. Incomplete exploration of experiences, events, and circumstances—including the feelings associated with them—may interfere with the development of a constructive working relationship and a positive outcome.

Therefore, as you look for strengths, keep the client's perspective and the timing of the exploration in mind. Typically, looking for strengths should occur after the worker has accurately communicated understanding of the client's views and experiences of the problems and issues, and relevant aspects of the person and environment.

Strengths may become apparent in clients' or others' responses to problems, issues, and other challenges. When they materialize within the situational or environmental context, strengths may be referred to as assets. We may look for strengths in the areas of competencies, assets and social support, successes, and life lessons (see Table 9.7).

All clients have many abilities, capacities, and talents. They also hold various beliefs about them. Social workers seek to help clients identify and explore strengths in both dimensions: *beliefs* as well as *realities*. For example, an optimistic attitude, a basic belief in one's own value and goodness, or a religious or philosophical perspective can contribute to a sense of inner peace or contentment under

TABLE 9.7 Looking for Strengths		
	Person	Situation and Environment
Competencies		
Assets and Social Support		
Successes		
Life Lessons		

the most trying of circumstances. By **looking for competencies**, you and your clients may discover an incredible array of useful traits and attributes. Unless you consciously seek them out, however, they may never become apparent.

You can look for competencies by asking questions such as "When people praise or compliment you about your talents and abilities, what things do they mention?" "If people were to brag about your special qualities and characteristics, what would they say?" "Some people have special talents or abilities that they keep pretty much to themselves; what are some of yours?" You can also help clients explore competencies by using "incomplete" sentences. You could ask clients to complete sentences that begin with phrases such as "I am very good at . . ." or "I am especially talented when it comes to. . . ." Extend the exploration by considering how clients' talents, abilities, and competencies become manifest in social roles and situations (for example, family, work, and other social systems or during times of stress, conflict, or crisis). "Of all the things you do with your family, what gets you the most praise or credit?" "What qualities or abilities do you possess that you wish your boss knew about?" "When it comes to relationships, which of your personal qualities help you the most?" Competencies also relate to the issue of concern. "Over the course of time that you've been dealing with this issue, what talents or abilities of yours have been most helpful?" "What things do you say to yourself that help you address or cope with problems such as these?"

Social workers tend to recognize the importance of assets and social support[10] in all aspects of human life. By **looking for assets and social supports**, we encourage clients to identify and reflect on those resources within the physical environment and those individuals and groups within the social environment that have been or could be resources. Ask questions such as "When you're physically exhausted, where do you go and what do you do to recover?" or "When you have a financial emergency and you cannot pay some of your bills, what do you do?" or "Over the course of your life, who have been the people that provided the greatest support?" or "Where do you feel the most support?" Of course you would also consider *how* those assets and social supports have been helpful in the past or might yet favorably affect the person and contribute to resolution of the issue of concern.

Experiences of accomplishment and achievement tend to contribute to feelings of competency and optimism. By **looking for successes** we try to identify and recognize those positive outcomes. Questions such as the following may help: "When you reflect back upon your life, what do you consider your greatest successes or achievements?" "When you were a child, what were your biggest accomplishments? When you were a teenager? When you were a young adult?" Discovery of successes may lead to the creation of a "success timeline."

Over time, people tend to gain perspective and make their significant life experiences meaningful in some way. Successes and failures, good times and bad, pain and pleasure, all become part of a personal philosophy. By **looking for life lessons**, you encourage clients to consider what they have learned and realized. In effect, you help clients to acknowledge their own wisdom. Frequently, lessons learned earlier, perhaps in different circumstances, can be applied to current issues and concerns. You can look for life lessons by asking questions such as "You've been through a great deal and somehow survived. What have you learned about life from these experiences? What have you learned about yourself? What have you learned about people?" As you proceed, you may find opportunities to look for life lessons that might apply to the current issue of concern. "Of all the things you've learned from these experiences, which lessons might help you address this issue?"

As people explore issues and share aspects of themselves and their situations with social workers, they often share their hypotheses or "theories" about causes and sometimes about "solutions." Indeed, once we have a solid grasp of the person or people involved, the issues, and the circumstances, we may encourage others to share their ideas, hypotheses, or theories about them.

---

[10] Please see the discussion of social support in Chapter 2.

TABLE 9.8	Explanatory and Change-Oriented Hypotheses	
	Explanatory Hypotheses	Change-Oriented Hypotheses
Client's		
Social Worker's		

Many clients readily offer ideas and explanations about "why" something happens or "how" a problem might be resolved. Let's refer to these as **explanatory hypotheses** and **change-oriented hypotheses**, respectively. Of course, social workers also generate hypotheses based upon our knowledge of theoretical models of human behavior, practice experience, and familiarity with relevant research studies. Our appreciation of risk and protective factors often leads us to generate implicit or explicit hypotheses based on the following assumption: If more risk factors and fewer protective factors are associated with the emergence of a problem, then a decrease in risk factors and an increase in protective factors may contribute to its prevention or resolution. If a society and its mainstream culture reflect systemic, institutionalized injustice, then we can hypothesize that similar (parallel) injustices will appear in our local communities, organizations, and even within our families as well. However, as Table 9.8 illustrates, we highly value clients' as well as our own hypotheses.

Clients' explanatory and change-oriented hypotheses frequently contribute to our understanding of risk and protective factors, as well as clients' ways of viewing themselves, the problems and goals, and their circumstances. Sometimes, however, their hypotheses appear unrelated to actual events or potential solutions. Regardless of their relevance, we take special note of clients' explanatory and change-oriented hypotheses because they may contribute to or hinder progress toward resolution. Indeed, some clients have fixed views about causes or solutions that represent genuine obstacles to change. For example, a teenage boy might view his mother's nagging as the cause of the problems for which he wants your help. His explanatory hypothesis is, "I drink a lot because she nags." Based upon his explanation for the problem, he may also identify his mother as the solution: His change-oriented hypothesis is, "If she stops nagging, I will drink less and my drinking will not be a problem."

From the boy's perspective, he is a "victim," his mother is a "persecutor," and you as the social worker are the potential "rescuer" who might convince mom to change her ways. While you should express your understanding of the teenager's hypotheses, you might be wise to test out their credibility. For example, suppose you had a separate conversation with his mother and learned that he had been arrested and convicted for possession, use, and sales of illicit substances; and, that his meetings with you are a required condition of his probation. Might that enlarge your perspective? Might the "mother's nagging" be viewed in another way—perhaps as a concerned attempt to help him acknowledge and recover from substance misuse, and keep him from additional legal trouble?

If the teenager retains his view, or if you and the mother unquestioningly accept the validity of his hypotheses, then the locus of responsibility and control shifts from the adolescent to the mother. The targeted problem changes from the teenager's "drinking a lot" to the "mother's nagging." She could conclude that, "Yes, I do nag too much. I'll stop that and he'll stop drinking." Unfortunately, the mother could work hard and succeed in eliminating the so-called "nagging" behavior without having any impact whatsoever on his drinking. If so, we can conclude that both the explanatory and the change-oriented hypotheses were invalid; both you and the mother wasted time and energy; and money was poorly spent. Indeed, by prematurely endorsing the boy's hypotheses, you might inadvertently reinforce the problematic behaviors that led to the agency visit in the first place.

Despite the obvious dangers of "validating invalid hypotheses," helping processes proceed more smoothly when the clients' and the workers' explanatory and change-oriented hypotheses

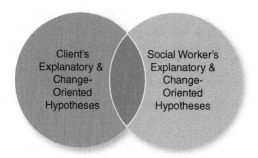

FIGURE 9.8 Congruence between Client and Social Worker's Explanatory and Change-Oriented Hypotheses

are identical, similar, or at least compatible. Take some time to explore others' hypotheses to identify relevant and reasonable observations. Whenever possible, combine as many aspects of their hypotheses with your own. Seek to maximize the overlap between the two sets of hypotheses (see Figure 9.8). The chances that a client and a social worker will have a positive and productive working relationship increase as their respective hypotheses converge. The probability of a favorable partnership and a successful outcome becomes markedly less likely when a client's and a worker's hypotheses diverge.

As you explore hypotheses with clients and others, recognize that excessive speculation about possible reasons for problems and issues may sometimes inhibit the exploratory process. Some clients and social workers prefer intellectual analysis over factual description and emotional expression about events and circumstances. Such a preference for speculation may contribute to inadequate consideration of details or inhibited expression of feelings about the issues of concern. Through a process called intellectualization, people sometimes attempt to protect themselves from or defend against powerful feelings by engaging in abstract, cognitive thought. In most cases, clients and social workers wisely explore descriptive information before examining possible reasons for phenomena. The quality of reflective thought tends to improve when a solid understanding of the facts and circumstances serves as a foundation. The worker postpones questions such as "Why do you think that happens?" or "What do you think causes that?" until the client has shared feelings and explored details about the person-issue-situation in sufficient depth and breadth. In general, descriptive exploration precedes and forms the basis and context for the development of hypotheses.

Usually, within the first meeting, you and the client have discussed the more pressing issues, explored a good deal about the client system and the circumstances, identified relevant risk and protective factors, and discovered various strengths, assets, and resources. At this point in the process, you can decide whether you and your agency have the authority, resources, and expertise necessary to provide the needed social work services to this particular client system. Because of a lack of familiarity with social service, health, and mental health networks, prospective clients sometimes contact providers and organizations that are not well prepared to help them address their particular issues. Through exploration of the person-issue-situation, you may be able to determine that another organization in the community would be better prepared to provide helpful service. Then, if the client concurs, you could contact the other agency to initiate a professional referral. Of course, you should conduct the referral process with great care, so that the client does not feel rejected by you or your agency. Furthermore, treat the other agency's personnel with professionalism and courtesy. The nature of your relationships with other community professionals often determines whether prospective clients receive a warm or cool reception. Therefore, approach your colleagues in other agencies with the same high degree of professionalism you show to clients.

When the issue of concern is congruent with your agency's mission and range of services and falls within your areas of expertise, you and your clients may appropriately continue the working relationship. Before long, the collaborative process of exploration should lead to a clear sense of direction for the work that you will do together.

◼ Asking Questions

Asking questions serves to elicit facts, ideas, and feelings concerning the person, the issue, the situation, and potential means or processes for resolution. Questions help identify risk and protective factors as well as strengths, competencies, assets, and resources. They often yield information necessary for mutual understanding, assessment, decision making, planning, working and evaluating, and ending. Indeed, we use questions throughout the entire process of work with and on behalf of clients. However, they are especially useful during the exploring phase.

The first primary use of the questioning skill typically occurs as you and the client conclude the beginning phase. By this time, you have introduced yourselves, reached a tentative understanding of the purpose for meeting and possibly your respective roles, discussed relevant policies and ethical principles, and sought feedback.[11] The initial exploratory question represents the first substantive consideration of the issue or problem that led to the contact (Perlman, 1957, p. 88). Commonly, we phrase the question in such a way as to allow clients maximum opportunity to express themselves freely, fully, and in their own way. For example, you might ask, "When you telephoned the other day, you mentioned something about family problems. What's happening with the family that concerns you?" It may also be useful to ask about precipitating events related to the presenting concern. For instance, you might ask, "What led you to contact us about the family problems at this time?"

Helping professionals occasionally phrase questions as requests or directives. For example, you could say, "Please share your concerns about the difficulties that trouble you at this time." In the case of an involuntary client, you might say, "I understand that the judge required you to come here for counseling. I know quite a bit about the situation, but I'd like to hear the full story from you. Please describe what happened." In general, however, questions are preferred because directives may implicitly suggest a power or status differential. "Tell me . . ." or "Describe . . ." is, in effect, a command that may subtly indicate that the social worker is the superior person in this encounter.

"Tell me . . ." requests also tend to imply that the primary reason for clients' sharing is for you, the social worker, to acquire information that you will then use to formulate an assessment and prescribe a solution—that is, to come up with "the answer." However, in most circumstances, social workers hope to foster a collaborative working relationship where clients function as full participants in the process. Indications that the social worker is the expert authority who provides answers and solutions often lead clients to assume a passive, subordinate role akin to a "doctor–patient" or "parent–child" relationship, rather than to a genuine partnership of equals.

As you might expect, the questioning skill is applicable at many points throughout the exploration phase and, of course, all other phases as well. We use questions to explore relevant aspects of the person-issue-situation, including the circumstances surrounding the origin, development, and status of the presenting concerns. Examples of some common questions include: "How did these difficulties begin?" "Who were the members of your family as you were growing up?" "What were your parents like?" "Who lives with you now?" "What did you feel when she left?" "What were

---

[11] The skill of seeking feedback represents a specialized form of questioning that social workers routinely use to ensure that participants clearly understand all facets of the process.

you thinking about when that happened?" "What would you like to be different?" "What did you do then?"

The questions you ask derive from your active pursuit of information regarding the person-issue-situation over time. There are two general types of questions: *closed-ended* and *open-ended*. **Closed-ended questions** (Goodman & Esterly, 1988, pp. 123–127) are phrased to elicit short responses, sometimes simply yes or no. Closed-ended questions can yield a great deal of information in a brief amount of time. They are especially useful in crises and emergency situations, when we need to gather vital information quickly.

Here are a few examples of closed-ended questions: "What is your phone number?" "What's your address?" "Do you have a car?" "Do you live at home?" "When were you born?" "How old are you?" "Where do you work?" "Who is your family doctor?" "When was your last physical exam?" "Does anyone live with you?" "Is somebody there in the house with you right now?" "Which do you prefer?" "Have you taken some medicine?" "How many pills did you take?"

"Either–or" and "multiple-choice" questions are also usually closed-ended: "Is your mother or father more supportive?" "Do you prefer Mr. Johnson or Mrs. Xavier?" "How difficult is it to complete that step: (1) extremely difficult, (2) difficult, (3) somewhat difficult, (4) not at all difficult?" Answers to such questions are usually quite brief. This can be advantageous or not, depending on the purpose of the meeting and the needs of the situation. Sometimes the rapid collection of specific information is so important that you postpone free and full exploration of other aspects of the person-issue-situation. However, too many closed-ended questions, asked one after another, may lead clients to feel like suspects in a criminal investigation. They may feel interrogated rather than interviewed, and the quality of the professional relationship may suffer. Therefore, unless the situation is immediately life threatening or otherwise urgent, you would usually be wise to intersperse closed-ended questions with many more open-ended questions and active-listening responses.

Some closed-ended questions are, in legal terminology, leading. A leading question is phrased in a way that elicits (that is, "leads to") a specific answer—one that the questioner wants to hear. For example, suppose a social worker asks a client, "Haven't you experienced lots of pain in your pelvic area? Yes? Haven't you felt that pain since you were a young child? Yes? Aren't these painful symptoms common among people who were sexually abused as children? Yes? So, isn't it likely that you were sexually abused as a child?" Such a series of questions would clearly lead or suggest to a client that a certain conclusion held by the social worker is the right and valid one. During the exploration phase, such leading questions are generally counterproductive because they tend to narrow a process that should usually be quite open and expansive. In particular, whenever you serve an investigative function in your service as a social worker, choose your words and the phrasing of questions carefully. If you frequently ask leading questions in such interviews, your courtroom testimony could easily be challenged and perhaps disallowed. During the exploring phase especially, try to avoid leading or suggestive questions.

Open-ended questions (Goodman & Esterly, 1988, pp. 127–137) are phrased in a manner that encourages people to express themselves expansively and extensively. Open-ended questions tend to further exploration on a deeper level or in a broader way. They are usually not leading because they enable the client to respond in any number of ways. We may phrase them as "how" questions, which nearly always yield open responses from clients. For example, "How did that come to happen?" "How did he react?" "How do you feel right now?" "How did he act in that situation?" "How did you respond?"

We may also use "what" questions to elicit expansive responses from clients. For example, "What is the nature of your concern?" "What is she like?" "What happened then?" "In what way did you . . . ?" "What did you say then?" Recognize, however, that certain "what" questions are closed-ended. "What is your phone number?" "What is your date of birth?"

"What" questions tend to yield descriptive information. To elicit feelings, you often have to ask directly for them. For example, "What feelings did you experience when you realized that?" or "What are you feeling right now?" encourage clients to identify and perhaps share emotions. Indeed, some evidence indicates that open questions about feelings may encourage clients to share more emotion than do active-listening responses (Hill & Gormally, 1977, 2001). In exploring feelings and emotions, it may help to combine active-listening responses with specific open questions about feelings.

Directives can serve the functions of open- or closed-ended questions. For example, "Please say more about that," "Please elaborate," "Please continue," "Please share more about that part of your life" all encourage open responses. "Please spell your name," "Please tell me your street address" serve as closed-ended requests for brief responses. Remember, however, our earlier caution about the potential negative effects of directives on the working relationship. In most circumstances, social workers seek to develop a collaborative partnership rather than a hierarchical relationship in which we are the "experts in charge." Use directives sparingly and try to avoid indications that you are the superior party in the relationship.

"Why" questions may also encourage clients to express themselves in a full and open fashion. However, they can also generate defensiveness. Clients may conclude that you are judging them negatively and feel compelled to justify some aspect of their behavior or circumstances. Therefore, be cautious about the use of "why" questions. Use them in a tentative fashion and adopt a gentle tone of voice combined with warm, open, and accepting facial expressions. The way you phrase "why" questions can also help. For example, you may moderate the defensiveness-eliciting quality of a "why" question by qualifying phrases such as "I wonder why (that is)?" or "Why do you think that happens?" In asking "why" questions, be certain to communicate attitudes of interest and acceptance; use Giraffe language and completely avoid Jackal when you ask "why."

During the exploration process, intersperse your questions with active-listening responses. Otherwise, an interview can quickly turn quite unpleasant. When clients must answer one question after another—even when they are open questions—they often begin to feel badgered rather than supported. Realize that questions can suggest blame, judgment, evaluation, or advice. They are not always simply neutral requests for information. For example, "Have you talked with your mother yet?" might imply that you expected a client to talk with his or her mother. "Have you completed that form?" may convey a similar message. Although it is sometimes useful to express a statement of opinion or preference in the form of a question, be aware that you are doing so. Sharing your personal or professional views within the context of a question does not relieve you of responsibility for the substance of the message. Also, try to avoid asking a string of questions at the same time. For example, "Are you still going with Jackie or have you given up on her and are now dating only Jill? And what about Cathy?" would confuse most clients. They would not know whether to respond to your first, second, third, or fourth question. Instead of a series of questions, ask one at a time and give people time to respond.

Questions can be extremely useful for providing a sense of coherence and continuity to the exploration process. As clients talk about themselves, the issues of concern, and their situational contexts, they quite understandably sometimes focus a great deal on one topic while avoiding or only briefly touching on important related information. When that occurs, you can ask questions that guide clients toward an exploration of other pertinent aspects of the person-issue-situation. For example, to gather information about an aspect of a client's family and social situation that had been neglected, you might ask, "How would you describe your relationship with your older sister?" Be careful, however, to respect clients' psychological and interpersonal sensitivities. This is particularly important during the exploring phase. When a client is especially tender about a particular topic or theme, we usually postpone inquiry into that specific dimension until our working relationship becomes more established. Then, when the client feels secure, we can return to areas that require further exploration.

You may use the exploring skill of asking questions to gather and consider information about the person-issue-situation and to look for strengths and resources. As you might imagine, however, we commonly ask questions throughout the entire helping process.

EXERCISE 9-1 Asking Questions

Refer to your earlier responses (see Exercises 7-8 and 8-1 through 8-6) as you begin to use the exploring skills in your initial meetings with Mr. K, Loretta, the S family, Mrs. F, and the "troubled agency."

1. It is now about 10 minutes into your first interview with Mr. K. You have exchanged introductions, agreed upon a tentative purpose, discussed policy and ethical issues, and addressed other aspects of the beginning phase of work. Mr. K appears anxious to share what's on his mind and you're now ready to encourage him to do so through the use of the exploring skills. Use the space below to write the words you would say and describe the actions you would take in asking an initial exploratory question. Please place quotation marks around the words you would use. Then, identify anything else you might say. Once written, specify whether the initial question is open- or closed-ended. Briefly discuss your rationale for choosing this particular question and anticipate how Mr. K might respond.

   Now, formulate three additional questions to encourage further expression and exploration of the issues from a person-in-environment perspective. Indicate whether each question is open- or closed-ended and anticipate how Mr. K might react to each question.

2. After a fairly lengthy beginning process, Loretta has begun to trust you. She appears ready to engage in an exploration of needs and problems, and perhaps other issues as well. Use the space below to write the words you would say and describe the actions you would take in asking an initial exploratory question. Please place quotation marks around the words you would use. Then, identify anything else you might say. Once written, specify whether the initial question is open- or closed-ended. Briefly discuss your rationale for choosing this particular question and anticipate how Loretta might respond.

Now, formulate three additional questions to encourage Loretta to explore the issues from a person-in-environment perspective. Indicate whether each question is open- or closed-ended and anticipate how Loretta might react to each question.

3. You have taken some time to begin with the S family. You especially wanted them to understand the nature and limitations of the policies and ethics that might impact your work together. At this point, however, Mr. and Mrs. S seem quite ready to share their concerns about the tension and conflict within the family. You too are eager to make the transition from the beginning to the exploring skills. Directing your first question to the family as a whole rather than to any particular person, you ask, "What do you see as the major issues within the family?" The father responds first. Then the mother answered, followed by other family members. Although the specific nature of the responses varied somewhat, there appeared to be considerable agreement that the strained relationship between the two teenage boys (biological children of the father) and their father's wife (the boys' stepmother) is a major issue. Their relationship appears to involve a great deal of tension, conflict, and anger. As the social worker, you now want to explore the origin and development of the difficulties in this relationship. Use the space below to record what you would say in doing so. Please place quotation marks around your words. After you have written your question, determine whether it is open- or closed-ended. Are you directing the question to the boys, the other children, Mrs. S, Mr. S, or the entire family? Outline your rationale for choosing this particular question and selecting the person or people you decided to address. How do you think the boys would react to the question? How might Mr. or Mrs. S respond?

Now, formulate three additional questions to further the family's exploration of the issues? For each one, determine whether it is open- or closed-ended and anticipate how various family members might react to each question.

4. Thus far in your initial meeting with Mrs. F, you have completed the introductions, addressed the policy and ethical factors, and established a tentative purpose for the meeting. It's clear that Mrs. F wishes to discuss the concerns she has about her 7- and 9-year-old daughters. According to Mrs. F, they are the only Latino children in their school, and several teenage boys have periodically harassed them. Mrs. F is worried that her children might be in physical danger. She is also concerned that these experiences may undermine their positive attitude toward school.

You are now ready to explore the issue further. Use the space below to write the words you would say in asking a relevant exploratory question. Place quotation marks around your question and then determine whether it is open- or closed-ended. Then, explain your rationale for the question you chose. Now, formulate three additional questions concerning the issue, the children, Mrs. F, the family system, or the school situation. Identify whether each question is closed- or open-ended. Outline your rationale for their selection. Finally, anticipate the reaction that Mrs. F might have to each question.

5. During the early part of your first consultation meeting with a troubled social service agency, you suggested that participants begin to share their concerns about the organization. Most are anxious to do so. Write the words you would say in asking an initial exploratory question to the group as a whole. Place quotation marks around your question and then determine whether it is open- or closed-ended. Then, explain your rationale for the question you chose. Now, formulate three additional questions concerning the agency, the issues, or the circumstances. Identify whether each question is closed- or open-ended. Describe your rationale for the questions you created.

Seeking Clarification

During an interview, clients and others sometimes make statements that seem unclear or that you do not fully understand. They may communicate in an apparently contradictory fashion, skim over a relevant issue, or neglect some significant aspect of themselves, the issue, or the circumstances. Such indirect, unclear, or incomplete messages often involve important aspects of the client's experience. Therefore, the manner in which you respond may substantially affect the nature of the relationship, the direction of your work together, and the outcome of the helping endeavor. In such instances, you may use the skill of **seeking clarification**. That is, you attempt to elicit a more complete expression of the meaning of particular words or gestures. In effect, you ask clients to elaborate about something they have just said or done. During the early portion of an interview, you seek clarification to generate more complete and comprehensible information about particular aspects of the person-issue-situation. Seeking clarification also subtly suggests that a particular term or topic may be of some special relevance.

Obviously, social workers do not always completely understand everything that clients say. Sometimes this is because we are not listening well. At other times, clients do not clearly express themselves because they are uncertain about what they actually think and feel. After all, one purpose of exploring is to help clients understand themselves better. Also, clients sometimes send indirect messages that they hope you will notice. Many people are reluctant to ask directly for help. Such hesitancy is quite common among members of some groups and may be greater if the social worker and clients are from different cultures. In addition, many issues are so embarrassing or emotional in nature that clients find them difficult to talk openly about. Therefore subtle or ambiguous communications are common. Be sensitive to indirect expressions in the form of hints, nonverbal gestures, or incomplete or mixed messages, and recognize that considerable anxiety may be associated with such communications. Some clients may send extremely significant messages in an indirect manner because they are not yet fully aware of or comfortable with some aspects of their thinking or feeling, or because they fear that you might judge and disapprove.

In responding to indirect expressions, move carefully toward a greater degree of specificity and clarity by asking for further information about the term, phrase, or topic. For example, during a first meeting, a 50-year-old client says to a 25-year-old social worker, "I've never had much luck with young social workers. You're all so innocent." The worker might respond to such a statement by asking, "When you talk about not having 'much luck' with other young social workers, it sounds like there have been some problems. What sorts of difficulties have you had with young social workers before?"

You may use the skill of seeking clarification to encourage clients to explain a term or elaborate about the specific aspects of a thought, feeling, action, or situation (Shulman, 1992). People often communicate in vague or general terms. Seeking clarification about detailed aspects of an experience or the specific meaning of a term may enable you and the client to gain a more complete and realistic understanding.

Seeking clarification may be especially helpful in circumstances where the social worker and the client reflect cultural differences. Words, phrases, and gestures commonly used in one culture may be nonexistent in another, or their meaning may differ dramatically. Although the client may know exactly what she or he means by a particular term, you may not—at least when it is first used. Even when a client uses a standard form of English, a term may have a unique meaning to him or her. Clients may use words that you have never heard before, or they may use a familiar term in an unusual manner. The skill of seeking clarification can help in these circumstances. In seeking clarification, you are looking for additional specific information about a particular word or phrase or some other aspect of a client's verbal or nonverbal communication.

Seeking clarification usually occurs as a discrete form of open questioning, although it may occasionally appear in the form of a closed question or a directive. Rather than encouraging clients to provide more general information about a current or new topic, its purpose is to gain further understanding of specific aspects of a previous message. To practice this skill, use the following format.

PRACTICE FORMAT | *Seeking Clarification*

What, specifically, do you mean when you say _____?

or

Would you please elaborate on _____?

or

Please explain what you mean by _____?

EXAMPLE | **Seeking Clarification**

Client: My spouse and I just don't get along. We haven't for years. The relationship stinks.

Worker: What do you mean when you say "The relationship stinks"?

As is the case with most exploring skills and the skill of seeking feedback, seeking clarification is useful throughout the entire helping process. It is especially relevant when exploring aspects of problems from a person-in-environment perspective, establishing goals, during the working and evaluating phases, and when concluding your relationship with clients. Often, you can effectively precede your request for clarification with an active-listening response.

EXERCISE 9-2   Seeking Clarification

Refer to your earlier responses as you continue to use exploring skills in your initial meetings with Mr. K, Loretta, the S family, Mrs. F, and the "troubled agency."

1. You are in the midst of the first interview with Mr. K, a recently divorced 55-year-old man. You are currently exploring the person-issue-situation. Mr. K says, "I feel so bad. It really hurts. I miss her terribly. I'm not sure I can go on." Write the words you would say in seeking clarification of what he has just said. Outline your rationale for the words you chose. How do you think he might react to this question? Now try preceding your attempt to seek clarification with an active-listening response. What effect does that have?

2. You are an outreach worker for homeless and "street" people in your city. You have begun to talk with Loretta. She responded to your initial exploratory question about her current situation by saying, "I've been like this since I lost my kids." Write the words you would use to seek clarification in this situation. Outline the rationale for the words you chose. How do you think Loretta might react to this attempt to gain greater clarity about her statement?

3. You are in the midst of exploring the nature and development of the problems that concern the S family when Theo, one of the father's teenage boys, angrily refers to their step-mother as a "home wrecker." In reaction, Mrs. S lowers her eyes and becomes very quiet. Write the words you would say in seeking clarification from the teenager. What is your rationale for the words you chose? How do you think he might react to your words? How might other members of the family? Now, write the words you would say in seeking clarification from Mrs. S concerning her nonverbal response to the term *home wrecker*.

How do you think she and the other family members might react to your request for clarification from her?

4. You are exploring Mrs. F's concern about the safety of her children at school. At one point she raises her voice and says, "White men control this whole country and don't care about anybody but themselves!" Write the words you might say in seeking clarification. Briefly describe your rationale for the words you selected. How do you think Mrs. F might react to your question? What is another way you might seek clarification in this situation?

5. Early in the first meeting with a fairly large group of agency employees, other stakeholders, and two consumers, the director says, "As you probably know, these problems are not new. They did not suddenly emerge when I became director about 3 months ago. Most of these issues began long ago under the previous administration." Write the words you might say in seeking clarification. Outline your rationale for the words you selected. What is another way you might seek clarification in this situation?

■ Reflecting Content

Reflecting content (Carkhuff, 1987) is the empathic skill of communicating your understanding of the factual, descriptive, or informational part of a message. In exercising this skill, a form of active listening, you paraphrase or restate the client's words. By accurately reflecting content, you demonstrate that you have heard and understood what the client is trying to convey.

This skill is most applicable when a client communicates factual or descriptive material, or shares ideas that lack an emotional dimension. If clients do not express feelings, do not add them to your content reflections. Stick with their message and accurately communicate your understanding of what clients say. This is crucial for several reasons. If clients do not believe that you understand their expressions, they may become less open and expressive, or they may even prematurely discontinue services. Accurate restatement of clients' expressions about the problems or issues that led to the contact demonstrates that you understand their concerns. Accurate reflections of content can also contribute to the development of a positive working relationship and promote a sense of collaborative partnership. Without accurate reflections, clients are likely to assume a passive, subordinate role in the process and view the social worker as an expert who asks questions, collects information, diagnoses problems, gives answers, and prescribes solutions.

To practice this skill, use the following format:

PRACTICE FORMAT *Reflecting Content*

You're saying _____.

EXAMPLE | **Reflecting Content**

Client: I'm a househusband. Every day, I cook the meals, clean the house, and do the laundry. That's my job now.

Worker: You're saying that your current responsibilities include taking care of the family needs and doing the household chores.

In using the practice format, recognize that repeated use of the same lead-in phrases might begin to sound artificial and mechanical. Imagine how it would seem to you if someone started six or seven sentences in a row with the words, "You're saying." Indeed, the phrase "I hear you saying" has become a cliché. Therefore, vary the lead-in phrases or avoid them altogether. If you accurately reflect the content of the person's message, such lead-in phrases are usually unnecessary.

Try to use your own words to reflect, restate, or mirror the information the client has conveyed. If you repeat too many of the client's words, he or she may begin to feel that you are "parroting" or "mimicking" rather than truly listening. You can sound more like a tape recorder than a concerned human being.

EXAMPLE | **Reflecting Content**

Client: Several years ago, I lost my job. They closed the plant where I had worked for years and years. There was a huge layoff. Most of my buddies and I were let go. Since then, my wife has worked part-time, and that keeps some food on the table. My unemployment compensation ran out long ago. We've not been able to pay the mortgage on the house for about the last 6 months. I think the bank is going to foreclose on us soon.

Worker: You haven't had an adequate income for a long time and it's beginning to look like you may lose your home.

The client is probably experiencing some emotion as he expresses himself. Although he has not actually mentioned his feelings, he may do so nonverbally by shedding tears or dropping his head and shoulders. In using the skill of reflecting content, you stay with the factual content of the message. Even when a client explicitly expresses emotions along with facts or opinions, you might choose to use the skill of reflecting content rather than a more complete form of active listening. By reflecting only the content of the message rather than both content and feeling, you highlight your understanding of the informational portion of the message. You might do so when the urgency of a situation requires you to elicit facts, ideas, or preferences quickly; when you determine that the content of a client's message is more relevant at that particular point than the feelings; or when you are trying to help a client maintain emotional self-control. In general, during the early stages of the exploration process, you should carefully respect clients' coping strategies. Follow their lead. If a client primarily expresses facts and opinions in an unemotional or intellectualized fashion, use the skill of reflecting content. At this stage, there is usually no pressing need to reflect feelings that clients have not directly expressed. In our example, the client may be trying to maintain control of his emotions by expressing himself in a matter-of-fact, businesslike fashion. He may not yet trust the worker enough to risk full and free expression of his true feelings. The worker could further develop the relationship by accurately reflecting the content of his stated message and then, perhaps later during the interview, return to an exploration and reflection of his feelings.

EXERCISE 9-3 Reflecting Content

Refer to your responses to earlier exercises as you continue to use exploring skills in your initial meetings with Mr. K, Loretta, the S family, Mrs. F, and the "troubled agency."

1. During the exploration process, Mr. K says, "The divorce was final about 3 weeks ago. She said she'd had enough of my constant criticism and sarcastic comments and that she was leaving me." Write the words you would say in reflecting the content of what he has said. Outline your rationale for the words you chose. How do you think he might react to your reflection?

2. In response to a question about her situation, Loretta says, "I've been sleeping in a wooded area near the west side park. I made up this sign because I needed food. I'm hungry but I'm willing to work." Write the words you would use in reflecting the content of Loretta's message. Briefly describe your rationale for the words you chose. How do you think Loretta might react to your content reflection?

3. As you continue the exploration process with the family, Mrs. S says, "I fell in love with Hank [Mr. S], and when we married I hoped that his children and mine would come to love one another as brothers and sisters. I also wanted his kids to know that I would love and treat them as if I had given birth to them myself." Write the words you would say to reflect the content of Mrs. S's message. Outline your rationale for the words you chose. How do you think Mrs. S might react? What is another way you might reflect the content of her message in this situation?

4. Following an exploratory question, Mrs. F says, "I have talked to the teachers and the guidance counselor. They listen politely but they don't care about what this does to my children. They won't do a thing about it." Write the words you might say in reflecting content. Outline your rationale for the words you selected. How do you think Mrs. F might react to your response? What is another way you might reflect the content of Mrs. F's message in this situation?

5. As you continue to explore the nature of the organizational problems facing the agency, one social worker says, "I haven't had a clinical supervision meeting in more than a year. In fact, unless it is my program coordinator, I don't even know who my supervisor is." Write the words you might say in reflecting content. Outline your rationale for the words you selected. How do you think the social worker would react to your response? What is another way you might reflect the content of the social worker's message in this situation?

Reflecting Feelings

Reflecting feelings (Carkhuff, 1987) is another of the empathic, active-listening skills. It usually consists of a brief response that communicates your understanding of the feelings expressed by a client. Some of the more effective responses consist of a simple sentence containing a single feeling word. For example, phrases such as "You feel ashamed," "You're really hurting," or "You're terrified!" can be powerful empathic reflections of feeling. Despite the brevity and utility of such phrases, some workers are hesitant to reflect clients' emotions. The skill of reflecting feelings requires that you, at least to some extent, feel those same emotions yourself. Empathy can be uncomfortable, even painful. Partly because of such discomfort, you may be tempted to convert feeling reflections into content reflections by neglecting to use words that convey emotions. For instance, suppose a client says, "I am devastated." You might reflect the feeling by saying, "You feel crushed." If, however, you were to respond by saying, "It feels like you've been hit by a freight train," you imply the feeling; you do not actually say it. The message conveys an idea rather than a feeling. Although *hit by a freight train* is an apt phrase to amplify the feeling of devastation, it is much more effective when used in conjunction with one or more feeling words. For example, "You feel crushed. It's like you've been hit by a freight train" includes both a feeling word and a powerful idea that amplifies the emotion. Certain lead-in phrases, such as "You feel like . . . ," tend to be followed by ideas, analogies, similes, or metaphors rather than words that connote actual feelings. Therefore, until you develop proficiency, practice by using a format such as the following:

PRACTICE FORMAT   *Reflecting Feelings*

You feel _____ (*appropriate feeling word*).

The single most important aspect in reflecting feelings is to capture accurately the primary emotion experienced by a person and mirror it back so that she or he *feels* your empathic understanding. When two feelings are in evidence, you may respond to both. For example: "You feel _____ and _____ ." Sometimes, you may be able to identify a single word that communicates both feelings. For example, *burdened* and *discouraged* might be reflected as *overwhelmed*.

EXAMPLE   **Reflecting Feelings**

Case Situation: His former wife remarried about a year ago. Last month she and her current husband left the area with the client's 5-year-old son. They moved 2,000 miles away. The client tried to stop their relocation by filing a motion with the court, but his former spouse won the right to move with her son.

Client: I just can't stand it. I miss my son terribly, I know that he'll gradually lose interest in me and I can't do a thing about it.

Worker: You feel sad and powerless.

EXAMPLE   **Reflecting Feelings**

Case Situation: A 16-year-old girl wanted desperately to be selected to the school's cheerleading team. However, she was not chosen.

Client: It's awful. I can't go back to school. I can't face them. I wanted to be on the team so bad. It hurts. It really hurts.

Worker: You feel terribly rejected and you're awfully disappointed.

During the early portions of our work together, we typically reflect only those feelings that clients verbally express. After establishing a foundation of accurate reflections, or when the nonverbal, emotional message is very clear, try to reflect what you perceive as the unspoken feeling message. Nonverbal messages in the form of facial expressions, body positions and movements, gestures, and tone of voice are important means for communicating emotions. Notice them. As forms of expression, you may appropriately use the reflecting feelings skill. However, when you do so, recognize that you are taking a modest risk. Use the skill in an especially tentative fashion because the client has not actually expressed the feelings in words. Also, a client may not be ready to acknowledge certain feelings even though she expresses them nonverbally. Of course, members of certain cultural groups may feel especially vulnerable when feelings are directly recognized. Therefore, please be cautious when reflecting unspoken emotions, particularly early in the working relationship. When you do so, use a gentle, tentative tone of voice. Be prepared to return to the skills of reflecting content, questioning, or seeking clarification if the client overtly or covertly indicates that your feeling reflections are premature or off target.

Effective use of the reflecting feelings skill requires a large and sophisticated vocabulary of terms that connote emotions. Without such a vocabulary, we would find it extremely difficult to mirror back or paraphrase the feelings, emotions, and sensations experienced and expressed by others. Of course, there are hundreds of words used to communicate feelings. Several scholars have proposed organizational schemes and some have attempted to identify fundamental emotions that are universal to humans from all cultures and societies. For example, Ekman[12] suggests that there are six universal emotions reflected in humans' facial expression: (1) happiness, (2) anger, (3) surprise, (4) sadness, (5) disgust, and (6) fear (Ekman, 1982; Ekman & Friesen, 1975).

As a social worker attempting to reflect clients' feelings accurately and at various levels of intensity, you should be familiar with a wide range of feeling words commonly used by the cultural groups in your community. Otherwise you could find it difficult to mirror the feelings expressed. For example, everyone experiences anger to one degree or another. A person who is mildly annoyed or slightly irritated would probably not feel understood if you were to say, "You feel enraged." The words you use should match both the kind as well as the intensity of the feelings expressed by clients. As in other forms of active listening, your reflection should be essentially equivalent to the client's message.

EXERCISE 9-4   Reflecting Feelings

Refer to your responses to earlier exercises as you continue to use exploring skills with Mr. K, Loretta, the S family, Mrs. F, and the "troubled agency."

1. As you continue your initial interview, Mr. K says, "I am absolutely lost. There is no reason to go on. I feel like someone reached into my gut and wrenched out my insides." Write the words you would say in reflecting the feelings Mr. K has expressed. Outline your rationale for the words you chose. How do you think he might react to your reflection? What are two alternative feeling reflections that might also apply in this situation?

---

[12] Subsequently, Ekman (1999, p. 52) expanded his array of basic emotions to include the following: amusement, anger, contempt, contentment, disgust, embarrassment, excitement, fear, guilt, happiness, pride in achievement, relief, sadness, satisfaction, sensory pleasure, shame, surprise.

2. As you continue to talk with Loretta, she says, "I am afraid sometimes. A few days ago, a man drove by and said he had work for me. He took me to some woods and made me do a sex act on him. I didn't want to but I couldn't fight him off. I hope that doesn't happen again. He did give me 20 bucks though." Write the words you would use in reflecting feelings contained in Loretta's message. Briefly describe your rationale for the words you chose. How do you think Loretta might react to your feelings reflection? What implicit feelings might Loretta experience that she does not express in actual words?

3. Following her expression of love for Hank and her hopes for a unified family, Mrs. S hangs her head as tears fall down her cheeks. Mr. S's eyes are also watery. Although specific feeling words were not used, write the words you would say in reflecting the feelings suggested by Mrs. S's non-verbal messages. Then do the same for Mr. S. Outline your rationale for the words you chose for each feeling reflection. How do you think Mrs. S might react to your response? Mr. S? What is another way you might reflect the feelings suggested by their communications in this situation?

4. At one point during your first meeting, Mrs. F says, "I'm so angry. Talking with the teachers and the guidance counselor does not help at all. It's so frustrating having to fight so hard for fair treatment. My kids deserve to be protected." Write the words you might say in reflecting her feelings. Outline your rationale for the words you selected. How do you think Mrs. F might react to your response? What is another way you might reflect the feelings indicated by Mrs. F's message in this situation?

5. Shortly after a social worker talked about a lack of supervision, an administrative assistant says, "The other secretaries and I are blamed for everything that goes wrong around here. The so-called professionals treat us like dirt. I cannot tell you how many times I've been yelled at for something that isn't my responsibility. I love the clients but every morning I dread coming to work!" Use the space below to write the words you might say in reflecting feelings. Outline your rationale for the words you selected. How do you think the administrative assistant would react to your response? What is another way you might reflect the feelings contained in the staff person's message?

■ Reflecting Feelings and Meaning

Reflecting feelings and meaning (Carkhuff & Anthony, 1979) is probably the most complete form of active listening. It is certainly the most complex. By reflecting both emotional and informational or ideational elements of a message, you convey a great deal of empathy.

For practice purposes, use the following formats:

PRACTICE FORMAT   *Reflecting Feelings and Meaning*

You feel _____ (*appropriate feeling word*)
because _____.
or
You feel _____ (*appropriate feeling word*)
and _____.
or
You feel _____ (*appropriate feeling word*)
but/yet/however _____.

Reflecting feelings and meaning mirrors clients' emotions along with the facts or beliefs associated with them. As with other reflections, your response should represent an accurate and equivalent form of the client's message. Do not speculate or interpret. Rather, paraphrase or mirror the feelings and meaning as expressed. Even when you personally believe that clients' views about the causes of feelings they experience are incomplete or inaccurate, reflect their perspectives anyway. Often the meanings that clients convey suggest external or situational causes for their feelings (for example, "My mother makes me feel guilty"). At other times, clients refer to aspects of themselves (for example, attitudes, habits, traits, psychological patterns, fears, or physiological conditions) as the reason for their feelings (for example, "I'm basically a lazy person"). Whether the meaning associated with the feelings is externalized or internalized, try to remain congruent with the client's expressed experience when you reflect feelings and meaning. Resist the temptation to modify the meaning. As with other empathic reflections, accuracy is fundamental. Your response should be essentially equivalent to the message communicated by the client. Here are two examples:

EXAMPLE | **Reflecting Feelings and Meaning**

Case Situation: A 60-year-old man who has just lost his job after 35 years of employment.
Client: I have nowhere to turn—no job—no income—no nothing. They just let me go after 35 years of pain and sweat for them. I'm scared and angry.
Worker: You feel desperate because the company has turned you out after so many years of hard work, and it does not look like you'll be able to find something else.

EXAMPLE | **Reflecting Feelings and Meaning**

Client: I'm a wreck. I can't sleep or eat; I can't concentrate. I know my head is really messed up.
Worker: You feel awful. You're anxious and confused, and you know you're not thinking straight right now.

EXERCISE 9-5   Reflecting Feelings and Meaning

Refer to your responses to earlier exercises as you continue to use exploring skills with Mr. K, Loretta, the S family, Mrs. F, and the "troubled agency."

1. As Mr. K continues to talk about his former wife, he says, "I was so used to her being there. I needed her but I never told her so. Now that she's gone, I realize just how much she meant to me." Write the words you would say in reflecting the feelings and meaning contained in what Mr. K has said. Outline your rationale for the words you chose. How do you think Mr. K might respond? What are two additional feelings and meaning reflections that could also apply to Mr. K's statement?

2. In response to a follow-up question about a recent sexual assault, Loretta says, "When that man forced me to give him sex I first felt terrified for my life. I thought he'd kill me if I didn't do what he wanted. Then, I felt disgusted about what I was doing. I've never been a whore and I tried oral sex only once before—and that was with my husband on our wedding night. After it was all done though, it didn't seem so bad and the guy did give me some money for food. That

was the first time in several days that I had something to eat." Write the words you would use in reflecting the feelings and meaning contained in Loretta's message. Create three or four different versions to capture the different feelings and meaning. Briefly describe your rationale for the words you chose. How do you think Loretta might react to your reflection of her feelings and meaning?

3. As Mr. and Mrs. S begin to cry, one of Mr. S's teenage sons says, "Well, it just seems that she came into the house expecting to be Mom. She'll never be my mother, and I resent it when she tries to be." Write the words you would say in reflecting the feelings and meaning contained in his statement. Outline your rationale for the words you chose. How do you think the teenager might react to your response? Mr. S? Mrs. S? What is another way you might reflect the feelings and meaning suggested by the boy's words?

4. While discussing the school that her daughters attend, Mrs. F says, "I'm frustrated with the whole system! This society is racist to the core! Money and power are the only things they respect." Write the words you might say in reflecting feelings and meaning. Outline your rationale for the words you selected. How do you think Mrs. F might react to your response? What is another way you might reflect the feelings and meaning indicated by Mrs. F's words?

5. Following statements by one social worker and then an administrative assistant, another social worker says, "I've worked here about 5 years now. When I first arrived I noticed that many of the social workers were way behind in their record keeping. In fact, some didn't even keep records. I asked the program coordinators and the agency director about the policies on record keeping and was told that 'all professionals are responsible for maintaining their own case

records and that if they are not doing so, they should be.' During that first year, I tried several times to organize staff meetings to discuss the issue of record keeping. I even developed a format and a sample to show everyone. Well, nothing happened. I continue to keep good-quality case records, but it's frustrating and frightening to know that not everybody does." Use the space below to write the words you might say in reflecting feelings and meaning. Outline your rationale for the words you selected. How do you think the social worker would react to your response? What is another way you might reflect the feelings and meaning of the social worker's message in this situation?

■ Partializing

The skill of **partializing** (Perlman, 1957; Shulman, 1992) is used to help clients break down multiple or complex aspects and dimensions of the person-issue-situation into more manageable units so you can address them more easily. Partializing is especially helpful during the exploration phase. If you and a client tried to deal with a multitude of facts, ideas, or feelings simultaneously, one or both of you would probably end up quite confused. Sometimes, there are simply too many phenomena to explore effectively all at once. The partializing skill helps you and clients to maintain a sense of coherence by considering smaller, more manageable units of information one at a time. For practice purposes, please use a format such as the following:

PRACTICE FORMAT | *Partializing*

You've addressed a number of topics here. You've talked about _____ , _____ , _____ , and _____ . There are so many aspects of what you've said that we could lose track if we try to consider them all at once. Could we explore them one at a time? (Yes)
Which would you like to consider first?
or
Would it make sense to start with _____ ? That seems to be very important to you right now.

EXAMPLE | **Partializing**

> **Client:** My whole life is a mess. My husband drinks two six-packs every night and even more on weekends. I think he's an alcoholic. He's out of work—again! My teenage son smokes dope. I've found marijuana in his room. And he has just been expelled from school for stealing money from another kid's locker. So, both of them are at home now. I'm the only one working and I'm falling apart. I'm a nervous wreck. And, I'm angry as hell!

(Continued)

> **Worker:** You sure have a lot happening all at once. It sounds like everybody in the family has their own share of problems—and you're affected by all of them. I wonder, because there are so many issues to address—your husband's behavior, your son's, and your own feelings about it all—could we start by looking at them one at a time? Does that make sense to you? Okay? Which of these concerns you most right now? Let's start with that one.

EXERCISE 9-6 Partializing

Refer to your responses to earlier exercises as you continue to use exploring skills with Mr. K, Loretta, the S family, Mrs. F, and the "troubled agency."

1. Mr. K says, "I think I'm on the brink of a nervous breakdown. I can't do my work. I can't sleep at night. I don't eat. All I do is think about her. I wonder what she's doing and whether she ever thinks of me. It's affecting my job. I think my boss is getting tired of my mistakes. I've also forgotten to pay some bills. Creditors are calling all the time. My life is a train wreck." First, separate and identify each of the elements in the client's message. List them in outline fashion. Which do you think is most important? Now write the words you would say in attempting to partialize what Mr. K has said. Outline your rationale for the words you chose. How do you think Mr. K might react to your words?

2. In response to a question about her current needs, Loretta says, "Well, first I need food. I'm really hungry. Then, I need to clean up, put on a decent outfit, and find a job. It would be nice to have a roof over my head—but I can stay at my little campsite for a while longer. Once I save enough money to travel, I'll continue on my way to visit my youngest daughter. She lives about 1,300 miles from here." First, separate and identify each of the elements in Loretta's message. List them in outline fashion. Which do you think is most important? Now write the words you would say in attempting to partialize what she said. Outline your rationale for the words you chose. How do you think Loretta might react to your words?

3. During the initial interview, Mr. S picks up where Mrs. S left off by saying, "Since we married, we've had troubles with both my kids and hers. Basically, they dislike each other, they seem to

hate us, and lately my wife and I have begun to fight. Finances have become a problem, and there's no time for anything. I don't think I've had a single minute to myself in 6 months. The woman I love and I haven't been out of the house on a weekend evening since our wedding." First, separate and identify each of the elements in the client's message. List them in outline fashion. Which do you think is most important? Now write the words you would say to partialize the complex message communicated by Mr. S. Outline your rationale for the words you chose. How do you think Mr. S might react to your words?

4. During the first meeting, Mrs. F says, "I've had troubles ever since I moved into this community. The school system is totally insensitive to the Latino population. My kids have begun to disrespect me and berate their own heritage. All the neighbors are white and haven't even introduced themselves to us. My mother is seriously ill in Peru, but I don't dare leave the children here alone while they're in danger." First, separate and identify each of the elements in the client's message. List them in outline fashion. Which do you think is most important? Now write the words you might say in partializing this message. Outline your rationale for the words you selected. How do you think Mrs. F might respond?

5. Following the remarks of a few staff members, an agency board member says, "As I see it, our agency has a long history of laissez-faire leadership, unprofessionalism at all levels of the organization, some incompetence, and a nearly complete absence of mission-driven, purposeful, and focused effort." Use the space below to separate and identify each of the elements in the client's message. List them in outline fashion. Which do you think is most important? Now write the words you might say in partializing this message. Outline your rationale for the words you selected. How do you think the board member might respond? How might other participants?

■ Going Beyond

Going beyond what is said (Hammond et al., 1977) occurs when you use your empathic understanding of clients' messages to extend slightly what they express. Instead of mirroring exactly what clients say, you use your knowledge, experience, logic, and intuition to add modestly to the feelings or meanings actually communicated. Through a process called additive empathy, you take a small leap beyond the expressed message to bring into greater awareness or clarity information that a client already knows. Your responses "go beyond what the client has explicitly expressed to feeling and meaning only implied in the client's statements and, thus, somewhat below the surface of the client's awareness" (Hammond et al., 1977, p. 137).

Going beyond sometimes involves combining what clients say verbally with what they express nonverbally. In this process, however, continue to remain congruent with clients' overall direction and perspective. Although departing somewhat from their actual words, stay within their frame of reference. Rather than changing directions, build on the agenda your client has previously established.

For example, during the early part of a first meeting, a client who recently immigrated to the United States from Haiti might say to a white worker, "Do they have any black social workers at your agency?" This may be an indirect communication (Shulman, 1992, pp. 42–44) by a client who wonders whether a white worker has the capacity to understand him and to value his culture. He might prefer a black social worker. Perhaps he has had a negative experience with a white social worker at some point in the past. A white worker might respond to this question by saying something such as "Yes, we have several black social workers [sharing information], although not as many as we should [sharing opinion]. Because you ask that question though, I wonder if you might be saying that you'd prefer to work with an African American social worker [going beyond]?"

EXAMPLE	**Going Beyond**

Client: About 6 months ago, my son was killed in a motorcycle crash. We had a fight just before he left home that morning. I yelled at him and called him a "spoiled brat." He swore at me and tore out of the yard on that bike.

Worker: You feel guilty because the last conversation with your son was so bitter. Do you sometimes think that your words had something to do with the accident?

Going beyond is not an interpretation, nor is it a speculation or guess. Rather, it involves putting into words those thoughts and feelings that a person probably thinks or feels but has not yet verbally expressed.

EXAMPLE	**Going Beyond**

Case Situation: A 12-year-old girl who was sexually molested by her mother's male friend.

Client: My mother loved him very much and now he's gone.

Worker: You sometimes wonder whether you should have said anything. You think that maybe your mom might be happier and still have her boyfriend if you had just kept quiet about what he did to you?

EXERCISE 9-7   Going Beyond

Refer to your responses to earlier exercises as you continue to use exploring skills with Mr. K, Loretta, the S family, Mrs. F, and the "troubled agency."

1. Mr. K continues by saying, "I guess I'm a real wimp! I'm desperate for her to come home. All I do is think of ways to get her back. I make these plans about how to contact her, how to persuade her to change her mind. I constantly wonder what she's doing and whether she ever thinks of me." Write the words you would say in going beyond what Mr. K has said. Outline your rationale for the words you chose. How do you think he might react to your response? What is another way you might go beyond what he said?

2. In response to a question about her youngest daughter, she says, "Well, I haven't seen or talked with her in more than 15 years. When my husband divorced me, he got custody of the children. That destroyed me and I began to slide downhill from there. He remarried and his wife became their mother." Write the words you would use in attempting to go beyond Loretta's verbal statement. What is your rationale for the words you chose? How do you think she might respond? What is an alternative means for going beyond what she said?

3. Following remarks by Mr. S, Mrs. S says, "Things are so bad between my kids and his kids that I've begun to wonder whether it's worth trying anymore. Maybe my children and I should just leave. We made it on our own before, and we can do it again." Write the words you would say in going beyond what Mrs. S has said. Outline your rationale for the words you chose. How do you think Mrs. S might react to your response? What is another way you might go beyond what she said?

4. At one point Mrs. F says, "Maybe it's not worth fighting this racist system. Maybe I should just accept things as they are. I'm just one person—just one woman—what can I do?" Write the words you might say in going beyond her verbal message. Outline your rationale for the words you selected. How do you think Mrs. F might respond? What is another way in which you might go beyond Mrs. F's statement?

5. Almost immediately after a board member spoke, the agency director says, "Look, I'm the director and, ultimately, I'm responsible for what happens here. I know things have been bad for a long time and I also know that in the 3 months I've been here I have not been active enough in addressing the problems. I have clearly been part of the problem and would like to be part of the solution. However, if it would help the agency, I would be willing to submit my resignation." Use the space below to write the words you might say in going beyond the director's verbal message. Outline your rationale for the words you selected. How do you think the director might respond? What is another way in which you might go beyond the director's statement?

Reflecting Issues

By **reflecting issues**, you demonstrate to clients that you understand their view of identified needs, problems, or other topics of concern. An important form of active, empathic listening, reflecting issues represents a more specific application of the reflecting content skill. In this case, you paraphrase and highlight those issues that clients wish to address in your work together. In effect, when you reflect issues, you take an early step toward the processes of assessment and contracting. When you empathically communicate your understanding of clients' experience of the issues that concern them, both the working relationship and clients' motivation to work with you tend to improve. By expressing empathic appreciation of the nature of the problems as clients see them, you simultaneously convey respect for clients as people of worth and value, and endorse their right to autonomy and self-determination.

Of course, reflection of an issue does not necessarily convey moral approval or professional agreement to work toward its resolution. Occasionally, clients identify problems or goals that social workers could not morally, ethically, or legally help to address. For instance, suppose you serve as a school social worker in a high school. One of the students—a 16-year-old girl—says she wants your advice. She states:

> *Everybody drinks at the school dances. It helps people feel better and have more fun. But the new regulations prevent us from going out to our cars during dances. It's a good policy. Everybody had to go out to the parking lot to drink and then come back into the gym to dance. It was, like, back and forth all night long. It would be so much better if we could just spike one bowl of punch with whiskey. It would be safer and we wouldn't have to leave the building.*

As a school social worker, you obviously could not condone this action. Indeed, as you consider the student's comments, you might wonder if they might represent a "test" to see if you are susceptible enough to consent to the idea or perhaps to see if you would react with anger or judgment. Indeed, her words might constitute an attempt to provoke an emotional or irrational response. Regardless of the student's motivation, however, you could easily communicate your understanding of the student's expressed view of the issue so that she feels heard and understood. You need not approve of her words to demonstrate empathy. Such understanding can form the basis for further exploration and perhaps reconsideration of the issue. Furthermore, if you respond in a nonreactive, nonjudgmental way, you might pass the student's "test."

Clients, especially those who voluntarily seek social services, are usually quite ready to share their issues and concerns. However, some clients in some circumstances may need considerable support, guidance, and encouragement to do so; and, sometimes, we may have to identify issues for them (see "Identifying Issues" in Chapter 10). In emergency and in some crisis situations, people may be too physically or emotionally injured to identify their basic human needs. For example, after months or years of oppression and deprivation in camps, refugees may find it difficult to even imagine that housing, employment, or education could be possible. You may also have to assume major responsibility for both issue identification and goal establishment in certain involuntary circumstances or when clients lack competence to participate in the process.

Regardless of the context, do not assume that the issues clients initially introduce will necessarily remain the primary focus. During exploration with an attentive social worker, clients often reveal different concerns that are more "real," more urgent, or more essential than those discussed earlier. Some clients test workers by trying out a relatively modest issue first. Based on the nature of your response, they may then move on to identify a problem of greater significance. In addition, the collaborative process of assessment may lead clients to reconsider and reformulate issues for work.

As you begin to practice the skill of reflecting issues, please use the format outlined here. Later, when you gain greater proficiency, experiment with alternate formats.

PRACTICE FORMAT *Reflecting Issues*

As you see it, one of the issues you'd like to address in our work together is _____ _____.

EXAMPLE | **Reflecting Issues**

Client: My wife left me—sure, for very good reasons—but I'm really down about it. She has left me before but always came back. This time I know she won't. She's gone for good, and I don't know what to do. I can't go on the way things are. I'm so sad and lost without her.

Worker: As you see it, there are two major issues you'd like to address in our work together. First, you feel terrible. You're lonely and depressed, and you find it hard to function well when you feel that way. Second, you're unsure of how to get on with your life without your wife.

As a form of active listening, if you accurately paraphrase the issue as experienced by clients, they are likely to respond with something like "Yeah, that's right" to verify your reflection. Nonetheless, it is often useful to precede issue reflections with reflections of feelings, content, or feelings and meaning to show you understand multiple aspects of clients' experiences. It may help to seek feedback following your reflection of the issue. For instance, a social worker might ask a client, "Are these the major issues you'd like to work on?"

EXERCISE 9-8   Reflecting Issues

Refer to your responses to earlier exercises as you continue to use exploring skills with Mr. K, Loretta, the S family, Mrs. F, and the "troubled agency."

1. During the second half of the initial interview, Mr. K begins to discuss the problems he would like to address in your work together. He says, "I guess my major problem is that I can't seem to get over her. I keep hoping when there is no hope." Write the words you would use in reflecting issues as Mr. K sees them.

2. As Loretta discusses her concerns, she says, "I guess I'm most afraid that when I finally arrive at my daughter's doorstep, she won't recognize me as her mother and will simply turn me away." Write the words you would use in reflecting issues as Loretta views them.

3. During the latter portion of the first family meeting, Mr. S says, "I guess I can say this in front of the children—they know so much already. Anyway, today at work, I learned that there will soon be massive layoffs. It's likely that I will lose my job within the next 3 or 4 weeks. It's just what we need, to top off the rest of our problems!" Write the words you would say in reflecting issues as Mr. S sees them.

4. During the second half of the initial meeting, Mrs. F says, "I guess I've never felt we truly belong in this town. Nobody really seems to like us or want us here. I guess we just don't fit in." Write the words you might say in reflecting issues as Mrs. F sees them.

5. As participants continue to share thoughts and feelings during the first meeting, one professional staff member says, "I'm almost 60 years old and have worked in eight different agencies since I received my social work degree 32 years ago. I can honestly say that my morale is the lowest it has ever been and that this place is toxic. Some people refuse to talk to others—even when it's needed for the job. Nasty rumors about people spread like wildfire, and I believe it's fair to say that some administrators have 'favorites' who receive special perquisites. Last year, a few of them received extremely large salary increases while the rest of us had our salaries frozen." Use the space below to write the words you would say in reflecting issues as the professional staff member sees them.

◼◼ Reflecting Hypotheses

Social workers use the skill of **reflecting hypotheses** to empathically communicate our understanding of clients' ideas and "theories" about "why" problems occur and "what to do" to resolve them. Indeed, clients' hypotheses often contribute to our collaborative understanding of the factors associated with the origin, development, and continuation of particular problems. **Explanatory hypotheses** are ideas used to understand or explain the reasons that a problem exists and the factors that contribute to its persistence. When you accurately communicate your understanding of clients' explanatory hypotheses, they feel heard, understood, and valued as genuine collaborators in the exploration process.

When you reflect clients' explanatory hypotheses, you demonstrate respect for the way they think about issues. Of course, like other forms of active listening, reflecting an explanatory hypothesis does not necessarily indicate endorsement of the "theory." Sometimes clients' explanatory hypotheses are based upon invalid assumptions and popular but unsubstantiated views about the causes of biopsychosocial and environmental phenomena. People sometimes adopt implausible or superstitious beliefs in their attempts to make sense of problems and concerns. For instance, clients sometimes hold themselves fully and unreasonably responsible for things clearly beyond their personal control. Though we may reflect our understanding of such views, we need not validate the invalid. However, to the degree that clients' hypotheses reflect consistency with research findings and empirically supported theories, we reflect their views and build upon them with compatible hypotheses of our own.

In addition to explanatory hypotheses, many clients have ideas about what should be done to resolve the problem. In effect, they generate **change-oriented hypotheses**. These are predictions about how resolution of problems or achievement of goals could or should occur. For example, some clients believe that they can resolve complex, long-standing multisystem problems through acts of personal willpower alone. Although we might sometimes wonder about their credibility, we empathically reflect clients' change-oriented hypotheses in our attempt to demonstrate understanding and respect.

Many clients have well-conceptualized explanatory and change-oriented hypotheses. However, some do not. In such cases, you may encourage clients to think aloud about "why" the problems occur and "what might work" to resolve them.

Regardless of the context, do not assume that clients' "hypotheses" necessarily remain fixed and unalterable. As do social workers, clients often develop more sophisticated, more accurate, and more relevant explanatory and change-oriented hypotheses as they collect additional information, reconsider facts, engage in change-focused activities, and monitor outcomes.

As you begin to practice the skill of reflecting hypotheses, please use the formats outlined here. Later, when you gain greater proficiency, experiment with alternate versions.

PRACTICE FORMAT | *Reflecting Explanatory Hypotheses*

As you see it, the reasons for this problem include _____

_____ .

or

As you see it, one explanation for this issue is _____

_____ .

EXAMPLE | **Reflecting Explanatory Hypotheses**

Client: My wife left me for another man. Of course, I drank too much, was away from home a lot, and neglected her needs. Basically, I was a lousy husband. I certainly cannot blame her for leaving me. It was my fault and I feel guilty as sin about it. I'm pretty sure that's why I'm so depressed. How could I have been so selfish?

Worker: As you see it, she left because of your selfishness. She was entirely justified because you drank heavily and frequently neglected her. You feel guilty about your self-centered behavior and the depression is a natural result of that realization.

PRACTICE FORMAT | *Reflecting Change-Oriented Hypotheses*

As you see it, you could address this particular problem by _____

_____

EXAMPLE | **Reflecting Change-Oriented Hypotheses**

Client: She had every right to leave. I was the one at fault and I feel so guilty and ashamed. This didn't have to happen. So far, I haven't given up hope for reconciliation, and I haven't forgiven myself for my selfish behavior. I guess if I'm going to get over this depression, I'll have to do both of those things.

Worker: So, you think that if you accept the fact that the marriage is truly over and you also begin to forgive yourself, the depression will start to lift and you could have a life again.

Reflecting clients' explanatory hypotheses and their change-oriented hypotheses represent, of course, forms of active listening. If you accurately paraphrase clients' hypotheses, they are likely to respond, "Yes. That's how I see it," or "Yeah, that's right," to confirm the accuracy of your reflection.

EXERCISE 9-9 Reflecting Hypotheses

Refer to your responses to earlier exercises as you continue to use exploring skills with Mr. K, Loretta, the S family, Mrs. F, and the "troubled agency."

1. As you approach the end of your initial meeting with Mr. K, he says, "I think the major reason that I can't get over her is that I don't truly believe it's over. I can't seem to accept the facts of the situation. The truth is that the marriage has ended and she will not take me back. Once I accept that reality, I'll begin to recover." Write the words you would say in reflecting hypotheses (explanatory, change oriented, or both) as Mr. K sees them. Outline your rationale for the words you chose. How do you think Mr. K might react to your reflections?

2. Toward the end of your first meeting with her, Loretta says, "If my daughter does reject me when I show up on her doorstep after all these years, I guess I'll be able to understand why. I've been a mess for so long that I thought it would be better for both my kids if I were simply out of their lives. Their father is a good man and I'm pretty sure he married a kind and decent woman. They've been better off without me. Despite that, I still hope that someday, somehow I'll be able to reconnect with them and perhaps even add something to their lives." Write the words you would say in reflecting explanatory and change-oriented hypotheses as Loretta expresses them. Outline your rationale for the words you chose. How do you think she might react to your reflections?

3. Toward the end of the initial meeting, Mr. S says, "I'm incredibly worried and stressed. I'll probably be laid off from my job in the next few weeks. I can't eat or sleep. I'm constantly irritated and often fly off the handle with my wife and children. As best I can tell, the only way out of this mess is to find another job—one that pays at least as much as this one does." Write the words

you would use to reflect Mr. S's explanatory and his change-oriented hypotheses. Outline your rationale for the words you chose. How do you think he might react to your reflections?

4. As you move toward winding up the first meeting together, Mrs. F says, "I guess I've had to acknowledge that there is a lot of prejudice and discrimination in this town and especially in this school. I think that's the reason for the abuse my kids have taken. I'm not optimistic that the school officials can or will do anything to correct the situation so I think my only option is to move away from this place." Write the words you would use to reflect Mrs. F's explanatory and her change-oriented hypotheses. Outline your rationale for the words you chose. How do you think she might react to your reflections?

5. Toward the end of the initial meeting, one of the staff members says, "I'm an employee here so I realize I'm taking a risk in saying what I'm about to say—but here it is anyway. All of these problems are a direct result of passive, indecisive, and sometimes incompetent leadership from both our past and present directors and from board members. In my opinion, active, hands-on, competent leadership is needed to resolve these long-standing problems." Write the words you would use to reflect the staff member's explanatory and change-oriented hypotheses. Outline your rationale for the words you chose. How do you think she might react to your reflections?

SUMMARY

During the exploration phase of social work practice, you encourage clients to share thoughts and feelings, and to describe experiences about the issues or concerns that led to the contact. Through the process of exploration, you and the client gather and review information regarding the needs, problems, or issues of concern from a biopsychosocial and person-in-environment perspective and from the dimension of time: present-past-future. Both the social worker and the client participate in an attempt to understand the development, maintenance, and status of the issues of concern.

You seek to determine their frequency, intensity, and duration, as well as the risk and protective factors that might increase or decrease the probability of occurrence. By looking for strengths, you and your client identify assets, talents, abilities, and resources that could help in resolution efforts. In particular, you look for strengths in the areas of competencies, social support, successes, and life lessons. When combined with your professional knowledge and the client's input, the information collected contributes to the development of an assessment and plans for work.

Although the exploring skills are especially useful for encouraging mutual consideration of information regarding the person, issue, situation, and strengths, they also apply throughout the entire helping process. Along with the beginning skill of seeking feedback, you may use the exploring skills repeatedly as you and your clients work together toward resolution of the issues of concern.

CHAPTER 9 Summary Exercises

1. At this point, you have prepared for and begun first meetings with the four clients described below (see the Summary Exercises in Chapters 7 and 8). Use word-processing software to *write the words* you would say and describe the actions you would take as you engage them in exploring the issues of concern. In other words, build upon your previous work to demonstrate how you would apply the requested exploring skills in these particular situations. Please *label* each of the skills that you use and place quotation marks around the words you would say. When finished, combine your work into a single "Four Explorations" document with a section for each of the four cases. Save the document to a file labeled "4_Exps." Include the file in your Social Work Skills Learning Portfolio.

   a. You are in the early part of the first meeting with a fairly large number of community members interested in addressing several pressing social problems. You've facilitated introductions and suggested that the purpose for the group might be to assess the state of the community, identify its problems and needs, and develop plans to address the issues and improve the social and economic conditions throughout the community. Now, use word-processing software to write the words you would say in (a) asking an initial exploratory question of the group. Then, (b) write five additional open-ended questions you would want to ask at some point during this first meeting.

   b. You are in the early part of the first meeting with a woman who telephoned the agency earlier in the day to request an appointment right away. You've introduced each other. She would like you to call her Danni. You responded by asking her to use your first name too. You have discussed policy factors, suggested a tentative purpose for the meeting, and described how she could most effectively participate in the process. She said, "That sounds good" but looked anxious to begin. You asked an opening question. She immediately began to cry and said, "Last Saturday night, I was raped; and it's my fault. I was so stupid!" Now, word-process the words you would say in (a) reflecting the feelings and meaning contained in her message. Then, (b) prepare an open-ended question to follow her statement. Next, write the words you would say in (c) seeking clarification of her words. Following your response to her statement, she says, "I met this guy in a bar. We had some drinks and talked. He seemed really nice. He offered to drive me home and I accepted. I invited him up to my apartment. Once we got inside the door, things changed; he changed. He grabbed me, threw me on the sofa, ripped off my panties, and raped me." Now, write the words you would say in (d) reflecting the content of her statement. Then she said, "I should have known better. I said to myself. 'Well, that's a mistake I won't repeat.' I thought I could cope and I did for about three days. Then, I just fell apart. Now, I cry all the time. I can barely sleep and when I do drift off, I wake up with a start—terrified that someone's there. I'm afraid that he'll come back." Next, write the words you would say in (e) reflecting the feelings and meaning contained in her message. Then, record what you would say in (f) going beyond the words she said. Finally, write the words you would say in (g) reflecting issues.

c. You are in the early part of the first meeting with a family of six (two parents and four children who range in age from 1 to 7 years) who had been sleeping in their dilapidated Chevy in a rest area on the highway. You've learned everyone's name and shared your own. You have discussed policy factors, suggested a tentative purpose for the meeting, and described how they could most effectively participate in the process. Following an open-ended, exploratory question, Mr. Z said that they are trying to get to another part of the country where they hope to find work. However, they ran out of money, food, and gasoline. At that point, Mrs. Z added, "We don't want charity. We just need enough to make it there." Use word-processing software to write the words you would say in (a) reflecting content following her statement. Then, (b) write two open-ended questions and one closed-ended question that might yield useful information in your effort to understand the family.

Following one of your open-ended questions, Mrs. Z said, "The baby hasn't been eating well. She's sleeping all the time and has a fever. She has diarrhea and yesterday she vomited three times. I think she must be sick. She needs a doctor and maybe a hospital … but … we don't have documents and I'm afraid we'll be arrested if we seek medical help." Write the words you would say in (c) reflecting the feelings and meaning in her message. Then, write what you would say in (d) seeking clarification. Then, (e) write two closed-ended questions and one open-ended question concerning the baby's health. Next, write the words you would say in (f) going beyond the words she said. Then, write the words you would say in (g) reflecting issues. Finally, record what you would say in (h) reflecting hypotheses.

d. You are in the early part of the first meeting with Mr. T. You've introduced yourself, discussed policy factors, suggested a tentative purpose for the meeting, and described how he could actively participate in the process. Following an open-ended, exploratory question, he said that he faces criminal charges of child molestation. He added, "I lived with the girl and her mother for more than a year. I paid the rent, the utilities, and bought most of the food. I thought things were fine. Now they have a restraining order against me. I can't even talk with them about this." First, write the words you would say in (a) reflecting feelings and meaning in response to his statement. Next, (b) write three open-ended questions that might follow his statement. Then, (c) go beyond the words he said. Following your response, Mr. T said, "I don't know why she said that I did those things. It really hurts me. I've been good to her and her mother. She's just lying and I don't know why. Maybe she's jealous." Write the words you would say in (d) reflecting the feelings and meaning contained in his statement. Then, record how you might (e) seek clarification concerning his message. Next, write the words you would say in (f) reflecting issues. Finally, write the words you would say to (g) reflect hypotheses.

Chapter 9 Experiential Interviewing Exercise

By the time of the first meeting, you should be well-prepared to assume the role of social worker. Since you already have your practice client's consent to record the interviews, turn on the equipment and then proceed to use the appropriate beginning skills. Be sure that the practice client knows your name and credentials and that you know hers (the pseudonym). Share a tentative purpose for your work together. You might suggest a social work role or roles that you could fulfill in your collaborative efforts. Orient the client to the process and discuss relevant policy and ethical factors. Be sure to seek feedback from the client at various points during the beginning process to ensure clear and accurate understanding.

Once you have completed the beginning tasks, proceed to ask exploratory questions about the issues of concern. As the client responds to questions, follow up with appropriate empathic and other exploring skills as you seek to enhance mutual understanding of the issues from a person-in-environment perspective. In this first meeting, limit the interview to the beginning and exploration phases only. Do not attempt to assess, contract, or in any way try to work toward resolution. Resist temptations to speculate about underlying reasons or causes. Do not offer theoretical interpretations and, at this point, refrain from giving advice.

As you proceed toward the conclusion of the meeting, be sure to arrange for another in the near future. In saying good-bye, you might suggest a tentative starting point for the next meeting. For example, if you are still exploring the identified issues or the person-in-environment context, you might say something such as, "Next time, let's continue to explore these issues and try to reach some understanding about why and how these things seem to occur. How does that sound?"

Although the interview is relatively brief, you and your colleague will probably gain some understanding of the issues as well as considerable information about their origin and development, and their impact upon the client and others in her world.

When you've finished the 30-minute interview, take another 15 minutes for the following:

1. Leave your respective social worker and client roles. Request that your colleague complete a copy of the Talking and Listening Skills Rating Form, the Preparing and Beginning Skills Rating Form, and the Exploring Skills Rating Form (see Appendix 6). When your colleague has done so, inquire about today's interview experience. Ask general open-ended questions so that you might get as much evaluative feedback as possible and, through that, enhance your learning. For example, you might ask your colleague questions such as:
   * What thoughts, feelings, or other reactions do you have about today's meeting?
   * What do you think about the process of working together that we discussed today?
   * What parts of the interview affected you the most—either positively or negatively?
   * What do you wish had happened during the interview that did not occur?
   * What suggestions do you have about how the interview could have been better, more helpful, or more constructive for you?
   * What suggestions do you have about how I could have been a better or more helpful social worker today?

   As you finish securing feedback from your practice client, thank her and tell her that you will see her soon.

   As soon as you can following the interview, use your word-processing software to prepare a report entitled "First Interview: Practice Client Feedback." Label the document file "Intvue_1_Client_Feed." Include the date and your name as the student social worker. Then summarize your practice client's feedback along with the results of the rating forms she completed. Include the document in the "Experiential Exercise Folder" of your Social Work Skills Learning Portfolio.

2. Next, play the audio or video recording. Review and reflect upon what you see or hear, and appraise your performance. Take written notes as you go along. Then do the following:
   a. Refer to the figures and tables presented earlier in this chapter: Outline of Selected Biopsychosocial and Environmental Dimensions (Table 9.1), Exploration Matrix

(Table 9.2), exploration of the issue (Table 9.3), timeline (Figure 9.5), genogram (Figure 9.6), eco-map (Figure 9.7), risk and protective factors (Tables 9.4, 9.5, 9.6), looking for strengths (Table 9.7), and explanatory and change-oriented hypotheses (Table 9.8). Use the labels in figures and the row and column headings in tables as guides to estimate the approximate degree to which you have explored various dimensions of the person-issue-situation over time. We are usually interested in information that helps both you and clients understand the primary issues of concern; any goals or aspirations the client may share; risk and protective factors; personal strengths and environmental assets; and any explanatory and change-oriented hypotheses. Use your estimates to identify aspects of the person-issue-situation that you would like to explore further in the next interview. Word-process a few open-ended questions for each dimension needing additional exploration. Incorporate them in a brief document entitled "First Interview: Additional Exploration Questions." Label the file "Intvue_1_More_Quests." Include the document in the "Experiential Exercise Folder" of your Social Work Skills Learning Portfolio.

b. Next, go to Appendix 10 and complete the talking and listening, the beginning, and the exploring sections of The Social Work Skills Interview Rating Form. Use your ratings as a stimulus to evaluate your performance of relevant skills. Complete the evaluation of your performance in a brief document entitled "First Interview: Self-Evaluation." In this summary, identify the skills you performed well, those that need improvement, and those that you should have used during the interview but did not. Also, make note of those skills that you used but probably should not have. Describe and discuss your own reactions to and appraisal of the interview. Summarize the notes you prepared as you watched or listened to the recording. Address questions such as "How prepared were you?" "How did you feel about the interview?" "What did you like and what did you dislike?" Discuss what you would do differently if you had a chance to conduct the interview again. Finally, reflect upon the entirety of the first interview experience and prepare summary comments. Save the document as "Intvue_1_Self-Eval" and store it in the "Experiential Interviewing Exercise" folder of your Social Work Skills Learning Portfolio.

3. You have now completed your evaluation of the first meeting and will soon begin to plan for a second. As soon as you can find the time, begin to organize information gathered during the first interview into a set of coherent notes. You will use them after the second session when you begin to prepare a formal word-processed case record that approximates the professional documentation required in an actual social service agency. Remember to disguise the identity of the practice client. Refer to the date and time of the first interview and make note of the date you completed the written record. Identify yourself as a student social worker. When finished, save the "First Interview Notes" in a document file labeled "Intvue_1_Notes." Include it within the "Experiential Interviewing Exercise" folder of your Social Work Skills Learning Portfolio.

4. Following your review and self-evaluation of the first interview, completion of your review and evaluation of performance, and preparation of your notations, use relevant preparing skills to get ready for the next meeting with your practice client. Draw upon what you learned from the first interview to prepare tentative plans for the next. Use your word processor to do so. Save your "Plans for the Second Interview" in a document file labeled "Intvue_2_Plans" and deposit it in the "Experiential Interviewing Exercise" folder of your Social Work Skills Portfolio.

CHAPTER 9 Self-Appraisal

As you finish this chapter, please reflect on your learning by using the following space to identify any ideas, terms, or concepts addressed in Chapter 9 that remain confusing or unclear to you:

Next, respond to the following items by carefully reading each statement. Please use a 1-to-10-point rating scale (where *1 = strongly disagree* and *10 = strongly agree*) to indicate the degree to which you agree or disagree with each statement. Place a check mark at the point that best reflects your view at this particular point in time. If you're truly *undecided*, place your check at the midpoint (5.5) mark.

1. I can discuss the purposes and functions of exploring.

   1 2 3 4 5 6 7 8 9 10

2. I can explore relevant aspects of the person-issue-situation and look for strengths and assets in the person-in-environment.

   1 2 3 4 5 6 7 8 9 10

3. I can ask questions of others.

   1 2 3 4 5 6 7 8 9 10

4. I can seek clarification following others' words and gestures.

   1 2 3 4 5 6 7 8 9 10

5. I can reflect the content of others' communications.

   1 2 3 4 5 6 7 8 9 10

6. I can reflect the feelings expressed by others.

   1 2 3 4 5 6 7 8 9 10

7. I can reflect the feelings and meaning expressed by others.

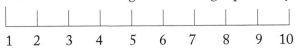

   1 2 3 4 5 6 7 8 9 10

8. I can partialize others' statements.

1	2	3	4	5	6	7	8	9	10

9. I can go beyond others' expressed communications.

1	2	3	4	5	6	7	8	9	10

10. I can reflect others' views of needs, problems, or issues.

1	2	3	4	5	6	7	8	9	10

11. I can reflect others' hypotheses about possible causes and potential solutions.

1	2	3	4	5	6	7	8	9	10

Assessing

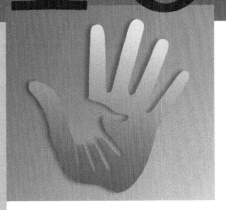

A spects of the assessment process typically begin during the exploring phase and continue on into the contracting phase as well. When the exploration process has progressed well, you and your clients have gathered and begun to reflect on a great deal of information about relevant people, issues, and circumstances. You have collaboratively traced the origin and development of problems, and found factors that might be associated with their occurrence. You have learned about aspects of the person-in-environment in both the present and the past, and may have considered various scenarios in the future. You have explored risk and protective factors as well as strengths and resources of various kinds. Some of the competencies, assets and social supports, successes, and life lessons you identified may become extremely useful later in planning actions to resolve problems and achieve goals. Importantly, you communicated your understanding of issues as presented by clients, and perhaps considered some of their preliminary explanatory and change-oriented hypotheses as well.

Chapter Goals

Following completion of this chapter, you should be able to:

- Discuss the purposes and functions of assessment.

- Identify issues.

- Share explanatory and change-oriented hypotheses.

- Confirm issues for work.

- Organize descriptive information.

- Prepare an assessment and case formulation.

Core Competencies

The content addressed in this chapter supports the following core EPAS competencies:

- Competency 4: Engage in Practice-Informed Research and Research-Informed Practice

- Competency 5: Engage in Policy Practice

- Competency 7: Assess Individuals, Families, Groups, Organizations, and Communities

Through the **assessing** skills, social workers and clients move toward clarification of the direction and focus for work (Jordan, 2008; Meyer, 1993; Perlman, 1957; Richmond, 1944; Sowers & Dulmus, 2008). Having reflected and considered client-generated hypotheses, you may now share your professionally based *explanatory hypotheses* about how personal and situational factors influence issues and vice versa—how needs and problems affect people and circumstances. You consider the relative urgency about which concerns should receive primary attention and often share your own *change-oriented hypotheses* about how issues might be addressed. In so doing, you frequently draw on strengths within the client system as well as assets and resources within the social and physical environments.

Understanding gained from these reflective processes usually leads to a relatively clear direction for the collaborative work that you and your client are about to undertake. Preferably, participants reach reasonable consensus about explanatory and change-oriented hypotheses, which form the basis for a **case formulation**.[1] The case formulation, in turn, logically leads to a service agreement or "contract" for your work together (Dziegielewski, 2008; Maluccio & Marlow, 1974; Seabury, 1975, 1976). Ideally, these processes reflect internal consistency (see Figure 10.1). Indeed, you should be able to discuss how the data support the hypotheses, the case formulation, and the service contract that contains goals, action plans, action steps, and plans for evaluation.

Assessment involves scientific inquiry, critical thinking, and lifelong learning as you bring your professional knowledge together with clients' firsthand experience in a collaborative process of reflection, analysis, and synthesis. Using theoretical and empirical knowledge within the context of biopsychosocial and person-in-environment perspectives, you conjointly assess needs and problems. You or your clients may adopt conceptual or assessment tools of various kinds. For example, concept maps and diagrammatic representations such as family genograms, eco-maps, or timelines could be helpful, as might some of the hundreds of valid and reliable instruments that pertain to potential topics of concern (Corcoran & Fischer, 2013a, 2013b; Hudson, 1982).

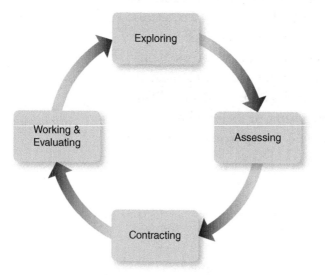

FIGURE 10.1 The Exploring, Assessing, Contracting, and Working & Evaluating Cycle

---

[1] In this context, the term *case formulation* applies to work with issues at the macro, mezzo, and microsystem levels. Indeed, in policy–practice and social action where social workers pursue mission-related causes such as eliminating poverty, reducing inequality, cleaning toxic waste areas, or challenging discrimination on the basis of class, race, sex, ethnicity, or sexual orientation, we also prepare "formulations." Whether "case" or "cause," the processes are equivalent.

You might examine a phenomenon in relation to a set of criteria or guidelines derived from research studies or validated protocols. For example, in assessing the relative risk of recidivism among people who have committed sexual offenses, you might consider findings from a meta-analysis conducted by Hanson and Morton-Bourgon (2009). If you are interested in the effectiveness of sex offender registries in reducing recidivism, you could review several relevant research studies (see, for example, Brewster, DeLong, & Moloney, 2013; Calkins, Jeglic, Beattey, Zeidman, & Perillo, 2014; Levenson, D'Amora, & Hern, 2007; Prescott & Rockoff, 2011; Sandler, Freeman, & Socia, 2008; Vásquez, Maddan, & Walker, 2008; Zgoba, Witt, Dalessandro, & Veysey, 2008, Dec.; Zgoba & Bachar, 2009, Apr. 9).

In assessing child sexual abuse, you might refer to *The Evaluation of Sexual Abuse in Children* (Kellogg & The American Academy of Pediatrics Committee on Child Abuse and Neglect, 2005). Although prepared for pediatricians, social workers benefit from an understanding of biophysical as well as psychosocial dimensions. In terms of psychosocial risk factors for child sexual abuse, you might review Levenson and Morin's article (2006). For the assessment of child abuse in general, you might consider empirical factors such as those summarized by Herring (1996). Certain conditions tend to be associated with a greater risk of child abuse. Among these are a history of child abuse or neglect reports, a parent who was abused as a child, a youthful parent, a single-parent or an extended-family household, domestic violence in the household, the lengthy separation of parent and child, substance abuse by parent or caretaker, impairment (for example, physical, intellectual, psychological) of the child, and impairment of the parent or caretaker (Brissett-Chapman, 1995, pp. 361–362). Using factors such as these as a guide, the worker thoughtfully considers the information learned during the exploring phase to estimate the risk of child endangerment. The outcomes of assessment tools and processes may powerfully affect, for better or worse, the well-being of a child and family. The consequences of both false positives (for example, where the worker concludes there is high risk but the true danger is low) and false negatives (for example, where the worker concludes there is low risk but the true danger is high) can be serious. In some cases, an inaccurate assessment may endanger lives or ruin reputations.

Of course, social workers serve couples, families, groups, organizations, and communities as well as individuals, and we also pursue social, economic, and environmental justice. Assessment guidelines and instruments are just as useful in work with medium and larger size client systems as well as for national and global issues. For example, the Inventory of Family Protective Factors (Gardner, Huber, Steiner, Vazquez, & Savage, 2008) may help families identify factors that foster resilience. Moos and Moos' (2009) Family Environment Scale has long been used in family-environment-related research. In work with groups, scales such as the Group Attitude Scale (Evans & Jarvis, 1986) or the Perceived Group Cohesion Scale (Chin, Salisbury, Pearson, & Stollak, 1999) may be quite useful. In terms of organizational culture, Cooke and Lafferty's Organizational Culture Inventory (Szumal, 2003), the Organizational Culture Survey (Glaser, Zamanou, & Hacker, 1987), or Cameron and Quinn's (1999) Organizational Culture Assessment Instrument can complement individual and small group interviews.

The Community-Oriented Programs Environment Scale (Moos & Otto, 1972) may be used to evaluate change in communities. The World Values Survey (2009) and several of the indices used by the United Nations are helpful in assessing large communities and societies. Perspectives related to the concepts of social capital, social cohesion, and "well-being" may be useful in both large and small-community contexts. Based in large part on the work of Robert Putnam (1995, 2001, 2002; Putnam & Campbell, 2010; Putnam, Feldstein, & Cohen, 2003), the Saguaro Seminar on Civic Engagement in America at Harvard University's Kennedy School of Government created a Social Capital Community Benchmark Survey (2000, 2002, Sept.). The Saguaro Seminar completes large-scale national studies (2000, 2006). Other tools include the Social Capital Inventory

(Narayan & Cassidy, 2001), the Social Capital Integrated Questionnaire, and the Social Capital Assessment Tool—the latter two developed by the World Bank Social Capital Thematic Group (2009, 2011, July).

As social workers become more interested in issues related to peace and violence, we might refer to the Global Peace Index (GPI) as prepared each year by the Institute for Economics and Peace (IEP). The IEP uses 23 distinct indicators to appraise the peacefulness of some 162 nations. According to the 2015 GPI report, the three most peaceful nations in the world at that time were Iceland, Denmark, and Austria—ranked 1, 2, and 3, respectively. The three least peaceful should come as no surprise: Afghanistan, Iraq, and Syria—160, 161, and 162, respectively. The United States ranked 94th, between Guyana and Peru which tied for 92nd and Saudi Arabia at 95th (2015a).

The IEP also prepares a U.S. Peace Index (USPI) for the nation and each of its 50 states. As of 2012, Maine, Vermont, and New Hampshire ranked as the 1st, 2nd, and 3rd most peaceful states, respectively. The three least peaceful are Nevada at 48th, Tennessee at 49th, and Louisiana at 50th. Based on policing practices, access to firearms, rates of violent crime and homicide, incarceration rates, and other relevant factors within the nation, the 2012 USPI for the nation as a whole reflected the greatest level of peacefulness in the last two decades. Recall, however, that within the global context the United States in 2015 ranked 94th of 162 countries in peacefulness. Neighbor Canada in 7th place was much more peaceful than the United States while Mexico at 144th was considerably less so (2015a).

Although social work assessments tend to have much in common, the specific approaches vary considerably according to client system characteristics and size as well as practice setting, agency or program purpose, and presenting issues. For example, a social worker serving an elderly client might refer to government guidelines to help determine whether a nursing home has adequate physical facilities and sufficient social stimulation to meet the basic needs of aged people. In health care contexts, a social worker might help determine if a client can function safely and independently. You might use an **Activities of Daily Living (ADL)** tool or instrument to estimate clients' ability to shop, prepare food, cook, keep house, arrange for transportation, manage medications, use the telephone, bathe, dress, and feed themselves (Lawton & Brody, 1969), as well as their continence, mobility, and ability to go to the bathroom independently (Katz, Down, Cash, & Grotz, 1970). A psychiatric or clinical social worker might refer to criteria published in a recent edition of the *Diagnostic and Statistical Manual (DSM)* (American Psychiatric Association, 2000a, 2013) to help consider whether a client might reflect symptoms associated with a mental disorder (Williams, 2008). A social worker serving in a crisis and suicide-prevention program might use guidelines to estimate a distraught client's risk of suicidal action as low, moderate, or high (American Psychiatric Association, 2003; Berman, Jobes, & Silverman, 2006; Rogers, Lewis, & Subich, 2002; Rutter & Behrendt, 2004; Verwey et al., 2010).

A social worker working with community members seeking to enhance conditions in their neighborhood might conduct a needs assessment—which, not surprisingly—mirrors the processes and procedures of scientific inquiry (Reviere, Berkowitz, Carter, & Ferguson, 1996; Samuels, Ahsan, Garcia, & Coalition, 1995; Wambeam, 2015; Watkins, Meiers, & Visser, 2012; Witkin & Altschuld, 1995). You might even integrate the processes of needs assessment with those of asset strengthening and capacity building (Altschuld, 2015; Assessment Capacities Project & Emergency Capacity Building Project, 2014).

Needs assessments are not limited to communities. Indeed, as social workers, our primary professional mission guides us to consider human needs and well-being at the individual, national, and global levels as well.

In Chapter 2, we discussed Maslow's original and Kenrick's revised version of a **human needs** hierarchy (Kenrick et al., 2010; Maslow, 1943, 1968). Other scholars have contributed conceptual schemes that might apply in some assessment contexts as well. In *A Theory of Human Need*, Len Doyal and Ian Gough (Doyal & Gough, 1991) propose a listing of needs and their respective **need satisfiers** (that is, what is required to satisfy those needs) along with social indicators that might be used as evidence of progress toward need satisfaction among a population.

Similarly, Braybrooke (1987) introduces a two-part "List of Matters of Need." The first part (1–6) primarily involves physical needs while the second part (7–12) is more social in nature:

1. The need to have a life-supporting relation to the environment
2. The need for food and water
3. The need to excrete
4. The need for exercise
5. The need for periodic rest, including sleep
6. The need (beyond what is covered under the preceding needs) for whatever is indispensable to preserving the body intact in important respects
7. The need for companionship
8. The need for education
9. The need for social acceptance and recognition
10. The need for sexual activity
11. The need to be free from harassment, including not being continually frightened
12. The need for recreation (Braybrooke, 1987)

Some of the dimensions addressed by Gough and Braybrooke are similar to those incorporated within the United Nations Human Development Index (HDI) that we explored in Chapter 2. In fact, the HDI was largely an outgrowth of the "capabilities approach" originated by Amartyr Sen (2005) and extended by Sudhir Anand (Anand & Sen, 2000), James Foster (2006), and Martha Nussbaum (Nussbaum & Glover, 1995; Nussbaum & Sen, 1993).

In regard to the **capabilities approach**, Nussbaum suggests that:

This approach to quality-of-life measurement and the goals of public policy holds that we should focus on the question: What are the people of the group or country in question actually able to do and to be? Unlike a focus on opulence (say, GNP per capita), this approach asks about the distribution of resources and opportunities. In principle, it asks how each and every individual is doing with respect to all the functions deemed important. (p. 34)

This idea of capability is remarkably consistent with social work's person-in-environment perspective. Nussbaum seems to say that each of us has various capabilities that we might choose to fulfill if the surrounding physical and social environment provides adequate resources, opportunities, and encouragement, and does not obstruct us from our quest. Examples abound. A child has extraordinary intellectual gifts but is born into a family and community where reading, learning, and thinking independently are devalued and opportunities for their pursuit denied. A girl is born with the capability for a pleasurable sexual life in adulthood but her clitoris is removed at the age of 10. A young African American man who has a capability for a relatively long life is shot and killed on the doorstep of his church. A 35-year-old parent who has the capability of seeing a firstborn graduate from college dies when an improvised bomb explodes nearby.

Nussbaum argues that if we truly aspire to provide people with the freedom and opportunity to do and to be what they are capable of doing and being, then certain essential—perhaps even universal—conditions are required. She refers to these as the **Central Human Functional Capabilities** (2000):

1. *Life.* Being able to live to the end of a human life of normal length; not dying prematurely or before one's life is so reduced as to be not worth living.
2. *Bodily Health.* Being able to have good health, including reproductive health; to be adequately nourished; to have adequate shelter.
3. *Bodily Integrity.* Being able to move freely from place to place; to be secure against violent assault, including sexual assault and domestic violence; having opportunities for sexual satisfaction and for choice in matters of reproduction.
4. *Senses, Imagination, and Thought.* Being able to use the senses, to imagine, think, and reason—and to do these things in a 'truly human' way, a way informed and cultivated by an adequate education, including, but by no means limited to, literacy and basic mathematical and scientific training. Being able to use imagination and thought in connection with experiencing and producing works and events of one's own choice, religious, literary, musical, and so forth. Being able to use one's mind in ways protected by guarantees of freedom of expression with respect to both political and artistic speech, and freedom of religious exercise. Being able to have pleasurable experiences, and to avoid non-necessary pain.
5. *Emotions.* Being able to have attachments to things and people outside ourselves; to love those who love and care for us, to grieve at their absence; in general, to love, to grieve, to experience longing, gratitude, and justified anger. Not having one's emotional development blighted by fear and anxiety.
6. *Practical Reason.* Being able to form a conception of the good and to engage in critical reflection about the planning of one's life.
7. *Affiliation*
   a. Being able to live with and toward others, to recognize and show concern for other human beings, to engage in various forms of social interaction; to be able to imagine the situation of another and to have compassion for that situation; to have the capability for both justice and friendship.
   b. Having the social bases of self-respect and non-humiliation; being able to be treated as a dignified being whose worth is equal to that of others. This entails protections against discrimination on the basis of race, sex, sexual orientation, religion, caste, ethnicity, or national origin.
8. *Other Species.* Being able to live with concern for and in relation to animals, plants, and the world of nature.
9. *Play.* Being able to laugh, to play, to enjoy recreational activities.
10. *Control over One's Environment*
    a. *Political.* Being able to participate effectively in political choices that govern one's life; having the right of political participation, protections of free speech and association.
    b. *Material.* Being able to hold property (both land and movable goods); having the right to seek employment on an equal basis with others; having the freedom from unwarranted search and seizure. In work, being able to work as a human being, exercising practical reason and entering into meaningful relationships of mutual recognition with other workers. (pp. 231–233)

Assessment processes that include consideration of human needs (Doyal & Gough, 1991; Gough, 2003, Mar.; Gough, 2014), human motivations, or human capabilities (Comim & Nussbaum, 2014) from a person-in-environment perspective contribute to a contextual understanding of clients, families, organizations, communities, and societies. Indeed, many common social problems directly or indirectly result from unmet human needs.

Certain kinds of needs and problems routinely surface in many social work practice settings. Violence toward self or others, child physical and sexual abuse, domestic abuse, exploitation of vulnerable people, poverty, inequality, prejudice and discrimination, and mental health or substance misuse issues are likely to emerge as concerns wherever you serve. All social workers, therefore, need to be alert to their possible presence. Indeed, some agencies make it standard operating procedure to screen for substance abuse, child abuse and domestic violence, and risk of suicide or violence against others. It also makes sense to inquire about clients' needs for food, water, shelter, and safety.

Social workers also routinely consider clients' personal problems in the context of parallel processes in the larger social and physical environments. For instance, when we meet with a client who has been arrested and convicted of a violent crime, we do not limit our assessment to the person and the immediate circumstances alone. Recognizing that false arrests and convictions regularly occur—especially to African Americans, Hispanic Americans, and persons reflecting symptoms of mental illness—social workers analyze community policing, judicial, and incarceration processes and practices in terms of fairness, basic human needs, and human rights (Benforado, 2015; Casselman, 2015; Cohen, 2012; Gould, 2008; Gross et al., 2005; Gross et al., 2014; Huff, Rattner, & Sagarin 1996; Northwestern University Law School, 2015; Petro & Petro, 2014; The Innocence Project, 2015; The Innocence Project, 2015, Sept. 3; The National Registry of Exonerations, 2013; The National Registry of Exonerations, 2015; Turvey & Coole, 2014; Uphoff, 2006; Warden, 2001). We also consider social and environmental factors in our client's developmental history and at the time of pertinent incidents. If a client did engage in violent action, we certainly examine that behavior—perhaps through a functional analysis. However, we also assess the nature and extent of violence within his communities and cultures, within the larger society, and between the larger society and other societies. A country that quickly resorts to violence with other nations or groups is likely to reflect parallel processes within its borders. Its police forces are likely to use violence as a primary option when dealing with atypical or oppositional behavior—including expressions of nonconformity, difference, or dissidence. Given such contexts, we can anticipate that individual people, families, and other small groups will adopt violent words and actions in their relations with others. In other words, we can expect that our behaviors will often parallel those extant in the larger society and our cultures.

Indeed, processes that parallel one another at the micro-, mezzo-, and macro-system level are so ubiquitous that people—even social workers—sometimes neglect them. Consider, for example, the processes associated with prejudice. Most of us notice when someone uses a racial epithet, tells a sexist or homophobic joke, blames a rape victim for being sexually assaulted, or holds a homeless person exclusively responsible for his homelessness. Their societal parallels, however, often remain unacknowledged, unspoken, or unaddressed. In many societies, institutionalized racism, sexism, victim blaming, and heterosexism are pervasive in the political and legal systems, private and public policies and programs, the mass media, and within many subcultures. And, as most social workers in the United States know, privileged groups at the very top of the power structure who gain the most from a money-driven political structure and a largely unregulated economic system, seek to ensure that wages from workers' labor remain as low as possible to maximize profits for investors; and to embellish executives' salaries, bonuses, and perks. Most poor people work—but remain in poverty because they lack full-time jobs that pay a living wage. Similarly, most unemployed people want to work—but remain jobless because jobs have been technologically automated or exported to even lower-wage countries. In addition, several political, economic, and cultural ideologies serve to maintain the status quo by holding poor people individually responsible for their inadequate incomes while excusing privileged individuals, corporations, and governments for their economic exploitation of other humans and the natural environment.

As social workers, let's remain alert for parallel processes—those political, economic and cultural beliefs, social structures, and processes that correspond to needs and problems among the individuals, families, and communities we serve. Remember to look for "the macro in the micro" in settings where you primarily serve people dealing with personal issues, and certainly in settings where individualized "labels" are assigned to people or their problems. Similarly, if you work primarily at the macro-system level, remain aware that policy and program changes affect real people in different ways. Some benefit while others do not.

Many social workers serve in settings where assignment of certain diagnostic labels and procedural codes is expected. The *DSM* is by far the most widely used classification manual of "mental disorders" in the world. The *DSM-5* (American Psychiatric Association, 2013) is the most recent edition and, like its predecessor the *DSM-IV-TR* (American Psychiatric Association, 2000a), should sell more than a million copies within a few years. Many social workers own copies of the latest "psychiatric bible" (Kirk & Kutchins, 1992; Kutchins & Kirk, 1997) and use the classification codes contained in both the *DSM-5* and the *International Classification of Diseases, Tenth Revision, Clinical Modification* (ICD-10-CM) (National Center for Health Statistics, 2015) in their work. In order to secure medical insurance reimbursement for certain mental health services, some clinical social workers also incorporate procedural codes from the *International Classification of Diseases, Tenth Revision, Procedural Coding System* (ICD-10-PCS) (Centers for Medicare & Medicaid Services, 2015).

Although the *DSM-5* and its earlier editions are extremely well known and widely used by practitioners from several professions, it remains a controversial classification system (Cooper, 2014; Demazeux & Singy, 2015; First, 2014; Frances, 2013; Greenberg, 2013; Paris & Phillips, 2013; Stijn Vanheule, 2014). According to the *DSM-5*, a "mental disorder is a syndrome characterized by clinically significant disturbance in an individual's cognition, emotion regulation, or behavior that reflects a dysfunction in the psychological, biological, or developmental processes underlying mental functioning" (American Psychiatric Association, 2013, p. 20). Such a broad definition could result in inconsistent interpretations and applications. Indeed, findings from numerous studies raise questions about the validity and reliability of the *DSM* system (Dalal & Sivakumar, 2009; Kirk & Kutchins, 1992, 1994; McLaren, 2008; Spitzer, Williams, & Endicott, 2012).

Social workers might ask questions such as, "What distinguishes a 'clinically significant disturbance' from one that is not clinically significant?" "How likely is it that someone without a mental disorder could be incorrectly classified with one? Indeed, how common are false-positive classifications?" "How likely is it that people struggling with various forms of social, economic, and environmental injustice and those engaged in social action to address them might be identified as 'significantly disturbed' or 'mentally disordered' and assigned a diagnosis?"

We might also ask, "What biological evidence supports the existence (that is, the validity) of the nearly 300 mental disorders listed in the *DSM-5*?" "Do people with a particular mental disorder reflect 'chemical imbalances' that differ from the 'chemical imbalances' present in those without any disorder?" "Are there genetic, blood, urine, or electronic scanning tests than can confirm or reject the judgments of mental health providers who assign classifications on the basis of observed or reported disturbances? If not, how can these mental disorders be considered valid, medical conditions?"

We might also ask about the variability within each diagnosis. In the *DSM* system, some classifications may be assigned when a certain proportion of individual symptoms (for example, any 5 of 9) within the cluster of symptoms that comprise a mental disorder are observed or reported. As a result, people who receive an identical diagnosis may experience or exhibit quite different arrays of symptoms. For example, two 12-year-old children, Juan and John, are each assigned a *DSM-5* diagnosis of conduct disorder (312.81). The criteria for that particular mental disorder includes evidence of "A repetitive and persistent pattern of behavior in which the basic rights of others or major age-appropriate societal norms or rules are violated, as manifested by the presence of at least three of . . . 15 criteria in the past 12 months . . . with at least one criterion present in the past 6 months" (American Psychiatric Association, 2013, p. 469). Juan meets these three criteria: He (1) "Often stays out at night despite parental prohibitions," (2) "Has run away from home overnight at least twice . . . or once without returning for a lengthy period," and (3) "Is often truant from school" (American Psychiatric Association, 2013, p. 470). John reflects these three criteria: He (1) "Often bullies, threatens, or intimidates others," (2) "Often initiates physical fights," and (3) "Has used a weapon that can cause serious physical harm to others" (American Psychiatric Association, 2013, p. 469).

Social workers might reasonably challenge the credibility of the diagnosis if two children, each reflecting such different behaviors, can both be legitimately classified with conduct disorder. We might also wonder if, in fact, these particular behaviors might be better explained in social and behavioral terms rather than as a mental disorder, psychiatric illness, or medical condition.

Social workers might also ask about the inter-rater reliability correlation or coefficient of agreement for various disorders. In other words, "What are the chances that two or more providers will assign the same psychiatric diagnosis when presented with the same information?"

Cohen's kappa[2] is typically used in studies of inter-rater reliability. A kappa of 1 indicates 100 percent or perfect agreement among all providers, and a kappa of 0 indicates the amount of agreement expected on the basis of random chance alone. When Spitzer and Fleiss (1974) first used Cohen's kappa to assess inter-rater reliability in studies of psychiatric diagnosis, they considered a kappa equal to or greater than 0.90 as indicative of an excellent level of reliability; those between 0.70 and 0.90 as good; and those less than 0.70 as unacceptable. Interestingly, the kappa values used in the *DSM-5* field trials were much more lenient. For the *DSM-5*, a kappa value equal to or greater than 0.80 was considered excellent; values between 0.60 and 0.79 were very good; those between 0.40 and 0.59 were good; values between 0.20 and 0.39 were questionable; and those less than 0.20 were unacceptable (Vanheule et al., 2014). Social workers might ask, "Why did the American Psychiatric Association choose to change what constitutes unacceptable reliability from less than 0.70 to less than 0.20?"

Vanheule and colleagues (2014) conclude that:

> reliabilities in the year 2013 are not better than those observed in 1974, and actually remain in the same range. While some disorders are now diagnosed more reliably (e.g. psychophysiological reaction/complex somatic disorder), the reverse is true of other conditions (e.g. alcoholism/ alcohol use disorder). Moreover, the diagnosis of mood/affective disorders remains a big concern. (2014, p. 313)

Concerns about the credibility and reliability of the *DSM* classification are amplified by questions about conflicts of interest. The massive amounts of money directly or indirectly associated with the health care, pharmaceutical, and health insurance industries may influence the appearance, reformulation, and disappearance of particular disorders in the *DSM*. Indeed, some investigators have identified financial conflicts of interest associated with the identification and incorporation of *DSM* disorders for which pharmaceutical drugs may be produced and marketed, and medical and psychiatric treatments prescribed (Cosgrove, 2011; Cosgrove & Krimsky, 2012; Cosgrove, Krimsky, Vijayaraghavan, & Schneider, 2006; Wakefield, 2012).

---

[2] Cohen's kappa is calculated through the formula $(p_o - p_c)/(1 - p_c)$. The chance proportion (p_c) of agreement is subtracted from the observed proportion (p_o) of agreement and the result divided by $(1 - p_c)$. Let's say, for example, multiple mental health providers in possession of the same information about a potential patient, arrive at the same diagnosis some 55% of the time. However, given the number of providers, we can expect that such agreement will occur 20% of the time on the basis of random chance alone. We apply the formula as follows: $(0.55 - 0.20)/(1 - 0.20)$ to obtain a Cohen's kappa of 0.44. In other words, after accounting for agreement due to random chance, less than one-half of the providers agree on the diagnosis.

Given our person-in-environment perspective, many social workers challenge the medicalization of social problems and common life challenges, and their description as psychiatric illnesses. By focusing so much on individuals' mental status and functioning, we may underestimate or entirely neglect the relevance of social and physical environments as causal factors as well as the potential locus of solutions. Rather than viewing psychosocial problems as at least partly a result of social, economic, or environmental injustice, they become defined in individual terms as mental disorders. As the range of psychiatric classifications increases and the number of people diagnosed with various mental disorders grows, we can anticipate that the health care–related professions and the medical and pharmaceutical industries will expand accordingly (Caplan, 2012, Apr. 27; Kirk & Kutchins, 1992; Kutchins & Kirk, 1997).

According to the *DSM-5*, "Mental disorders are usually associated with significant distress or disability in social, occupational, or other important activities" (American Psychiatric Association, 2013, p. 20). Despite this acknowledgment, the primary focus in the *DSM* system remains on the individual—not on the person-in-environment and certainly not on the social and physical environment. The person receives the diagnosis; the situation does not. Corrupt economic and political systems, racism and sexism, and other forms of systemic social and environmental injustice are not recognized as distressed, disordered, or disabled.

The *DSM-5* does contain cautionary statements such as the following:

An expectable or culturally approved response to a common stressor or loss, such as the death of a loved one, is not a mental disorder. Socially deviant behavior (e.g., political, religious, or sexual) and conflicts that are primarily between the individual and society are not mental disorders unless the deviance or conflict results from a dysfunction in the individual, as described above. (American Psychiatric Association, 2013, p. 20)

Despite these warnings, symptoms associated with many mental disorders listed in the *DSM-5* classification manual are clearly linked to social, economic, and cultural circumstances. Mental disorders cannot all be explained as brain defects or deficits within individual people. Indeed, many symptoms appear to be entirely "normal" reactions to "abnormal" situations. Should feelings of sadness following the death of a loved one be viewed as symptoms of a mental disorder? Should extreme stress and agitation following exposure to violence? Should anger and outrage at oppression and discrimination?

Despite its flaws and limitations, many social workers will continue to use the *DSM-5* to secure reimbursement for mental health services. Of course, the *DSM* system is not all "bad." There are potential benefits as well. Like other kinds of labels, *DSM* classifications are used in the conduct of research studies about the treatment of individuals experiencing debilitating personal symptoms that result from or relate to social or environmental conditions. For example, many people who suffer from acute stress disorder or posttraumatic stress disorder were affected by wartime conflict, violent assault, or by natural and human-made crises and disasters. Many who experience depressive symptoms have routinely been exposed to prejudice, discrimination, and covert and overt forms of oppression. Just as social workers use various keywords to search for and discover information and guidelines for service to victims and perpetrators of child sex abuse and other social and environmental assaults, we can use *DSM* classifications as keywords to locate relevant research studies about individual clients' personal issues, symptoms, and sometimes effective interventions.

In addition, the *DSM-5* (American Psychiatric Association, 2013) may be less complicated to use than the *DSM-IV-TR* (American Psychiatric Association, 2000a). The multi-axial system has been replaced, and both mental disorders and physical conditions or illnesses can be identified on a single dimension. Relevant information about psychosocial, contextual, and environmental factors may be presented in narrative descriptions. Level of functioning or degree of overall disability may also be addressed.

In the previous edition, the *DSM-IV-TR*, mental disorders and "other conditions that may be the focus of attention" were recorded on Axis I. Personality disorders and forms of "mental retardation" appeared on Axis II (American Psychiatric Association, 2000a, p. 27). General medical conditions were recorded on Axis III. "Psychosocial and Environmental Problems" were recorded on Axis IV and could be organized according to several subcategories: problems with primary support group, problems related to the social environment, educational problems, occupational problems, housing problems, economic problems, problems with access to health care services, problems related to interaction with the legal system/crime, and other psychosocial and environmental problems (American Psychiatric Association, 2000a, p. 32). A "Global Assessment of Functioning" (GAF) scale score was entered on Axis V. The GAF was used to rate a person's "psychological, social, and occupational functioning on a hypothetical continuum of mental health—illness" (American Psychiatric Association, 2000a, p. 34).

Some social workers hoping to maintain a person-in-environment perspective when using the *DSM-5* are disappointed by the loss of Axis IV. In the *DSM-IV-TR*, Axis IV could be used to identify Psychosocial and Environmental Problems that affect the person or contribute to distress. However, the *DSM-5* does incorporate several *ICD-10-CM* classifications under the category of "Other Conditions That May Be a Focus of Clinical Attention." According to the American Psychiatric Association, these "other conditions" should not be viewed as "mental disorders" (American Psychiatric Association, 2013, p. 715). Rather, they involve circumstances, issues, and phenomena that may be considered within the following general categories:[3]

- Adult and child abuse, neglect, and other maltreatment (T74, T76);
- Education and literacy (Z55);
- Employment and unemployment (Z56);
- Occupational exposure to risk factors (Z57);
- Housing and economic circumstances (Z59);
- Social environment (Z60);
- Upbringing (Z62);
- Primary support group, including family circumstances (Z63);
- Certain psychosocial circumstances (Z64);
- Other psychosocial circumstances (Z65);
- Mental health services for victim and perpetrator of abuse (Z69); and
- Counseling related to sexual attitude, behavior, and orientation (Z70). (National Center for Health Statistics, 2015)[4]

Instead of the Axis V: Global Assessment of Functioning scale (incorporated within the *DSM-IV-TR*), social workers using the *DSM-5* may adopt the World Health Organization Disability Assessment Schedule (WHODAS 2.0) (World Health Organization, 2010a, 2010b) to appraise overall functioning and ability. The WHODAS was developed to complement the *International Classification of Functioning, Disability, and Health* (ICF) (World Health Organization, 2001) and the *International Classification of Functioning, Disability, and Health: Children and Youth Version*

---

[3] More specific conditions are subsumed under each of these categories.

[4] Note that the *DSM-5* uses the *ICD-10-CM* numerical codes. Most of the "Other Conditions That May Be a Focus of Clinical Attention" involve "Z-Codes." However, the terminology in the *DSM-5* may differ from that in the *ICD-10-CM*. For example, in the *DSM-5*, the Z62.820 code refers to a "Parent–Child Relational Problem." In the *ICD-10-CM*, the same code indicates a "Parent–Biological Child Conflict." Social workers in mental health services should probably have access to both classification systems.

(ICF-CY) (World Health Organization, 2007). The **WHODAS 2.0** comes in 12- and 36-item forms and addresses six "**Domains of Functioning**." These include:

- Cognition—understanding & communicating
- Mobility—moving & getting around
- Self-care—hygiene, dressing, eating & staying alone
- Getting along—interacting with other people
- Life activities—domestic responsibilities, leisure, work & school
- Participation—joining in community activities. (World Health Organization, 2010b, para. 2)

Ratings on these dimensions may be of use to clients and social workers alike. A self-administered instrument, people appraise themselves. Such active participation in the assessment process represents a genuine advantage of the WHODAS 2.0 over the GAF scoring scale—which was based on professionals' observations and sometimes subjective impressions.

To illustrate how the *DSM-5* may be applied, consider the following, fictionalized example of 13-year-old Daniella Washington. Two weeks earlier, Daniella witnessed the police shooting of her unarmed 10-year-old brother. Wounded, he fell and began to bleed. She rushed to his side. Police used racial epithets as they pulled her away from her brother, pushed her to the ground, and cuffed her hands behind her back. Then, they locked her in a patrol car until other officers and an ambulance arrived. She suffered abrasions and bruises to her face, arms, and wrists but was not offered nor provided medical attention. Her brother, however, was transported to a hospital for emergency care. Several days later, he died from the gunshot wounds.

Three weeks later, the family had yet to receive the results of an internal police investigation into the incident. Frustrated, the family filed formal complaints with the city and the federal government about the killing of their unarmed son. Although all members of the family remain grief-stricken, angry, and sleepless, Daniella appears more distraught than others. Her mother reports that her daughter is now agitated, highly emotional, and often enraged. She frequently curses the police, white people, and God—even though she had previously been extremely devout and highly religious. She has not attended church services since her brother's death and no longer prays.

If you served as a social worker in a mental health center and interviewed Daniella, you might consider a *DSM-5* mental classification of *acute stress disorder* 308.3 (F43.0).[5] Daniella meets the diagnostic criteria because (A) she directly witnessed the violent death of a close family member; (B) she experiences at least 9 of 14 relevant symptoms; (C) the symptoms have occurred between 3 days and 1 month after witnessing her brother's death; (D) she experiences "clinically significant distress or impairment in social . . . or other important areas of functioning"; and (E) the symptoms do not result from substance use, "another medical condition," or a "brief psychotic disorder" (American Psychiatric Association, 2013). The pertinent symptoms (B) include:

1. Recurrent, involuntary, and intrusive distressing memories of the traumatic event(s).
2. Recurrent distressing dreams in which the content and/or affect of the dream are related to the event(s).
3. Dissociative reactions (e.g., flashbacks) in which the individual feels or acts as if the traumatic event(s) were recurring.
4. Intense or prolonged psychological distress or marked physiological reactions in response to internal or external cues that symbolize or resemble an aspect of the traumatic event(s).

---

[5] The *DSM-5* classification code for acute stress disorder is 308.3. The *ICD-10-CM* code for acute stress reaction is F43.0.

5. Persistent inability to experience positive emotions (e.g., inability to experience happiness, satisfaction, or loving feelings).

6. An altered sense of the reality of one's surroundings or oneself (e.g., seeing oneself from another's perspective, being in a daze, time slowing).

7. Inability to remember an important aspect of the traumatic event(s) (typically due to dissociative amnesia and not to other factors such as head injury, alcohol, or drugs).

8. Efforts to avoid distressing memories, thoughts, or feelings about or closely associated with the traumatic event(s).

9. Efforts to avoid external reminders (people, places, conversations, activities, objects, situations) that arouse distressing memories, thoughts, or feelings about or closely associated with the traumatic event(s).

10. Sleep disturbance (e.g., difficulty falling or staying asleep, restless sleep).

11. Irritable behavior and angry outbursts (with little or no provocation), typically expressed as verbal or physical aggression toward people or objects.

12. Hypervigilance.

13. Problems with concentration.

14. Exaggerated startle response. (American Psychiatric Association, 2013, p. 281)

Daniella meets many of the 14 listed criteria for *acute stress disorder*—a *DSM-5* mental disorder. However, she also reflects aspects of "Other Conditions That May Be a Focus of Clinical Attention." For example, Daniella appears to be struggling with "distressing experiences that involve loss or questioning of faith . . . or questioning of spiritual values" (American Psychiatric Association, 2013, p. 725). As a consequence, the category *Religious or Spiritual Problem* (Z65.8) might apply. If Daniella's coercive confinement by police was unjustified and illegal, the classification *Victim of Crime* (Z65.4) might be warranted. Indeed, her detention might be considered a form of *Child Physical Abuse* (T74.12XA) in that she experienced a "nonaccidental physical injury" at the hands of police officers who, as public servants, were at least partly responsible for her safety. "Such injury is considered abuse regardless of whether the caregiver intended to hurt the child" (American Psychiatric Association, 2013, p. 717).

As African Americans, she and her brother could also be *Targets of Adverse Discrimination or Persecution* (Z60.5). This classification may apply "when there is perceived or experienced discrimination against or persecution of the individual based on his or her membership (or perceived membership) in a specific category. Typically, such categories include gender or gender identity, race, ethnicity, religion, sexual orientation, country of origin, political beliefs, disability status, caste, social status, weight, and physical appearance" (American Psychiatric Association, 2013, pp. 724–275).

As a social worker using the *DSM-5*, you might include one or more of these "other conditions" in the classification process. They may reflect some of the social and environmental factors that affect Daniella. Indeed, they may help in generating both explanatory and change-oriented hypotheses. In addition, some aspects could become specific targets for intervention. As Luhrmann (2015, Jan. 17) suggests, "social experience plays a significant role in who becomes mentally ill, when they fall ill and how their illness unfolds. We should view illness as caused not only by brain deficits but also by abuse, deprivation and inequality, which alter the way brains behave. Illness thus requires social interventions, not just pharmacological ones" (para. 12).

As an alternative or supplement to the *DSM*, and *ICD* approaches, social workers may also consider the Person-in-Environment (PIE) classification system (Karls & O'Keefe, 2008; Karls & Wandrei, 1994; Williams, Karls, & Wandrei, 1989). The *PIE* approach gives practitioners, presumably with the input and participation of clients, an opportunity to classify or code problems within the following dimensions or factors (Karls & O'Keefe, 2008, p. 1):

- Factor I: Social Functioning Problems: type, severity, duration, coping ability, and strengths
- Factor II: Environmental Problems: severity, duration, and resources or strengths
- Factor III: Mental Health Problems and Strengths
- Factor IV: Physical Health Problems and Strengths

Problems in *Factor I—Social Functioning* (for example, family roles, other interpersonal roles, occupational roles, special life situation roles) may be identified and then classified and coded by type (for example, power conflict, ambivalence, obligation/responsibility, dependency, loss, isolation, oppression, mixed, other) as well as severity, duration, coping ability, and strengths (Karls & O'Keefe, 2008).

Social workers may then use the classifications within the *Factor II: Environmental Problems* dimension to identify those situational conditions that affect or are affected by the identified problems in social role functioning (Factor I). Environmental problems are categorized according to the following major systems (Karls & O'Keefe, 2008, p. 17):

1. Basic Needs System
2. Education and Training System
3. Judicial and Legal System
4. Health, Safety, and Social Services System
5. Voluntary Association System
6. Affectional Support System

Each of these major systems contains problem areas (for example, food/nutrition, shelter, employment, economic resources, transportation, and discrimination) and each problem area contains a list of specific problems. For example, the discrimination problem area includes discrimination on the basis of age, ethnicity, color, language, religion, gender, sexual orientation, lifestyle, noncitizen status, veteran status, dependency, disability, marital status, body size, political affiliation, and other. Once an environmental condition or problem has been identified, its severity, duration, and strengths index are determined and coded (Karls & O'Keefe, 2008).

Factor III: Mental Health Problems and Strengths may be presented through narrative descriptions or coded using the *DSM-5* or the *ICD-10-CM* classification systems. *Factor IV: Physical Health Problems and Strengths* may also be described or coded using the *ICD-10-CM* system. Notice that strengths as well as problems may be identified and described.

The *PIE* classification system has generated considerable interest among social work academicians and researchers. Social work practitioners, however, appear to be less intrigued. Many may not be aware of the system, and others, especially those in health and mental health settings, may not see the value of additional classification beyond the *DSM* and *ICD* systems. The potential utility of the *PIE* classification scheme may become apparent only in years to come, when epidemiological and demographic studies establish the incidence and prevalence rates of various problems involving social role functioning and environmental conditions. Like the *DSM*, the *PIE* classification system is primarily problem focused in nature. To be truly useful to helping professionals and consumers, each problem classification or disorder must reflect both validity and reliability, and effective interventions for each must be established.

In using the *DSM-5* or the *ICD-10-CM*, recognize that helping professionals without medical licenses may not practice medicine. In some contexts, social workers are not legally permitted to "diagnose" medical conditions. If you include medical diagnoses in client records or medical insurance claims, identify the licensed MD who assigned them or indicate that they are "self-reported" by the client. In some locales, certain helping professionals are also legally prohibited from assigning *DSM* classifications. Check the laws in your area. Even when social workers are legally authorized to use the *DSM*, let's propose classifications in a tentative, provisional fashion—as hypotheses for consideration. In that way, we avoid excessive focus on individual pathology and balance our attention to the person with equal or greater attention to the situation. In other words, we seek to maintain our person-in-environment perspective.

In addition to classification manuals such as the *DSM* and the *PIE* systems, **Rapid Assessment Instruments (RAIs)** of various kinds may complement the assessment process and sometimes serve as potential indicators or measures of progress (Corcoran & Fischer, 2013a, 2013b; Hudson, 1982; Rush Jr., First, & Blacker, 2008; Schutte & Malouff, 1995). In the case of substance abuse issues, instruments such as the CAGE Screening Test for Alcohol Dependence (Ewing, 1984), the Michigan Alcoholism Screening Test (MAST) (Selzer, 1971; Selzer, Vinokur, & van Rooijen, 1975), or the Drug Abuse Screening Test (Skinner, 1982), in conjunction with other information, can be used to estimate if a client might be physically addicted, perhaps indicating a need for detoxification in a hospital setting. Judgments of this nature and magnitude require perspective, objectivity, and well-developed critical thinking skills. A great deal of lifelong learning is also required because of continuing advances in the scientific knowledge on which assessment criteria are based.

Indeed, during the last decade or two, many helping professionals have become concerned that exclusive or excessive focus on problems may interfere with clients' motivation and impede progress toward resolution. Several scholars (De Jong & Berg, 2002; de Shazer, 1988; de Shazer et al., 1986; Miller, Hubble, & Duncan, 1996) have questioned the assumption that detailed exploration of clients' personal and social histories and in-depth understanding of the contributing causes of psychosocial problems are necessary for effective resolution of those problems. Partly because of these concerns, professional helpers have become extremely interested in concepts and perspectives related to strengths, capacities, protective factors, assets, resiliencies, and solutions.

Dozens of books, book chapters, and journal articles have been published on the topic of strengths in social work practice (Chapin, 2007; Cowger, 1994, 1996; Dybicz, 2011; Gilgun, 2004a, 2004b; Greene & Lee, 2011; Rapp & Goscha, 2006; Saleebey, 2009). Indeed, Saleebey (2001) advocates for the development of a diagnostic strengths manual to counterbalance the symptom perspective reflected in the American Psychiatric Association's *DSM* classification system.

Locating, enhancing, and promoting resilience and hardiness have generated similar interest (Fraser et al., 1999; Gilgun, 2005; Kamya, 2000; Maddi, Wadhwa, & Haier, 1996; Peters, Leadbeater, & McMahon, 2005; Smokowski, 1998; Walsh, 2006; Whittaker, 2001), as has solution-focused or solution-oriented practice (Baker & Steiner, 1996; Berg & De Jong, 1996; Berg & Reuss, 1998; De Jong & Berg, 2002; Greene & Lee, 2011; Lee, 1997; Mattaini & Thyer, 1996; Miller et al., 1996; O'Connell, 2005; Sundman, 1997). The positive psychology initiative represents an analogous trend. Stimulated initially by Martin Seligman (2002, 2011), virtues and strengths are emerging in psychology as a focus for both research and practice. Numerous publications reflect this phenomenon (Carr, 2003; Compton, 2004; Csikszentmihalyi & Csikszentmihalyi, 2006; Frisch, 2005; Linley, Joseph, & Seligman, 2004; Ong & Dulmen, 2006; Peterson, 2006; Peterson & Seligman, 2004; Seligman & Csikszentmihalyi, 2000; Snyder & Lopez, 2005). In addition, Peterson and Seligman (2004) offer a classification handbook of character virtues and strengths. They provide an overall list of 24 strengths that support the following six **character virtues** (pp. 29–30):

1. **Wisdom and knowledge**—cognitive strengths that entail the acquisition and use of knowledge
2. **Courage**—emotional strengths that involve the exercise of will to accomplish goals in the face of opposition, external or internal

    manity—interpersonal strengths that involve tending and befriending others
    tice—civic strengths that underlie healthy community life

5. **...mperance**—strengths that protect against excess
6. **Transcendence**—strengths that forge connections to the larger universe and provide meaning

Hardly a threat to the dominance of the *DSM* among helping professionals, this effort to classify virtues and strengths nonetheless represents a significant opportunity to acknowledge positive aspects of human behavior and experience. The strengths reflected in these virtues may represent protective or resilience factors of relevance to many people, problems, and aspirations.

Another theme or trend in contemporary psychosocial services involves the assessment and enhancement of motivation, particularly as it relates to the **Transtheoretical Model (TTM)** or "stages of change" perspective (Miller & Rollnick, 2002; Prochaska, 1999; Prochaska & Norcross, 2007; Prochaska et al., 1994; Prochaska & Velicera, 1998; Rollnick & Miller, 1995). According to the TTM, long-term change tends to proceed in a more or less sequential five-stage fashion (Prochaska, 1999):

1. Precontemplation
2. Contemplation
3. Preparation
4. Action
5. Maintenance

Prochaska and Norcross (2007) suggest that people who make significant changes in their behavior proceed through all stages of the Transtheoretical Model (TTM). Although the process may sometimes be spiral rather than linear in nature, they conclude that people who make durable change eventually address each stage (Norcross, Loberg, & Norcross, 2012; Prochaska, Norcross, & DiClemente, 2013).

Precontemplation is the first TTM stage of change. People in this stage tend to reflect ambivalence, uncertainty, disinterest, or denial. For example, suppose you had agreed to help an unemployed, paraplegic client find a job. Your client is highly motivated and has already taken numerous steps. He's in the action stage. When you first contact a prospective employer who has never employed someone who uses a wheelchair, you might anticipate a precontemplative response. Despite the Americans with Disabilities Act, the employer could be quite reluctant to take the request seriously. As a social worker, your first step toward change might be to help the employer consider the idea of moving toward the next stage—contemplation.

Contemplation is the second stage of the change process. People in this stage tend to engage in data collection, reflection, and analysis. The possibility of change is considered. There may even be a general sense of direction or a vague plan. Let's return to the situation of your paraplegic client (action stage) and the "reluctant employer." Suppose you supply the employer with scholarly papers that outline the benefits of a diverse workforce and describe businesses that became successful after employing disabled workers. When the "precontemplative employer" reads those materials and entertains the idea of hiring a person affected by a spinal cord injury, you might begin to see signs of contemplation and reflection. Unfortunately, thinking about change in general terms does not usually produce it. In trying to serve your client, you encourage the employer toward the preparation stage.

Preparation is the third stage of change. The transition from contemplation to preparation is associated with at least two notable shifts in thinking. First, there is a significant increase in thinking about solutions and resolutions, accompanied by a decrease in contemplation about the problem, issue, or need. Second, thoughts about the future increasingly replace those about the past and present. "The end of the contemplation stage is a time of anticipation, activity, anxiety, and excitement" (Prochaska et al., 1994, p. 43). Plan making characterizes the onset of the preparation stage. People might outline specific steps and set short-term dates. Importantly, they share with others and publicly "announce" their intent to change. You would notice signs of preparation when the "contemplative" employer tells colleagues, "We will hire at least one disabled worker this month and at least one more each month for the next 6 months." However, even extremely well-conceived plans do not automatically lead to change. Change requires action of some kind.

Action, the fourth stage, is characterized by motivation, purposefulness, activity, and optimism. You notice actual differences in the person, the situation, or aspects of both. Indeed, the most long-lasting change tends to occur when action involves several dimensions of the person and the environment. However, the activities of this stage may not lead to durable change. The intensity may fade, sometimes remarkably quickly, and change-related activities may not continue. The action stage can be short-lived and disappointing. Despite the public announcements, the plans, and the flurry of initial activity, your client may not be hired or, if he is, additional disabled workers may not become employed. "Many people . . . erroneously equate action with change, overlooking not only the critical work that prepares people for successful action but the equally important (and often more challenging) efforts to maintain the changes following action" (Prochaska et al., 1994, p. 44).

Maintenance is the fifth stage in the change process. In some ways, it represents the greatest challenge of all. Requiring ongoing motivation, commitment, stamina, persistence, and follow-through, maintenance lacks the excitement of the preparation stage and the intensity of the action stage. Maintaining lasting change usually requires ongoing, detailed attention to small steps on a day-to-day and week-to-week basis. Human systems tend to reflect powerful forces of inertia that return them to traditional behaviors and processes. Without continuous attention and consistent routines designed to maintain change, you may anticipate a return to previously established patterns. The recently "enlightened employer," who appears so motivated and "ready" to diversify the workforce, can easily become distracted by unrelated problems and challenges, and fail to monitor progress on a day-to-day basis. The person leading the effort to employ disabled workers may leave the company or be transferred to another area. There may be a downturn in the economy. When there is a surplus of applicants, workforce diversification may not seem as important or attractive as it does when a scarcity of dependable workers exists. Unless you persistently attend to maintenance, change is unlikely to last. However, if maintenance activities continue, the potency of the older forces of inertia gradually decreases as the once-new changes become part of the established and traditional routine, reflecting their own forces of inertia. At that point, they would be quite difficult to change (Prochaska et al., 1994).

West (2005) and others have challenged the TTM stages of change on theoretical and empirical grounds. Indeed, it is not certain that all people proceed through all five "stages," and the descriptions of the stages are far from precise. These issues call for further development and additional research. Nonetheless, the TTM represents a potentially useful addition to the array of conceptual models available to social workers and clients in their efforts to understand how change occurs, and to incorporate such understanding in their plans.

In addition to the TTM, social workers may be interested in aspects of the Health Belief Model (Applewhite, 1996; Becker, 1974; Harrison, Mullen, & Green, 1992; Rosenstock, 1990; Rosenstock, Strecher, & Becker, 1994; Rosenstock, Strecher, & Becker, 1988), the Theory of Reasoned Action (TRA) and its successor the Theory of Planned Behavior (TPB) (Ajzen, 1991; Ajzen & Fishbein, 1980; Albarracin, Johnson, Fishbein, & Muellerleile, 2001; Fishbein & Middlestadt, 1989; Fishbein, Middlestadt, & Hitchcock, 1994), and "self-efficacy" (Bandura, 1977, 1992, 1995a, 1997, 1995b;

Holden, 1991; Schwarzer, 1992; Schwarzer & Fuchs, 1995) to help us and our clients consider aspects of the change process that relate to psychosocial factors. As social workers know, motivation to change is not the exclusive result of personal qualities. Situational factors also affect clients' expectations about eventual outcomes as well as their readiness to take action.

Failure to consider motivational dimensions may lead social workers to presume that once clients discuss an issue, they are necessarily ready to make changes. Given social workers' long-standing belief in "starting where the client is," we recognize that people often experience conflicting feelings about problems, and especially about steps needed to resolve them. Furthermore, when clients experience multiple problems, their degree of motivation to address one problem may differ substantially from that of another. When we fail to incorporate clients' readiness, motivation, and beliefs and expectations regarding change, we may inadvertently obstruct rather than enhance problem resolution. Clearly, many clients are not "ready" or "motivated" to make changes when they first meet with a social worker. In such cases, we should respect our clients "where they are" rather than where we might prefer them to be.

Different levels of readiness and motivation call for different helping activities—ones that "match" the stage of change. For example, people who are "preparing to change" typically experience marginal benefit from additional exploration into historical events or examination of the problems of concern. They are ready to consider potential solutions and begin the process of formulating plans. Helping them to develop plans and identify steps is likely to match their stage of change and contribute to goal-oriented action.

Conversely, people who are only beginning to contemplate the possibility and value of change would probably find examination of relevant intervention strategies premature and perhaps even insulting. Helping them to explore problems or issues and facilitating discussion about the pros and cons associated with change would better match their level of readiness.

Recognition of the stages of change helps social workers appreciate clients' readiness, motivation, beliefs, and expectations. Focusing on psychological factors may help clients assume greater responsibility for addressing the issues they identify. Such processes reflect a traditional social work theme of "helping clients to help themselves." Let's remember, however, to attend to situational and environmental factors as well as the personal. What happens "outside" the person is often much more of a problem than what occurs "inside." Indeed, social workers frequently take social or political action with or on behalf of clients to effect changes in the environment. In such circumstances, our own motivation becomes highly relevant to the change process. By adopting a person-in-environment perspective, social workers attend to situational and contextual factors, as well as to personal and psychological factors, that relate to client-identified issues. Of course, motivation is not limited to clients and social workers. Other people and social systems in the "environment" also reflect varying degrees of readiness.

Interestingly, more than 60 years ago, leading social work scholars in the School of Social Service at the University of Chicago proposed a triadic model of assessment that included *motivation*, *capacity*, and *opportunity* (Ripple, 1955; Ripple & Alexander, 1956; Ripple, Alexander, & Polemis, 1964). Using this framework (Figure 10.2), social workers and clients may consider ways and means to understand issues and pursue goals by assessing and intervening within these intersecting and interacting dimensions of the person-in-environment.

As social workers, we resist the tendency to view motivation, capacity, or opportunity as residing exclusively or even primarily within individuals. *Motivation* may be as much a characteristic of a society or a culture as it is for a person. Therefore, let's consider both the personal and the environmental aspects of motivation. *Capacity* also involves both dimensions. Some environments have limited capacity to feed, employ, educate, or protect their populations. In such contexts, even those individuals with great motivation and enormous potential would be unlikely to reach their

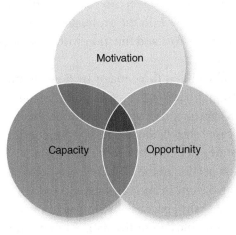

FIGURE 10.2   The University of Chicago Motivation-Capacity-Opportunity Model

aspirations. However, just as people can strengthen their personal abilities and enlarge their individual capacities, social assets and environmental capacities can also grow and expand to better meet human wants and needs.

Finally, social workers view *opportunity* as multidimensional as well. Just as people think critically and creatively to open their minds and dramatically increase the array of potential options, environments also reflect different kinds, degrees, or levels of opportunity. Indeed, some environments reflect enormous capacity but severely limit opportunities for political, economic, ideological, or cultural reasons.

In contemporary practice, social workers may apply the stages of change model and various other assessment perspectives. Let's recognize, however, that knowledge is increasing at an exponential rate and the conceptual tools, classification systems, and theoretical perspectives used today will probably change within a few years as researchers advance our scientific knowledge.

Approach assessment processes as professional rather than technical endeavors, as collaborative rather than singular undertakings, and as dynamic rather than static processes. Avoid "top-down" or bureaucratic approaches. Whenever possible, adopt an interactional style that reflects the core facilitative conditions of empathy, respect, and genuineness. Use professional knowledge and judgment to determine the particular nature and style of assessment. Different clients and circumstances call for different assessment processes. The unique nature of each person-issue-situation virtually requires certain adaptations or innovations. When possible, incorporate valid and reliable assessment instruments. However, be sure to consider their cultural implications and other potential limitations. Regularly seek feedback and encourage clients to participate with you in formulating assessments. When people genuinely collaborate in the assessment experience, their sense of empowerment and self-efficacy tends to grow and their motivation for change increases.

Although social work assessments are ongoing processes rather than finished products, formal records are usually required. Records may be handwritten, digitally recorded, or word-processed. Keep in mind, however, that assessments change, sometimes frequently and occasionally dramatically, during work with or on behalf of our clients. Also remember to exercise caution with terminology that may unnecessarily label or stigmatize people.

Assessment records serve many purposes. Documents may be organized or formatted in ent ways in accord with various organizational schemes. For learning purposes, we propose prehensive integrated format that could be used in several, but certainly not all, social work Indeed, you will probably discover that some sections of the Description, Assessment, and

(DAC) outline are irrelevant for some clients or certain practice settings. In addition, recognize that numerous other formats are readily accessible in the professional literature. Some may be especially applicable to your particular social work role and function with specific population groups or in assessing specific problems of concern.

As its title suggests, the DAC includes three major sections. First, you organize the information gained through the exploration process into a description. Second, you translate the ideas and hypotheses concerning plausible causes and potential solutions that you and the client generated into a tentative assessment and case formulation. Third, you summarize the agreement about goals and plans that you and the client negotiated into a service contract.[6]

Completion of the description portion of the DAC helps to organize a great deal of information about a client system, the situational context, and the issues of concern. The assessment section contains information that you and the client generate through analysis, synthesis, and the formulation of questions or hypotheses concerning the descriptive data. At first glance, the DAC may appear exhaustingly inclusive. It certainly does include a large array of sections. However, several of these are obviously inappropriate for work with many clients, certain issues, and various settings. When that is so, simply ignore irrelevant sections and adapt the format of the DAC to fit the unique needs and functions of your specific social work setting. Realize that numerous alternate schemes are available. Ultimately, in consultation with your supervisors and agency colleagues, you determine the utility of any format for the particular needs and circumstances of your social work practice.

Identifying Issues

On occasion, social workers may identify needs, problems, or other issues that clients do not. Sometimes, you must assume primary responsibility for **identifying issues** and perhaps even for establishing goals. For instance, when the situation is immediately life threatening (for example, a client may be suicidal, homicidal, psychotic, unconscious, or heavily intoxicated), when clients must meet with you on an involuntary basis (for example, a client may be required to attend counseling sessions or face felony charges), or when they remain unwilling or unable to share their views, you may identify at least some of the issues and goals. Once you do so, however, seek feedback so that clients may suggest other issues or goals, or propose modifications.

Even when the situation is neither life threatening nor involuntary, you may legitimately share your professional views. Based on your observations and hypotheses, you could suggest that the client consider a different perspective or perhaps an additional problem for your work together. You may have professional knowledge or prior experience that indicates the presence of a potentially relevant issue. For example, suppose a client describes feelings of constant fatigue, difficulty sleeping, loss of appetite, decreased interest in pleasurable activities, and diminished social involvement. You would probably wonder whether the client might be mourning the loss of someone or something, be physically ill (for example, suffer from a diabetic or infectious condition), or perhaps be reacting to an event in the external world.

Social workers naturally form opinions about factors that might contribute to clients' presenting issues. Clients often appreciate it when you share these ideas. However, if and when you do so, express them in the same way you share all your professional opinions. That is, communicate them as ideas to consider rather than as indisputable facts. In addition, acknowledge clients' right to agree, disagree, or suggest alternatives. As a part of this process, routinely seek feedback concerning newly identified or redefined issues.

---

[6] We explore the description and assessment portions of the DAC in this chapter and the contract part in the next.

In practicing the skill of identifying issues, follow the format outlined here. Notice how we incorporate the skill of seeking feedback at the end.

PRACTICE FORMAT *Identifying Issues*

As we have talked about you and your situation, I have been wondering about _____

_____

_____ (*identifying needs, problems, or issues*). What do you think? Is that a concern we should consider too (*seeking feedback*)?

EXAMPLE | **Identifying Issues**

Case Situation: Lisa and Ruth have sought help to address problems in their relationship.

Client: We argue all the time. We have a knock-down drag-out fight virtually every single day. We moved in together 2 months ago. Ever since we've fought like cats and dogs. We were so great together before we decided to share the apartment. We don't hit each other, but there sure is a lot of yelling and screaming.

Worker: As we've talked about your relationship and how moving in together has affected it, I've been wondering about the question of expectations. It seems to me that moving from a dating relationship to a live-in relationship represents a very significant change—one that might leave each of you uncertain about what the other wants and needs in this new form of relationship. What do you think—could this issue of expectations be something we should also address?

EXERCISE 10-1 Identifying Issues

Refer to your earlier exchanges with Mr. K, Loretta, the S family, Mrs. F, and the "troubled agency" (see Exercises 7-8, 8-1 through 8-6, and 9-1 through 9-9) as you make the transition into the next phase and begin to use the assessing skills.

1. You have spent nearly a full hour talking with Mr. K. He has explored a number of issues, expressed feelings, and shared ideas about how and why the divorce occurred and what he might do to recover from the loss. Based on this summary of concerns and a review of exchanges that occurred earlier, write the words you would use in identifying one or more issues that Mr. K did not explicitly mention but, based upon your social work perspective, you conclude might apply to him or his situation.

2. You have spent several hours with Loretta, a homeless woman. You first arranged for her to eat a large meal. Then, you drove her to your agency office where you continued to explore issues from a person-in-environment perspective. She has mentioned a number of concerns, some aspirations, and shared thoughts and feelings about various aspects of her life and circumstances. Based on this summary of concerns and a review of exchanges that occurred earlier, write the words you would use in identifying one or more issues that Loretta did not explicitly mention but, based upon your social work perspective, you think might apply to her and her situation.

3. You have spent approximately 75 minutes talking with the seven-member blended S family. You and the family members have identified several issues: strain and conflict between Mr. S's children and Mrs. S, financial difficulties, marital distress, and most recently the threat to Mr. S's job. Based on this summary of concerns and a review of exchanges that occurred earlier, write the words you would use in identifying one or more issues that members of the S family did not explicitly mention but, based upon your social work perspective, you believe might apply to them or their situation.

4. You have now talked with Mrs. F for quite some time. You've explored several issues, including her doubts that she and her family could fit in this community, her children's apparently increasing disrespect for her and for their heritage, and, most importantly, the concern for her children's safety at school. Based on this summary of concerns and a review of exchanges that occurred earlier, write the words you would use in identifying one or more issues that Mrs. F did not explicitly mention but, based upon your social work perspective, you believe might apply to her or her family and their situation.

5. In your role as organizational consultant to a troubled social service agency, you have now met with a large group of staff, consumers, board members and other stakeholders in an attempt to identify and clarify several problem areas and then develop plans to resolve them. Numerous issues have already been identified and you have observed people as they interacted with each other during earlier meetings. Based on these issues, your observations, and a review of previous exchanges, write the words you would use in identifying one or more issues that participants did not explicitly mention but, based upon your social work perspective, you believe might apply to the agency; its personnel, structure, or administrative processes; or to current circumstances.

Sharing Hypotheses

Like many clients, social workers also have ideas and "theories"[7] about "why" problems occur and "what to do" to resolve them. Unlike many clients, however, social workers usually possess sophisticated knowledge of scientific theories and empirical research about the causes for and the risk and protective factors associated with various social issues. We also often understand the research-based evidence about the policies, programs, practices, and interventions that serve to prevent, ameliorate, or resolve social problems. Many social workers keep up-to-date with systematic reviews and meta-analyses of service effectiveness. Indeed, our professional education and our emphasis on scientific inquiry, critical thinking, and lifelong learning help to prepare us to view phenomena from theoretical lenses and perspectives that are supported by research-based evidence. Embracing a person-in-environment perspective, we also tend to generate explanatory and change-oriented hypotheses[8] that reflect multiple dimensions, including situational as well as personal factors. Some may involve aspects of the client system, elements of the environment, and, of course, facets of the issues themselves. Social workers use the skill of **sharing hypotheses** when we express our theoretical or research-based opinions about "why" or "how" issues occur and persist, and "what" to do to resolve them.

As social workers engage in assessment processes, we apply the primary critical thinking skills of *analysis* and *synthesis*. In reviewing information about the client system, the issues, and the circumstances, we attempt to understand the functional aspects and consequences of pertinent phenomena. **Functional analysis** builds upon the data collected during the exploring phase when the

---

[7] When used scientifically, the term *theory* has a much different meaning than it has in everyday life. When your neighbor says, "I have a theory about why kids today are so messed up," he is not referring to a theory in the scientific sense. Scientific theories are limited to those that (1) have not been proven false (never "falsified") and (2) are supported by an extraordinary amount of tangible, empirical evidence. Examples include the "theory of gravity" and "germ theory." When conversing with clients, social workers sometimes use the term in a colloquial rather than a scholarly manner. However, we fully recognize the difference.

[8] Later, when we explore the working and evaluating skills, we discuss "educating." Sharing explanatory and change-oriented hypotheses that have solid foundation in scientific theory and research evidence as well as critical thought and analysis represents a specific form of the skill of educating.

worker and client addressed questions about the history and evolution of the issue of concern. These include dimensions such as:

- "How did the issue begin?" "When?" "Under what circumstances?" "What seemed to trigger the initial occurrence?"
- "How has the issue changed since it first began?" "When has it been better?" "When has it been worse?"
- "How often does the issue occur now?"
- "Where and when does the issue occur?"
- "How intense, serious, or severe is the issue?"
- "How long does an episode of the issue last?"

In addition to information about the origin, development, and current status, we also organize functional data about current episodes of the issue of concern. These data emerged during the exploring phase when you and your clients addressed questions such as:

- "Where do current episodes of the issue typically take place?"
- "What happens in the situation or context just before, during, and after an episode occurs?"
- "What thoughts and images go through your mind just before, during, and after an episode of the issue?"
- "What are you doing (what actions are you taking) just before, during, and after an occurrence of the issue?"
- "What feelings or emotions do you experience just before, during, and after an occurrence of the issue?"
- "What bodily sensations[9] do you experience just before, during, and after an episode of the issue?"

Let's consider how a social worker might organize relevant data for the purpose of sharing hypotheses with John C, a client who is genuinely concerned about a current pattern of excessive drinking and wants to make changes now "before he becomes a drunk like his father."

John C reports that he drinks excessively when he feels stressed, angry, or sad when he returns home after work. He has these feelings daily and drinks each evening while sitting in his recliner watching TV. John believes that the problems began when his long-term marriage ended some 18 months earlier. In addition to feelings of distress, he frequently experiences thoughts of helplessness and hopelessness, and believes he will end up alone and miserable—like his father. He is now socially isolated, physically inactive, and disengaged from relatives and former friends.

Based on these data as gathered during exploration, a social worker might organize information about the onset, origin, development, and current status of the focal issue as described by John C. We can do so in the form of a simple table (Table 10.1).

In work with individuals alone or as members of a family or group, it may help to organize your functional analysis in tabular form (see Table 10.2). You may prepare a similar table for those times or circumstances when the focal issue "does not occur," "occurs less often, less intensely, or of shorter duration," or when clients are "coping well."

Based upon their collaborative exploration, John and the social worker recognize that John is ready and highly motivated to take action. In other words, he is in the preparation stage; he is *prepping* for change. John and the social worker plan to address the excessive drinking issue first. John wants to resolve it, and the drinking pattern is currently the most critical and urgent focal issue.

---

[9] Clients' experience of their own bodily sensations is sometime overlooked as a significant aspect of feelings and emotions, and as precursors to thoughts or actions.

TABLE 10.1	Focal Issue: Excessive Alcohol Consumption—John C Onset, Development, Current Status	
Onset	Onset 18 months ago.
Original Situational or Environmental Context	Spouse initiated divorce proceedings.
Development and Evolution	Gradual worsening. It was better for about 1 week when he and spouse attempted reconciliation. Worsened again when reconciliation failed. Does not drink at work or when away from home.
Current Situational or Environmental Context	Drinks exclusively while watching TV in his living room in the evening after work. Typically falls asleep in a recliner afterward. Socially isolated and physically inactive.
Frequency	Nightly episodes.
Intensity/Severity	7–10 ounces of vodka each episode.
Duration	Each episode lasts about 4–5 hours.

TABLE 10.2	Functional Analysis Focal Issue: Excessive Alcohol Consumption—John C			
	Before		During	After
	Distant or Historical Antecedent Factors	Proximate Antecedent Factors	Co-occurring Factors	Subsequential Factors
Situational and Environmental Factors	John C's wife divorced him 18 months earlier. His father and mother divorced when he was a child. He was often left alone much of the time because his mother had to work at minimum wage jobs to support them.	Arrives home from work in the early evening. Alone in the house. Stays home on weekends.	Sits and watches TV in large reclining chair.	Falls asleep.
Cognitive Factors (Thoughts, Beliefs, Images)	Remembers what happened during his childhood when his parents divorced. "It was awful." "I was alone all the time."	"I'm alone again." "I'll always be alone." "Life is unbearable without my wife." "When can I get a drink—it will help me feel better?" Pictures his father's bitterness and unhappiness.	"Ahh, that feels better." "It's her (my wife's) fault." "Someday she'll realize what she's done."	"I'm not an alcoholic." "I'm not going to end up like my father. This is just temporary with me."

(Continued)

TABLE 10.2 (Continued)			
	Before	**During**	**After**
Bodily Sensations	Remembers headaches, stomachaches, and tension during childhood.	Agitation, tension, tearfulness.	Senses become dulled; bodily tension seems to lessen; tears stop.	Awakens next morning feeling somewhat hung over with increasingly strong urge for an alcoholic drink.
Feelings and Emotions	Remembers feeling pity for his father and anger at his mother for initiating the divorce.	Anger, loneliness, stress, sadness.	Becomes less angry and stressed. Sadness remains but becomes less intense.	Guilt and remorse upon awakening.
Physical Behaviors	Remembers unsuccessful attempts to comfort his father—who sat every night in front of the TV drinking beer.	Enters living room.	During weekdays, he drinks vodka with tonic water continuously from about 6:00 P.M. until he falls asleep at about 11:00 P.M. On weekends, he begins drinking at about 1:00 P.M.	Loses consciousness and falls asleep.

After a thorough exploration of the problem, consideration of its developmental history and completion of a functional analysis, the social worker might share an explanatory hypothesis such as, "John, when you're alone and especially when sitting in your recliner watching TV, you seem to drink. Those things seem to go together right now—like a habit. Does that make sense to you?" When John says, "Yes," you might build upon that explanation with a change-oriented hypothesis: "John, I wonder what would happen if when you returned home after work, you intentionally did something different than sitting and watching TV? Things that are kind of opposite of what you do now; things that might start to break up the pattern and weaken the habit. For example, instead of sitting alone in front of the TV, you might take a walk, jog, or bike ride or invite a friend for coffee. Instead of watching TV you might read a book, write a letter, or do something that involves mental or physical activity. What do you think?"

Let's consider another case situation. Imagine that you are meeting with a 30-year-old woman who reports that she "feels anxious in the presence of men and wants to change that as soon as possible." Together, you consider how different dimensions of anxiety interact. After collecting information about what the client thinks, feels, senses, imagines, and does when she experiences anxiety, you track the sequence of events leading up to and following the upsetting feelings. Such a functional analysis might reveal that the anxious feelings usually occur in the presence of men who are her own age or older, are confident and appear successful, and whom she thinks are eligible and available for romantic consideration. Further analysis reveals that the client does not feel anxious when she interacts with men in business or professional contexts, men who are married or gay, or those who are much younger or less successful. You and your client might also discover that when she first notices the early signs of anxiety, she immediately begins to say certain things to herself. For example, in such contexts, she might think, "I must not become anxious right now; if I become anxious, I will not say what I want to say and I will embarrass myself." She also seems to focus intently on physiological symptoms of anxiety such as flushing, perspiration, hyperventilation, and rapid heart rate.

Analysis often leads you and the client to pinpoint critical elements from among the various pieces of information. These become cornerstones in the formulation of *explanatory hypotheses* and, subsequently, *change-oriented hypotheses* as well. Synthesis builds on what you gain from analysis. It involves assembling significant pieces of information into a coherent whole by relating them to one another and to elements of your theory, knowledge, and experience base. For example, you might hypothesize that the client's anxiety in the presence of certain men may reflect a learned pattern resulting from her experience of growing up as an only child, attending girls-only grammar and high schools, and later enrolling in a college for women only. Such an explanatory hypothesis might help address the "why" question that many clients (and many social workers) ask themselves. However, we are usually even more interested in formulating hypotheses that involve contemporary factors. Often enlightening, factors from the past are not as amenable to change as are those in the present.

Consider, for example, the case of a neighborhood community that reflects a growing crime rate, an increase in high school dropout rates, and an upward spike in food stamp (SNAP) applications. You and community members hypothesize that the recent closing of a local manufacturing plant and the resulting loss of employment contribute to these phenomena. Such a hypothesis would help to explain, in part, "why" the incidence rates of these social problems have increased. Later, based upon our explanatory hypotheses, we also seek to generate *change-oriented hypotheses* to guide our efforts to resolve problems and achieve goals. In this instance, you might hypothesize that returning jobs to the community could help to alleviate the identified social problems and contribute to community development.

Similarly, members of an African American community may begin to hypothesize that the "the system is rigged" or the "deck is stacked" due to institutionalized racism; social and economic discrimination; and political corruption. We might observe that African Americans are disproportionately underrepresented in all major influential systems: the city-county council, the mayor's office, the police department, local government, the education department and school board, the state legislature, the governor's office, state government, and banks, businesses, and corporations in the region. Based on our "rigged system" hypothesis, we may begin to generate change-oriented hypotheses to target aspects of the systemic problems of racial discrimination and political corruption. For example, to counter the gerrymandering and voter suppression practices that severely limit the number of African Americans who can vote or could possibly be elected to office, we might organize and mobilize underrepresented groups to advocate for fair, impartial, and nonpolitical redesign of political districts and to undertake "the right for all to vote" or "black votes matter too" initiatives. Similarly, to challenge discriminatory hiring practices in government and business, we might plan social media campaigns and take political, economic, and legal action.

In generating explanatory and change-oriented hypotheses, social workers use scientific inquiry and critical thinking skills. After analyzing information about the needs, problems, or other issues from a person-in-environment perspective, we take pertinent bits of information and synthesize them into coherent themes. We often use our research-based knowledge and professional expertise in generating relevant, plausible hypotheses. In doing so, however, we can never neglect or ignore others' knowledge, experience, and wisdom. Clients and other stakeholders have ideas, opinions, and theories of their own. Based as they are on firsthand experience, their contributions often add realism, practicality, and depth to both explanatory and change-oriented hypotheses.

Assessment leads to greater understanding by both worker and client. Reasonable explanatory hypotheses about how and why identified problems occur also tend to enhance motivation and encourage optimism. However, our primary purpose for assessment goes well beyond understanding, hope, and readiness. As social workers, our fundamental purpose is to help clients meet needs, resolve problems, and achieve goals.

In the case of the woman who becomes anxious in the presence of certain men, you might consider a two-part explanatory hypothesis such as the following: (1) distorted thoughts and beliefs trigger anxious feelings, and (2) an intense focus upon physiological sensations serves to exacerbate them. In other words, when our client is in the presence of an "eligible, available" man, she experiences thoughts and beliefs that have the following effects:

1. They inflate the importance of "having a romantic relationship with a man" or "being married to a man."
2. They exaggerate the significance of each moment of each encounter with any and all potential romantic partners.
3. They intensify her focus on herself (how she appears, what she says, what she does) so that she becomes highly self-conscious.
4. They increase her attention to her own physiological signs and bodily sensations of anxiety.

Such explanatory hypotheses involve contemporary rather than historical factors and naturally lead to ideas about how to resolve the problem. That is, they logically guide us toward change-oriented hypotheses for possible inclusion in a case formulation. We might hypothesize that if she learns to think and focus somewhat differently in the presence of "eligible men," she will probably experience fewer signs and symptoms of anxiety. Therefore you and the client might well consider intervention strategies designed to change (1) the distorted thoughts and beliefs she has about herself, men and relationships, and the future; and (2) the pattern of intensely focusing on interoceptive signs and symptoms of anxiety. The approach would probably also include increasing the frequency and duration of interaction with "eligible" men. Increased exposure to the anxiety-provoking stimuli (the "men") might help to desensitize her and help her to think, feel, and focus differently in their presence.

In this particular instance, we use cognitive and behavioral concepts in conjunction with our functional analysis to develop change-oriented hypotheses. These hypotheses are central to our formulation and reflect our "theory of the case." They logically lead to change-oriented predictions such as the following:

1. If she places less intense emphasis upon "having a romantic relationship with a man" or "being married to a man," she will experience less anxiety in the presence of men she finds attractive.
2. If she places less significance on each moment of each encounter with a potential romantic partner, she will experience less anxiety in the presence of men she considers "eligible."
3. If she focuses less on herself (how she appears, what she says, what she does) and more on people she's with, she will be less self-conscious and less anxious in their presence.
4. If she pays less attention to the physiological sensations and symptoms of anxiety when they occur, she will experience fewer of them and at lower levels of intensity.
5. If she spends more time in the presence of attractive, "eligible" men (that is, more "exposure"), she will, over time, experience fewer and less intense signs and symptoms of anxiety.

In addition to cognitive and behavioral perspectives, however, there are dozens of theoretical models and thousands of research studies that might apply to particular people, issues, and situations. Indeed, scholarly social workers typically first consider change-oriented hypotheses and intervention approaches that reflect research-based evidence of relevance and effectiveness. That is, we start with those intervention models shown through research studies to be safe and effective in helping people like our clients address problems similar to those they hope to resolve. If sufficient high-quality research-based evidence exists—as it does in the case of psychosocial services for people affected by anxiety and panic—we call the approach evidence-based. Currently, however, we do not have evidence-based practices (EBP) for all human needs, all social problems, all population groups, and all circumstances. There does not seem to be a single "silver-bullet" practice theory or policy approach that works well for everybody everywhere. Indeed, helping professionals will probably never be able to rely on a single theoretical perspective in our attempts to help diverse populations, living in diverse circumstances, and affected by diverse problems. Consequently, we must continue to review research studies that pertain to the clients we serve and the problems they address; and we must think critically about which theoretical perspectives and conceptual models best apply to particular clients.

On those occasions when we lack strong research-based evidence of the effectiveness of services for particular people, issues, and situations, we may generate hypotheses from strong scientific theories. For example, when certain interpersonal relationship issues are the target of concern, you might apply concepts from social learning theory. When strain and conflict within or between groups or organizations are the focus of attention, we might apply aspects of social systems theory. Fundamental concepts within social role theory—role ambiguity, role change, role strain, and role conflict—may be considered in relation to signs of frustration and distress. Crisis theory may help during emergencies, such as natural disasters, violent experiences, and other circumstances that involve sudden change. Family systems concepts may lead you to consider the effects of enmeshed boundaries or the absence of feedback processes within a family unit. Family structural models help us appreciate the significance of power and function. Understanding development theories may allow you to identify tasks necessary for further growth in individual, family, group, organizational, and community systems. Ecological and evolutionary perspectives may help explain how a particular phenomenon could represent an understandable adaptation to social and environmental circumstances. Behavior theories may enrich our understanding of the power of negative reinforcement (that is, the removal of aversive stimuli) in addictive processes and how the absence of reinforcement opportunities may contribute to emotional issues (such as depression), existential issues (such as alienation and despair), and social issues (such as criminal or antisocial activities). Economic models, particularly contemporary versions that incorporate social and behavioral elements (Belsky & Gilovich, 2000), are often extremely relevant. Indeed, a plethora of theories may prove useful as you and your clients seek to understand and synthesize significant information about the concerns and circumstances. When supported by and combined with research-based knowledge, such theoretical understanding can contribute to the preparation of well-reasoned and well-supported hypotheses and the case formulations that emerge from them.

In the early stages of work with clients, the analysis and synthesis processes of assessment are tentative and speculative. You and your client do not usually have conclusive support or confirmation for a particular "theory of the case." Therefore, continue to view the results of your critical analysis as hypotheses or questions rather than as conclusions. When viewed in this tentative way, your hypotheses serve to guide the collection of additional information and often help to identify possible interventions. Notice, for example, how a closed factory and a rise in associated social problems might lead to change-oriented hypotheses such as the following: (1) if community leaders and city officials offer a recently closed factory building to a local worker-cooperative[10] at a discounted rent with a temporary tax credit, that organization will occupy the vacant facility and expand its operations; and (2) if recently unemployed adults receive education and training in needed skills, they will secure employment and become partial owners in the cooperative. If the rate of community employment and local business ownership grows, then there will be an increase in economic activity, a reduction in unemployment, a drop in SNAP (food stamp) applications, and concomitant decreases in high school dropout rates and crime.

During the assessment process, resist the temptation to conclude that you have "the key" or "the solution." Very few problems have one right answer. Most of the time, there are many plausible hypotheses and numerous potential solutions. Collaborate with clients to identify those change-oriented hypotheses most likely to be relevant and useful for each unique client system and the stage of change, and each set of circumstances.

---

[10] A worker-cooperative ("coop" or "co-op") is a business that is owned and managed by its employees (or "members"). The members function as both owners and workers, and share in the co-op's profits.

Frequently, clients express hypotheses that both make logical sense and reflect reasonable consistency with your professional knowledge. When that occurs, you may adopt or perhaps slightly adapt them for use in your work together. Sometimes, however, clients' explanatory hypotheses and perhaps especially their change-oriented hypotheses constitute an obstacle to progress. For example, many clients, and many social workers for that matter, tend to view another person's (mis)behavior as the cause of a presenting problem. It logically follows then that if and when that other person does change the troublesome behavior, the problem should disappear. Attempting to change others' behavior rather than one's own is, indeed, a popular but often futile pastime. Sometimes, however, it actually makes sense. Influencing your elected representative to vote for fair and just policies, teaching your child a second language, or persuading your 18-year-old son to adopt safe-sex practices would usually represent useful changes in another's behavior. At other times, however, an attempt to change others constitutes a profoundly counterproductive and disempowering endeavor. Suppose, for instance, that a woman holds herself in positive regard only when other people view her as physically attractive. Consequently, she regularly engages in compulsive and sometimes frantic behavior to elicit favorable reactions from others. That is, she tries to change others as a way to help herself feel better. However, her approach places the locus of power in the hands of other people rather than in her own. Through their behavior toward her, other people control her views and feelings about herself. Obviously, this places her in an extremely vulnerable position. Clothing, makeup, extreme diet and exercise, and cosmetic surgeries may become routine, as may various forms of seductive or manipulative behavior. Nonetheless, when others do not notice or fail to acknowledge her attractiveness, or when another woman garners greater attention, her self-regard plummets and despair sets in. In such instances, the woman might benefit from other hypotheses—ones that shift the locus of control and power from outside to inside. She might, for example, hypothesize that if she could truly believe that she is inherently valuable simply because she exists, she might feel better about herself regardless of what others think about her desirability. Or, she might hypothesize that if she could conclude that one's attractiveness is simply irrelevant to beliefs about one's self-worth, she might pay more attention to her own self-judgment and less to the judgments of others.

Although many client-generated hypotheses contribute to understanding and change, others get in the way. Fixed explanatory perspectives and limited ideas about potential solutions can sometimes be as problematic as the problems themselves. Indeed, humans frequently attempt to resolve issues by repeating familiar problem-solving approaches—despite their previous negative outcomes. In habit-like fashion, we often reprise those very strategies that failed us miserably in the past. In other words, we tend to do the same thing over and over again while expecting different outcomes. When clients' explanatory and change-oriented hypotheses constitute part of the problem rather than part of the solution,[11] you may share one or more alternate hypotheses for their consideration. However, adopt a tentative and cautious approach. If your hypotheses obviously conflict with those of the client, they can negatively affect the working relationship—which introduces another issue to address. Clients may strongly believe that their views are correct or true and yours are incorrect, false, or even "silly." Indeed, people often vigorously defend their positions and may come to view social workers who hold different perspectives as adversaries rather than as collaborators. Sometimes, social workers also strongly believe that we are right; that our hypotheses are true; and that clients ought to give up their beliefs, defer to us, and accept our point of view. Unfortunately, when we adopt such positions, we risk damage to the cooperative, collaborative nature of our work with others.

Therefore, before you share your hypotheses, first reflect those of your clients' so that they know that you truly understand what they mean (see Chapter 9). Then, use the exploring skills to help

---

[11] In 1967, Charles Rosner wrote the following slogan for the Volunteers in Service to America (VISTA) program as part of a recruitment campaign: "If you're not part of the solution, you're part of the problem."

clients examine their hypotheses in greater depth. Encourage them to question the credibility and utility of their explanations about why and how the issues occur, and what to do to resolve them. In other words, encourage them to think critically about their own thinking. As a result of such exploration, clients may begin to see flaws in their hypotheses and become more receptive to alternate views. Then, you may ask them if they would be interested in hearing about another "theory." The simple act of asking, especially when preceded by hypothesis reflections and exploratory questions, can often increase clients' openness and cognitive flexibility.

Finally, before you share your explanatory hypotheses ensure that they actually do a better job of explaining phenomena than do those of your clients. Insufficient, easily refuted explanations do not usually contribute to the process or to progress. Similarly, when you offer change-oriented hypotheses make sure that they are considerably more likely to contribute to goal attainment than are those of your clients. Ideally, any change-oriented hypotheses that social workers share should reflect a strong logical rationale and a solid foundation in scientific theory, critical thought, or empirical evidence. And, as you share hypotheses, do so in a tentative manner, as something for clients to consider. Convey them in such a way that others may freely evaluate their relevance and usefulness for themselves and their particular circumstances. Recognize clients' right to accept, reject, or propose alternative hypotheses. One way to emphasize clients' autonomy is to immediately follow the skill of sharing hypotheses with the skill of seeking feedback.

As you begin to practice the skill of sharing hypotheses, please use the formats outlined here. Later, when you gain greater proficiency, experiment with alternate versions.

PRACTICE FORMAT | *Sharing Explanatory Hypotheses*

Would you be interested in considering another "theory" about how and why problems such as this one might occur? Yes? Okay. Well, we might also look at the problem in this way: _____ _____. How does that sound to you?

EXAMPLE | Sharing Explanatory Hypotheses

Client: I'm sorry to say so but our 4-year-old son is basically a lazy and selfish child who does whatever he wants whenever he feels like it. He has just started preschool and the teachers report that he doesn't pay attention and often misbehaves. He's disobedient at home now too.

Worker: (*reflecting explanatory hypotheses*) As you see it, your son has at least two fundamental flaws in his character. First, he's selfish and, second, he's lazy; and those two characteristics lead to problematic behavior both at home and in preschool. (*seeking feedback*) Is that accurate? Yes? Your theory about your son makes some sense—many children do seem to exhibit traits during childhood that continue on throughout their lives. (*closed-ended question*) However, I wonder if you might be interested in considering another possible explanation for such misbehavior? Yes? Okay. (*sharing explanatory hypotheses*) Well, if it's alright with you, I'd like to offer an alternate explanation for your son's behavior at home and school, an explanation that might also include what you consider to be his selfish and lazy traits. Briefly, I wonder if it might be possible that your 4-year-old son could be reacting to the fact that he has recently begun to attend preschool; that this represents a major change from the first 3 years of his life; and that the adjustment to that change might be reflected in what appears to be selfishness, laziness, and misbehavior? (*seeking feedback*) How does that sound to you?

PRACTICE FORMAT   *Sharing Change-Oriented Hypotheses*

(*closed-ended question*) Would you be interested in considering another theory about how we might attempt to resolve this issue? Yes? Okay. Well, there are, of course, many ways to make changes and sometimes we must engage in a process of trial and error. However, in the case of addressing problems such as those you identified, there's a theory that seems to apply quite well. In brief, the theory goes something like this: (*sharing change-oriented hypotheses*)_____. (*seeking feedback*) How does that sound to you?

EXAMPLE | Sharing Change-Oriented Hypotheses

Client: I think it's time to use the belt—just as my grandfather did with my father, and my father did with me. What's that biblical saying, "Spare the rod and spoil the child?"[12] I think we need to get serious here and punish him until he gets the message.

Worker: (*reflecting change-oriented hypotheses*) So, you think that if you punish your 4-year-old son with a belt, he will become more obedient and improve his behavior. (*seeking feedback*) Is that accurate? Yes? (*reflecting change-oriented hypotheses*) Well, it's certainly possible that more severe punishment might help. (*closed-ended question*) I wonder, though, would you be interested in a different theory about how parents might help their children learn to control their behavior? Yes? Okay. (*sharing change-oriented hypotheses; educating*) Well, this theory is based on research studies of childhood discipline. Some of that research does suggest that punishment can reduce misbehavior—especially in young children and particularly when the people who delivered the punishment are present. Following severe punishment, children usually become fearful of the people delivering the punishment, the location where the punishment takes place, and the instrument of punishment (for example, a paddle or belt). If the people who punished them are close by, the punished children may be able to refrain from misbehavior; although they often display signs of fear and agitation when doing so. Sometimes the children become so anxious about not misbehaving that they slip up and do so anyway. It's similar to people who are so concerned about making mistakes when speaking in public that they keep saying to themselves, "Don't make a mistake! Don't make a mistake!" The added stress and the emphasis on "mistakes" often increase the likelihood of making those very errors.

On the other hand, when parents routinely look for, notice, and praise their children's positive behaviors and their growing abilities and do so in an enthusiastic manner, kids often learn to manage their own behavior even in the absence of their parents. Of course, consequences for misbehavior are needed. The consequences that seem to work best for young children are relatively modest ones—such as brief 2- to 3-minute periods in a chair that faces a blank wall. Instead of focusing only on rewards or only on punishments, a combination of both may be more effective. If that

---

[12] Although the phrase "spare the rod and spoil the child" is not an exact quote from the King James Bible, Proverbs 13:24 does read: "He that spareth his rod hateth his son: but he that loveth him chasteneth him betimes." Proverbs 23: 13–14 reads: "Withold not correction from a child: for if thou beatest him with the rod, he shall not die. Thou shalt beat him with a rod, and shalt deliver his soul from hell." And Proverbs 29:15 reads: "The rod and reproof give wisdom; but a child left to himself bringeth his mother to shame."

> makes sense to you, we would figure out ways to deliver brief, modest consequences for misbehavior and provide lots and lots of enthusiastic praise for positive behavior. In fact, the emphasis would be on "catching him being good." (*seeking feedback*) How does that sound to you?

When sharing explanatory and change-oriented hypotheses, let clients know that you do not expect them to accept uncritically whatever you say. Always incorporate the skill of seeking feedback. When you ask clients for their thoughts about your ideas, they may pleasantly surprise you with responses such as, "Oh, that's interesting" or "I've never thought about it like that before" or "Let me think about that for a while" or, even, "My, that makes a lot of sense. The way I've been approaching this problem obviously hasn't worked; maybe your ideas might help."

EXERCISE 10-2   Sharing Hypotheses

Refer to your responses to earlier exercises as you continue to use assessing skills with Mr. K, Loretta, the S family, Mrs. F, and the "troubled agency."

1. Reflect on the exchanges that occurred earlier in your interactions with Mr. K, and then write the words you would use in sharing at least one explanatory and at least one change-oriented hypothesis that differ distinctly from any that Mr. K expressed. The hypotheses you share should relate to a problem, issue, or phenomenon reflected in the earlier exchanges and can reasonably be supported on the basis of strong logical, theoretical, or empirical grounds.

2. Reflect on your earlier exploration with Loretta, and then write the words you would use in sharing at least one explanatory and at least one change-oriented hypothesis that differ distinctly from any that Loretta expressed. The hypotheses you share should relate to a problem, issue, or phenomenon reflected in the earlier exchanges and can reasonably be supported on the basis of strong logical, theoretical, or empirical grounds.

3. Reflect on your earlier exploration with the S family, and then write the words you would use in sharing at least one explanatory and at least one change-oriented hypothesis that differ distinctly from any that members of the S family expressed. The hypotheses you share should relate to a problem, issue, or phenomenon reflected in the earlier exchanges and can reasonably be supported on the basis of strong logical, theoretical, or empirical grounds.

4. Reflect on your previous exchanges with Mrs. F, and then write the words you would use in sharing at least one explanatory and at least one change-oriented hypothesis that differ distinctly from any that Mrs. F expressed. The hypotheses you share should relate to a problem, issue, or phenomenon reflected in the earlier exchanges and can reasonably be supported on the basis of strong logical, theoretical, or empirical grounds.

5. Reflect on your earlier exchanges with associates of the troubled agency, and then write the words you would use in sharing at least one explanatory and at least one change-oriented hypothesis that differ distinctly from any that participants expressed. The hypotheses you share should relate to a problem, issue, or phenomenon reflected in the earlier exchanges and can reasonably be supported on the basis of strong logical, theoretical, or empirical grounds.

Confirming Issues

Confirming issues constitutes the first definitive indication that you and the client agree to work together toward meeting certain needs or resolving particular problems. **Focal issues** (confirmed issues) are those that participants agree to address. By confirming issues with your clients, you formalize and indeed emphasize that agreement. Derived from the needs, problems, aspirations, or other issues that the client identifies, those you contribute, or some negotiated combination of the two, the focal issues are central to the change process. They provide the direction and context for all subsequent professional activities. Indeed, in our work with clients, social workers must have extremely good professional reasons to depart from the confirmed issues. You can imagine a supervisor raising this question with a social worker: "Exactly why aren't you working on the issues that you and the client agreed to address together?" Because of their importance, the focal issues assume a prominent place in the contract portion of the Description, Assessment, and Contract (DAC). Whenever possible, state the focal issues for work in clear and descriptive terms.

Confirming issues for work follows naturally from the processes of exploration and assessment. Typically, you use the skills of reflecting and identifying issues before you and clients jointly agree on the specific problems or issues to address. When you confirm issues, you make a commitment that your work together will focus primarily on these particular areas. In practicing this skill, consider the format outlined below.

PRACTICE FORMAT *Confirming Issues for Work*

I think we agree about the primary issues that we will address in our work together. Let's review them, and write them down so that we can refer to them as we go along. First, there is the issue of _____. Second, the issue of _____ _____. Third, _____.
What do you think? Is this an accurate list of the issues that we'll focus upon?

EXAMPLE | Confirming Issues for Work

Case Situation: A woman has identified two major issues that she would like to address. You have contributed a third issue. You have explored them all in considerable detail and done so from a person-in-environment perspective.

Client: Well, that's my story. I hope you can help with the mess I'm in.

Worker: I hope so too. It seems to me that we have identified three major issues to address during our work together. Let's review them once more, and write them down so that we can refer to them as we go along. First, there is the issue of housing. You have been living on the street now for 3 weeks and the weather is beginning to turn cold. Second, there is the diabetes. You have been without medicine for a week now and you have no insurance or money to pay for it. Third, you lost your job 2 months ago and need to find work so you can make a living. What do you think? Is this an accurate list of the issues that we'll address together?

FIGURE 10.3 Sample Concept Map of Confirmed (Focal) Issues

As you and your clients confirm the issues for work, record them in a coherent fashion for ready reference. You could prepare a simple outline, a table, or a concept map (see Figure 10.3). Such forms serve that purpose well. Be sure to provide a copy to all clients—even to those who have drawn them in their own notebooks.

EXERCISE 10-3   Confirming Issues for Work

Refer to your responses to earlier exercises as you confirm issues with Mr. K, Loretta, the S family, Mrs. F, and the "troubled agency." You may use the format suggested earlier in the chapter. However, feel free to be somewhat creative in your responses. You cannot actually exchange ideas with these clients, so you must adopt a certain amount of flexibility in confirming issues for work.

1. Reflect upon earlier exercises, and then write the words you would use to confirm issues for work as they might apply to Mr. K's situation.

2. Reflect upon earlier exercises, and then write the words you would use to confirm the issues for work as they might apply to Loretta's situation.

3. Reflect upon earlier exercises, and then write the words you would use to confirm the issues for work as they might apply to the seven-member S family.

4. Reflect upon earlier exercises, and then write the words you would use to confirm the issues for work as they might apply to Mrs. F and her family's situation.

5. Reflect upon earlier exercises, and then write the words you would use to confirm the issues for work as they might apply to the troubled social service agency that retained you as a social work consultant.

▮▮ Organizing Descriptive Information

Most social work interviews do not occur in such a logical fashion that a transcript of the interaction between worker and client would represent a coherent description of the available information. Therefore, your first step in the assessment process is **organizing descriptive information** gathered during the exploration process into a form that allows for easy understanding and efficient retrieval.

Typically, this involves arranging data into sections and subsections according to certain categories that you and agency professionals consider significant. In other words, you adopt a rational format to organize relevant information.

Regardless of the organizational format used, however, be sure to recognize that descriptive information involves reported and observed information. That is, things that others say and things that you observe. Ideas or conclusions resulting from speculation or inference are opinions or hypotheses. Differentiate them from descriptive data. Assertions, opinions, and hypotheses are not facts, and we should never present them as such. Save hypotheses for the assessment portion of the DAC.

As you organize information into a document, make note of the date and source. In settings where the DAC format is applicable and a particular individual is identified as the formal client,[13] you may include descriptive data in accordance with the guidelines contained in Box 10.1. Remember, however, that many portions of the DAC format will not apply to some of the individuals, dyads, families, groups, organizations, and communities that you serve. Ultimately, our purpose for the descriptive section is to organize relevant data gathered during the exploration phase into a coherent, understandable representation of the client system; the issues; and relevant situational and environmental factors. The structure of any particular format used to organize the descriptive data is not especially important. What is critical, however, is that the data be presented in a coherent, easily understood, and readily accessible fashion.

Box 10.1 GUIDELINES FOR COMPLETION OF THE DAC DESCRIPTION: INDIVIDUAL

I. Description

A. Identification and Contact Information

In this section, place information that identifies the client and other relevant members of the person-in-environment systems. Data such as names and ages of household members, birth dates, insurance identification numbers, home addresses, places of work, telephone numbers, e-mail addresses, names and contact information of family doctors, and people to notify in case of emergency may be included. Note the date and place of the interview. Record your own name as the interviewer.

B. Person, Family and Household, and Community Systems

1. Person System

In this section, provide additional biopsychosocial information about the client. Whenever possible, use information that comes from clients, referral sources, and your direct observations, rather than from your inferences. Also, identify the source of the information (for example, "Mr. M stated that he has been a member of the local congregational church since he was a child and serves as an elder on the church board of directors." Or, "I observed that the client walked with a limp. She seems to have some difficulty with her left leg." Or, "Mrs. Jimenez says that she has a heart condition."). Quote significant words or phrases that the client uses in self-description. Be careful to use language that enhances the description rather than stereotypes the person. For example, the statement "Mary is a 45-year-old, white, divorced female" tends to emphasize age, race, and marital

(*Continued*)

---

[13] In many contexts, an entire family may be served even though only one member of that family is formally designated as "the client" (for example, a child or a teenager). Similarly, each participant in a social work group is commonly considered an "individual client," and relevant descriptive, assessment, and contracting information about him or her is included in a case record. Perhaps unfortunately, many social workers do not maintain a separate case record for "the family unit" or the "group as a whole."

status in a manner that could unnecessarily narrow the focus. Contrast that with this description, "Mary describes herself as a person with a 'great deal of energy and zest for life.' She describes herself as 'single and happy to be so.' She says she 'just turned 45 years old but feels 30.'"

Information based on your own observations of clients, such as their approximate height and weight, physical appearance, striking or characteristic features, speech patterns, and clothing may be included in this section. However, ensure that such information is actually relevant for the purpose of assessment and mention that it derives from your own observations.

2. **Family and Household System**

In this section, describe the client's family and household, or primary social system. If you have not included them elsewhere, include names, ages, and telephone numbers and addresses of significant people. Family genograms and household eco-maps are useful tools for organizing this information. Cite the source of information and quote significant words and phrases. It may be easier to attach a genogram to the document rather than trying to include it within the description. When you do so, simply insert a notation such as "See attached genogram dated January 13."

3. **Community System**

In this section, describe the community system within which the identified client functions. Indicate the source of the information and include systems such as school, work, medical, recreational, religious, neighborhood, ethnic, cultural, and friendship affiliations whenever appropriate. The eco-map is an especially valuable tool for presenting this kind of information and can be included in this section. It may be easier to attach an eco-map to the document rather than trying to include it within the description. When you do so, simply insert a notation such as "See attached eco-map dated January 13."

C. **Presenting Issues**

In this section, describe the presenting needs, problems, aspirations, or other issues of concern as identified by the client or responsible party (for example, parent, guardian, judge, teacher, or medical doctor). Clearly identify the source of the information and summarize the origin, development, and status of each primary issue. Quote significant words and phrases that help to describe needs, problems, concerns, or aspirations. In this section, briefly describe how the prospective client came to seek social services at this time. Also, if identified, record the initial, desired outcome or goal as envisioned by the client or responsible party. Unless the situation is of such an urgent or life-threatening nature that you must take immediate action, postpone your own view of issues and goals until you and the client undertake a more thorough exploration and assessment.

D. **Assets, Resources, and Strengths**

In this section, record information concerning the assets, resources, and strengths available within the client-and-situation systems. You may make note of competencies, social supports, successes, and life lessons, along with specific resources such as the involvement of concerned relatives, sufficient financial assets, optimistic attitudes, or high energy levels. Be sure to include those aspects that might influence or moderate the presenting problems and issues. Identify the source of this information about assets, strengths, and resources. The source might be the client, a family member, a previous social worker, or your own observations. Where possible, quote significant descriptive words and phrases. As a social worker, you encourage identification of strengths and resources to provide a balanced picture—one not solely characterized by needs, problems, concerns, and deficiencies. In addition, certain assets, strengths, competencies,

(Continued)

and resources often become extremely relevant later when we seek to identify and use protective factors during the assessing, contracting, and the working and evaluating phases of work.

E. Referral Source and Process; Collateral Information

Summarize information concerning the source of the referral (who suggested or required that the identified client make contact with you) and the process by which the referral occurred. You may present information provided by sources other than the identified client or the client system (for example, family member or a close friend) here. Cite the source by name, role, or position, and phone number. Try to quote specific words and phrases used in describing the person-issue-situation and the events that prompted the referral (for example, "When her medical doctor, Dr. Muhammad, called to refer Mrs. Malbi, he said she is severely depressed.").

F. History

In this section, include summary information about the identified client's social history and current social circumstances. You may include or attach one or more timelines in this section. Include data that is relevant to the purpose for your involvement. Do not include extraneous information just because "it is interesting." It should relate to the issues. Cite the source of the information (for example, the client, a family member, or your own observations) and quote significant words and phrases wherever possible. In describing historical information, recognize that experiences may have consequences that are energy enhancing, growth promoting, liberating, and empowering, as well as energy depleting, growth limiting, disempowering, disenfranchising, or traumatic. As you describe historical information, be sure to include, where indicated, those aspects that represent strengths or successes. You may use a "successes timeline" in this context. Other kinds of timelines may be used to summarize relevant historical information (for example, developmental, relationship, familial, critical events, sexual, alcohol or drug use, educational, or employment).

Depending on the agency program, your social work function, and the specific circumstances of the person-issue-situation, this section could contain some or all of the following subsections.

1. Developmental

If relevant to the presenting issues, you might include a description of a client's developmental history. You might provide information such as the nature of the client's birth, infancy, childhood, adolescent, and adult developmental processes. Specific information regarding events or experiences might be included here.

2. Personal, Familial, and Cultural

You may summarize here information concerning the significant past and present personal and familial relationships, and cultural affiliations. You may include significant processes and events that influenced the client's biopsychosocial development and behavior.

3. Critical Events

Summarize events or situations that might have been significant to the issues in some way. Identify liberating, empowering, or growth-enhancing processes and events such as successes, accomplishments, achievements, and experiences that may have enhanced psychosocial functioning. Also identify critical events such as violence, abuse, rape or molestation, suicides or suicide attempts, victimization, oppression, and discrimination that may have had traumatic effects. Describe how these experiences affected the client.

(Continued)

4. **Sexual**

   You may include here, if relevant to the presenting issues, information related to the person's sexual development and history.

5. **Alcohol and Drug Use**

   Because alcohol and drug abuse is so prevalent in our society, unless this topic is clearly irrelevant to the social work purpose, it is frequently useful to explore and summarize clients' history in these areas.

6. **Medical/Physical/Biological**

   If pertinent to the presenting issues, summarize here the person's medical and physical history. This might include identification of illnesses, injuries, disabilities, and current physical health and well-being. If relevant, you may refer to the medical history of family members or conditions that appear to have some genetic or hereditary influence. When applicable, you could include or attach a family medical genogram or pedigree. Be sure to include the date and results of the client's most recent physical examination. If not recorded earlier, the client's family doctor or source of medical care should be identified.

7. **Legal**

   Include here, as relevant, history of involvement in the criminal justice and legal system as well as pertinent information such as citizen or residency status, custody, or guardianship.

8. **Educational**

   Summarize the client's educational history as it pertains to the presenting issues. Both formal and informal educational experiences may be noted.

9. **Employment**

   If relevant, include here the client's employment history, including military and volunteer experiences.

10. **Recreational**

    Where applicable, summarize recreational and avocational activities that the client has undertaken over the years. Often, these endeavors constitute strengths or resources.

11. **Religious, Spiritual, Philosophical**

    If relevant, summarize current and past religious and spiritual affiliations and activities, and their significance for the client. Some clients adopt a nonreligious or nonspiritual philosophical worldview that holds great meaning for them. Include those as well. Aspects of this dimension often represent strengths or resources, but certainly not always. For some clients, certain religious beliefs or practices are more problematic than helpful and directly pertain to the focal issues.

12. **Prior Psychological, Social, or Medical Services**

    Summarize here previous involvement with psychological, social, and medical services that may relate to the presenting issues. Record the names, addresses, and telephone numbers of agencies and service providers.

13. **Other**

    Include here any additional, relevant historical and developmental information.

Appendix 9 contains an example of a completed DAC. You may review it now to see how information about the case of Mrs. Lynn Chase might be organized into the description section of the DAC. Please recognize, however, that most individual or family descriptions are not nearly as comprehensive in nature as the one created for Mrs. Chase. You should not view the format as a guide for data collection. Rather, the format represents one possible way to organize relevant data that has been gathered. There are many other formats. Indeed, several of the subsections contained in this particular format could easily be merged into one or two, or omitted altogether. Also, remember that a key focus for the organization of data remains the needs, problems, or other issues as presented by clients. Our clients' concerns and aspirations remain central. As a result, many dimensions suggested as possible subsections in Box 10.1 would be irrelevant to clients concerned with different issues.

In working with larger systems (for example, naturally formed groups, organizations, and communities) and when pursuing causes related to social, economic, or environmental justice, different formats may help us organize relevant information. Box 10.2 contains one—but only one—possible structure for work with larger systems.

BOX 10.2 GUIDELINES FOR COMPLETION OF THE DAC DESCRIPTION: NATURAL GROUP, ORGANIZATION, OR COMMUNITY

I. Description

A. Identification and Contact Information

In this section, place information that identifies the people with whom you first interact and those expected to join you in your collaborative work together. In the case of a community organization or a social action group, it might be the formal leaders or a subgroup that initiated contact or responded to your invitation. Data such as names, home addresses, places of work, telephone numbers, and e-mail addresses may be included. Sometimes, for example, in work with a group of street-based sex workers or members of a youth gang, participants may prefer to remain partially or completely anonymous. Note the date and, if useful, the place of the interview. Record your own name as the interviewer.

B. Client System

In this section, provide additional psychosocial information about the natural group, organization, or community with which you expect to work. Include information that comes from others as well as your direct observations. In the descriptive section, avoid opinions, conclusions, or hypotheses based on your own inferences. Also, identify the source of the information (for example, "Ms. P stated that she and several other sex workers in the 11th Street area have been hit with stones thrown by passersby. She said it has happened about three or four times weekly for the last month or so." Or, "I observed that as we talked about the stone throwing, the women routinely scanned the street and sidewalks. Sometimes, one or two would briefly step away to talk with potential customers."). Quote significant words or phrases that people use in self-description. Be sure to use language that enhances the description rather than stereotypes people or groups.

You may include social network maps or organizational charts. Cite the source or sources of information. It may be easier to attach graphical data to the document rather than trying to include it within the description. When you do so, simply insert a notation such as "See attached organizational chart dated October 24."

Information based on your own observations of the people involved may be included in this section. However, ensure that such information is actually relevant for the purpose of assessment and mention that it derives from your own observations.

(Continued)

C. **Social and Physical Environment**

In this section, describe the social and physical environment within which the natural group, organization, or community functions. Indicate the source of the information and include systems such as competing and cooperating groups, organizations, and communities with which the client system does or could interact. Eco-maps are often valuable tools for presenting this kind of information and can be included in this section. Geographical maps may be included (for example, to identify the territory of a particular gang or the boundaries of a community). It may be easier to attach maps to the document rather than trying to include it within the description. When you do so, simply insert a notation such as "See attached maps dated January 13."

D. **Presenting Issues**

In this section, describe the presenting needs, problems, aspirations, or other issues of concern as identified by members of the client system. Clearly identify the source of the information and summarize the origin, development, and status of each primary issue. Quote significant words and phrases that help to describe or illustrate the issues. In this section, outline how contact was initiated and by whom; also, if identified, record the initial, desired outcome or goal as envisioned by members of the client system. Unless the situation is of such an urgent or life-threatening nature that you must take immediate action, postpone your own view of issues and goals until you and members of the natural group, organization, or community undertake a more thorough exploration and assessment.

E. **Assets, Resources, and Strengths**

In this section, record information concerning the assets, resources, and strengths available within the client system and the social and physical environment. You may make note of competencies, social supports, successes, and life lessons, along with specific resources such as the involvement of concerned others, sufficient financial assets, optimistic attitudes, or high energy levels. Be sure to include those aspects that might influence or moderate the presenting problems and issues. Identify the source of this information about assets, strengths, and resources. The source might be one or more members of the client system or others who value them. It might be a previous social worker or consultant, or your own observations. Where possible, quote significant descriptive words and phrases. As social workers, we encourage identification of strengths and resources to provide a balanced picture—one not solely characterized by needs, problems, concerns, and deficiencies. In addition, certain assets, strengths, competencies, and resources often become extremely relevant later when we seek to identify and use protective factors during the assessing, contracting, and the working and evaluating phases of work.

F. **Referral Source and Process; Collateral Information**

Sometimes others make the first contact with you or your agency on behalf of a natural group, organization, or community. When that occurs, summarize information concerning the source of the referral and the process by which it occurred. You may present information provided by referral sources. Cite the source by name, role, or position, and phone number. Try to quote specific words and phrases used in describing the problems, situation, and the events that prompted the referral (for example, "When Rabbi Cohen called to express his concern about a group of youths congregating near the Hebrew Academy, he mentioned that several of the boys wore Nazi swastikas.").

G. **History**

In this section, include summary information about the history and current circumstances of the natural group, organization, or community. You may include or attach one or more

(Continued)

timelines in this section. Include data that are relevant to the purpose for your involvement. Do not include extraneous information just because "it is interesting." It should relate to the client system, the identified issues, or goals. Cite the source of the information and quote significant words and phrases wherever possible. In describing historical information, recognize that past experiences may have present-day or potential consequences that are energy enhancing, growth promoting, liberating, and empowering, as well as energy depleting, growth limiting, disempowering, disenfranchising, or traumatic. As you describe historical information, be sure to incorporate, where indicated, those aspects that represent strengths or successes. You may use a "successes timeline" in this context. Other kinds of timelines may be used to summarize relevant historical information (for example, developmental, critical events, or "eras").

Depending on the agency program in which you serve, your social work function, and the specific circumstances of the client system, this section could contain some or all of the following subsections.

1. **Developmental**

   You might include a description of the origin and development of the group, organization, or community. You might provide information about the original formation of the group, establishment of the organization, or foundation of the community. Specific information regarding notable development-related events or experiences might be included here.

2. **Social and Cultural**

   You may summarize here information concerning the cultural aspects of the client system. For example, a natural group of young people hanging out outside a neighborhood thrift store may be of working-class background. Many of their fathers or mothers lost their jobs in a recent plant closure. The group of sex workers on 11th Street may be first- or second-generation immigrants—perhaps from a particular region of the world. Members of a church may seek to open a "soup kitchen" for hungry members of the neighborhood. An organization's board of directors may reflect a single ethnic group, the executive director another, whereas the staff members may reflect considerable ethnic diversity. A community may include three more or less distinct neighborhoods. One is predominantly European American, Catholic, and working class in composition. A second is racially, ethnically, and religiously mixed and includes people from both working and professional classes. The third is almost exclusively European American, Protestant, and well-to-do.

3. **Critical Events**

   If not described earlier, you may summarize events or situations of significance to the client system in some way. Identify liberating, empowering, or growth-enhancing processes and events such as successes, accomplishments, achievements, and experiences that may have enhanced social functioning. Also identify events that negatively affected the system. In work with youth gangs, for example, the murder of a beloved leader may have triggered a war with a rival gang believed responsible for his death. An organization may have once laid off 25 percent of its staff to forestall bankruptcy. A neighborhood may have been flooded by a hurricane, flattened by a tornado, or destroyed by a fire. A community may have been hit by a dangerous epidemic of influenza. These and other such events may have seriously affected the group, organization, or community. Include descriptive information about these critical events.

(Continued)

4. Legal

If not included in other sections, describe relevant contact with the criminal justice and legal system as well as pertinent information such as citizen or residency status of members of the client system. For example, a previous director of an organization may have embezzled funds and a trial is about to start. Key members of a gang may be in jail or prison, or a police task force may be targeting violent youth gangs for special attention, arrest, and prosecution. Two homes in a neighborhood may have been foreclosed by banks and another may recently have been burglarized. A community association may have filed a lawsuit to restrain the city from building a highway that would split a neighborhood in half—fragmenting a community that originated nearly two centuries earlier.

5. Financial

If relevant to the purpose for your involvement, you may include here the client system's sources of and amounts of income as well as expenditures. Sometimes financial factors are associated with the onset or continuation of problems or could be involved in the achievement of goals. For example, a youth gang may acquire money through drug sales, theft, or the "protection" of businesses and neighborhoods. An organization may secure funding through grants and fees, or sales of goods and services. A community may depend upon a local factory for employment.

6. Prior Social Services

Summarize here previous involvement with social or consultative services that may relate to the client system and its presenting issues and goals. Where relevant, identify the names, addresses, and telephone numbers of service providers.

7. Other

Include here any additional, relevant information.

EXERCISE 10-4 Organizing Descriptive Information

For this exercise, assume that you are your own client. Use a word-processing program to draft the description section of a written DAC as if you are a social worker who learned what you know about yourself as a person and about your situation. Identify an issue for which you might conceivably consult a social worker. All humans confront problems and issues of various kinds throughout the course of life. Such challenges are inevitable and social workers are not exempt. Social workers benefit when we remember that clients are not "them" and "we" are not "us." Clients and social workers simply assume different roles and functions at different times. Indeed, you may anticipate that you will have social workers as your clients at some point in the future, and other social workers may well have you as theirs. By preparing our own DACs, we gain an appreciation for all we ask of our clients.

Begin by organizing relevant information about yourself, your circumstances, and an issue that concerns you. Use the DAC format to word-process the description portion of a personal case record for inclusion in a separate part of your Social Work Skills Learning Portfolio. Include whatever information you need to describe the issue and its relationship to relevant personal and environmental factors in the past and present. You might find it useful to incorporate one or more timelines, a genogram, an eco-map, the results of various assessment instruments, or perhaps baseline data. In creating your case record, it might be prudent to disguise your own identity. After all, these materials reflect a great deal about yourself and your own personal life. Instead of your full name, you might create pseudonyms to identify yourself and the significant people in your life. Entitle the document "My DAC: Description" and save the file as "My_DAC_Desc." Include it in your Social Work Skills Learning Portfolio in a separate electronic folder.

Preparing an Assessment and Case Formulation

After recording the available descriptive information in an organized fashion, we begin to prepare an **assessment and case formulation** (that is, a "theory of the case"). As you do with descriptive data, organize the results of your analysis and synthesis into a coherent structure. The particular format varies from agency to agency, program to program, issue to issue, and indeed from client to client. Nonetheless, virtually all social work assessment schemes refer in one way or another to various theoretical dimensions and include consideration of the client system; needs, aspirations, problems, and other issues; and, of course, environmental circumstances. The organizing structure may be derived from a single theoretical perspective or, eclectically, from several. On occasion, the assessment may even be atheoretical in nature. Indeed, sometimes you and your clients apply practical logic to develop (1) explanatory hypotheses to understand particular problems, people, and circumstances, and (2) change-oriented hypotheses that lead to goals and plans for action and evaluation.

Whether theoretical or atheoretical in nature, the assessment process enables you and others to reach agreement about a "theory of the case." You develop explanatory hypotheses about risk factors and those conditions that affect and maintain problems. You hypothesize about strengths, assets, competencies, resources, and protective factors that could help in resolution. In addition, you seek to determine clients' or others' current readiness and motivation to address particular issues (that is, their stage of change).

Building upon your explanatory hypotheses, you and your clients develop change-oriented hypotheses and identify other people or systems that could and should be involved in the helping process. You conjointly determine potential targets for change—those aspects that, if altered, might resolve the issue. You identify potential obstacles or barriers to progress as well. You predict probable consequences if things remain the same and assess risk to determine how urgently intervention must be undertaken. In addition, you consider applicable intervention approaches, modalities, strategies, techniques, activities, and tasks; and assess their relative probability of success. Finally, you negotiate a time frame for work and develop ways and means to evaluate progress.

Box 10.3 contains guidelines for completing the assessment and case formulation parts of the DAC (see Appendix 9 for a completed example). The assessment derives from information presented in the description portion of the DAC. However, do not use the assessment section to repeat material. Instead, refer to descriptive information to support explanatory and change-oriented hypotheses that you and the client generate. In a sense, the assessment and case formulation portion of the DAC represent an argument that involves "claims" supported by descriptive evidence.

Appendix 9 contains an example of a tentative assessment and case formulation, organized as part of a DAC. As you review the example in the appendix, realize that most written assessments and case formulations are not as lengthy as the example and do not contain as many sections and subsections. Often, you will be able to integrate the results of analysis and synthesis into a simpler organizational format. Furthermore, if your client system is a natural group, an organization, or a community, the assessment and case formulation would look quite different from the one completed with Mrs. Lynn B. Chase. Similarly, in life-threatening or other crisis situations, the processes and documentation would be quite different.

BOX 10.3   GUIDELINES FOR COMPLETION OF THE DAC ASSESSMENT
AND CASE FORMULATION

II. Tentative Assessment

A. Focal Issues

1. **Nature, Duration, Frequency, Severity, and Urgency**

   Analyze information gained during the exploration phase and reported in the description section to capture the nature and essence of the focal issues. Go beyond the earlier description to offer explanatory hypotheses about "why" they are of concern and "how" they came to be so at this particular time. Include the client's as well as your own explanatory hypotheses about the focal issues. Incorporate professional and scientific knowledge to enhance understanding of the identified problems or issues.

   Where available, include the results of questionnaires, surveys, and other assessment instruments as well as "pretest" or baseline rating data (for example, frequency or intensity of problem occurrence during the interval between initial contact and first face-to-face meeting). In your assessment of issues, incorporate or make reference to tables or concept maps and to narrative discussion about their duration, frequency, severity, and urgency (see Table 10.1 for an example).

2. **Risk and Protective Factors; Exceptions**

   In this section, propose explanatory hypotheses about risk factors and conditions that contribute to the onset, development, or continuation of the issues. Specify factors that seem to trigger, accompany, and follow episodes. You may incorporate or attach a functional analysis table as a summary (see Table 10.2 for an example).

   If relevant, assess the risk of suicide, homicide, violence, abuse, neglect, and substance misuse. Generate hypotheses about risks to the client system, and to other people and social systems if things continue as they are. That is, what is likely to happen if the problems or issues remain unresolved? Also, anticipate potential consequences of successful resolution. How will the client system change when the problems are resolved? How will other people and social systems react to those changes? Recognize that certain negative effects may accompany positive change.

   Hypothesize about circumstances and conditions that inhibit, impede, or prevent emergence or reemergence of the issues. Refer to protective factors, strengths and assets, and exceptions—those times when and where the issues do not occur—and offer explanatory hypotheses about these exceptions. Support your explanatory hypotheses by incorporating or referencing tables, concept maps, or narrative information contained in the descriptive section. However, avoid unnecessary repetition of descriptive content.

   Hypothesize about aspects of the client system and circumstances that represent challenges, obstacles, or barriers to resolution of the issues. When applicable, make reference to deficiencies in basic needs for money, shelter, food, clothing, and social and intellectual stimulation, as well as to social, political, and cultural obstacles such as oppression and discrimination. As needed, hypothesize about the impact of environmental conditions such as overcrowding, inadequate or excessive stimulation, and the presence of toxic materials.

B. Contributing Factors

1. **Client System Factors**

   If the focal issues involve specific individuals (for example, someone is unemployed, a family member misuses alcohol or drugs, a person has been victimized and traumatized),

(Continued)

personal factors may require assessment.[14] In such circumstances, you and your client may appropriately generate explanatory hypotheses about the relationship between relevant individual factors and the focal issues.

When the client system includes more than one person (for example, family, formed group, natural group, organization, or community), you and your clients may generate explanatory hypotheses about the relationship between client system factors and the focal issues. Hypothesize about aspects of the client system that relate to the concerns, and incorporate concepts from theoretical and research-based knowledge. Include your own hypotheses as well as those of the client. The nature of the professional knowledge that might apply varies according to the unique characteristics of the problems, client system, and circumstances. At times, hypotheses about an individual's personality style and characteristics, or a client system's approach to problem solving, may be useful. At other times, hypotheses about self-efficacy or family, group, organizational, or community functioning can further understanding. Sometimes, interpersonal or relational styles or social skill deficits may apply. Frequently, hypotheses about familial, cultural, social, and occupational role identities, along with the extent of congruence or conflict among them, may be noted. Hypotheses about a person's (or group's) beliefs about oneself (or itself), others, the world, and the future may serve both to explain the how and why of a particular issue and to provide some indication about how to proceed and what to do.

Hypothesize about how client system factors may affect the issues and, in turn, how the issues affect the client system's thinking, feeling, and doing. If relevant, hypothesize about possible biochemical or physical factors and effects. Consider personal or group assets, strengths, and competencies vis-à-vis the issues and the preliminary goals. Hypothesize about the effects and effectiveness of strategies the client system tends to adopt to cope with or respond to the issues. Anticipate potential effects if the issues are resolved as well as if they remain unresolved. Where applicable, consider the issues in relation to the client system's spiritual, religious, and other cultural beliefs.

At times, the relative flexibility or rigidity of a client system's boundaries and decision-making strategies, as well as the nature, strength, and functionality of defensive and coping processes may be considered. Sometimes the client system's relative ability to control desires and impulses and to manage temptations may apply. Often, explanatory hypotheses about the client system's emotional states and traits are useful, as are those about the phase of life cycle development and maturity level. At times, it helps to consider hypotheses about the client system's competence to make significant life decisions, fulfill time and situation-appropriate roles and tasks, function autonomously, and participate in the helping process.

Sometimes, the results of specific assessment processes such as mental status or substance abuse examinations, questionnaires, surveys, and baseline ratings may warrant analysis and elaboration. Hypotheses about such results may further understanding about the client system, the focal issues, and the social and physical circumstances.

2. **Situational, Environmental, and Systemic Factors**
Propose explanatory hypotheses about the relationship between the issues and situational and systemic factors. Look for parallel processes. Hypothesize about potential effects of

(Continued)

---

[14] In work with natural groups, organizations, and communities, "personal" or "individual" factors may not be relevant for the purposes of assessment and case formulation. If so, you may simply exclude that section.

the issues upon the client system, other people and social systems, and the environment. Analyze the systemic patterns, structures, and processes of social systems associated with the promotion and maintenance of the issues. Appraise the strategies used to cope with or adapt to the issues. Assess the degree of energy, cohesion, and adaptability of primary social systems. Analyze relevant life cycle developmental issues and the maturity of pertinent social systems. Consider how the needs and aspirations of other people and social systems relate to the issues and the people involved.

When pertinent, propose explanatory hypotheses about the social system's predominant emotional climate; operating procedures; communication styles and process; affection and support patterns; distribution of power and availability of resources; assignment of roles; boundaries between members, subsystems, and other systems; and processes of decision making. Similarly, hypotheses about systemic structures, patterns, and processes; developmental life cycle issues; external stressors; and other situational factors may be relevant.

You may refer to genograms, eco-maps, concept maps, and timelines presented in the description section, as they often provide evidentiary support for explanatory hypotheses. Tables that present risk and protective factors and strengths, and especially functional analysis tables, may be particularly relevant. If applicable, consider the legal and ethical implications that may pertain to service in this case.

Hypotheses about assets, capacities, abilities, strengths, competencies, and resources within the social and environmental context may add depth to the assessment; and so might those about the spiritual, religious, and cultural beliefs and practices of significant others, groups, organizations, and communities. Include hypotheses about the potential effects on the client system and on significant others if the focal issues (1) remain as they are, (2) worsen, and (3) become resolved.

3. **Motivation and Readiness; Stage of Change**

Generate hypotheses about the client system's motivation to address and resolve the issues, and to work collaboratively toward change. In your assessment, refer to assets, strengths, and competencies and determine the transtheoretical stage that best reflects the client system's current readiness for change vis-à-vis each identified issue. Hypothesize about factors associated with the readiness level and, if applicable, those that might serve to enhance motivation. Hypothesize about significant other people and social systems' motivation to contribute to resolution of the issues. You might try using a 10-point subjective rating scale *(1 = low; 10 = high)* to estimate various aspects of motivation (for example, motivation to address particular issues, motivation to take action, motivation to work with you). Realize that an individual's or group's level of motivation to address one issue may differ dramatically from their motivation to address another. Such information can be invaluable in conjointly deciding which issues to address first.

C. **Case Formulation**

The earlier portions of the assessment section primarily involve analysis. The case formulation, however, tends to require synthesis. We piece together various elements derived from analysis to identify or create one or more strategies for change. We seek to identify those factors within the client system and the social and physical environment that, if changed in some way, might help to resolve the identified problems. In other words, we propose change-oriented hypotheses.

The case formulation typically follows logically from the analyses of the issues, the client system, and the social and physical environment. As social workers, we commonly target factors

(Continued)

> both within the client system (for example, individual, family, group, organization, or community) and outside the client system (for example, social and physical environment) for change. Occasionally, however, the focus may be primarily on the people or primarily on the situation.
>
> We can think of the case formulation as a set of change-oriented hypotheses or strategic predictions. Based upon our analytic assessment, we predict that, working together, the social worker and client will resolve the issues by changing one or more aspects of the client system, one or more aspects of the environment, or some combination of the two. We often include an estimate of the probability that our predictions will turn out to be true or accurate. That is, we provide a prognosis that the issues can be successfully resolved through our strategic actions.

If the issue is societal in nature, a macro-system assessment, community needs assessment, or perhaps a policy analysis may be required. For example, suppose you participate in a group seeking to reduce economic inequality and eliminate poverty in the United States. You would identify and retrieve scientific evidence concerning the nature, extent, impact, and effects of the problems; factors associated with their origin and continuation; and scientific theses concerning their remediation. The process might lead to the development of hypotheses that logically lead to social action and policy–practice plans.[15]

EXERCISE 10-5 Preparing an Assessment and Case Formulation

For this exercise, please review the information that you organized into the description section of your case record as part of Exercise 10-4. Based on what you know about yourself and what you included in the description portion of your DAC, proceed to word-process a tentative assessment and case formulation through analysis and synthesis of the available data to add to your personal DAC. In completing your assessment and case formulation, remember that much of what you record remains tentative and speculative—even in this case, where you are assessing yourself and your situation. These hypotheses await later support and confirmation. Present your ideas in accord with the format provided in the assessment and case formulation section of the DAC. Continue to disguise your identity and any people you might reference in the record. Identify your completed word-processed document as "My DAC: Assessment." Save the file as "My_DAC_Assess" file for inclusion in a separate "My DAC" section of your Social Work Skills Learning Portfolio.

SUMMARY

During the assessment phase of social work practice, you and the client attempt to make sense of the data gathered during the exploration phase. The assessment and especially the case formulation provide collaborating parties a perspective from which to initiate the process of contracting.

CHAPTER 10 Summary Exercises

1. You are continuing your work with the four clients described below (see the Summary Exercises in Chapters 7, 8, and 9). Use word-processing software to *write the words* you would say and discuss the actions you would take as you engage them in the assessment processes. In other words, build upon your previous work to demonstrate how you would apply the requested assessing

---

[15] See the section on "Policy–Practice" in Chapter 4.

skills in these particular situations. Please *label* each of the skills that you use and place quotation marks around the words you would say. When finished, combine your work into a single document with a section for each of the "Four Assessments." Save the document to a file labeled "4_Assessments" and include the file in your Social Work Skills Learning Portfolio.

a. You are well into the process of encouraging community leaders to explore the nature and scope of the social issues that most concern residents. Recently, participants decided to separate the large group into subgroups according to five targeted social issues. One subgroup is focusing on unemployment, a second on gangs, a third on drug sales, a fourth on drug use, and a fifth on youth prostitution. Because the problems overlap, representatives from each smaller group meet periodically so that everybody is aware of their respective activities.

First, (a) propose at least one explanatory hypothesis for each of the following issues: high unemployment; many children and adolescents from the community join neighborhood gangs; many youth and young adults sell drugs; many more youngsters buy drugs; and some adolescent girls and boys perform sexual acts in exchange for money. Use scientific theories, empirical research findings, and logical analysis to formulate plausible hypotheses. After creating explanatory hypotheses, build upon them to (b) propose at least one change-oriented hypothesis for each of the social issues. In other words, "theorize" about how each issue might be resolved.

b. You are now working with Danni as she struggles to recover from the traumatic effects of rape and its repercussions. Write the words you might use to (a) identify at least two psychosocial issues that rape victims often experience and might also apply to Danni. You might locate common problems through a quick review of the relevant research literature. Alternately, you might use your own knowledge and experience to anticipate possible problems. Once you have identified at least two issues, (b) propose explanatory hypotheses about how or why they might occur. Base your hypotheses on scientific theories, empirical research findings, or logical analysis.

Now, with at least two issues and associated explanatory hypotheses in mind, (c) formulate change-oriented hypotheses about how the problems might be resolved. You might conduct a brief search for research studies that pertain to the effectiveness of programs, practices, or interventions that target those particular problems. Alternately, you might apply concepts from a relevant practice theory. Or, you could base the change-oriented hypotheses upon logic and reason. If you do the latter, be sure to include a rationale that remains consistent with the circumstances Danni described.

c. You are working with the Z family of six who had been sleeping in their car in a rest area on the highway. They exhausted their funds on their way to another part of the country, where they hoped to find work. During your exploration with the parents, you learned that Mrs. Z has disabling diabetes and Mr. Z lost his job in part due to an economic slowdown in his industry and in part due to increased police and governmental efforts to identify and deport undocumented workers. He has been unsuccessful in his search for work during the last few months. You also learned that the family does not have friends or relatives in their intended location. Rather, they based their hopes for employment on rumors that jobs are available there. Write the words you would say to (a) identify issues apparent from this and earlier discussions. Then, (b) generate at least one explanatory hypothesis about how or why each issue might occur. Next, (c) formulate a change-oriented hypothesis for each issue. Make sure that they flow logically from the issues and the explanatory hypotheses.

d. You are working with Mr. T. Accused of molesting the 13-year-old daughter of his woman friend, he is participating in counseling services with you at the urging of his attorney. Mr. T must not have any contact with the woman and her daughter during this period.

During the first several meetings, Mr. T consistently said that the girl is lying about the mo-lestation. He swore that he never touched her. At this point, you cannot determine if Mr. T is telling the truth about the molestation, lying, or deluding himself. Write the words you would say in (a) proposing at least two explanatory hypotheses about how or why Mr. T might lie about the child sex abuse. Now, with your explanatory hypotheses in mind, (b) generate at least two change-oriented hypotheses about how the issue of deception might be resolved.

Chapter 10   Experiential Interviewing Exercise

Building on the previous meeting with your practice client, conduct the second interview. Once again, ensure that the interview setting is private and record the meeting. You might begin by briefly referring to what you explored during the first meeting and identifying a tentative purpose or agenda for this one. Be sure to seek feedback from the client about your ideas for today's meet-ing. If the practice client agrees, proceed to use exploring, assessing, and other relevant skills in your interview. In addition to seeking feedback, the most applicable exploring skills might be asking questions, seeking clarification, reflecting content, reflecting feelings, reflecting feelings and mean-ing, partializing, going beyond what is said, reflecting issues, and reflecting hypotheses. The most applicable assessing skills might be identifying issues, sharing hypotheses, and confirming issues for work. Toward the end of the session, arrange for another meeting in a week or so. You might also share your preliminary ideas about what may happen in the next meeting.

When you've finished the 30-minute interview, take another 15 minutes for the following:

1. Leave your respective social worker and client roles. Request that your colleague com-plete a copy of the Exploring Skills Rating Form and the Assessing Skills Rating Form (see Appendix 6). Aspects of the Talking and Listening Skills Rating Form may also apply. When your colleague has completed the rating forms, inquire about today's interview experi-ence. Ask general open-ended questions to obtain as much evaluative feedback as possible and, through that, enhance your learning. For example, you might ask your colleague ques-tions such as:

   • What thoughts, feelings, or other reactions do you have about today's meeting?
   • What do you think about the problems or issues we identified as the primary focus for our work together?
   • What parts of the interview affected you the most—either positively or negatively?
   • What do you wish had happened during the interview that did not occur?
   • What suggestions do you have about how the interview could have been better, more helpful, or more constructive for you?
   • What suggestions do you have about how I could have been a better or more helpful social worker today?

   As you finish securing feedback from your practice client, thank her and tell her that you will see her soon.

   Later, when you have time, create a word-processed report entitled "Second Interview: Practice Client Feedback." Label the document file "Intvue_2_Client_Feed." Include the date and your name as the student social worker. Then summarize your practice client's feedback along with the results of the rating forms she completed. Include the document in the "Expe-riential Exercise Folder" of your Social Work Skills Learning Portfolio.

2. Next, play the audio or video recording. Review and reflect upon what you see or hear, and appraise your performance. Take written notes as you go along. Then, go to Appendix 10 and complete the talking and listening, beginning, exploring, and assessing sections

of The Social Work Skills Interview Rating Form to evaluate your performance of the social work skills. Use your ratings as a stimulus to evaluate your performance of relevant skills. Identify those skills you performed well, those that need improvement, those that you might or should have used during the interview, and those that you used but probably should not have. Reflect upon how you feel about the interview. Describe what you like and what you dislike. Also, discuss the quality of the assessment and identify additional aspects of the person-issue-situation that might contribute to a more complete assessment. You might have a chance to explore those in a subsequent meeting. Finally, discuss what you would do differently if you had a chance to conduct the interview again and outline what you might do in the next interview to improve the quality of your work. Complete the evaluation of your performance in a brief document entitled "Second Interview: Self-Evaluation." Save the file as "Intvue_2_Self-Eval" in the "Experiential Interviewing Exercise" section of your Social Work Skills Learning Portfolio.

3. Find the time to record information gathered during the second interview into a formal practice client case record. Record the date of the interview as well as the date you prepare the record. At this point you are acquainted with the first two sections of the Description, Assessment, and Contract (DAC). Adopt the DAC format to word-process a succinct and coherent record of the descriptive data gathered during the first and second meetings. Identify yourself as the social worker but continue to disguise the identity of the practice client. Then, begin to formulate a tentative assessment through thoughtful reflection about the available data. After analyzing and synthesizing the information, word-process an assessment entry for the case record. Use the DAC format for that as well. Remember, much of what you enter into the assessment section remains tentative and speculative. These are ideas or hypotheses, not facts. Generated by the client or the social worker, or collaboratively by both, they nonetheless require further support and confirmation. When you have completed the description and assessment sections of the DAC, title the document "Description and Assessment" and save it in a file labeled "Intvue_2_DAC." Store the file in the "Experiential Interviewing Exercise" folder of your Social Work Skills Learning Portfolio.

4. Next, reflect upon the entirety of the second interview experience and use relevant preparing skills to prepare for the third meeting with the practice client. Draw upon what you learned and the documents you created to word-process "Plans for the Third Meeting." Label the document file "Intvue_3_Plans" and save it in the "Experiential Interviewing Exercise" folder of your Social Work Skills Learning Portfolio.

CHAPTER 10 Self-Appraisal

As you finish this chapter, please reflect on your learning by using the following space to identify any ideas, terms, or concepts addressed in Chapter 10 that remain confusing or unclear to you:

Next, respond to the following items by carefully reading each statement. Please use a 1-to-10-point rating scale (where *1 = strongly disagree* and *10 = strongly agree*) to indicate the degree to which you agree or disagree with each statement. Place a check mark at the point that best reflects your view at this particular point in time. If you're truly *undecided*, place your check at the midpoint (5.5) mark.

1. I can discuss the purposes and functions of assessment.

   | | | | | | | | | | |
   1   2   3   4   5   6   7   8   9   10

2. I can identify issues.

   | | | | | | | | | | |
   1   2   3   4   5   6   7   8   9   10

3. I can share explanatory and change-oriented hypotheses.

   | | | | | | | | | | |
   1   2   3   4   5   6   7   8   9   10

4. I can confirm issues for work.

   | | | | | | | | | | |
   1   2   3   4   5   6   7   8   9   10

5. I can organize descriptive information.

   | | | | | | | | | | |
   1   2   3   4   5   6   7   8   9   10

6. I can prepare an assessment and case formulation.

   | | | | | | | | | | |
   1   2   3   4   5   6   7   8   9   10

Contracting

Contracting[1] follows integrally from the exploration and assessment processes and leads to the development of a service agreement or "contract" between the worker and the client. This chapter will help you develop proficiency in contracting skills. Competent use of these skills enables social workers and clients to establish goals, develop plans to pursue and achieve those goals, and create plans to evaluate progress toward goal achievement.

Chapter Goals

Following completion of this chapter, you should be able to:

- Discuss the purposes and functions of contracting.
- Establish goals.
- Develop action plans.
- Identify action steps.
- Plan for evaluation.
- Summarize the contract.

Core Competencies

The content addressed in this chapter supports the following core EPAS competencies:

- Competency 4: Engage in Practice-Informed Research and Research-Informed Practice
- Competency 5: Engage in Policy Practice
- Competency 7: Assess Individuals, Families, Groups, Organizations, and Communities
- Competency 8: Intervene with Individuals, Families, Groups, Organizations, and Communities
- Competency 9: Evaluate Practice with Individuals, Families, Groups, Organizations, and Communities

---

[1] We use the term *contracting* to describe an interactional process between worker and client that leads to a more or less formal agreement concerning the nature, scope, and focus of the services to be provided. Although it is not, strictly speaking, a legal document, we refer to the written or unwritten outcome of this process as a *service agreement* or *service contract*.

Establishing Goals

Following confirmation of issues, consideration of how and why they occur, and generation of ideas about how best to address and resolve them, social workers encourage clients to participate in **establishing goals** for their work together. Setting effective goals is a critical element in the change process. First, social workers and clients agree upon the focal issues to address and then we develop goals that, if accomplished, would resolve those issues. Goals are the aims toward which the social worker and client direct their cognitive, emotional, behavioral, and situational actions. They are essential.[2] Consider this book title: *If You Don't Know Where You're Going, You'll Probably End Up Somewhere Else* (Campbell, 1974). Without clear goals, you and your clients are indeed likely to end up somewhere other than where you intend.

In co-constructing goals with clients, we often adopt a SMART format. SMART stands for:

- Specific
- Measurable
- Action oriented
- Realistic
- Timely

Objectives defined in a SMART manner are usually easier to understand, undertake, accomplish, and evaluate. As Egan (1982) suggests, effective goals are:

- Stated as accomplishments.
- Stated in clear and specific terms.
- Stated in measurable or verifiable terms.
- Realistic (that is, have a reasonable chance of success).
- Adequate, if achieved, to improve the situation.
- Congruent with clients' value and cultural systems.
- Time-specific (that is, include a time frame for achievement).

According to Egan, effective goals meet the criteria just outlined. First, well-formed goals appear as accomplishments rather than processes. "To lose weight" is a process. "To achieve a weight of 125 pounds and maintain that weight for 6 months" is an accomplishment. Second, effective goals are clear and specific. They are not vague resolutions or general mission statements. "Securing employment" is nonspecific. "To secure employment as a waiter in a restaurant within 6 weeks" is much more clear and specific. Third, well-stated goals appear in easily understood, measurable, or verifiable terms. Clients can easily recognize when they have reached their goals. "To feel better" is hard to recognize and not sufficiently measurable. "To feel better as indicated by sleeping the night through (at least 7 hours per night on at least five nights per week), completely eating three meals daily, and scoring at least 15 percent better on the Hamilton Depression Rating Scale (HAM-D)" is much more measurable. Fourth, effective goals are realistic and reasonable. Given the motivations, opportunities, strengths, resources, and capacities of the person-issue-situation systems, the established goals reflect a reasonably high probability of attainment. A goal "to get all straight A's" would not be realistic for a student who has never before received a grade better than a C. Something such as, "Pass all courses and get a B or higher in at least one course" is more reasonable. Fifth, effective goals are adequate. A goal is adequate to the degree that its accomplishment would represent

---

[2] Social workers and their clients benefit by periodically asking themselves and each other: "Exactly what goals are we working toward here?" It is truly surprising how many clients, and how many of their social workers, cannot directly identify the goals for their work together.

progress toward the resolution of an agreed-upon problem or issue. Goals that do not contribute to problem resolution are therefore inadequate. Sixth, effective goals are congruent with the client's value and cultural systems. Unless a life-threatening situation exists, you should generally neither ask nor expect clients to forsake their fundamental personal or cultural values. Seventh, effective goals include a time frame. Both you and your clients need to know when achievement of the goals is expected.

Although specification of goals in a SMART manner consistent with Egan's criteria represents a useful ideal, it is not always desirable nor feasible. Some clients are in such a state of uncertainty and confusion that pushing too hard toward goal specificity would exacerbate their state of distress. It would not match their stage of change. Do not become so focused on defining goals in a precise manner that you lose touch with the client's reality. As we discussed earlier in relation to the Transtheoretical Model (Prochaska, 1999; Prochaska et al., 1994; Prochaska & Velicera, 1998), people are at different levels of readiness and motivation to take action. Pushing for SMART goals with clients who are just beginning to contemplate the idea that a problem might exist could interfere with the process of exploring and identifying issues. In such circumstances, simply postpone precise goal specification and instead establish a general direction for work. Indeed, sometimes the general direction involves "working toward clarifying goals for our work together" or "figuring out where we want to go from here." Later, when the confusion and ambiguity subside, you may appropriately return to encourage identification of clear and precise goals that conform more closely to a SMART format.

The probability of constructive progress markedly decreases when there is a mismatch between clients' goals and their stage of change. The same holds true for action plans and action steps. **Stage matching** applies to the processes of establishing goals, developing action plans, and establishing action steps that correspond to clients' level of motivation and readiness.

Clients who are in a stage of precontemplation tend to deny or minimize issues that other people notice. For example, Jared drinks at least two 750-ml bottles of wine each and every night. During the first meeting with a social worker, he says drinking is not a problem for him. "The only problem is that my wife Bethea constantly complains about my drinking." Imagine what would happen if a social worker suggested the following goal: "Jared will completely abstain from the ingestion of all alcohol within 4 weeks and maintain that abstinence for at least 12 months thereafter." The mismatch between his stage of change and the goal is so extreme that Jared would probably not return for a second meeting. Instead of directly challenging Jared about the drinking issue, a social worker might suggest that he consider a goal such as this: "Within 4 weeks, I (Jared) will learn more about Bethea's concerns and better understand her perspective about the drinking issue."

People in a stage of contemplation are generally well aware of needs and problems. Indeed, many spend a great deal of time and energy thinking, worrying, or obsessing about an issue, its causes, and sometimes even how to address it. However, contemplators are usually not ready to make a serious pledge to change. Like those in the precontemplation stage, introduction of a goal that calls for immediate action would constitute a mismatch. Contemplators are more likely to respond appreciatively to general goals that involve, for example, achieving a better understanding of the nature and scope of the problem, increased self-understanding, or perhaps greater insight into the reasons they have denied or minimized the issue for so long. A goal such as the following more closely matches the stage of change for Bo—who is concerned about what he calls "rage attacks." "Three weeks from today, I (Bo) will have collected and recorded 21 days of data concerning the frequency, intensity, and duration of his "rage attacks." Notice that this goal matches the stage of change and also appears in SMART format.

Clients in the preparing stage are usually eager to create plans for change. Insightful, they typically hold themselves partially or wholly responsible for either or both the cause or the solution of a problem of concern. Motivated to take action in the near future, many people in this stage have attempted to make changes in the past but without much success. Goals that correspond most directly with the preparation change often involve dimensions such as (1) increased knowledge about "what works" and "what doesn't," (2) commitment to take action, and (3) a plan to take action.

Issa, for example, has made several unsuccessful attempts to overcome a long-term problem of procrastination at work. He jokes that he even procrastinates about the problem of procrastination. The following goal would represent wonderful long-term progress: "Within 1 year, I (Issa) will have completed 95 percent or more of all time-sensitive work-related projects on or before their respective due dates for at least the previous 6 months." People in the preparation stage would typically embrace such an ultimate goal. Issa might say something such as, "Wow! That would be great!" However, the goal is so large and distant that smaller, shorter-term goals might better match his level of motivation and readiness. Since Issa has made several false starts, let's help him establish initial goals that reflect a high probability of success within a manageable period of time. One goal might be this: "Within 2 weeks, I (Issa) will understand how to modify those aspects of myself and my situation that can help me reduce my habit of procrastination at work." Another might be: "Within 1 week, I (Issa) will prepare a written plan that outlines how I will change my habit of procrastination at work." A third could be: "Within 1 week, I (Issa) will make a public commitment to at least five of my closest friends that I intend to overcome my habit of procrastination at work, and ask them for their help in the process."

People in the action stage are already taking steps and making changes. Most have identified goals and are investing time and energy in their pursuit. If the goals appear reasonable, achievable, and measurable, and clients are making progress, then social workers enthusiastically support the process. In effect, we stay out of the way and offer support and encouragement. If, however, progress has stalled or a problem worsened, the goals may need to be reexamined, clarified, or even reformulated. Sometimes, of course, plateaus or relapses may have little to do with the goals and more to do with the plan for change and its implementation, or with the environmental circumstances.

Whether stated in general or specific terms, effective goal statements follow logically from and relate directly to the confirmed issues for work. Typically social workers and clients identify at least one goal for each focal issue. We often begin the process by turning a focal issue into its logical opposite. For example, a social worker and client could readily convert a couple's ignorance about family planning (a knowledge deficit) into a goal such as, "to increase our (the clients') knowledge of family planning." Indeed, many issues appear as surpluses or deficits of knowledge, skill, motivation, capacity, opportunity, or resources. A client-identified issue of excessive anxiety (that is, a surplus of anxiety) could be converted into a client goal such as, "I will decrease my excessive anxiety by 50 percent within 6 weeks." Similarly, a problem of inadequate or insufficient time with an intimate partner could become a goal: "I will increase my one-to-one time with Laurie by 25 percent within 2 months."

Sometimes, achievement of one goal naturally resolves more than one focal issue. Because of the interactive and systemic nature of problems and goals, it may not always be necessary to create a separate goal for each focal issue. Nonetheless, be sure that accomplishing the service goals actually resolves all the agreed-upon issues for work. Be cautious, however, about attempting to pursue too many goals all at once. A large number of goals can diminish motivation and decrease the probability of success (Dalton & Spiller, 2012).

Consistent with our professional values, social workers define goals through a collaborative process with clients and gain full, informed consent to work toward their achievement. In effect, when you and a client establish goals, you implicitly agree to a contract in which both parties commit to work toward their accomplishment. Clients are usually quite capable of active participation in goal identification. As part of that process, encourage them to identify a goal for each focal issue. In doing so, however, recognize that some clients focus so intently on problems that they simply cannot respond to a direct question such as "What is your goal for this problem?" or even "What would you like to see happen?" In such circumstances, we may engage clients in the goal-setting process by asking how they will know when a particular problem is no longer a problem (Berg, 1994; De Jong & Berg, 2002; Lipchik, 2002; O'Connell, 2005). In addition to encouraging goal identification, questions such as these serve another extremely important function. They tend to enhance clients' hope and optimism. Such questions encourage clients to envision, in considerable detail, a future in which the issue has indeed been resolved. In so doing, clients often begin to feel better, more energized, and more motivated to work toward goal attainment. To yield such results, however, we phrase these questions in a certain way. We adapt the exploring skill of seeking clarification to encourage clients to both establish a goal and to imagine a future without the problem or issue. As a way to practice, you may use the following format to phrase goal-identification questions in a future-focused manner:

PRACTICE FORMAT   *Encouraging Goal Identification*

In specific terms, how will you know when the issue of _____ is truly resolved?

or

What would indicate to you that this problem is truly a thing of the past?

EXAMPLE | **Encouraging Goal Identification and Establishing Goals**

Worker: Now that we have a pretty clear list of the problems, let's try to establish specific goals for each one. The first issue we've identified is that your 14-year-old son skips school 2 or 3 days each week. Let's imagine that it is now some point in the future and this issue has been completely resolved. What would indicate to you that your son's truancy is truly a thing of the past?[3]

Client: Well, I guess I'll know when Johnny goes to school every day and his grades are better.

Worker: (*reflecting goal; seeking feedback*) When Johnny goes to school daily and improves his grades, you will feel that it's no longer an issue. Is that right?

Client: Yes.

Worker: (*seeking clarification*) Okay, now let's try to be even more specific. When you say, "Johnny will go to school every day," do you also mean that he will attend all his classes when he's there?

Client: Yes.

Worker: (*seeking clarification*) What do you think would be a reasonable period for accomplishing this goal?

Client: Well, I don't know. I'd like him to start now.

(Continued)

---

[3] Note that this example involves problems or issues and goals for Johnny—a person who is not present. And, the goals are derived from problems in Johnny's behavior as identified by his mother, not by Johnny himself. If Johnny does not view his school-related behavior as problematic, and if he does not concur with these goals, the chances for progress diminish. He may not be motivated or ready (that is, he may be in a precontemplation or contemplation stage of change). Of course, it is often perfectly reasonable for parents to express concern about their children's behavior and to establish goals for improvement. However, when children are old enough to participate and it is safe for them to do so, social workers encourage parents to involve the children themselves. In this case, the social worker and client would probably seek 14-year-old Johnny's input and reaction to the identified issues and proposed goals, and attempt to secure his voluntary and active participation—in a manner that is consistent with his stage of change.

> **Worker:** (*sharing opinion; seeking feedback*) That would be great progress! But I wonder if that might be expecting too much. Let's see, it's now 1 month into the school year. As I understand it, Johnny skipped school some last year too and this year he is skipping even more. What do you think about a 2-month period for accomplishing the goal?
>
> **Client:** That sounds really good.
>
> **Worker:** (*establishing goal*) Okay, how does this sound as our first goal? "Within 2 months from today's date, Johnny will go to school every day and attend all his classes. The only exception would be when he's so sick he has to visit the doctor." Let's take a moment to write that down.... Now about the grades, as I understand, he is currently failing most of his courses. How will you know when that is no longer a problem?

As should be apparent from this example, social workers are sometimes quite active in encouraging goal identification. Notice that the questions reflect an implicit optimism. They require the client to envision a future in which the issue is indeed resolved. Therefore, in seeking goal identification, try to avoid phrases such as, "If the issues were resolved...." This could suggest pessimism about the chances for success. In expressing optimism, however, be careful to avoid making promises that you cannot keep. Most of the time social workers cannot guarantee that our services will result in successful outcomes.

Sometimes, in response to your questions, clients formulate clear goals with which you can readily concur. When this happens, you may simply reflect the goal by paraphrasing the client's words. You may use a format such as the following.

PRACTICE FORMAT | *Reflecting Goals*

As you see it, one goal for our work together is _____.

EXAMPLE | Reflecting and Establishing Goals

Client: (*responding to worker's request to state a goal*) Well, I guess I'd like to improve the quality of the communication between us.

Worker: (*reflecting goals*) As you see it then, one goal for our work together is for the two of you to become better at talking pleasantly and respectfully with one another. (*seeking feedback*) Is that right?

Client: Yes.

Reflecting goals involves communicating your empathic understanding of clients' views about goals that they would like to pursue. As are all reflecting skills, it is a form of active listening. When you reflect their goals, you demonstrate that you have heard and understood the direction clients want to go. In reflecting goals, you may paraphrase or mirror the client's words even when they are expressed in general terms. Alternately, you can modestly extend what the client said by phrasing your response so that the goal is clear and specific.

Sometimes, despite your active encouragement, a client cannot or will not identify a goal. In such instances, you may simply postpone the goal-setting process and engage in additional exploration of the person-issue-situation. Or, you could propose a tentative goal, which the client may accept, reject, or modify. In **proposing goals**, you may adopt a format such as the following:

PRACTICE FORMAT | *Proposing Goals*

I wonder, would it make sense to establish this as one goal for our work together:

_____?

EXAMPLE | **Proposing Goals**

Worker: Now that we have a pretty clear understanding of the issues and a sense of the direction we'd like to go, let's establish goals for our work together. We've agreed that your habit of watching Internet porn is a significant problem that we'll address in our work together. If I understand correctly, it's a habit that you'd like to break completely—since it affects your marriage. I wonder then, would it make sense to establish as one goal for our work together to abstain completely from any and all pornography?

EXAMPLE | **Proposing and Establishing Goals**

Client: Yes. It does feel like I've lost everything I had hoped for. I guess it's normal to feel sad when a marriage fails.

Worker: (*reflecting feelings and meanings*) Your dreams for the future of the marriage have been shattered, and you feel a powerful sense of loss and sadness.

Client: Yes, my marriage meant a lot to me.

Worker: (*encouraging goal identification*) I wonder if it might be possible for us to identify a goal in relation to these feelings of sadness and loss. Let's imagine that it's now sometime in the future when you have fully recovered. What will you be thinking, feeling, and doing when these depressed feelings are no longer a problem for you?

Client: Gee, I don't know exactly. I guess when I'm finally over her I'll feel a lot better.

Worker: (*reflecting content; encouraging goal specificity*) So it will be a positive sign when you begin to feel better. And what will indicate to you that you're feeling better?

Client: I guess once I'm over this, I'll be able to sleep and eat again and not think about her so much, and I might even be dating someone else.

Worker: (*reflecting content; proposing a goal; seeking feedback*) So when you begin to eat and sleep better, and you think about her less, we'll know that things have taken a positive turn. Let's make the goals even more specific so that we will know when you have completely achieved them. How does this sound to you? "Within 6 months, to (1) sleep 6 or more hours per night at least five nights per week, (2) regain the weight that you lost, (3) think about things other than your wife at least 75 percent of the time, and (4) go out on at least one date." What do you think?

Client: Real good. Right now, I probably think about her 95 percent of the time, and the idea of going on a date sounds just awful. If I were thinking about other things, doing other things, and dating someone else, I'd know that I'd finally be over her.

Worker: (*establishing goal*) Okay. Let's jot that down so we can remember it.

In the same way you previously recorded the focal issues for work, we now do the same for goals. As we discussed earlier, the goals often bear a close relationship to the identified needs, problems, or issues of concern. Table 11.1 reflects the relationship between several focal issues and their corresponding, general service goals. If we converted the general goals reflected in Table 11.1 into SMART goals, they might appear as those presented in Box 11.1.

TABLE 11.1 Sample: Relationship of Service Goals to Focal Issues	
Focal Issues (Confirmed Issues for Work)	**General Service Goals**
• Currently homeless	• Client has permanent housing
○ Lives on the street	○ Client has shelter
○ Winter approaching	○ Client has warm shelter
• Diabetes	• Client manages diabetic symptoms
○ Without medicine for a week	○ Client has medicine
○ Lacks medical care	○ Client has medical care
• Currently unemployed	• Client is employed
○ Lacks money	○ Client has stable income
○ Lacks medical insurance	○ Client has medical insurance

Box 11.1 SERVICE GOALS IN SMART FORMAT

1. Housing
   a. I (the client) have warm temporary shelter by 7:00 P.M. this evening.
   b. I have warm, permanent housing within 3 months of today's date.

2. Diabetes
   a. I obtain at least 1-week's supply of diabetes medication within 4 hours of this time.
   b. I meet with a medical doctor within 1 week of today's date.
   c. I develop an ongoing relationship with a health care system within 3 months of today's date.

3. Employment
   a. I secure regular employment within 3 months of today's date.
   b. I receive income from employment within 3-1/2 months of today's date.
   c. I obtain medical insurance within 5 months of today's date.

EXERCISE 11-1 Establishing Goals

Refer to your earlier exchanges with Mr. K, Loretta, the S family, Mrs. F, and the "troubled agency" (see Exercises 7-8, 8-1 through 8-6, 9-1 through 9-9, and 10-1 through 10-3) as you make the transition from the assessing to the contracting phase. Of course, the nature of this exercise does not allow you to interact with actual clients in establishing goals. Therefore, you must use some creativity to imagine each client system, formulate appropriate questions, and share your view of goals that might match the focal issues. The primary purpose for this exercise is to practice asking questions that encourage goal identification and to gain experience in preparing goal statements.

1. Refer to the earlier exchanges with Mr. K, then use the space below to (a) write the words you would say in asking questions that encourage Mr. K, the 55-year-old man who experienced post-divorce issues, to identify goals for your work together. Then, on behalf of Mr. K,

write (b) a general goal statement and, following that, (c) a SMART goal statement that relate to one or more of the focal issues as confirmed in Exercise 10-3-1.

2. Refer to the earlier exchanges with Loretta, then use the space provided to write the words you would say in asking questions to (a) encourage Loretta, the homeless woman, to identify goals for your work together. Then, on behalf of Loretta, write (b) a general goal statement and, following that, (c) a SMART goal statement that relate to one or more of the focal issues as confirmed in Exercise 10-3.2.

3. Refer to the earlier exchanges with the S family, then use the space below to write the words you would say in (a) asking questions to encourage members of the S family to identify goals for your work together. Then, on behalf of the S family, write (b) a general goal statement and, following that, (c) a SMART goal statement that relate to one or more of the focal issues as confirmed in Exercise 10-3.3.

4. Refer to the earlier exchanges with Mrs. F, then use the space provided to write the words you would say in asking questions that (a) encourage Mrs. F to identify goals for your work together. Then, on behalf of Mrs. F, write (b) a general goal statement and, following that, (c) a SMART goal statement that relate to one or more of the focal issues as confirmed in Exercise 10-3.4.

5. Refer to the earlier exchanges with people associated with the troubled social service agency, then use the space below to write the words you would say in asking questions that (a) encourage members of the social service agency group with whom you provide consultation services to identify goals for your work together. Then, on behalf of the social service agency group, write (b) a general goal statement and, following that, (c) a SMART goal statement that relate to one or more of the focal issues as confirmed in Exercise 10-3.5.

When you have completed these exercises, review the SMART goal statements that you wrote and then ask yourself the following questions. Have I described the goals as accomplishments rather than processes? Are the goals clear and specific? Are they measurable or verifiable in some way? Are they realistic, given the circumstances? Are they adequate? Are they consistent with the fundamental values and cultural preferences that you might expect of these clients? Finally, ask yourself if the goals are truly congruent with the focal issues as confirmed in Exercises 10-3.1 through 10-3.5? If your answer to any of these questions is no, revise your SMART goal statements to meet Egan's ideal form.

▉ Developing Action Plans

Once you and your clients establish goals, engage them in the process of **developing action plans**. Sometimes called "service plans," "treatment plans," or "intervention plans," action plans address the questions of who, what, where, when, and especially how you and the client will pursue the agreed-upon goals. In planning action, you and the client identify pertinent others who will meet with you and who or what will be the target for change. Together, you also determine who will be involved in the change efforts and how those efforts might affect others.

Consider, for example, a case in which the mother of an 8-year-old boy expresses concern about his disobedience and aggression. You and the mother would determine who could and who should be involved and in what context. Will it be the mother and boy together; the mother independently; the boy separately; sometimes one, sometimes the other, sometimes both; the boy in a group with other boys; or the mother in a group with other mothers? Possibilities abound, and many decisions are required. Clients participate in the process and, of course, must provide informed consent before any intervention or action may be undertaken.

Lifelong learning, scientific inquiry, and critical thinking abilities become particularly relevant in the action-planning process. At times, you might be extremely knowledgeable about recent outcome studies of the effectiveness of services intended to address problems and pursue goals such as those you and your clients identify. In such circumstances, you need to think critically about how that knowledge applies to this particular person-in-environment. At other times, you may need to search, review, and analyze current research studies before you can even begin to competently explore potential action plans.

You and clients also determine what social work role or roles you will play (for example, advocate, broker, case manager, counselor, educator, evaluator, facilitator, investigator, mediator, therapist, consultant, researcher, or policy analyst and policy planner). If, for example, you and a client decide that you will serve in the role of counselor, you also need to select a theoretical model or practice approach, a change strategy, or an intervention protocol that will guide your actions (for example, task centered, family systems, behavioral, problem solving, solution-focused, strengths-based, cognitive, or some combination thereof). You also determine the optimal counseling formats (for example, individual, dyadic, family, small group, or some combination of them). You and the client also decide how to implement the change efforts. As the social worker, how active should you be? How direct? Should you encourage the client to take the initiative, or should you assume primary leadership responsibility? You and the client decide how fast to proceed with change efforts and how to approach other people who could or should be involved.

You and the client decide where and when to hold your meetings and where and when the change efforts will occur. Sometimes it is easier for clients or potentially more effective, to meet in their homes rather than in an agency office. On other occasions, an entirely neutral location may be the best choice. You and the client also determine when you will meet (for example, morning, afternoon, evening; on which days), how often (for example, once per week, three times weekly, once per month), and how long (for example, 15 minutes, 30 minutes, 1 hour, 2 hours). Usually, you and the client establish a time frame for your work together. Will you plan to work together toward these goals for 6 weeks, 9 sessions, 3 months, 12 meetings, 6 months, or longer?

In addition, social workers and clients discuss the nature of a typical meeting so that those involved understand the general expectations. In an extension of the skill of orienting clients, you might initiate such a discussion by saying, "Here's what we usually do in our meetings. ..." It also helps to discuss expectations about activities between meetings. Some clients are unaware that much of the work toward goal attainment actually occurs during the time between one meeting and another. You could introduce this topic by saying, "Between meetings, we'll each engage in various tasks or activities and take steps to accomplish these goals. In fact, we'll do much of our work between meetings. Some people call this 'homework.'"

As you flesh out aspects of the plan, engage the client in identifying possible obstacles as well as potential resources that might affect outcomes. You might think of these as risk and protective factors for the service plan. Importantly, you also review and reflect on the likely benefits of a successful conclusion.

Most social work action plans involve change of some kind—change that would help resolve an issue and achieve a goal. Sometimes a single decision or action is sufficient. More commonly, however, we focus on change that requires several decisions and numerous actions. We may direct these change efforts toward some biological or psychological aspect of a person, toward some part of the social or physical environment, or, as is usually the case, toward elements of both the person and the situation. For instance, change in a person's thinking might be a focus (for example, to think more favorably about oneself, to develop a more optimistic attitude, or even to accept that certain things will probably remain pretty much as they are). Alternately, change in a client's feelings (for example, to reduce the frequency and intensity of angry feelings or to become more relaxed) might be the focus. Often, we attempt to produce a change in a client's behavior (for example, speak more often in a group context or become more proficient in certain parenting skills). As social workers, we also focus a great deal on situational, policy, and environmental change of various kinds. For instance, you might attempt to secure housing for a homeless person or to improve the quality of care for someone living in a foster home. You might try to find employment for someone out of work or obtain an exception for someone deemed ineligible for the SNAP (food stamps) program, health insurance, or Social Security benefits. You might even engage in policy–practice activities to challenge an unjust policy or improve the effectiveness of a social program. Regardless of the focus of change, recognize that individuals, dyads, families, groups, organizations, communities, or societies that are not ready for planned change or motivated to take action rarely do so. If you expect that change naturally and easily results from a cooperative process of goal setting and action planning, you will be sorely disappointed. Social workers realize that human beings and social systems vary in their readiness and motivation for change (Prochaska, 1999; Prochaska et al., 1994; Prochaska & Velicera, 1998). Indeed, an individual client might be anxious to take action to resolve one problem but reluctant to consider the possibility of change with regard to another.

Earlier, we considered the Transtheoretical Model (TTM) stages of change as they might apply to a particular goal. The original model referred to five stages: *precontemplation, contemplation, preparation, action,* and *maintenance* (Prochaska et al., 1994; Prochaska & Velicera, 1998). More recently, Norcross adapted the earlier scheme to emphasize the self-help nature of much change. In the revised model, Norcross continues to emphasize the non-linear nature of most change. The notion of a **spiral of change** recognizes that people frequently lapse in their attempts at change, return to and redo previous stages, and recycle the process—often several times—before change becomes habituated (Norcross et al., 2012).

Norcross refers to the steps or processes in the revised model as *psych, prep, perspire, persevere,* and *persist*. Whereas the original model was primarily descriptive in nature, the *5-P* approach is more prescriptive (Norcross et al., 2012).

Psych refers to the process of contemplating change or becoming *psyched*. In directing self-change, the person identifies and sets realistic goals, and begins to get ready for action. **Prep** refers to planning or *prepping*. The self-changer explores and selects ways and means to pursue and achieve the goals. A well-conceived plan is vital to positive outcomes. Indeed, the self-changer's motivation grows when a goal is set and a plan formulated. The plan should make sense to the person and reflect a reasonably high probability of success. Premature action—that is, taking steps before establishing a coherent plan—diminishes motivation and reduces the long-term likelihood of goal attainment.

Perspire involves action. The self-changer puts the plan into effect and begins to work at it—sometimes through large, dramatic action; but often through small, incremental changes. **Persevere** involves dealing with slips, lapses, relapses, or plateaus in the change process. The self-changer has prepared (or *prepped*) for these possibilities and has a plan for managing guilt, shame, fatigue, and pessimism if or when they occur. Perseverance frequently involves recycling the psyching and prepping steps before resuming action.

Persist involves maintaining the desired change over a sustained period of time. Indeed, some changes are so desirable that people wish to maintain them for as long as they live. In fact, once people become skilled in these self-directed change processes, they frequently know what to do if old problems reemerge or new ones arise (Norcross et al., 2012).

In developing action plans, you and your clients address a number of factors, including the focal issues and established goals, the stages of change, and your explanatory and change-oriented hypotheses as you develop an approach to guide your work together. Box 11.2 contains an example of how action plans might appear as part of the contract portion of the DAC.

BOX 11.2 EXAMPLE: ACTION PLANS

Florence Dupre (client) and I (Susan Holder—social worker) plan to meet together for weekly 1-hour sessions over the course of the next 8 weeks. Our purpose is to accomplish the goals identified above. In particular, we will work to secure a full-time job for Florence that pays $15 or more per hour and includes medical and retirement benefits. We will approach this work as a cooperative effort with each of us contributing ideas and suggestions and each of us taking steps toward goal achievement. I (Susan Holder) will serve in the roles of counselor, educator, and advocate in attempting to help Florence Dupre reach the established goals. Sometimes we will meet at the agency, sometimes at

(Continued)

Ms. Dupre's apartment, and sometimes at other locations within the community. In approaching this work, we will adopt a collaborative problem-solving approach in which we will jointly analyze the potential pros and cons associated with various courses of action and undertake various actions or steps intended to pursue the agreed-upon goals. Throughout the 8-week period, we will keep track of the tasks we undertake and their impact, and generally monitor progress toward goal achievement. At the end of that time, we will determine whether to conclude our work, consult with or refer to someone else, or contract with each other for further work together.

Susan Holder
Licensed Social Worker

EXERCISE 11-2   Developing Action Plans

For these exercises, assume that you are continuing your work with Mr. K., Loretta, the S family, Mrs. F, and the troubled social service agency. Review your responses to Exercises 10-3 (confirming issues for work) and 11-1 (establishing goals). Then, use a word-processing program to outline "Action Plans for Five Clients." The plans should be congruent with the focal issues and the established goals, and consistent with other dimensions discussed earlier. Save the five action plan outlines in separate sections within a single document. Save it to a file labeled "Action_Plans_for_5_Clients" and include it within your Social Work Skills Learning Portfolio.

When you have completed a first draft of the action plans, review them carefully and ask yourself if they adequately describe who is to be involved; who or what are the targets of change; where, when, and how long the meetings are to occur; how active or direct you are to be; what role or roles you are going to assume; what strategy or approach is to be used; and what the time frame is to be. Also, determine if the plan matches the stage of change for each client system's goals. In addition, consider whether the action plans could infringe on the personal values and cultural preferences you might expect of these particular clients. Decide if the action plans are logically congruent with the previously confirmed focal issues and the established goals for your work together. Finally, estimate the probability that successful implementation of the plans will lead to the achievement of the goals. Reflect upon your answers to these questions and, if needed, revise the action plans accordingly.

Identifying Action Steps

The goals that social workers and clients establish and plan to pursue through their action plans are usually too large to accomplish at one time. Therefore, we typically engage clients in identifying smaller tasks or action steps that, when completed, constitute progress to goal achievement (Reid, 1992).

In **identifying action steps**, you and clients use information gained and hypotheses generated during the exploration and assessment phases. We foster a creative, brainstorming atmosphere and use the skills of questioning, seeking clarification, reflecting, going beyond, and seeking feedback to generate possible tasks. As a collaborative partner in the process, you may also share your own professional knowledge and experience. Indeed, several evidence-based practice approaches include specific intervention activities, exercises, or techniques that often serve as excellent action steps. The explanatory and change-oriented hypotheses generated during assessment often suggest action steps that logically flow from a "theory of the case." Nonetheless, critical thinking is needed even when one or more action steps logically follow from both the research literature and your explanatory and change-oriented hypotheses. We think through issues such as, "Is the action step within a particular client's capacity?" "Are there opportunities for a client to attempt the task?" "Are there sufficient resources?" Importantly, we also ask, "What is the client's motivation and readiness (that is, the stage of change) to undertake this particular activity at this particular time?" As we discussed earlier, action steps that do not match a client's change stage are unlikely to be attempted and completed.

Tasks or action steps are sometimes referred to as **instrumental objectives**[4] because they are *instrumental* to the achievement of the established service goals. For example, people who believe they are powerless or helpless in certain life circumstances often become passive, inactive, reclusive, and withdrawn. They might even be called depressed. Numerous research studies suggest that when people who feel depressed increase their level of physical activity, become more engaged in meaningful personal and social endeavors, and begin to change what and how they think about themselves and their circumstances, they usually become less depressed and more content (Nieuwsma et al., 2012). Based upon such research-based evidence, social workers might encourage clients whose goals include becoming less depressed and more satisfied with life to consider actions steps that involve increasing the frequency and duration of (1) physical activity, (2) meaningful pursuits, (3) social interaction, and (4) thoughts of personal self-efficacy. We hypothesize that these changes would be instrumental in achieving clients' goals.

Of course, there are many ways to resolve issues and achieve goals. Some approaches require changes in the person, others involve changes in the social or physical environment, and many entail changes in multiple dimensions. Changes such as increasing one's knowledge about parenting or increasing one's skill in assertive communication are examples of person-focused change. Securing adequate food and shelter or organizing a tenants' union to lobby for improved building conditions exemplify situation-focused change. Sometimes unjust policies and practices, or toxic environments are targets of change. In social work practice, changes are rarely limited to an individual person. We usually seek changes in the social or physical environment as well. When you engage in policy–practice, participate in social or political action, and when you serve as an advocate, broker, or mediator, you are working toward situational or environmental change. For example, an unemployed client's situation could improve dramatically if you intercede with a prospective employer to help the client secure a new job; if you engage in collective efforts to improve the overall health of the economy and create many new jobs; or, if you change national economic policy so that every family is guaranteed a basic income.

Consider the example of a client living with a man who physically and emotionally abuses her, and does so on a frequent basis. With your help, several situational changes might be possible. Her male companion—clearly a critical part of her primary social system and a key element of her social environment—might be encouraged to join in a process of relationship counseling designed to enhance direct verbal communication and decrease the risk of future violence. He might begin to participate in a program for abusive men. Alternately, a criminal charge might be filed with the police or a restraining ordered obtained through the courts. She might leave the household for a safe shelter. All these steps involve changes in the situation, and all affect the person as well. Although an action step in any given case may be primarily person-focused or primarily environment-focused, you should be aware of the following systemic principle: Changes in one aspect of the person-in-environment nearly always result in changes in other aspects as well. In other words, person-focused change tends to affect the environment in some way—just as environment-focused change affects the person.

Involving relatively small tasks, action steps tend to have a relatively high probability of success. Unless broken down into smaller segments, large goals can seem overwhelming. Consider

---

[4] The terms *action step*, *task*, and *instrumental objective* refer to the same thing. They are synonymous.

this example: Suppose you are 50 pounds overweight and want to lose that much to improve your health. You commit to a goal of losing 50 pounds as soon as possible. Except through surgery, it is physically impossible to lose that much weight all at once. Reducing by one pound, then another, and then another, however, is conceivable. It is similar to the "one day at a time" principle of Alcoholics Anonymous (AA). Abstaining from alcohol for the rest of one's life is indeed a large order for anyone who has drunk large quantities of alcohol every day for many years. Abstaining for one day, one hour, or even for one minute is more manageable and certainly more probable. By putting together and accomplishing several small tasks (instrumental objectives), a large goal that otherwise would seem insurmountable may be achieved. Imagine how challenging it would be to address major social issues such as racial and sexual discrimination, political corruption, economic inequality, or environmental assaults on mother earth in single large steps. If we hope to have an impact, we usually must break down or partialize goals to address huge, amorphous, and insidious problems into precise targets and manageable tasks.

Identifying action steps involves determining what will be done, when, and by whom. These include actions that you or the client will take in your work toward goal achievement. Various action steps may be referred to as *client tasks, worker tasks, in-session tasks, between-session tasks* (Tolson, Reid, & Garvin, 1994), or *maintenance tasks*. **Client tasks** or **between-session tasks** are action steps that clients take during the intervals between your meetings. Sometime social workers refer to client tasks as "homework" activities. However, the term *task* may better convey that the worker and client jointly determine the activity. The social worker does not usually "assign" a task as a teacher might assign homework to a student. Rather, social workers and clients together decide what tasks to undertake. Furthermore, not all actions steps are completed by clients alone. We also complete tasks in our efforts to help.

Worker tasks are those that social workers complete outside the context of meetings with clients. **In-session tasks** are procedures, activities, or intervention techniques that you or clients undertake during your meetings together. **Maintenance tasks** are those regularly occurring personal or situational activities that become routine or institutionalized by clients to promote long-term change. Although maintenance tasks may occur within sessions, clients usually complete them between sessions and following conclusion of the working relationship.

In attempting to specify tasks or action steps, you and clients engage each other in generating small steps toward the goal. You may initiate this process by asking questions such as "What would represent a first step toward achieving this goal?" or "What will be the first sign that you are beginning to make progress toward this goal?"

Questions of this sort help to generate action steps. They may also suggest ways to evaluate progress. Notice the emphasis on identifying actions to take. Our focus is on doing something that represents movement toward goal achievement. Depending on the nature of the established goals, you may encourage clients to identify steps leading to changes in their thoughts, feelings, sensations, or behaviors, or in their social or physical environments.

When the agreed-upon established goals require long-term change (for example, maintain a 50-pound weight loss for 1 year or abstain from all alcohol use for 6 months), you engage the client in identifying action steps that directly relate to the maintenance of durable change. We do not require maintenance tasks in circumstances where a single decision or short-term action is the goal. Lasting change, however, usually requires ongoing attention. Therefore, social workers and clients identify ways and means to maintain change over the long term. Durable change becomes more likely when personal or environmental policies, practices, or activities become routine or institutionalized. The most effective maintenance tasks occur regularly (for example, hourly, daily, weekly, or biweekly) and function as reminders, incentives, or rewards for the affected individuals, families, groups, organizations, communities, or societies.

To identify maintenance tasks, you and clients envision a future where positive changes have already occurred and goals have been achieved. Together you address the question, "How do we maintain these changes over the long term?" You ask yourselves, "How can these changes become a natural and routine part of everyday life?" Building on the mutual understanding gained earlier, you jointly generate possible maintenance tasks within each relevant sphere of the person-in-environment.

During the contracting phase, you ask questions and share information that leads to the establishment of manageable tasks that, when completed, contribute to the accomplishment of one or more goals. As you and clients reach consensus concerning action steps, reflect them in clear terms and then seek feedback. When clients confirm your understanding, record the agreed-upon action steps in your case notes.

Tasks or action steps may emerge in various ways. People often have a wonderful sense of what it would take to make some progress toward goals. However, some may require encouragement in the form of "step-seeking questions." The following are some examples of typical processes by which social workers might engage clients in identifying action steps.

PRACTICE FORMAT   *Seeking Action Steps*

Okay, we've set a goal of _____. What do you think would represent a good first step toward that goal? (or) Let's imagine that you've already begun to make progress. What will be the first signs that things are improving?

EXAMPLE | **Seeking Action Steps**

Worker: (*reflecting a goal; seeking an action step*) You hope to improve your sleeping patterns. Right now, you sleep through the night only about 1 out of every 7 days. Your goal is to do so at least 5 days per week. Going from 1 to 5 nights is a pretty large jump. It might be helpful to start with something a bit smaller. What would represent a good first step toward achieving the goal?

EXAMPLE | **Seeking Action Steps**

Worker: (*reflecting a goal; seeking an action step*) At this point, you and your group have identified 126 people in the community who want to work but can't find jobs. You've established a goal of securing employment for at least 50 percent of them within the next year. You've also identified numerous obstacles to employment. What's one change that would make it easier for folks to find jobs and keep them?

If the client cannot or does not respond to your encouragement by identifying a small step, you may tentatively propose one for consideration. You may be familiar with relevant tasks, activities, or interventions from the professional literature and empirical research studies. Sometimes, you can logically generate relevant action steps based on previously identified explanatory and change-oriented hypotheses. Regardless of their source, be sure—as always—to seek your client's reactions to the idea. In proposing a task, you might use a format such as the following:

PRACTICE FORMAT | *Proposing Action Steps*

As a first step toward the goal of _____, what do you
think about _____ (client task, worker task, or
in-session task as needed)?

EXAMPLE | **Proposing Action Steps**

> **Worker:** (*reflecting goal; proposing a client task*) You hope to complete your General
> Education Diploma (GED) within the next 12 months. Since you completed 9
> years through public schools, I wonder if it might be useful to review your records to
> identify your stronger and weaker subjects. What do you think about contacting your
> previous schools to request your academic records?

EXAMPLE | **Proposing Action Steps**

> **Worker:** (*reflecting goal; proposing a worker task*) You hope to complete your General
> Education Diploma (GED) within the next 12 months. As one step toward that goal,
> I'd like to contact the department of education on your behalf and ask for information
> about local GED programs and other options. How does that sound to you?

EXAMPLE | **Proposing Action Steps**

> **Worker:** (*proposing an in-session task*) Here's a copy of the application form for a nearby
> GED program. I thought we might try to complete it together during our meeting
> today. What do you think?

Once action steps have been identified by a client or social worker and consensus reached, you
formalize the agreement by establishing an action step.

In practicing the skill, you may use a format such as the following:

PRACTICE FORMAT | *Establishing Action Steps*

So, the (first or next) step that (you, I, or we) will take is _____
_____. (You, I, or We) will complete this task by (date) and
talk about it at our next meeting.

EXAMPLE | **Establishing Action Steps**

> **Client:** (*identifying an action step*) I'll go ahead and talk with her to see if she'd be
> interested in the idea of joint counseling.
> **Worker:** (*establishing an action step*) Okay, the next step that you will take is to talk with
> your partner and ask her if she might be interested in joining us for a few meetings.
> You'll talk with her within the next few days in order to give her a chance to think
> about it and make a decision before our next meeting. How does that sound? Fine,
> let's jot that down so we can keep it in mind.

TABLE 11.2 Action Steps Associated with Established Service Goals

Service Goals	Action Steps
• I (client) have warm temporary shelter by this evening.	**Client Task:** Gather together belongings. **Worker Task:** Contact temporary housing shelters; make arrangements for short-term shelter.
• I have warm, permanent housing within 3 months of today's date.	**Client Task:** Complete necessary application forms. **Worker Task:** Locate low-cost or subsidized housing.
• I obtain at least 1 week's supply of diabetes medication by this evening.	**Client Task:** Describe medical condition. **Worker Task:** Contact medical clinic to secure interim supply of medication.
• I meet with a medical doctor within 1 week of today's date.	**Client and Worker Tasks:** Schedule appointment with medical clinic; arrange for transportation if needed.
• I develop an ongoing relationship with a health care system within 3 months of today's date.	**Client Task:** Arrange for follow-up visit with medical clinic. **Worker Task:** Facilitate arrangement of follow-up visit if needed.
• I secure regular employment within 3 months of today's date.	**Client Task:** Search for job openings; make application; secure employment, preferably with company that provides health insurance. **Worker Task:** Search for job openings; help client with application and preparation for job interview; help arrange for transportation if needed.
• I receive income from employment within 3-1/2 months of today's date.	**Client Task:** Share information with worker. **Worker Task:** Seek information from client.
• I obtain medical insurance within 5 months of today's date.	**Client Task:** If employment does not include health insurance, make application with low-cost carrier. **Worker Task:** Locate low-cost health insurer—if employment does not include health insurance.

Agreement about action steps commonly increases clients' motivation to make changes—especially if the tasks are relevant to the goals, within each person's resources and capacities, and consistent with the explanatory and change-oriented hypotheses. Social workers typically assume responsibility for entering the jointly agreed-upon tasks or action steps into the formal case record (see Table 11.2). In the entry, we identify the person or people responsible for undertaking each task and the time frame for completion. Record keeping is our professional responsibility. We must maintain accurate documentation. However, many clients also make notes for themselves. In doing so, they often feel a greater sense of active participation in the process. To encourage this, some social workers provide notebooks to clients during their first meeting together.

EXERCISE 11-3 Identifying Action Steps

Refer to your responses to Exercises 11-1 (establishing goals) and 11-2 (developing action plans) as you continue to use contracting skills with Mr. K, Loretta, the S family, Mrs. F, and the "troubled agency."

1. Write the words you might say to (a) encourage Mr. K to identify one or more action steps. Then, record what you might say in (b) proposing a client task, (c) a worker task, and (d) an in-session task.

2. Write the words you might say to (a) encourage Loretta to identify one or more action steps. Then, record what you might say in (b) proposing a client task, (c) a worker task, and (d) an in-session task.

3. Write the words you might say to (a) encourage members of the S family to identify one or more action steps. Then, record what you might say in (b) proposing a client task, (c) a worker task, and (d) an in-session task.

4. Write the words you might say to (a) encourage Mrs. F to identify one or more action steps. Then, record what you might say in (b) proposing a client task, (c) a worker task, and (d) an in-session task.

5. Write the words you might say to (a) encourage the group at the troubled social service agency to identify one or more action steps. Then, record what you might say in (b) proposing a client task, (c) a worker task, and (d) an in-session task.

When you have completed these exercises, review each of the tasks or action steps you have identified and ask yourself if the steps actually involve somebody doing something. Are the steps clear and specific? Would they in any way infringe on the personal values and the cultural preferences that you might expect of these clients? Do the steps match the client's stage of change? Are the action steps congruent with the specified issues, the goals, and the action plans previously prepared? Are they consistent with the strategies and interventions used in evidence-based practices and services? In particular, what is the probability that, if completed, the action steps would indeed contribute to and maintain the achievement of the identified goals? Reflect upon your answers to these questions and, if needed, revise the action steps accordingly.

◼ Planning for Evaluation

As helping professionals, we are responsible for evaluating progress toward problem resolution and goal achievement. Regardless of the nature of the agency setting, the presenting issues, or the client's circumstances, you should be able to identify some means to measure progress. In **planning for evaluation**, be sure to consider the "goodness of fit" between the measurement tools or procedures and clients' capacities and resources. For example, some clients are unable to create frequency charts or to complete lengthy paper-and-pencil instruments. Nonetheless, start with the presumption that you can locate or create some reasonable and relevant form of evaluation. In many practice contexts, failure to evaluate progress could constitute negligence and perhaps malpractice.

You can measure progress toward goal achievement in several ways. One of the more applicable methods is called goal attainment scaling (Kiresuk & Sherman, 1968; Kiresuk, Smith, & Cardillo, 1994). **Goal attainment scaling (GAS)** is particularly well suited to social work practice because the dimensions for measurement are not predetermined, as is the case with standardized tests and questionnaires. In GAS, the dimensions for assessment evolve from the goals negotiated by you and the client. Therefore they are specific to each unique client system, focal issue, and goal. Kagle and Kopels (2008) provide a useful summary of GAS procedures. In addition, Marson and Dran (2006) sponsor an extraordinary website on the topic of goal attainment scaling.

In developing a Goal Attainment Scale (see Table 11.3), social workers and clients identify and "weight" or "value" the importance of each established goal. Use a 1-to-10-point scale, where 10 reflects the "most important." Record each goal in the appropriate cell. Then collaborate with the client to generate a series of five descriptive predictions concerning the possible outcomes of work toward achievement of each goal. Record those in the appropriate cells as well. These predictions provide you and your client with markers on which to base your evaluation of progress. The possible outcomes range from "most unfavorable" to "most favorable."

Other means for evaluating progress toward goal achievement include frequency counting and subjective rating. In **frequency counting**, you, the client, or another person in the client's environment

| TABLE 11.3 | Blank Goal Attainment Scale Form | | | | |

Client: _____ Session Number or Date _____

Outcomes	Goal 1 Weight (1–10) _____	Goal 2 Weight (1–10) _____	Goal 3 Weight (1–10) _____	Goal 4 Weight (1–10) _____	Goal 5 Weight (1–10) _____
−2 Most unfavorable results thought likely					
−1 Less than expected success					
0 Expected level of success					
+1 More than expected success					
+2 Most favorable results thought likely					

keeps track of the frequency of a goal-related phenomenon (see Table 11.4). For example, people who have low self-regard often think disparaging and critical thoughts about themselves. You and such a client might identify as a final goal to increase the frequency of self-approving thoughts. You might provide the client with a small notepad in which to keep track of the number of self-approving thoughts during a given period (for example, each day for 1 week). You could then transfer the frequency counts onto graph paper, with the expectation that the change program will lead to a higher frequency of self-approving thoughts per day. We often use frequency counting to establish a baseline for the targeted phenomenon, before implementing intervention plans. Then, we use the baseline as a benchmark for evaluating the effectiveness of the service approach. You can apply frequency-counting procedures to many different phenomena in various person-in-environment dimensions.

| TABLE 11.4 | Frequency Count Form: Self-Approving Thoughts per Day |

Client: _____

Date	Frequency
Day 1	2
Day 2	5
Day 3	4
Day 4	8
Day 5	11
Day 6	9
Day 7	12
Day 8	14
Day 9	14
Day 10	15

TABLE 11.5	Sample Subjective Rating Form: Quality of Relationship Encounters	
Client: _____		
Date/Time	Encounter	Subjective Rating (1–10)
Day 1: 7:30 A.M.	Early morning conversation	8
Day 1: 11:30 A.M.	Phone conversation	3
Day 1: 6:17 P.M.	Early evening conversation	5

Subjective rating requires that you, clients, or other people make relative judgments concerning the extent, duration, frequency, or intensity of a targeted phenomenon. For example, you might ask a client to create an imaginary 10-point scale that runs from "worst" or "least" (number 1) to "best" or "most" (number 10). The client may then use this subjective scale to rate the target phenomenon. For example, suppose a client is concerned about the quality of the relationship with her partner. You could make a request in this fashion: "Would you please imagine a scale that runs from 1 to 10, with 1 being the lowest possible and 10 being the highest possible? Now let's rate the quality of each encounter you had with your partner yesterday. We'll use this form [see Table 11.5] to record your ratings." By using the form with the client during your meeting, you increase the likelihood that she will both understand how to use it and that she actually will use it between sessions to record the quality of daily encounters. Suppose the client reports she had four interactions with her partner yesterday. The first interaction was positive (Level 8), the second was unpleasant (Level 3), the third was okay (Level 5), and the last was extremely positive (Level 9). You could then ask the client and perhaps her partner as well to use subjective ratings forms to track the quality of their interactions throughout the day. You could phrase the request in this manner: "I'll give you several blank copies of the Subjective Rating Form. Following each encounter with your partner, use a row in the form to indicate the date and time, provide a brief description of the interaction, and record your rating of its quality. Please do not share your ratings with your partner until we meet together again. When we have several weeks' worth of ratings, we will create a graph so we can determine how your views change as we work toward improving the quality of the relationship. How does that sound?"

Subjective ratings also work well for problems that involve the intensity of unpleasant personal feelings or sensations. We often call this a **Subjective Units of Distress Scale (SUDS)**. For example, suppose you working with a teenage high school student. The teenager reports intense anxiety when she talks in front of her peers in classroom contexts. In this case, we plan to track progress by recording subjective ratings of the relative intensity of her anxious feelings in various classroom situations. A SUDS rating of *1* indicates the lowest possible level of anxiety (that is, a reasonable degree of calmness); *10* represents the highest possible level of anxiety. The teenager indicates that she can manage anxiety levels up to about *4* without losing her ability to function. Indeed, her goal is to maintain levels of *4* or less in all classroom situations. Table 11.6 illustrates how you might use subjective ratings of distress for evaluation purposes.

Subjective ratings can be used in relation to almost all forms of human phenomena (for example, physiological, psychological, or social). Of course, because they are subjective by definition, they are susceptible to individual bias and other forms of human error. Nonetheless, subjective ratings can be extremely useful when used to complement objective measures or when objective tools are inappropriate or impractical.

Frequency counts and subjective rating tables can easily be converted into graphic form through computerized spreadsheet software programs. Figure 11.1 reflects a graphic illustration of the data contained in Table 11.4.

TABLE 11.6	Sample Subjective Units of Distress Scale (SUDS)	

Client: _____ **Issue: Classroom Anxiety**

Date/Time	Situation	SUDS Rating (1–10)
Day 1: 9:15 A.M.	English class: Teacher calls on me to answer a question. I know the answer.	7
Day 1: 11:20 A.M.	Math class: Teacher asks me to complete a problem on the board in front of the entire class.	9
Day 1: 1:12 P.M.	Speech class: I give a 1-minute preview of a 10-minute speech I'm supposed to give in 2 weeks.	9
Day 1: 2:30 P.M.	Science Class: Teacher calls on me to answer a question from today's required reading. I don't know the answer.	10
Day 14: 9:35 A.M.	English class: Teacher calls on me to answer a question. I know the answer.	2
Day 14: 11:45 A.M.	Math class: Teacher asks me to complete a problem on the board in front of the entire class.	3
Day 14: 1:25 P.M.	Speech class: I give a 10-minute speech.	4
Day 14: 2:15 P.M.	Science Class: Teacher calls on me to answer a question from today's required reading. I don't know the answer.	5

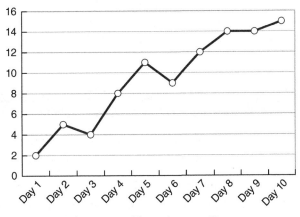

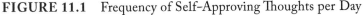

FIGURE 11.1   Frequency of Self-Approving Thoughts per Day

In addition to frequency counts and subjective ratings, social workers may also select from a vast array of widely available, valid, and reliable paper-and-pencil measurement tools—often called rapid assessment instruments (RAIs). For example, *The Clinical Measurement Package: A Field Manual* (Hudson, 1982) contains nine scales that are useful to social workers. These scales relate to phenomena that often affect our clients. The Clinical Measurement Package (CMP) scales address dimensions such as self-esteem, generalized contentment, marital satisfaction, sexual satisfaction, parental attitudes, child attitudes toward mother, child attitudes toward father, family relations, and peer relations. Each of the scales may be completed and scored quickly.

Measures for Clinical Practice: A Sourcebook (Corcoran & Fischer, 2013a, 2013b) is another extraordinary resource. The sourcebook contain two volumes of rapid assessment instruments relevant for many aspects of social work practice. Volume 1 contains more than 100 measures for assessing various dimensions of couples, families, and children. Volume 2 includes more than 200 instruments relevant for adults. Among the measures are those that aid in the assessment of various kinds of abuse, acculturation, addiction, anxiety and fear, assertiveness, beliefs, children's behavior, client motivation, coping, couple and marital relationships, death concerns, depression and grief, ethnic identity, family functioning, geriatric issues, guilt, health issues, identity, impulsivity, interpersonal behavior, locus of control, loneliness, love, mood, narcissism, pain, parent–child relationship, perfectionism, phobias, posttraumatic stress, problem solving, procrastination, psychopathology and psychiatric symptoms, rape, satisfaction with life, schizotypal symptoms, self-concept and esteem, self-control, self-efficacy, sexuality, smoking, social functioning, social support, stress, suicide, treatment satisfaction, and substance abuse. The two volumes of *Measures for Clinical Practice* represent a rich resource of easily administered and rapidly scored instruments.

Social workers sometimes incorporate RAIs as part of an assessment process. For the purposes of evaluation, however, we administer each RAI at least twice (in before-and-after fashion). Many social workers ask clients to complete them on a periodic basis to obtain data points throughout the course of their work together. Changes in scores over time can then be tracked and graphed in the same way as frequency counts and subjective ratings.

In policy–practice and advocacy work, social workers often rely on general indices such as those discussed in Chapter 4. Rates of child and adult poverty, employment and unemployment, voting, high school and college graduation, social mobility, and crime and incarceration may be pertinent. Statistics related to health and well-being, mortality, average family incomes, racial and gender equality, and those related to environmental health such as average global temperatures, sea levels, and air quality can serve as indirect indicators for the purposes of evaluation. Under most circumstances, of course, we cannot conclude that changes in such general indices over time result from a particular policy, program, or initiative. Nonetheless, if social workers remain aware of their limitations, they can be extremely helpful for policy–practice and advocacy purposes.

EXERCISE 11-4 Planning for Evaluation

Refer to the goals, action plans, and action steps you established in earlier exercises as you continue to use contracting skills with Mr. K, Loretta, the S family, Mrs. F, and the "troubled agency."

1. Prepare brief plans by which you might (a) subjectively evaluate progress toward goal attainment in your work with Mr. K. Then, outline plans by which you might (b) objectively evaluate progress toward goal achievement in your work with him. If you can locate one or more relevant RAIs, (c) include each instrument's name and identify where it can be obtained.

2. Prepare brief plans by which you might (a) subjectively evaluate progress toward goal attainment in your work with Loretta. Then, (b) outline plans by which you might objectively evaluate

progress toward goal achievement in your work with her. If you can locate one or more relevant RAIs, (c) include each instrument's name and identify where it can be obtained.

3. Prepare brief plans by which you might subjectively (a) evaluate progress toward goal attainment in your work with the S family. Then, (b) outline plans by which you might objectively evaluate progress toward goal achievement in your work with them. If you can locate one or more relevant RAIs, (c) include each instrument's name and identify where it can be obtained.

4. Prepare brief plans by which you might (a) subjectively evaluate progress toward goal attainment in your work with Mrs. F. Then, (b) outline plans by which you might objectively evaluate progress toward goal achievement in your work with her and her family. If you can locate one or more relevant RAIs, (c) include each instrument's name and identify where it can be obtained.

5. Prepare brief plans by which you might (a) subjectively evaluate progress toward goal attainment in your work with the troubled social service agency. Then, (b) outline plans by which you might objectively evaluate progress toward goal achievement in your work with the organization. If you can locate one or more relevant RAIs, (c) include each instrument's name and identify where it can be obtained.

When you have completed these exercises, please consider the means of evaluation you have identified and ask yourself the following questions: How subject to evaluator bias and other forms of error are these evaluation procedures? What are the ethical implications of these forms of evaluation? Do the procedures appear to be respectful of the personal values and the cultural preferences you might expect of these clients? Finally, are the procedures likely to yield an accurate indication of progress toward the goals established in Exercise 11-1? When complete, reflect upon your responses to these questions and, if needed, revise the evaluation plans accordingly.

■ Summarizing the Contract

Summarizing the contract or **service agreement** involves a concise review of the essential elements of the service agreement as endorsed by both the client and social worker. The service contract includes focal issues for work, goals, action plans, tasks or action steps, and the means by which you and the client intend to evaluate progress. Written agreements are generally preferred so that all involved parties may have copies and can refer to them as needed (Hanvey & Philpot, 1994). The service agreement may be organized in accordance with the framework shown here (see Box 11.3) and incorporated into a DAC. Alternately, they may be prepared separately as formal contracts, using letterhead paper, with spaces for clients and social workers to sign. Whether formal or informal,

---

Box 11.3 GUIDELINES FOR COMPLETION OF THE SERVICE CONTRACT

III. Service Contract

A. Issues

1. Client-Identified Issues

In this section, clearly outline the issues that the client identifies.

2. Worker-Identified Issues

In this section, outline the issues that you identify.

3. Confirmed (Focal) Issues

In this section, outline the issues that both parties agree to address. These are the issues that remain the focus for work unless subsequently renegotiated by you and the client. Of course, either party may request revisions to the service agreement.

B. Service Goals

In this section, outline the final outcome goals that you and the client select. Of course, they should relate directly to the problems or issues for work. If possible, define the final goals in a SMART format. Sometimes, of course, only general goal statements are possible or advisable. Whether specific or general, you may record the service goals in this part of the contract.

C. Plans

1. Action Plans/Service Approach

In this section, build upon the case formulation to summarize the general parameters of the action plans or service plans that you and your client have devised. Make note of factors such as who will be involved; where, when, and how often the work will occur, and for how long; and how the process will unfold. Identify, where applicable, the social work role or roles you will assume, and the theoretical approach, perspective, or model selected for use in work with this particular client as you collaboratively pursue the service goals.

(Continued)

> **a. Client Tasks/Action Steps**
>
> In this section, outline the initial tasks or action steps that the client agrees to undertake in his or her attempt to achieve the agreed-upon goals.
>
> **b. Worker Tasks**
>
> In this section, outline the initial tasks or activities that you plan to undertake in your effort to help achieve the agreed-upon goals.
>
> **c. In-Session Activities**
>
> In this section, outline the initial tasks or activities that you and the client agree to undertake during your meetings together.
>
> **d. Maintenance Tasks**
>
> If the goals involve long-term change, use this section to outline the tasks or activities that you agree will occur on a regular, ongoing basis to promote lasting change.
>
> **2. Plans to Evaluate Progress**
>
> In this section, outline the means and processes by which you and the client will evaluate progress toward goal accomplishment. Whenever possible, incorporate valid and reliable objective evaluation instruments to accompany subjective means and processes.

written or unwritten, the service agreement reflects your commitment to work together with the client toward achievement of the agreed-upon goals. Of course, the specific dimensions of the DAC format shown here may not be relevant for practice in all social work settings or with all clients, issues, or situations. As a professional social worker, you are responsible for adopting contract guidelines that best match the needs and functions of your agency program and your clients. Regardless of the setting, however, you will probably find that service agreements or contracts represent a key component of effective social work practice.

Social workers typically prepare service contracts or service agreements in narrative form for inclusion in the case record. However, the addition of graphic representations (for example, logic models, concept maps, or tables) to the agreement can serve multiple purposes (Alter & Egan, 1997; Alter & Murty, 1997; Julian, 1997; Julian, Jones, & Deyo, 1995; Mattaini, 1993a, 1993b, 1995). Indeed, preparation of an **Action-Planning Table (APT)** enables you and your clients to refer regularly to the focal issues and service goals, and to the action plans and the evaluation plans for each goal. You can also incorporate specific action steps, the results of those steps, and the results of various outcome indicators (for example, subjective rating scores, frequency counts, or scale scores). In a sense, such a planning table is another kind of "concept map" or "logic map." However, we typically arrange the components in a linear fashion to highlight the relationship of problems to goals, goals to plans, plans to action steps, and action steps to outcomes.

An abbreviated Action-Planning Table to guide service activities in work with Mrs. Chase might look something like the one presented in Table 11.7.

EXERCISE 11-5 Summarizing the Contract

For this exercise, please review the information you organized into the description and assessment sections of your own DAC (see Exercises 10-4 and 10-5). Based on what you know about yourself and what you included in the description and assessment sections, word-process a written contract as if you are your own social worker. In creating your contract, be aware that you, despite your considerable self-understanding, may miss one or more key issues that a professional social worker might help you to identify. Therefore—even though it concerns you rather than someone

TABLE 11.7	Action-Planning Table: Mrs. Chase		
Issues	**Service Goals**	**Action Plans**	**Evaluation Plans**
Issue 1: Arguments with son and husband	Goal 1a: Decrease frequency of arguments by 50% within 4 weeks.	Service Plans 1a: 8 weekly cognitive-behavioral and task-centered service sessions	Evaluation Plans 1a: Argument log (completed daily)
	Goal 1b: Increase frequency of satisfying exchanges with son and husband by 50% within 4 weeks.	Service Plans 1b: 8 weekly cognitive-behavioral and task-centered service sessions	Evaluation Plans 1b: Satisfying exchanges log (completed daily)
Issue 2: Irritable, critical, angry feelings toward son and husband	Goal 2a: Decrease frequency and intensity of negative feelings of irritation and anger toward son and husband by 50% within 4 weeks.	Service Plans 1a: 8 weekly cognitive-behavioral and task-centered service sessions	Evaluation Plans 1a: Argument log (completed daily)
	Goal 2b: Increase frequency and intensity of positive feelings of comfort and acceptance of son and husband by 50% within 6 weeks.	Service Plans 1b: 8 weekly cognitive-behavioral and task-centered service sessions	Evaluation Plans 1b: Satisfying exchanges log (completed daily)

else—view the contract as a dynamic document, subject to later revision. Word-process your contract in accordance with the format provided in the DAC guidelines. When complete, save the "My DAC: Contract" document to a file labeled "My_DAC_Contract." Include it in the relevant section of your Social Work Skills Learning Portfolio. At this point, you have completed all three sections of your own DAC—the Description, the Assessment, and the Contract.

SUMMARY

Based on the exploration and assessment processes, social workers collaborate with clients to reach consensus about a service agreement that specifies the goals for work, the plans to pursue them, and the plans to evaluate progress. Agreement about the contract constitutes the formal start of the active change process—when social workers and others begin to work toward and measure progress toward goal achievement.

CHAPTER 11 Summary Exercises

1. You continue to work with the four clients described below (see the Summary Exercises in Chapters 7 through 10). You have engaged them, explored relevant issues and circumstances and, as part of the assessment processes, generated several explanatory and change-oriented hypotheses. Use word-processing software to *write the words* you would say and discuss the

actions you would take as you engage them in the contracting process. In other words, build upon your previous work to demonstrate how you would apply the requested contracting skills in these particular situations. Please *label* each of the skills that you use and place quotation marks around the words you would say. When finished, combine your work into a single document with a section for each of the four cases. Save the "Four Contracts" document to a file labeled "4_Contracts." Include the file in your Social Work Skills Learning Portfolio.

  a. Participants have formed subgroups to address five targeted social problems: unemployment, gangs, drug sales, drug use, and prostitution. Today, you're meeting with the subgroup on youth prostitution. Build upon the exploration and assessment processes you have previously undertaken to write the words you would say in (a) establishing at least one SMART goal for the following issue: some adolescent girls and boys perform sexual acts in exchange for money. After formulating one or more goals, use a word-processing program to (b) develop an action plan to pursue the goal or goals; (c) identify at least two action steps for each goal; (d) prepare plans for evaluation; and (e) summarize the contract.

  b. Danni is continuing her efforts to explore, process, and transcend the experience of victimization. In her mid-20s, she is college educated and has an excellent, well-paying job. Nevertheless, she remains somewhat surprised that she has been unable to "get over this incident by now." In today's meeting, build upon the exploration and assessment processes you have undertaken to (a) establish final goals for the needs, problems, or issues you identified (in Chapter 10). After formulating one or more goals, use a word-processing program to complete the following for each goal: (b) develop an action plan; (c) identify action steps; (d) prepare plans for evaluation; and (e) summarize the contract.

  c. You have developed a strong working relationship with the Z family. At this point you hope build upon the exploration and assessment processes you have previously undertaken to (a) establish final goals for the needs, problems, or issues you identified (in Chapter 10). After establishing final goals, use a word-processing program to complete the following for each goal: (b) develop an action plan; (c) identify action steps; (d) prepare plans for evaluation; and (e) summarize the contract.

  d. You have continued to work with Mr. T in advance of his trial date. In this meeting, build upon the exploration and assessment processes you have undertaken to (a) establish final goals for the needs, problems, or issues you previously identified. After establishing final goals, use a word-processing program to complete the following for each goal: (b) develop an action plan; (c) identify action steps; (d) prepare plans for evaluation; and (e) summarize the contract.

CHAPTER 11 Experiential Interviewing Exercise

At this point, you have completed two interviews with a practice client and are about to undertake a third. Thus far, you probably used some or all of the beginning skills and many or most of the exploring skills as well. As a result, you have probably demonstrated a high level of empathic understanding of the practice client from a person-in-environment perspective. You might have acknowledged several strengths and abilities as well as assets and resources. You have probably also collaboratively examined the client-identified problems or issues of concern and know a good deal about how they originated, when and how they occur, and their impact on the client's life. You may have summarized the practice client's ideas or hypotheses about why or how those issues occur.

Building on the previous meetings with your practice client, conduct the third interview. Ensure that the setting is private, and again record the meeting. As usual, you might propose a tentative agenda and then, of course, seek feedback from the client about it. When you and the practice client agree upon a direction for today's meeting, proceed to use exploring, assessing, and contracting skills with an aim of reaching consensus about a few primary goals for your work together. Goals phrased in SMART format are usually preferable. However, some clients are not yet ready for or amenable to that degree of specificity. If so, general goals or directions will certainly suffice. In addition to exploring and assessing skills, the most applicable contracting skills include establishing goals, developing action plans, identifying action steps, planning for evaluation, and summarizing the contract. Be sure to seek feedback from the practice client about all aspects of the service agreement (contract). If the practice client's views about the goals and plans differ from yours, continue discussion until you reach genuine consensus. Major difficulties occur when social workers adopt one set of goals and plans, and clients adopt another. As you conclude, arrange for another meeting and share with the practice client your preliminary ideas about what may happen in the next meeting.

When you've finished the 30-minute interview, take another 15 minutes for the following:

1. Leave your respective social worker and client roles. Request that your colleague complete a copy of the Contracting Skills Rating Form (see Appendix 6). Aspects of the Talking and Listening, Exploring, and Assessing Skills Rating Forms may also be applicable. When your colleague has completed the rating forms, inquire about today's interview experience. Ask general open-ended questions so that you might get as much evaluative feedback as possible and, through that, enhance your learning. For example, you might ask your colleague questions such as:
   - What thoughts, feelings, or other reactions do you have about today's meeting?
   - What do you think about the goals that we established?
   - What do you think about the plans we discussed?
   - What parts of the interview affected you the most—either positively or negatively?
   - What do you wish had happened during the interview that did not occur?
   - What suggestions do you have about how the interview could have been better, more helpful, or more constructive for you?
   - What suggestions do you have about how I could have been a better or more helpful social worker today?

   As you finish securing feedback from your practice client, thank her and tell her that you will see her soon.

   As soon as you can following the interview, use your word-processing software to prepare a report entitled "Third Interview: Practice Client Feedback." Label the document file "Intvue_3_Client_Feed" and deposit it in the "Experiential Exercise Folder" of your Social Work Skills Learning Portfolio.

2. Next, play the audio or video recording. Review and reflect upon what you see or hear, and appraise your performance. Take written notes as you go along. Then, go to Appendix 10 and complete the contracting section of The Social Work Skills Interview Rating Form to evaluate your performance of the social work skills. You may find items within the talking and listening, beginning, exploring, and assessing sections relevant as well. Use your ratings as a stimulus to evaluate your performance of relevant skills. Identify those skills you performed well, those that need improvement, those that you might or should have used during the interview, and those that you used but probably should not have. Reflect upon how you feel about the interview. Describe what you like and what you dislike. Also, discuss the quality of the assessment and identify additional aspects of the person-issue-situation that might contribute to a more complete assessment. You might have a chance to explore those in a subsequent meeting.

Finally, discuss what you would do differently if you had a chance to conduct the interview again and outline what you might do in the next interview to improve the quality of your work. Complete the evaluation of your performance in a brief document entitled "Third Interview: Self-Evaluation." Save the file as "Intvue_3_Self-Eval" in the "Experiential Interviewing Exercise" section of your Social Work Skills Learning Portfolio.

3. Next, proceed to prepare material for the formal practice client case record. Record information gained during this meeting into relevant sections of the DAC. Note the date of the interview as well as the date you prepare the record. Identify yourself as the social worker but continue to disguise the identity of the practice client. If you have gathered additional descriptive information, you may incorporate it into the description section that you prepared earlier. The same holds true for additional analysis and synthesis. Incorporate that into the assessment section. Based on the third meeting, you should have considerable information for the "Contract" section of the DAC for the formal case record. Label the document file "Intvue_3_DAC" and save it in the experiential exercise folder of your Social Work Skills Learning Portfolio.

4. Next, reflect upon the entirety of the third interview experience and use relevant preparing skills to prepare for the next meeting with the practice client. Draw upon what you learned and the documents you created to word-process "Plans for the Fourth Interview." Label the document file "Intvue_4_Plans" and deposit it in the "Experiential Interviewing Exercise" folder of your Social Work Skills Learning Portfolio.

CHAPTER 11   Self-Appraisal

As you finish this chapter, please reflect on your learning by using the following space to identify any ideas, terms, or concepts addressed in Chapter 11 that remain confusing or unclear to you:

Next, respond to the following items by carefully reading each statement. Please use a 1-to-10-point rating scale (where *1 = strongly disagree* and *10 = strongly agree*) to indicate the degree to which you agree or disagree with each statement. Place a check mark at the point that best reflects your view at this particular point in time. If you're truly *undecided*, place your check at the midpoint (5.5) mark.

1. I can discuss the purposes and functions of contracting.

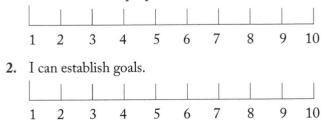

```
|   |   |   |   |   |   |   |   |   |
1   2   3   4   5   6   7   8   9   10
```

2. I can establish goals.

```
|   |   |   |   |   |   |   |   |   |
1   2   3   4   5   6   7   8   9   10
```

3. I can develop action plans.

   1   2   3   4   5   6   7   8   9   10

4. I can identify action steps.

   1   2   3   4   5   6   7   8   9   10

5. I can plan for evaluation.

   1   2   3   4   5   6   7   8   9   10

6. I can summarize the contract.

   1   2   3   4   5   6   7   8   9   10

Working and Evaluating

CHAPTER 12

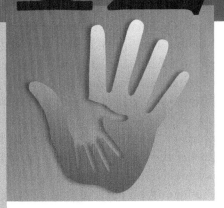

As you engage clients in the process of working toward the goals you jointly agree to pursue, you make a transition. Until this point in the helping process, you use social work skills primarily for collecting information, developing a relationship, formulating an assessment, and negotiating a service contract. Once you agree on a contract, however, you may legitimately use skills to promote change within various aspects of the person-issue-situation. The **working and evaluating** skills build on clients' experience and frames of reference by introducing, in a much more active and expressive fashion, your professional knowledge and expertise.

The skills covered in earlier chapters are primarily empathic, exploratory, and contractual

(Continued)

Core Competencies

The content addressed in this chapter supports the following core EPAS competencies:

- Competency 3: Advance Human Rights and Social, Economic, and Environmental Justice

- Competency 4: Engage in Practice-Informed Research and Research-Informed Practice

- Competency 5: Engage in Policy Practice

- Competency 6: Engage with Individuals, Families, Groups, Organizations, and Communities

- Competency 8: Intervene with Individuals, Families, Groups, Organizations, and Communities

- Competency 9: Evaluate Practice with Individuals, Families, Groups, Organizations, and Communities

Chapter Goals

Following completion of this chapter, you should be able to:

- Discuss the purposes and functions of the working and evaluating skills.

- Rehearse action steps.

- Review action steps.

- Evaluate.

- Focus.

- Educate.

- Advise.

- Respond with immediacy.

- Reframe.

- Observe inconsistencies.

- Represent.

- Link.

- Point out endings.

- Record progress.

in nature. You use them to clarify policies under which you operate; explore factors associated with the origin, development, and maintenance of the issues of concern; learn about and understand clients' experience from their own perspective; collaboratively develop an assessment; and agree on plans to pursue and evaluate progress toward the jointly determined goals for work. Throughout these processes, you listen actively to convey empathic understanding, reflect hypotheses, ask questions, and seek feedback. This encourages further self-expression and self-exploration by clients while also strengthening your working relationship. You may sometimes go slightly beyond clients' literal statements, but your primary focus is on their experience and frame of reference.

The working and evaluating skills are significantly different. Here, you may appropriately proceed from your social work frame of reference; your professional knowledge, experience, and expertise; and your capacity to think critically, rationally, and free from superstition and prejudice. These skills tend to be more active and expressive than empathic in nature. Through the working and evaluating skills, you express your professional agenda, your thoughts, feelings, beliefs, opinions, hypotheses, deductions, and conclusions. You first use such an active and expressive skill during the beginning phase of practice, when you suggest a tentative purpose for meeting and outline relevant policy and ethical factors. You also express your knowledge and experience when you identify an issue, suggest a goal, or propose an action step during the assessing and contracting processes.

Occasionally, the expressive skills bear little obvious relationship to clients' words or actions. However, most of the time, use of the expressive skills reflects an attempt to expand or extend clients' experience. You take what you have learned from the client and process it through your knowledge of research findings and science-based theoretical perspectives. Then, you apply the results in words and actions that you reasonably anticipate will help clients progress toward their goals.

Because the working and evaluating skills tend to be expressive rather than empathic, you must have a clear and justifiable rationale for their use. Your motivations should be professional, not personal. Resist temptations to share your knowledge, feelings, or opinions simply because they occur to you in the moment. Rather, the working skills you apply should consistently relate to the contract for work. That is, use your knowledge, intelligence, and expertise to help clients in their pursuit of agreed-upon goals. Indeed, unless you can demonstrate a clear relationship to the goals, it would be quite difficult to establish a logically defensible rationale for the use of an expressive skill. To determine whether an expressive work-phase skill is appropriate and applicable, you might critically consider the following questions:

- Have we adequately explored the person or people, the issue or issues, and the circumstances?
- Have I sufficiently communicated empathic understanding of the client's experience so that I may now reasonably consider using an expressive work-phase skill?
- Do we have a clear service agreement or contract?
- What is my objective in choosing a particular expressive work-phase skill at this particular time?
- Will my use of one or more expressive work-phase skills at this point help the client progress toward resolution of at least one focal issue and achievement of at least one goal?
- Will the use of a particular work-phase skill convey respect for the client's personal values and cultural preferences?
- How will the client likely react to my use of a particular expressive work-phase skill?

- What is the risk that using an expressive work-phase skill at this point in this context might endanger the client's personal or social well-being?
- What might be the risks that using an expressive work-phase skill now might endanger other people?
- How might my personal thoughts and feelings about this client at this time influence my selection or application of an expressive work-phase skill?
- Am I tempted to use an expressive work-phase skill now to express a personal view of my own, satisfy an individual need, or fulfill my own impulses?

If you think critically about these questions and consider their implications, you should be able to determine the appropriateness and applicability of a particular expressive work-phase skill. If you remain uncertain, however, you may choose a skill that is clearly more appropriate or return to an empathic exploring skill until you and the client are ready to take change-oriented action.

During the work and evaluation phase, social workers continue to use many of the empathic skills previously discussed. However, we increasingly use expressive skills such as rehearsing, reviewing, evaluating, focusing, educating, advising, responding with immediacy, reframing, observing inconsistencies, representing, linking, and pointing out endings. In using expressive work-phase skills, maintain your focus on the assessment and service contract. In particular, shape your efforts according to the agreed-upon goals and the service approach you and the client have established. Each application of a working skill should relate in some way to one or more of the identified goals or their associated instrumental objectives and action steps.

Rehearsing Action Steps

As part of the contracting process, clients often agree to attempt an action step. In the work phase, social workers prepare and encourage clients to carry out agreed-upon tasks. Unfortunately, clients' good intentions during a meeting are not always realized. Life's demands and challenges sometimes get in the way so that certain action steps remain incomplete or unattempted. When this happens, you and your clients identify and confront those biopsychosocial or environmental obstacles that interfere with task accomplishment. You may do several things within the context of your meetings with clients to increase the chances that steps will be taken. Various in-session activities such as role play, guided practice, and visualization bridge the gap between the special circumstances of the social work interview and the more common environment of everyday life. Involving more than talk alone, rehearsal activities constitute action step practice. By engaging several dimensions of experience (for example, thinking, feeling, and doing) in the rehearsal activity, clients move closer to what is necessary in the real-world context.

Rehearsing action steps decreases anxiety associated with the idea of taking action, enhances motivation, and increases the probability that the task will be undertaken. It also improves the chances that the action step will be successful. Through rehearsal, social workers help clients identify what needs to take place, anticipate what could happen, consider probable scenarios, and prepare various ways and means to complete the task. Although many clients are quite capable of creatively generating alternate scenarios and potential courses of action, some are not. When clients need such help, you may appropriately assume a more active role to anticipate possible circumstances and identify various options. You might propose a few different ways to undertake the step or present examples of how other people might do so. As part of the rehearsal process, you could model an action step for clients by saying or doing what they could say or do in various circumstances. In similar fashion, you might engage clients in role play. For example, you could assume the role of a person who will be involved in a client's action step. During or following the role play, you provide the client with guidance, feedback, support, and encouragement.

Another form of rehearsal involves clients visualizing themselves undertaking an agreed-upon action step (Lazarus, 1984). Before encouraging clients to engage in visualization, however, first determine whether they have the capacity to create mental images or "pictures." You might explore this by asking, "If I were to ask you to imagine in your mind's eye the kitchen in the place where you live, could you do so?" If the client says, "Yes," you could then say, "Good, some people aren't able to imagine as well as you do. Your mental capacity in this area will help in our work together." You might then say, "Please assume a relaxed position and take a few slow, deep breaths. You may close your eyes if you wish but closing your eyes is not essential—many people can visualize just as well with their eyes open." Then you might go on to ask, "Please imagine a movie screen on which you can see the context where the step you'll take will occur. Now see yourself actually taking the action we have discussed." You might pause for a moment to ask the client to study the visualized scene in detail, noticing all aspects of the action step.

You may use visualization to identify clients' fears and to anticipate potential obstacles to successful action, as well as for the purpose of rehearsal. Once your clients generate clear ideas (that is, mental pictures) about what needs to be done, you may ask them to imagine overcoming obstacles and successfully completing the action step. Following that, you may also ask clients to identify the positive thoughts and feelings that accompany imaginary completion of the action step.

The following is an excerpt from an interview in which Susan Holder helped Lynn Chase to rehearse an action step through role play.

EXAMPLE | **Rehearsing an Action Step**

Worker: (*identifying an action step; seeking feedback*) One of the steps we identified is to express your affection for both Robert and Richard at least once each day. If I understand the usual patterns correctly, this would represent a change from the way you have recently related. Is that right?

Client: (*Mrs. Chase*) Yes, it would be a big change.

Worker: Making changes such as this usually requires some preparation and planning. By practicing ahead of time, we increase the likelihood that we will actually do it. With that in mind, what do you think about taking a little time to plan and practice with me what you are going to say and do each day with Robert and Richard?

Client: Okay.

Worker: Thanks. Now, when you think of where and when you might make your first caring statement to Robert, what comes to mind?

Client: Well, I think that I'd like to start off the day with something positive.

Worker: Good idea! Where do you think you will be when you make your first affectionate statement?

Client: Well, I think it will probably be in the kitchen.

Worker: In the kitchen. . . . Okay, let me assume the role of Robert. And, if you would, let's imagine that it is now tomorrow morning and we are in your kitchen. What will you say to him?

Client: Well, I think I'll say something like, "Robert, I know that we have been on each other's nerves lately. I now recognize that a lot of it has been my fault. I guess I've been more stressed out than I realized. Anyway, I want to say I'm sorry and I want you to know that I have never loved you more than I do now."

Worker: (*As Robert*) Geez. Thanks, Mom. I love you too.

Worker: (*As Herself*) Thanks, Lynn. When you say those words to Robert, I can really see your love for him. It shows especially when you look right into his eyes with gentleness and affection. How does it feel to you?

Client: It feels really good. I feel warm inside. I feel loving toward him and also better about myself.

Worker: How do you think Robert will respond to your words?

Client: I'm not sure. But I do think he'll like it, and it should bring us closer.

Worker: That's exactly what you want to happen, isn't it?

Client: Yes, it sure is.

Worker: How do you feel when you realize that Robert will probably appreciate your comments and feel very loved?

Client: Really good. I can't wait until tomorrow morning!

The following excerpt illustrates how Ms. Holder, the social worker, helps Mrs. Chase rehearse an action step using visualization.

EXAMPLE | **Rehearsing an Action Step**

Worker: (*identifying the step; exploring probability of action; seeking feedback*) One of the steps we identified as a means to decrease stress and increase feelings of personal comfort is to spend 15 minutes each day planning for or working in your garden. I must admit to wondering about your ability to actually do that. You are very busy. You do so many things that I wonder whether you will really take the time to do the 15 minutes of gardening each day. What do you think?

Client: (*Mrs. Chase*) Well, to be honest, I have known for some time that I need to get back to gardening and I just haven't done it. I keep on making promises to myself and I keep on breaking them.

Worker: Thanks for being frank with me. If we're going to get anywhere with these issues, honesty and openness with each other is the best policy. If you don't think you will actually take a step that we identify, please share that so we can make better plans.

Client: Okay, I will.

Worker: Thanks, Lynn. Making changes such as this usually requires some preparation and planning. Unless we practice ahead of time, things tend to stay the same. With that in mind, shall we try a little experiment that may make it a little easier to actually do the gardening that you'd like to do?

Client: Well, I guess so. What kind of experiment?

Worker: I'm sure that you've heard the old saying "Practice makes perfect." Well, for many people, practicing in one's imagination is nearly as effective as actually practicing in real life. If you happen to be one of the people who can form mental pictures, then we can use that capacity to visualize the steps you plan to take. Through visual practice, you increase the likelihood that you will actually begin to garden for real. Does that make sense to you?

Client: Yes, I think so. How do I do it?

(*Continued*)

Worker: First, let's find out about your picture-making ability. Please try now to imagine your garden as it used to be when it was in full bloom. Can you picture it?

Client: Yes. I can see it now.

Worker: Can you see it in color or is it black and white?

Client: It's in color.

Worker: Wonderful. Now, please imagine yourself in the garden tilling the soil around the growing plants. Is that the sort of thing you might be doing?

Client: Yes. I'd be down on my knees, working the soil.

Worker: Can you visualize that in your mind's eye?

Client: Yes.

Worker: Now, please describe what you are feeling, what you are experiencing, as you work the garden.

Client: Well, I feel warm and relaxed. I feel content. I feel happy. Working the soil is, well, it's pleasurable.

Worker: Now, please picture yourself in the garden this very evening. Can you do that?

Client: Yes.

Worker: And does that feel as good as the other picture did?

Client: Yes.

Worker: Now, let's shift to a different picture. Suppose it rains. Can you imagine planning or preparing for the garden in a way that would also be relaxing or pleasurable?

Client: Yes. I can work on my drawings of the garden. I draw a kind of map to show which plants, fruits, and vegetables go where in the garden. I also work out what to plant, when to plant, and the approximate dates they should be harvested.

Worker: And what do you feel in this picture?

Client: I feel just as relaxed and content as when I'm in the garden itself.

Worker: Let's create a picture of you actually doing that on rainy days when you cannot go out into the garden.

Client: Okay.

As a result of rehearsing—whether through role play, guided practice, visualization, or some combination—clients are more likely to carry out the activity in their own natural environment.

EXERCISE 12-1   Rehearsing Action Steps

Review the earlier exercises that involve Mr. K, Loretta, the S family, Mrs. F, and the troubled agency (see Exercises 7-8, 8-1 through 8-6, 9-1 through 9-9, 10-1 through 10-3, and 11-1 through 11-4) as you move from the contracting to the working and evaluating phase of service. Pay close attention to the action steps you previously identified as you use the skill of rehearsing with our five clients.

1. You are in the midst of an interview with Mr. K. You have agreed on the issues and goals for work and have identified an action step. In the following space, describe what you would

do and say in rehearsing the action step with this client. In formulating your description, anticipate what the client might say or do in response to your statements and actions.

2. You are in the midst of an interview with Loretta. You have agreed on the issues and goals for work and have identified an action step. In the following space, describe what you would do and say in rehearsing the action step with this client. In formulating your description, anticipate what the client might say or do in response to your statements and actions.

3. You are in the midst of an interview with the seven-member blended S family. You have agreed on the issues and goals for work and have identified an action step. In the following space, describe what you would do and say in rehearsing the action step with this client system. In formulating your description, anticipate what the clients might say or do in response to your statements and actions.

4. You are interviewing Mrs. F. You have agreed on the issues and goals for work and have identified an action step. In the following space, describe what you would do and say in rehearsing the

action step with this client. In formulating your description, anticipate what the client might say or do in response to your statements and actions.

5. You are meeting with the executive director of the agency for which you are providing social work consultative services. You and the director have agreed on the issues and goals for work and have identified an action step. In an initial effort to turn the troubled agency in a positive direction, the director intends to make a presentation to the board of directors outlining the major components of a strategic plan. In the following space, describe what you would do and say in rehearsing the action step with the agency director. In formulating your description, anticipate what the director might say or do in response to your words and actions.

Reviewing Action Steps

There are three possible outcomes when a client agrees to undertake an action step: (1) the client may complete it, (2) the client may partially complete it, or (3) the client may not attempt any portion of the action step. The first two outcomes typically represent progress; the third does not. Even the third outcome, however, may be useful if you and the client carefully review and analyze the process to improve the chance of success in the future. In working with clients, try to increase the probability that they will attempt and complete agreed-upon action steps. If clients rehearse an action step before attempting it for real, they are more likely to try it. Clients may also become more motivated to take action when they understand that they will subsequently review the action step with you. Demonstrate your interest in the process and outcome of their action steps by asking about them. By reviewing what happened following the attempt, you also gather information that contributes to the evaluation of progress toward goal achievement and the identification of subsequent action steps.

In **reviewing action steps**, adopt an attitude of supportive curiosity. Share your pleasure when clients partially or fully complete the task or activity. On the other hand, avoid disapproval or criticism when clients fail to attempt an action step. Rather, convey your interest through questions such as "What do you think got in the way of the attempt?" In such circumstances, explore with clients the thinking and feeling experiences that led them to defer action. Also inquire about situational factors that may have contributed to a change in plans. Often, it will become clear that unanticipated obstacles interfered with completion of the action step. You and your clients can use that information to devise alternate plans that address the obstacles. Then, you can rehearse the revised action steps. When clients complete an action step, you may appropriately express both pleasure and curiosity as you inquire about the factors contributing to the accomplishment. "What was different this time that enabled you to take this step?" For clients who have partly completed the activity, inquire with pleasure and interest about those differences that made it possible to take this "step in the right direction." Later, you may explore what factors blocked a more complete attempt and then collaborate to adjust the plans. When clients partially or fully complete the action step, encourage them to identify and express the satisfying thoughts and feelings that accompany action toward goal achievement. In most circumstances, you may also appropriately share your positive impressions about the client's efforts. Following such encouragement, you and your clients may then proceed to identify and rehearse additional action steps.

EXAMPLE | **Reviewing a Completed Action Step**

Worker: (*Ms. Holder*) Last time we talked, you planned to spend 15 minutes each day in gardening activities. If you recall, we went through the process of visualizing those activities in your mind's eye. How did that work out?

Client: (*Mrs. Chase*) It was great! I gardened every day, sometimes more than 15 minutes, and I enjoyed it enormously. It spread out into other parts of my life too. I felt more calm and content throughout the day.

Worker: Wonderful! So, it was truly effective in increasing your feelings of contentment?

Client: Yes. It really worked. I had only one headache all week, and I felt much better.

Worker: Terrific! Now is there anything about the gardening activity that we should change to make it better?

Client: No. It's working just fine. Let's not change anything about it.

Worker: Agreed. Let's keep the gardening activity just the same. That is, each day you will spend 15 minutes in a gardening activity. Is that right?

Client: Yes.

EXAMPLE | **Reviewing a Partially Completed Action Step**

Worker: (*Ms. Holder*) Last time we talked, you planned to spend 15 minutes each day in gardening activities. If you recall, we went through the process of visualizing those activities in your mind's eye. How did that work out?

Client: (*Mrs. Chase*) Well, I gardened on 2 days this week but I couldn't find the time to do any more than that. I was just too busy.

Worker: You were able to find time to do the gardening on 2 of the 7 days. That's a very good beginning. On the 2 days that you gardened, what was it like?

Client: Well, I guess at the beginning of the week I was just determined to do the gardening. I did it and I liked it. It's a lot to do, to start up a garden when you haven't worked on it for a long time. But I enjoyed it a lot and I felt good on those 2 days. On the third day, I just couldn't find the time.

Worker: It sounds like the 2 days that you did the gardening were very good days for you. You enjoyed those days at lot. On the third day when you did not garden you didn't feel as well. Would I be correct in saying that the gardening is definitely a helpful activity?

(Continued)

Client: Oh, yes! If only I would do it!

Worker: Let's see if we can figure out some way to make it easier for you to do the gardening and gain the benefits from it. What was different about the days that you did garden from the days that you didn't?

Client: Well, I was really motivated on the first 2 days. On the third day, I had a tough time at work, and I was exhausted when I got home. I just slumped onto the sofa and went to sleep. I guess I was tired every night after that.

Worker: Let's assume then that when you come home from work really tired, it's much harder for you to do the gardening, even though it leads to relaxing and contented feelings. I wonder, when you fall asleep on the sofa after work, do you awaken feeling as rested and relaxed as you do when you garden?

Client: Actually, I feel much worse after dozing on the sofa. I'm kind of grouchy for the rest of the evening. And I don't sleep very well at night. It's better when I garden.

Worker: Now that we know that, let's see what we can do to help you garden even when you're tired and exhausted from work. Imagine that you have just come home from a stressful day at work. You're exhausted. Your usual pattern has been to crash on the sofa. This time, however, imagine instead that you take a drink of ice water and walk out to the garden. You sit in a chair and look at your garden while drinking the ice water. You don't do anything. You just sit there. After 10 minutes or so, you can feel the stress and exhaustion begin to lessen. You decide to do just a little bit of gardening. After 15 minutes, you pause, and notice that you feel calm and relaxed. You're no longer tired. Instead, you're ready to go on with the rest of your evening.

How about it, Mrs. Chase, could you imagine that pretty clearly?

Client: Yes. And I can see myself really relaxing during the gardening. I don't relax as well when I sleep on the sofa.

Worker: In that case, what do you think about trying the 15 minutes of gardening again during this next week—only, let's go for 4 days instead of all 7?

Client: That sounds good. I think I'll do it this week.

EXAMPLE | **Reviewing an Unattempted Action Step**

Worker: (*Ms. Holder*) Last time we talked, you planned to spend 15 minutes each day in gardening activities. If you recall, we went through the process of visualizing those activities in your mind's eye. How did that work out?

Client: (*Mrs. Chase*) Well, I thought about it but I couldn't find the time to do any gardening at all. I was just too busy.

Worker: You were unable to find time to do the gardening at all during this past week. Tell me, during this past week, have there been any signs that things are getting better?

Client: Well, no. Things are about the same. I did feel a lot better after talking with you last time, but that lasted only a day or so.

Worker: It sounds like there was some temporary relief from talking about the problems with me, but there hasn't been any real progress, is that right?

Client: Yes, I'm afraid so.

Worker: Let's talk some about the gardening activity itself. In our discussion last time, you were quite sure that when you begin to garden again, even for a little bit, you will soon feel better. Do you think that still holds true, or have you reconsidered whether gardening would actually be helpful to you?

Client: Well, I know it would help me, but I just can't find the time.

Worker: If you still think the gardening would be helpful, let's see if we can identify what gets in the way of taking time to do it. During this past week, what did you end up doing instead of the gardening?

Client: Well, on the first evening I planned to garden, Robert injured his knee playing basketball and I had to take him to the emergency room. He has been in bed all this week. I've been nursing him each evening after I get home from work.

Worker: Your son's injury got in the way. How is his knee now?

Client: Well, it's much better. He should be able to get out of bed about the middle of next week. Then he'll start walking around the house. By the first part of the following week, he should be able to return to school.

Worker: It sounds as if your son is well on the way to recovery, and you will soon have more time once he can get around on his own. Do you think that when he does start to walk again, you will be more likely to do the gardening?

Client: I think so. It depends upon how much help he needs.

Worker: It sounds like you'll be nursing him at least for another several days. What is involved when you care for him in the evening?

Client: Well, first I make him supper and then I take it to his room. Then we talk for a while. Then I clean up the kitchen and do the dishes. Then I check on Robert again. We usually talk some more. By that time, it's time for bed.

Worker: Lynn, it seems to me that we have a choice to make here. First, if you really believe that once Robert is better you will begin the gardening, we can simply delay our start date for the gardening activities. If you believe, however, that if it were not Robert's injury it would be something else that would prevent you from gardening, then perhaps we should take this opportunity to challenge the pattern of excessive caretaking. When we explored this before, we used the phrase "over-mothering" to refer to the way you sometimes care so much for others, especially Richard and Robert, that it interferes with their ability to care for themselves. If your decision not to garden is a matter of neglecting yourself and over-mothering rather than simply a matter of unusual circumstances, then perhaps we might begin to address that right now while Robert is still injured. What do you think?

Client: Well, honestly, I think it's some of both. Robert's injury gives me an opportunity to care for him. I'm not sure it's over-mothering but I certainly do more than is really necessary. And, focusing so much on him this past week kept me away from the gardening activities that I was truly looking forward to.

Worker: Then, what do you think? Should we delay the start date for the gardening activities, or should we start now in order to challenge the tendency to avoid caring for yourself?

Client: Well, I guess I'd like to start right now. Even with Robert's injury, I should be able to find 15 minutes at some point during the evening.

Worker: All right. I wonder, though, because of the extra responsibilities caused by Robert's injury, should we change the plans from 15 minutes every single day to 15 minutes three times during the next week? That might be more reasonable, given the current circumstances.

Client: Yes, yes. I think that would be just about right. I know I can garden three times during the next 7 days.

Worker: Okay. We've changed the plans for gardening from once every day to three times during the next week. Now, what do you think about rehearsing this a little bit?

As a result of reviewing action steps, clients are more likely to believe that you genuinely care about between-session tasks and are serious about helping them progress toward agreed-upon goals. Reviewing increases the probability that clients will attempt and complete more tasks in the future.

EXERCISE 12-2 Reviewing Action Steps

Review the action steps you previously identified to create simulated dialogues between yourself and each of our five clients to demonstrate the skill of reviewing action steps. Feel free to be somewhat creative as you imagine how the exchanges might occur.

1. You are in the midst of reviewing action steps that you previously rehearsed with Mr. K. He reports that he has fully completed the action step (client task) as agreed. What might you say in reviewing the action step with this client?

2. You are in the midst of reviewing action steps that you previously rehearsed with Loretta. She reports that she attempted but did not fully complete the action step (client task). What might you say in reviewing the action step with this client?

3. You are in the midst of reviewing action steps that you previously rehearsed with the seven-member S family. The family members unanimously indicate—with slight chuckles—that they partially but not completely carried out the action step (client task). What might you say in reviewing the action step with them?

4. You are in the midst of reviewing action steps that you previously rehearsed with Mrs. F. She somberly reports that she simply did not attempt the action step (client task). What might you say in reviewing the action step with this client?

5. You are working with the executive director of the social service agency where you are providing social work consultative services. The director reports completion of the action step (client task) that you had previously agreed upon and rehearsed. What might you say in reviewing the action step with the director? Anticipate what the director might say or do in response to your statements and actions.

▉ Evaluating

Evaluation of progress is crucial during the work and evaluation phase. It often occurs while you are reviewing action steps. Through the skill of **evaluating**, you engage the client in reviewing progress toward goal attainment. You and the client may identify progress through changes in such indicators as goal attainment scales, frequency counts, individualized or subjective rating scales, rapid assessment instruments, or other paper-and-pencil and online instruments. Include the results of evaluations in case records. Also, track results so that you may note the presence or absence of progress as well as the rate of change. If you use a spreadsheet software program, you can readily convert numerical scores into tables, line graphs, pie charts, bar graphs, forest plots, and other graphic forms that clients can easily understand. Such graphic evidence of progress may enhance clients' self-efficacy and increase their motivation to take further action. Over time, if evaluation reveals little or no progress, or suggests a deteriorating trend, you and your clients can reconsider the assessment, the contract, and the action steps that you planned. Obviously, when progress toward goal achievement is not forthcoming, you need to reexamine the approach to change.

Through the skill of evaluating, you engage clients in examining data in accordance with the plans for evaluating progress. You determine whether the evaluation data reflect progress toward goal attainment, no change, or a change in the wrong direction. As you do when reviewing action steps, you may appropriately express your pleasure when there is clear evidence of progress. Encourage clients to identify those factors that contribute to positive change. When there is no evidence of progress, enlist clients in a collaborative exploration of the reasons why. Then, jointly consider

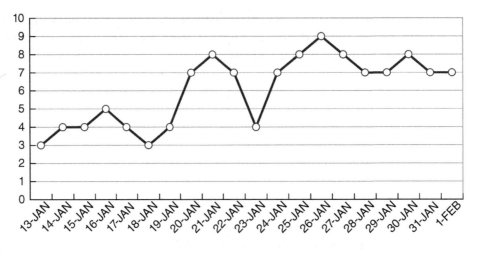

FIGURE 12.1 Lynn Chase: Hours of Sleep per Night

whether you need to make a major revision to the plans or whether relatively minor adjustments might suffice. Frequently, the evaluation instruments provide useful information to supplement clients' experiences and your own observations. When problems worsen, an intensive reanalysis is needed. You and your clients attempt to determine if the planned action steps, rather than help- ing, actually contribute to the deteriorating situation. Occasionally, initial negative effects are an expected but temporary phenomenon, subsequently followed by positive results. Because of the systemic nature of many issues, at first "things may sometimes become worse before they get better." However, this phenomenon—if it occurs at all—should be short-lived. If it continues for any length of time, it represents a problem that must immediately be addressed. Also, negative effects are not always the result of either your professional efforts or the action steps undertaken by clients. Rather, they may be the effects of changes in circumstances. Of course, sometimes the change program itself produces negative consequences. When this occurs, a thorough review of the contract is imperative.

As an example, consider Mrs. Chase's sleep log, in which she records the number of hours she sleeps each night. Susan Holder, the social worker, has reviewed these daily logs and converted the sleep data into the graph displayed in Figure 12.1.

As the line graph reveals, Mrs. Chase slept approximately 4 hours nightly during the period between January 13 and January 19. According to her, 4 hours has been the approximate amount she slept each night over the last several months. On the evening of January 20, following the sec- ond interview with Susan Holder, Mrs. Chase implemented the change program they had jointly devised. From that night on, Mrs. Chase's daily log reflects general progress toward the goal of sleeping 8 hours nightly. She slept less than 7 hours on only one night.

In evaluating progress, Mrs. Chase and Susan can reasonably infer that, in regard to the goal of sleeping more, the plans are working successfully. Of course, they would also review Mrs. Chase's subjective ratings concerning how refreshed she feels when she awakens each morning. Susan could also convert these subjective ratings into graphic form for ready review.

EXAMPLE | **Evaluating**

Worker: (*Ms. Holder*) As one measure of progress, you've been keeping track of the number of hours you sleep each night. I've taken your data and created a graph (see Figure 12.1) so we could easily see how your sleep patterns have changed during our work together. As you can see, you averaged a bit less than 4 hours per night during the first week. Since the time you completed your first action steps, however, things have improved. Beginning in the second week, you slept at least 7 hours every night but one. What does this graph suggest to you?

Client: (*Mrs. Chase*) Well, you can see I'm smiling. I sleep the whole night through now and feel refreshed when I awake in the morning. It's truly remarkable. In just a few weeks, I'm feeling and doing so much better—not only in terms of sleep and energy, but also in other areas as well.

Worker: Wonderful! So, the measurement data and your personal experience point in the same direction. It looks like you're making progress. Do you agree?

Client: I certainly do!

As they review the evaluation data, Mrs. Chase and Susan can feel pleased with the outcomes of their collaborative efforts. However, even if the data indicate little or no progress, or suggest deterioration, they can help the worker and client to identify obstacles and make necessary changes. Application of the evaluating skill differs according to the nature of the trend lines. The process is similar to our adaptation of the reviewing action steps skill according to whether a step was completed, partially completed, or not attempted. Let's imagine that the data presented in Figure 12.1 were reversed so that Mrs. Chase reflected an average of 7 hours per night during the first week (the baseline) but much less sleep since then. She now averages about 4 hours per night—a substantial decrease from before she began to work with you.

In a deteriorating situation, the exchange between Susan Holder and Mrs. Chase might go something like this:

EXAMPLE | **Evaluating**

Worker: (*Ms. Holder*) As one measure of progress, you've been keeping track of the number of hours you sleep each night. I've taken your data and created a graph so we could easily see how your sleep patterns have changed during our work together. As you can see, you averaged between 7 and 8 hours per night during the first week. Since the time you completed your first action steps, however, you slept a lot less. Beginning in the second week, you slept, on average, less than 4 hours each night. What does this graph suggest to you?

Client: (*Mrs. Chase*) Well, I'm really disappointed. I sleep less now than before. I am exhausted every day and I'm also more irritable with others. In fact, I think I'm worse since I first met you.

Worker: Yes. That's how it looks to me too. Both the measurement data and your personal experience point in the same direction. Things are getting worse.

Client: Yes they are!

Worker: Okay. Since our plans aren't working out the way we hoped, let's see if we can figure out what needs to change so that things begin to improve rather than worsen. Does that make sense to you?

Client: It certainly does. I can't go on like this much longer!

Whether the data suggest deterioration, progress, or a lack of progress, the skill of evaluating enables social workers and clients to incorporate evidence in their work together. Indeed, evaluation data generated by clients themselves are perhaps the most important forms of evidence in evidence-based social work practice.

EXERCISE 12-3   Evaluating

In the spaces provided, create simulated dialogues between yourself and our five clients. Showing how you might use the skill of evaluating progress toward goal attainment. Use your responses to earlier exercises to recall how you planned to evaluate progress for each of our five clients: Mr. K, Loretta, the S family, Mrs. F, and our troubled agency.

1. You are in the midst of evaluating progress toward goal attainment with Mr. K. The measurement data clearly reflect overall progress toward goal achievement. However, during the past week, the scores reflected a sharp decline. In fact, the data suggest that things are worse. Write the words you would use to initiate a review of the data and discuss the implications with him.

2. You are in the midst of evaluating progress toward goal attainment with Loretta. The measurement data clearly indicate that some progress toward goal achievement has occurred. However, the extent of progress is modest. Write the words you would use to initiate a review of the data and discuss the implications with Loretta.

3. You are in the midst of evaluating progress toward goal attainment with the S family. The measurement data for the previous week indicate that progress toward goal achievement has not occurred. In earlier weeks, there had been consistent positive improvement. However, last week the data suggest that there was no change in either a positive or a negative direction. It appears that there is a plateau. Write the words you would use to initiate a review of the data and discuss the implications with the S family.

4. You are in the midst of evaluating progress toward goal attainment with Mrs. F. The measurement data clearly indicate that progress toward goal achievement has occurred. There is a definitive change in a positive direction. Write the words you would use to initiate a review of the data and discuss the implications with Mrs. F.

5. You are in the midst of evaluating progress toward goal attainment with the board of directors of the agency for which you are providing social work consultation services. The measurement data clearly reflect progress toward goal achievement. There is a definitive change in a positive direction. Communications among staff members have improved, staff members now receive weekly supervision, the agency director is pursuing an active and engaged approach to leadership, and morale is improving. Write the words you would use to initiate a review of the data and discuss their implications with the board.

▮ Focusing

Focusing (Perlman, 1957) is a skill used to direct or maintain attention to the work at hand. Occasionally, both workers and clients wander away from agreed-upon agendas. These diversions are sometimes productive, leading to greater understanding and improving chances for effective change. At other times, however, such departures are clearly unproductive. Through the skill of focusing, you redirect energy to relevant topics. Also, clients sometimes miss the significance of phenomena that relate to targeted problems and goals. By directing attention to them, you may heighten their awareness. For example, in working with a family, you may observe that just as plans for an action step are about to be finalized, one sibling interrupts with a complaint about another family member's past misbehavior. As a social worker, you might hypothesize that the interruption may represent a defensive or self-protective act, ambivalence about change, or perhaps an attempt to maintain family-system equilibrium. However you regard it theoretically, you may use the skill of focusing to respond to the interruption. You could say to the family member who interrupts, "Would you please hold on to that thought so that we can come back to it later? Let's complete our plans first. Thanks." Through such a form of focusing, you guide the family back to the work at hand. To accomplish a different purpose, that of enhancing process awareness, you might focus in a different way: "I noticed that just about the time we were reaching consensus on a step to address one of the issues, Johnny brought up his concern about Sheila's past behavior. Johnny, I wonder, what do you think led you to raise the topic at this particular time?"[1]

PRACTICE FORMAT *Focusing*

"Sorry to interrupt but I wonder if we could come back to this topic later. We were just beginning to explore _____. Let's complete our discussion of that first. Thanks."

EXAMPLE | Focusing

Case Situation: You are working with a young couple (an Arab American man and a European American woman) who have sought counseling in advance of their forthcoming marriage. The three of you are discussing the fears and worries that their respective parents and siblings have about the marriage.

Woman: It's just awful. I don't think his father will come to the wedding. And, if he doesn't, then neither will his mother or his siblings. (*At this point, she breaks into tears and begins to sob uncontrollably.*)

Man: (*As she sobs, the young man looks extremely uncomfortable. He turns away from her and looks at you.*) Did you receive the check I sent for our last session?

Worker: Amir, thanks for asking but I wonder if we might go back to what Jerri was saying about her worry that your family might not attend the wedding.

EXERCISE 12-4   Focusing

For this exercise, use the social work skill of focusing with our five clients: Mr. K, Loretta, the S family, Mrs. F, and our troubled agency.

1. You are reviewing action steps with Mr. K. In the midst of this process, he begins to reminisce about a childhood friend. Based upon the service goals, you believe that he would benefit if you were to complete the process of reviewing action steps. You intend to return later to his childhood memories. Write the words you would say in using the skill of focusing with Mr. K.

2. You are meeting with Loretta to discuss her current circumstances. In the midst of this, she mentions her eldest daughter. However, she stops abruptly and returns to the topic of her new housing arrangement. Based upon the service goals, you believe that she would benefit if you

---

[1] This form contains elements of the "observing inconsistencies" and "responding with immediacy" skills.

were to encourage her to continue to talk about her daughter. Write the words you would say in using the skill of focusing with Loretta.

3. You are in the midst of exploring a new topic of importance to the S family. Only the parents and the teenage children are present for this meeting. The subject involves the emerging sexuality of the adolescents. As the discussion begins, you observe that Mrs. S changes the subject to a less anxiety-provoking issue. This pattern seems to occur whenever the adolescent family members begin to express sexual concerns. Based on your professional judgment, you conclude that continuing with the topic of adolescent sexuality would be congruent with the values and cultural background of the family, would be helpful to the family, and would represent a step toward goal achievement. You therefore decide to use the skill of focusing. Write the words you would say to redirect the discussion back to the topic of adolescent sexuality. Then indicate how you might refocus to enhance the family's awareness of the pattern of shifting away from difficult topics.

4. You are in the midst of role-playing an action step with Mrs. F. She has assumed the role of her own daughter. A few moments after taking the part of her daughter, Mrs. F's eyes begin to water, and then tears start to fall onto her cheeks. Mrs. F shrugs and continues in the role of her daughter. You make a professional judgment that Mrs. F would benefit from a more complete expression of her feelings and an exploration of the meaning of the tears. You also realize that such steps would be entirely consistent with the contract for work. In the space provided, write the words you would say in using the skill of focusing to call attention to the tears as well as to the thoughts and feelings behind them.

5. You are in the midst of evaluating progress toward goal attainment with the board of directors of the agency for which you are providing social work consultation services. Following your summary presentation of data regarding progress, the board members begin an active discussion of the implications of these positive findings. Suddenly, one of the participants introduces the topic of the former director's misbehavior. In your professional judgment, a shift away from the current discussion at this time would detract from the board's work. Write the words you would say to help the board members continue to discuss the implications of the positive evaluation data.

Educating

During the work phase, it may become apparent that clients lack valid information or relevant skills needed to progress toward goal achievement. In such circumstances, you may appropriately assume the role of teacher or educator. The skill of **educating** involves several dimensions. Often, you share relevant knowledge. For example, you might describe the eligibility requirements to a family interested in an innovative program for their youngest son, who suffers from multiple sclerosis. You could outline the substance of a piece of legislation that could adversely affect the human rights of nonreligious residents. Or, you might inform parents about major developmental milestones to anticipate in an infant's first year of life. You could share professional knowledge about how parents might facilitate childhood development through, for instance, mutual play activities. In educating, convey the information in such a way that clients may freely consider its relevance for their particular situation and decide whether to accept it. This is particularly true when sharing professional opinions rather than facts. Even when you present factual information, however, continue to respect the right of clients to disagree and choose their own course of action.

In educating clients, realize that all people do not learn in the same way. There are several different learning styles; some of your clients are likely to have learning styles that differ from your own preferred manner of teaching or learning. Therefore, individualize your educational approach so you can reach each client. For example, some clients have an affinity for deductive thinking. They enjoy theoretical concepts and principles. Once they comprehend an abstract principle, they can apply it through deductive reasoning to everyday life. Other clients possess strength in inductive thinking. They can take a specific incident or situation and reach a clear understanding of it. Sometimes, they can apply this understanding to similar circumstances in the future, but at other times, these clients may have to go through the learning process all over again. Such clients often benefit more from examples, illustrations, and specific guidelines than from abstract principles. Many clients also learn better when you tell a story, use a metaphor, or share an analogy. For example, in working with an adult male client who feels trapped by circumstances, you might realize—having thoroughly explored the situation with the client—that he is, in many ways, trapping himself. There are options, but the client has not really seen or seriously considered them. At such a time, you might tell a story in the following fashion.

EXAMPLE | Educating

I remember a comic strip I once saw. In the first frame, there is a desperate-looking man, staring out between the iron bars of a jail. His eyes and head are absolutely still. He looks only through the bars and nowhere else. He seems to be highly anxious, afraid, and depressed all at the same time. In the second frame, we see the scene from a more distant perspective. Again we notice the desperate man looking out from between the bars. But then we realize that there are iron bars on one side of the room only. The other three sides don't have bars at all; there aren't even any walls. It's completely open. The prisoner, if he would only move his head out from between the bars and look in another direction, could easily see that he could walk away any time he wanted.

Some clients learn best by hearing, others by seeing, and others through a multisensory learning approach (a combination of hearing, seeing, and physically experiencing). Some people learn best by working independently and some by working cooperatively with others, receiving guidance and feedback throughout the process. Certain individuals are more receptive to learning during the morning, others during the afternoon, and still others during the evening hours. Some people enjoy moving around while learning, whereas others prefer stillness. Some prefer to have stimulation in the form of music or background noise, whereas others learn best when it is absolutely quiet. As you try to educate clients, discover their preferred learning styles and adapt your teaching approach accordingly.

Sometimes, you can serve important educational functions by sharing personal feelings and experiences. It is very much like telling a story, but it is a story about yourself. This process is known as self-disclosure. In **self-disclosing**, you typically become a more genuine human being to the client. In addition, the personal experience may carry special meaning to the client, who might attribute considerable significance to the message or moral of your personal story. In sharing your personal feelings and experiences, however, be careful not to become the client's client. There should be a clear relationship between your self-disclosures and the identified problems and established goals for work. Also, do not take so much time in sharing your experiences and feelings that it detracts significantly from clients' opportunities for self-expression. If you share too much of yourself, especially personal difficulties or tragedies, clients may begin to view you as troubled or needy rather than as competent. If your clients begin to see you in this light, it could seriously diminish your effectiveness. Clients might abruptly end the relationship with you and look for a "healthier" professional. Alternately, clients may start to take care of you, assuming the role of caretaker or surrogate parent. In addition, your clients might begin to protect you from the full impact of the truth about their situations. Therefore be cautious about speaking of yourself too often or at too great a length. Remember, social work services are primarily for others, not for us.

The skill of educating is, of course, hardly limited to work with individuals, families, or small groups. Social workers also seek to educate organizations, communities, the general public, policy influencers, and policy makers. As part of our policy–practice activities, we often engage in consciousness-raising activities and may do so in many different ways and means. Social workers may write papers for scholarly journals, articles for popular magazines, or letters to newspaper editors. We may provide written or oral testimony to legislative committees, give talks or workshops at conferences, or share our knowledge with community members. Sometimes we attempt to raise conscious awareness through public demonstrations, marches, protests, or boycotts, and occasionally through civil disobedience. Increasingly, however, social workers use e-mail and social media services as a means to educate our friends, colleagues, and members of the public who might benefit from the information.

Popular social networking sites such as Facebook, Twitter, LinkedIn, Pinterest, Google Plus+, and Tumblr enable social workers to educate others and raise consciousness about issues involving human rights and social, economic, and environmental justice. We often participate with others through online communities. Some social workers publish their own blogs as do several organizations.

Deona Hooper, for example, publishes "The Social Work Helper" at **www.socialworkhelper .com**, and the NASW sponsors the "Social Work Blog" at **www.socialworkblog.org**. Gary Holden of New York University publishes the extraordinary "Information for Practice" at **http://ifp.nyu .edu/**. On Tumblr, you may find outlets such as "Intersectional Feminism for Beginners" at **http:// intersectionalfeminism101.tumblr.com/**, "Microaggressions: Power, Privilege, and Everyday Life" at **http://www.microaggressions.com/**, and "This ... is White Privilege" at **http://thisiswhiteprivilege.tumblr.com/**. The University at Buffalo School of Social Work sponsors the "inSocialWork" audio-streaming podcast series at **www.insocialwork.org**, and social worker Jonathan Singer hosts "The Social Work Podcast" at **http://socialworkpodcast.blogspot.com/**.

Numerous videos available through "**YouTube.com**" can serve educational purposes as can massive open online courses (MOOCs) accessible via **www.edx.org** and other sites. Many social activists have Twitter accounts to inform others and coordinate consciousness-raising and policy–practice initiatives. For example, community organizer Alicia Garza and her colleagues Patrisse Cullors and Opal Tometi created #BlackLivesMatter to mobilize African Americans and others concerned about the February 26, 2012, shooting death of unarmed 17-year-old Trayvon Martin by a Florida security guard. The guard was neither charged nor prosecuted. Following the August 9, 2014, killing of unarmed 18-year-old Michael Brown in Ferguson, Missouri, by a police officer; the subsequent deaths of dozens more young black men; and the brutal beatings of hundreds more, #BlackLivesMatter (Garza, 2014, Oct. 7) has grown from Twitter account into a mass social movement with a website at **http:// blacklivesmatter.com/** and a Facebook community at **www.facebook.com/BlackLivesMatter**.

In the contemporary world, social workers educate and are educated by colleagues, constituents, stakeholders, people affected by poverty and injustice, and, of course, scientists and researchers. Although we often share knowledge in our direct service work with clients in contexts of privacy and confidentiality, social workers also frequently engage in consciousness-raising and other forms of educating through electronic means. When we educate through social networking services and other public forums, we can reach a large and diverse audience and do so quickly. In our public education initiatives, whether they occur through Twitter, Facebook, a blog, podcast, streaming video, or an online course, let's remember that our digitized communications remain forever stored somewhere in cyberspace. Once published, they can never be truly erased. As a result, we must remain acutely conscious of the nature, accuracy, and potential impact of our words and images.

In educating, social workers apply the universal intellectual virtues along with our critical thinking, scientific inquiry, and lifelong learning skills to ensure that we truly inform rather than misinform others. Endorsing or re-posting suspect material and various forms of propaganda is inconsistent with our professional values and ethics. Let's be sure to share valid and reliable information that contributes to the well-being of our clients and advances the common good.

EXERCISE 12-5 Educating

For this exercise, use the social work skill of educating with our five clients: Mr. K, Loretta, the S family, Mrs. F, and our troubled agency. You may find it helpful or necessary to conduct a search of the relevant professional literature to ensure that your words are based on credible theory and research.

1. You are in the midst of exploring the current status of some of Mr. K's symptoms. You notice that he has lost quite a bit of weight in the last few weeks. He reports that his appetite has disappeared. Foods that he had previously enjoyed are no longer pleasurable. He says he drinks

a lot of coffee and makes sandwiches. He hasn't eaten in a restaurant since the divorce. He says that he hates to eat alone but hasn't felt motivated to either invite friends or to accept invitations from others to join him for meals. You and Mr. K agree that his poor appetite and restricted eating patterns, and perhaps especially his social isolation, may be symptomatic of grief or perhaps depression. You then begin to educate him about the role of social engagement and social activity in reducing depressive symptoms. Write the words you would say as you begin to educate Mr. K about these protective factors.

2. You are talking with Loretta about her plans to secure employment. You notice that she has begun to prepare her hair differently, apply some makeup, and wear appealing clothing that she obtained from charitable sources. You celebrate her progress and mention that employers sometimes (rightly or wrongly) consider applicants' appearance during job interviews. She says that she'd like to know more about what employers want and how she should prepare for job interviews. You say that you'd be happy to talk with her about these things and then begin to use the skill of educating to do so. Write the words you would say as you begin to educate Loretta about the qualities that contemporary employers look for in their employees and about how to prepare for job interviews.

3. You are in the midst of an individual meeting with Gloria, a teenage member of the S family and Mrs. S's daughter. She reports to you in confidence that she is sexually active and "will continue to have sex with my boyfriend no matter what my mother says!" She reports that she and her boyfriend do not practice birth control but that she would like to have some protection. What would you like to communicate to her? How would you begin to educate the teenager about birth control possibilities and about medical care?

4. You have just rehearsed an action step with Mrs. F. She assumed the role of her daughter while you played the part of Mrs. F. Through this experience, Mrs. F became aware of her feelings of extreme guilt about the way she has reared her children. She sobs and says, "I tried not to repeat the bad things my parents did to me, but it looks like I did so anyway." How might you educate her about the human tendency to repeat intergenerational family patterns even when trying to avoid them?

5. You are in the midst of evaluating progress toward goal attainment with the board of directors of the agency for which you are providing social work consultation services. The measurement data clearly indicate that progress toward goal achievement has occurred. The board members report their satisfaction with this news. However, you are well aware that maintenance of positive organizational change usually requires continued attention over a considerable period of time. Without clear, continuing plans to maintain change, reversion to previous, long-established patterns is quite likely. How might you educate the board members about the potential to return to previous, dysfunctional organizational patterns and the need for continued engagement?

▆ Advising

In working with clients and other constituents, it is sometimes proper for you to provide advice. Making a suggestion or recommendation can be a perfectly appropriate action by a social worker. In using the skill of **advising**, social workers almost always convey that others may freely accept or reject our advice. As Maluccio (1979) observes, many clients very much value and appreciate professional advice. Nonetheless, particularly during the early stages of your professional development, you may experience conflict about advising. You may be tempted to give too much advice or perhaps too little. As a social worker, you are probably keenly aware of the values of autonomy and self-determination. In interpreting these values, you might conclude that you should never offer any advice at all. Conversely, you might decide that clients are entitled to all the expertise you possess; you might therefore provide a great deal of advice, whether or not clients request or need it. These two positions represent extremes of a continuum. Most likely, you will take a more moderate stance, giving advice in certain circumstances but not in all.

Some advice is usually appropriate and helpful. The challenge for social workers is to know when to, when not to, and especially how to give advice.

Resist the temptation to offer advice based on your own personal feelings, attitudes, ideology, and preferences. This can be difficult in situations when a client asks, "What should I do?" or "What would you do if you were in my place?" For example, suppose you have worked for several weeks with a 19-year-old man who is gay. Through your exploration together, the young man has become much more self-accepting and comfortable with his sexual orientation. Recently, he raised the issue of whether to tell his parents the truth about his sexuality. He asks you, "Should I tell them?"

You could, of course, deftly avoid answering his question by responding with a question of your own: "What do you think?" Alternately, you could respond directly and share your personal opinion: "Of course. Tell them. You have nothing to be ashamed about." Or, not knowing what to do or say, you might become confused and uncertain. On the one hand, you might expect that the client would probably feel less distressed and more personally integrated if he were to tell his parents about his sexual orientation. On the other hand, you might also anticipate that such an encounter between the young man and his parents could be extremely stressful. It could conceivably lead to the loss of his parents' approval and support; he might even lose all contact with them. You might conclude that this decision is ultimately his and his alone to make. Following that line of thinking, you might respond directly to his question, but without advising him what to do: "I'd be more than glad to explore this issue with you and help you make a decision. However, I cannot simply give you an easy, direct answer to that question. I cannot advise you exactly what to do. The final decision is yours and yours alone to make."

Of course, there are also many occasions when you clearly should offer direct and specific advice. For example, suppose that you have been helping an adult female client become more assertive with her lover. You and the client have rehearsed assertive communication during your meetings together. The client is about to take a step toward greater assertion in her intimate relationship. Based upon your understanding of relationship theory and research, you believe that soft or caring expressions tend to strengthen relationships and provide a basis for moving toward hard or confrontational assertions. You therefore advise the client to begin with affectionate, caring assertions and later, after some experience, to initiate assertive expressions that involve requests that her partner make changes.

Advising is involved in many aspects of practice. For example, you might advise an adult male client who grew up in a household where his father was regularly intoxicated and abusive to read selected books on the topic of children of alcoholic families. You might advise a client to seek medical care. You might appropriately give advice concerning a variety of life events. In so doing, you would phrase the advice in slightly different ways to accomplish different objectives. Unless life-threatening circumstances exist, however, you should nearly always express advice in the form of a suggestion or perhaps a strong recommendation. Avoid communicating advice as commands or directives, such as an authoritarian boss might deliver to a subordinate employee or an angry parent might say to a disobedient child.

As you begin to practice the skill of advising, please use the format outlined here. As you become more proficient in using the skill, experiment with alternate formats.

PRACTICE FORMAT *Advising*

I have an idea for you to consider. I'd like to suggest that you _____
_____.

EXERCISE 12-6   Advising

For this exercise, use the skill of advising with our five clients: Mr. K, Loretta, the S family, Mrs. F, and our troubled agency.

1. You have educated Mr. K about the role of social engagement and social activity in reducing depressive symptoms. However, Mr. K seems uncertain and ambivalent about becoming more socially active. In the space provided, write the words you would say in advising Mr. K to do so.

2. As you role play practice job interviews with Loretta, you observe that when she talks about her positive characteristics and abilities she tends to tilt her face downward, lower her eyes, and clasp her hands together. She also begins to speak in a softer voice and in a less expressive manner. In the space provided, write the words you would say in advising Loretta about body posture, facial expression, eye contact, and speaking voice when trying to "sell oneself" to potential employers.

3. During an individual meeting with Gloria, a teenage member of the S family, she mentions that she has recently begun to feel some unusual itching and discomfort "down there" (in her vaginal area). As she continues to describe the symptoms, you wonder if she might have contracted a sexually transmitted disease (STD). In the space provided, write the words you would say in advising the teenager.

4. As you and Mrs. F have explored more about the relationship between her parenting patterns and the childhood experiences in her own family of origin, you conclude that she might benefit

from the construction of a family genogram. In the space provided, write the words you would say in advising Mrs. F to help you complete her family genogram.

5. You are in the midst of evaluating progress toward goal attainment with the board of directors of the agency for which you are providing social work consultation services. The measurement data clearly indicate that progress toward goal achievement has occurred. However, there is one area where the positive trend is not apparent. On average, clients' satisfaction with the agency and the quality of services has not improved. Of course, if clients were highly satisfied before changes were implemented and their degree of satisfaction simply continued as before, you and the board members might not be concerned. Unfortunately, in general, clients were not very satisfied and that has not changed—despite clear improvement in other areas. The board members ask for your advice. They want to know what you think should be done to improve client satisfaction with the agency and the services they receive. Use the space below to write what you would say in advising the board of directors in this matter.

Responding with Immediacy

The skill of **responding with immediacy** (Carkhuff & Anthony, 1979) involves exploring clients' thoughts and feelings about you, your relationship with each other, or your work together as they occur. In responding with immediacy, you focus on clients' experience of what is occurring right here and right now between you. These thoughts and feelings become the subject for immediate exploration. Responding with immediacy makes things real. It intensifies the relationship and encourages clients to explore relational concerns as they emerge. When you respond in an immediate manner, you also demonstrate or model an open communication style. Such openness may promote greater honesty and authenticity on the part of clients, increase their understanding of interpersonal patterns, and reduce their hesitation to address issues and goals. One format for responding with immediacy is as follows.

PRACTICE FORMAT *Responding with Immediacy*

Right here and now with me you seem to be (thinking/feeling/doing/experiencing) _____
_____.

Usually, the skill is applied directly to clients' immediate experience about you, your relationship, or the nature and utility of your work together. Your response becomes less immediate and less powerful as you move away from the context of "right here and right now with me." Responding with immediacy occurs in the present tense, in the immediate moment. Whenever the discussion shifts into the past or future tense, the interaction becomes less immediate. For example, if you comment about something that happened a week or two earlier, clients may recall it differently or not at all, or they may process the information intellectually without feeling its full impact. Although it may still be a useful comment to make, exploring a previous exchange rarely has the powerful effect of responding immediately to something that is occurring right here and right now.

In some cases, the manner in which clients relate to you is representative of their general pattern of relating with people. Clients sometime recreate in the working relationship the same patterns that appear in other relationships. By focusing on and responding immediately to such relational patterns as they emerge with you, you can help clients learn to recognize them and perhaps develop new, more useful styles of interaction.

Responding with immediacy is not appropriate for use with all clients. It depends on the nature of your contract, including the goals for work and your plans for change. In general, you would not respond with immediacy unless clients' reactions are clearly relevant to the issues and goals for work. Also, social workers differ in the degree to which they emphasize and attend to immediate interactions in their relationships with clients. Some social work practice approaches regard worker–client relational factors as extremely important, whereas others consider them less so. Nonetheless, most social workers recognize that client reactions within the working relationship are often relevant to the helping process. Responding with immediacy is a skill for addressing and exploring client experiences as they occur.

For example, suppose that you have begun to work with an adult female client who is troubled because her spouse reports that he does not like to spend time with her. Indeed, her spouse confirms this: "It's true. I'm sorry to say that I don't like her company. Every time we start to talk, she drifts off into the ozone—into some daydream world." During your meetings with this client, you notice that her attention frequently does seem to wander in a fashion similar to her spouse's description. She seems to focus on her own thoughts and listens just enough to your comments to stay distantly aware of the conversation. You begin to observe and to feel that when you talk, she essentially tunes you out. Because this pattern relates to the agreed-upon focal issues and goals, you might appropriately respond with immediacy: "Right here and now as I'm talking, I notice that your eyes are turned away from me. You seem to be looking off into the distance and thinking about something else. What are you experiencing right now?"

Responding with immediacy often results in a significant increase in energy between you and your clients. Both social workers and clients are likely to become much more oriented to the present moment and more engaged with one another. Because immediate responses often heighten intensity and interpersonal intimacy within the professional relationship, use the skill only after rapport is well established and, of course, a contract has been negotiated. Also, refer to observable phenomena in descriptive terms. Avoid judgmental terms; use Giraffe language instead. "You're ignoring me" involves a judgment about another's behavior. "I notice that your eyes are directed away from my eyes" is descriptive. Your clients should know that you genuinely have their interest at heart before you move into the intimate realm of immediacy.

EXERCISE 12-7 Responding with Immediacy

For this exercise, use the skill of responding with immediacy during exchanges with our five clients: Mr. K, Loretta, the S family, Mrs. F, and our troubled agency.

1. Mr. K begins to cry as he tries unsuccessfully to express his feelings about the way you advocated for him and arranged for the meeting with his former wife. Although he cannot put his emotions into words, it is apparent that he is touched by your loyalty to him and feels extremely grateful to you for your efforts on his behalf. Write the words you would say in responding with immediacy to Mr. K's nonverbal expressions.

2. During a discussion with Loretta, you ask a question about her eldest daughter. At that point, Loretta abruptly jumps up from her chair and begins to pace back and forth. She seems agitated and extremely uncomfortable with the topic, and appears annoyed with you for mentioning her daughter. Write the words you would say in responding with immediacy to Loretta's reaction.

3. In the midst of an individual meeting with Gloria, a teenage member of the S family, she confides to you that although she is sexually active with her boyfriend, she often fantasizes about another person. As she says that, she looks deeply into your eyes, blushes, and then looks away in an apparently embarrassed reaction. You suspect that she has sexual fantasies about you. You know that it would be quite consistent with your contract to discuss this directly. In the space provided, write the words you would say in responding with immediacy to the teenager's expression.

4. As Mrs. F talks with you about her own parenting practices and those that she experienced as a child in her own family of origin, you observe that she sits back in her chair, crosses her arms in front of her, and appears to frown. You're not entirely certain what this reaction means, but you suspect that she may be feeling ashamed and vulnerable. You think she is afraid that you might be critical of her. In the space provided, write the words you would say in responding with immediacy to Mrs. F.

5. As part of your consultation with the troubled agency, you meet regularly with the executive director to review actions taken, consider the results of evaluation data, and plan next steps to take. During today's meeting you and the director discuss findings from client satisfaction evaluation data. Some of the data reflect unfavorably upon the agency's current administration. Learning of this, the director's facial expression and body language begin to change, and both the volume and pace of speech increase as the director says, "You're encouraging clients to criticize agency administration in general and me in particular. I don't think that's fair. As a consulting social worker, you're supposed to be helping—not making things harder for me." Use the space below to write the words you would say in responding with immediacy to the director's words.

Reframing

The term **reframing** (Bandler & Grinder, 1979, 1982; Hartman & Laird, 1983; Tingley, 2001) refers to the words you say and the actions you take in introducing clients to a new way of looking at some aspect of themselves, the issue, or the situation. Usually, reframing involves sharing a different perspective from that which clients currently hold. Clients sometimes embrace a point of view in such a determined fashion that the viewpoint itself constitutes an obstacle to goal achievement. Of course, fixed views are not always problematic. Do not indiscriminately attempt to reframe clients' perspectives. The skill is applicable when clients' viewpoints constitute a fundamental part of the issue for work. Similar to the skill of educating, it differs in that the overall purpose of reframing is to liberate the client from a dogmatic perspective that interferes with progress. As a result of reframing, clients may reconsider strongly held beliefs. This may, in turn, affect their feelings and behavior as well.

There are several forms of reframing. One of the more common is **reframing a negative into a positive**.

EXAMPLE | Reframing a Negative into a Positive

When you say that you're "stupid" and "indecisive" because you find it difficult to choose from among various courses of action, I feel confused. I mean, what you refer to as indecisive appears to me to be the ability to see different points of view. It seems to me that you're willing to consider many perspectives and options. This sounds like curiosity, flexibility, and open-mindedness rather than indecisiveness. And what you call stupidity sounds a great deal to me like carefulness, thoroughness, and patience. These are attributes that I find extremely appealing and functional. Are you sure they are so bad?

Personalizing meaning (Carkhuff & Anthony, 1979) is another form of reframing through which you encourage clients to shift the attribution of responsibility away from other people, organizations, or external forces (that is, the situation) and toward themselves (that is, the person). Personalizing meaning can help people assume greater responsibility for effecting change. It can be liberating, even empowering. Personalizing meaning can help clients see a relationship between their own beliefs, values, attitudes, and expectations, on the one hand, and the feelings they experience or the behavior they enact on the other. This form of reframing involves going beyond the communication directly expressed by the client. You slightly alter the client's expression to shift an externalized meaning toward a more internalized or personalized meaning. As a consequence, the client is likely to feel greater responsibility, personal power, and control. In personalizing meaning, you may use a format such as the following.

PRACTICE FORMAT | *Personalizing Meaning*

You feel (do/experience) _____ because you think
(believe/value/perceive/expect) _____.

Phrase your comments in a tentative manner. After all, the skill of personalizing meaning derives from your frame of reference rather than from clients. Personalizing meaning suggests that others' thoughts, feelings, or actions are more associated with conscious individual processes than with external or situational factors. Occasionally, it may leave clients feeling greater guilt or more burdened with responsibility. Conversely, however, it may also convey a sense of considerable optimism, because such feelings result from one's own values, beliefs, or thoughts. These are aspects of a person that are not necessarily permanent. One's beliefs and attitudes can and do change and, unlike many situational factors, they are largely within one's own control. Such a view reflects an enormous potential for change—much more so than do explanations that people feel a certain way because they are jinxed, have a deficient superego structure, had a lousy childhood, suffer from a mental disorder, or have a biochemical deficiency.

Here is an example of a social worker talking with a client who happens to be a social work student.

EXAMPLE | Personalizing Meaning

Client: I'm devastated! I got a C+ in my social work field placement. I'll never make it through the program. I'm a total failure.

Worker: You're disappointed in yourself because you believe you should do better than C+ work, and you're afraid that getting a C+ means that you won't be able to graduate?

Situationalizing meaning is another form of reframing through which you change the meaning suggested by clients' expressions. Although there is certainly an empathic element, in this form of reframing you also slightly alter the meaning as presented by others. In the case of situationalizing meaning, you reflect understanding of the client's feelings or behaviors but then suggest that they may also be viewed as a result of external, societal, systemic, situational, or other factors beyond the client's individual control or responsibility. Frequently, situationalizing meaning results in an expansion of clients' perspectives and a lessening of their sense of guilt, self-blame, or personal responsibility. In situationalizing meaning, you may use a format such as the following:

PRACTICE FORMAT *Situationalizing Meaning*

You feel (do/experience) _____. I wonder though, might these (thoughts/feelings/actions) be related to current (or past) circumstances? Could we view such (thoughts/feelings/actions) as a more or less reasonable response to these (unreasonable/unjust/unexpected) conditions?

EXAMPLE | Situationalizing Meaning

Client: I'm a wreck. I can't sleep or eat; I can't concentrate. I know my head is really messed up. I've been kind of crazy.

Worker: You feel awful; you're anxious and depressed and you have lots of issues. I wonder, though, might these feelings be an understandable reaction to the recent changes in your life? Wouldn't even the best-adjusted person feel out of sorts and have some difficulty sleeping after losing a good job without any immediate prospects for another?

EXERCISE 12-8   Reframing

For this exercise, use the skill of reframing with our five clients: Mr. K, Loretta, the S family, Mrs. F, and our troubled agency.

1. During a meeting with you, Mr. K says, "The fact that she's gone hurts a lot less than before and I actually went on a date! I know I'm making progress but, it's clear to me that I'll never ever find anyone that I'll love as much as I loved her." Write the words you would say in reframing Mr. K's statement so that it reflects a personalized meaning.

2. Loretta is sharing, tentatively, some new information about her personal and family history. She says, "The fact is that I was terribly mean to my husband and I abused my kids—especially my oldest. They are all better off without me but I'm sure the girls will be emotionally damaged for

the rest of their lives." Write the words you would say in reframing Loretta's statement so that it reflects a personalized meaning.

3. You are in the midst of an individual meeting with Gloria, a teenage member of the S family. She says, "My mother is always on my case. She's so controlling. I can't do anything I want to do. She thinks that I'm 5 years old." Reframe her statement from a negative to a positive. Then, reframe her statement so that it has a personalized meaning.

4. During a meeting with Mrs. F, she confirms that she is indeed feeling guilty and ashamed that she may have harmed her children. She says, "I feel so ashamed. I've done just what I've always criticized my parents for." Reframe Mrs. F's statement so that it reflects a situationalized meaning. Then reframe her statement so that it has a personalized meaning. Finally, reframe it from a negative into a positive.

5. As part of your consultation with the troubled agency, you meet regularly with a group of about eight professional social workers. During today's meeting, one social worker expresses concern that the recent changes (for example, more active and engaged leadership by the agency director, clear and complete communications throughout the agency, regular supervisory meetings, and emphasis on quality control) may limit the professional autonomy of the social work staff. She says, "I'm becoming increasingly concerned and worried about these changes. If these trends continue, before long the other social workers and I will become little more than glorified technicians and bureaucrats. We'll have to check with a supervisor before we take any action with clients. We won't be able to exercise our

independent professional judgment and do what we think is best for our clients." Reframe the social worker's statement so that it reflects a situationalized meaning. Then, reframe it so that it has a personalized meaning. Finally, use the skill of reframing a negative into a positive.

Observing Inconsistencies

In **observing inconsistencies**[2] (Carkhuff & Anthony, 1979), you directly and without judgment point out discrepancies, incongruities, or contradictions in clients' words, feelings, and actions. In observing inconsistencies, you gently encourage clients to consider apparently incongruent aspects of themselves or their behavior, and sometimes their circumstances. For example, suppose an adult male client has requested help from you regarding a troubled marriage. The client says, "I am willing to do whatever is necessary to improve this relationship." Following a joint meeting with you and his spouse, during which he promised "to go out for a date with my spouse this week," he voluntarily worked overtime at his job and arrived home 3 hours late—too late for the date. After the client subsequently misses another planned date night, you might use the skill of observing inconsistencies by saying, "You said you want to improve the relationship and you agreed to two dates with your spouse. However, you worked late on the nights you had planned to go out with your wife. What do you think this might mean?"

Adopt a peaceful attitude and demeanor before you observe inconsistencies. If you are irritated by someone's words or gestures, access a place of peace and center yourself first. Otherwise, you could easily communicate annoyance, irritation, or judgment in a confrontational or even combative manner. The purpose of observing inconsistencies is to enhance others' awareness and self-understanding. It is definitely not intended as a means for social workers to vent our frustrations at clients' expense.

In observing inconsistencies, you may use the following format (Carkhuff & Anthony, 1979, p. 117).

PRACTICE FORMAT   *Observing Inconsistencies*

On the one hand you say (feel, think, or do) _____ but (and/yet) on the other hand you say (feel/think/do) _____.

Observing inconsistencies can have a powerful effect on clients. It has the potential to cause severe disequilibrium in people who are highly stressed or have fragile coping skills. Therefore, before pointing out inconsistencies with a particular client, be certain that person has the psychological

---

[2] In earlier editions, the term *confrontation* or *confronting inconsistencies* was used to refer to this skill. The term *confrontation*, however, is now so associated with judgment, criticism, and sometimes anger that a change to *observing inconsistencies* helps to capture the more empathic, gentle, and nonviolent perspective adopted here.

and social resources to endure the impact. Certainly you should have a solid relationship with the client before using the skill. When you do observe inconsistencies, try to be descriptive about the incongruities or discrepancies that you observe. Avoid judgmental or evaluative speculations and conclusions; use Giraffe language. Finally, try to incorporate empathic comments before and after observing inconsistencies (Hammond et al., 1977).

EXERCISE 12-9   Observing Inconsistencies

For this exercise, use the skill of observing inconsistencies during exchanges with Mr. K, Loretta, the S family, Mrs. F, and people from our troubled agency.

1. As you and Mr. K continue to review his efforts to recover from the effects of the divorce so that he can become emotionally as well as legally separated from her, he says, "I'm getting closer to putting my dreams of getting back with her behind me. It should be very interesting. When I no longer need or want her so desperately, I wonder if she'll view me in a different way. If I'm not so needy, she might even give me another chance."

2. As you talk with Loretta about her new job, she says, "I really enjoy my work. The other employees are great and the boss—well, he's okay too." As she spoke about the boss she, apparently quite unconsciously, shook her head side-to-side and pursed her lips in what seemed to be an expression of disgust. Write the words you would say in using the skill of observing inconsistencies in regard to Loretta's communication.

3. You are in the midst of an individual meeting with Gloria, a teenage member of the S family. She reports that her physician had prescribed medication for treating the sexually transmitted disease. The doctor told her to abstain from sexual intercourse during the 2-week period she is to take the medication. She was also told to inform her boyfriend that he should see his doctor and be treated before he resumes any sexual relations. Otherwise Gloria and her boyfriend would continue to infect each other. The girl says that her boyfriend will not go to the doctor and continues to want to have sex with her. She says, "I'll probably just let him have what he wants because if I don't, he'll go somewhere else." Write the words you would

say in using the skill of observing inconsistencies between what Gloria knows and what she thinks she will do.

4. During the course of your interaction with the principal of the school where Mrs. F's daughters have been harassed by several teenage boys, the principal says, "There is no racism at this school. The F girls are simply too sensitive. They are the only Latino students we have in the school, and they will just have to learn to deal with the boys. We never had any trouble before they enrolled here." Write the words you would say in using the skill of observing inconsistencies in regard to the principal's words and the apparent reality of the situation.

5. As part of your consultation with the troubled agency, you meet regularly with the executive director. During today's meeting, the director says, "I'm blamed and criticized whatever I do. I'm viewed as weak and incompetent because of the situation I inherited from the former director. He defrauded the agency, treated people unfairly, and failed to fulfill his responsibilities. I've been doing the best I can and I'm still guilty by association." Write the words you would say in using the skill of observing inconsistencies in regard to the agency director's words and his aspirations as a leader.

▇ Representing

The skill of **representing** includes those actions social workers take on behalf of clients in pursuit of agreed-upon goals. We usually engage in representational activities to facilitate clients' interaction with members of various social systems. Representing incorporates the roles of social broker, case advocate, and mediator (Compton et al., 2005). Building on many of the skills of the preparing, beginning, and exploring phases, as well as those of assessing, contracting, and working, it can be a complex process indeed. When representing, you intervene with other people or social systems on behalf of your clients or constituents. For example, suppose an unemployed adult woman is currently homeless and desperately needs immediate shelter, food, clean clothes, and financial support. Based on your joint assessment, you and the client concur that a particular resource agency would probably deny her application if she applied directly and in person. Therefore, the client asks you to represent her in this matter. You agree to make an initial contact with the appropriate agency. Then, with the support of the client, you sketch out several action steps. As you would use the preparing skills in advance of a first meeting with a client, you also carefully prepare for the contact with the agency to improve your chances of effectively representing the client.

During the course of your social work career, collect the names, phone numbers, and e-mail addresses of other social workers and representatives of various community resources. Get to know people at churches, temples, mosques, community centers, hospitals, neighborhood associations, government and nongovernmental organizations, and other systems that might serve as resources for clients. Make notes about resource people and keep them in a card file or computerized database for easy access. Periodically send them friendly thank-you notes and forward letters of praise to their supervisors and agency administrators. Such actions tend to enhance your value within the helping community and improve the chances that your clients will receive the high-quality service they deserve.

In the instance of the woman in need of food and shelter, you might decide that a good first step would be to contact a social work colleague at the agency in question. Once you make telephone contact, proceed in much the same manner as if you were beginning with a client. Introduce yourself and secure an introduction in return. Depending on the circumstances, you might make a few informal, friendly remarks to put your colleague at ease. Then outline the purpose for the contact: "I have a client here with me who needs assistance. She is unemployed, without money. She hasn't eaten for 2 days and has no place to stay tonight. I'm calling to determine whether she might be eligible to receive some help from your agency." Following this description of purpose, you may seek feedback to confirm that your message has been understood. At this point in the process, you could invite your colleague to provide information about eligibility requirements or to inquire further about your client's circumstances.

Representing clients in such cases is often extremely satisfying. Interactions with resource people may be both pleasant and productive. Your clients may be treated well and receive what they need. If you cultivate positive relationships with resource people and know something about the mission and programs of various service organizations, you are more likely to be effective in representing your clients.

However, representing clients is not always enjoyable. Sometimes, you must become an assertive advocate on behalf of clients that receive unfair or poor-quality treatment. It can be frustrating. For example, consider the situation of a client who seeks your help in dealing with a property owner. In the middle of a cold winter, heat, which all tenants are supposed to receive as part of their rent, is not reaching into the client's apartment. Despite several complaints, the property owner has taken no action to correct the situation. The client then asks you to represent her by contacting the property owner on her behalf.

First, you would use preparing skills to formulate preliminary plans. You explore the situation more fully with the client, securing detailed facts about the heating problem and learning about her experience as a tenant there. You might then consult city officials who are knowledgeable about housing regulations and landlord–tenant laws, expanding your own knowledge base. You also prepare for the initial contact with the property owner. In this instance, suppose you decide to telephone first. You might telephone, give your name, and say, "I am a social worker with the tenants' advocacy program of the city social services agency. One of your tenants, Mrs. Wicker, has contacted us about a problem with the heating system. It seems that the family has been without heat for 5 days. Could you tell me what's being done to repair the problem and how much longer it will be before their apartment is warm enough for them to live there safely?"

If the property owner does not acknowledge the problem and, for example, begins to denigrate the client, you might respond, "Regardless of the complaints you have about Mrs. Wicker and her family, they still need heat. As you know, it's dangerously cold, and the lives of the family members could be in serious jeopardy if heat is not restored soon." If the landlord remains unresponsive, you might outline the steps you could take should the heating system remain unrepaired and the family continues to be in danger. In several respects, your comments are similar to those you might share in beginning with a client. You state your purpose, describe your role as client advocate, and discuss the actions you could take should your client continue to be in need or at risk (that is, your policies and procedures). You also make a specific request for action from the property owner (that is, you outline the property owner's role).

If the property owner acknowledges the problem, outlines plans and a timetable for repair, and makes a commitment to provide the family with sufficient heat, you may appropriately express your thanks and credit him for being responsive to your request. You would then apprise the client of the property owner's proposal and request that she notify you about the outcome. If the property owner follows through as promised, you might communicate appreciation for the positive action. If the property owner does not do so, however, you would probably contact him again, report that the apartment is still dangerously cold, and inform him specifically about the steps you will now take to ensure the safety and well-being of your client.

You will probably represent clients quite frequently as a regular part of social work practice, to link clients with needed community resources and to secure fair and equitable treatment, as part of the processes of mediation and conflict resolution. In representing, ensure that you have clients' informed consent to act on their behalf, always keep their best interests in mind, and regularly update them about your activities.

As discussed earlier (see the Policy–Practice section in Chapter 4), many social workers routinely engage in class advocacy and other forms of policy–practice. When we seek to correct social, economic, and environmental injustices; restore and safeguard human rights; and promote fair and just policies and practices, we represent and advocate for large numbers of people—including hundreds, thousands, or more whom we have never met and will probably never know.

EXERCISE 12-10 Representing

For the following exercise, outline the steps you might take in representing our five clients in the following situations. Describe how you would prepare to represent each one, and then write the words you would say in beginning with the person, people, or organization you contact on your clients' behalf.

1. With his consent, you are representing Mr. K in relation to his former wife. He believes that if he could apologize to her, express his sincere hope that her future will be bright, and say good-bye, it would help him complete the process of truly accepting the fact that the marriage is over. You are about to contact the former Mrs. K. to advocate for a meeting that would include her, Mr. K, and you in your role as his social worker. In the space provided, outline the steps

you would take before making contact, and then write the words you would say as you begin to represent Mr. K with the former Mrs. K.

2. With her consent, you are representing Loretta in regard to a possible job opportunity. The position involves answering phones and serving as a receptionist for a nonprofit, nongovernmental agency. You are about to contact an administrator of the agency on Loretta's behalf. In the space provided, outline the steps you would take before making contact, and then write the words you would say as you begin to represent Loretta and advocate for her employment with the agency.

3. With his consent and that of his parents, you will represent Theo and his parents—Mr. and Mrs. S—in a discussion with high school officials. Apparently, Theo is suspected of participating in a recent incident of vandalism and has been suspended from school. You have jointly decided that you will meet with school officials to gather facts and obtain information about the accusation, the suspension, and the ongoing processes. You have a formal letter signed by Theo and his parents authorizing you to act on their behalf. Outline the steps you would take before making contact with school officials, and then write the words you would say in beginning to represent Theo and his parents in this matter.

4. With the informed consent of Mrs. F and her daughters, you are representing the family in discussions with the principal of the school where her daughters report that several teenage boys have harassed them. According to the girls, the boys spit on them and used ethnic epithets in

referring to their Latino heritage. Outline the steps you would take in preparing for contact with the principal and then write the words you would say in representing Mrs. F and her daughters.

5. As part of your consultation with the troubled agency, you recruited a group of about 10 current and former clients to meet together with you and with the agency's newly appointed "consumer advocate" at least once per month in an effort to improve service quality and advocate for agency consumers. During the most recent consumers' group meeting, one participant—a current client—expressed her disappointment and frustration with the fact that her social worker has not returned any of the several telephone calls she has made over the course of the past 2 weeks. She wanted to schedule an appointment to discuss a pressing issue involving her 8-year-old daughter. First, you ask the client if she would prefer to handle the matter herself or might she want the help of the agency's consumer advocate. The client says she would love the help and provides permission for the advocate to represent her in this matter. Then, you turn to the consumer advocate and ask, "What might be done to help in this matter?" What do you think the agency's consumer advocate might say in outlining preliminary plans to represent the client in (a) providing feedback regarding her dissatisfaction and (b) securing an early appointment with a social worker to help her with the urgent matter involving her 8-year-old daughter?

Linking

Linking occurs when social workers seek to establish, maintain, or restore connections between two or more people; between one or more persons and a social group, organization, or community; or between elements of two or more social systems. The skill is widely needed and frequently used in social work. For example, in working with couples, families, groups, and organizations, a social worker might encourage one person to talk or listen to another. A mother might be frustrated with her 14-year-old daughter's silence and solitary behavior—until a social worker encourages the teenager to describe how she is harassed and bullied nearly every day in school as well as on her way to and from home. The social worker simply asks, "Talia, would you look at your mom and explain to her what happens when you go to school?"

In many contexts, we use other skills in conjunction with linking. For example, we might introduce ourselves, seek introductions from others, or facilitate introductions between people who do not yet know each other. As part of linking, we might propose an initial purpose, orient others about expectations, seek feedback, and offer advice. Linking may involve educating others about how to talk, how to listen, how to attend, how to express empathic understanding through active listening, how to ask questions, and how to make assertive requests. Helping others engage and communicate with one another is a key aspect of linking, and most social workers are well versed in this information. We have practiced these basic communication skills many times over and use them constantly in our personal and professional lives. Indeed, we may even help people learn to communicate in the Giraffe language to enhance their ability to relate intimately and compassionately with one another.

Social workers also use the skill of linking when we help a client secure an appointment at a medical clinic or obtain food at a local pantry. Indeed, linking is a central aspect of the broker role. However, we also engage in linking when we help someone interested in a human rights or justice issue join a group or organization dedicated to its resolution through social and political action. Occasionally, social workers might help to establish better connections and improved communication between units or departments within an organization, or between consumers and service providers of an agency.

At times, we might even seek to establish collaborative ties between two or more community action groups interested in policy change about the same or similar issues. For example, the "Forward Together"[3] movement in North Carolina is famous for its demonstrations outside the state's legislative buildings on "Moral Mondays." Spearheaded by the North Carolina State Conference of the National Association for the Advancement of Colored People (NAACP) under the leadership of Dr. William Barber, "Forward Together" is the result of an organizational effort that began in December 2006 and now includes more than 170 coalition partners. The partner organizations include those interested in justice for immigrants, human and civil rights, workers' rights (including farmworkers), women's rights, LGBT rights, health care access and affordability, economic justice and development, environmental justice, educational justice, youth organizations, community organizations and neighborhood associations, spiritual and religious groups, fraternities and sororities, and peace advocacy groups. This extraordinarily diverse array of coalition partners gradually came together in solidarity when people from one organization reached out to establish linkages with other organizations in pursuit of similar goals.

EXAMPLE | Linking

Situation: A support group for mothers whose sons or daughters suffered serious brain injuries during U.S. military combat operations in Afghanistan or Iraq.

Worker: (*group facilitator*) Hello everyone and welcome back! Tonight we'll continue where we left off last time. But before we begin, I'd like to introduce you all to Gayle. She'll be joining us for the first time tonight. Let's give her a warm welcome. Now, let's go around the circle so that each of you can introduce yourself to Gayle. Please identify yourself by your first name only and, if you wish, share a few words about what we do during our time together each week. Felicia, would you start?

Felicia: Sure. Hello Gayle. My name is Felicia and I've been meeting with these women for about 4 months now. We're all in the same boat. We help each other cope with the frustrations of doctors, hospitals, the VA, and with thoughts and feelings that almost nobody else could possibly appreciate. These women can and do understand,

(Continued)

---

[3] The official name of "Forward Together" is "Historic Thousands on Jones Street (HKonJ) People's Assembly Coalition." Learn about it at **www.hkonj.com/**. Learn about the North Carolina NAACP at **www.naacpnc.org/**.

and we care about each other. They've helped me keep it together for my daughter, and I love them for it. I think you will too.

I have to confess though that I really did not want to come to that first meeting. At that time, I just couldn't imagine how it would help. Later on Gayle when you have a chance to speak, I'd love to know what you were thinking about the group before you arrived.

Worker: (*after the other group members complete their introductions*) Thanks everyone for your words of welcome.

Gayle, I think you get a sense of what we're like here and a bit about how we share our troubles, our successes, our thoughts and our feelings with each other. Somehow, it seems to help. I wonder though, if you'd care to respond to Felicia's request.

If you remember, Felicia was the first one to introduce herself, and she told us how at first she hadn't really wanted to join the group. She didn't think it would help. She wanted to know what you were thinking about the group before you came tonight. Would you care to share that with us?

EXAMPLE | Linking

Case Situation: Jon, a teenage boy who stole a laptop computer from the apartment of a 72-year-old disabled Vietnam era veteran, is meeting face-to-face with the man as part of a restorative justice program. The meeting occurs at the site of the theft.

Worker: Jon, I'd like to introduce you to Mr. Sagin.

Mr. Sagin: (*offers to shake hands*) Hello, Jon, I'm glad you came to see me today.

Jon: Hello, Mr. Sagin.

Worker: Jon, I believe you have something to say to Mr. Sagin. Would you care to tell him what's on your mind?

EXERCISE 12-11 Linking

Use the skill of linking in the following situations involving our five clients: Mr. K, Loretta, the S family, Mrs. F, and the troubled agency.

1. You are just beginning a meeting with Mr. K and his former wife. They have not talked with each other for quite some time now. Prior to and just after the divorce, Mr. K contacted her frequently—in almost stalking-like fashion—until her brothers paid him a personal visit to inform him in somewhat threatening terms that there would be "consequences" if he continued to harass their sister. Just as you are about to begin the meeting, Mr. K turns to his former wife and says, "Josie, thanks so much for joining us today. I was so afraid that you wouldn't come and I'm truly grateful that you did. First of all, I want to tell you face-to-face that I was a terrible husband, that I'm sorry, and that I hope at some point you'll forgive me." As Mr. K speaks, Josie first looks stunned, then drops her head as she stares at her own hands. She remains silent. Write the words you would say to Josie in attempting to establish a link between Mr. K and her. Outline your rationale for the words you chose. How do you think Josie might react to your response? Now, imagine that instead of responding to Josie, you respected her silence. Write the words you

might say to Mr. K in linking him to her. Again, provide reasons for your choice of words and predict both Mr. K's and Josie's response to your words.

2. You are in the middle of a meeting with Loretta when she says, "I've located my youngest daughter's address and phone number. I'd like to call her but I'm terrified. I don't know what to say, how to say it, and I think she'll just hang up on me. That's what I'd do if I were in her shoes." In response you say, "It's so wonderful that you were able to find Joni! And, you want to make contact. I wonder though, might it make sense to write her a letter first before making the phone call? That way, your daughter will have some time to prepare for the call. What do you think?" Loretta nods her head vigorously and says that she agrees completely. Write the words you would use in helping Loretta prepare a letter intended as a first step toward reconnecting with her daughter Joni. What is your rationale for the words you chose? How do you think Loretta might respond to your words?

3. Earlier in a meeting with the seven-member, blended S family, Mrs. S said, "Things are so bad between my kids and his kids that I've begun to wonder whether it's worth trying anymore. Maybe my children and I should just leave. We made it on our own before, and we can do it again." Sometime after you responded to her comments and the discussion continued, you decided to return the focus to the relationship between her children and his. You direct your attention to Gloria and Theo, two of the older children. You hope to encourage them to talk directly with one another about their feelings. Write the words you would say in linking Gloria and Theo. Outline your rationale for the words you chose. How do you think they might react to your response? What is another way you might seek to link the two youngsters?

4. Toward the end of a meeting during which Mrs. F seemed especially discouraged, you jointly agreed to request a meeting with Dr. M, a member of the school board, to share concerns and explore options. You telephone the official to provide background and arrange for a meeting. Dr. M readily agrees to schedule an appointment. When the time comes, you and Mrs. F are invited into Dr. M's office. Introductions are shared and you're about to begin. You'd prefer that Mrs. F express her concerns directly to Dr. M. You think it will be more impactful if she describes what's happening than if you do. Write the words you might say in linking Mrs. F and Dr. M in such a way that she will share her knowledge and experience about her daughters' treatment at the school. How do you think Mrs. F will respond to your attempt at linkage? How about Dr. M? What is another way in which you might link Mrs. F with Dr. M, or, Dr. M with her?

5. Following several meetings with various personnel in a troubled social service agency that has a number of organizational problems, you arrange for a meeting between a small group of current and former consumers and the new agency director. You've suggested to the director that the primary purpose for the meeting could be to encourage the consumers to describe their experiences, share their concerns and complaints, and offer suggestions. Although somewhat reluctant, the director agreed, saying "I'll look at it as an opportunity to collect information, to learn, and especially to let them know that we care about them and want to improve the quality of our services." You respond by saying, "That sounds really good."

   The time for the meeting has arrived. Everyone is gathered together in a comfortable room. You facilitate introductions and then, before you speak, look around the group making eye contact with each person. Write the words you might say in linking the consumers with the director and the director with the consumers. Outline your rationale for the words you selected. How do you think the consumers might respond? How might the director respond? What might be another way you could link the director with the rest of the group?

◼ Pointing Out Endings

In **pointing out endings**, you remind clients "some time before the last session that the working relationship is coming to a close" (Shulman, 1992, p. 206). In most cases when you and clients agree to work together and establish a service contract, you also determine a time frame. This occurs as a significant part of the goal setting and planning processes (see Chapter 11). Periodically during the work phase, you refer to this time frame. Of course, you and clients may renegotiate the timetable when the situation warrants. Ideally, however, you and the client carefully consider and openly discuss any such revision. Extending a time frame does not necessarily increase the probability of goal achievement. Additional time could imply that the goals are just too difficult to accomplish. Also, time extensions may leave an impression that your work together can go on indefinitely. Of course, in several practice settings (for example, hospitals, residential facilities, prisons), there are natural ending points that are partially or completely beyond either clients' or social workers' control.

Ending processes may involve legal as well as practice considerations ("Lawsuit seeks discharge treatment-planning at NYC jails," 1999). For example, discharge planning following a stay in a medical or psychiatric facility is a complex ending process that often involves additional assessment, contracting, and working activities (Christ, Clarkin, & Hull, 1994; Cox, 1996; Morrow-Howell, Chadiha, Proctor, Hourd-Bryant, & Dore, 1996; Proctor, Morrow-Howell, & Kaplan, 1996; Tuzman & Cohen, 1992).

By pointing out endings, you may help motivate clients to work hard on the action steps so as to complete them within the established period. As Perlman (1957) suggests, the social work relationship is time limited. After all, as a social worker you are not marrying or adopting your clients. You are a professional helper, not a member of clients' families. By establishing time limits and pointing out endings, you help clients to prepare psychologically for the process of concluding the working relationship. If you and a client avoid the topic of ending the relationship, both of you can deny the immediacy of the feelings. Such denial may allow temporary emotional respite from strong feelings, but it also prevents the parties from psychologically anticipating and preparing themselves for ending. Therefore, despite feelings of discomfort, you should occasionally refer to the upcoming conclusion to the working relationship.

You may point out endings in several ways. Regardless of the specific form it takes, this skill helps clients begin to prepare consciously and emotionally for the conclusion of your work together. Whether it involves a transfer, a referral, or a termination, you gently remind clients that there will soon be an ending and that they may very well have some thoughts and feelings about the change.

For example, suppose you and several family members contract to meet for eight sessions. The agreed-upon goal is to improve communication within the family. The work has proceeded quite well. By the fourth meeting, the family members have progressed to such an extent that they are able to express differences of opinion without feeling devalued or rejected. There has also been a noticeable decrease in tension and an increase in humor. Toward the end of the session, you say, "We're now finishing up our fourth session. There are four meetings left. We're halfway there."

Following such a reminder, you might explore thoughts and feelings associated with the idea of ending. You might ask, "As we think about concluding our relationship, some thoughts or feelings may come up. I wonder, what comes to mind when you think about finishing our work together?" Or you might ask, "How will things be different once we have concluded our work together?" Although a specific format is not universally applicable, the primary element in pointing out endings is the reminder. Statements such as "We have _____ meetings left" or "We will be meeting for another _____ weeks" serve this function. In the case of transfers or referrals, clarify what will happen following your ending with the client. You might say, "We have _____ meetings left before you begin to work with _____," or "We will be meeting for another _____ weeks before you begin the program at _____."

EXERCISE 12-12   Pointing Out Endings

For this exercise, use the skill of pointing out endings with our five clients: Mr. K, Loretta, the S family, Mrs. F, and the troubled agency.

1. You have been working with Mr. K for approximately 2 months. He has met with his former wife and said good-bye, and has begun dating someone. His appetite has improved and he has become more active socially and recreationally. He exercises daily and, in a decisive gesture, donated his television to a charity. He says he now listens to music and reads books. He reports that when he thinks about his former wife, he does so fondly but no longer hopes they will get back together. A few weeks earlier, as you and Mr. K discussed his progress, you collaboratively decided that you would conclude your relationship in 1 month. Today's meeting is the next-to-last one. Your next meeting will conclude your work together. Write the words you would say in pointing out endings with Mr. K.

2. Over the course of the last few months, Loretta has blossomed. She is doing extremely well in her job, has been saving money, and enjoying life. She has friends that she spends time with and activities outside of work. She has submitted an application to serve as a volunteer to help homeless women in the community. She thinks they'll approve her request and she looks forward to helping others reclaim their lives. A few weeks earlier, as you evaluated progress with her, you wondered aloud about when you should conclude your work together. She said, "Three more times and I should be good to go." Today's meeting represents the second of the three. Your next meeting will conclude your work together. Write the words you would say in pointing out endings with Loretta.

3. You are in the midst of the next-to-last meeting with the S family. During the past several months, many productive changes have occurred. Two sessions before, the family members

indicated that they were well on their way to accomplishing their goals. At that time, you had agreed to meet three more times. Next week you will have the concluding session. Write the words you would say in pointing out endings with the S family.

4. Through a joint discussion 2 weeks earlier, you and Mrs. F concluded that she could best complete work toward goal attainment by participating in a 10-week assertiveness training group sponsored by another community agency. The group begins in 3 weeks. Next week will be your last meeting together. Write the words you would say in pointing out endings with Mrs. F.

5. For the past several months, you have provided consultation services to an agency that is trying to recover from incompetent management and fraudulent behavior under a previous administration. About every 5 or 6 weeks, you meet with a group of agency personnel, board members, consumers, and other key stakeholders to apprise them of progress, seek their feedback, and gather their input. Your 12-month contract with the agency expires in 3 months' time. You will meet with this group one more time after today's meeting. What would you say in pointing out endings with the group in this next-to-last meeting?

Recording Progress

As a professional social worker bound by numerous legal and ethical obligations, you must keep records throughout all phases of practice. During the work phase, social workers keep track of any revisions to the initial assessment and contract and maintain notes about action steps and progress toward goal achievement. When **recording progress**, incorporate the results of evaluation procedures such as goal attainment scaling, individual or subjective rating scores, rapid assessment instrument and other test scores, as well as graphics that reflect trends. Describe phenomena and events and identify issues or themes that might relate to the process of working toward goal accomplishment. In many instances, you would provide a rationale for an action you take or a recommendation you make.

Suppose, for example, you were to learn from an adult male client that he sexually molested his infant son. Of course, you must report this information to relevant authorities. Usually, this means a telephone call to the child-protection services division of the department of welfare or human services. Because you acquired this information during a meeting protected by laws and ethics concerning client confidentiality, you should meticulously record the data (that is, the words the client said) that led you to conclude that the child may have been abused. You should also record what you said to the client in response. You may have informed him that you, as a professional social worker, have a legal obligation to report this information to child-protection authorities. You should note this. You may also have indicated that you would like to continue to serve as his social worker during this time; you should record this as well. When you make the phone call to the relevant authorities, be sure to record the date and time, the person contacted, and the contents of the conversation. Of course, unless the client provides informed consent to do so, you refrain from sharing information about the client beyond that which is relevant to the issue of possible child abuse.

In many settings, social workers use a **problem-oriented recording (POR)** approach during the work phase (Biagi, 1977; Burrill, 1976; Johnson, 1978; Martens & Holmstrup, 1974). The well-known **SOAP** format (subjective data, objective data, assessment, and plan) is commonly used in medical settings and has been widely used in social services as well. The **DAR** (data, action, and response) and **APIE** (assessment, plan, implementation, and evaluation) are fairly common, and there are several variations to the traditional SOAP structure. For example, **SOAPIE** stands for subjective, objective, assessment, plan, implementation or interventions, and evaluation. **SOAPIER** adds "revisions" to the format. The **SOAIGP** format represents another derivation (Kagle & Kopels, 2008). SOAIGP stands for:

S—*supplemental* information from clients or family members
O—your *observations* and, if applicable, those of other agency staff
A—*activities* that you, the client, or others undertake
I—your *impressions*, hypotheses, assessments, or evaluations
G—current *goals*
P—*plans* for additional activities or action steps

In the *supplemental* category, you may include new or revised information provided by clients, family members, or other people in the client's primary social systems. In the *observation* section, you may describe your own observations of the person, issue, and situation. If applicable, you may also include observations of other agency staff members. In the *activities* category, you may summarize client tasks, worker tasks, and in-session tasks that have occurred. In *impressions*, you may summarize your current evaluation of progress toward goal achievement and make note of your tentative impressions and hypotheses. You may also summarize results of frequency counts, subjective ratings, and test results in this section. Under *goals*, you may record goals that are the current focus of work or revise original goals. In the *plans* section, you may make note of changes in your approach and identify additional action steps that you or your client intend to take. For example, following an interview with Mrs. Chase, Susan Holder might prepare a SOAIGP entry as shown in Box 12.1.

Problem-oriented recording formats serve many valuable functions. The SOAPIE, SOAPIER, and SOAIGP adaptations improve on the earlier SOAP system with their greater

---

Box 12.1 EXAMPLE: PROGRESS RECORDING—SOAIGP

SOAIGP Entry for Meeting with Lynn Chase, February 10

Supplemental Mrs. Chase indicated that she had accomplished the action step we had identified for this week. She reported that it was a great help. She stated that she has felt in better spirits than she has for months. Before the meeting, Mr. Chase had telephoned to report that things are much better at home. He said, "Everybody has begun to help out at home, and we're all much happier. Thanks a lot."

Observations Mrs. Chase does indeed appear to be in much better spirits. She speaks with energy and expressiveness. When talking about her family life and her gardening, her face becomes bright and animated. When she discusses work, there is a slight change to a more "businesslike" quality.

Activities During today's meeting, Mrs. Chase and I talked at length about her childhood. On several occasions, she referred to her mother's drinking and the mixed feelings she experienced as a child when she dealt with her intoxicated mother. She sobbed when she talked of the embarrassment and rage she felt when a friend visited while her mother was drunk and verbally abusive. She also revealed that she felt "somehow to blame" for her mother's drinking. She said, "I used to feel that if I were somehow better or less of a problem, then Mother wouldn't need to drink so much."

I reminded Mrs. Chase that we had three more meetings together. She said that she would miss me, but already "things were much better."

Impressions Mrs. Chase's daily logs (attached) reflect progress toward two of the goals: sleeping better and arguing less with Robert and Richard. It is my impression that the change program continues to be viable. There is no need to revise it at this time.

Goals The previously established goals remain in effect.

Plans We identified a new action step. In addition to those already identified last week, Mrs. Chase agreed to read Janet Woititz's book *Adult Children of Alcoholics* (1983) within 2 weeks of today's date.

Susan Holder, BSW, MSW
Licensed Social Worker

---

emphasis on implementation or intervention and evaluation and, in the case of SOAIGP, specific recognition of the importance of goals. To further that trend, please consider the preliminary, experimental version of a goal-focused format, tentatively called **GAAP**, as shown in Box 12.2.

Box 12.2 EXAMPLE: PROGRESS RECORDING—GAAP GUIDELINES

Goals Summarize the goals and objectives reflected in the contract.

Activities Describe the tasks, activities, and interventions undertaken by participants (for example, social worker, client, others) during or in between meetings in pursuit of the goals.

Assessment Report the results of assessment and evaluation processes related to effects and outcomes of activities and progress toward goal achievement. Incorporate or attach the results of subjective and objective evaluation instruments (for example, RAIs, frequency counts, subjective ratings).

Plans Based on the assessment and evaluation, outline plans for additional goal-related tasks and activities including, when necessary, changes to the agreed-upon goals and objectives.

Progress recordings are legal as well as professional documents. Prepare them as if they could become public knowledge—perhaps in the context of a review committee or even a courtroom hearing or trial. Organize them in a coherent manner. Prepare them in a well-written, legible, and timely fashion. Include descriptive and factual information that pertains to the purposes and goals for work. Avoid complex abstractions that cannot be substantiated. Ensure that your records reflect accurate, objective, unbiased reporting, along with respect for the individual and cultural characteristics of clients and their active participation in decisions and processes. While maintaining the confidentiality rights of third parties, identify the sources of information and support the reasons for decisions and actions. Finally, ensure that your records reflect compliance with legal and agency policies (Kagle, 2002; Kagle & Kopels, 1994, 2008).

EXERCISE 12-13   Recording Progress

1. Use a word-processing program to prepare simulated progress notes about interviews with our five clients: Mr. K, Loretta, the S family, Mrs. F, and the troubled agency. Prepare the notes as if you intended to include them within a formal case record. When finished, include the progress notes as separate sections with a single document. Save the "Progress Notes for Five Clients" document with a filename "ProgNotes_for_5_Clients" and deposit it in your Social Work Skills Learning Portfolio.

    a. Today's meeting with Mr. K is the next-to-last one. Next time, you will conclude your work together. During this meeting, he discussed the meeting with his former wife with considerable satisfaction and pride. He was especially pleased with himself for sincerely experiencing and truthfully sharing his pleasure that his wife seemed happier than she had for years and that she was enjoying life. Initially cautious, she also said that he looked and seemed better than he had for a long time as well. Although you had been somewhat concerned that the meeting might reactivate feelings of loss and remorse, it turned out well. Mr. K used the meeting to say good-bye to both his former wife and to the marriage itself. In today's meeting, he said that when he thinks about his former wife now, he does so fondly but no longer hopes they will get back together. He seems quite resolved about this. He reported that he is now dating someone, is eating better, and is active socially and recreationally. He said that he exercises daily and reads books—something that he loved to do as a child but had not done for the past 40 years. Prepare a progress note regarding the interview. Use the SOAIGP format.

    b. Today's meeting with Loretta is the next-to-last one. Next time, you will conclude your work together. During this meeting, she described how well she is doing in her job and in her life outside of work as well. She said that she spends time with friends and regularly takes long walks with two other women. She mentioned that she submitted an application to serve as a volunteer to help homeless women in the community. She thinks they'll approve her request and she looks forward to helping others reclaim their lives as she has her own. Loretta also described an encounter that she had with her boss. She said that she had felt uncomfortable around him since she began work there but she desperately wanted the job and did not want to "rock the boat." She reported that it became clear during the previous week exactly why she felt uneasy with him. She said the boss "came on to her" and asked her to have a drink with him after work. At that point, she thought to herself, "Oh, I remember this kind of thing from many, many years ago." She quoted the words she used in responding to him: "Thanks so much for the invitation. That's very nice of you but I know you need to get home to your wife and family, and I want to keep our relationship friendly and professional. So, thanks again but no thanks." She giggled as she described the shocked look on his face and reported that since that encounter he has treated her with courtesy and respect, and perhaps a little fear. Prepare a progress note regarding the interview. Use the SOAIGP format.

c. Earlier today, you completed an interview with Gloria, a teenage member of the S family. She reported that following your last meeting together, she had told her boyfriend that he would have to see his doctor and receive treatment before she would again have sex with him. She appeared to be pleased that she could report this to you. You praised her for taking that action and asked about her boyfriend's response. She said that he had left in a huff, but she thought that he might be back. Prepare a progress note regarding the interview. Use the SOAIGP format.

d. Earlier today, you completed a meeting with Mrs. F, her daughters, and the principal of their school. During the course of the meeting, the girls described in detail what the teenage boys had said and done to them. They talked of the boys spitting at them and calling them names that referred to their Latino heritage. The girls were able to identify the boys by name. The principal appeared surprised and disturbed by what the girls had to say. He apparently believed the girls because he said that he was indeed sorry that this had happened. Furthermore, he said that he would talk with the boys later that day. He also asked the girls to tell him right away if anything like this ever happened again. Prepare a progress note regarding the interview. Use the GAAP format.

e. For approximately 11 months, you have been providing social work consultation services to an agency attempting to recover from the consequences of incompetent management and fraudulent behavior under a previous administration. Change in a positive direction is now apparent. Communications among staff members have improved and they now receive weekly supervision. The agency director is pursuing an active and engaged approach to leadership, and morale is improving. Today, you met with the board of directors to review these positive trends and to outline your intentions to support the executive director, the administrators and supervisors, and other staff members in their efforts to improve. Although the board members were extremely pleased with your report and encouraged you to continue your fine work, they requested that you complete an evaluation of the executive director's performance and submit a recommendation to the board concerning his fitness to continue in that role. Prepare a progress note regarding the meeting. Use the SOAIGP format.

SUMMARY

During the work and evaluation phase of social work practice, you and clients or other constituents take action toward resolving focal issues and pursuing established goals. In this process, you use both empathic skills and work-phase expressive skills, and systematically evaluate progress toward goal achievement. You also point out that your work together will be coming to an end at a particular point in the relatively near future.

CHAPTER 12 Summary Exercises

1. You continue to work with the four clients described below (see the Summary Exercises in Chapters 7 through 11). At this point you have established goals and created plans for action and evaluation. You are now ready to implement those plans. Use word-processing software to *write the words* you would say and discuss the actions you would take as you engage them in the working and evaluating processes. In other words, build

upon your previous work to demonstrate how you would apply the requested skills in these particular situations. Please *label* each of the skills that you use and place quotation marks around the words you would say. When finished, combine your work into a single "Working with Four Clients" document with a section for each of the cases. Save the document to a file labeled "Work_w_4_Clients." Include the file in your Social Work Skills Learning Portfolio.

a. You are meeting again with the subgroup on prostitution. The community members are ready to take action. Despite the obvious dangers, a group of 10 women have committed to reach out to young sex workers where they gather on the streets. They plan to make contact with each youngster to offer help with food, shelter, education or employment, health care, or to meet other basic needs they might have. They have decided to adopt an attitude of peace and acceptance without judgment. The women are especially concerned about insulting, offending, or otherwise "turning off" those youngsters who might need aid. During the meeting you offer to help them practice making contact before they actually do so—beginning the very next evening. First, (a) write the words you would say and describe the actions you would take in helping them rehearse the action step of initiating contact with youthful sex workers.

The following night and each night thereafter, pairs of women have been taking turns visiting the sex workers to let them know they are available to help. A few youngsters asked them to leave the area because they are "bad for business." Others have thanked the women and advised them to wait in the local Dairy Queen where it is safer. The women have begun to buy coffee for the young men and women, and each night one or two more accept a cup and listen to what they have to say.

About 1 month later in a meeting with the group, you help them review their efforts. Write what would you say and do in (b) helping the women review the action step of initiating contact with the youthful sex workers.

Early on, the women decided to refer to individual sex workers by their "street names." They avoid using actual names, even if known. Starting on the very first night, they also began to track how many sex workers they observe, how many they talk with over coffee, how many they engage on the street, and how the youngsters respond to their offer to help (for example, yes, no, maybe). They also monitor the number of prostitution arrests in the area, as contained in police reports. At this point, the women have tracking data for 28 straight days. Their review and analysis of the data suggest that during the first month, a total of approximately 65 young sex workers operated in the neighborhood. On an average night, 10 to 15 were active. Thus far, the women have at least said hello to 50 and had more substantial talks with 35—most over coffee. Some 15 have accepted offers for some kind of help, and 8 have given up sex work when they secured other employment. Write the words you would say in (c) evaluating progress toward the goal or goals you established earlier (see Summary Exercise 11-1).

b. You are meeting again with Danni. Last time, she thought it might help if she brought her older brother with her so that she could talk with at least one family member about the rape. She has always admired him as a kind, generous, and supportive big brother. Although he knew nothing about the assault, he readily agreed to join her for today's meeting. He sat next to her holding her hand.

Danni began by saying, "Joey, thanks so much for joining me today. I can't tell you how much it means to me. I've been meeting with this wonderful social worker for a few weeks now. I started coming because . . . (at this point she breaks into tears and begins to sob) . . . because . . . 5 weeks ago I was raped by a man I invited into my own apartment."

Danni begins to sob again and as her crying continues, Joey's skin turns ashen and his body stiffens. His facial expression changes. He looks stern and angry, and he lets go of his sister's hand. He then looks out of the window in a silent stare.

Write what you would say and do in using the skill of (a) responding with immediacy to Joey. Then, record what you would say and do in (b) educating Danni and Joey about what just happened, and then use the skill of (c) reframing Joey's reaction. Finally, use the skill of (d) linking to encourage a reconnection between the brother and sister.

c. During the last several days, you have secured temporary housing, food, and medical care for the Z family. However, Mr. Z has been incarcerated in the local jail. He has been charged with the crimes of driving an unregistered and unsafe vehicle and doing so without automobile insurance. He cannot afford the bail bond, so he must wait in jail until the case either goes to trial or is settled through a plea agreement. You are about to meet with the public defender assigned to Mr. Z's case. In effect, you're serving on Mr. Z's behalf as an advocate with his attorney. Before the meeting, (a) outline the steps you would take in preparing to meet with the attorney and advocate for Mr. Z. Then write the words you would say in (b) representing the father and family with the public defender.

d. During the course of today's meeting, Mr. T begins to describe his relationship with the girl and her family. At one point, he starts to cry and says, "I feel so bad for her and for her folks. They don't deserve to suffer for this—for something that is not their fault." He pauses for several moments and then looks directly into your eyes as he says, "I wish I knew if I could trust you." Write the words you would say in (a) responding with immediacy to Mr. T's statement about you. Following your response, Mr. T continues by saying, "I'm really afraid that if I tell you the whole truth, you'll have to testify in court." Now, write the words you would say to (b) go beyond what he said, and then to (c) reframe Mr. T's message by personalizing its meaning. After going beyond and then reframing his message, he says, "I'd like to help out the girl and her family, and I want to clear my conscience. But, I don't want to go to jail. Innocent or guilty, I know if I end up in prison, I'll die there." Write the words you would say in (d) observing inconsistencies in regard to Mr. T's message.

Following your observations, Mr. T seems to relax. He says, "The prosecutor has offered a plea settlement. I've just decided—thanks to you—to accept the deal and plead guilty as charged." Write the words you would say in (e) reflecting feeling and meaning.

After that he continues by saying, "If the court approves the arrangement, I will begin my prison term in about 10 days." As he says that, you realize that you will be able to meet one more time before he is incarcerated. Write the words you would say in (f) pointing out endings with Mr. T.

Chapter 12 Experiential Interviewing Exercise

At this point, you have completed three interviews with a practice client and are planning to undertake the fourth. Thus far, you have used numerous social work skills and probably have a clear conception of the agreed-upon issues for work, the goals, and plans to pursue those goals as well as means to evaluate progress toward their accomplishment. By this time, you and the practice client may have considered various explanatory and change-oriented hypotheses and perhaps shared some ideas in common. As a result of your frequent communication of empathic understanding and open-ended questions, you may have established a warm and trusting relationship. The practice client may feel quite safe and secure with you and may have shared thoughts, feelings, and observations freely and fully. Indeed, she might have made a commitment to undertake one or more action steps during the interval between meetings. She may have also planned to monitor and measure progress toward the agreed-upon service goals.

Building on the previous meetings with your practice client, conduct the fourth interview. In this meeting, proceed to use the working and evaluating skills during the meeting. Of course, seeking feedback, many of the exploring skills and possibly some of the assessing skills, and the contracting skills may be applicable as well. As you know, the working and evaluating skills include rehearsing action steps, reviewing action steps, evaluating, focusing, educating, advising, responding with immediacy, reframing, observing inconsistencies, representing, linking, and pointing out endings. Remember that you will complete a progress recording shortly after the meeting.

When you've finished the 30-minute interview, take another 15 minutes for the following:

1. Leave your respective social worker and client roles. Request that your colleague complete a copy of the Working and Evaluating Skills Rating Form (see Appendix 6). If items from other rating forms such as the Talking and Listening, the Exploring, the Assessing, or the Contracting Skills Rating Forms are applicable, you may use those as well. When your colleague has completed the ratings, inquire about today's interview experience. Ask general open-ended questions to obtain as much evaluative feedback as possible and, through that, enhance your learning. For example, you might ask your colleague questions such as:
   - Did we work on what you wanted to work on today?
   - Do you think that the approach we took today in working toward the goals was effective?
   - What do you think about the way we evaluated progress today?
   - What parts of the interview affected you the most—either positively or negatively?
   - What do you wish had happened during the interview that did not occur?
   - What suggestions do you have about how the interview could have been better, more helpful, or more constructive for you?
   - What suggestions do you have about how I could have been a better or more helpful social worker today?

   As you finish securing feedback from your practice client, thank her and tell her that you will see her soon.

   As soon as you can following the interview, use your word-processing software to prepare a report entitled "Fourth Interview: Practice Client Feedback." Label the document file "Intvue_4_Client_Feed" and deposit it in the "Experiential Exercise Folder" of your Social Work Skills Learning Portfolio.

2. Next, play the audio or video recording. Review and reflect upon what you see or hear, and appraise your performance. Take written notes as you go along. Then, go to Appendix 10 and complete the working and evaluating section of The Social Work Skills Interview Rating Form to evaluate your performance of the social work skills. You may find items within several other interview ratings sections relevant as well. Use your ratings as a stimulus to evaluate your performance. Identify those skills you performed well, those that need improvement, those that you might or should have used during the interview, and those that you used but probably should not have. Reflect upon how you feel about the interview. Describe what you like and what you dislike. Also, discuss how well you used the working and evaluating, and any other social work skills during the meeting. Finally, discuss what you would do differently if you had a chance to conduct the interview again and outline what you might do in the next interview to improve the quality

of your work. Complete the evaluation of your performance in a brief document entitled "Fourth Interview: Self-Evaluation." Save the file as "Intvue_4_Self-Eval" in the "Experiential Interviewing Exercise" section of your Social Work Skills Learning Portfolio.

3. As soon as you can, prepare "Progress Notes" for the formal case record. You might use the SOAIGP format. Record the date of the interview as well as the date you prepare the record. Identify yourself as the social worker but continue to disguise the identity of the practice client. When finished, save the progress notes to a document file labeled "Intvue_4_Notes" and deposit it into the "Experiential Interviewing Exercise" folder of your Social Work Skills Learning Portfolio.

4. Next, reflect upon the entirety of the interview experience and use relevant preparing skills to prepare for the fifth and final meeting with the practice client. Draw upon what you learned and the documents you created to word-process "Plans for the Fifth Interview." Label the file "Intvue_5_Plans" and save it in the "Experiential Interviewing Exercise" folder of your Social Work Skills Learning Portfolio.

CHAPTER 12 Self-Appraisal

As you finish this chapter, please reflect on your learning by using the following space to identify any ideas, terms, or concepts addressed in Chapter 12 that remain confusing or unclear to you:

Next, respond to the following items by carefully reading each statement. Please use a 1-to-10-point rating scale (where *1 = strongly disagree* and *10 = strongly agree*) to indicate the degree to which you agree or disagree with each statement. Place a check mark at the point that best reflects your view at this particular point in time. If you're truly *undecided*, place your check at the midpoint (5.5) mark.

1. I can discuss the purposes and functions of the working and evaluating skills.

    1 2 3 4 5 6 7 8 9 10

2. I can rehearse action steps with clients and constituents.

    1 2 3 4 5 6 7 8 9 10

3. I can review action steps with clients and constituents.

    1 2 3 4 5 6 7 8 9 10

4. I can evaluate progress in collaboration with clients and others.

```
|  |  |  |  |  |  |  |  |  |  |
1   2   3   4   5   6   7   8   9   10
```

5. I can focus conversations on agreed-upon topics.

```
|  |  |  |  |  |  |  |  |  |  |
1   2   3   4   5   6   7   8   9   10
```

6. I can educate others.

```
|  |  |  |  |  |  |  |  |  |  |
1   2   3   4   5   6   7   8   9   10
```

7. I can advise others.

```
|  |  |  |  |  |  |  |  |  |  |
1   2   3   4   5   6   7   8   9   10
```

8. I can respond with immediacy.

```
|  |  |  |  |  |  |  |  |  |  |
1   2   3   4   5   6   7   8   9   10
```

9. I can reframe others' messages.

```
|  |  |  |  |  |  |  |  |  |  |
1   2   3   4   5   6   7   8   9   10
```

10. I can observe inconsistencies in others' thoughts, words, and actions.

```
|  |  |  |  |  |  |  |  |  |  |
1   2   3   4   5   6   7   8   9   10
```

11. I can represent clients in case and class advocacy.

```
|  |  |  |  |  |  |  |  |  |  |
1   2   3   4   5   6   7   8   9   10
```

12. I can link people to people, people to social systems, and social systems to other social systems.

```
|  |  |  |  |  |  |  |  |  |  |
1   2   3   4   5   6   7   8   9   10
```

13. I can point out endings.

```
|  |  |  |  |  |  |  |  |  |  |
1   2   3   4   5   6   7   8   9   10
```

14. I can complete professional quality progress recordings.

```
|  |  |  |  |  |  |  |  |  |  |
1   2   3   4   5   6   7   8   9   10
```

Ending

This chapter should help you develop proficiency in the **ending** processes. Social workers use ending skills as we conclude our working relationships with clients. Although the particular form of ending may vary, a number of skills are important to the process. Drawing on the work of Schwartz (1971, 1976) and Kubler-Ross[1] (1969), Shulman (1992) discusses several that are associated with the dynamics of ending. The skills presented here derive in part from those. The social work ending skills include (1) reviewing the process, (2) final evaluating, (3) sharing ending feelings and saying goodbye, and (4) recording the closing summary.

Chapter Goals

Following completion of this chapter, you should be able to:

- Discuss the purposes and functions of ending.
- Review the process.
- Undertake a final evaluation.
- Share ending feelings and say good-bye.
- Record the closing summary.

Core Competencies

The content addressed in this chapter supports the following core EPAS competencies:

- Competency 4: Engage in Practice-Informed Research and Research-Informed Practice

- Competency 5: Engage in Policy Practice

- Competency 8: Intervene with Individuals, Families, Groups, Organizations, and Communities

- Competency 9: Evaluate Practice with Individuals, Families, Groups, Organizations, and Communities

---

[1] The validity of the Kubler-Ross "Stages of Grief" model has been challenged in several research studies. We cannot assume that clients necessarily respond to loss according to any or all of the five stages of denial, anger, bargaining, depression, and acceptance—or do so in any particular sequence (Konigsberg, 2011).

The four most common forms of concluding relationships with clients are (1) **transferral**, (2) **referral**, (3) **termination**, and (4) **client discontinuation**. In the first three, you and your clients openly discuss the ending process and jointly determine the best course of action given the circumstances. These are the preferred modes of ending. The fourth form, quite common in many agency settings, is exclusively client initiated. Often with good reason, clients may decide to stop meeting with you. They may do so by informing you during a meeting, in a telephone conversation, or even by letter. They may also discontinue without notification, perhaps by failing to attend a scheduled meeting. Their absence conveys the message. In such cases (assuming that you can make contact by phone or in person), it is often very useful to seek clarification from clients who discontinue in this manner. However, you should be extremely sensitive to clients' indirect expressions during these contacts. Sometimes, in response to your inquiry, clients might say they will resume meeting with you "because you were so nice as to call," when in fact they have decided to discontinue. If you listen carefully during such contacts, you may learn something about the ways you presented yourself or how you intervened that played a role in their decision to discontinue. This information may be helpful with other clients in the future. Providing clients with an opportunity to provide feedback about the nature and quality of service may also help them conclude the relationship in a more satisfying manner. It may sufficiently expand their view of you, the agency, and the experience to enable them to seek services again at some point in the future.

Clients are more likely to discontinue without notification at certain times. There is an increased probability of client discontinuation whenever changes occur. Changing from a customary meeting time or relocating from one meeting place to another may lead clients to discontinue. The transfer of a client to another social worker within the same agency can also involve a stressful transition, which the client may resolve through discontinuation. Perhaps the most difficult of all involves a referral to another professional in a different agency. This involves many changes—a new location; another agency with at least somewhat different policies, procedures, and mission; a new meeting schedule; and, of course, a different helping professional. Many clients, perhaps quite understandably, cope with these changes through discontinuation. Although the dynamics of transfers and referrals are similar, transfers are generally easier to manage. Referrals involve more change, and the psychosocial demands on the client are greater. Nonetheless, transfers and referrals, like termination and discontinuation, bring about a conclusion to the relationship between you and the client.

Ending a significant relationship is often a difficult and painful experience. It is certainly challenging for social workers. Concluding a relationship with a client can stimulate strong feelings of sadness, loss, and other emotions as well. For clients, the process of ending may be even more intense. By this time, clients usually view you as a kind, caring, and understanding person who listens well and has their best interests at heart. Often, clients have shared personally intimate thoughts and feelings. This may lead them to feel both safe and vulnerable. They may have entrusted their secrets to you, a person with whom they may never again have contact. They may have successfully addressed a major issue, turned their lives around, or reached a significant goal. They may experience intense gratitude and want to express it to you—perhaps with a tangible or symbolic gift. The conclusion of the relationship may elicit a host of deep feelings. Some clients may feel intensely sad, as if they had lost a best friend, which may in fact be the case. They may feel frightened and dependent as they ask themselves, "How can I make it without you?" They may feel guilty that they did not work as hard as they might have or that they did not take as much advantage of the opportunities for change and growth as they could have. They may feel rejected by you or angry that the relationship is ending. They may think, "If you really cared about me, you wouldn't end the relationship—you must not care about me at all. You're glad to be rid of me!" Clients may also deny or minimize feelings that lie just beneath the surface of awareness.

They may present themselves as being quite ready to terminate, when they are actually struggling with strong feelings that they do not acknowledge or express. There are many manifestations of the psychological and social processes associated with ending—a transition that often provokes significant reactions from both you and your clients. Ideally, we explore these responses as part of the ending process.

■ Reviewing the Process

Reviewing the process involves a summary retrospection of what has occurred between you and your clients during the time you have worked together. It is a collaborative endeavor; all parties participate in the review. Typically, you invite clients to share their reflections about the work you have undertaken together and perhaps identify some exchanges or events that were especially significant or meaningful or had the greatest impact.

Following the responses to your request, you might ask about additional thoughts and feelings. This often stimulates discussion of other experiences. After the client shares, take a few moments to mention some of your own significant recollections. When you do so, highlight something the client realized, said, or did that contributed to progress or made a difference of some kind.

PRACTICE FORMAT *Reviewing the Process (Encouraging Clients)*

I've been thinking about the work we've done together during these last several months. We've covered a lot of ground, and you have made changes in your feelings and emotions, the way you think about things, and how you approach others and the world. You've also made changes in your situation. As you think back over all that we've done together, what strikes you as especially significant or meaningful?
or
As I look back on our work together, one of the things that stands out for me is the time that you (concluded, realized, said, did) _____. I was really struck by that and it's something I'll remember forever.

Reviewing the process may be useful and potentially beneficial even when progress has been modest or nonexistent. Encourage the client to share significant moments—positive or negative—and then explore those to highlight lessons that can be learned. When you share, try to find strengths or positive aspects in the client's actions and experiences that might, in the future, serve as stepping stones for further progress or growth.

EXERCISE 13-1　Reviewing the Process

Review the earlier exercises that involve Mr. K, Loretta, the S family, Mrs. F, and the troubled social service agency as you move from the working and evaluating phase to the ending phase of service. For this exercise, use the skill of reviewing the process with each of our five clients.

1. You have been working with Mr. K for more than 2 months. When he first met with you, he said that his major problem was that he couldn't seem to "get over" his former wife; that he kept hoping for reconciliation when the chances were virtually nonexistent. During the time of your work together, he has made considerable progress. He has resolved the major

problem—he no longer obsesses about his ex-wife and has cognitively and emotionally accepted the fact that the marriage is truly over. He is moving forward in several areas, including his social and recreational life. He is extremely pleased with the resolution of the original problems and the achievement of the goals that you collaboratively identified. He is also proud of his own personal growth. He views himself as a more complete person who now feels quite content with himself and his life. You are also pleased with the work you have done together. As this is your last meeting, please write the words you would say in encouraging Mr. K to review the process with you. After that, refresh your memory about previous exchanges to write the words you might say in sharing something about your work together that you believe might have been especially significant, meaningful, or impactful for Mr. K.

2. You have now worked with Loretta for nearly 4 months. During that time, she has found a job—where she now regularly receives excellent evaluations—secured an apartment, made friends, and is enjoying an active social and recreational life. When you first met, Loretta said that she was traveling to visit her youngest daughter whom she hadn't seen, spoken, or corresponded with in more than 15 years. She has decided to postpone her travel plans until she determines if either of her daughters is truly interested in resuming some kind of a relationship. As this is your last meeting, please write the words you would say in encouraging Loretta to review the process with you. After that, refresh your memory about previous exchanges to write the words you might say in sharing something about your work together that you believe might have been especially significant, meaningful, or impactful for Loretta.

3. You are in the midst of the final meeting with the S family. During the past several months, many productive changes have occurred. Mr. and Mrs. S are happier with each other and have adopted a consistent approach to parenting. They enjoy the children much more than they had before and the children, in turn, seem to have gained respect for their parents and each other. The children are also doing well, perhaps especially Gloria who is growing into a self-confident, independent, and assertive young woman. As this is your last meeting, please write the words you would say in encouraging the S family to review the process with you. After that, refresh your memory about previous exchanges to write the words you might say in sharing something about your work together that you believe might have been especially significant, meaningful, or impactful for the family as a whole or for individual members.

4. This is your concluding session with Mrs. F. The school situation has dramatically improved. In large part due to Mrs. F and the girls, the school has initiated an anti-racist, anti-bullying program which has been embraced by the community at large. Within the family, Mrs. F and her daughters are communicating in a much more satisfying way. In 2 weeks, the three of them will begin a 10-week assertiveness-training group sponsored by another community agency. As this is your last meeting, please write the words you would say in encouraging Mrs. F to review the process with you. After that, refresh your memory about previous exchanges to write the words you might say in sharing something about your work together that you believe might have been especially significant, meaningful, or impactful for Mrs. F or her daughters.

5. For about a year now, you have been providing social work consultation services to an agency that is trying to recover from the consequences of incompetent management and fraudulent behavior under a previous administration. During that time a number of positive changes have occurred and the agency is ready to attempt to continue on without your direct involvement. As this is your last meeting, please write the words you would say in encouraging the agency group to review the process with you. After that, refresh your memory about previous exchanges to write the words you might say in sharing something about your work together that you believe might have been especially significant, meaningful, or impactful for the group as a whole or for individual participants.

Final Evaluating

In addition to reviewing the process, social workers also engage clients in a final evaluation of progress toward problem resolution and goal attainment. In **final evaluating**, you encourage clients to share their reactions to the results of measurement instruments such as questionnaires, various individual or subjective rating scales, and the graphic reflections of trends and patterns (for example, line graphs). You may also share your own impressions of progress toward goals, or overall growth and development. Be sure to seek feedback from clients when you summarize evaluative data or make observations. Although they usually concur, clients sometimes hold different views that deserve consideration and acknowledgment.

As part of this process, express your pleasure concerning positive changes that have occurred. Credit clients for the work they have undertaken and help them identify issues that have not been completely resolved, goals that have been only partially achieved, and new aspirations that may have emerged during the course of your time together. Work toward such goals does not have to stop because you and your client are ending your working relationship. Clients, often with the support of friends, family members, and colleagues may continue to take action steps toward desirable outcomes—including those that involve overall quality of life. By the time clients conclude the working relationship with a social worker, many have become competent problem solvers in their own right. They are often quite capable of defining goals and identifying and taking action on their own. This phenomenon, when it occurs, is enormously satisfying for clients and social workers alike. When clients become effective problem solvers who are skilled at self-help, you may reasonably conclude that you have made a significant impact. If, because of their association with you, clients acquire skills with which to address future issues and pursue additional aspirations, they have gained a great deal indeed.

Like most of the ending skills, final evaluating is a cooperative process. You and clients share your respective evaluations of progress and jointly identify areas for additional work. As part of the process, provide clients with a summary of the results of subjective and objective evaluation instruments, in graphical form if possible. When clients see tangible evidence of progress in a graphic illustration, they often experience feelings of success and accomplishment in a different way than they do when we talk only verbally about their progress.

PRACTICE FORMAT   *Final Evaluating*

Let's now take a final look at where we stand in regard to progress toward the goals that we identified. One of our major goals was _____. Let's look at our evaluation data. How far do you think we have come toward achieving that one?

Join clients in celebrating largely or completely accomplished goals with appropriate pleasure and satisfaction. Encourage them to experience and enjoy the sense of personal competence, self-efficacy, and satisfaction that accompanies goal achievement. Help clients in **considering the future** by identifying areas that need additional work and encourage them to plan additional action steps to take after you conclude your relationship together. Of course, this discussion is not nearly as extensive or as detailed as when you and clients established action steps as part of the contracting and work processes. Rather, you encourage clients to look forward to future activities that can support continued growth and development. You may initiate this process by asking a question such as "What kinds of activities do you think might help you to continue the progress you've made so far?"

PRACTICE FORMAT   *Final Evaluating (Considering the Future)*

Now that we're concluding our time together, you may have some ideas about goals you'd like to pursue or steps you'd like to take in the future. What do you think you'll do next?

As part of the final evaluation, you may ask for honest feedback from clients about things you said or did that were helpful and things that were not. This kind of evaluation may help clients to identify behaviors they can adopt for their own future use. It may also provide an opportunity for clients to share their gratitude to you for your help. However, an important purpose for obtaining feedback about helpful and unhelpful factors is to aid you in your own professional growth and development. In a sense, you request that clients evaluate your performance as a social worker. By **asking for evaluative feedback**, you may gain valuable information about yourself that may prove useful in your work with other current and future clients.

PRACTICE FORMAT | *Final Evaluating (Asking for Evaluative Feedback)*

Now that we're finishing up, I would really appreciate it if you would tell me about those things that I said or did that were particularly helpful to you during our work together. What comes to mind?

or

Thanks so much! I'd really like to get better at what I do, so anything you can tell me about mistakes I made or things I said or did that were upsetting or unhelpful would also be a big help to me. What comes to mind on that score?

EXERCISE 13-2   Final Evaluating

For this exercise, engage each of our five clients in the process of final evaluating. Prepare statements and questions to encourage each client to identify future action steps. Then, write the words you might say in seeking evaluative feedback concerning what has been helpful and what has not.

1. This is your last meeting with Mr. K. He has made considerable progress. He no longer obsesses about his ex-wife and has cognitively and emotionally accepted the fact that the marriage is truly over. He is more socially active and engages in several recreational pursuits as well. He feels quite content with himself and his life. You are also pleased with the work you have done together. You have evaluation data in graphic form that reflect significant decrease in the frequency and intensity of disturbing thoughts about the divorce, improvement in overall mood, and increase in personal satisfaction. You also have several evaluative observations about his progress as well as his personal growth and development. With this information in mind, please write the words you would say to engage Mr. K in the process of final evaluating.

2. Loretta has made remarkable progress during the time you have worked together. This is your last meeting together. She now has secure and satisfying employment, a decent and safe apartment, and she enjoys an active social and recreational life. She has accomplished virtually all of the basic goals of securing income, food, and shelter and has grown personally as well. You provide Loretta with a Goal Attainment Scale that summarizes progress toward these goals. The single major goal that remains involves the relationship with her daughters. Originally, Loretta

said that she was traveling to visit her youngest daughter whom she hadn't seen, spoken, or corresponded with in more than 15 years. Partly as a result of your work together, she has decided to postpone her plans to visit her youngest daughter and has slightly revised her goals. She realized she was afraid to meet her eldest daughter because she felt so guilty about her behavior as a mother. Her current plan is to decide if either of her daughters is genuinely interested in resuming some kind of a relationship. Once she makes that decision, she'll take action. With this information in mind, please write the words you would say to engage Loretta in the process of final evaluating.

3. You are meeting for the last time with the S family. During the past several months, many productive changes have occurred. At times, modest strain is apparent between some of the children. In general, however, the family seems to be coping well with the complex demands of blending and growing together. You have observed numerous ways in which they are communicating more directly and honestly with one another, and experiencing more satisfying relationships. In addition, weekly scale scores reveal a modest but consistent trend toward greater family cohesion and satisfaction. In addition, the family has achieved more than half of their agreed-upon goals. You have graphics that reflect both data sets. With this information in mind, write the words you would say to engage the S family in the process of final evaluating.

4. You are meeting for the last time with Mrs. F. She and her daughters have made noticeable gains. The school and community have embraced the anti-racist, anti-bullying initiative that the F family instigated. The F daughters are now actively involved in school and after-school

activities, and have developed a strong, inclusive, and accepting social network. The subjective scales that Mrs. F rated each week reveal a marked improvement in overall quality of life, family life, work life, and social life scores. You have a line graph that displays upward trends in all four areas. The F family is extremely satisfied with the changes that have occurred and they are looking forward to the assertiveness-training group they will join in another week or so. With this information in mind, write the words you would say to engage Mrs. F in the process of final evaluating.

5. This is your last meeting as a social work consultant with a social service agency that is recovering from the consequences of incompetent management and fraudulent behavior under a previous administration. The agency has made substantial progress toward achievement of almost all goals. You have a Goal Attainment Scale that summarizes these results. You also have observed numerous ways in which the agency has progressed—notably in its relationships with the community and especially in the way agency personnel interact with and engage current and former clients as ongoing "consultants" in their efforts at continuous improvement of service quality. Data from client satisfaction surveys have begun to show substantial improvement. Write the words you would say in initiating the process of final evaluating with the agency group.

▊▊ Sharing Ending Feelings and Saying Good-bye

The nature and intensity of the feelings clients experience as they conclude a relationship with you vary according to their personal characteristics, the duration of service, the issue and goals, the roles and functions you served, and the degree of progress (Hess & Hess, 1999). Because ending is a significant event in the lives of many clients, social workers often engage others in **sharing ending feelings and saying good-bye**.

Clients may experience several emotional responses as they end their relationship with you: anger, sadness, loss, fear, guilt, rejection, ambivalence, gratitude, and affection. Clients may hesitate to express their emotions freely at this time. If they conclude the relationship without sharing some of these feelings, they may experience a sense of incompleteness. This "unfinished" quality may impede the appropriate process of psychological separation from you and inhibit the client's movement toward increased autonomy and independence. Therefore, we usually encourage clients to express their ending feelings.

PRACTICE FORMAT *Sharing Ending Feelings (Encouraging Clients)*

We've reviewed our work together and evaluated progress, but we haven't yet shared our feelings about ending our relationship with one another. As I realize that this is our final meeting together, I am touched by so many things and feel several different emotions. I wonder if you might have some feelings about this as well.

Social workers, of course, also experience various feelings as we end our working relationships with clients. You may have spent several weeks or months with a person, a couple, a family, or a group. During your work together, a client may have shared painful emotions, discussed poignant issues, or made significant progress. Despite your professional status and commitment to an ethical code, you are also human. It is entirely understandable and appropriate that you experience strong feelings as you end your relationships with clients. During the ending process, you may find yourself feeling guilty, inadequate, proud, satisfied, sad, angry, ambivalent, relieved, or affectionate. The nature and intensity of your feelings may vary because of many factors. Like many clients, you will probably experience some kind of emotional reaction during the ending phase. It is often useful to share some of these feelings. Unlike clients, however, you retain your professional responsibilities, even in ending. You cannot freely express whatever feelings you experience. You must consider the potential effects on others. For example, suppose you feel annoyed at an adult male client because he did not work as hard toward change as you had hoped he would. You should not share these or any other such feelings, unless to do so would help the client progress toward any remaining goals or conclude the relationship in a beneficial manner. Even during the final meeting, you consciously choose which feelings to express and how to express them. However, do not simply suppress feelings that are inappropriate to share with clients. Rather, engage in the skills of accessing a place of peace, self-exploration, and centering to address them in a personally and professionally effective fashion at another time and place.

When they are relevant and appropriate, you may share your personal feelings about ending the relationship. Often, when you do share your feelings, clients respond by sharing additional emotions of their own. You may then reflect their feelings and perhaps share more of your own. Finally, however, you and the client complete the ending process by saying good-bye.

PRACTICE FORMAT *Sharing Ending Feelings (Worker)*

When I think about the fact that we will not meet anymore, I feel _____
_____.

(Continued)

| EXAMPLE | Sharing Ending Feelings (Worker) |

Worker: Now that we're concluding our work together, I feel a real sense of loss. I have truly valued our time together and have come to admire you and the way you're approaching life's challenges. I'm not only feeling sad about saying good-bye but also happy that you're moving forward. I'm really going to miss you.

EXERCISE 13-3   Sharing Ending Feelings and Saying Good-Bye

For this exercise, encourage each of our five clients to share feelings about ending. Also, share your own ending feelings. As part of your own sharing, please specify those feelings that you think you might experience had you actually worked with each client. Identify those that would be appropriate to share and those that would not. Finally, say your good-byes.

1. After working with Mr. K for more than 2 months, you have completed your review of the process and conducted a final evaluation. You have approximately 15 minutes left in this very last meeting. Write the words you would say to encourage Mr. K to share his feelings about ending; to express your own feelings; and finally to say good-bye to Mr. K.

2. After working with Loretta for several months, you have completed your review of the process and conducted a final evaluation. You have approximately 15 minutes left in this very last meeting. Write the words you would say to encourage her to share her feelings about ending; to express your own feelings; and finally to say good-bye to this fascinating woman.

3. You have reviewed the process and engaged in a final evaluation of progress with the S family. In the last several minutes remaining in this final meeting, you would like to share ending feelings

and say good-bye. Write the words you would say to encourage family members to share their feelings about ending; to express your own feelings; and finally to say good-bye to the S family.

4. You are in the process of winding down your final session with Mrs. F. You have reviewed the process and engaged in a final evaluation of progress. Now it is time to move toward closure. Write the words you would say to encourage her to share her feelings about ending; to express your own feelings; and finally to say good-bye to Mrs. F.

5. For the past year, you have been providing social work consultation services to an agency that is trying to recover from the consequences of incompetent management and fraudulent behavior under a previous administration. You are meeting with a large group of agency personnel, board members, and key stakeholders for the last time. You are in the process of winding down this final meeting. You have reviewed the process and engaged in a final evaluation of progress. Now it is time to finish up. Write the words you would say to encourage group members to share their feelings about ending; to express your own feelings; and finally to say good-bye to the people you've worked with for nearly a year.

▮ Recording the Closing Summary

Following your final meeting with a client, you synthesize what occurred into a written closing summary. **Recording the closing summary** involves somewhat more effort than that required for common progress notes. When the ending session has included a review of the process, a final evaluation, and a sharing of ending feelings, you will probably have most of what you need to complete a closing summary. Include the following information in the final record: (1) date of final contact; (2) your name and title as well as the name of the client; (3) beginning date of service; (4) the reason contact between you and the client was initiated; (5) the agreed-upon issues and goals for work; (6) the approach taken, the nature of the services that you provided, and the activities that you and the client undertook; (7) a summary evaluation of progress and an identification of issues and goals that remain unresolved or unaccomplished; (8) a brief assessment of the person-issue-situation as it now exists; and (9) the reason for closing the case (Wilson, 1980).

You may use the following section headings to organize your closing summary:

- Process and issues
- Evaluation
- Continuing goals
- Current assessment
- Ending process

As an illustrative example, consider how social worker Susan Holder might prepare a closing summary following the final interview with Mrs. Chase (see Box 13.1).

Box 13.1 EXAMPLE: RECORDING—CLOSING SUMMARY—LYNN CHASE

Process and Issues Mrs. Lynn B. Chase and I, Susan Holder, MSW, met together today for the eighth and final time. Mrs. Chase and I first met almost 3 months ago. At that time, we agreed on the following issues for work: (1) frequent arguments with and feelings of irritability and anger toward son and husband; (2) stress, tension, and anxiety; (3) sleep disturbance; (4) ambivalence about job; (5) thoughts and feelings of excessive responsibility and possibly of control; and (6) role strain and possibly conflict among the roles of mother, wife, homemaker, and employee. Based on these issues, we established several related goals and developed an 8-week plan by which to approach our work together.

Evaluation In reviewing the work process and evaluating progress, Mrs. Chase reported today that the feelings of stress and anger have decreased substantially since the time of the first contact. She also indicated that relations between her and her son, her and her husband, and even her husband and her son have greatly improved since the family more evenly redistributed housework responsibilities. Her reports are consistent with the other evaluation measures we used.

She also said that she assumes less of a caretaker role with her husband and son. She said that she now believes that they have actually benefited from the assumption of greater family and household responsibility. She stated that she now sleeps fine and rarely has a headache. Mrs. Chase reported that her job at Fox Manufacturing is now quite satisfying; she said she is glad she kept it. And she has been engaging in more playful and pleasurable activities, particularly gardening.

Mrs. Chase indicated that the single most helpful aspect of our work together was when I said to her that "doing too much for your husband and son may prevent them from developing their full potential."

(Continued)

> *Continuing Goals* Mrs. Chase indicated that she is still working on issues related to excessive caretaking and intends to do further reading. She reported that she might attend an Adult Children of Alcoholics meeting to see what it's like. She said that she is also considering taking an assertiveness-training course.
>
> *Current Assessment* Based on the available evidence, Mrs. Chase, her son, and her husband are communicating more directly, sharing household responsibilities, and experiencing considerable satisfaction in their relationships with one another.
>
> Robert seems to be negotiating the demands of adolescence in a constructive fashion, and Mrs. Chase has made considerable progress in reversing her long-held patterns of excessive responsibility and control. Mrs. Chase and her family reflect numerous personal strengths that should serve them well in the future. I anticipate that Mrs. Chase will continue to grow and develop now that she has permitted herself to consider more expansive and flexible personal and familial roles.
>
> *Ending Process* Mrs. Chase and I concluded our work together in a positive manner. She expressed her gratitude, and I shared my affection for her as well as my pleasure at the progress she has made. We closed the case in the 8-week time frame as contracted.
>
> February 27
>
> Susan Holder, BSW, MSW
> Licensed Social Worker

EXERCISE 13-4 Recording the Closing Summary

1. For this exercise, use a word-processing program to prepare brief closing summaries for Mr. K, Loretta, the S family, Mrs. F, and our troubled agency. The numerous earlier exercises about these five clients should provide most of the needed information related to issues, goals, action steps, and progress. Prepare the closing summaries as if you intended to include them within a formal case record. When finished, include the "Closing Summaries for Five Clients" as separate sections within a single document. Save the document with a filename "Sums_for_5_Clients" and deposit it in your Social Work Skills Learning Portfolio.
   a. You have just completed your final meeting with Mr. K. Use information from previous exercises to prepare a closing summary of your work with him.
   b. You have just completed your final meeting with Loretta. Use information from previous exercises to prepare a closing summary of your work with her.
   c. You have completed the final meeting with the S family. Use information from previous exercises to prepare a closing summary of your work with the family.
   d. You have concluded the last session with Mrs. F. Use information from previous exercises to prepare a closing summary of your work with her.
   e. You have concluded your last meeting with members of the troubled social service agency. Use information from previous exercises to prepare a closing summary of your work with the group.

SUMMARY

The ending phase of social work practice provides an opportunity for you and your clients to look back on your relationship and the work you undertook together. You have a chance to evaluate overall progress and to identify directions for future work. Of course, concluding these working relationships can be both a joyful and a painful experience for you and your clients. Each of you may experience satisfaction concerning the progress achieved, regret about actions that were not taken, and sadness at the departure of a person who has been important. In optimal circumstances, you can explore these feelings as part of the ending process.

CHAPTER 13 Summary Exercises

1. You are about to conclude your work with the four clients described below (see the Summary Exercises in Chapters 7 through 12). Over the course of time, you and your clients established goals and created plans for action and evaluation. You and they implemented those plans and evaluated progress. Use word-processing software to *write the words* you would say and discuss the actions you would take as you engage them in the ending processes. Please *label* each of the ending skills that you use and place quotation marks around the words you would say. When finished, combine your work into a single "Ending with Four Clients" document with a section for each of the four cases. Save the document to a file labeled "End_w_4_Clnts." Include the file in your Social Work Skills Learning Portfolio.

    a. This is your final meeting with the subgroup on prostitution. You are about to employ several ending skills with the group of 10 extraordinary women who have for slightly more than one full year reached out on a daily basis to young sex workers to help them secure food, shelter, education or employment, health care, or other basic needs. You are completing your role as a social worker and community organizer with them. In fact, the women are entirely capable of continuing this project on their own or, for that matter, planning and carrying out others. According to the tracking data for the previous 365 days, the total number of young sex workers active on the streets in the neighborhood has dropped from 65 to 30. In the beginning, approximately 10 to 15 were conducting business on an average night. That figure has dropped to 5 to 8. The number of arrests for prostitution in the neighborhood has dropped from about 35 to less than 10 per month. Thus far, the women have now met and talked with more than 200 young sex workers. More than 120 have accepted offers for some kind of help, and 40 have given up sex work for other employment. Write the words you would say and describe the actions you would take with them in (a) reviewing the process, (b) final evaluating, and (c) sharing ending feelings and saying good-bye. Following that, identify the kinds of information you would include in (d) a closing summary of your work with these extraordinary women.

    b. You are meeting for the last time with Danni, the young woman who sought counseling following a rape. She has made great progress. She has completed one course in martial arts and plans to take another soon. She has also taken a course in assertive skills training for women. Meanwhile, she and her brother Joey have become closer than ever before. He told her that he's grown more as a result of her experience than he thought possible. At that point, she teared up as she said, "He thanked me for letting him be a part of this process." As you conclude your work together, record the words you would say and the actions you would take with her in (a) reviewing the process, (b) final evaluating, and (c) sharing ending feelings and saying good-bye. Following that, identify what you would include in (d) a closing summary of your work with this courageous woman.

    c. You are meeting for the last time with the Z family. Over the course of several weeks, with the help of the public defender, other community organizations, and your advocacy on his behalf, Mr. Z has been released from jail. He is completing a modest period of community service and has found a fairly well-paying job. The family decided they like this city. The family has secured permanent housing and the older children are now enrolled in school. To supplement their family income, Mrs. Z babysits on a part-time basis. You have also linked them to an immigration attorney. Mr. and Mrs. Z hope that since three of their four children were born in the United States, they might be able to stay in this country.

As you conclude your work with the Z family, write the words you would say and describe the actions you would take with them in (a) reviewing the process, (b) final evaluating, and (c) sharing ending feelings and saying good-bye? Following that, identify what you would include in (d) a closing summary of your work with this family.

d. You are meeting for the last time with Mr. T. Tomorrow, he will begin his prison sentence for child molestation. He said, "I hope my confession helps the girl and her family. I want them to know it is not her fault. It's mine and mine alone. I'm so sorry that I couldn't control myself with that poor child." He went on to say, "Yes, I'm really frightened about what will happen to me. I've heard awful stories about what happens to sex offenders in prison. But, I'm still glad I told the truth. Whatever happens, I can remember that I did one good thing."

Record the words you would say and describe the actions you would take with Mr. T in (a) reviewing the process, (b) final evaluating, and (c) sharing ending feelings and saying good-bye. Following that, describe what you would include in (d) a closing summary of your work with him?

EXERCISE 13 Experiential Interviewing Exercise

Conduct the fifth and final interview with the person who served as your practice client during these past several weeks. As you did previously, ensure that the interview setting is private, and once again record the meeting. Using empathic, working, and especially ending skills, interview your colleague with a view toward concluding the relationship. This is your last meeting. Therefore use the relevant ending skills of reviewing the work process, final evaluating, and sharing ending feelings and saying good-bye. Remember that you will complete a closing summary shortly after the meeting.

When you've finished the 30-minute interview, take another 15 minutes for the following:

1. Leave your respective social worker and client roles. Request that your colleague complete a copy of the Ending Skills Rating Form (see Appendix 6). If items from other rating forms such as the Talking and Listening, the Exploring, the Assessing, the Contracting Skills, or the Working and Evaluating Rating Forms are applicable, you may use those as well. When your colleague has completed the ratings, inquire about today's interview experience. Ask general open-ended questions to obtain as much evaluative feedback as possible and, through that, enhance your learning. For example, you might ask your colleague questions such as:
   - Did we work on what you wanted to work on today?
   - Do you think that the approach we took today in working toward the goals was effective?
   - What do you think about the way we evaluated progress today?
   - What parts of the interview affected you the most—either positively or negatively?
   - What do you wish had happened during the interview that did not occur?
   - What suggestions do you have about how the interview could have been better, more helpful, or more constructive for you?
   - What suggestions do you have about how I could have been a better or more helpful social worker today?

   Because this is your last meeting together as part of this exercise, also ask your partner to provide you with feedback concerning the entire five-session experience. You may adapt the session-focused open-ended questions (above) so that they refer to the complete series of meetings. For example, you might ask:

- Over the course of our five meetings together, did we work on what you wanted to work on? Are there issues that you would have preferred to address that we did not address? If so, what do you think caused that?
- How effective was the approach we took in addressing the problems and pursuing the goals that we identified for our work together?
- What do you think about the way we evaluated progress toward the goals we identified?
- What parts of the five-session experience affected you the most—either positively or negatively?
- What do you wish had happened during our five interviews that did not occur?
- What suggestions do you have about how our meetings could have been better, more helpful, or more constructive for you?
- What suggestions do you have about how I could have been a better or more helpful social worker in our work together?

As you finish receiving feedback, thank her for all the time and effort she expended in serving as your practice client for these many weeks.

As soon as you can following the interview, use your word-processing software to prepare a report entitled "Fifth Interview: Practice Client Feedback." Label the document file "Intvue_5_Client_Feed" and deposit it in the "Experiential Exercise Folder" of your Social Work Skills Learning Portfolio.

2. Next, play the audio or video recording. Review and reflect upon what you see or hear, and appraise your performance. Take written notes as you go along. Then, go to Appendix 10 and complete the ending section of The Social Work Skills Interview Rating Form to evaluate your proficiency in the social work skills. You may find items within several other interview ratings sections relevant as well. Use your ratings as a stimulus to evaluate your performance. Identify those skills you performed well, those that need improvement, those that you might or should have used during the interview, and those that you used but probably should not have. Reflect upon how you feel about the interview. Describe what you like and what you dislike. Also, discuss the quality of performance of the ending skills. Finally, discuss what you would do differently if you had a chance to conduct the interview again and improve your performance. Complete the evaluation in a brief document entitled "Fifth Interview: Self-Evaluation." Save the file as "Intvue_5_Self-Eval" in the "Experiential Interviewing Exercise" section of your Social Work Skills Learning Portfolio.

3. As soon as possible, prepare a "Closing Summary for the Case Record." Use the guidelines outlined in this chapter. Label the document file "Intvue_5_Sum" and save it in the "Experiential Interviewing Exercise" folder of your Social Work Skills Learning Portfolio.

4. Now consider the entire series of five interviews. Summarize your overall impressions and reflections about the experience, and especially what you learned in a report entitled "Reflections on an Experiential Learning Exercise: Five Interviews with a Practice Client." When finished, save the document file as "Reflections" for deposit into the "Experiential Interviewing Exercise" folder of your Social Work Skills Learning Portfolio.

CHAPTER 13   Self-Appraisal

As you finish this chapter, please reflect on your learning by using the following space to identify any ideas, terms, or concepts addressed in Chapter 13 that remain confusing or unclear to you:

Next, respond to the following items by carefully reading each statement. Please use a 1-to-10-point rating scale (where *1 = strongly disagree* and *10 = strongly agree*) to indicate the degree to which you agree or disagree with each statement. Place a check mark at the point that best reflects your view at this particular point in time. If you're truly *undecided*, place your check at the midpoint (5.5) mark.

1. I can discuss the purposes and functions of ending.

   | 1 | 2 | 3 | 4 | 5 | 6 | 7 | 8 | 9 | 10 |

2. I can review the process of working together with clients and other constituents.

   | 1 | 2 | 3 | 4 | 5 | 6 | 7 | 8 | 9 | 10 |

3. I can engage clients and others in a process of final evaluation.

   | 1 | 2 | 3 | 4 | 5 | 6 | 7 | 8 | 9 | 10 |

4. I can share ending feelings and say good-bye.

   | 1 | 2 | 3 | 4 | 5 | 6 | 7 | 8 | 9 | 10 |

5. I can record a closing summary.

   | 1 | 2 | 3 | 4 | 5 | 6 | 7 | 8 | 9 | 10 |

PART 2 SUMMARY EXERCISE: Social Work Skills

Final Lessons

Congratulations! You have now completed all the chapters in the workbook, undertaken many, many exercises, and created a large Social Work Skills Learning Portfolio. You have done a lot! Acknowledge the extraordinary amount of time and effort you expended completing various activities. Please give yourself some well-deserved credit!

Completion of this workbook represents a kind of ending too. In a way, it resembles the ending processes that social workers and clients experience. Some of the skills you recently practiced may be adapted for this last set of exercises—the "Final Lessons." Use a word-processing program to respond to each of the tasks described below. Create section headings to organize the document in a coherent fashion. When finished, label the file "Final_Lessons" and deposit it as the final document for inclusion in your Social Work Skills Learning Portfolio.

1. Compare the contents of your Social Work Skills Learning Portfolio with the checklist contained in Appendix 1. These documents represent tangible evidence of your learning. Identify any documents that are missing from the portfolio. Also, make note of those documents that could be improved through careful revision.

2. The portfolio materials, however, are only a part of the skills development story. From the time you first opened this workbook until now, you undertook a great many learning exercises. You practiced the social work skills a number of times and did so in various ways. Reflect about what you have learned. Then, briefly discuss the most important lessons gained from the various learning experiences.

3. Following your identification of important lessons learned, conduct a final evaluation of your proficiency in the social work skills. To do so, please turn to Appendix 2 and complete Part I of the Social Work Skills Test. The items are geared toward the comprehension level of understanding and are derived directly from the text. At this point in time, most learners who have carefully read the text and completed many of the exercises will correctly answer 70 percent or more of the items.[2] If you completed the test previously, the exam should be much easier to complete and your score should be considerably higher.

   Later, at a point when you have a few free hours—perhaps during a between-term or summer break—complete Part II of the Social Work Skills Test. That can serve as a learning booster, and help you to retain in longer-term memory some of the skills you learned earlier.

4. Now go to Appendix 3 and complete the Social Work Skills Self-Appraisal Questionnaire. You may have completed the questionnaire earlier. If you did, you will be able to compare your item ratings and overall scores from the two events in pretest–posttest fashion. As such, it should provide you with a reasonable indication of the degree to which you gained increased proficiency in the social work skills. If this is the first time you completed the entire instrument, you may compare your items ratings and scores from the self-appraisal exercises that conclude each chapter with those in the relevant sections of the Social Work Skills Self-Appraisal Questionnaire in Appendix 3. The end-of-chapter appraisals represent sections of the questionnaire as a whole.

5. After you have analyzed the results of the Social Work Skills Test and the Social Work Skills Self-Appraisal Questionnaire, identify those skills that require a lot of additional practice, those that need some, and those for which you have developed high levels of proficiency. Identify a list of relevant learning goals and develop plans to pursue them.

---

[2] The correct answers to the items in Part 1 of the Social Work Skills Test may be found through a careful review of the text. These items are written at the comprehension level and should not require much thought; knowledge of the text alone should suffice. The items in Part 2, however, do require application, analysis, synthesis, or evaluation. Determining the correct answers to those items may require discussion with professors or colleagues—after, of course, you have completed the test.

The Social Work Skills Learning Portfolio

Portfolios are widely used in many contexts to demonstrate talents, competence, achievement, and potential. Artists and photographers, for example, commonly maintain selections of their creative work in portfolios. Then, when looking for jobs, bidding on contracts, applying to graduate schools or institutes, or seeking to display their work in art galleries, they may present examples of their artistic products as part of the process. You may use portfolios within learning contexts as well. A collection of written products, especially those that have been assessed or evaluated, can contribute to and reflect the depth and breadth of your learning. The documents you prepare as you complete the exercises contained in this workbook are especially well suited for incorporation into your own Social Work Skills Learning Portfolio.

Prepare the Social Work Skills Learning Portfolio in word-processed, computerized format. It should contain several completed exercises, assignments, self-assessments, and products that reflect and represent your learning. At various points during the learning process, "interim portfolios" may be self-assessed or submitted to someone else (for example, a social work colleague, a professor, or a supervisor) for evaluation and feedback. You may later prepare a "final" portfolio that includes a selected collection of products that you have carefully revised and reworked to reflect your very best work. Such final portfolios may be used for various purposes, including job interviews. Most importantly, however, they can represent a foundation for ongoing lifelong learning and skill development throughout your social work career.

As a first step in creating a Social Work Skills Learning Portfolio, please consider the products you might include. The following represents a list of selected learning exercises contained in the workbook. You may circle "Y" ("Yes") or "N" ("No") in the first column to keep track of those products you decide (or are assigned) to include in your portfolio. Where applicable, you may also use the rating scale in the "Document Quality" column. Circle the number that best reflects the quality of each relevant document.

The Social Work Skills Learning Portfolio: Contents

Document Enclosed?		Documentation	Document Quality (5 = Excellent; 4 = Superior; 3 = Good; 2 = Fair; 1 = Poor; N/A = Not Applicable)
Yes	No		Rating
Y	N	Chapter 1 (Reflective Exercise 1): "Reflections on the Social Work Mission" (SWK_Mission_Reflections)	5 4 3 2 1 N/A
Y	N	Chapter 2 (Reflective Exercise 1): "How We Could Do Better" (Better_SWK)	5 4 3 2 1 N/A
Y	N	Chapter 2 (Reflective Exercise 2): "Preliminary Self-Appraisal of Social Work Knowledge and Abilities" (Prelim_Self-Eval_K_and_A)	5 4 3 2 1 N/A
Y	N	Chapter 2 (Reflective Exercise 3): "Self-Regulation for Social Work" (Self-Reg_for_SWK)	5 4 3 2 1 N/A

(Continued)

The Social Work Skills Learning Portfolio: Contents (*Continued*)			

Document Enclosed?		Documentation	Document Quality (5 = Excellent; 4 = Superior; 3 = Good; 2 = Fair; 1 = Poor; N/A = Not Applicable)
Yes	No		Rating
Y	N	Chapter 3 (Reflective Exercise 1): "Critical Thinking, Scientific Inquiry, and Lifelong Learning in Social Work" (CritThink_in_SWK)	5 4 3 2 1 N/A
Y	N	Chapter 4 (Reflective Exercise 1): "Implicit Attitudes and Quick Judgment in Social Work" (IAT_in_SWK)	5 4 3 2 1 N/A
Y	N	Chapter 4 (Reflective Exercise 2): "Valuing Diversity and Difference" (Val_Div_and_Dif)	5 4 3 2 1 N/A
Y	N	Chapter 4 (Reflective Exercise 3): "What Social Workers Can Do about Injustice" (Soc_Action_in_SWK)	5 4 3 2 1 N/A
Y	N	Chapter 5 (Reflective Exercise 1): "Confidentiality and the Couple" (Couple_Confidentiality)	5 4 3 2 1 N/A
Y	N	Chapter 5 (Part I: Summary Exercise 1): "Summary Assessment of My Motivation, Readiness, and Suitability for the Profession of Social Work" (My_Readiness_for_SWK)	5 4 3 2 1 N/A
Y	N	Chapter 6 (Exercise 6-3.1): "Reflections on a Nonverbal Exercise" (Nonverb_Ex)	5 4 3 2 1 N/A
Y	N	Chapter 6 (Exercise 6-4.1): "Outreach Script" (Outreach_Script)	5 4 3 2 1 N/A
Y	N	Chapter 6 (Exercise 6-4.2): "Letter" (Draft_Letr_1) and "Memorandum" (Draft_Mem_1)	5 4 3 2 1 N/A
Y	N	Chapter 6 (Exercise 6-5.1): "Reflections on a Listening Exercise" (Listen_Ex)	5 4 3 2 1 N/A
Y	N	Chapter 6 (Summary Exercise 1): "Transcript of an Early Interview" (Early_Intvue_Transcript) and "An Early Interview: Self-Evaluation Report" (Early_Int_Self-Eval)	5 4 3 2 1 N/A
Y	N	Chapter 6 (Summary Exercise 2): "Letter to Self" (Letter_to_Self)	5 4 3 2 1 N/A
Y	N	Chapter 7 (Exercise 7-8): "Preliminary Plans for Five Clients" (Plans_for_5_Clients)	5 4 3 2 1 N/A
Y	N	Chapter 7 (Summary Exercise 1): "Preparing for Four Meetings" (Prep_for_4_Mtgs)	5 4 3 2 1 N/A
Y	N	Chapter 8 (Summary Exercise 1): "Four Beginnings" (4_Beginnings)	5 4 3 2 1 N/A
Y	N	Chapter 8 (Experiential Exercise): "Plans for the First Interview" (Intvue_1_Plans)	5 4 3 2 1 N/A
Y	N	Chapter 9 (Summary Exercise 1): "Four Explorations" (4_Exps)	5 4 3 2 1 N/A
Y	N	Chapter 9 (Experiential Exercise 1): "First Interview: Practice Client Feedback" (Intvue_1_Client_Feed)	5 4 3 2 1 N/A
Y	N	Chapter 9 (Experiential Exercise 2-a): "First Interview: Additional Exploration Questions" (Intvue_1_More_Quests)	5 4 3 2 1 N/A
Y	N	Chapter 9 (Experiential Exercise 2-b): "First Interview: Self-Evaluation" (Intvue_1_Self-Eval)	5 4 3 2 1 N/A
Y	N	Chapter 9 (Experiential Exercise 3): "First Interview Notes" (Intvue_1_Notes)	5 4 3 2 1 N/A

The Social Work Skills Learning Portfolio: Contents (*Continued*)			
Document Enclosed?		**Documentation**	**Document Quality** (5 = Excellent; 4 = Superior; 3 = Good; 2 = Fair; 1 = Poor; N/A = Not Applicable)
Yes	**No**		**Rating**
Y	N	Chapter 9 (Experiential Exercise 4): "Plans for the Second Interview" (Intvue_2_Plans)	5 4 3 2 1 N/A
Y	N	Chapter 10 (Exercise 10-4): "My DAC: Description" (My_DAC_Desc)	5 4 3 2 1 N/A
Y	N	Chapter 10 (Exercise 10-5): "My DAC: Assessment" (My_DAC_Assess)	5 4 3 2 1 N/A
Y	N	Chapter 10 (Summary Exercise 1): "Four Assessments" (4_Assessments)	5 4 3 2 1 N/A
Y	N	Chapter 10 (Experiential Exercise 1): "Second Interview: Practice Client Feedback" (Intvue_2_Client_Feed)	5 4 3 2 1 N/A
Y	N	Chapter 10 (Experiential Exercise 2): "Second Interview: Self-Evaluation" (Intvue_2_Self-Eval)	5 4 3 2 1 N/A
Y	N	Chapter 10 (Experiential Exercise 3): "Assessment" (Intvue_2_DAC)	5 4 3 2 1 N/A
Y	N	Chapter 10 (Experiential Exercise 4): "Plans for the Third Interview" (Intvue_3_Plans)	5 4 3 2 1 N/A
Y	N	Chapter 11 (Exercise 11-2.1): "Action Plans for Five Clients" (Action_Plans_for_5_Clients)	5 4 3 2 1 N/A
Y	N	Chapter 11 (Exercise 11-5): "My DAC: Contract" (My_DAC_Contract)	5 4 3 2 1 N/A
Y	N	Chapter 11 (Summary Exercise 1): "Four Contracts" (4_Contracts)	5 4 3 2 1 N/A
Y	N	Chapter 11 (Experiential Exercise 1): "Third Interview: Practice Client Feedback" (Intvue_3_Client_Feed)	5 4 3 2 1 N/A
Y	N	Chapter 11 (Experiential Exercise 2): "Third Interview: Self-Evaluation" (Intvue_3_Self-Eval)	5 4 3 2 1 N/A
Y	N	Chapter 11 (Experiential Exercise 3): "Contract" (Intvue_3_DAC)	5 4 3 2 1 N/A
Y	N	Chapter 11 (Experiential Exercise 4): "Plans for the Fourth Interview" (Intvue_4_Plans)	5 4 3 2 1 N/A
Y	N	Chapter 12 (Exercise 12-13.1): "Progress Notes for Five Clients" (ProgNotes_for_5_Clients)	5 4 3 2 1 N/A
Y	N	Chapter 12 (Summary Exercise 1): "Working with Four Clients" (Work_w_4_Clients)	5 4 3 2 1 N/A
Y	N	Chapter 12 (Experiential Exercise 1): "Fourth Interview: Practice Client Feedback" (Intvue_4_Client_Feed)	5 4 3 2 1 N/A
Y	N	Chapter 12 (Experiential Exercise 2): "Fourth Interview: Self-Evaluation" (Intvue_4_Self-Eval)	5 4 3 2 1 N/A
Y	N	Chapter 12 (Experiential Exercise 3): "Progress Notes" (Intvue_4_Notes)	5 4 3 2 1 N/A
Y	N	Chapter 12 (Experiential Exercise 4): "Plans for the Fifth Interview" (Intvue_5_Plans)	5 4 3 2 1 N/A
Y	N	Chapter 13 (Exercise 13-4.1): "Closing Summaries for Five Clients" (Sums_for_5_Clients)	5 4 3 2 1 N/A

The Social Work Skills Learning Portfolio: Contents (*Continued*)

Document Enclosed?		Documentation	Document Quality (5 = Excellent; 4 = Superior; 3 = Good; 2 = Fair; 1 = Poor; N/A = Not Applicable)
Yes	No		Rating
Y	N	Chapter 13 (Summary Exercise 1): "Ending with Four Clients" (End_w_4_Clients)	5 4 3 2 1 N/A
Y	N	Chapter 13 (Experiential Exercise 1): "Fifth Interview: Practice Client Feedback" (Intvue_5_Client_Feed)	5 4 3 2 1 N/A
Y	N	Chapter 13 (Experiential Exercise 2): "Fifth Interview: Self-Evaluation" (Intvue_5_Self-Eval)	5 4 3 2 1 N/A
Y	N	Chapter 13 (Experiential Exercise 3): "Closing Summary" (Intvue_5_Sum)	5 4 3 2 1 N/A
Y	N	Chapter 13 (Experiential Exercise 4): "Reflections on an Experiential Learning Experience: Five Interviews with a Practice Client" (Reflections)	5 4 3 2 1 N/A
Y	N	Chapter 13 (Part II: Summary Exercises) "Final Lessons" (Final_Lessons)	5 4 3 2 1 N/A

The Social Work Skills Test

APPENDIX 2

The Social Work Skills Test[1] contains two major parts. Part 1 includes true-false and multiple-choice items that refer directly to descriptive content contained within the book. These items are written primarily at the comprehension level of intellectual development. In order to answer such items correctly, you must have read, understood, and remembered material presented in the book.[2]

Part 2[3] includes short-answer items in which you must apply what you have learned to practice scenarios. More intellectually challenging than Part 1, these items are framed at the application, analysis, synthesis, and evaluation levels of intellectual development. Many of these items approximate contexts and exchanges that commonly occur in social work practice. You must invest considerable thought, judgment, and care in responding to items in Part 2 of The Social Work Skills Test.

The Social Work Skills Test—Part 1

Carefully read each of the following true-false and multiple-choice items and choose the best response from among the available answers. Circle the letter that reflects the best response to each item. Record the date you completed this part of the test.

1. There is more genetic variation within races than exists between them. Indeed, DNA studies in the Human Genome Project suggest that distinct, identifiable subspecies or "races" do not appear among modern human beings.
   A. True
   B. False

2. Failure to discuss relevant policy and ethical factors with clients may be grounds for malpractice action.
   A. True
   B. False

3. All employees in the United States must receive at least the federal minimum hourly wage.
   A. True
   B. False

4. Social workers often attribute their career satisfaction to factors such as the variety of work challenges, the creativity needed to address those challenges, and the opportunity to work closely with and on behalf of people—especially people in need.
   A. True
   B. False

---

[1] The Social Work Skills Test (Ver. 1.3). Copyright © 2009, 2013, and 2016 by Barry R. Cournoyer. For information about the test, email the author at bcourno@iupui.edu.

[2] In order to enhance learning, correct answers to Part 1 of The Social Work Skills Test are not provided here. Since the true-false and multiple-choice items are primarily comprehension-level in nature, answers may be found within the text itself.

[3] The items in Part 2 of The Social Work Skills Test are short-answer in nature. They involve critical thinking and the application of knowledge. Although we can usually distinguish superior from inferior responses, various short answers could be "correct" or "partially correct." Your professor may provide you with "model" responses for comparison with your own; or, after you have completed all items, you may compare your responses with those of your colleagues and discuss which ones are better or worse.

5. Usually appearing in the form of negative or unfavorable opinions about a person, phenomenon, or group, prejudice may occur in a positive or favorable direction as well.
   A. True
   B. False

6. Several experimental research studies have demonstrated that false memories are quite difficult to produce.
   A. True
   B. False

7. Perhaps because of the comparatively better quality of its health care system, the average life expectancy in the United States (78.9 years in 2014) is 3 to 4 years longer than, for example, in Australia or Switzerland.
   A. True
   B. False

8. If researchers do not obtain favorable findings through the statistical procedures incorporated as part of the original research design, they may obtain credible results by running the figures through a series of various other statistical procedures to determine if the anticipated findings can be established through one or more of them.
   A. True
   B. False

9. As conceptualized in the Educational Policy and Accreditation Standards (EPAS) of the Council on Social Work Education (2015), social work competence is the ability to integrate and apply social work knowledge, values, and skills to practice situations in a purposeful, intentional, and professional manner to promote human and community well-being.
   A. True
   B. False

10. Based on their studies of happiness, Lyubomirsky and colleagues suggest that very little of a person's happiness results from voluntary, intentional activities.
    A. True
    B. False

11. In our professional work, social workers must think critically about human needs and social problems. Such deep, complex intellectual processes that involve concentration and considerable mental effort are sometimes referred to as "slow" or "strong" forms of thinking. Daniel Kahneman calls this "System 1 Thinking."
    A. True
    B. False

12. Researchers who seek to determine the efficacy of policies, programs, and change-oriented interventions are increasingly expected to include _____ statistics in addition to more traditional statistics in their published studies.
    A. significance level
    B. demographic
    C. effect size
    D. epidemiological

13. The *duty of care* applies to social workers and other helping professionals. This legal principle requires the professional to
    A. adopt practice methods, models, and procedures that reflect the best research-based evidence of safety and effectiveness.
    B. meet a minimal standard of care.
    C. meet a reasonable standard of care.
    D. possess advanced expertise in a practice method, model, technique, or procedure before using it with clients.

14. People tend to adjust their aspirations to current conditions. For example, within a few years following the windfall, many major lottery winners who do not spend everything, adapt to their newfound lifestyle and adjust their aspirations upward—so that the "gap" between

what is and what they aspire to remains about the same. This process is sometimes
described as

A. aspirational adaptation.
B. the ambition differential.
C. the hedonic treadmill.
D. the have-want gap.

15. Suppose a social worker asked a client, "Haven't you experienced lots of pain in your pelvic area? So, isn't it likely that you were sexually abused as a child?" Such questions would best be characterized as

A. leading.
B. closed-ended.
C. open-ended.
D. theme building.

16. Multiple content areas are addressed in the standardized social work licensing examinations used throughout the 50 states, the District of Columbia, Puerto Rico, the U.S. Virgin Islands, and several Canadian provinces. In the Bachelor's Exam, the _____ content domain contains the largest percentage of items; in the Master's exam, the largest percentage falls within the _____ content domain.

A. Professional Relationships, Values and Ethics . . . Assessment and Intervention Planning
B. Human Development, Diversity, and Behavior in the Environment . . . Direct and Indirect Practice
C. Direct and Indirect Practice . . . Professional Relationships, Values and Ethics
D. Assessment . . . Human Development, Diversity, and Behavior in the Environment

17. During the beginning phase of the working relationship, many clients and other constituents are quite unclear about what is expected of them. Many do not know what they are "supposed to do." When social workers describe what's likely to happen and how clients and others may participate as active, collaborative partners in the change-making process, we are using the social work skill of

A. *orienting.*
B. *outlining expectations.*
C. *socialization.*
D. *clarifying processes.*

18. Suppose a client (a high school senior) says, "I've been accepted to two universities. One offers the academic program that perfectly matches my career goals and interests. The other is located close to where my boyfriend will go to school. I'm hopelessly torn between the two options." The social worker responds to the client's statement by saying, "You don't know whether to pursue your academic goals or your relationship goals." In responding in this way the social worker is probably using the skill of

A. *focusing.*
B. *reflecting content.*
C. *reflecting feelings and meaning.*
D. *reflecting feelings.*

19. Belief in one's ability to organize or plan a course of action, implement that plan, and achieve a successful outcome is best described as

A. problem-solving.
B. ego-strength.
C. self-esteem.
D. self-efficacy.

20. In advance of all meetings and especially before initial meetings, social workers try to envision clients' current circumstances, their perspectives, and their expectations. We attempt to experience what our clients are likely to sense, feel, think, imagine, and do in the encounter. Through _____ social workers seek to better appreciate others' subjective experience related to seeking or receiving social service and to this particular meeting.

A. *preparatory planning*
B. *preparatory anticipation*
C. *anticipatory assessment*
D. *preparatory empathy*

21. A client says, "The company laid me off about 8 months ago and I haven't been able to make the mortgage payments on the house for the last 6 months. I've looked and looked for work but I can't find anything. I'm so discouraged that I've just about given up." In response, the social worker says, "As you see it, there are at least three major issues you'd like to address in our work together. First, you're unemployed and can't find work. Second, you haven't paid your home mortgage in several months. Third, you're close to giving up hope that things will improve." In this situation, the social worker is probably using the skill of
    A. *focusing.*
    B. *reflecting feelings and meaning.*
    C. *reflecting issues.*
    D. *going beyond what is said.*

22. As human beings, we tend to see what we hope or expect to see and find what we hope or expect to find. In research, these human tendencies may lead to misapplication of research designs or misinterpretation of data such that the anticipated findings are "discovered." When such tendencies are not controlled or managed in some way, researchers would likely be subject to the effects of
    A. confirmation bias.
    B. attrition.
    C. maturational bias.
    D. reactivity.

23. Occasionally, persons who believe they were negatively affected by a social worker's professional behavior submit grievances to the National Association of Social Workers (NASW) or a government-sponsored licensing bureau. Most claims of ethical misconduct are filed by
    A. clients or their family members.
    B. supervisees or employees of the social worker.
    C. supervisors or employers of the social worker.
    D. coworkers or colleagues.

24. Well-designed, practice-relevant, outcome studies often produce information about the relative probability that a certain program, practice, policy, protocol, or interventive action will lead to a particular outcome. These studies typically involve good size samples and random assignment of participants into "treatment" and "comparison" or "control groups." Such studies often produce _____ of great value to social workers and clients as we consider how to address problems and pursue goals.
    A. nomothetic evidence
    B. predictive evidence
    C. projective evidence
    D. idiographic evidence

25. Toward the end of a series of 12 scheduled meetings, a social worker draws on the results of measurement instruments such as questionnaires, various individual or subjective rating scales, and the graphic reflections of trends and patterns (e.g., line graphs) to present estimates of progress toward achievement of the agreed-upon goals for work. In doing so, the social worker is probably using the skill of
    A. *pointing out endings.*
    B. *seeking clarification.*
    C. *final evaluating.*
    D. *reviewing the process.*

26. Among the classification schemas that some social workers use as part of an assessment process are the *DSM* and
    A. the *PIE system.*
    B. *Bloom's Taxonomy.*
    C. *Gorman's Grid.*
    D. the *GARP Scale.*

27. When social workers seek advice from a social work supervisor or colleagues concerning an upcoming visit with a prospective client or other persons, we are engaged in
    A. *preparatory advice-seeking.*
    B. *preparatory exploring.*

C. *preparatory consulting.*

D. *anticipatory supervision.*

28. A(n) _____ is a simple graphical representation that reflects, in shorthand fashion, important events or experiences in chronological order during a designated period.
    A. chronograph
    B. ecogram
    C. genomap
    D. timeline

29. Triangles of various kinds may emerge in families, groups, organizations, communities, and societies. Many of these reflect moral judgments and metaphors. The famous "dramatic triangle" involves three roles or positions. Which of the following is *not* one of them?
    A. persecutor
    B. victim
    C. rescuer
    D. mediator

30. *Hearing* or *receiving* others' words, speech, and language; *observing* their nonverbal gestures and positions; *encouraging* them to express themselves fully; and *remembering* what they communicate are elements of the social work skill of
    A. listening.
    B. registering.
    C. understanding.
    D. reflecting.

31. In legal terms, malpractice, or *mal praxis*, by professional social workers is
    A. a felony.
    B. a violation of contract law.
    C. a misdemeanor.
    D. a tort.

32. When social workers encourage clients to consider occurrences of problems in terms of their distant as well as proximate antecedent factors, co-occurring factors, and subsequential factors, we are probably engaged in a process of
    A. factor analysis.
    B. situational assessment.
    C. systems analysis.
    D. functional analysis.

33. The term _____ may be used to refer to the uses and abuses of power by those of higher status in relation to those of lower status. The feelings of shame, humiliation, indignity, or inferiority felt by a "nobody" when abused, oppressed, enslaved, imprisoned, or exploited, or even when addressed with superiority, arrogance, or condescension by a "somebody" are often similar whether it appears as racism, sexism, ageism, ableism, lookism, heterosexism, or other insidious "isms."
    A. xenophobia
    B. elitism
    C. ethnocentrism
    D. rankism

34. _____ includes formal and informal relations and activities that address and often meet significant human needs for inclusion, social identity, socialization, understanding, and encouragement.
    A. Social support
    B. Social intelligence
    C. Social consensus
    D. Social welfare

35. The idea that individual happiness is based, in part, upon genetic and biological factors, and tends to remain quite stable over time may lead to a hypothesis that each person has a
    A. happiness ceiling.
    B. relatively fixed happiness quotient.

    C. happiness floor.

    D. happiness set-point.

36. A social worker is meeting with Sharon Oh. The client says, "I'm glad I've come here. Last time I needed help, I went to the North Central Social Services Center. They were just awful. They didn't know what they were doing and didn't help me at all." Which of the following would be the best example of a social worker's optimum use of active listening in response to this client's statement?

    A. "Yes, I've heard other people say they have had bad experiences at that agency."

    B. "Ms. Oh, you're hoping that we're more competent than that other agency."

    C. "You didn't have a positive experience when you sought help before and you're hoping for good service here."

    D. "Sharon, I'm glad you've come here too."

37. A social worker says to a client, "I think we agree about the primary issues that we'll address in our work together. Let's review them, and I'll write them down so that we can refer to them as we go along. First, there is the problem of unemployment and finding work. Second, there's the problem of the overdue mortgage payments. Third, there's the problem of your own discouragement. How about it—is this an accurate list of the problems that we should address in our work together?" In this situation, the social worker is probably using the skill of

    A. *confirming issues for work.*

    B. *identifying issues.*

    C. *partializing.*

    D. *reflecting issues.*

38. As described in the Educational Policy and Accreditation Standards (EPAS) of the Council on Social Work Education (2015), the purpose of the social work profession is actualized through the profession's "quest for social and economic justice, the prevention of conditions that limit human rights, the _____, and the enhancement of the quality of life for all persons, locally and globally."

    A. elimination of poverty

    B. development of job and educational opportunities

    C. promotion of democratic political processes

    D. distribution of food and material resources

39. Suppose a new client says to a social worker, "I'm facing a whole lot of problems all at the same time. One of my kids needs surgery but I just lost my job and my health insurance. My husband just left us and moved across the country with a woman half my age. Good riddance to him but, of course, he's not providing us any financial support. I'm hoping to get another job—one with insurance—but my 18-year-old car just broke down and I can't go anywhere. I don't know what to do. I'm frightened and desperately need your help." After first responding empathically to ensure that the client feels respected and understood, the social worker would probably next use the skill of

    A. *reflecting content.*

    B. *focusing.*

    C. *partializing.*

    D. *reflecting feelings and meaning.*

40. A client says, "Well, I guess the first thing I'd like to accomplish is to get a job so I can pay some bills." The social worker responds by saying, "As you see it then, your most important goal is to find work." In this situation, the social worker is probably using the skill of

    A. *proposing goals.*

    B. *establishing goals.*

    C. *going beyond what is said.*

    D. *reflecting content.*

41. When considering moral and ethical issues or dilemmas, a social worker would wisely consider dimensions such as *motives, means, ends,* and _____.

    A. *settings*

    B. *persons*

    C. *effects*

    D. *measures*

42. During the early phases of practice, social workers often seek to explore clients' reasons for making contact with the agency at this particular time. For example, in some circumstances, a social worker might ask, "What led you to call us at this particular time—rather than, say, 6 months or a year ago?" Such a question would best be characterized as
    A. leading.
    B. open-ended.
    C. closed-ended.
    D. explanatory.

43. The concept of "inclusive cultural empathy" involves at least three central processes. Which of the following is *not* one of the three?
    A. *Intellectual Understanding:* Know something about others' cultures.
    B. *Appropriate Interaction:* Engage others in ways that convey respect for their cultural affiliations.
    C. *Cultural Matching:* Adopt the gestures, speech patterns, and slang or jargon of the diverse cultural groups with whom we interact.
    D. *Affective Acceptance:* Accept and value those who belong to different cultural groups.

44. During the assessment phase of work, social workers and clients commonly generate a "theory of the case" that includes two kinds of hypotheses:
    A. Ad Hoc and Predictive.
    B. Explanatory and Change-Oriented.
    C. Causal and Correlational.
    D. Description and Diagnostic.

45. During the exploration phase of work, social workers and their clients commonly review two general aspects or dimensional areas in addition to the need, problem, issue, or goal. The two include (1) the person and (2) the _____.
    A. family
    B. person's history
    C. situation
    D. development of the problem

46. Arguments typically contain a claim or a conclusion along with one or more premises. Consider the following argument:
    • The bodies of all human males contain testosterone.
    • Testosterone causes violence.
    • Therefore all human males are violent.

    This particular argument is
    A. valid but unsound.
    B. invalid but sound.
    C. valid and sound.
    D. invalid and unsound.

47. Typically, the last entry in a completed case record is a
    A. *final evaluation.*
    B. *final progress note.*
    C. *terminal assessment.*
    D. *closing summary.*

48. Human beings are generally remarkably resilient. In time, following stressful life events and difficult circumstances, most people return to or close to their previous levels of happiness. This phenomenon is often referred to as the _____.
    A. positivity bias
    B. adaptation theory of well-being
    C. rebound hypothesis
    D. strengths perspective

49. When social workers introduce clients to a new way of looking at some aspect of a phenomenon, we probably are using the skill of
    A. *paraphrasing.*
    B. *going beyond what is said.*

    C. *reflecting meaning.*

    D. *reframing.*

50. Many clients readily offer ideas about "why" something happens. We can refer to these ideas as their _____.

    A. explanatory hypotheses

    B. conceptual hypotheses

    C. theoretical hypotheses

    D. causal hypotheses

51. Which one of the following states reflected the highest prison population (per 100,000 residents) in 2013?

    A. New York

    B. Arizona

    C. New Jersey

    D. Massachusetts

52. In *The Social Work Skills Workbook*, the author outlines seven phases of practice that elaborate the four introduced in the Educational Policy and Accreditation Standards (EPAS) of the Council on Social Work Education. The second of the seven phases is

    A. Exploring.

    B. Beginning.

    C. Assessing.

    D. Working and Evaluating.

53. A single statistical measure or indicator can never adequately capture the complexities associated with income and wealth inequality. The Gini is a useful but far from perfect index. Other types of measures help to complement the Gini. These include, for example, indicators of economic

_____.

    A. regression

    B. progression

    C. mobility

    D. equilibrium

54. After a client and social worker agree upon goals and plans for work, the social worker may appropriately engage in the skill of _____ if it becomes apparent that members of the client system lack useful or valid information or abilities that could contribute to the achievement of the agreed-upon goals for work.

    A. *interpreting.*

    B. *advising.*

    C. *educating.*

    D. *informing.*

55. The probability that a particular statistical procedure will correctly detect a difference in a sample when such a difference actually exists in the larger population is often referred to as

    A. statistical significance.

    B. statistical power.

    C. the effect size.

    D. an accuracy estimate.

56. Social workers sometimes have an opportunity to talk with referral sources or previous helpers before meeting clients for the first time. When social workers do ask questions about incoming clients' needs and circumstances, or about other relevant topics before actually meeting with them, we are probably engaged in

    A. *preliminary questioning.*

    B. *preparatory exploring.*

    C. *preparatory investigating.*

    D. *preparatory reviewing.*

57. When social workers encourage clients to explore experiences and feelings that are occurring right here and right now between the client and the social worker, we are probably using the skill of

    A. *responding with immediacy.*

    B. *exploring.*

C. *questioning.*

D. *focusing.*

58. Occasionally, social workers and clients wander away from the agreed-upon issues and goals. These diversions are sometimes productive, leading to greater understanding and improving the chances for effective change. At other times, however, such departures are clearly unproductive. When social workers redirect attention and energy to relevant topics, we are probably using the skill of

A. *focusing.*

B. *reframing.*

C. *attending.*

D. *restructuring.*

59. Sponsored by the United Nations Development Programme, the Gender Inequality Index (GII) measures three general dimensions: (1) health—as measured by the mortality and adolescent fertility rates, (2) empowerment—as measured by level of education and percentage of parliamentary seats, and (3) labor—as measured by participation in the workforce. Which of the following nations reflected the highest level of gender equality (that is, the lowest level of gender inequality) in 2013 as measured by the GII?

A. Germany

B. Canada

C. Mali

D. United States

60. During a meeting with a client, a social worker says, "When we began this process, we decided to meet 12 times. At first, we met twice per week, then once per week, and recently once per month. According to my calendar, we have two more meetings to go: one in another month and the last one a month after that." In this situation, the social worker is probably using the skill of

A. *confronting.*

B. *pointing out endings.*

C. *focusing.*

D. *clarifying.*

61. Toward the conclusion of their work together, social workers typically provide clients an opportunity to express their feelings about the experience, their relationship, and about ending. Social workers also often share our own feelings as we conclude our work with clients. In doing so, social workers are probably using the skill(s) of

A. *pointing out endings.*

B. *self-disclosure, questioning, and educating.*

C. *reviewing the process.*

D. *sharing ending feelings and saying good-bye.*

62. The United Nations's Human Development Index (HDI) is a composite indicator of three measures of human development. Which of the following is *not* one of the three?

A. health and longevity

B. knowledge

C. standard of living

D. personal property

63. A social worker says, "We've agreed that finding work is the first and most important goal for our work together. As a step toward that goal, I'd like to ask one of our employment consultants to review your resume and provide suggestions for improvement. How does that sound to you?" In this situation, the social worker is probably using the skills of

A. *educating* and *seeking feedback.*

B. *proposing a goal* and *seeking feedback.*

C. *planning* and *seeking feedback.*

D. *proposing an action step* and *seeking feedback.*

64. During the initial stages of exploring the need, problem, or other issue, social workers most often encourage clients to
    A. imagine how others would resolve the issue.
    B. describe their previous attempts to resolve or cope with the problem or issue.
    C. talk with their friends and family members to gain alternate perspectives about the problem or issue.
    D. consider epidemiological research findings concerning the problem or issue.

65. During the exploration phase of work, social workers and their clients commonly explore temporal aspects of the problem or issue. That is, they consider the problem as it was in both the past and the present. In this context, they may also consider the problem or issue
    A. as it could appear in the future.
    B. as if it were a strength.
    C. as if it had never appeared.
    D. as if another person or people experienced it.

66. Bloom's taxonomy is often used in the preparation of learning objectives. The taxonomy proceeds through six categories or levels of learning. The first or basic level involves *recollection* and the sixth level involves *evaluation*. The third level involves
    A. *synthesis.*
    B. *analysis.*
    C. *comprehension.*
    D. *application.*

67. The standardized social work licensing examinations used throughout the 50 states, the District of Columbia, Puerto Rico, the U.S. Virgin Islands, and several Canadian provinces are developed under the aegis of and sponsored by the
    A. International Federation of Social Workers.
    B. Association of Social Work Boards.
    C. National Association of Social Workers.
    D. Council on Social Work Education.

68. When you share your name and profession, and your agency or departmental affiliation, you are using the social work skill of
    A. *self-identification.*
    B. *self-disclosure.*
    C. *introducing yourself.*
    D. *orientation.*

69. Suppose a social worker visits a household to determine if a child has been abused by her parents or older siblings. Based upon the available evidence, the social worker concludes that child abuse has not occurred. Subsequent information, however, reveals that the social worker's conclusion was incorrect. In fact, the child had been abused on several occasions. The social worker's inaccurate conclusion represents a
    A. false negative.
    B. false positive.
    C. true positive.
    D. true negative.

70. Which category of social work skills builds on clients' experience and frames of reference by introducing, in a much more active and expressive fashion, social workers' professional knowledge and expertise?
    A. the *contracting skills*
    B. the *working and evaluating skills*
    C. the *assessing skills*
    D. the *exploring skills*

71. Five categories of common, nonspecific factors account for much of the variation in counseling and psychotherapy outcomes. These categories include (1) client and situational factors, (2) helper

and relationship factors, (3) _____, (4) technique and allegiance factors, and (5) evaluative feedback factors.

A. hope and expectancy factors
B. socioeconomic factors
C. education and experience factors
D. professional identify factors

72. During the exploration phase of practice, social workers often engage clients in *looking for strengths*. In doing so, social workers and clients typically look for (1) *competencies*, (2) *assets and social support*, (3) *successes*, and (4) _____

A. *happiness.*
B. *fortunate events.*
C. *life lessons.*
D. *dreams.*

73. When social workers schedule appointments, secure interview rooms, locate interpreters, or reposition furniture to better accommodate incoming clients who speak a foreign language or are accompanied by service dogs, we are most likely using the skill of

A. *preparatory planning.*
B. *preparatory organizing.*
C. *preparatory arranging.*
D. *environmental preparation.*

74. Suppose a social worker responds to a client's statement in this way: "You mention that you and your partner are no longer intimate. What do you mean by the phrase, 'no longer intimate'?" In responding in this way the social worker is probably using the skill of

A. *questioning.*
B. *focusing.*
C. *seeking clarification.*
D. *going beyond what is said.*

75. A group of agency social workers are consulting with each other to improve the quality of their service to clients. One social worker discusses a family she's serving. She describes a situation in which three young children were physically and sexually abused by their mother's boyfriend. The boyfriend is now in jail. Which of the following would be the most accurate way for the social worker to refer to the boyfriend?

A. "I think he's a pedophile."
B. "He's a predator."
C. "He's a sex offender."
D. "He abused the children."

76. During an initial meeting, a social worker learns that a client has recently begun to consider the possibility that she may have an alcohol abuse problem. Although she has not yet altered her drinking habits and has not developed a plan for change, she has begun to keep a record of when, where, what, and how much alcohol she drinks each day. In relation to the issue of alcohol consumption at this point in time, you and the client would probably consider her to be in the _____ stage of change.

A. contemplation
B. action
C. maintenance
D. preparation

77. The following graphic representation indicates that

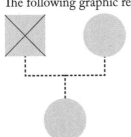

A. a casual relationship resulted in the birth of a male child who died.
B. the biological father of a female child is deceased.
C. the biological mother of a male child is deceased.
D. a marital relationship that ended in divorce produced a female child.

78. Toward the end of a series of 16 scheduled meetings, a social worker says to a client, "As we conclude our work together, I've been thinking about what we've done during these last several months. We've covered a lot of ground together, and you have made changes in both your own behavior as well as in your situation. As you think back over our work together, what things seem especially significant?" In this context, the social worker is probably using the skill of
    A. *pointing out endings.*
    B. *final evaluating.*
    C. *seeking clarification.*
    D. *reviewing the process.*

79. According to the U.S. Census Bureau, the nation's racial and ethnic composition will change dramatically during the 21st century. When combined, members of minority ethnic groups will probably constitute a majority of the U.S. population by the year
    A. 2024
    B. 2064
    C. 2044
    D. 2084

80. Within the U.S. criminal justice system, there are many causes of wrongful convictions. However, more than 60 percent of defendants who were wrongfully convicted but subsequently exonerated involved _____, making it the single most common cause of wrongful convictions.
    A. witness perjury
    B. eyewitness misidentification
    C. prosecutor misconduct
    D. defense attorney incompetence

81. During the previous meeting, a client agreed to engage in a specific goal-directed behavior at least once each day. In today's meeting, the social worker says, "Last time we met, you said that each day before you went to sleep, you would get out your notebook and write down five things that you're grateful for. How did that work out?" In this situation, the social worker is probably using the skill of
    A. *responding with immediacy.*
    B. *reviewing action steps.*
    C. *evaluating.*
    D. *focusing.*

82. To encourage others to express themselves as fully and as freely as possible, social workers typically seek to communicate nonverbally that we are open, nonjudgmental, and interested in and accepting of them as people. This process is commonly referred to as
    A. matching.
    B. proxemics.
    C. empathy.
    D. attending.

83. During a meeting with a long-time client, a social worker says, "On the one hand you say you want to improve the relationship with your children and on the other hand you report that you cannot spend time with them because of your work responsibilities." In this situation, the social worker is probably using the skill of
    A. *observing inconsistencies.*
    B. *reflecting meaning.*
    C. *reframing.*
    D. *going beyond what is said.*

84. Evidence-based practice (EBP) involves five sequential steps. The second step in the EBP process involves the
    A. analysis of evidence in light of clients' needs, goals, culture, and preferences.
    B. application of the evidence in practice with clients.
    C. search for and discovery of relevant research-based evidence.
    D. evaluation of the effects of the application in collaboration with clients.

85. Humans' tendency to view their own racial, ethnic, cultural, or national group as superior to others' is called
    A. ethnocentrism.
    B. discrimination.
    C. prejudice.
    D. bias.

86. During a meeting, a social worker and client examine a graphic representation of the number of caring gestures the client made toward his teenage son each day. As they review the graph (below) together, the social worker is probably using the skill of

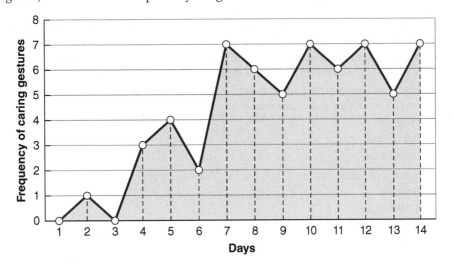

    A. *reviewing action steps.*
    B. *reframing.*
    C. *evaluating.*
    D. *educating.*

87. To identify the potential effects of their own personal histories, characteristics, needs, biases, emotional tender spots, philosophical or religious views, and behavioral patterns, social workers often engage in _____ in advance of meetings with others.
    A. *preparatory self-management*
    B. *preparatory self-exploration*
    C. *preparatory sensitization*
    D. *preparatory self-control*

88. In its *Educational Policy and Accreditation Standards* (EPAS), the Council on Social Work Education (CSWE) endorses the six core values identified in the *Code of Ethics* of the National Association of Social Workers (NASW) and adds two more. These two are
    A. knowledge and expertise.
    B. human rights and scientific inquiry.
    C. honesty and professionalism.
    D. equality and community.

89. The following graphic representation is an element of

    A. a social systems map.
    B. a famframe.
    C. an eco-map.
    D. a genogram.

90. A social worker has been working with a client for a few weeks now. At this point, they are discussing factors associated with the client's current unemployment. In exploring possible reasons for her unemployment, the client shares a theory, "I believe I'm unemployed because I did not complete my degree in engineering. If I had, I'd still have a job or I'd have an easier time finding one." The social worker says, "As you see it, one of the reasons you're unemployed is because you didn't finish your college degree in engineering." In this situation, the social worker is probably using the skill of
    A. *reflecting hypotheses.*
    B. *reflecting issues.*
    C. *identifying issues.*
    D. *going beyond what is said.*

91. A social worker's responsibility to *warn and protect* a potential victim of violence may be distinguished from the *duty to report* child abuse in terms of the standard or level of evidence required to breach client confidentiality. For example, the standard of evidence needed to take protective action in the case of an adult male client's threat to kill or harm his boss would _____ that required to report possible child abuse.
    A. sometimes be higher and sometimes lower than
    B. be lower than
    C. be higher than
    D. be the same as

92. There are three common forms of malpractice. Which of the following is *not* one of the three?
    A. misfeasance
    B. masfeasance
    C. malfeasance
    D. nonfeasance

93. As it had for the preceding several years, the federal minimum wage for 2015 remained at _____ per hour.
    A. $6.75
    B. $7.25
    C. $8.50
    D. $9.25

94. In *The Social Work Skills Workbook*, the author introduces several formats that social workers might use to organize written progress notes. Which of the following is *not* one of these formats?
    A. APIE
    B. GRAF
    C. SOAPIER
    D. GAAP

95. When social workers engage other people or social systems on behalf of clients in pursuit of agreed-upon goals, we are typically using the skill of
    A. *educating.*
    B. *representing.*
    C. *interpreting.*
    D. *advising.*

96. A social worker agrees to help a client find employment. Together, they have developed a plan for pursuing that goal and are now engaged in planning ways to evaluate progress toward its achievement. They identify a range of possible outcomes from "most unfavorable" to "most favorable." In doing so, they are probably generating a
    A. subjective rating scale.
    B. individualized rating scale.
    C. goal attainment scale.
    D. rapid assessment instrument.

97. In 2013, the average annual household income of the top 5 percent in the United States was approximately _____. By contrast, the average annual household income for the bottom 20 percent was about _____.

    A. $87,900 . . . . $25,400
    B. $185,200 . . . . $8,400
    C. $322,300 . . . . $11,600
    D. $752,100 . . . . $17,800

98. In the context of social work practice, professionalism involves (1) sophisticated knowledge, expertise, and self-efficacy in the provision of social work services; (2) respect for and adherence to the values of the social work profession and its code of ethics; and (3) personal and professional integrity, self-understanding and self-control, and social support. Among the remaining aspects of professionalism identified in *The Social Work Skills Workbook* are

    A. confidence, hope, and optimism.
    B. critical thinking, scientific learning, and lifelong learning.
    C. appearance, style, and presentation.
    D. honesty, determination, and dedication.

99. When we encourage others to identify themselves by name and perhaps to share something about themselves, social workers are using the social work skill of

    A. *engaging others.*
    B. *seeking introductions.*
    C. *preliminary exploration.*
    D. *identifying others.*

100. Before meetings, contacts, and interviews with individuals, families, groups, organizations, and communities, social workers commonly engage in _____. In doing so, social workers often address questions such as: "Why is this meeting occurring? What is its overall purpose? What do I hope to accomplish through this meeting? What is my tentative agenda? What might be the agenda of the people who will be involved or affected by the meeting? What might they hope to accomplish? What would I consider a successful meeting? What might they? What are my functions or roles in this meeting? How do I wish to begin? What things should I say? What questions should I ask? What might they want to ask of me? What kind of interactional process would I like to see? What kind might they? How would I like the meeting to conclude? How might they like to see it end?"

    A. *agenda setting*
    B. *clarification*
    C. *focusing*
    D. *preliminary planning*

101. Suppose a client (a high school senior) says, "I've been accepted to two universities. One offers the academic program that perfectly matches my career goals and interests. The other is located close to where my boyfriend will go to school. I'm hopelessly torn between the two options." The social worker responds to the client's statement by saying, "You're afraid that if you go to the school that you want to, the relationship with your boyfriend could end." In responding in this way the social worker is probably using the skill of

    A. *reflecting feelings.*
    B. *going beyond what is said.*
    C. *reflecting feelings and meaning.*
    D. *reflecting content.*

102. Despite noble, idealistic, and altruistic motives, social workers who lack _____ might unwittingly act out unresolved personal issues or enact ideological, emotional, or behavioral patterns that harm the very people we hope to help.

    A. self-awareness and self-control
    B. integrity and commitment
    C. knowledge and skill
    D. confidence and self-efficacy

103. The overall dependency ratio in the United States is expected to _____ from 60.25 in 2014 to _____ in 2060.

    A. decrease 57.14
    B. increase 76.37

    C. decrease 49.66

    D. increase 63.18

104. A major theme or trend in contemporary psychosocial services involves the assessment of motivation—particularly as it relates to the transtheoretical model (TTM) or the five "stages of change." The third of these five TTM stages is called

    A. contemplation.

    B. maintenance.

    C. preparation.

    D. action.

105. Suppose a client (a high school senior) says, "I've been accepted to two universities. One offers the academic program that perfectly matches my career goals and interests. The other is located close to where my boyfriend will go to school. I'm hopelessly torn between the two options." The social worker responds to the client's statement by saying, "You're ambivalent because you don't know whether to pursue your academic goals or your relationship goals." In responding in this way the social worker is probably using the skill of

    A. *reflecting content.*

    B. *reflecting feelings and meaning.*

    C. *focusing.*

    D. *reflecting feelings.*

106. When social workers suggest a possible focus or function for a meeting, we are probably using the social work skill of

    A. *orienting others.*

    B. *describing initial purpose.*

    C. *focusing.*

    D. *agenda setting.*

107. In advance of meetings, social workers seek to organize and manage our own personal thoughts, feelings, and physical sensations so that they do not interfere with our professionalism, performance, and delivery of social services. This skill is often referred to as

    A. *centering.*

    B. *clarifying.*

    C. *focusing.*

    D. *calibrating.*

108. The positive or negative treatment of people based on characteristics such as race, gender, religion, ethnicity, age, physical appearance or ability, or sexual orientation constitutes

    A. ethnocentrism.

    B. bias.

    C. discrimination.

    D. prejudice.

109. Individual or environmental markers associated with an increased likelihood that a negative outcome will occur are often called

    A. negative probabilities.

    B. risk factors.

    C. adverse effect factors.

    D. effect sizes.

110. Although ethical decision making is challenging in most circumstances, those that _____ _____ represent the greatest intellectual challenge of all. They require the most advanced critical thinking skills.

    A. involve several relevant legal and ethical obligations that are consistent with each other

    B. oblige social workers to subordinate their own personal views to those of the social work profession

    C. involve several relevant legal and ethical obligations that conflict with each other

    D. remind social workers of their own personal mistakes or failings

111. In work with client systems of different sizes at various phases or stages of practice, social workers should consistently demonstrate the essential facilitative qualities of (1) empathy, (2) respect, and (3) _____.

    A. support
    B. understanding
    C. authenticity
    D. compassion

112. In which stage of Cross et al.'s Cultural Competency Continuum (1989) do individuals, families, groups, organizations, and communities actively respect, affirm, and value the culture of diverse others through their beliefs, attitudes, policies, practices, words, and behaviors?
    A. Stage 7
    B. Stage 4
    C. Stage 6
    D. Stage 5

113. A(n) _____ is a diagrammatic representation of a person, family, or household in its social context—highlighting energy-enhancing and energy-depleting relationships between members of a primary social system (e.g., family or household) and the outside world.
    A. genogram
    B. eco-map
    C. social systems map
    D. famframe

114. Suppose a client who has been involved for several years with a violent and abusive man says, "I'm afraid to leave and I'm afraid to stay. If I stay, he'll beat me again. If I leave, he'll find me and beat me even more. He might even kill me." The social worker responds by saying, "You're terrified." In responding in this way the social worker is probably using the skill of
    A. *reflecting feelings and meaning.*
    B. *focusing.*
    C. *responding with immediacy.*
    D. *reflecting feelings.*

115. Specific measures of various kinds may complement the assessment process and sometimes serve as indicators of goal attainment. One group of such measures are called RAIs—an acronym that stands for
    A. *Readiness Assessment Indicators.*
    B. *Rapid Assessment Instruments.*
    C. *Rational Analysis Indices.*
    D. *Readable Assessment Indicators.*

116. When people regularly make definitive assertions or claims based upon an assumption that the positions of authorities or the statements contained in authoritative sources represent absolute truth, they are probably engaged in
    A. relativistic thinking.
    B. magical thinking.
    C. multiplistic thinking.
    D. dualistic thinking.

117. Individual or environmental safeguards that enhance a person's ability to resist stressful life events, risks, or hazards and promote adaptation and competence are often called
    A. protective factors.
    B. positive probabilities.
    C. effect sizes.
    D. favorable effect factors.

118. A social worker asks a client, "Although you haven't mentioned it as a problem, as we've talked, I've been wondering about your sleep patterns. If my calculations are correct, you're only sleeping 2 or 3 hours each night." In this situation, the social worker is probably using the skill of
    A. *advising.*
    B. *identifying an issue.*
    C. *observing inconsistencies.*
    D. *reflecting issues.*

119. In its 2015 Educational Policy and Accreditation Standards (EPAS), the Council on Social Work Education (CSWE) identifies _____ core competencies (the last of which address the processes of *engagement, assessment, intervention*, and *evaluation*).
   A. 12
   B. 9
   C. 6
   D. 10

120. In 2013, approximately _____ million children lived in poverty in the United States.
   A. 5.2
   B. 21.2
   C. 14.7
   D. 103

121. During a meeting with a social worker, a client makes a commitment to undertake an action step during the next 7 days. In order to increase the probability of completion, the social worker engages the client in
   A. *anticipatory evaluation.*
   B. *probability enhancement.*
   C. *reviewing the action step.*
   D. *rehearsing the action step.*

122. Of the various claims of ethical misconduct filed against social workers, the largest single category involves
   A. incompetence.
   B. poor quality practice.
   C. boundary violations.
   D. fraud or dishonesty of some kind.

123. DAC is an acronym that stands for *Description, Assessment*, and
   A. *Circumstances.*
   B. *Conceptualization.*
   C. *Conditions.*
   D. *Contract.*

124. As described in *The Social Work Skills Workbook*, a social work skill is a discrete set of _____ and _____ actions that are consistent and congruent with (1) social work values, ethics, and obligations; (2) research-based knowledge; (3) the dimensions of professionalism; and (4) a legitimate social work purpose within the context of a phase or process of practice.
   A. professional . . . . interpersonal
   B. cognitive . . . . behavioral
   C. psychological . . . . social
   D. intrapersonal . . . . interpersonal

125. A social worker is meeting with Janna Olazavitz for the first time. The client says, "I'm Mrs. Olazavitz and I'd like your advice about how to help my 16-year-old son. He's gotten involved with the wrong crowd and his school grades have suffered. I'm worried he won't be able to get into college." Which of the following would be the best example of a social worker's optimum use of the active listening skills in responding to this client's statement?
   A. "Mrs. Olazavitz, you think your son's new friends have led him astray. His grades have dropped and you're worried that he might be drinking or using drugs."
   B. "Janna, you're terrified that your son is ruining his chances for a better life."
   C. "Mrs. Olazavitz, you're concerned about your son's new friends and his poor academic performance, and you'd like some guidance about how you might help him change things to improve his chances of going on to college."
   D. "So Janna, you'd like my help in helping your son."

126. Many clients readily offer ideas and explanations about "how" a problem might be resolved. We can refer to them as their

    A. explanatory hypotheses.
    B. theoretical hypotheses.
    C. exploratory hypotheses.
    D. change-oriented hypotheses.

127. In conducting a detailed exploration of a problem or issue, social workers often encourage clients to discuss its onset, evolution or development, and the situational contexts in which it occurs. When applicable, social workers also commonly seek to determine the frequency, intensity or severity, and _____ of each episode.
    A. prognosis
    B. implications
    C. duration
    D. variability

128. The skill of _____ involves examining and considering information available to you and your agency before an initial contact with another person or persons.
    A. *preparatory reviewing*
    B. *preliminary assessing*
    C. *preparatory reflection*
    D. *preliminary preparation*

129. Perhaps the most widely known and used measure of income inequality is the Gini index, also known as the Gini ratio or Gini coefficient. Which of the following Gini scores would reflect the highest level of equality (that is, the lowest level of inequality)?
    A. 0
    B. 1
    C. 10
    D. 100

130. Currently, one of the most popular trait approaches to personality assessment involves attention to the "big five" personality factors. These five aspects or dimensions of personality are captured in the following acronym:
    A. OCEAN
    B. MULTI
    C. CEASE
    D. FIVES

131. According to the Council on Social Work Education (2015), pursuit of the social work profession's purpose is guided by a person-in-environment framework, a global perspective, respect for human diversity, and
    A. knowledge based on scientific inquiry.
    B. international law.
    C. Judeo-Christian values.
    D. basic humanitarian principles.

132. The skill of *active listening* involves three steps: The first is *inviting*. The other two are
    A. *listening* and *reflecting*.
    B. *mirroring* and *providing feedback*.
    C. *receiving* and *registering*.
    D. *hearing* and *talking*.

133. After a client and social worker agree upon goals and plans for work, the social worker may appropriately engage in the skill of _____ if it becomes apparent that the client would probably benefit from a suggestion or recommendation that could contribute to the achievement of the agreed-upon goals for work.
    A. *informing*.
    B. *interpreting*.
    C. *educating*.
    D. *advising*.

134. In its *Code of Ethics*, the National Association of Social Workers (NASW) identifies a set of six core values. These core values serve as the foundation of social work's unique purpose and perspective. The first of these is
    A. dignity and worth of the person.
    B. integrity.
    C. service.
    D. social justice.

135. When social workers resist tendencies to approach complex issues in an overly confident, intellectually superior manner and instead approach them with open-mindedness, we demonstrate
    A. intellectual courage.
    B. intellectual empathy.
    C. intellectual autonomy.
    D. intellectual humility.

136. Proficient use of the *preparing* skills contributes to a productive engagement between clients and social workers. Their use helps to reduce the high rates of premature discontinuation of needed services. Social workers who adequately prepare in advance of meetings are more likely to express accurate understanding of clients' views of the problem or issue that concerns them. Failure to do so _____ the probability of early dropout.
    A. triples
    B. increases by half
    C. quadruples
    D. doubles

137. During the assessment phase of practice, social workers and clients attempt to make sense of the data gathered during the exploration phase. The assessment gives the parties involved a perspective from which to formulate goals and develop plans for action. Five skills are especially pertinent to the assessment phase. Two of the five are
    A. *data collection* and *interpretation*.
    B. *exploring* and *reviewing*.
    C. *proposing* and *finalizing*.
    D. *sharing hypotheses* and *confirming issues*.

138. During the early phases of practice, social workers sometimes seek to gather specific information. For example, in some circumstances, a social worker might ask questions such as, "What is your phone number?" "What's your address?" "What's your date of birth?" Such questions would best be characterized as
    A. closed-ended.
    B. data-gathering.
    C. open-ended.
    D. detail-oriented.

139. When social workers seek to establish, maintain, or restore connections between two or more people; between one or more persons and a social group, organization, or community; or between elements of two or more social systems, we are probably using the skill of
    A. *relationship building*.
    B. *networking*.
    C. *engaging*.
    D. *linking*.

140. In providing professional service, social workers usually seek to engage others in a physical setting where people can communicate freely and expressively without fear of harm. Importantly, we also access a place of peace within ourselves. _____ is a skill that can help social workers adopt a balanced, peaceful attitude as we prepare to meet a client or other constituent.
    A. *Preparatory empathy*
    B. *Centering*
    C. *Preparatory exploring*
    D. *Preliminary planning*

■ The Social Work Skills Test—Part 2

Carefully read each of the following short-answer items. Use a word processor to record your responses to the following short-answer items. Label and date the file so that you can quickly determine when you completed each administration of this portion of the test. Number each of your answers so that you may easily refer to the test items themselves. Identify the document as "The Social Work Skills Test—Part 2" and save the file as "Skills_Test_Pt2_[date]" for inclusion in your Social Work Skills Learning Portfolio and for later comparison with responses to subsequent test administrations.

After you have completed this part of the test, you may track the quality of your responses on a scale where *1 = Unsatisfactory*, *2 = Inferior*, *3 = Satisfactory*, and *4 = Proficient*. Alternately, you could use a traditional grading system where *A = Excellent*, *B = Good*, *C = Satisfactory*, *D = Poor*, and *F = Unsatisfactory*.

After some time has passed, you might review your original answers and attempt to create better responses—especially for those you consider unsatisfactory.

1. A 17-year-old male client says, "I don't know what's wrong with me. I can't get a date to save my life. Nobody will go out with me. Every girl I ask out says no. I don't have any real guy friends either. I am so lonely. Even my folks hate my guts! My mother and I fight all the time, and my stepdad will have nothing to do with me. I spend most of my time alone in my room listening to music. I know I'm real depressed, but I don't know what to do about it."

    Write the words you would say in using the skill of *partializing* in your attempt to focus the client's exploration following this client's statement.

2. You have been serving as a social worker in a counseling role with a voluntary client for about 6 months. The client has reached virtually all of the goals that you jointly identified during the contracting phase of work. You enjoy your visits with this client, and the client also appears to enjoy the meetings with you. You have extended the time frame for work once already, and as a professional you realize that it would be unwise to do so again. You therefore suggest to the client that you meet once more to conclude your working relationship.

    When you make this suggestion, the client pauses for a moment and then says, "That sounds about right. You have helped me a great deal, and I think I am ready to try it on my own. In fact, you've become extremely important to me and I've come to like and respect you a great deal. I'd like it very much if we could become friends once I'm no longer a client. Instead of meeting one more time, I'd like to take you to dinner. What kind of food do you like?"

    Identify and discuss the social work values, legal duties, and ethical principles, if any, that might apply in this situation. If applicable, develop a case-specific values hierarchy to help you resolve any conflicts. Then describe what you would say and do in this situation to behave in an ethical manner.

3. A 21-year-old male client says, "My father began to molest me when I was about 9 years old. When I think about it, I just shudder. It was so disgusting, so humiliating. Even today, whenever I think about it, I still feel dirty and damaged. My father kept doing it until I was 14. After that he'd try sometimes but I was too strong for him by that time."

    Write the words you would say in using the skills of (a) *reflecting feelings*, (b) *reflecting feelings and meaning*, and (c) *going beyond what is said* in your attempt to encourage further client exploration following this client's statement.

4. Briefly explain how and why members of a long dominant, majority group might be unaware of the privileges associated with their position in society.

5. Why should social workers regularly engage in scientific inquiry?

6. How might a lack of professionalism by a few social workers negatively affect the profession as a whole?

7. Briefly describe or create an action undertaken by a social worker that would reflect a high level of *professional integrity*.

8. How might a social worker's well-developed sense of professional self-efficacy contribute to positive client outcomes?

9. Yesterday, Mrs. Little telephoned the family service agency where you work to express concern that her husband of 6 months might be abusing her 7-year-old daughter, Shari. Although she loves her new husband, she's extremely worried about Shari—whose biological father abandoned the family several years earlier. In your agency, you serve as a social worker specializing in helping couples and families. You will be talking with Mrs. Little when she visits the agency later today.

Demonstrate your knowledge of and ability to use the applicable preparing skills (*preparatory arranging, preparatory empathy, preliminary planning, preparatory self-exploration,* and *centering*) in advance of your first meeting with Mrs. Little. Be sure to label each of the skills by making a brief notation beside it.

10. Assume that you are a social worker who has already prepared for an initial meeting with Mrs. Little (see previous item). The time for her appointment arrives. You walk up to her in the waiting room and then escort her to a private office or interview room.

    Write the words you would say in beginning with Mrs. Little. If applicable, use any or all of the beginning skills that would be relevant in this situation. When you've finished writing the words you would say, label each of the skills you choose to use by making a brief notation beside it. If you determine that a particular beginning skill would not be applicable as you begin in this situation, provide a brief rationale for omitting it.

11. Discuss how and why valuing diversity and difference is a central element of professionalism in the context of social work practice.

12. How and why might a social worker who lacks a strong, positive social support network be susceptible to boundary violations with clients?

13. Use your own words to explain the meaning of the phrase "intersectionality of multiple factors" within the context of diversity and difference.

14. In discussing social justice, John Rawls suggests that people adopt a "veil of ignorance" in thinking about, proposing, or considering potential policies and actions. What does this notion of "veil of ignorance" mean in the context of social justice?

15. An adult male client of African ancestry says, "Sometimes it seems so phony. I grew up hearing whites call me "boy" and "nigger." I was poor as dirt and sometimes I was beaten just because of the color of my skin. But I fought on through it all. I kept my pride and made it to college. I did really well too. When I graduated, a lot of the big companies wanted to meet their minority quota so I was hired right away at a good salary. I've been at this company now for five years, and I have contributed a great deal. I've been promoted twice and received raises. But so far, not one white person in the company has ever asked me to his home. Now what does that say to you?"

    Write the words you would say in using the skill of *going beyond what is said* in your attempt to encourage further client exploration following this client's statement.

16. Use your knowledge and critical thinking to identify two or three explanatory hypotheses about how a several hundred year history of slavery, oppression, and discrimination against black people in the United States might affect the beliefs, attitudes, and behavior of contemporary African Americans.

17. Generate two or three explanatory hypotheses about how a several hundred year history of slavery, oppression, and discrimination against black people in the United States might affect the beliefs, attitudes, and behavior of contemporary white people.

18. In your own words, describe what is meant by the terms *inherent, universal, inalienable,* and *indivisible* within the context of human rights.

19. Draw an abbreviated genogram of a family headed by a lesbian couple who have adopted a 7-year-old boy and a 6-year-old girl. Each of the adoptive parents had heterosexual parents. Their mothers are living. However, both of their fathers have died during the past 7 years.

20. Draw an abbreviated eco-map to illustrate positive, energy-enhancing relationships between a four-member nuclear family and their religious community, their neighborhood, and the workplaces of the parents. Also, depict conflicted, energy-depleting relationships between the parents and their respective in-laws and between the children and their school.

21. A client who has been married for 1 year says, "We fight all the time about his teenage son—the one from his first marriage. My husband doesn't think I should discipline the boy at all. He doesn't want me to correct him or to punish him in any way. But, I'm around the boy much more than my husband is and I have to deal with the brat!"

    Write the words you would say in using two forms of the skill of asking questions in your attempt to encourage further client exploration following this client's statement. Make your first question *open-ended* and the second, *closed-ended*.

22. A 14-year-old male client says, "Sometimes I wonder whether there is something wrong with me. Girls just turn me off. But boys . . . when I'm close to a good-looking boy, I can feel myself becoming excited. Does that mean I'm gay?"

    Write the words you would say in using the skill of *reflecting content* in your attempt to encourage further client exploration following this client's statement.

23. A 14-year-old male client asks (see previous item), "If I am gay, what will I do? If my mother finds out, she'll be crushed. She'll feel that it's her fault somehow. I'm so scared and so worried. If my friends learn that I'm gay, what will they do?"

    Write the words you would say in using the skills of (a) *reflecting feelings*, (b) *reflecting feelings and meaning*, and (c) *going beyond what is said* in your attempt to encourage further client exploration following this client's statement.

24. A 15-year-old female client in foster care says, "This family treats me like dirt. They call me names and don't let me do anything I want to do. Half the time they don't even feed me. I just hate it there!"

    Write the words you would say in using the skill of *seeking clarification* in your attempt to encourage further client exploration following this client's statement.

25. Generate two or three explanatory hypotheses about how and why so many men physically and emotionally abuse their intimate female partners.

26. Generate two or three explanatory hypotheses about how and why parents would physically and emotionally abuse their children.

Case Study *Use a word processor to record your responses to the items that refer to the following case study. Label and date the file so that you can quickly determine when you completed this part of the test.*

Presume that you are a social worker in the Child Protective Services (CPS) unit of a Department of Child Welfare. Your job is to investigate allegations of child abuse and neglect to determine if the child or children involved require protective service. When a child is determined to be in need of care, you sometimes follow up by providing ongoing counseling and case management services.

A county resident has telephoned CPS to report that she has observed severe bruises on the back and the legs of Paul N, an 8-year-old neighborhood child. The neighbor has heard loud arguments in the child's home and believes that the child has been beaten on several occasions. You are called to respond to the allegation. You drive to the neighborhood and go to the N home, where the abuse is reported to have occurred. The door is answered by a woman who confirms that she is Mrs. N, the child's mother.

After you introduce yourself by name and profession, you describe your purpose and role and outline the relevant policy and ethical factors.

Mrs. N says, "I know why you're here—it's that damn nosy neighbor down the street. She's always butting into other people's business. She called you, didn't she?"

You respond to Mrs. N's expression by saying, "I'm not allowed to reveal how information regarding allegations of child abuse or neglect come to us. My job is to investigate the reports however they occur and to determine whether a child is in danger. Is that clear?"

Mrs. N says, "Yeah. Come on in. I guess you want to see Paul." She loudly calls for Paul (who has been playing in another room).

Paul enters the room with a quizzical look on his face. Using terms he can easily understand, you introduce yourself and outline your purpose and role. You take Paul to a quiet area, well away from his mother (who abruptly goes to the kitchen). Then you say, "I'm here to make sure that you are safe from harm and to find out whether anyone might have hurt you in any way. Paul, do you understand what I am saying? Yes? Okay, then, I'd like to ask you some questions. First, who lives in this house with you?"

Paul says, "Well, my mom lives with me. And, uh, uh, her boyfriend stays here a lot too."

You ask, "What is he like?"

Paul hesitates, looks questioningly toward the kitchen, and then looks back into your eyes. It looks to you that he's afraid to say anything more.

You respond by communicating your understanding about how difficult and frightening it is to be interviewed in this way.

Paul responds to your empathic communication by saying, "Yeah, it sure is."

You follow that by asking, "Paul, does anyone ever hurt you?"

Paul again hesitates, but then says, "Yeah. Charlie, that's my mom's boyfriend, sometimes hits me with his belt."

You reflect his statement. Paul responds to your empathic communication by saying, "Yeah. He and my mom get drunk and yell and hit each other. I get so scared. If I make any noise at all, Charlie starts yelling at me. Then he takes off his belt and beats me with it."

You communicate your understanding of the feeling and meaning inherent in his message. Then you ask an open-ended question concerning the nature of the beatings and the location of any bruises that might exist.

Paul responds to your question by saying, "I have bruises all over my legs and back and my bottom. It hurts real bad. Sometimes when Charlie beats me, I start to bleed. I hate him! I hate him! I wish he'd just leave and never come back."

You then ask Paul to elaborate. He responds by saying, "Things were fine until Charlie showed up. Mom and I got along great! See, my real dad was killed in a car wreck before I was born and so it has always been just Mom and me—that is, until Charlie moved in."

---

27. Respond to Paul's statements by using the skill of *reflecting an issue*.

28. After you reflect the issue, Paul says, "Yeah, that's it all right."

    Following that exchange, you excuse yourself from Paul and join Mrs. N in the kitchen. You indicate that you have seen severe bruises and abrasions on Paul's legs and back. There is also a deep gash on one thigh. You inform Mrs. N that you will first obtain medical care for Paul and then place him in temporary foster care until a more complete investigation can be conducted. You indicate that the final decision about Paul's custody will be in the hands of Judge Dixon, who will conduct the hearing. But before leaving with Paul, you add that you would like to share with her your view of the problem.

    Record the words you would say in using the skill of *identifying an issue* with Mrs. N.

29. At this point, you provide Mrs. N with a written summary of her rights and contact information so that she knows exactly who is responsible for Paul's care and safety during this time. You then arrange for Paul's temporary foster care, introduce him to the caretaking family, and facilitate his entry into the home.

    After saying good-bye to Paul and the foster care family, you return to your office to prepare the case record. Outline the kinds of information that you might include in the *description section* of a case record as you consider organizing information concerning the N family.

30. Outline, in general, what you might address in the *assessment section* of a case record that relates to the N case.

31. Identify what you would include in the *contract section* of a case record as it relates to the N family.

32. Based on your earlier description, formulate a goal that reasonably follows from the issue you identified with Mrs. N. Do so in two ways: First, write a *general goal statement*. Then, write a *specific goal statement* in SMART format.

33. Building on your view of the issue and the goals just described, identify at least one way in which you could *evaluate progress* toward attainment of the *general* goal and then at least one way to evaluate progress vis-à-vis the *specific* goal.

34. Next, in a manner that is congruent with the issue, goals, and evaluation methods, *formulate an action plan* by which you and the client in this case might work together toward goal achievement.

35. Several weeks have passed. Charlie has been charged with various crimes associated with child abuse and left the N household. He may have fled the area. Mrs. N has progressed from an initial state of confusion to a point where she has stopped drinking and is now actively engaged in counseling. Indeed, she seems to find the conversations interesting and stimulating as well as helpful. She has already successfully completed several between-session tasks and activities.

    Paul remains in temporary foster care, but he may be able to return home within this next week. Mrs. N has visited him daily, and those visits have gone very well.

    During one of your meetings, Mrs. N says to you (while tears stream down her cheeks), "You know, when I was a child, my stepfather used to beat me too. He made me pull down my pants and he beat me with a razor strap. I used to cry and cry but he kept doing it, and my mother never could or would stop him. They never listened to me and nobody ever protected me. In fact, and it's strange to think about it this way, but when you came to this house to make sure that Paul was all right, that was the first time I had ever seen anybody try to protect a child from harm. And you are the first and only person who has ever seemed interested in me and in what I think and feel. Thank you so much for that."

Write the words you would say in responding to Mrs. N's verbal and nonverbal expression with the skill of *responding with immediacy*.

36. Following that exchange, you continue to explore with Mrs. N her history of relationships with alcoholic and abusive men. It's a pattern that seems remarkably similar to the relationship she observed between her own mother and her stepfather. In the midst of this discussion, she says, "I guess I must be masochistic. I must like to be beaten and degraded. Boy, am I ever sick!"

Respond to Mrs. N's statement with the skill of *reframing a negative into a positive*.

37. Now, respond to Mrs. N's statement (above) with the form of *reframing* that *personalizes the meaning*.

38. This time, respond to Mrs. N's statement (above) with the form of *reframing* that *situationalizes the meaning*.

39. Now, respond to Mrs. N's statement (above) with the skill of *observing inconsistencies*.

40. Following your *reframing* and *observing inconsistencies* responses to Mrs. N's statements, it seems appropriate that you use the skill of *educating* in an attempt to help Mrs. N understand how adults who were abused as children tend to think, feel, and behave. Write the words you might use in educating her about this topic.

41. Following your attempt to *educate* Mrs. N, it appears that she might benefit from some specific advice on how to be a better parent to her son Paul. Record the words you might use in *advising* her in this area.

42. Approximately 1 week goes by. Paul has returned home, and he and his mother are delighted. In a session with the two of them, you discuss one of the goals Mrs. N has identified for herself: becoming a more loving parent and a better listener.

You ask Paul, "How would you like your mother to show you she loves you?"

Instead of answering the question, Paul grabs a ball and begins to bounce it.

Write the words you might say to Paul in responding with the skill of *focusing*.

43. Later during the visit, Paul, Mrs. N, and you are "playing a game" of drawing on large pieces of paper. With crayons, each of you draws a picture of the N family. Interestingly, Paul's drawing reflects a mother and a child who are both large in size—that is, the child (Paul) is every bit as tall and as large as his mother (Mrs. N).

Please respond to your observation about the relative size of the mother and son by using whatever social work skill you believe to be the most applicable. Record the words you might say in using the skill. Following that, discuss the rationale for your choice.

44. Following your observation to Paul and Mrs. N about the approximately equal size of the mother and son in Paul's drawing (see previous item), you hope to encourage Paul and Mrs. N to discuss their reactions to the drawing with each other. Record the words you might say in using the *linking* skill.

45. A few more weeks go by. Paul and Mrs. N appear to be thriving. Paul is clearly no longer in danger. You have been authorized by the court to provide no more than four additional counseling sessions.

Write the words you might say to Paul and Mrs. N in *pointing out endings*.

46. A month goes by. You, Paul, and Mrs. N are meeting for the last time. Things are better than ever. They have achieved all of the identified goals and are extremely pleased with their progress. They are also grateful to you.

Write the words you might say in initiating a *review of the process* as part of ending your work with Paul and Mrs. N.

47. Write the words you might say in encouraging Paul and Mrs. N to engage in a *final evaluation* as part of ending your work together.

48. Write the words you might say in *encouraging* Paul and Mrs. N to *share their feelings* as you conclude your work together.

49. Write the words you might say in *sharing your own ending feelings* before you, Paul, and Mrs. N say your respective good-byes.

50. Write the words you might say in *saying good-bye* to Paul and Mrs. N.

The Social Work Skills Self-Appraisal Questionnaire

Compiled from the exercises that conclude each chapter, this questionnaire yields an estimate of your self-appraised proficiency in the knowledge, values, and skills addressed in the workbook. Read each statement carefully. Then, rate the degree of agreement or disagreement by checking the box below the number that most closely reflects your view. Notice that a **higher** number indicates a greater degree of agreement.

4 = Strongly Agree   3 = Agree   2 = Disagree   1 = Strongly Disagree

				Chapter 1 Self-Appraisal: Introduction
4	**3**	**2**	**1**	**Rating Statement**
				At this point in time, I can
☐	☐	☐	☐	1. Describe the mission and purposes of the social work profession.
☐	☐	☐	☐	2. Discuss the concepts of social work skills and competencies.
☐	☐	☐	☐	3. Identify the phases or processes of social work practice.
☐	☐	☐	☐	4. Identify the dimensions of professionalism addressed in *The Social Work Skills Workbook*.
				Subtotal
				Chapter 2 Self-Appraisal: Introduction to Professionalism
4	**3**	**2**	**1**	**Rating Statement**
				At this point in time, I can
☐	☐	☐	☐	1. Discuss the topic of professionalism within the context of social work practice.
☐	☐	☐	☐	2. Discuss integrity as an integral aspect of professionalism.
☐	☐	☐	☐	3. Discuss self-understanding and self-control as essential for professionalism in social work.
☐	☐	☐	☐	4. Discuss the relationship of professional knowledge, expertise, and self-efficacy to effective social work practice.
☐	☐	☐	☐	5. Discuss the relationship of social support and well-being to professionalism in social work.
				Subtotal
				Chapter 3 Self-Appraisal: Critical Thinking, Scientific Inquiry, and Lifelong Learning
4	**3**	**2**	**1**	**Rating Statement**
				At this point in time, I can
☐	☐	☐	☐	1. Discuss the processes of critical thinking, scientific inquiry, and lifelong learning and their implications for effective social work practice.
☐	☐	☐	☐	2. Use critical thinking skills to assess the credibility of a claim, conclusion, or argument and to evaluate the quality of a research study.
☐	☐	☐	☐	3. Recognize logical fallacies in my own and in others' written and verbal communications.

4	3	2	1	Rating Statement
☐	☐	☐	☐	4. Use scientific inquiry skills to formulate a precise question and search for, discover, and analyze one or more research studies related to a practice or policy-relevant topic.
☐	☐	☐	☐	5. Incorporate the universal intellectual virtues in my scholarly and professional activities.
☐	☐	☐	☐	6. Assess my lifelong-learning needs, establish learning goals, prepare learning plans, and document learning progress.
				Subtotal
				Chapter 4 Self-Appraisal: Diversity and Difference; Human Rights; Social, Economic, and Environmental Justice; and Policy–Practice
4	3	2	1	Rating Statement
				At this point in time, I can
☐	☐	☐	☐	1. Discuss the topic of diversity and difference in human relations.
☐	☐	☐	☐	2. Discuss intersectionality.
☐	☐	☐	☐	3. Discuss the processes of accepting others and respecting autonomy in service with others.
☐	☐	☐	☐	4. Discuss human rights in the context of social work practice.
☐	☐	☐	☐	5. Discuss the topics of social, economic, and environmental justice.
☐	☐	☐	☐	6. Discuss the topic of policy-practice as a means to advance human rights and promote social, economic, and environmental justice.
				Subtotal
				Chapter 5 Self-Appraisal: Social Work Values and Ethical Decision Making
4	3	2	1	Rating Statement
				At this point in time, I can
☐	☐	☐	☐	1. Identify and discuss the legal duties that apply to helping professionals.
☐	☐	☐	☐	2. Access laws that affect the practice of social work in my locale.
☐	☐	☐	☐	3. Discuss the fundamental values of the social work profession.
☐	☐	☐	☐	4. Discuss the moral values that guide professional helping activities.
☐	☐	☐	☐	5. Discuss the ethical principles and standards that inform social work practice.
☐	☐	☐	☐	6. Identify the relevant values, legal duties, and ethical principles that apply in various professional contexts and situations.
☐	☐	☐	☐	7. Determine the relative priority of competing legal and ethical obligations when ethical dilemmas arise in specific circumstances.
☐	☐	☐	☐	8. Use critical thinking skills and scientific inquiry skills to reach ethical decisions and plan appropriate action.
				Subtotal
				Chapter 6 Self-Appraisal: Talking and Listening
4	3	2	1	Rating Statement
				At this point in time, I can
☐	☐	☐	☐	1. Access a place of peace.
☐	☐	☐	☐	2. Engage diversity and difference with cultural sensitivity.

4	3	2	1	Chapter 6 Self-Appraisal: Talking and Listening
4	3	2	1	**Rating Statement**
☐	☐	☐	☐	3. Discuss the talking and listening skills.
☐	☐	☐	☐	4. Communicate nonverbally in social work contexts.
☐	☐	☐	☐	5. Communicate verbally and in writing for social work purposes.
☐	☐	☐	☐	6. Listen (hear, observe, encourage, and remember) in social work practice.
☐	☐	☐	☐	7. Listen actively in professional contexts.
				Subtotal
				Chapter 7 Self-Appraisal: Preparing
4	3	2	1	**Rating Statement**
				At this point in time, I can
☐	☐	☐	☐	1. Discuss the purposes and functions of preparing.
☐	☐	☐	☐	2. Engage in preparatory reviewing.
☐	☐	☐	☐	3. Engage in preparatory exploring.
☐	☐	☐	☐	4. Engage in preparatory consultation.
☐	☐	☐	☐	5. Engage in preparatory arranging.
☐	☐	☐	☐	6. Engage in preparatory empathy.
☐	☐	☐	☐	7. Engage in preparatory self-exploration.
☐	☐	☐	☐	8. Center myself.
☐	☐	☐	☐	9. Engage in preliminary planning and recording.
				Subtotal
				Chapter 8 Self-Appraisal: Beginning
4	3	2	1	**Rating Statement**
				At this point in time, I can
☐	☐	☐	☐	1. Discuss the purposes and functions of beginning.
☐	☐	☐	☐	2. Introduce myself.
☐	☐	☐	☐	3. Seek introductions from others.
☐	☐	☐	☐	4. Describe an initial purpose for meetings and interviews.
☐	☐	☐	☐	5. Orient others to the process.
☐	☐	☐	☐	6. Discuss policy and ethical factors.
☐	☐	☐	☐	7. Seek feedback.
				Subtotal
				Chapter 9 Self-Appraisal: Exploring
4	3	2	1	**Rating Statement**
				At this point in time, I can
☐	☐	☐	☐	1. Discuss the purposes and functions of exploring.
☐	☐	☐	☐	2. Explore relevant aspects of the person-issue-situation and look for strengths and assets in the person-in-environment.
☐	☐	☐	☐	3. Ask questions of others.
☐	☐	☐	☐	4. Seek clarification following others' words and gestures.

4	3	2	1	Rating Statement
☐	☐	☐	☐	5. Reflect the content of others' communications.
☐	☐	☐	☐	6. Reflect the feelings expressed by others.
☐	☐	☐	☐	7. Reflect the feelings and meaning expressed by others.
☐	☐	☐	☐	8. Partialize others' statements.
☐	☐	☐	☐	9. Go beyond others' expressed communications.
☐	☐	☐	☐	10. Reflect others' views of needs, problems, or issues.
☐	☐	☐	☐	11. Reflect others' hypotheses about possible causes and potential solutions.
				Subtotal
				Chapter 10 Self-Appraisal: Assessing
4	**3**	**2**	**1**	**Rating Statement**
				At this point in time, I can
☐	☐	☐	☐	1. Discuss the purposes and functions of assessment.
☐	☐	☐	☐	2. Identify issues.
☐	☐	☐	☐	3. Share explanatory and change-oriented hypotheses.
☐	☐	☐	☐	4. Confirm issues for work.
☐	☐	☐	☐	5. Organize descriptive information in the form of a written record.
☐	☐	☐	☐	6. Prepare an assessment and case formulation.
				Subtotal
				Chapter 11 Self-Appraisal: Contracting
4	**3**	**2**	**1**	**Rating Statement**
				At this point in time, I can
☐	☐	☐	☐	1. Discuss the purposes and functions of contracting.
☐	☐	☐	☐	2. Establish goals.
☐	☐	☐	☐	3. Develop action plans.
☐	☐	☐	☐	4. Identify action steps.
☐	☐	☐	☐	5. Plan for evaluation.
☐	☐	☐	☐	6. Summarize the contract.
				Subtotal
				Chapter 12 Self-Appraisal: Working and Evaluating
4	**3**	**2**	**1**	**Rating Statement**
				At this point in time, I can
☐	☐	☐	☐	1. Discuss the purposes and functions of the working and evaluating skills.
☐	☐	☐	☐	2. Rehearse action steps with clients and constituents.
☐	☐	☐	☐	3. Review action steps with clients and constituents.
☐	☐	☐	☐	4. Evaluate progress with clients and others.

4	3	2	1	Chapter 12 Self-Appraisal: Working and Evaluating
				Rating Statement
☐	☐	☐	☐	5. Focus conversations on agreed-upon topics.
☐	☐	☐	☐	6. Educate others.
☐	☐	☐	☐	7. Advise others.
☐	☐	☐	☐	8. Respond with immediacy.
☐	☐	☐	☐	9. Reframe others' messages.
☐	☐	☐	☐	10. Observe inconsistencies in others' thoughts, words, and actions.
☐	☐	☐	☐	11. Represent clients in case and class advocacy.
☐	☐	☐	☐	12. Link people to people, people to social systems, and social systems to other social systems.
☐	☐	☐	☐	13. Point out endings.
☐	☐	☐	☐	14. Prepare professional-quality progress recordings.
				Subtotal
				Chapter 13 Self-Appraisal: Ending
4	**3**	**2**	**1**	**Rating Statement**
				At this point in time, I can
☐	☐	☐	☐	1. Discuss the purposes and functions of ending.
☐	☐	☐	☐	2. Review the process of working together with clients and other constituents.
☐	☐	☐	☐	3. Engage clients and others in a process of final evaluation.
☐	☐	☐	☐	4. Share ending feelings and say good-bye.
☐	☐	☐	☐	5. Record a closing summary.
				Subtotal
				TOTAL

This questionnaire provides you with an indication of your self-appraised proficiency in the social work skills. Because it is based on your own beliefs about your proficiency, absolute scores are relatively unimportant. Rather, use the results as a stimulus both to ask yourself further questions concerning your competency with various skills and to develop plans by which to improve your proficiency in those skill areas that need additional study and practice. You may complete the questionnaire at various points throughout the learning process. Increased proficiency may be reflected in changing scores over time. In considering your results, please remember that a higher rating suggests a higher level of appraised proficiency.

To score the Social Work Skills Self-Appraisal Questionnaire, simply sum the total of your ratings to the 94 items. Your score should range somewhere between 94 and 376. A higher score suggests a higher level of appraised proficiency. In theory, a score of 282 (or an average of 3 on each of the 94 items) would indicate that, on average, you "agree" with statements suggesting that you are proficient in the 94 items. Please note, however, that such an average score does not necessarily indicate that you are proficient in all of the skills. You might obtain such a score by rating several items at the "4" or "strongly agree" level and an equal number at the "2" or "disagree level." Therefore, you should look carefully at your rating for each item, as well as the subtotals for each skill area.

Finally, you should recognize that this questionnaire reflects your own subjective opinions. You may consciously or unconsciously overestimate or perhaps underestimate your proficiency in these skills. Therefore, please use the results in conjunction with other evidence to appraise your abilities.

The Critical Thinking Questionnaire

Please read each of the statements contained in the following questionnaire.[1] Rate the degree of agreement or disagreement by checking the box below the number that most closely reflects your view. Notice that a **lower** number indicates a greater degree of agreement. Please use the following rating system:

1 = Strongly Agree **2 = Agree** **3 = Disagree** **4 = Strongly Disagree**

				Critical Thinking Questionnaire
1	2	3	4	**Rating Statement**
☐	☐	☐	☐	1. I rarely make judgments based solely upon intuition or emotion.
☐	☐	☐	☐	2. I almost always think before I speak or act.
☐	☐	☐	☐	3. I almost never express opinions as if they were facts.
☐	☐	☐	☐	4. I always identify the assumptions underlying an argument.
☐	☐	☐	☐	5. I carefully consider the source of information in determining validity.
☐	☐	☐	☐	6. I rarely reach conclusions without considering the evidence.
☐	☐	☐	☐	7. I regularly think in terms of probabilities.
☐	☐	☐	☐	8. I rarely think in terms of absolutes.
☐	☐	☐	☐	9. I always question the validity of arguments and conclusions.
☐	☐	☐	☐	10. I rarely assume that something is valid or true.
☐	☐	☐	☐	11. I regularly identify my own biases and preferences.
☐	☐	☐	☐	12. I regularly think about issues of reliability.
☐	☐	☐	☐	13. I routinely identify my own logical fallacies.
☐	☐	☐	☐	14. I rarely say that something is true unless I have supporting evidence.
☐	☐	☐	☐	15. I regularly use a thinking process routine to reach decisions.
				Total CT Questionnaire Score (Sum Ratings of Items 1–15)

To score the questionnaire, simply sum the total of your ratings for all 15 items. Your overall score should range somewhere between 15 and 60. Lower scores suggest greater levels of critical thinking. Remember, however, that the questionnaire is still under development and its psychometric properties have not yet been determined. View the instrument and your results with caution. As a tentative indicator, however, you might compare your score with those of a convenience sample of 21 members of a foundation-year, MSW-level social work practice class. That sample yielded an average score of 32.38 (range 20–42; SD 6.26) on the critical thinking questionnaire (Cournoyer, 1999). Another sample of more than 90 foundation- and concentration-year MSW students combined reflected an average score of 31.79 ($n = 95$; range 20–51; SD 4.51) (Cournoyer, 2003).

---

[1] The Critical Thinking Questionnaire (CTQ). Copyright © 2000 by Barry R. Cournoyer.

The Lifelong Learning Questionnaire

Please read each of the statements contained in the following questionnaire.[1] Rate the degree of agreement or disagreement by checking the box below the number that most closely reflects your view. Notice that a **lower** number indicates a greater degree of agreement. Please use the following rating system:

1 = Strongly Agree   2 = Agree   3 = Disagree   4 = Strongly Disagree

1	2	3	4	Lifelong Learning Questionnaire
				Rating Statement
☐	☐	☐	☐	1. I regularly read professional journals in my field.
☐	☐	☐	☐	2. I genuinely enjoy learning.
☐	☐	☐	☐	3. I always do more than the minimum requirements in courses, seminars, or workshops.
☐	☐	☐	☐	4. I regularly pursue opportunities to advance my knowledge and expertise.
☐	☐	☐	☐	5. I never become defensive when someone offers feedback that could improve my skill.
☐	☐	☐	☐	6. I like to study.
☐	☐	☐	☐	7. I know my personal learning style.
☐	☐	☐	☐	8. I am actively involved in learning experiences.
☐	☐	☐	☐	9. I take personal responsibility for my own learning.
☐	☐	☐	☐	10. I view examinations as a way to learn.
☐	☐	☐	☐	11. I know how to conduct a professional literature review.
☐	☐	☐	☐	12. I sometimes contact national and international experts in my learning efforts.
☐	☐	☐	☐	13. I have a list of learning goals.
☐	☐	☐	☐	14. I have specific plans to advance my learning.
☐	☐	☐	☐	15. I enjoy teaching others.
				Total LLL Questionnaire Score (Sum Ratings of Items 1–15)

To score the questionnaire, simply sum the total of your ratings for all 15 items. Your overall score should range somewhere between 15 and 60. Lower scores suggest greater levels of lifelong learning. Remember, however, that the questionnaire is still under development and its psychometric properties have not yet been determined. View the instruments and your results with caution. As a tentative indicator, however, you might compare your score with those of a convenience sample of 21 members of a foundation-year, MSW-level social work practice class. That sample yielded an average score of 33.10 (range 20–43; SD 7.44) on the lifelong learning questionnaire (Cournoyer, 1999). Another sample of more than 90 foundation- and concentration-year MSW students combined reflected an average score of 29.12 ($n = 97$; range 16–41; SD 5.44) (Cournoyer, 2003).

---

[1] The Lifelong Learning Questionnaire (LLQ). Copyright © 2000 by Barry R. Cournoyer.

The following rating form allows clients to provide constructive feedback about their social workers' professional skills. Social workers use these ratings to improve the quality of their service to you and other clients. You can be most helpful in this process by thinking carefully about each statement and providing the most accurate rating possible. Use the five-point scale to rate the degree of your agreement with each item. Notice that a **higher** number indicates a greater degree of agreement. Place a check mark in the box below the number that most closely reflects your view.

5 = Strongly Agree   4 = Agree   3 = Undecided   2 = Disagree   1 = Strongly Disagree

					Talking and Listening Skills Rating Form
5	**4**	**3**	**2**	**1**	**Statement**
☐	☐	☐	☐	☐	S6.1 The interviewer was sensitive to and respected my cultural beliefs and practices even when they differed from her or his own.
☐	☐	☐	☐	☐	S6.2 The interviewer's facial expressions, head movements, tone of voice, body positions, and physical gestures indicated that she or he was truly interested in me and everything I had to say.
☐	☐	☐	☐	☐	S6.3 The interviewer spoke clearly and audibly so that I easily heard everything she or he expressed during the conversation.
☐	☐	☐	☐	☐	S6.4 The interviewer used familiar words and language so that I understood everything she or he expressed during the conversation.
☐	☐	☐	☐	☐	S6.5 During the conversation, the interviewer listened attentively, respectfully, and nonjudgmentally to everything I expressed
☐	☐	☐	☐	☐	S6.6 The interviewer remembered what I said during the interview so that she or he sometimes made reference to things I mentioned earlier.
☐	☐	☐	☐	☐	S6.7 The interviewer periodically summarized my messages in her or his own words so that I knew she or he accurately understood what I was trying to say.
☐	☐	☐	☐	☐	S6.8 Overall, I felt accepted, respected, valued, heard, and understood during this interview.
					TOTAL

Following a meeting in which the interviewer consistently demonstrated proficient use of the talking and listening skills, interviewees would usually assign ratings of 4 or 5 on each item. Possible total scores for the eight items range from 8 to 40. Scores between 32 and 40 indicate overall proficiency. However, make note of any items that receive ratings of less than 4. Additional practice may be needed to strengthen competency in those skills.

The following rating form allows clients to provide constructive feedback about their social workers' professional skills. Social workers use these ratings to improve the quality of their service to you and other clients. You can be most helpful in this process by thinking carefully about each statement and providing the most accurate rating possible. Use the five-point scale to rate the degree of your agreement with each item. Notice that a **higher** number indicates a greater degree of agreement. Place a check mark in the box below the number that most closely reflects your view.

5 = Strongly Agree   4 = Agree   3 = Undecided   2 = Disagree   1 = Strongly Disagree

5	4	3	2	1	Preparing and Beginning Skills Rating Form
					Statement
☐	☐	☐	☐	☐	S7.1 The interviewer was well acquainted with information that had previously been provided.
☐	☐	☐	☐	☐	S7.2 The interviewer conveyed a sense of professionalism.
☐	☐	☐	☐	☐	S7.3 The interviewer was calm and confident.
☐	☐	☐	☐	☐	S7.4 The interviewer made arrangements in advance so the room, materials, and equipment were all ready for use.
☐	☐	☐	☐	☐	S7.5 The interviewer was eager to hear what I had to say.
☐	☐	☐	☐	☐	S7.6 The interviewer was open-minded and nonjudgmental.
☐	☐	☐	☐	☐	S7.7 The interviewer was well prepared for the meeting.
☐	☐	☐	☐	☐	S7.8 The interview was conducted in a competent manner.
☐	☐	☐	☐	☐	S8.1 The interviewer introduced herself or himself by name and profession.
☐	☐	☐	☐	☐	S8.2 The interviewer learned my name, pronounced it correctly, and used my name at several times during the meeting.
☐	☐	☐	☐	☐	S8.3 The interviewer suggested a general purpose or agenda for this meeting.
☐	☐	☐	☐	☐	S8.4 The interviewer asked me for feedback about the proposed agenda.
☐	☐	☐	☐	☐	S8.5 The interviewer suggested how I could actively participate in this process.
☐	☐	☐	☐	☐	S8.6 The interviewer informed me about relevant laws, ethics, and policies that might affect our work together.
☐	☐	☐	☐	☐	S8.7 The interviewer asked me if I was unclear about anything or had any questions about anything discussed thus far.
☐	☐	☐	☐	☐	S8.8 Through tone of voice, facial expressions, nonverbal communications, and spoken words the interviewer conveyed a clear message that I am a valued and respected person who can contribute as an equal partner in our work together.
					TOTAL

Following a meeting in which the interviewer was prepared and consistently demonstrated proficient use of the beginning skills, interviewees would usually assign ratings of 4 or 5 on each item. Possible total scores for the 16 items range from 16 to 80. Scores of between 64 and 80 indicate overall proficiency. However, make note of any items that receive ratings of less than 4. Additional practice may be needed to strengthen competency in those skills.

The following rating form allows clients to provide constructive feedback about their social workers' professional skills. Social workers use these ratings to improve the quality of their service to you and other clients. You can be most helpful in this process by thinking carefully about each statement and providing the most accurate rating possible. Use the five-point scale to rate the degree of your agreement with each item. Notice that a **higher** number indicates a greater degree of agreement. Place a check mark in the box below the number that most closely reflects your view.

5 = Strongly Agree   4 = Agree   3 = Undecided   2 = Disagree   1 = Strongly Disagree

5	4	3	2	1	Exploring Skills Rating Form / Statement
☐	☐	☐	☐	☐	S9.1 The interviewer encouraged me to discuss in considerable detail the issues that most concern me.
☐	☐	☐	☐	☐	S9.2 The interviewer encouraged me to discuss aspects of myself that relate to the issues that concern me.
☐	☐	☐	☐	☐	S9.3 The interviewer encouraged me to discuss aspects of my situation that relate to the issues that concern me.
☐	☐	☐	☐	☐	S9.4 The interviewer recognized some of my positive abilities, successes, and wisdom.
☐	☐	☐	☐	☐	S9.5 The interviewer recognized some of the assets, resources, and sources of social support in my life.
☐	☐	☐	☐	☐	S9.6 The interviewer asked relevant questions that helped me to express myself more fully.
☐	☐	☐	☐	☐	S9.7 The interviewer periodically summarized my words in her or his own words so that I knew she or he accurately understood what I was trying to say.
☐	☐	☐	☐	☐	S9.8 The interviewer communicated understanding of my feelings.
☐	☐	☐	☐	☐	S9.9 The interviewer communicated understanding of the reasons behind my feelings.
☐	☐	☐	☐	☐	S9.10 The interviewer communicated understanding of something I truly thought or felt but had not yet actually said.
☐	☐	☐	☐	☐	S9.11 In her or his own words, the interviewer summarized the issues that I am most concerned about.
☐	☐	☐	☐	☐	S9.12 In her or his own words, the interviewer summarized my ideas about how or why these issues occur.
☐	☐	☐	☐	☐	S9.13 In her or his own words, the interviewer summarized my ideas about how these issues could be resolved.
					TOTAL

Following a meeting in which the interviewer was prepared and consistently demonstrated proficient use of the exploring skills, interviewees would usually assign ratings of 4 or 5 on each item. Possible total scores for the 13 items range from 13 to 65. Scores of between 52 and 65 indicate overall proficiency. However, make note of any items that receive ratings of less than 4. Additional practice may be needed to strengthen competency in those skills.

The following rating form allows clients to provide constructive feedback about their social workers' professional skills. Social workers use these ratings to improve the quality of their service to you and other clients. You can be most helpful in this process by thinking carefully about each statement and providing the most accurate rating possible. Use the five-point scale to rate the degree of your agreement with each item. Notice that a **higher** number indicates a greater degree of agreement. Place a check mark in the box below the number that most closely reflects your view.

5 = Strongly Agree   4 = Agree   3 = Undecided   2 = Disagree   1 = Strongly Disagree

5	4	3	2	1	Assessing Skills Rating Form
					Statement
☐	☐	☐	☐	☐	S10.1 The interviewer introduced a possible problem or issue that I had not previously considered.
☐	☐	☐	☐	☐	S10.2 The interviewer introduced a possible way of thinking about how or why these issues occur.
☐	☐	☐	☐	☐	S10.3 The interviewer introduced a possible way of thinking about how these issues could be resolved.
☐	☐	☐	☐	☐	S10.4 The interviewer and I clearly identified and agreed upon the issues that we would work together to resolve.
					TOTAL

Following a meeting in which the interviewer was prepared and consistently demonstrated proficient use of the assessing skills, interviewees would usually assign ratings of 4 or 5 on each item. Possible total scores for the 4 items range from 4 to 20. Scores of between 16 and 20 indicate overall proficiency. However, make note of any items that receive ratings of less than 4. Additional practice may be needed to strengthen competency in those skills.

The following rating form allows clients to provide constructive feedback about their social workers' professional skills. Social workers use these ratings to improve the quality of their service to you and other clients. You can be most helpful in this process by thinking carefully about each statement and providing the most accurate rating possible. Use the five-point scale to rate the degree of your agreement with each item. Notice that a **higher** number indicates a greater degree of agreement. Place a check mark in the box below the number that most closely reflects your view.

5 = Strongly Agree   4 = Agree   3 = Undecided   2 = Disagree   1 = Strongly Disagree

					Contracting Skills Rating Form
5	**4**	**3**	**2**	**1**	**Statement**
☐	☐	☐	☐	☐	S11.1 The interviewer and I clearly identified and agreed upon the goals that we would work together to achieve.
☐	☐	☐	☐	☐	S11.2 The interviewer and I agreed upon action plans to pursue our agreed-upon goals.
☐	☐	☐	☐	☐	S11.3 The interviewer and I identified one or more action steps that I plan to take.
☐	☐	☐	☐	☐	S11.4 The interviewer and I identified one or more action steps that she or he plans to take.
☐	☐	☐	☐	☐	S11.5 The interviewer and I agreed upon one or more ways to measure or evaluate progress toward our goals.
☐	☐	☐	☐	☐	S11.6 The interviewer summarized our agreement so that we both understand our goals and how we plan to accomplish them.
					TOTAL

Following a meeting in which the interviewer was prepared and consistently demonstrated proficient use of the contracting skills, interviewees would usually assign ratings of 4 or 5 on each item. Possible total scores for the 6 items range from 6 to 30. Scores of between 24 and 30 indicate overall proficiency. However, make note of any items that receive ratings of less than 4. Additional practice may be needed to strengthen competency in those skills.

The following rating form allows clients to provide constructive feedback about their social workers' professional skills. Social workers use these ratings to improve the quality of their service to you and other clients. You can be most helpful in this process by thinking carefully about each statement and providing the most accurate rating possible. Use the five-point scale to rate the degree of your agreement with each item. Notice that a **higher** number indicates a greater degree of agreement. Place a check mark in the box below the number that most closely reflects your view.

5 = Strongly Agree   4 = Agree   3 = Undecided   2 = Disagree   1 = Strongly Disagree

5	4	3	2	1	Working and Evaluating Skills Rating Form
					Statement
☐	☐	☐	☐	☐	S12.1 The interviewer helped me get ready to take an action step by practicing it with me in a kind of rehearsal.
☐	☐	☐	☐	☐	S12.2 The interviewer encouraged me to discuss in detail each action step I had agreed to undertake so that I could learn from the experience and improve in the future.
☐	☐	☐	☐	☐	S12.3 The interviewer and I measured, reviewed, and evaluated progress toward goals so that we both know how things stand.
☐	☐	☐	☐	☐	S12.4 When I wandered, the interviewer sometimes got us back on track so that we focused on what I really wanted to address.
☐	☐	☐	☐	☐	S12.5 When I didn't know about something, the interviewer shared information that helped me understand.
☐	☐	☐	☐	☐	S12.6 The interviewer sometimes offered advice but did so in a way that left me free to accept or reject it.
☐	☐	☐	☐	☐	S12.7 The interviewer sometimes served as my representative or advocate.
☐	☐	☐	☐	☐	S12.8 The interviewer sometimes made tentative observations about what was happening in our relationship (that is, between him or her and me) at the very moment it occurred.
☐	☐	☐	☐	☐	S12.9 The interviewer sometimes helped me to think about something in a new or different way.
☐	☐	☐	☐	☐	S12.10 The interviewer sometimes gently pointed out inconsistencies in my thoughts, words, feelings, or actions so that I could consider their implications.
☐	☐	☐	☐	☐	S12.11 The interviewer reminded me about how many more meetings we would have together.
					TOTAL

Following a meeting in which the interviewer was prepared and consistently demonstrated proficient use of the working and evaluating skills, interviewees would usually assign ratings of 4 or 5 on each item. Possible total scores for the 11 items range from 11 to 55. Scores of between 44 and 55 indicate overall proficiency. However, make note of any items that receive ratings of less than 4. Additional practice may be needed to strengthen competency in those skills.

The following rating form allows clients to provide constructive feedback about their social workers' professional skills. Social workers use these ratings to improve the quality of their service to you and other clients. You can be most helpful in this process by thinking carefully about each statement and providing the most accurate rating possible. Use the five-point scale to rate the degree of your agreement with each item. Notice that a **higher** number indicates a greater degree of agreement. Place a check mark in the box below the number that most closely reflects your view.

5 = Strongly Agree   4 = Agree   3 = Undecided   2 = Disagree   1 = Strongly Disagree

					Ending Skills Rating Form
5	4	3	2	1	**Statement**
☐	☐	☐	☐	☐	S13.1 In our final meeting, the interviewer helped me to review what we had done during our time together.
☐	☐	☐	☐	☐	S13.2 In our final meeting, the interviewer helped me to evaluate overall progress.
☐	☐	☐	☐	☐	S13.3 In our final meeting, the interviewer helped me to anticipate how I might apply what I've learned to other issues or to those that might possibly emerge sometime in the future.
☐	☐	☐	☐	☐	S13.4 The interviewer sincerely shared her or his thoughts and feelings about concluding our work together.
☐	☐	☐	☐	☐	S13.5 The interviewer helped me to share my thoughts and feelings about concluding our work together.
☐	☐	☐	☐	☐	S13.6 The interviewer said good-bye to me in a way that conveyed respect and appreciation for me.
☐	☐	☐	☐	☐	S13.7 The interviewer let me say good-bye in a way that felt real and sincere to me.
					TOTAL

Following a meeting in which the interviewer was prepared and consistently demonstrated proficient use of the ending skills, interviewees would usually assign ratings of 4 or 5 on each item. Possible total scores for the 7 items range from 7 to 35. Scores of between 28 and 35 indicate overall proficiency. However, make note of any items that receive ratings of less than 4. Additional practice may be needed to strengthen competency in those skills.

Experiential Interview Exercise—Guidelines and Forms

Experiential Interviewing Exercise: Guidelines for Interviewing a Practice Client

You are about to embark upon a series of 30-minute interview sessions with a "practice client." You will serve in the role of "social worker" with a classmate, colleague, or "standardized client" who agrees to assume the role of practice client. Your course or practicum instructor, or another professional social worker, must agree to serve the dual roles of (1) your supervisor and (2) advocate for the practice client.

Social workers always benefit from constructive feedback about their performance, and lifelong learners usually want to maximize the impact of educational activities. Contact with an instructor during the course of the experiential interviewing exercise makes good sense. Her ideas and suggestions might increase your learning, enhance your social work skills proficiency, improve the quality of your performance, and perhaps heighten the practice client's satisfaction with the experience. Sometimes, however, practice clients also want or need to discuss an encounter with someone other than the person assuming the role of social worker. For instance, during the exercise, a practice client might realize something about herself that warrants consideration of a referral to a licensed social worker or other professional helper. At other times, a practice client might feel adversely affected by an exchange and want advice from an advocate to help reduce or eliminate the damage. The supervisor/client advocate fulfills those functions and helps ensure the safety and well-being of the people involved—those in the role of practice client as well as those in the role of social worker.

The person who serves in the role of practice client should understand that the learning exercise requires about 60 minutes of time for each of five meetings spread over the course of several weeks. Each formal interview is scheduled for 30 minutes. Immediately after that, each of you step out of your respective roles of social worker and practice client and, for 10–15 minutes, you become active teachers and learners. Take the initiative to seek constructive evaluative feedback from your partner about the nature and quality of the interview, your performance, and her thoughts and feelings about the interview. Take notes during the post-interview feedback session so that you can reflect upon them at a later time.

The practice client should choose an actual need, problem, or other issue to address during the five-session process. However, the issue should be one that is relatively modest and manageable. The practice client should not choose a serious problem, one that is of an urgent nature, or one that is especially tender. Colleagues who are currently dealing with severe issues, those in an especially fragile state, and those in highly vulnerable circumstances probably should not participate as practice clients.

Approach the experiential exercise as if you actually are a social worker and your practice client really is your client. That will improve realism and enhance learning. Recognize, however, the primary purpose for the learning experience is to help you gain proficiency in the social work skills. Although your colleague may benefit from the experience of assuming the role of practice client, any such benefits would be incidental. The primary purpose for this activity is educational in nature; it is not intended nor should it be interpreted as a therapeutic or professional service. Nonetheless, social work values and ethics apply before, during, and following the learning exercise. Adopt a professional attitude and demeanor throughout the experience. Maintain your role as social worker and encourage your practice client to do the same. Be sure to maintain the practice client's privacy and confidentiality, and adopt a fictitious name for the practice client to help disguise her identity when you make audio or video recordings, take notes, and prepare case records.

Secure the formal consent of your colleague to serve in the role of practice client and maintain the signed document in a safe place. Also, keep audio or video recordings in a private, locked location. As you word-process documents for use during the exercise, ensure that they are accurate and carefully prepared at a professional level of quality; however, disguise information that might reveal the identity of the practice client.

Create electronic folders to keep your preliminary plans for meeting as well as any notes and documents you prepare throughout the course of the exercise. Password-protect your document files and ensure that all exercise-related materials are stored in secure locations.

Each meeting requires that you engage in the social work skills associated with one or more phases of practice. For example, you would use the preparing skills before you first contact and attempt to recruit a colleague, and then in advance of all subsequent interviews. Such preparation enhances your readiness to engage people from the moment of first contact. During the first meeting, use the beginning skills as well as the basic skills of talking and listening, and do so in a culturally sensitive manner. Several exploring skills might be applicable as well. As part of your planning, anticipate how you might begin and how you might conclude each session. Use relevant exploring and assessing skills during the second meeting, and exploring, assessing, and contracting skills in the third. Use the working and evaluating skills in the fourth meeting, and the ending skills in the fifth. Seeking feedback and most of the exploring skills may be applicable in all interviews.

Keep professional quality records throughout. Following the third meeting, you should be able to finalize a Description, Assessment, and Contract (DAC) to guide the goal-directed efforts of both the practice client and you as the social worker. Following the fourth meeting, word-process a progress record; and after the final interview, prepare a closing summary. When combined, these documents along with additional relevant materials such as genograms, eco-maps, timelines or concept maps, your planning notes, and client satisfaction and outcome-related measurement data constitute the formal "Practice Client Case Record."

In summary, the specific tasks and activities for the Experiential Interviewing Exercise are as follows:

- **Enlist a Professor or Professional Social Worker to Serve as Supervisor and Client Advocate**
  If you are completing *The Social Work Skills Workbook* as part of a course or a practicum experience, the experiential interviewing exercise may be a required assignment. If so, double check to ensure that your professor or field practicum instructor agrees to serve as your supervisor during the experience and as an advocate for the practice client as well. If you are undertaking the experiential interviewing exercise as part of your own career learning, locate a professional social worker and secure his or her consent to fulfill those functions. Do not begin the learning exercise until a professional social worker formally agrees to serve as your supervisor and as an advocate for the practice client.

- **Prepare for a Recruitment Contact**
  Sometimes practice clients are assigned by instructors. At other times, you must recruit someone to serve in that role. However, before asking a classmate or colleague to participate in the experiential interviewing exercise, use applicable preparing skills—including developing preliminary plans and securing copies of relevant documents (such as a description of the exercise, guidelines for the practice client, and a consent to participate form). In preparing for a recruitment contact, you might use some or all of the following preparing skills: (1) preparatory reviewing, (2) preparatory exploring, (3) preparatory consultation, (4) preparatory arranging, (5) preparatory empathy, (6) preparatory self-exploration, (7) centering, and (8) preliminary planning and recording.

- **Recruit a Practice Client**
  If your professor or practicum instructor has not assigned a practice client to you, contact a classmate or colleague and use applicable beginning skills to describe the experiential interviewing learning exercise and invite her to join you in the educational experience. Obtain her informed consent to participate as a practice client over the course of several weeks. In the recruitment contact, you might use some or all of the following beginning skills: (1) introducing yourself, (2) seeking introductions, (3) describing initial purpose, (4) orienting clients or others, (5) discussing policy and ethical factors, and (6) seeking feedback.

- **Prepare for the First Meeting with a Practice Client**
  Before the first meeting with your practice client (a standardized client, colleague, or classmate who has been introduced to the learning exercise and provided informed consent), use applicable preparing skills. In the process of preparing for the first meeting, you might use some or all of the following skills: (1) preparatory reviewing, (2) preparatory exploring, (3) preparatory consultation, (4) preparatory arranging, (5) preparatory empathy, (6) preparatory self-exploration, (7) centering, and

(8) preliminary planning and recording. Word-process your preliminary plans and deposit them in the "Practice Client Case Record Folder." Be sure to disguise the identity of the practice client.

● ● ● ● ● ● ● ● ● ● ●

1. **First Meeting with a Practice Client: Beginning and Exploring**
   During the first meeting with your practice client, use applicable beginning and exploring skills. You might use some or all of the following beginning skills: (1) introducing yourself, (2) seeking introductions, (3) describing initial purpose, (4) orienting clients, (5) discussing policy and ethical factors, and (6) seeking feedback. You may find that seeking feedback is useful at many points throughout all interviews. Many of the exploring skills are also almost universally applicable. These include (1) asking questions, (2) seeking clarification, (3) reflecting content, (4) reflecting feelings, (5) reflecting feelings and meaning, (6) partializing, (7) going beyond what is said, (8) reflecting issues, and (9) reflecting hypotheses. Following the meeting, begin to word-process a preliminary draft of descriptive information gathered during the first meeting.

2. **Second Meeting with a Practice Client: Exploring and Assessing**
   During the second meeting with your practice client, use applicable exploring skills. These include (1) asking questions, (2) seeking clarification, (3) reflecting content, (4) reflecting feelings, (5) reflecting feelings and meaning, (6) partializing, (7) going beyond what is said, (8) reflecting issues, and (9) reflecting hypotheses. Some of the assessing skills may also apply. These include (1) identifying issues, (2) sharing hypotheses, and (3) confirming issues for work. Following the meeting, use the skills of (4) organizing descriptive information as you prepare a word-processed case record. In some instances, you may begin to draft portions of (5) an assessment and case formulation.

3. **The Third Meeting: Exploring, Assessing, and Contracting**
   During the third meeting with your practice client, continue to use applicable exploring skills along with relevant assessing skills such as (1) identifying issues, (2) sharing hypotheses, and (3) confirming issues for work. Incorporate relevant contracting skills into the interview. These include (1) establishing goals, (2) developing action plans, (3) identifying action steps, and (4) planning for evaluation, Following the meeting, use the skills of organizing descriptive information, preparing an assessment and case formulation, and summarizing the service contract to word-process the description, assessment, and contract (DAC) into a coherent case record.

4. **The Fourth Meeting: Working and Evaluating**
   During the fourth meeting with your practice client, use applicable exploring, assessing, or contracting skills as needed. Incorporate relevant working and evaluating skills into the interview. These include (1) rehearsing action steps, (2) reviewing action steps, (3) evaluating, (4) focusing, (5) educating, (6) advising, (7) responding with immediacy, (8) reframing, (9) observing inconsistencies, (10) representing, (11) linking, and (12) pointing out endings. Following the meeting, use the SOAIGP format to prepare a word-processed progress note.

5. **The Fifth Meeting: Ending**
   During the fifth and final meeting with your practice client, use applicable skills from the working and evaluating phase as you incorporate ending skills into the final meeting with the practice client. The ending skills include (1) reviewing the process, (2) final evaluating, and (3) sharing ending feelings and saying good-bye. Following the meeting, word-process a closing summary about the final interview and the experience as a whole.

Student Social Worker Consent Form
for Experiential Interviewing Exercise

I _____ (insert your name as the student social worker) understand the requirements of the multiweek experiential interviewing exercise. This includes my ethical obligation to ensure the practice client's personal safety, privacy, and well-being and the confidentiality of any and all relevant verbal and written communications.

_____   _____
(Signature of Student Social Worker)   (Date)

Summary Outline of the Multiweek Experiential Interviewing Exercise

Summary of the Multiweek Experiential Interviewing Exercise			Word-Processed Documents	
Meeting	Phase/Assignment	Tasks and Activities	Interview Evaluation Reports	Practice Case Record
Pre-	Chapter 7: Experiential Interviewing Exercise Preparing for a Recruitment Contact (if necessary)	Before attempting to recruit someone to participate in the experiential interviewing exercise, use applicable preparing skills—including developing a preliminary plan, securing copies of needed documents (such as the description of the exercise, guidelines for the practice client, and an agreement to participate form—Appendix 7).		
Pre-	Chapter 8: Experiential Interviewing Exercise Recruit a Practice Client (if necessary) Preparing for the First Meeting	Attempt to recruit a practice client. If she genuinely understands the nature of the assignment and agrees to participate, provide a consent form that includes your signature as well as your colleague's. Store the consent form in a secure location. In advance of the first formal meeting with your practice client, prepare a preliminary plan for the meeting. Create electronic folders in a private and secure location to keep all notes and documents related to the experiential interviewing exercise.		Plans for First Interview (Intvue_1_Plans)
1.	Chapter 9: Experiential Interviewing Exercise Beginning	Protect the actual identity of your practice client. Use applicable beginning skills and exploring skills during the first 30-minute interview. Step out of roles and engage in a 10- to 15-minute post-interview feedback session. Prepare an evaluation of your performance in the first interview. Summarize relevant content from the first interview in the form of a coherent set of notes. Prepare plans for the second meeting.	First Interview: Practice Client Feedback (Intvue_1_Client_Feed) First Interview: Additional Exploration Questions (Intvue_1_More_Quests) First Interview: Self-Evaluation (Intvue_1_Self-Eval)	First Interview Notes (Intvue_1_Notes) Plans for the Second Interview (Intvue_2_Plans)
2.	Chapter 10: Experiential Interviewing Exercises Exploring and Assessing	Use applicable exploring skills and assessing skills during a 30-minute interview. Step out of roles and engage in a 10- to 15-minute post-interview feedback session. Prepare an evaluation of your performance in the second interview. Prepare the description and assessment sections of a DAC. Prepare plans for the third meeting.	Second Interview: Practice Client Feedback (Intvue_2_Client_Feed) Second Interview: Self-Evaluation (Intvue_2_Self-Eval)	Description and Assessment (Intvue_2_DAC) Plans for the Third Interview (Intvue_3_Plans)

#	Chapter	Activity	Interview	Forms
3.	Chapter 11: Experiential Interviewing Exercise Assessing and Contracting	Use applicable assessing skills and contracting skills during a 30-minute interview. Several exploring skills may be useful as well. Step out of roles and engage in a 10- to 15-minute post-interview feedback session. Prepare an evaluation of your performance in the third interview. Prepare the contract section, update the description and assessment sections, and finalize the DAC for the case record. Prepare plans for the fourth meeting.	Third Interview: Practice Client Feedback (Intvue_3_Client_Feed) Third Interview: Self-Evaluation (Intvue_3_Self-Eval)	Contract (Intvue_3_DAC) Plans for Fourth Interview (Intvue_4_Plans)
4.	Chapter 12: Experiential Interviewing Exercise Working and Evaluating	Use applicable working and evaluating skills during a 30-minute interview. Several exploring skills may be useful as may skills from other phases. Step out of roles and engage in a 10- to 15-minute post-interview feedback session. Prepare an evaluation of your performance in the fourth interview. Prepare a progress note in SOAIGP or equivalent form. Prepare plans for the fifth and final meeting.	Fourth Interview: Practice Client Feedback (Intvue_4_Client_Feed) Fourth Interview: Self-Evaluation (Intvue_4_Self-Eval)	Progress Note (Intvue_4_Notes) Plans for the Fifth Interview (Intvue_5_Plans)
5.	Chapter 13: Experiential Interviewing Exercise Ending	Use applicable ending skills during a 30-minute interview. Several exploring skills and working and evaluating skills may be useful as well. Step out of roles and engage in a 10- to 15-minute post-interview feedback session. Prepare an evaluation of your performance in the final interview and another report reflecting on the entire multiweek learning experience. Prepare a closing summary and finalize the practice client case record.	Fifth Interview: Practice Client Feedback (Intvue_5_Client_Feed) Fifth Interview: Self-Evaluation (Intvue_4_Self-Eval) Reflections on an Experiential Learning Exercise: Five Interviews with a Practice Client (Reflections)	Closing Summary for the Case Record (Intvue_5_Sum)

Social Work Supervisor and Practice Client Advocate: Agreement Form

As a _____ (insert title; for example, social work professor, practicum instructor, professional social worker), I agree to serve as both a **social work supervisor** for you _____ (insert student's name) in your role of student social worker and as a **client advocate** for the person serving in the role of your role of practice client. Questions, concerns, complications, and grievances that you as the student social worker or that your colleague as the practice client have at any point before, during, or after the multiweek experiential interviewing exercise should be addressed to me. In this learning exercise, the safety and well-being of the participants take precedence over the educational objectives.

_____   _____
(Signature of Supervisor/Advocate)   (Date)

_____   _____
(Phone Numbers)   (E-mail Address)

_____   _____
(Signature of Student Social Worker)   (Date)

_____   _____
(Phone Numbers)   (E-mail Address)

Experiential Interviewing Experience: Guidelines for the Practice Client

1. Choose one or two real but relatively modest issues, problems, or concerns that you can personally manage. Do not choose any that have the potential to overwhelm your coping capacities. Be prepared to discuss in considerable detail the identified issues as well as personal and situational aspects that relate to them. Because social workers adopt a person-in-environment perspective, it is quite likely that the interviews could be broad in scope and quite in-depth—especially when it comes to the origin, development, duration, and severity of the issues themselves.

2. Adopt a fictitious name (pseudonym) that you and the student social worker can use throughout the process. Although the student social worker is ethically committed to maintaining your privacy and confidentially throughout the process, please adopt pseudonyms for yourself as well as for family members, friends, colleagues, and other people that you might discuss during the interviews. That provides some added protection. Also, disguise those characteristics that might readily identify you. For example, if you mention that your mother is the city's mayor, your identity might be compromised, as it would be if you provided your actual home address during a recorded interview.

3. Honesty about other aspects of yourself, including the identified issues, your history, and your life circumstances helps to add realism to the learning experience.

4. Realize that the exercise is educational in nature and is intended to provide the student social worker with opportunities to practice the social work skills. Do not expect that the social worker will actually be of any service whatsoever! She may be, but the primary purpose is not therapeutic or service oriented. Rather it is fundamentally educational in nature.

5. Understand that the experiential interviewing exercise will require you to meet five times with a student social worker over the course of several weeks. Each interview is about 30 minutes in length. At the end of that time, you and the student social worker will step out of your roles to engage in a 10- to 15-minute discussion about the interview. Be prepared to provide constructive evaluative feedback to the student social worker during these post-interview discussions. As a practice rather than an actual client, you are in a valuable position to provide extraordinarily helpful feedback to a colleague who is learning to serve as a social worker. Maximize the learning potential by frankly sharing your thoughts and feelings about each meeting and about the student social worker's performance.

6. Learn how to contact your client advocate and feel free to do so if you have questions about the multiweek learning exercise; about either the practice client or social worker roles; about any excessive personal distress that arises during the exercise; or about anything about the experience that concerns you. Make note of the client advocate's name and contact information.

7. Learn how to contact your practice social worker and feel free to do so if you have questions or need to reschedule a meeting. Make note of his or her name and contact information.

Client Advocate's Name: _____

Office Address: _____

_____

Phones: _____

E-mails: _____

Student Social Worker's Name: _____

Phones: _____

E-mails: _____

Practice Client Consent Form for the Experiential Interviewing Exercise

I understand the requirements of this multiweek experiential interviewing exercise and agree to participate as a practice client for five meetings—each of which is scheduled to last no longer than 1 hour. I also understand that this is an educational activity intended to help the student social worker practice and develop proficiency in essential social work skills.

_____   _____

(Signature of Practice Client)   (Date)

abandoned	agreeable	arcane	beckoning
abased	aimless	archaic	becoming
abashed	alarmed	ardent	bedazzled
abdicated	alarming	ardor	bedeviled
abducted	alienated	arduous	bedraggled
abhor	alive	argumentative	befuddled
abominable	alleviate	arresting	begrudging
abrasive	alluring	arrogant	beguiling
abrupt	alone	artificial	beholden
accepted	aloof	ashamed	belittled
acclaimed	altruistic	assailed	bellicose
accused	amazed	assaulted	belligerent
accustomed	ambiguous	assertive	belonging
achieved	ambitious	assuaged	bemoan
acknowledged	ambivalent	assured	beneficent
acquiesced	ameliorate	astonished	benign
acrimonious	amicable	astounding	berated
adamant	amused	attached	bereaved
adapted	anemic	attentive	bereft
adept	angelic	attracted	bested
adjusted	angry	attuned	betrayed
admired	angst	audacious	beware
admonished	anguish	auspicious	bewildered
adored	animosity	aversive	bewitched
adrift	annoyed	awarded	biased
adventurous	anomie	awful	bidden
adverse	anonymous	back-sided	bigoted
advocated	antagonistic	backstabbed	bitter
affected	antagonized	bad	blah
affectionate	anticipation	balanced	blamed
affinity	antsy	balked	bleary
afraid	anxious	bamboozled	blessed
aggravated	apathetic	banking	blissful
aggressive	apocalyptic	barrage	blocked
aggrieved	apologetic	bashful	blue
aghast	appalling	basic	blunted
agile	appetizing	battered	blushed
agitated	apprehensive	bawdy	bogged-down
aglow	approachable	beaming	boggled
agonized	approving	beaten	bolstered
agony	arbitrary	beautiful	bonded

bored
botched
bothered
boundless
bountiful
boxed-in
braced
branded
brave
brazen
breached
bright
brilliant
brisk
broached
broken
browbeaten
bruised
brushed-off
brutalized
bucking
buck-passing
bugged
bulldozed
bullied
buoyant
burdened
burned
burned-out
busted
butchered
cakewalk
calculating
calling
callous
callow
calm
cancerous
candid
canned
capitulated
capricious
capsulated
captivated
captive
care
carefree
careful
careless
caretaking
caring
caroused

carping
cast-off
cataclysmic
catalyst
catapulted
catastrophic
catharsis
caught
caustic
cautious
celibate
cemented
censored
censured
certain
challenged
chancy
changeable
charismatic
charitable
charmed
charming
chased
chaste
cheap
cheapened
cheeky
cheered
cheerful
cheesy
cherished
chivalrous
chummy
chump
civil
clammy
clandestine
clean
cocksure
coherent
cohesive
coincidental
cold
cold-blooded
cold-shouldered
collared
collusive
combative
combustible
come-on
comfortable
coming-out

commanded
committed
compartmentalized
compassionate
compelling
compensated
competent
complacent
complementary
complete
compliant
complicated
complimented
composed
comprehensible
comprehensive
compressed
compromised
concentrating
concerned
conciliatory
conclusive
concocted
condemned
condescending
condoned
conducive
confident
confined
conflicted
congenial
congratulated
congruent
connected
conquered
conscientious
considerate
considered
consoled
consoling
conspiratorial
constant
consternation
constrained
constricted
constructive
contaminated
contemplative
contented
contentious
contributory
convenient

convinced
convincing
cool
corrected
corroborate
corrosive
cosmetic
counted
countered
courageous
courteous
covered
cowardly
cozy
crabby
crafty
craggy
crappy
credible
creepy
crestfallen
cried
cringe
critical
criticize
crooked
cross
crossed
crucified
cruddy
crummy
crushed
crystallized
curative
curious
cursed
cutoff
dangerous
debased
dejected
demeaned
demure
denigrated
depressed
detached
determined
devoted
disappointed
disapproval
disbelief
disgust
dismal

dismayed
displeased
distant
distasteful
distrust
disturbed
doubtful
dubious
ecstatic
elated
elevated
embarrassed
empty
enamored
energetic
enervated
enraged
enriched
enthusiastic
entrusted
envious
euphoric
exasperated
excited
exhausted
fantastic
fearful
fearless
ferocious
flighty
flustered
fondness
forgiveness
forgotten
forsaken
frazzled
friendly
frightened
frustrated
gagged
galvanized
gamy
garrulous
gawky
generous
genial
gentle
genuine
glad
glee
glib
gloomy

glow
glum
golden
good
graceful
graceless
gracious
grand
great
greedy
green
gregarious
grief
grim
gross
grubby
gruesome
gruff
grumpy
grungy
guarded
guiltless
guilty
gullible
gutsy
gutted
haggard
hammered
hamstrung
handcuffed
handicapped
handy
hang-dogged
hapless
happy
harassed
hard
hard-boiled
hard-edged
hardheaded
hardy
harmful
harmless
harried
hate
hated
haunting
hazardous
hazy
healthful
healthy
heartache

heartbroken
heartless
heartsick
heartwarming
helpful
helpless
hesitant
high-spirited
hoggish
hog-tied
homesick
honorable
hope
hopeful
hopeless
horny
horrendous
horrible
horrified
hostile
hot
hotblooded
hotheaded
huffy
humble
hungry
hung up
hurried
hurt
hyped
hysterical
ice-cold
idiotic
idyllic
ignominious
ill-at-ease
impatient
impersonal
impetuous
impotent
impressive
impulsive
inadequate
incoherent
incompetent
incomplete
inconsiderate
indebted
indecisive
independent
indestructible
indifferent

indignant
indiscreet
indispensable
indulgent
inept
infantile
infatuated
inferior
inhibited
injurious
innocent
insane
insatiable
insolent
inspirational
intense
interested
intimate
intolerable
intolerant
intoxicated
intrusive
invincible
irate
irritable
irritated
itchy
jaded
jagged
jaundiced
jaunty
jealous
jerky
jolly
joyful
joyless
joyous
jubilant
judged
judgmental
just
keen
kind
kindhearted
kinky
kooky
laborious
lenient
light-headed
lighthearted
limited
lonely

lonesome
loss
lost
lousy
lovable
love
lovely
lovesick
love-struck
low
loyal
luckless
lucky
ludicrous
lukewarm
mad
maddening
magical
magnanimous
magnetic
magnificent
majestic
maladjusted
malaise
malicious
malignant
manic
manipulated
manipulative
martyred
masterful
mature
mean
meaningful
meaningless
mean-spirited
mediocre
meditative
melancholy
mellow
melodramatic
mercurial
methodical
mind-boggling
mindful
mindless
mischievous
miserable
mistrust
misty
misunderstood

monotonous
monstrous
monumental
moody
mortified
motivated
mournful
muddled
murky
mushy
mysterious
nasty
natural
naughty
nauseous
necessary
needful
needy
negative
neglected
neglectful
nervous
nice
noble
normal
nostalgic
nosy
noteworthy
notorious
oafish
obdurate
obedient
object
obligated
obnoxious
obscene
obstinate
obstructionist
odd
odious
offensive
onerous
optimistic
ornery
outrage
outrageous
pained
panic
panic-stricken
paranoid
passionate

passive
patchy
patient
peaceful
penalized
permissive
perplexed
persecuted
persistent
personable
pessimistic
petty
petulant
phobic
phony
picky
pitiful
pivotal
pleasing
pleasurable
plentiful
poetic
poignant
poisonous
polluted
pout
praised
praiseworthy
prejudicial
pressure
presumptuous
prickly
pride
prideful
protective
proud
prudish
pulled
pushed
put-off
puzzled
quake
qualified
qualm
quandary
quarrelsome
queasy
quizzical
radiant
radiate
radical

rage
ragged
rancor
raped
rapture
rash
raucous
raunchy
rebellious
rebuffed
recalcitrant
reckless
reclusive
refreshed
regretful
reinvigorate
rejected
rejoice
rejuvenated
relaxed
released
relentless
relieved
relish
reluctant
remorse
remorseful
remorseless
remote
renewed
repellent
repentant
reprehensible
reprimanded
reproached
repugnant
repulsive
resentful
resentment
reserved
resigned
resilient
resistant
resolute
resolved
resourceful
respectful
responsible
responsive
restful
restless

restricted	serious	strung-out	ticked
reticent	settled	stuck	ticked-off
retiring	severe	stumped	timid
revolting	sexual	stunned	tingle
revulsion	shady	sullen	tingling
rewarding	shaggy	sunk	tired
ridiculed	shaken	super	tireless
risky	shaky	supported	tiresome
rosy	shame	supportive	tolerate
rotten	shameful	surly	torment
rough	shameless	surprised	torpid
rude	sheepish	suspicious	touched
rueful	shifty	sympathetic	tough
rugged	shocked	taboo	toxic
ruined	shortchanged	taciturn	tragic
rundown	shunned	tacky	tranquil
rush	sick	tactful	transcendent
rushed	sickening	tactless	transformed
sacked	sincere	tainted	trapped
sacred	sinful	taken	trashed
sacrificial	singled-out	taken-in	traumatic
sacrilegious	sinister	tangled	treacherous
sacrosanct	skeptical	tattered	tricked
sad	sleazy	teased	tricky
saddled	sleepless	tedious	triggered
safe	sleepy	teed-off	tripped
sanctified	slick	tempted	triumphant
sanctimonious	smug	tempting	trivial
sanguine	soiled	tenacious	troubled
satisfied	solemn	tender	troubling
scandalized	solid	tension	trust
scandalous	sordid	tenuous	tuckered
scapegoated	sorrow	terminal	turbulent
scarce	spacey	terrible	turned-off
scared	spellbound	terrific	turned-on
scarred	spiritual	terrified	twinkling
scattered	spiteful	terrorized	tyrannized
scrambled	splendid	testy	ubiquitous
scrapped	split	thankful	ugly
scrawny	spoiled	therapeutic	umbrage
searching	spooky	thick-skinned	unabashed
seasoned	squeamish	thin-skinned	unaccepted
secure	stable	thoughtful	unaccustomed
sedated	stalked	thoughtless	unacknowledged
seductive	steady	thrashed	unappealing
seedy	stern	threatened	unappreciated
seeking	stilted	threatening	unashamed
sensational	stodgy	thrifty	unbearable
sensitive	stressed	thrilled	uncared-for
sensual	stretched	thrilling	uncertain
sentimental	strong	thunderstruck	unclean

uncomfortable
undaunted
undecided
understood
undesirable
undisturbed
unequal
unfaithful
unfavorable
unglued
unified
unimportant
united
unjust
unkind
unlucky
unpleasant
unproductive
unreasonable
unrelenting
unrepentant
unresponsive
unsafe

unselfconscious
unselfish
unstable
upbeat
uprooted
upstaged
uptight
urgent
vacant
vain
valiant
valued
vandalized
vengeful
victimized
victorious
vigilant
vigorous
vindicated
virtuous
violated
violent
vital

vitriolic
vituperative
vulnerable
wacky
wane
wanted
wanting
washed-out
washed-up
wasted
weak
weakened
well-adjusted
well-balanced
well-intentioned
well-meaning
well-rounded
wicked
wide-awake
wide-eyed
wild
wild-eyed
wily

winced
winded
wiped-out
wired
wishful
withdrawn
wobbly
wonderful
wondrous
worried
worthless
worthwhile
worthy
wounded
wretched
wrought-up
xenophobic
yielded
yielding
zealous
zestful

I. Description

   A. Client Identification and Contact Information

      1. Date/Time of Interview: January 13/3:30–5:00 P.M.; Interviewed by Susan Holder, LSW
      2. Person Interviewed: Lynn B. Chase, Date of Birth: October 5, Age: 34
      3. Residence: 1212 Clearview Drive, Central City
      4. Home phone: 223-1234
      5. Employment: Assembler at Fox Manufacturing Co.
      6. Business phone: 567-5678
         a. Household Composition: Lynn Chase is married to Richard S. Chase, 35-year-old carpenter with Crass Construction Company—work phone 789-7890. They have a 12-year-old son, Robert L. Chase, sixth-grade student at Hope Middle School.
         b. Referral Source: Sandra Fowles (friend of Lynn Chase)

   B. Person, Family and Household, and Community Systems

      1. Person System
      Lynn Chase prefers to be addressed as "Lynn." She described herself as "Irish-American" and said she was "raised as a Roman Catholic." She indicated that her maiden name was Shaughnessy. She looked to me to be approximately 5 feet 6 inches tall and of medium build. On the date of this interview, I noticed that she wore contemporary slacks and blouse. I observed what appeared to be dark circles under her eyes, and the small muscles in her forehead looked tense. She seemed to walk slowly and expressed an audible sigh as she sat down. She spoke in an accent common to this area—although in a slow and apparently deliberate fashion. I noticed that she occasionally interrupted her speech to pause for several seconds, then sighed before resuming her speech.

      2. Family and Household System
      As reflected in the attached intergenerational family genogram [see Figure 9.6 in Chapter 9] that Mrs. Chase and I prepared during the initial interview, the household is composed of Lynn, Richard, Robert, and a mongrel dog, "Sly." They have lived on Clearview Drive for 5 years and "like it there." Their family life is "busy." During the week, Monday through Friday, both Lynn and Richard work from 8:00 A.M. to 5:00 P.M. One parent, usually Lynn, helps Robert ready himself for school and waits with him until the school bus stops at a nearby street corner at about 7:15 A.M. Then she drives herself to work. After school, Robert takes the bus home, arriving at about 3:45 P.M. He stays alone at home until his parents arrive at about 5:45 P.M. Mrs. Chase indicated that Robert and his father have a very positive relationship. They go to sporting events together and both enjoy fishing. Robert was a member of a Little League baseball team this past summer. His dad went to every game. She described her own relationship with Robert as "currently strained." She also indicated that although she "loves her husband, there is not much joy and romance in the relationship at this time."

3. Community System

As reflected in the attached eco-map [see Figure 9.7 in Chapter 9], Mrs. Chase indicated that the Chase family is involved with several other social systems. Mrs. Chase reported that the family regularly attends the First Methodist Church, although "not every week." She said that she occasionally helps with bake sales and other church activities. She indicated that Robert goes to Sunday school almost every week. Mrs. Chase said that her husband Richard does not engage in many social activities. "He doesn't really have close friends. Robert and I are his friends." She said that Richard attends Robert's sporting events and goes fishing with him. Outside of work and those activities with Robert, Richard spends most of his time working on the house or in the yard. She said that Richard has a workshop in the basement and constructs furniture for the home.

Mrs. Chase reported that Robert has generally been a good student. She said that his teachers tell her that he is shy. When called upon in class, they said, he speaks in a quiet and hesitant voice but usually has thoughtful answers to questions. Mrs. Chase indicated that Robert had played very well on his Little League baseball team this past summer. She said that his coach thought highly of him and believed that he would make the high school team in a few years. Mrs. Chase said that her son has two or three close friends in the neighborhood.

Mrs. Chase reported that the family lives in a middle-class neighborhood. She indicates that, racially, it is minimally integrated and that the rate of crime is low and the neighbors friendly. She indicated that most of the home owners tend to maintain their property carefully. Mrs. Chase said that her family is friendly with several families in the neighborhood, and perhaps once every month or so, two or three of the families get together for dinner or a cookout.

Mrs. Chase reported that her job is "okay" and she likes the people there. She indicated that her husband truly loves his work: "Being a carpenter is what he's made for."

C. Presenting Issues

Mrs. Chase said that she has been concerned lately because she and her son have been getting into arguments "all the time." She said that she does not know what causes the trouble. She reported that she becomes critical and angry toward Robert at the slightest provocation. She said that Robert is "not misbehaving" and that "it's really my own problem." She indicated that about 6 months ago she began to become more irritable with Robert and, to some extent, with Richard as well. She reported that she hasn't slept well and has lost about 10 pounds during that 6-month period. She indicated that she took up smoking again after quitting some 5 years ago and has begun to have terrible headaches several times each week. Mrs. Chase reported that these issues began about the time that she took the job at Fox Manufacturing 6 months ago. "Before that I stayed at home to care for Robert and the household."

When asked what led her to take the job, she said, "We don't have any real savings and we'll need money for Robert's college education. I thought I'd better start saving while we have a few years before he leaves. Also, one of my friends said there was an opening at Fox and that she'd love me to work there with her." Mrs. Chase indicated that she hoped these services would help her to feel less irritable, sleep better, have fewer headaches, discontinue smoking, and have fewer arguments with her son and husband.

D. Assets, Resources, and Strengths

Mrs. Chase acknowledged that she has an above-average intellect and a capacity to consider thoughtfully various aspects and dimensions of needs and problems/issues. She reported that she is extremely responsible: "At times, too much so." She said that she is dependable in fulfilling her various roles. Mrs. Chase said that the family has sufficient financial resources and that her job has provided them with a "little bit more than we actually need." She indicated that the family lives in a "nice home in a safe and pleasant neighborhood." She said that her job is secure. She indicated that even though she has worked there for only 6 months, her employer values her work highly and her colleagues enjoy her company. Mrs. Chase reported that she has several close women friends who provide her with support and understanding. She mentioned, however, that "most of the time I am the one who provides support to them." She said that she feels loved by her husband and indicated that both her husband and son would be willing to do anything for her.

E. Referral Source and Process; Collateral Information

Ms. Sandra Fowles, friend and neighbor, referred Mrs. Chase to this agency. Ms. Fowles is a former client of this agency. In talking about Mrs. Chase, Ms. Fowles said that she is "an incredibly kind and thoughtful woman who would give you the shirt off her back. She may be too kind for her own good." Ms. Fowles made preliminary contact with the agency on behalf of Mrs. Chase and asked whether agency personnel had time to meet with her. Subsequently, Mrs. Chase telephoned the agency to schedule an appointment for this date and time.

F. History

1. Developmental

Mrs. Chase reported that she believed that her mother's pregnancy and her own birth and infancy were "normal." She described her childhood as "unhappy" (see personal and familial section below).

2. Personal, Familial, and Cultural

As reflected in the attached intergenerational genogram [see Figure 9.6 in Chapter 9], Mrs. Chase reported the following about her personal and family history. She comes from a family of five. Her mother and father married while in their late teens. Her mother became pregnant with Lynn right away. Mrs. Chase is the eldest sibling. She has a brother 1 year younger and a sister 5 years her junior. Her parents are alive and, she said, "Somehow, they are still married." Mrs. Chase reported that during her childhood her father "was, and still is, a workaholic" who was rarely home. She described her mother as an "unstable, angry, and critical woman who never praised me for anything and always put me down." Mrs. Chase said that she "raised her younger sister" because her mother was then drinking all the time. Mrs. Chase indicated that her mother has refrained from drinking alcohol for the past 3 years and now goes to Alcoholics Anonymous meetings. She described the relationship between her mother and father as "awful—they have hated each other for years." She said, "They don't divorce because they're Catholic." Mrs. Chase said that her mother disapproved of her marriage to Richard because he had been married once before. She said that her mother would not attend her wedding. She said that her mother continues to berate Richard and "frequently criticizes the way I am raising Robert too."

Mrs. Chase reported that she rarely sees her mother, who lives 200 miles away, but does visit her sister about once a month. She said that her sister frequently needs emotional support, advice, and sometimes financial assistance as well. Mrs. Chase said that her sister had formerly abused alcohol and drugs, but the problem is "now under control."

Mrs. Chase said that her husband's family was "even more messed up than mine—if that's possible." She indicated that Richard came from a family of five. She reported that his father abandoned the family when Richard was 9 and his sisters were 10 and 7. Mrs. Chase said that Richard's father had a serious drinking problem and that Richard remembered his father frequently beating both his mother and himself. Mrs. Chase indicated that Richard grew up in destitute circumstances and learned to value money. She reported that even today he closely watches how the family's money is spent and worries that "we'll end up broke."

Mrs. Chase reported that her childhood was an unhappy one. She said that she remembers feeling "different" from other children. She indicated that as a child she was very shy, often afraid, and easily intimidated. She reported that she often felt guilty and ashamed when parents or teachers criticized or corrected her. She indicated that she always tried to be "good" and, she continued, "for the most part—at least until my teenage years—I was." She said that she received excellent grades in school, although she remembered that other children sometimes taunted her by calling her a "teacher's pet." She said that she was slightly overweight during childhood and always thought of herself as "fat." She indicated that she had only a few friends during her younger years. She remembered one or two close childhood friends and described them as "shy and unattractive too." She recalled occasions when other children she had hoped would become friends "rejected" her. She remembered feeling sad and depressed on many occasions throughout her childhood.

3. Critical Events

As reflected in the attached critical events timeline [see Figure 9.5 in Chapter 9], Mrs. Chase described an incident that occurred when she was about 12 years old. She said that a boy she had liked said she was "fat" in front of a group of her peers. She said that she felt humiliated and "stayed at home and cried for days." She also recalled a time when she was about 14 or 15. She said she had begun to explore her body and to experiment with masturbation. She indicated that she found it pleasurable but believed that such behavior was sinful. She said that she discussed it with a priest during a regular confession. Mrs. Chase said that the priest became "very angry" at her and told her in a "loud and judgmental voice" to "stop abusing herself in that disgusting way." She said that she felt horribly guilty and ashamed. She reported that this experience in particular led her to leave the Catholic Church a few years later. Mrs. Chase indicated that she has never been the victim of rape or any other violent crime. She did recall, however, several occasions when a male relative (maternal uncle) forcibly kissed her and fondled her breasts. She said that each time, she almost immediately pushed him away but she remembered that she felt dirty and disgusted anyway. She said she wondered, "What is it about me that makes him think I'd be interested in that?" She said she was approximately 12 or 13 years old at the time and never told anyone about what had happened.

4. Sexual

Mrs. Chase reported that she did not date until her senior year in high school, when she went out with one boy a few times. She said that she "lost her virginity" in this relationship. She reported that she had sex with "lots of boys" after that but that she "never really enjoyed it." She indicated that she met her future husband Richard about 2 years after graduation from high school and that, she was "pleased to say," has since found sex to be pleasurable and satisfying. She said that her sex life has been "great throughout our marriage" but that she has not had much interest during the last several months.

5. Alcohol and Drug Use

Mrs. Chase stated that she does not now have an alcohol or drug use problem but recalled drinking heavily as an 18-year-old. She said that after she graduated from high school, she ran around with a crowd that "partied all the time." She said that she drank a lot of alcohol then. She reported that she sometimes drank in order to "belong" and to feel comfortable in sexual relations with boys.

6. Medical/Physical/Biological

Mrs. Chase reported that she has not had any major medical or physical problems except for an enlarged cyst in her uterus. She had that surgically removed approximately 8 years ago. She said that since that time she has been "unable to get pregnant again," although "both Richard and I wished we could have another child." She said that she has concluded that "it's not going to happen," and "I guess that's what's meant to be."

Mrs. Chase said that she "gained control of the weight problem" during the early years of her marriage by going to Weight Watchers. She indicated that she had recently spoken with her medical doctor about her occasional feelings of extreme fatigue, her change in sleep patterns, the unwanted loss of weight, and the periodic headaches. Her doctor could find nothing physically wrong and raised the question of "stress-related symptoms."

7. Legal

Mrs. Chase indicated that she and her family have not had any difficulties with the legal or criminal justice systems.

8. Educational

Mrs. Chase reported that she has a high school education and has taken approximately 2 years of college courses. She said that she had taken a course each semester until about 6 months ago, when she discontinued an evening course to "be at home more."

9. Employment

Mrs. Chase reported that she had worked in both secretarial and administrative positions following graduation from high school. She said that when Robert was born, she quit working outside the home to care for him. When he went to grammar school, she went back to work part-time. She said that she was laid off from that job about 3 years ago and was unable to find another part-time job that would enable her to be home at the end of Robert's school day. She indicated that a little more than 6 months ago, she and Richard decided that Robert was old enough to be at home alone for a couple of hours each day. She therefore applied for and secured the full-time position at Fox Manufacturing.

10. Recreational

Mrs. Chase reported that over the years she has found great pleasure in gardening. She also said, however, that during the last year or so she has discontinued that activity. She indicated that she thought she could rekindle that sense of satisfaction if she were to resume gardening again at some point in the future.

11. Religious, Spiritual, Philosophical

Mrs. Chase reported that she quit going to the Catholic Church at the age of 18 when she graduated from high school. She said she did not attend any church until the birth of her child. She indicated that she and her husband then decided that they wanted their children to have some religious involvement. She remembered joining the neighborhood Methodist Church because "it was nearby."

12. Prior Psychological, Social, or Medical Service

Mrs. Chase reported that she had not sought or received social or psychological services before and has not taken medication for depression. She reported that her mother has been in "therapy" for approximately 4 years.

II. Tentative Assessment

A. Focal Issues

1. Nature, Duration, Frequency, Severity, and Urgency

The issues of irritability and argumentativeness toward her son and husband, shame and guilt following expressions of anger or arguments, sleeplessness, weight loss, headaches, and resumption of cigarette smoking appeared to emerge at about the time Mrs. Chase accepted full-time employment outside the home. She indicated that she had not experienced these symptoms previously, although she did say that her adolescent years were painful. At this point, it is not certain that her job is or will be as satisfying to her as child rearing and homemaking have been. The fact that she discontinued her regular routine of taking evening college courses may also be a factor. There may be role strain or conflict among the family, work, educational, and personal roles. As we attempted to analyze this issue, Mrs. Chase and I wondered if the symptoms might be indicative of increased stress associated with expanded demands on her time and energy and changes in roles and role identities. Although she now works at least 40 hours per week at her paid job, she also continues to perform all of the family and household duties she fulfilled before taking the outside job. Mrs. Chase appears to assume a protective, hard-working, caretaker role with her husband and son, siblings, and friends. Indeed, she seems to hold herself responsible for the thoughts, feelings, and behaviors of all members of her family.

2. Risk and Protective Factors; Exceptions

In a general sense, assumption of the full-time job seems to have precipitated the onset of the issues of concern. Mrs. Chase and I wondered if the symptoms may represent an indirect attempt to secure greater attention, appreciation, gratitude, and support from her husband and son or, if they worsen, to provide reasonable cause to quit the job and return to her previous family and household roles. The immediate precursors to the symptoms appear related to Mrs. Chase's beliefs and expectations about herself and perhaps others. She reports that she frequently worries about various things she "should" or "ought" to be doing and feels guilty that she is not fulfilling her parental, spousal, and household (homemaker) roles as well as she previously did.

According to Mrs. Chase, there were two occasions during the past 6 months when she felt a sense of contentment and happiness. The first occurred when Richard, Robert, and she went on a weekend trip to another city. They stayed in a hotel, ate in restaurants, went to a baseball game, and spent time talking and joking with each other. On the other occasion, Richard and she went on an overnight trip to attend a family friend's wedding.

The issues of concern have existed for about 6 months. Mrs. Chase and I estimated the severity of the problems and symptoms to be in the moderate range. She continues to fulfill all of her responsibilities in a competent manner. Mrs. Chase herself seems to experience the greatest discomfort from the issues—although Robert and to some extent, Richard, are also affected by the irritability and argumentativeness. Mrs. Chase and I concur that the issues are not life threatening and do not require immediate, emergency, or intensive intervention.

B. Contributing Factors

1. Client System Factors

Mrs. Chase reflects a strong ethic of obligation and responsibility, especially toward her son and husband, but to most other people as well. She holds herself to extremely high standards and often feels guilty or worried that she's not doing well enough. She feels ashamed when she makes mistakes or believes she has hurt someone's feelings. She rarely engages in free and spontaneous play, relaxation, or recreation, and often feels quite uncomfortable when she does so. She previously enjoyed gardening, but since she took the full-time job at Fox Manufacturing, she has become reluctant to allow herself time for "unproductive" leisure and relaxation. Shortly after we began to explore the nature and scope of her expectations and caretaking activities, she wondered aloud if she might be doing too much for others. We wondered if she might feel stressed and guilty about the possibility that she might be unable to fulfill her responsibilities in the superior manner that she expects of herself. Indeed, she may feel guilty that she now spends less time with her son Robert and worried she may be unable to protect him from potentially dangerous circumstances. We wondered if this idea about protecting Robert might relate to her recollections of her own childhood, when she had not felt loved and protected. We also wondered if she might worry that Robert was approaching the age at which she, as a senior in high school, first had sex and began to drink—sometimes heavily. We wondered if she might be, in a sense, overprotecting her adolescent son at a time when he might be dealing with issues related to identity and the development of autonomy. Mrs. Chase, directly or indirectly, may be uneasy and unclear concerning her parenting role during this time. Her own adolescent experiences and the shame she felt may continue to affect her today in relation to her son Robert. She may wonder about his unfolding sexuality and be concerned about how he will deal with adolescent changes.

Mrs. Chase seems to view herself primarily as a wife and mother and as a hard-working, responsible member of the community. She appears to assume the role of a parent-like big sister with her siblings. She seems open to input from others and from me and has a well-established sense of personal identity in relation to family roles such as wife, mother, daughter, and eldest sibling. She and her husband had wanted more children, but a medical condition (the cyst or the surgery to remove it) prevented that. She seems less clear and secure, however, when it comes to other, more playful or recreational roles. In these areas, she appears more uncertain and less inner-directed. She has yet to formulate personal life goals that are distinct from those of her family.

Application of the *DSM-5* (American Psychiatric Association, 2013) criteria might suggest a "Z Code" classification. Z Codes are issues of concern but do not necessarily indicate or relate to a psychiatric disorder or mental illness. The Z Codes that seem applicable to the person-issue-situation seem to be "Z62.820 Parent–Child Relational Problem" in recognition of the current strain between Mrs. Chase and her son. Because of Mrs. Chase's work-related stress, the Z56.9 Code "Other Problem Related to Employment" might apply. The Z60.0 Code "Phase of Life Problem" could reflect the complications associated with the change in role identity from primarily homemaker to homemaker plus full-time paid worker outside the home—at a time when her teenage son is undergoing changes of his own.

Other Z Codes that could conceivably apply include Z62.810 "Personal History (Past History) of Sexual Abuse in Childhood" or Z62.811 "Personal History (Past History) of Psychological Abuse in Childhood." These might be used because of Mrs. Chase's uncle's assaults and her mother's behavior toward her throughout her childhood, adolescence, and young adulthood.

The *DSM-5* mental disorder diagnosis of "309.28 (F43.23) Adjustment Disorder with Mixed Anxiety and Depressed Mood" might also be considered. It does appear that Mrs. Chase's distress did emerge shortly after an identifiable stressor (that is, the assumption of the full-time job outside the home). Usually, however, most adjustment disorders are resolved—with or without professional aid—within 6 months of onset.

Application of the PIE Manual criteria (Karls & O'Keefe, 2008a) to Mrs. Chase and her situation might yield the following classification:

Factor I: Homemaker Role—Home, mixed type (ambivalence, responsibility, dependency), moderate severity, duration of 6 months to 1 year, adequate coping skills. Also consider parental role or perhaps spousal role problems.

Factor II: Other Affectional Support System Problem, low severity, more than 5 years' duration.

Might the fact that Robert is alone, unsupervised, and unprotected during 2 hours after school each weekday represent an important trigger to Mrs. Chase's feelings of stress, irritability, and guilt? Might she feel a conflict between earning money for her son's college education and being unavailable to him when he returns from school? Might she be afraid that he could be in some danger? Might Mrs. Chase believe that she is less able to protect Robert from the influence of the neighborhood boys now that she works outside the home? Does she feel an obligation to keep Robert entirely away from all potentially negative or risky phenomena? Does she suspect that Robert might be especially susceptible to negative peer pressure and that he might be unable to make responsible decisions or to resist temptations? Might she be associating Robert's adolescence with her own teenage experience? Could she be worried that Robert might indeed be fully capable of making mature decisions and might not need her as much anymore? What would Mrs. Chase need to conclude that Robert is reasonably safe during the 2-hour "latchkey" period?

How much does she really want to work outside the home? Does she truly enjoy the work? How does her husband feel about her job? How similar is Mrs. Chase to her father in terms of a workaholic, or compulsive, approach to life? Might her reactions to working outside the home be in some way related to her view of her father as "a workaholic who was never at home"? Might she feel guilty that "she's like her father"? Have the symptoms of irritability and argumentativeness led to a comparison with her mother—whom she views as angry, critical, and unstable? Might Mrs. Chase worry that if she does not do for others, they might not love or approve of her?

What was the impact of discontinuing the evening college courses that Mrs. Chase regularly took before resuming full-time employment? How much did she enjoy those courses? Was the role of college student part of an emerging personal identity? What was her long-term educational goal? Could the loss of the college student role relate to her biopsychosocial symptoms?

Based on information from the initial interview, Mrs. Chase and her immediate family have a lengthy history of competent functioning. Individually and as a system, the family members appear to be coherent and stable. However, Mr. Chase, Robert, and especially Mrs. Chase have begun to experience strain associated with changing demands. It appears that Mrs. Chase has tried to continue to "do it all" and may feel worried and guilty that she is not as available to her son as he might need or want her to be.

Several factors may have relevance to the identified issues. First, Mrs. Chase comes from a family of origin where she assumed adult responsibilities from an early age. She reported that her mother abused alcohol and her father was a workaholic. It is possible that Mrs. Chase tends to assume substantial responsibility for others—perhaps especially family members. She apparently learned to do so from an early age. Working full-time outside the home may represent a major psychological conflict for her. One part of her, perhaps like her father, may be strongly tempted to invest a great deal of time and energy in her employment. Another part may feel much anxiety and uncertainty when she is away from the home. She is so familiar with the role of caretaker for her husband and son that she may sometimes feel anxious when she is away from home and unable to meet their needs. Second, Mrs. Chase wanted to have more children, but a medical condition has prevented that. She may have yet to explore fully and grieve for the loss of her dream for additional children. She may also invest even greater emotional energy in her son Robert, because "he's my only child; and the only one I'll ever have." Third, as an early adolescent, Robert is probably experiencing numerous physical, psychological, and social changes. Along with Mrs. Chase's employment and the disruption of her evening college course routine, these changes may also add considerable stress to the family system. As a person emotionally attuned to the family, Mrs. Chase is understandably affected during this transition period. She may soon become aware of the limitations associated with an exclusively, family-centered role identification.

The current issues of concern may represent a kind of positive signal to Mrs. Chase to make some personal changes that could both liberate her from inhibitions that originated in childhood, and prepare her for a more peaceful and enjoyable second half of life. Although assumption of the full-time paid job outside the home seems associated with the onset of the issues of concern, it is plausible that the family system needed something to help her, her husband, and her son to proceed to the next stage of individual and family development. Application of Erikson's psychosocial theory of life cycle stages (Erikson, 1963, 1968) might suggest that Mrs. Chase could be engaged in "generativity versus stagnation" issues as she begins to pursue greater meaning in life and a more coherent sense of personal identity. Some issues related to certain earlier life cycle stages may require exploration (for example, autonomy versus shame and doubt, initiative versus guilt, identity versus role confusion). Application of Gilligan's theoretical approach to women's development might suggest that Mrs. Chase could be seeking enhanced intimacy and greater attachment to the most important people in her life (Gilligan, 1979, 1982). Although her commitment to and relationship with others have been strong, the degree of intimacy and closeness may have been inhibited by the dominance of the parent-like, caretaking role.

Mrs. Chase seems to reflect a high level of competence and possesses well-developed coping skills and defense mechanisms, which have served her well over the years. She has coped well with numerous life challenges, transitions, and issues. At present, however, her usual coping capacities appear less functional as she experiences atypical irritation and anger. At some level, she may fear that she is becoming more like her mother, whom she described as "unstable, angry, and critical."

In spite of the current concerns, however, she continues to function well in most social roles. She appears to possess a coherent and integrated personality. She reflects superior thinking capacities, probably possesses above-average intelligence, and is insightful and articulate. She has excelled in her role as part-time college student. Since the time of her marriage to Richard, her lifestyle has been stable and congruent. In addition, she seems highly motivated to function well in the role of client and agent of change in her life.

Mrs. Chase and I wondered if certain cognitive beliefs could contribute to the identified problems. She commonly makes statements to herself (self-talk) such as "Think about others before oneself," "Do for others before doing for yourself," "Don't make mistakes," "Don't be a burden to others," "Don't think about yourself," and "Don't be selfish." These may be related to the gender-related role expectations of her family of origin, her religious training and experiences, and her cultural background. During the first interview, she concluded that there was a relationship between such beliefs and the current issues. This hypothesis seemed to heighten her motivation to reconsider what she believes and how she talks to herself.

2. Situational, Environmental, and Systemic Factors

Based on information gained in the first interview, the Chase family system appears organized in such a way that Mrs. Chase serves as the primary executive or manager, or perhaps "parent figure." She seems to have responsibility for the bulk of the household and family chores, functions, and activities. Mr. Chase apparently assumes few household duties with the exception of yard work, as well as home and auto repairs. She is the primary housekeeper and parent. She prepares the meals, does the shopping and cleaning, coordinates transportation for Robert, and pays the bills. Until Mrs. Chase began full-time work outside the home, the family rules and role boundaries were clear. Mrs. Chase sought ideas and input from Richard and Robert, but she made and implemented most family decisions. Now that she is home less often and there are increased demands on her, some of the rules and roles may be in flux. At this point, it seems that Mrs. Chase is trying to maintain her previous family and community duties while adding additional occupational responsibilities. She also appears concerned about certain "troubled teenage boys" in the neighborhood and worries that Robert might be negatively influenced by them. We wondered if she might especially be worried that Robert might begin to use alcohol or drugs.

It appears that communication and relational patterns within the Chase family are relatively open but inhibited and constrained. The family members are mutually affectionate and seem to like each other. According to Mrs. Chase, however, the male family members sometimes appear to "hint at" rather than clearly state their preferences. Mrs. Chase seems to respond to such indirect expressions by guessing what they really want. She cited an example where, at a recent family dinner, Robert "made a face" when he was served his meal. Mrs. Chase then asked, "What's the matter?" Robert said, "Nothing." Mrs. Chase asked, "Don't you like the meal? I'll get you something else." Robert said, "Don't bother, this is okay." Mrs. Chase said, "No, I'll get you something else to eat." Robert said, "Oh, okay. Thanks." At this point, Mrs. Chase interrupted her own meal, got up, and prepared something that Robert would prefer.

When we considered the communication patterns in the family, we wondered if Richard and Robert realized that they sometimes express themselves indirectly through facial expressions and nonverbal gestures. Do they understand that Mrs. Chase often tries to "read their minds"—which may, indirectly, serve to encourage and maintain their patterns of indirect communication? What might be the consequence of more direct and full verbal expression within the family system? What would each family member stand to gain or lose?

Members of the Chase family appear to have adopted many of the stereotypic rules and roles of men, women, and children projected by the dominant North American culture. Robert's adolescence and Mrs. Chase's full-time outside employment probably represent the most significant stressors the family system now faces.

As a system, the Chase family may be approaching a phase when an adolescent child often stimulates a number of issues and decisions for all the family members and the family system as a whole. According to Mrs. Chase, Robert has begun to experience bodily changes and has become more self-conscious and self-centered. These changes may be affecting the nature of the relationship between Robert and Mrs. Chase and perhaps that with his father as well.

We wondered what might happen if Richard and Robert began to demonstrate a capacity to care for themselves and assume responsibility for some of the household chores. Might the frequency and intensity of Mrs. Chase's symptoms decrease if she had fewer family and household demands? Or might they increase if she concluded that she was not as "needed" by Robert and Richard? I wondered if Mrs. Chase would be willing to let her husband and son assume greater responsibility for household and family chores. Would they be willing to take on these duties? If they did shift the family structure and roles in such a manner, how would the family members respond?

What specific issues and dilemmas, if any, is Robert confronting during his adolescent years? How comfortable is Mrs. Chase with her son's desire for increasing freedom and personal responsibility? If she is not, might she reconsider her views about adolescent development? How does Mr. Chase relate to his son during this time? What hopes and dreams do Mr. and Mrs. Chase have for Robert's future? What doubts and fears do they have about him?

There seem to be sufficient resources to meet basic and urgent needs of the Chase family. They have adequate assets and opportunities to pursue their aspirations. They have not been subject to overt oppression or discrimination. Mrs. Chase appears to have the affection and support of her husband and son. Although her mother, father, and siblings do not appear to provide much in the way of interest, understanding, or support, she has several friends who care about her a great deal. In these relationships as in most others, she seems to "give more than she receives" and "knows more about others than others know about her." She also believes strongly that her husband and son, as well as numerous friends, would be willing to do anything they could to help her.

3. Motivation and Readiness; Stage of Change

Before the end of our first meeting together, Mrs. Chase concluded that throughout most of her life she has adopted a protective, parent-like, caretaking, and people-pleasing role toward people in general and the members of her family in particular. She also said that "not only has this pattern left me feeling guilty and stressed, it may have interfered to some extent with

Richard and Robert's ability to care for themselves." She smiled as she said, "I might have to become more selfish—for the sake of my husband and son."

By the end of our first meeting, Mrs. Chase appeared highly motivated to make personal changes to allow her to lighten her burdens of responsibility and permit others to assume more control over their own lives. She looked forward to feeling more relaxed and playful and more able to experience joy and pleasure. She indicated that this is very important to her, as it could help her overcome her "family legacy" of anger, criticism, shame, guilt, and workaholism. Mrs. Chase seemed comfortable with and confident in my ability to help her address these issues and willing to work collaboratively with me in the process.

In regard to Prochaska's transtheoretical scheme (Prochaska, Norcross, & DiClemente, 1994), Mrs. Chase probably fits within the latter portions of the contemplation and the early parts of the preparation stages of change. She appeared motivated by the idea that she might change patterns of thinking, feeling, and behaving that had their origins during her childhood. She also seemed encouraged by the idea that making those changes could not only make her life easier and more enjoyable, but also be of help to her husband and son.

Mrs. Chase believed that Richard and Robert would be enthusiastic about any efforts to help her. She felt secure and confident in their love and affection for her and thought they would place a high priority on helping to address the issues of irritability, argumentativeness, shame and guilt, sleeplessness, smoking behavior, and excessive weight loss. She also believed that they would join in an attempt to alter the family structure so that she could become less of the "mommy" for both of them. She anticipated, however, that there might be times when all of them might be tempted to slip back into old familiar patterns.

She was less optimistic about her parents' and siblings' willingness to acknowledge problems or help to address them. She also seemed worried about the reactions of people at her job and friends within the church and community. She wondered if they might become confused and perhaps annoyed if she began suddenly to do less for them. However, she smiled when she said, "I'll talk with them about my issues, and we'll see what happens when I start to change."

4. Challenges and Obstacles

One aspect that may represent a personal challenge involves control. Mrs. Chase and I have not yet discussed the possible relationship between taking care of others and feelings of control. I wondered about the possibility that as she worries less about others and reduces her caretaking behavior, she may experience increased anxiety associated with a decreased sense of control. Indeed, she sometimes feels quite uncomfortable when she engages in playful or recreational activities.

In addition, some elements of her primary and secondary social systems may resist the changes she hopes to make. Despite their love and support, Richard and Robert might experience some resentment if they were expected to do more for themselves and take on additional household chores. Mrs. Chase's parents and siblings might also respond in a similar fashion, as might some of her work colleagues and church and community friends.

5. Risk Assessment

Despite the indications of distress and perhaps depression, Mrs. Chase and I concur that she does not represent a danger to herself or others. In response to a question concerning suicidal thoughts and actions, she indicated that she has never taken any self-destructive action and does not have suicidal thoughts. Similarly, she reported that she has never experienced thoughts about or taken actions intended to hurt another person. She also confirmed that she does not use drugs of any kind—only rarely takes an aspirin—and drinks at most one glass of wine per week.

C. Case Formulation

Based upon our assessment, Mrs. Chase and I hypothesized that changes in certain aspects of her personal and family life might help to resolve the identified issues. We thought that:

1. If Mrs. Chase logically examined the beliefs she developed during her childhood, she might decide to change some in a way that would enable her to feel less excessively responsible for the safety, well-being, and happiness of her son, her husband, and most other people she

knows. We predicted that changes in her thinking would probably lead to changes to her feelings, emotions, and bodily sensations and would probably help her to sleep better as well.

2. If Mrs. Chase assumed somewhat less responsibility for the family and household work and her son Robert and husband Richard assumed somewhat more, Mrs. Chase would probably feel less stressed—if she simultaneously changed some of her beliefs and self-statements.

3. If Mrs. Chase encouraged Robert to assume more responsibility for his thoughts and actions and granted him somewhat greater freedom and autonomy, he would probably find it easier to address his adolescent development needs and the two of them would probably argue less and find their encounters more enjoyable.

Mrs. Chase's intelligence, maturity, insight, and motivation—along with the affection and support of her husband and son—suggest a high likelihood that the family will be able to address the identified issues effectively. I estimate that the probability of full and successful resolution is greater than 85 percent. I also anticipate a satisfactory outcome in 1 to 2 months of weekly meetings with Mrs. Chase and her immediate family.

III. Service Contract

A. Issues

1. Client-Identified Issues
Mrs. Chase identified the following issues:
a. Frequent arguments with her son Robert and, less often, with her husband Richard
b. Increased irritability, criticism, and anger toward Robert and, to a lesser degree, toward Richard
c. Shame and guilt following arguments with her son
d. Unplanned weight loss (10 pounds) over the past 6 months
e. Sleep disturbance
f. Resumption of cigarette smoking after 5 years' abstinence
g. Fatigue
h. Headaches

2. Worker-Identified Issues
Following the first interview, I tentatively identified the following as potential issues:
a. Ambivalence about job at Fox Manufacturing
b. Feelings of depression
c. Ambivalence about Robert's adolescence
d. Feelings of loss, disappointment, and grief about:
    (1) the apparent physical inability to have a second child
    (2) giving up the part-time college courses she had taken for many years
e. Stress and tension; anxiety
f. Thoughts and feelings of excessive responsibility and possibly of control
g. Role strain and possibly role conflict among the roles of mother, wife, homemaker, employee, and college student
h. Issues related to childhood experiences (that is, growing up in a family system with a parent who reportedly abused alcohol; largely absent and possibly workaholic father; unhappy incidents with childhood peers; feeling overweight and unattractive; church-related issues; reported episodes of attempted molestation by maternal uncle)
i. Interactional styles that may be classified as predominantly nonassertive with occasional periods of aggressive verbal expression

3. Confirmed (Focal) Issues
Mrs. Chase and I agreed on the following issues for work. These will provide us with a focus for our work together:
a. Frequent arguments with her son Robert and, less often, with her husband Richard
b. Irritability, criticism, and anger toward Robert and, to a lesser degree, toward Richard
c. Disproportionate feelings of shame and guilt
d. Sleep disturbance

      e. Ambivalence regarding job at Fox Manufacturing

      f. Stress and tension; anxiety

      g. Thoughts and feelings of excessive responsibility and possibly of control

      h. Role strain and possibly role conflict among roles of mother, wife, homemaker, employee, and college student

B. Service Goals

Mrs. Chase and I agreed to work toward accomplishment of the following goals:

1. Within 6 weeks, decrease by 50 percent the frequency of unwarranted arguments with Robert and Richard and increase the frequency of satisfying interactions with them by 50 percent.

2. Within 6 weeks, decrease by 50 percent the frequency and intensity of inappropriate feelings of irritability, criticism, and anger toward Robert and Richard and increase appropriate feelings of comfort and acceptance of them by 50 percent.

3. Within 6 weeks, decrease by 50 percent the frequency and intensity of disproportionate feelings of shame and guilt, and increase feelings of self-acceptance and self-forgiveness by 50 percent.

4. Within 6 weeks, sleep 8 full hours per night and awaken feeling refreshed at least four of seven mornings a week.

5. Within 6 weeks, decrease the ambivalence about the job at Fox Manufacturing by deciding whether she really wants to keep the job.

6. Within 6 weeks, decrease the stress, tension, and anxiety and increase feelings of personal comfort and calmness by 50 percent.

7. Within 2 weeks, complete an in-depth exploration of the issue of excessive responsibility and control; by the end of that time, decide whether maintaining or lessening the current level of responsibility and control is desirable.

C. Plans

1. Action Plans/Service Approach

To achieve the final goals, Mrs. Chase and I agreed on the following action plans:

Mrs. Lynn Chase and I (Susan Holder, social worker) will meet for eight 1-hour sessions during the next 2 months. Our purpose is to work together toward achievement of the final goals identified above. We will approach this work as a cooperative effort, with each party contributing ideas and suggestions. I will serve as counselor and facilitator and approach our work together from an integrated combination of cognitive-behavioral, problem-solving, family-systems, and task-centered approaches. On at least some occasions, we will ask Mrs. Chase's husband and son to join us. Throughout the 2-month period, we will monitor the rate and degree of progress. At the end of that time, we will determine whether to conclude our work, consult with or refer to someone else, or contract with each other for further work together.

a. Client Tasks/Action Steps

Mrs. Chase and I agreed that she would undertake the following steps during the first week of our work together. Other tasks will be identified and implemented later in the program.

- As a first step toward decreasing her stress, tension, and anxiety and increasing feelings of personal comfort and calmness, Mrs. Chase agreed to spend 15 minutes each day during the next week (1) planning for or working in her garden, and (2) planning for or working on a personal learning goal that might support her long-term educational aspirations.

- As a first step toward decreasing the frequency of her inappropriate feelings of irritability, criticism, and anger toward Robert and Richard and increasing appropriate feelings of comfort, understanding, and acceptance of them by 50 percent, Mrs. Chase agreed to do two things during the course of the next week. First, she agreed to resist temptations to "stuff" her feelings. Whether by writing them down on paper, verbally expressing them in a place where no one can hear, or expressing them directly to the relevant person or people, she agreed to express whatever feelings she experiences within a few minutes of the time that she first becomes aware of them. Second, she agreed to take 5 minutes every day to engage Robert and Richard pleasantly by inquiring about their thoughts, feelings, and activities.

- As a first step toward addressing the goal of determining whether a lessening of responsibility and control in some areas might be helpful, Mrs. Chase agreed to identify and write down as many reasons as she could why she should continue to maintain her current level of responsibility and control. Following that, Mrs. Chase agreed to identify as many reasons as she could why a lessening of her responsibility and control might be beneficial to her, her husband, and her son at this time. We agreed to review the two lists of reasons in our next meeting.

b. Worker Tasks

- I, Susan Holder, agreed to prepare this service agreement in written form and provide a copy to Mrs. Chase.
- I agreed to assume responsibility for planning tentative agendas for our meetings together and to consult with Mrs. Chase concerning the implementation of the action steps and their effects.
- I agreed to provide Mrs. Chase with a notebook and related materials for completing written tasks and monitoring progress.

c. In-Session Tasks

Mrs. Chase and I agreed that during our meetings together, we would undertake some or all the following activities (additional in-session tasks are to be identified and implemented later in the program):

- Value-clarification exercises intended to aid Mrs. Chase in addressing various issues about which she experiences ambivalence
- Self-talk analysis to help Mrs. Chase identify the "things she says to herself" that appear associated with attitudes of excessive responsibility and with the feelings of irritability, criticism, anger, depression, stress, and tension
- Strength-oriented, "bragging" exercises to help Mrs. Chase develop a stronger sense of individuality and autonomy—separate from her identity as wife, mother, and friend

d. Maintenance Tasks

Mrs. Chase and I agreed that the goals involve long-term change and require ongoing attention. Mrs. Chase indicated that she would recite the serenity prayer at least once per day for the next 365 days.

2. Plans to Evaluate Progress

We will evaluate progress toward goal achievement in several ways. First, Mrs. Chase agreed to keep a daily log in her notebook, where she intends to record the time and date of all "arguments" and all "satisfying interactions." Second, Mrs. Chase also agreed to log the time and date of all inappropriate feelings of "irritability, anger, and criticism" toward Richard or Robert, as well as all feelings of "comfort, understanding, and acceptance" of them. Third, Mrs. Chase agreed to use the logbook to record the number of hours slept each night and to rate, on a subjective scale of 1 to 10, how refreshed she feels upon awakening. Fourth, Mrs. Chase agreed to register completion of her daily 15 minutes of "gardening." Evaluation of progress toward other goals will occur by asking Mrs. Chase for self-reports. In regard to the issues of excessive responsibility and ambivalence about her job at Fox Manufacturing, progress will be indicated when Mrs. Chase reports that she has decided whether to lessen responsibility and control and whether she wants to keep her job. We concluded that a decision in either direction would represent progress. Finally, Mrs. Chase agreed to complete brief client satisfaction and session rating scales during each meeting to help improve service quality.

The Social Work Skills Interview Rating Form

You may use this rating form[1] as part of the process of evaluating your own or others' performance of the social work skills during interviews with clients. You may use it, for example, in rating your performance during an interview with an individual, couple, family, small group, organization, or community. You may also use the form to provide evaluative feedback to a colleague who is attempting to improve the quality of his or her performance.

In using the rating form, please use the following coding system:

N/A During the course of the interview, the skill in question was not appropriate or necessary and was therefore not used, having no effect on the interview.

−4 During the course of the interview, the skill in question was attempted at an inappropriate time and in an unsuitable context, and was performed in an incompetent manner. Its use represents a major problem in the interview.

−3 During the course of the interview, the skill in question was used at an inappropriate time or in an unsuitable context, seriously detracting from the interview.

−2 During the course of the interview, the skill in question was attempted at an appropriate time and in a suitable context, but was done so in an incompetent manner, significantly detracting from the interview.

−1 During the course of the interview, the skill in question was not used at times or in contexts when it should have been, detracting from the interview.

0 During the course of the interview, the skill in question was used and demonstrated at a minimal level of competence. Its use did not detract from nor contribute to the interview.

+1 During the course of the interview, the skill in question was attempted at an appropriate time and in a suitable context, and was generally demonstrated at a fair level of competence. Its use represented a small contribution to the interview.

+2 During the course of the interview, the skill in question was attempted at an appropriate time and in a suitable context, and was generally demonstrated at a moderate level of competence. Its use represented a significant contribution to the interview.

+3 During the course of the interview, the skill in question was attempted at an appropriate time and in a suitable context, and was generally demonstrated at a good level of competence. Its use represented a substantial contribution to the interview.

+4 During the course of the interview, the skill in question was attempted at an appropriate time and in a suitable context, and was demonstrated at a superior level of performance. Its use represented a major contribution to the interview.

The Social Work Skills Interview Rating Form	
Skill	**Rating**
Talking and Listening: The Basic Interpersonal Skills	
TL001 Accessing a place of peace	+4 +3 +2 +1 0 −1 −2 −3 −4 N/A
Comments:	

---

[1] Because this rating form is intended for the purpose of evaluating social work skills used during face-to-face interviews, some skills related to professionalism, ethical decision making, assessing, and recording are not included.

TL002 Engaging diversity and difference with cultural sensitivity	+4 +3 +2 +1 0 −1 −2 −3 −4 N/A
Comments:	

TL003 Communicating nonverbally (attending)	+4 +3 +2 +1 0 −1 −2 −3 −4 N/A
Comments:	

TL004 Talking: Communicating verbally	+4 +3 +2 +1 0 −1 −2 −3 −4 N/A
Comments:	

TL005 Listening: Hearing, observing, encouraging, and remembering	+4 +3 +2 +1 0 −1 −2 −3 −4 N/A
Comments:	

TL006 Active listening: Combining talking and listening	+4 +3 +2 +1 0 −1 −2 −3 −4 N/A
Comments:	

Beginning Skills	
BG001 Introducing yourself	+4 +3 +2 +1 0 −1 −2 −3 −4 N/A
Comments:	

BG002 Seeking introductions	+4 +3 +2 +1 0 −1 −2 −3 −4 N/A
Comments:	

BG003 Describing initial purpose	+4 +3 +2 +1 0 −1 −2 −3 −4 N/A
Comments:	

BG004 Orienting	+4 +3 +2 +1 0 −1 −2 −3 −4 N/A
Comments:	

BG005 Discussing policy and ethical factors	+4 +3 +2 +1 0 −1 −2 −3 −4 N/A
Comments:	

BG006 Seeking feedback	+4 +3 +2 +1 0 −1 −2 −3 −4 N/A
Comments:	

Exploring Skills	
EX001 Asking questions (open- and closed-ended)	+4 +3 +2 +1 0 −1 −2 −3 −4 N/A
Comments:	

EX002 Seeking clarification	+4 +3 +2 +1 0 −1 −2 −3 −4 N/A
Comments:	

EX003 Reflecting content	+4 +3 +2 +1 0 −1 −2 −3 −4 N/A
Comments:	

EX004 Reflecting feelings	+4 +3 +2 +1 0 −1 −2 −3 −4 N/A
Comments:	

EX005 Reflecting feelings and meaning	+4 +3 +2 +1 0 −1 −2 −3 −4 N/A
Comments:	

EX006 Partializing	+4 +3 +2 +1 0 −1 −2 −3 −4 N/A
Comments:	

EX007 Going beyond what is said	+4 +3 +2 +1 0 −1 −2 −3 −4 N/A
Comments:	

EX008 Reflecting issues	+4 +3 +2 +1 0 −1 −2 −3 −4 N/A
Comments:	

EX009 Reflecting hypotheses	+4 +3 +2 +1 0 −1 −2 −3 −4 N/A
Comments:	

Assessing Skills	
AS001 Identifying issues	+4 +3 +2 +1 0 −1 −2 −3 −4 N/A
Comments:	
AS002 Sharing hypotheses	+4 +3 +2 +1 0 −1 −2 −3 −4 N/A
Comments:	
AS003 Confirming issues	+4 +3 +2 +1 0 −1 −2 −3 −4 N/A
Comments:	
AS004 Organizing descriptive information	+4 +3 +2 +1 0 −1 −2 −3 −4 N/A
Comments:	
AS005 Preparing an assessment and case formulation	+4 +3 +2 +1 0 −1 −2 −3 −4 N/A
Comments:	
Contracting Skills	
CN001 Establishing goals	+4 +3 +2 +1 0 −1 −2 −3 −4 N/A
Comments:	
CN002 Developing action plans	+4 +3 +2 +1 0 −1 −2 −3 −4 N/A
Comments:	
CN003 Identifying action steps	+4 +3 +2 +1 0 −1 −2 −3 −4 N/A
Comments:	
CN004 Planning for evaluation	+4 +3 +2 +1 0 −1 −2 −3 −4 N/A
Comments:	

Working and Evaluating Skills	
WE001 Rehearsing action steps	+4 +3 +2 +1 0 −1 −2 −3 −4 N/A
Comments:	
WE002 Reviewing action steps	+4 +3 +2 +1 0 −1 −2 −3 −4 N/A
Comments:	
WE003 Evaluating	+4 +3 +2 +1 0 −1 −2 −3 −4 N/A
Comments:	
WE004 Focusing	+4 +3 +2 +1 0 −1 −2 −3 −4 N/A
Comments:	
WE005 Educating	+4 +3 +2 +1 0 −1 −2 −3 −4 N/A
Comments:	
WE006 Advising	+4 +3 +2 +1 0 −1 −2 −3 −4 N/A
Comments:	
WE007 Responding with immediacy	+4 +3 +2 +1 0 −1 −2 −3 −4 N/A
Comments:	
WE008 Reframing	+4 +3 +2 +1 0 −1 −2 −3 −4 N/A
Comments:	
WE009 Observing inconsistencies	+4 +3 +2 +1 0 −1 −2 −3 −4 N/A
Comments:	
WE010 Representing	+4 +3 +2 +1 0 −1 −2 −3 −4 N/A
Comments:	

WE011 Linking	+4 +3 +2 +1 0 −1 −2 −3 −4 N/A
Comments:	

WE012 Pointing out endings	+4 +3 +2 +1 0 −1 −2 −3 −4 N/A
Comments:	

Ending Skills	
EN001 Reviewing the process	+4 +3 +2 +1 0 −1 −2 −3 −4 N/A
Comments:	

EN002 Final evaluating	+4 +3 +2 +1 0 −1 −2 −3 −4 N/A
Comments:	

EN003 Sharing ending feelings and saying good-bye	+4 +3 +2 +1 0 −1 −2 −3 −4 N/A
Comments:	

Table of Social Work Skills

The skills addressed in this edition of *The Social Work Skills Workbook* are identified in the table below. Each skill may be classified according to the dimension or phase of practice. Such a system enables assessors and learners to "code" the use of a particular skill during observed or recorded interviews, or in transcripts of meetings.

	The Social Work Skills	ID
Professionalism (PF)	PF001 Demonstrating integrity	PF001
	PF002 Applying knowledge, expertise, and self-efficacy	PF002
	PF003 Demonstrating self-understanding and self-control	PF003
	PF004 Demonstrating empathy	PF004
	PF005 Demonstrating respect	PF005
	PF006 Demonstrating authenticity	PF006
	PF007 Giving and receiving social support	PF007
	PF008 Thinking critically and inquiring scientifically	PF008
	PF009 Engaging in lifelong learning	PF009
	PF010 Valuing diversity and difference	PF010
	PF011 Accepting others and respecting autonomy	PF011
	PF012 Advancing human rights and social well-being	PF012
	PF013 Promoting social, economic, and environmental justice	PF013
	PF014 Engaging in policy–practice	PF014
Ethical Decision Making (ED)	ED001 Recognizing legal duties	ED001
	ED002 Applying fundamental social work values and ethics	ED002
	ED003 Identifying ethical and legal implications	ED003
	ED004 Addressing ethical dilemmas	ED004
Talking and Listening Skills (TL)	TL001 Accessing a place of peace	TL001
	TL002 Engaging diversity and difference with cultural sensitivity	TL002
	TL003 Communicating nonverbally (attending)	TL003
	TL004 Talking: Communicating verbally and in writing	TL004
	TL005 Listening: Hearing, observing, encouraging, and remembering	TL005
	TL006 Active listening: Combining talking and listening	TL006
Preparing Skills (PR)	PR001 Preparatory reviewing	PR001
	PR002 Preparatory exploring	PR002
	PR003 Preparatory consultation	PR003
	PR004 Preparatory arranging	PR004
	PR005 Preparatory empathy	PR005
	PR006 Preparatory self-exploration	PR006
	PR007 Centering	PR007
	PR008 Preliminary planning and recording	PR008

Beginning Skills (BG)	BG001 Introducing yourself	BG001
	BG002 Seeking introductions	BG002
	BG003 Describing initial purpose	BG003
	BG004 Orienting	BG004
	BG005 Discussing policy and ethical factors	BG005
	BG006 Seeking feedback	BG006
Exploring Skills (EX)	EX001 Asking questions	EX001
	EX002 Seeking clarification	EX002
	EX003 Reflecting content	EX003
	EX004 Reflecting feelings	EX004
	EX005 Reflecting feelings and meaning	EX005
	EX006 Partializing	EX006
	EX007 Going beyond what is said	EX007
	EX008 Reflecting issues	EX008
	EX009 Reflecting hypotheses	EX009
Assessing Skills (AS)	AS001 Identifying issues	AS001
	AS002 Sharing hypotheses	AS002
	AS003 Confirming issues	AS003
	AS004 Organizing descriptive information	AS004
	AS005 Preparing an assessment and case formulation	AS005
Contracting Skills (CN)	CN001 Establishing goals	CN001
	CN002 Developing action plans	CN002
	CN003 Identifying action steps	CN003
	CN004 Planning for evaluation	CN004
	CN005 Summarizing the contract	CN005
Working and Evaluating Skills (WE)	WE001 Rehearsing action steps	WE001
	WE002 Reviewing action steps	WE002
	WE003 Evaluating	WE003
	WE004 Focusing	WE004
	WE005 Educating	WE005
	WE006 Advising	WE006
	WE007 Responding with immediacy	WE007
	WE008 Reframing	WE008
	WE009 Observing inconsistencies	WE009
	WE010 Representing	WE010
	WE011 Linking	WE011
	WE012 Pointing out endings	WE012
	WE013 Recording progress (documenting)	WE013
Ending Skills (EN)	EN001 Reviewing the process	EN001
	EN002 Final evaluating	EN002
	EN003 Sharing ending feelings and saying good-bye	EN003
	EN004 Recording the closing summary	EN004

Table of Social Work Skills Supporting the EPAS Competencies

The following table illustrates the relationships of the social work skills to the 43 knowledge and value dimensions (KVs) and the 31 practice behaviors (PBs) subsumed within the nine EPAS competencies (C) identified in the Educational Policies and Accreditation Standards (EPAS) of the Council on Social Work Education (CSWE) (2015). Each social work skill supports aspects of the knowledge and values, or the practice behaviors associated with one or more competencies.

Social Work Skills Supporting the 9 EPAS Competencies, the 43 Knowledge and Value Descriptors, and the 31 Practice Behaviors

EPAS Competencies KVs and PBs	The Social Work Skills
Competency 1: Demonstrate Ethical and Professional Behavior	**Chapter 2: Professionalism; Chapter 3: Critical Thinking, Scientific Inquiry, and Lifelong Learning; Chapter 5: Social Work Values and Ethical Decision Making; Chapter 6: Talking and Listening; Chapter 7: Preparing**
KV1.a: Social workers understand the value base of the profession and its ethical standards, as well as relevant laws and regulations that may impact practice at the micro, mezzo, and macro levels.	PF001 Demonstrating integrity
KV1.b: Social workers understand frameworks of ethical decision-making and how to apply principles of critical thinking to those frameworks in practice, research, and policy arenas.	PF002 Applying knowledge, expertise, and self-efficacy
	PF003 Demonstrating self-understanding and self-control
	PF008 Thinking critically and inquiring scientifically
KV1.c: Social workers recognize personal values and the distinction between personal and professional values.	PF009 Engaging in lifelong learning
	ED001 Recognizing legal duties
KV1.d: They also understand how their personal experiences and affective reactions influence their professional judgment and behavior.	ED002 Applying the fundamental social work values and ethics
	ED003 Identifying ethical and legal implications
KV1.e: Social workers understand the profession's history, its mission, and the roles and responsibilities of the profession.	ED004 Addressing ethical dilemmas
	TL001 Accessing a place of peace
KV1.f: Social workers also understand the role of other professions when engaged in inter-professional teams.	TL002 Engaging diversity and difference with cultural sensitivity
	TL003 Communicating nonverbally (attending)
KV1.g: Social workers recognize the importance of life-long learning and are committed to continually updating their skills to ensure they are relevant and effective.	TL004 Talking: Communicating verbally and in writing
	TL005 Listening: Hearing, observing, encouraging, and remembering
KV1.h: Social workers also understand emerging forms of technology and the ethical use of technology in social work practice.	TL006 Active listening: Combining talking and listening
PB1.a: Make ethical decisions by applying the standards of the NASW Code of Ethics, relevant laws and regulations, models for ethical decision-making, ethical conduct of research, and additional codes of ethics as appropriate to context;	PR003 Preparatory consultation
	PR006 Preparatory self-exploration
PB1.b: Use reflection and self-regulation to manage personal values and maintain professionalism in practice situations;	PR007 Centering
PB1.c: Demonstrate professional demeanor in behavior; appearance; and oral, written, and electronic communication;	
PB1.d: Use technology ethically and appropriately to facilitate practice outcomes; and	
PB1.e: Use supervision and consultation to guide professional judgment and behavior.	

(Continued)

EPAS Competencies KVs and PBs	The Social Work Skills
Competency 2: Engage Diversity and Difference in Practice	**Chapter 2: Professionalism; Chapter 4: Diversity and Difference; Chapter 6: Talking and Listening; Chapter 7: Preparing; Chapter 8: Beginning; Chapter 9: Exploring**
KV2.a: Social workers understand how diversity and difference characterize and shape the human experience and are critical to the formation of identity. The dimensions of diversity are understood as the intersectionality of multiple factors including but not limited to age, class, color, culture, disability and ability, ethnicity, gender, gender identity and expression, immigration status, marital status, political ideology, race, religion/spirituality, sex, sexual orientation, and tribal sovereign status. KV2.b: Social workers understand that, as a consequence of difference, a person's life experiences may include oppression, poverty, marginalization, and alienation as well as privilege, power, and acclaim. KV2.c: Social workers also understand the forms and mechanisms of oppression and discrimination and recognize the extent to which a culture's structures and values, including social, economic, political, and cultural exclusions, may oppress, marginalize, alienate, or create privilege and power. PB2.a: Apply and communicate understanding of the importance of diversity and difference in shaping life experiences in practice at the micro, mezzo, and macro levels; PB2.b: Present themselves as learners and engage clients and constituencies as experts of their own experiences; and PB2.c: Apply self-awareness and self-regulation to manage the influence of personal biases and values in working with diverse clients and constituencies.	PF001 Demonstrating integrity PF002 Applying knowledge, expertise, and self-efficacy PF003 Demonstrating self-understanding and self-control PF004 Demonstrating empathy PF005 Demonstrating respect PF006 Demonstrating authenticity PF010 Valuing diversity and difference PF011 Accepting others and respecting autonomy TL001 Accessing a place of peace TL002 Engaging diversity and difference with cultural sensitivity TL004 Talking: Communicating verbally and in writing TL005 Listening: Hearing, observing, encouraging, and remembering PR002 Preparatory exploring PR006 Preparatory self-exploration PR007 Centering BG006 Seeking feedback EX008 Reflecting issues EX009 Reflecting hypotheses
Competency 3: Advance Human Rights and Social, Economic, and Environmental Justice	**Chapter 2: Professionalism; Chapter 4: Diversity and Difference; Chapter 6: Talking and Listening; Chapter 7: Preparing; Chapter 12: Working and Evaluating**
KV3.a: Social workers understand that every person regardless of position in society has fundamental human rights such as freedom, safety, privacy, an adequate standard of living, health care, and education. KV3.b: Social workers understand the global interconnections of oppression and human rights violations, and are knowledgeable about theories of human need and social justice and strategies to promote social and economic justice and human rights.	PF002 Applying knowledge, expertise, and self-efficacy PF010 Valuing diversity and difference PF011 Accepting others and respecting autonomy PF012 Advancing human rights and social well-being PF013 Promoting social, economic, and environmental justice PF014 Engaging in policy–practice TL002 Engaging diversity and difference with cultural sensitivity WE010 Representing WE011 Linking

KV3.c: Social workers understand strategies designed to eliminate oppressive structural barriers to ensure that social goods, rights, and responsibilities are distributed equitably and that civil, political, environmental, economic, social, and cultural human rights are protected. PB3.a: Apply their understanding of social, economic, and environmental justice to advocate for human rights at the individual and system levels; and PB3.b: Engage in practices that advance social, economic, and environmental justice.	
Competency 4: Engage in Practice-Informed Research and Research-Informed Practice KV4.a: Social workers understand quantitative and qualitative research methods and their respective roles in advancing a science of social work and in evaluating their practice. KV4.b: Social workers know the principles of logic, scientific inquiry, and culturally informed and ethical approaches to building knowledge. KV4.c: Social workers understand that evidence that informs practice derives from multi-disciplinary sources and multiple ways of knowing. KV4.d: They also understand the processes for translating research findings into effective practice. PB4.a: Use practice experience and theory to inform scientific inquiry and research; PB4.b: Apply critical thinking to engage in analysis of quantitative and qualitative research methods and research findings; and PB4.c: Use and translate research evidence to inform and improve practice, policy, and service delivery.	**Chapter 2: Professionalism; Chapter 3: Critical Thinking, Scientific Inquiry, and Lifelong Learning; Chapter 4: Diversity and Difference; Chapter 5: Social Work Values and Ethical Decision Making; Chapter 7: Preparing; Chapter 10: Assessing; Chapter 11: Contracting; Chapter 12: Working and Evaluating; Chapter 13: Ending** PF002 Applying knowledge, expertise, and self-efficacy PF008 Thinking critically and inquiring scientifically PF009 Engaging in lifelong learning PF010 Valuing diversity and difference ED002 Applying the fundamental social work values and ethics ED003 Identifying ethical and legal implications PR002 Preparatory exploring AS001 Identifying issues AS002 Sharing hypotheses AS005 Preparing an assessment and case formulation CN004 Planning for evaluation WE003 Evaluating EN002 Final evaluating

(Continued)

EPAS Competencies KVs and PBs	The Social Work Skills
Competency 5: Engage in Policy Practice	**Chapter 2: Professionalism; Chapter 3: Critical Thinking, Scientific Inquiry, and Lifelong Learning; Chapter 4: Diversity and Difference; Chapter 7: Preparing; Chapter 10: Assessing; Chapter 11: Contracting; Chapter 12: Working and Evaluating; Chapter 13: Ending**
KV5.a: Social workers understand that human rights and social justice, as well as social welfare and services, are mediated by policy and its implementation at the federal, state, and local levels.	PF002 Applying knowledge, expertise, and self-efficacy
KV5.b: Social workers understand the history and current structures of social policies and services, the role of policy in service delivery, and the role of practice in policy development.	PF008 Thinking critically and inquiring scientifically
	PF010 Valuing diversity and difference
	PF012 Advancing human rights and social well-being
	PF013 Promoting social, economic, and environmental justice
KV5.c: Social workers understand their role in policy development and implementation within their practice settings at the micro, mezzo, and macro levels and they actively engage in policy practice to effect change within those settings.	PF014 Engaging in policy–practice
	PR002 Preparatory exploring
	AS005 Preparing an assessment and case formulation
KV5.d: Social workers recognize and understand the historical, social, cultural, economic, organizational, environmental, and global influences that affect social policy.	CN001 Establishing goals
	CN002 Developing action plans
KV5.e: They are also knowledgeable about policy formulation, analysis, implementation, and evaluation.	CN003 Identifying action steps
	CN004 Planning for evaluation
PB5.a: Identify social policy at the local, state, and federal level that impacts well-being, service delivery, and access to social services;	WE001 Rehearsing action steps
	WE002 Reviewing action steps
PB5.b: Assess how social welfare and economic policies impact the delivery of and access to social services;	WE003 Evaluating
	WE005 Educating
	WE006 Advising
PB5.c: Apply critical thinking to analyze, formulate, and advocate for policies that advance human rights and social, economic, and environmental justice.	WE009 Observing inconsistencies
	WE010 Representing
	WE011 Linking
	EN002 Final evaluating

Competency 6: Engage with Individuals, Families, Groups, Organizations, and Communities	Chapter 2: Professionalism; Chapter 3: Critical Thinking, Scientific Inquiry, and Lifelong Learning; Chapter 4: Diversity and Difference; Chapter 5: Social Work Values and Ethical Decision Making; Chapter 6: Talking and Listening; Chapter 7: Preparing; Chapter 8: Beginning; Chapter 9: Exploring; Chapter 12: Working and Evaluating
KV6.a: Social workers understand that engagement is an ongoing component of the dynamic and interactive process of social work practice with, and on behalf of, diverse individuals, families, groups, organizations, and communities.	PF001 Demonstrating integrity
	PF002 Applying knowledge, expertise, and self-efficacy
	PF003 Demonstrating self-understanding and self-control
KV6.b: Social workers value the importance of human relationships.	PF004 Demonstrating empathy
	PF005 Demonstrating respect
KV6.c: Social workers understand theories of human behavior and the social environment, and critically evaluate and apply this knowledge to facilitate engagement with clients and constituencies, including individuals, families, groups, organizations, and communities.	PF006 Demonstrating authenticity
	PF007 Giving and receiving social support
	PF008 Thinking critically and inquiring scientifically
	PF009 Engaging in lifelong learning
KV6.d: Social workers understand strategies to engage diverse clients and constituencies to advance practice effectiveness.	PF010 Valuing diversity and difference
	ED002 Applying fundamental social work values and ethics
KV6.e: Social workers understand how their personal experiences and affective reactions may impact their ability to effectively engage with diverse clients and constituencies.	TL001 Accessing a place of peace
	TL002 Engaging diversity and difference with cultural sensitivity
	TL003 Communicating nonverbally (attending)
KV6.f: Social workers value principles of relationship-building and inter-professional collaboration to facilitate engagement with clients, constituencies, and other professionals as appropriate.	TL004 Talking: Communicating verbally and in writing
	TL005 Listening: Hearing, observing, encouraging, and remembering
	TL006 Active listening: Combining talking and listening
PB6.a: Apply knowledge of human behavior and the social environment, person-in-environment, and other multidisciplinary theoretical frameworks to engage with clients and constituencies; and	PR002 Preparatory exploring
	PR003 Preparatory consultation
	PR005 Preparatory empathy
PB6.b: Use empathy, reflection, and interpersonal skills to effectively engage diverse clients and constituencies.	PR006 Preparatory self-exploration
	PR007 Centering
	BG001 Introducing yourself
	BG002 Seeking introductions
	BG003 Describing initial purpose
	BG004 Orienting
	BG005 Discussing policy and ethical factors
	BG006 Seeking feedback

(Continued)

EPAS Competencies KVs and PBs	The Social Work Skills
Competency 6: Engage with Individuals, Families, Groups, Organizations, and Communities	**Chapter 2: Professionalism; Chapter 3: Critical Thinking, Scientific Inquiry, and Lifelong Learning; Chapter 4: Diversity and Difference; Chapter 5: Social Work Values and Ethical Decision Making; Chapter 6: Talking and Listening; Chapter 7: Preparing; Chapter 8: Beginning; Chapter 9: Exploring; Chapter 12: Working and Evaluating** EX001 Asking questions EX002 Seeking clarification EX003 Reflecting content EX004 Reflecting feelings EX005 Reflecting feelings and meaning EX006 Partializing EX007 Going beyond what is said EX008 Reflecting issues EX009 Reflecting hypotheses WE011 Linking
Competency 7: Assess Individuals, Families, Groups, Organizations, and Communities KV7.a: Social workers understand that assessment is an ongoing component of the dynamic and interactive process of social work practice with, and on behalf of, diverse individuals, families, groups, organizations, and communities. KV7.b: Social workers understand theories of human behavior and the social environment, and critically evaluate and apply this knowledge in the assessment of diverse clients and constituencies, including individuals, families, groups, organizations, and communities. KV7.c: Social workers understand methods of assessment with diverse clients and constituencies to advance practice effectiveness. KV7.d: Social workers recognize the implications of the larger practice context in the assessment process and value the importance of inter-professional collaboration in this process. KV7.e: Social workers understand how their personal experiences and affective reactions may affect their assessment and decision-making.	**Chapter 2: Professionalism; Chapter 3: Critical Thinking, Scientific Inquiry, and Lifelong Learning; Chapter 4: Diversity and Difference; Chapter 6: Talking and Listening; Chapter 7: Preparing; Chapter 9: Exploring; Chapter 10: Assessing; Chapter 11: Contracting** PF001 Demonstrating integrity PF002 Applying knowledge, expertise, and self-efficacy PF003 Demonstrating self-understanding and self-control PF008 Thinking critically and inquiring scientifically PF009 Engaging in lifelong learning PF010 Valuing diversity and difference PF011 Accepting others and respecting autonomy PF012 Advancing human rights and social well-being PF013 Promoting social, economic, and environmental justice PF014 Engaging in policy–practice TL001 Accessing a place of peace TL002 Engaging diversity and difference with cultural sensitivity PR006 Preparatory self-exploration

PB7.a: Collect and organize data, and apply critical thinking to interpret information from clients and constituencies; PB7.b: Apply knowledge of human behavior and the social environment, person-in-environment, and other multidisciplinary theoretical frameworks in the analysis of assessment data from clients and constituencies; PB7.c: Develop mutually agreed-on intervention goals and objectives based on the critical assessment of strengths, needs, and challenges within clients and constituencies; and PB7.d: Select appropriate intervention strategies based on the assessment, research knowledge, and values and preferences of clients and constituencies.	PR007 Centering BG006 Seeking feedback EX001 Asking questions EX002 Seeking clarification EX003 Reflecting content EX004 Reflecting feelings EX005 Reflecting feelings and meaning EX006 Partializing EX007 Going beyond what is said EX008 Reflecting issues EX009 Reflecting hypotheses AS001 Identifying issues AS002 Sharing hypotheses AS003 Confirming issues AS004 Organizing descriptive information AS005 Preparing an assessment and case formulation CN001 Establishing goals CN002 Developing action plans CN003 Identifying action steps CN004 Planning for evaluation **Chapter 2: Professionalism; Chapter 3: Critical Thinking, Scientific Inquiry, and Lifelong Learning; Chapter 4: Diversity and Difference; Chapter 6: Talking and Listening; Chapter 7: Preparing; Chapter 10: Assessing; Chapter 11: Contracting; Chapter 12: Working and Evaluating; Chapter 13: Ending**
Competency 8: Intervene with Individuals, Families, Groups, Organizations, and Communities	
KV8.a: Social workers understand that intervention is an ongoing component of the dynamic and interactive process of social work practice with, and on behalf of, diverse individuals, families, groups, organizations, and communities. KV8.b: Social workers are knowledgeable about evidence-informed interventions to achieve the goals of clients and constituencies, including individuals, families, groups, organizations, and communities. KV8.c: Social workers understand theories of human behavior and the social environment, and critically evaluate and apply this knowledge to effectively intervene with clients and constituencies.	PF002 Applying knowledge, expertise, and self-efficacy PF008 Thinking critically and inquiring scientifically PF009 Engaging in lifelong learning PF010 Valuing diversity and difference TL001 Accessing a place of peace TL002 Engaging diversity and difference with cultural sensitivity TL003 Communicating nonverbally (attending) TL004 Talking: Communicating verbally and in writing

(Continued)

EPAS Competencies KVs and PBs	The Social Work Skills
Competency 8: Intervene with Individuals, Families, Groups, Organizations, and Communities	**Chapter 2: Professionalism; Chapter 3: Critical Thinking, Scientific Inquiry, and Lifelong Learning; Chapter 4: Diversity and Difference; Chapter 6: Talking and Listening; Chapter 7: Preparing; Chapter 11: Contracting; Chapter 12: Working and Evaluating; Chapter 13: Ending**
KV8.d: Social workers understand methods of identifying, analyzing and implementing evidence-informed interventions to achieve client and constituency goals.	TL005 Listening: Hearing, observing, encouraging, and remembering
KV8.e: Social workers value the importance of inter-professional teamwork and communication in interventions, recognizing that beneficial outcomes may require interdisciplinary, inter-professional, and inter-organizational collaboration.	TL006 Active listening: Combining talking and listening
	PR003 Preparatory consultation
	AS005 Preparing an assessment and case formulation
PB8.a: Critically choose and implement interventions to achieve practice goals and enhance capacities of clients and constituencies;	CN001 Establishing goals
	CN002 Developing action plans
	CN003 Identifying action steps
PB8.b: Apply knowledge of human behavior and the social environment, person-in-environment, and other multidisciplinary theoretical frameworks in interventions with clients and constituencies;	CN004 Planning for evaluation
	CN005 Summarizing the contract
	WE001 Rehearsing action steps
	WE002 Reviewing action steps
PB8.c: Use inter-professional collaboration as appropriate to achieve beneficial practice outcomes;	WE003 Evaluating
	WE004 Focusing
	WE005 Educating
PB8.d: Negotiate, mediate, and advocate with and on behalf of diverse clients and constituencies; and	WE006 Advising
	WE007 Responding with immediacy
	WE008 Reframing
PB8.e: Facilitate effective transitions and endings that advance mutually agreed-on goals.	WE009 Observing inconsistencies
	WE010 Representing
	WE011 Linking
	WE012 Pointing out endings
	WE013 Recording progress (documenting)
	ED002 Applying fundamental social work values and ethics
	EN001 Reviewing the process
	EN002 Final evaluating
	EN003 Sharing ending feelings and saying good-bye
	EN004 Recording the closing summary

Competency 9: Evaluate Practice with Individuals, Families, Groups, Organizations, and Communities	Chapter 2: Professionalism; Chapter 3: Critical Thinking, Scientific Inquiry, and Lifelong Learning; Chapter 4: Diversity and Difference; Chapter 6: Talking and Listening; Chapter 7: Preparing; Chapter 8: Beginning; Chapter 11: Contracting; Chapter 12: Working and Evaluating; Chapter 13: Ending
KV9.a: Social workers understand that evaluation is an ongoing component of the dynamic and interactive process of social work practice with, and on behalf of, diverse individuals, families, groups, organizations and communities. KV9.b: Social workers recognize the importance of evaluating processes and outcomes to advance practice, policy, and service delivery effectiveness. KV9.c: Social workers understand theories of human behavior and the social environment, and critically evaluate and apply this knowledge in evaluating outcomes. KV9.d: Social workers understand qualitative and quantitative methods for evaluating outcomes and practice effectiveness. PB9.a: Select and use appropriate methods for evaluation of outcomes PB9.b: Apply knowledge of human behavior and the social environment, person-in-environment, and other multidisciplinary theoretical frameworks in the evaluation of outcomes; PB9.c: Critically analyze, monitor, and evaluate intervention and program processes and outcomes; and PB9.d: Apply evaluation findings to improve practice effectiveness at the micro, mezzo, and macro levels.	PF002 Applying knowledge, expertise, and self-efficacy PF008 Thinking critically and inquiring scientifically PF009 Engaging in lifelong learning PF010 Valuing diversity and difference PF014 Engaging in policy–practice TL002 Engaging diversity and difference with cultural sensitivity BG006 Seeking feedback CN001 Establishing goals CN004 Planning for evaluation WE002 Reviewing action steps WE003 Evaluating WE005 Educating WE010 Representing WE011 Linking WE013 Recording progress (documenting) EN001 Reviewing the process EN002 Final evaluating

Self-Appraisal of Proficiency: EPAS Competency-Based Knowledge and Values, and Practice Behaviors

Derived from the Educational Policy and Accreditation Standards (EPAS) of the Council on Social Work Education (CSWE) (2015), this instrument helps you estimate your proficiency in the competency-based knowledge, values, and practice behaviors currently required of social work graduates of accredited educational programs. These items are extracted directly from the descriptions that elaborate the nine current EPAS competencies:

1. Demonstrate Ethical and Professional Behavior
2. Engage Diversity and Difference in Practice
3. Advance Human Rights and Social, Economic, and Environmental Justice
4. Engage in Practice-Informed Research and Research-Informed Practice
5. Engage in Policy–Practice
6. Engage with Individuals, Families, Groups, Organizations, and Communities
7. Assess Individuals, Families, Groups, Organizations, and Communities
8. Intervene with Individuals, Families, Groups, Organizations, and Communities
9. Evaluate Practice with Individuals, Families, Groups, Organizations, and Communities

Subsumed within each of the competencies are descriptions of the specific knowledge and values as well as lists of the particular practice behaviors needed to apply them in practice. We have extracted 43 knowledge and value components (KV1.a through KV9.d)[1] and 31 practice behaviors (PB1.a through PB9.d) and combined them into a 74-item self-appraisal instrument.

---

[1] For identification purposes, we have identified the knowledge and value items (KV) and the practice behavior items (PB) according to the competencies they support. For example, KV1.a refers to the first knowledge and value descriptor in Competency 1, and KV7.c refers to the third KV within Competency 7. Similarly, PB2.b refers to the second practice behavior within Competency 2, and PB8.d refers to the fourth PB within Competency 8.

■ Self-Appraisal of Proficiency: EPAS Competency-Based Knowledge, Values, and Practice Behaviors

Read each item[2] carefully. Then, use the following 4-point rating scale to indicate the degree to which you agree or disagree with each statement. Mark a check in the box below the number that best reflections your opinion.

4 = Strongly Agree   2 = Disagree   3 = Agree   1 = Strongly Disagree

Self-Appraisal of Proficiency: EPAS Competency-based Knowledge, Values, and Practice Behaviors					
				EPAS Knowledge and Values	
4	**3**	**2**	**1**		**Rating Statement**
					At this point in time, I
☐	☐	☐	☐	KV1.a	1. Understand the value base of the profession and its ethical standards, as well as relevant laws and regulations that may impact practice at the micro, mezzo, and macro levels.
☐	☐	☐	☐	KV1.b	2. Understand frameworks of ethical decision-making and how to apply principles of critical thinking to those frameworks in practice, research, and policy arenas.
☐	☐	☐	☐	KV1.c	3. Recognize personal values and the distinction between personal and professional values.
☐	☐	☐	☐	KV1.d	4. Understand how my personal experiences and affective reactions influence my professional judgment and behavior.
☐	☐	☐	☐	KV1.e	5. Understand the profession's history, its mission, and the roles and responsibilities of the profession.
☐	☐	☐	☐	KV1.f	6. Understand the role of other professions when engaged in inter-professional teams.
☐	☐	☐	☐	KV1.g	7. Recognize the importance of life-long learning and am committed to continually updating my skills to ensure I am relevant and effective.
☐	☐	☐	☐	KV1.h	8. Understand emerging forms of technology and the ethical use of technology in social work practice.
☐	☐	☐	☐	KV2.a	9. Understand how diversity and difference characterize and shape the human experience and are critical to the formation of identity. I also understand the dimensions of diversity as the intersectionality of multiple factors including but not limited to age, class, color, culture, disability and ability, ethnicity, gender, gender identity and expression, immigration status, marital status, political ideology, race, religion/spirituality, sex, sexual orientation, and tribal sovereign status.
☐	☐	☐	☐	KV2.b	10. Understand that, as a consequence of difference, a person's life experiences may include oppression, poverty, marginalization, and alienation as well as privilege, power, and acclaim.
☐	☐	☐	☐	KV2.c	11. Understand the forms and mechanisms of oppression and discrimination and recognize the extent to which a culture's structures and values, including social, economic, political, and cultural exclusions, may oppress, marginalize, alienate, or create privilege and power.

---

[2] Items adapted from the Council on Social Work Education's "Educational Policy and Accreditation Standards" (Council on Social Work Education, 2015) available at **www.cswe.org**.

Self-Appraisal of Proficiency: EPAS Competency-based Knowledge, Values, and Practice Behaviors					
					EPAS Knowledge and Values
4	3	2	1		Rating Statement
☐	☐	☐	☐	KV3.a	12. Understand that every person regardless of position in society has fundamental human rights such as freedom, safety, privacy, an adequate standard of living, health care, and education.
☐	☐	☐	☐	KV3.b	13. Understand the global interconnections of oppression and human rights violations, and am knowledgeable about theories of human need and social justice and strategies to promote social and economic justice and human rights.
☐	☐	☐	☐	KV3.c	14. Understand strategies designed to eliminate oppressive structural barriers to ensure that social goods, rights, and responsibilities are distributed equitably and that civil, political, environmental, economic, social, and cultural human rights are protected.
☐	☐	☐	☐	KV4.a	15. Understand quantitative and qualitative research methods and their respective roles in advancing a science of social work and in evaluating my practice.
☐	☐	☐	☐	KV4.b	16. Know the principles of logic, scientific inquiry, and culturally informed and ethical approaches to building knowledge.
☐	☐	☐	☐	KV4.c	17. Understand that evidence that informs practice derives from multi-disciplinary sources and multiple ways of knowing.
☐	☐	☐	☐	KV4.d	18. Understand the processes for translating research findings into effective practice.
☐	☐	☐	☐	KV5.a	19. Understand that human rights and social justice, as well as social welfare and services, are mediated by policy and its implementation at the federal, state, and local levels.
☐	☐	☐	☐	KV5.b	20. Understand the history and current structures of social policies and services, the role of policy in service delivery, and the role of practice in policy development.
☐	☐	☐	☐	KV5.c	21. Understand my role in policy development and implementation within my practice settings at the micro, mezzo, and macro levels; and actively engage in policy–practice to effect change within those settings.
☐	☐	☐	☐	KV5.d	22. Recognize and understand the historical, social, cultural, economic, organizational, environmental, and global influences that affect social policy.
☐	☐	☐	☐	KV5.e	23. Know about policy formulation, analysis, implementation, and evaluation.
☐	☐	☐	☐	KV6.a	24. Understand that engagement is an ongoing component of the dynamic and interactive process of social work practice with, and on behalf of, diverse individuals, families, groups, organizations, and communities.
☐	☐	☐	☐	KV6.b	25. Value the importance of human relationships.
☐	☐	☐	☐	KV6.c	26. Understand theories of human behavior and the social environment, and critically evaluate and apply this knowledge to facilitate engagement with clients and constituencies, including individuals, families, groups, organizations, and communities.

4	3	2	1		Rating Statement
☐	☐	☐	☐	KV6.d	27. Understand strategies to engage diverse clients and constituencies to advance practice effectiveness.
☐	☐	☐	☐	KV6.e	28. Understand how my personal experiences and affective reactions may impact my ability to effectively engage with diverse clients and constituencies.
☐	☐	☐	☐	KV6.f	29. Value principles of relationship-building and inter-professional collaboration to facilitate engagement with clients, constituencies, and other professionals as appropriate.
☐	☐	☐	☐	KV7.a	30. Understand that assessment is an ongoing component of the dynamic and interactive process of social work practice with, and on behalf of, diverse individuals, families, groups, organizations, and communities.
☐	☐	☐	☐	KV7.b	31. Understand theories of human behavior and the social environment, and critically evaluate and apply this knowledge in the assessment of diverse clients and constituencies, including individuals, families, groups, organizations, and communities.
☐	☐	☐	☐	KV7.c	32. Understand methods of assessment with diverse clients and constituencies to advance practice effectiveness.
☐	☐	☐	☐	KV7.d	33. Recognize the implications of the larger practice context in the assessment process and value the importance of inter-professional collaboration in this process.
☐	☐	☐	☐	KV7.e	34. Understand how my personal experiences and affective reactions may affect my assessment and decision-making.
☐	☐	☐	☐	KV8.a	35. Understand that intervention is an ongoing component of the dynamic and interactive process of social work practice with, and on behalf of, diverse individuals, families, groups, organizations, and communities.
☐	☐	☐	☐	KV8.b	36. Know about evidence-informed interventions to achieve the goals of clients and constituencies, including individuals, families, groups, organizations, and communities.
☐	☐	☐	☐	KV8.c	37. Understand theories of human behavior and the social environment, and critically evaluate and apply this knowledge to effectively intervene with clients and constituencies.
☐	☐	☐	☐	KV8.d	38. Understand methods of identifying, analyzing and implementing evidence-informed interventions to achieve client and constituency goals.
☐	☐	☐	☐	KV8.e	39. Value the importance of inter-professional teamwork and communication in interventions, recognizing that beneficial outcomes may require interdisciplinary, inter-professional, and inter-organizational collaboration.
☐	☐	☐	☐	KV9.a	40. Understand that evaluation is an ongoing component of the dynamic and interactive process of social work practice with, and on behalf of, diverse individuals, families, groups, organizations and communities.
☐	☐	☐	☐	KV9.b	41. Recognize the importance of evaluating processes and outcomes to advance practice, policy, and service delivery effectiveness.

					Self-Appraisal of Proficiency: EPAS Competency-based Knowledge, Values, and Practice Behaviors
					EPAS Knowledge and Values
4	**3**	**2**	**1**		**Rating Statement**
☐	☐	☐	☐	KV9.c	42 Understand theories of human behavior and the social environment, and critically evaluate and apply this knowledge in evaluating outcomes.
☐	☐	☐	☐	KV9.d	43. Understand qualitative and quantitative methods for evaluating outcomes and practice effectiveness.
					Subtotal EPAS Knowledge and Values
					EPAS Practice Behaviors
4	**3**	**2**	**1**		**Rating Statement**
					At this point in time, I can or do
☐	☐	☐	☐	PB1.a.	1. Make ethical decisions by applying the standards of the NASW Code of Ethics, relevant laws and regulations, models for ethical decision-making, ethical conduct of research, and additional codes of ethics as appropriate to context;
☐	☐	☐	☐	PB1.b.	2. Use reflection and self-regulation to manage my personal values and maintain professionalism in practice situations;
☐	☐	☐	☐	PB1.c.	3. Demonstrate professional demeanor in my behavior, appearance, and oral, written, and electronic communication;
☐	☐	☐	☐	PB1.d.	4. Use technology ethically and appropriately to facilitate practice outcomes; and
☐	☐	☐	☐	PB1.e.	5. Use supervision and consultation to guide my professional judgment and behavior.
☐	☐	☐	☐	PB2.a.	6. Apply and communicate understanding of the importance of diversity and difference in shaping life experiences in practice at the micro, mezzo, and macro levels;
☐	☐	☐	☐	PB2.b.	7. Present myself as a learner and engage clients and constituencies as experts of their own experiences; and
☐	☐	☐	☐	PB2.c.	8. Apply self-awareness and self-regulation to manage the influence of my personal biases and values in working with diverse clients and constituencies.
☐	☐	☐	☐	PB3.a.	9. Apply my understanding of social, economic, and environmental justice to advocate for human rights at the individual and system levels; and
☐	☐	☐	☐	PB3.b.	10. Engage in practices that advance social, economic, and environmental justice.
☐	☐	☐	☐	PB4.a.	11. Use practice experience and theory to inform scientific inquiry and research;
☐	☐	☐	☐	PB4.b.	12. Apply critical thinking to engage in analysis of quantitative and qualitative research methods and research findings; and
☐	☐	☐	☐	PB4.c.	13. Use and translate research evidence to inform and improve practice, policy, and service delivery.
☐	☐	☐	☐	PB5.a.	14. Identify social policy at the local, state, and federal level that impacts well-being, service delivery, and access to social services;

4	3	2	1		Rating Statement
☐	☐	☐	☐	PB5.b.	15. Assess how social welfare and economic policies impact the delivery of and access to social services;
☐	☐	☐	☐	PB5.c.	16. Apply critical thinking to analyze, formulate, and advocate for policies that advance human rights and social, economic, and environmental justice.
☐	☐	☐	☐	PB6.a.	17. Apply knowledge of human behavior and the social environment, person-in-environment, and other multidisciplinary theoretical frameworks to engage with clients and constituencies; and
☐	☐	☐	☐	PB6.b.	18. Use empathy, reflection, and interpersonal skills to effectively engage diverse clients and constituencies.
☐	☐	☐	☐	PB7.a.	19. Collect and organize data, and apply critical thinking to interpret information from clients and constituencies;
☐	☐	☐	☐	PB7.b.	20. Apply knowledge of human behavior and the social environment, person-in-environment, and other multidisciplinary theoretical frameworks in the analysis of assessment data from clients and constituencies;
☐	☐	☐	☐	PB7.c.	21. Develop mutually agreed-on intervention goals and objectives based on the critical assessment of strengths, needs, and challenges within clients and constituencies; and
☐	☐	☐	☐	PB7.d.	22. Select appropriate intervention strategies based on the assessment, research knowledge, and values and preferences of clients and constituencies.
☐	☐	☐	☐	PB8.a.	23. Critically choose and implement interventions to achieve practice goals and enhance capacities of clients and constituencies;
☐	☐	☐	☐	PB8.b.	24. Apply knowledge of human behavior and the social environment, person-in-environment, and other multidisciplinary theoretical frameworks in interventions with clients and constituencies;
☐	☐	☐	☐	PB8.c.	25. Use inter-professional collaboration as appropriate to achieve beneficial practice outcomes;
☐	☐	☐	☐	PB8.d.	26. Negotiate, mediate, and advocate with and on behalf of diverse clients and constituencies; and
☐	☐	☐	☐	PB8.e.	27. Facilitate effective transitions and endings that advance mutually agreed-on goals.
☐	☐	☐	☐	PB9.a.	28. Select and use appropriate methods for evaluation of outcomes;
☐	☐	☐	☐	PB9.b.	29. Apply knowledge of human behavior and the social environment, person-in-environment, and other multidisciplinary theoretical frameworks in the evaluation of outcomes;
☐	☐	☐	☐	PB9.c.	30. Critically analyze, monitor, and evaluate intervention and program processes and outcomes; and
☐	☐	☐	☐	PB9.d.	31. Apply evaluation findings to improve practice effectiveness at the micro, mezzo, and macro levels.
					Subtotal EPAS Practice Behaviors
					Total

To score the Self-Appraisal of Proficiency in the EPAS Competencies instrument, simply sum your ratings to the 43 items in the knowledge and values section. Your raw score should range somewhere between 43 and 172. In theory, a raw score of 129 (or an average of 3 on each of the 43 items) would indicate that, on average, you "agree" with the statements concerning your current proficiency in the EPAS knowledge and values. You may divide your score by 43 to obtain your item average. Next, sum your ratings to the 31 items in the practice behaviors section. Your raw score should range somewhere between 31 and 124. In theory, a score of 93 (or an average of 3 on each of the 31 items) would indicate that, on average, you "agree" with the statements concerning your current proficiency in the EPAS practice behaviors. You may divide your score by 31 to obtain your item average on that section of the instrument.

Together, the two portions of the instrument contain 74 items. When you combine your raw scores on the knowledge and values section with your raw score on the practice behavior section, your total should range between 74 and 296. A score of 222 (or an average of 3 on each of the 74 items) would indicate that, on average, you "agree" with the statements concerning your current proficiency in the EPAS. Divide your raw score by 74 to obtain your overall item average.

Please note, however, that raw scores at or above 129 on the knowledge and values portion, at or above 93 on the practice behaviors section, or 222 or above in both sections combined, does not necessarily mean that you consider yourself proficient in all dimensions. You might obtain such scores by rating several items at the "4" or "strongly agree" level and an equal number at the "2" or "disagree level." Therefore, look carefully at your rating for each item, as well as your raw scores. Find those knowledge and value areas, and practice behaviors that require additional study or practice.

Because the instrument is based on your own judgment about your current level of knowledge and skill, total scores and average item ratings are relatively unimportant. The best use of the instrument is as a stimulus for learning. Review the items and critically question yourself concerning your proficiency and then develop plans to improve. You might even complete the instrument at various points over several years. Increased proficiency may be reflected in changing scores over time. In considering your results, please remember that higher raw scores and higher average item rating suggest a greater level of appraised proficiency.

A useful tool for appraising your own proficiency and stimulating personal learning, it can also be used for course or programmatic purposes. For example, if all learners in your course or program anonymously shared their item ratings and total scores with a professor or program administrator, responses can be aggregated. When analyzed, they may reveal areas where students believe they are quite proficient as well as those they think require additional study or practice. When pre- and post-item raw scores and average item ratings of student cohorts are available for analysis, teachers can use findings to guide and promote learning.

Self-Appraisal of Proficiency in the ASWB Knowledge, Skills, and Abilities (Bachelor's Level)

APPENDIX 14

Derived from the content addressed in the bachelor's level licensing examination of the Association of Social Work Boards (ASWB) (2011), this self-appraisal instrument helps you do an estimate of your self-appraised proficiency in the knowledge, skills, and abilities currently reflected in social work practice. Read each item[1] carefully. Then, use the following 4-point rating scale to indicate the degree to which you agree or disagree with each statement. Mark a check in the box below the number that best reflections your opinion.

4 = Strongly Agree   3 = Agree   2 = Disagree   1 = Strongly Disagree

Self-Appraisal of Proficiency in the ASWB Bachelor's Level Social Work Licensing Exam Knowledge, Skills, and Abilities			
4	3	2	1	**Rating Statement**
				In my functioning as a social worker, I can or do apply a genuine understanding of
☐	☐	☐	☐	1. Typical and atypical physical growth and development
☐	☐	☐	☐	2. Typical and atypical cognitive growth and development
☐	☐	☐	☐	3. Typical and atypical social growth, development, and the socialization process
☐	☐	☐	☐	4. Typical and atypical emotional growth and development
☐	☐	☐	☐	5. Typical and atypical sexual growth and development
☐	☐	☐	☐	6. Spiritual growth and development
☐	☐	☐	☐	7. Child behavior and development
☐	☐	☐	☐	8. Adolescent behavior and development
☐	☐	☐	☐	9. Young adult behavior and development
☐	☐	☐	☐	10. Middle adult behavior and development
☐	☐	☐	☐	11. Older adult behavior and development
☐	☐	☐	☐	12. The impact of physical, mental, and cognitive impairment on human development
☐	☐	☐	☐	13. The interplay of biological, psychological, social, and spiritual factors

---

[1] Items adapted from "Content Outlines and KSAs: Social Work Licensing Examinations" (Association of Social Work Boards, 2011) available at **www.aswb.org**.

				Self-Appraisal of Proficiency in the ASWB Bachelor's Level Social Work Licensing Exam Knowledge, Skills, and Abilities
4	**3**	**2**	**1**	**Rating Statement**
☐	☐	☐	☐	14. Attachment and bonding
☐	☐	☐	☐	15. Basic human needs
☐	☐	☐	☐	16. Strengths-based and resilience theories
☐	☐	☐	☐	17. Defense mechanisms and human behavior
☐	☐	☐	☐	18. The psychosocial model
☐	☐	☐	☐	19. Group theories
☐	☐	☐	☐	20. Family theories and dynamics
☐	☐	☐	☐	21. Systems and ecological perspectives
☐	☐	☐	☐	22. Social change and community development theories
☐	☐	☐	☐	23. The influence of social context on behavior
☐	☐	☐	☐	24. Role theories
☐	☐	☐	☐	25. Gender roles
☐	☐	☐	☐	26. The interaction of culture, race, and/or ethnicity with behaviors, attitudes, and identity
☐	☐	☐	☐	27. The interaction of sexual orientation and/or gender with behaviors, attitudes, and identity
☐	☐	☐	☐	28. The interaction of age and/or disability with behaviors, attitudes, and identity
☐	☐	☐	☐	29. The interaction of spirituality and religion with behaviors, attitudes, and identity
☐	☐	☐	☐	30. The interaction of socioeconomic status with behaviors, attitudes, and identity
☐	☐	☐	☐	31. The dynamics and effects of stereotypes and discrimination
☐	☐	☐	☐	32. The relationship of diversity and communication styles
☐	☐	☐	☐	33. The impact of the physical environment on client systems
☐	☐	☐	☐	34. The impact of the political environment on policy making and client systems
☐	☐	☐	☐	35. The impact of the social environment on client systems
☐	☐	☐	☐	36. The impact of the cultural environment on client systems
☐	☐	☐	☐	37. How to gather a biological, psychological, social, and spiritual history
☐	☐	☐	☐	38. How to gather and evaluate collateral information
☐	☐	☐	☐	39. Types of information available from employment, medical, psychological, psychiatric, and educational records
☐	☐	☐	☐	40. The components of a sexual history
☐	☐	☐	☐	41. The components of a family history

4	3	2	1	Rating Statement
☐	☐	☐	☐	42. The process used in problem formulation
☐	☐	☐	☐	43. The methods of involving the client system in identifying the problem
☐	☐	☐	☐	44. The process of identifying the client system needs
☐	☐	☐	☐	45. The process of referring the client for additional evaluations (for example, medical, psychological, and educational)
☐	☐	☐	☐	46. The use of assessment instruments in practice
☐	☐	☐	☐	47. Assessment of the client system's communication skills
☐	☐	☐	☐	48. Assessment of the client system's strengths, resources, and challenges
☐	☐	☐	☐	49. Assessment of the client system's ability and motivation to engage in the intervention process
☐	☐	☐	☐	50. Assessment of the client system's coping abilities
☐	☐	☐	☐	51. Assessment of the client's needed level of care (for example, supportive services, residential placement, and continuum of care)
☐	☐	☐	☐	52. Assessment of group functioning
☐	☐	☐	☐	53. Assessment of community functioning
☐	☐	☐	☐	54. Assessment of the functioning of organizations
☐	☐	☐	☐	55. The differentiation of the use of, abuse of, and dependency on substances
☐	☐	☐	☐	56. The effects of addiction on the client
☐	☐	☐	☐	57. The effects of addiction on the family system and other relationships
☐	☐	☐	☐	58. The indicators of addictions to gambling, sex, food, media, and so on
☐	☐	☐	☐	59. The co-occurrence of addiction and other disorders
☐	☐	☐	☐	60. The symptoms of mental and emotional illness across the lifespan
☐	☐	☐	☐	61. The symptoms of neurologic and organic conditions
☐	☐	☐	☐	62. The indicators of behavioral dysfunction
☐	☐	☐	☐	63. Prescription medications and other substances
☐	☐	☐	☐	64. The indicators, dynamics, and impact of sexual abuse across the lifespan
☐	☐	☐	☐	65. The indicators, dynamics, and impact of emotional abuse and neglect across the lifespan
☐	☐	☐	☐	66. The indicators, dynamics, and impact of physical abuse and neglect across the lifespan
☐	☐	☐	☐	67. The indicators, dynamics, and impact of intimate partner violence
☐	☐	☐	☐	68. The indicators, dynamics, and impact of other forms of exploitation across the lifespan (for example, financial, immigration status, and sexual trafficking)
☐	☐	☐	☐	69. The dynamics and effects of life stage and life-cycle crises

Self-Appraisal of Proficiency in the ASWB Bachelor's Level Social Work Licensing Exam Knowledge, Skills, and Abilities				
4	**3**	**2**	**1**	**Rating Statement**
☐	☐	☐	☐	70. The impact of physical and mental illness
☐	☐	☐	☐	71. The dynamics and effects of trauma
☐	☐	☐	☐	72. The dynamics and effects of loss, separation, and grief
☐	☐	☐	☐	73. The impact of care giving on families
☐	☐	☐	☐	74. Indicators of and response to client danger to self and others
☐	☐	☐	☐	75. Stages of crises
☐	☐	☐	☐	76. The development and maintenance of a helping relationship
☐	☐	☐	☐	77. The development, evaluation, and establishment of a measurable intervention plan
☐	☐	☐	☐	78. Techniques used to engage and motivate client systems
☐	☐	☐	☐	79. Work with involuntary client systems
☐	☐	☐	☐	80. How to contract with client systems
☐	☐	☐	☐	81. Clarification of the roles and responsibilities of the client system
☐	☐	☐	☐	82. Termination and follow-up in social work practice
☐	☐	☐	☐	83. The effect of caseload management on client systems
☐	☐	☐	☐	84. The crisis intervention approach
☐	☐	☐	☐	85. Cognitive and/or behavioral interventions
☐	☐	☐	☐	86. Strengths-based and empowerment practice
☐	☐	☐	☐	87. Problem-solving approaches
☐	☐	☐	☐	88. Techniques used to teach skills to client systems (for example, role play and modeling)
☐	☐	☐	☐	89. Provision of education and information to client systems (for example, parenting and psychosocial aspects of health and illness)
☐	☐	☐	☐	90. How to teach coping strategies to client systems (for example, assertiveness, conflict resolution, and stress management)
☐	☐	☐	☐	91. Group work approaches
☐	☐	☐	☐	92. Family practice approaches
☐	☐	☐	☐	93. Community practice approaches
☐	☐	☐	☐	94. Social policy development and analysis
☐	☐	☐	☐	95. Advocacy for micro-, mezzo-, and macro-client systems
☐	☐	☐	☐	96. Intervention with organizations (for example, organizational policy development, hierarchy, and formal and informal power structures)
☐	☐	☐	☐	97. Determination of which individual, family, group, or combined modality meets the needs of client systems

4	3	2	1	Rating Statement
☐	☐	☐	☐	98. Determination of which community or organizational approach meets the needs of client systems
☐	☐	☐	☐	99. The effect of the client system's abilities on the selection of an intervention (for example, literacy, employability, developmental level, cognitive ability, and physical ability)
☐	☐	☐	☐	100. The effect of the client system's culture on the selection of an intervention
☐	☐	☐	☐	101. The effect of the client system's life stage on the selection of an intervention
☐	☐	☐	☐	102. Provision of case management services
☐	☐	☐	☐	103. How to refer client systems for services
☐	☐	☐	☐	104. Determination of the client's eligibility for services
☐	☐	☐	☐	105. Scope of practice and basic terminology of professions other than social work
☐	☐	☐	☐	106. The use of consultation and case conferences
☐	☐	☐	☐	107. Interdisciplinary and intradisciplinary team approaches
☐	☐	☐	☐	108. Establishment, maintenance, and utilization of formal and informal service networks or community resources and supports
☐	☐	☐	☐	109. The use of objective and subjective data in written assessments and case notes
☐	☐	☐	☐	110. How to write and maintain client records (for example, client progress notes)
☐	☐	☐	☐	111. Development of reports for external organizations (for example, the courts)
☐	☐	☐	☐	112. Development of administrative reports (for example, grant reports, outcomes and evaluations, program proposals, and accreditation reports)
☐	☐	☐	☐	113. How to record and monitor assessments and service plans
☐	☐	☐	☐	114. How to obtain and record service-related forms (for example, informed consent for services, consent for release of information, advanced directives, and Do Not Resuscitate [DNR])
☐	☐	☐	☐	115. Legal and ethical issues regarding documentation
☐	☐	☐	☐	116. How to obtain information relevant to a given situation
☐	☐	☐	☐	117. The use of verbal and nonverbal communication techniques
☐	☐	☐	☐	118. Identification of the underlying meaning of communication
☐	☐	☐	☐	119. The use of active listening and observation
☐	☐	☐	☐	120. Interview techniques (for example, supporting, clarifying, confronting, validating, feedback, and reflecting)
☐	☐	☐	☐	121. Elicitation of sensitive information (for example, substance abuse and sexual abuse)
☐	☐	☐	☐	122. How to interview clients with communication barriers (for example, language differences and use of interpreters)

				Self-Appraisal of Proficiency in the ASWB Bachelor's Level Social Work Licensing Exam Knowledge, Skills, and Abilities
4	**3**	**2**	**1**	**Rating Statement**
☐	☐	☐	☐	123. Use of bias-free language in interviewing
☐	☐	☐	☐	124. How to respond to clients' resistant behaviors
☐	☐	☐	☐	125. Evaluation of one's own practice (for example, single-subject designs, goal-attainment scaling, task-achievement scaling, and use of scales and instruments)
☐	☐	☐	☐	126. Critical evaluation of relevant research and statistical data (that is, understanding basic research design and methods)
☐	☐	☐	☐	127. Selection of interventions based on research
☐	☐	☐	☐	128. The use of data to inform and influence organizational and social policy
☐	☐	☐	☐	129. The use of program evaluation (for example, needs assessment, formative and summative, cost-effectiveness, cost–benefit analysis, and outcomes assessment)
☐	☐	☐	☐	130. Ethical issues and boundaries in the social worker–client relationship (for example, dual relationships, power differences, and conflicts of interest)
☐	☐	☐	☐	131. The influence of (my personal) values on the social worker–client system relationship
☐	☐	☐	☐	132. Ethical and legal issues regarding termination
☐	☐	☐	☐	133. Identification and resolution of ethical dilemmas
☐	☐	☐	☐	134. Ethical and legal issues regarding mandatory reporting (for example, abuse, threat of harm, and impaired professionals)
☐	☐	☐	☐	135. Professional values and ethics (for example, competence, social justice, integrity, and worth of the individual)
☐	☐	☐	☐	136. Legal and ethical issues regarding confidentiality
☐	☐	☐	☐	137. The secure use of client records, including electronic information
☐	☐	☐	☐	138. Legal and ethical issues regarding confidentiality and the competency of the client
☐	☐	☐	☐	139. Legal and ethical issues regarding confidentiality and minors
☐	☐	☐	☐	140. Protection and enhancement of client system self-determination
☐	☐	☐	☐	141. The client's right to refuse services (for example, medication, medical treatment, counseling, and placement)
☐	☐	☐	☐	142. Minors and self-determination (for example, emancipation, age of consent, and permanency planning)
☐	☐	☐	☐	143. Competence and self-determination (for example, financial decisions and treatment decisions)
☐	☐	☐	☐	144. How to balance self-determination and client risk (for example, suicidal, homicidal, and grave danger)
☐	☐	☐	☐	145. The use of empathy in the social worker–client relationship

4	3	2	1	Rating Statement
☐	☐	☐	☐	146. The concepts of transference and countertransference
☐	☐	☐	☐	147. The use of acceptance in the social worker–client relationship
☐	☐	☐	☐	148. The appropriate use of self-disclosure
☐	☐	☐	☐	149. Recognition and management of burnout, secondary trauma, and compassion fatigue
☐	☐	☐	☐	150. Transference and countertransference within supervisory relationships
☐	☐	☐	☐	151. Supervisee's role in supervision (for example, identifying learning needs, self-assessment, and prioritizing)
☐	☐	☐	☐	152. The use of ongoing professional development to improve practice and stay current (for example, in-service training, licensing requirements, reviews of literature, and workshops)
☐	☐	☐	☐	153. Differential use of consultation, peer support, and supervision
				Total

This instrument can help you estimate your self-appraised proficiency in the knowledge, skills, and abilities addressed in the ASWB-sponsored bachelor's-level social work licensing examination. Because it is based on your own appraisal, absolute scores are relatively unimportant. Rather, use the results as a stimulus to ask yourself questions concerning your knowledge, skills, and abilities, and to develop plans by which to improve your proficiency. You may complete the instrument at various points throughout the learning process. Increased proficiency may be reflected in changing scores over time. In considering your results, please remember that a higher rating suggests a higher level of appraised proficiency.

To score the Self-Appraisal of Proficiency in the ASWB Knowledge, Skills, and Abilities instrument, simply sum the total of your ratings to the 153 items. Your score should range somewhere between 153 and 612. In theory, a score of 459 (or an average of 3 on each of the 153 items) would indicate that, on average, you "agree" with statements suggesting that you are quite proficient. Please note, however, that such an average score does not necessarily indicate that you are proficient in all dimensions. You might obtain such a score by rating several items at the "4" or "strongly agree" level and an equal number at the "2" or "disagree level." Therefore, you should look carefully at your rating for each item, as well as the total score.

If all learners in your program share their item ratings and total scores, perhaps anonymously, with a professor or program administrator, responses can be aggregated. When analyzed, they may reveal areas where students believe they are proficient and areas that require additional study or practice. Comparison of pre- and post-test scores of individual students or those of student cohorts represents another way to use this self-appraisal to assess progress and promote learning.

Finally, you should recognize that this instrument reflects your own subjective opinions. You may consciously or unconsciously overestimate or perhaps underestimate your proficiency. Therefore, please use these results in conjunction with other evidence to establish a more balanced approximation of your current knowledge, skills, and abilities.

Self-Appraisal of Proficiency in the ASWB Knowledge, Skills, and Abilities (Master's Level)

Derived from content addressed in the master's level licensing examination of the Association of Social Work Boards (ASWB) (2011), this self-appraisal instrument helps you do an estimate of your self-appraised proficiency in the knowledge, skills, and abilities currently reflected in social work practice. Read each item[1] carefully. Then, use the following 4-point rating scale to indicate the degree to which you agree or disagree with each statement. Mark a check in the box below the number that best reflections your opinion.

4 = Strongly Agree   3 = Agree   2 = Disagree   1 = Strongly Disagree

Self-Appraisal of Proficiency in the ASWB Master's Level Social Work Licensing Exam Knowledge, Skills, and Abilities			
4 **3** **2** **1**	**Rating Statement**		
	In my functioning as a social worker, I can or do apply a genuine understanding of		
☐ ☐ ☐ ☐	1. Developmental theories		
☐ ☐ ☐ ☐	2. Systems theories		
☐ ☐ ☐ ☐	3. Family theories		
☐ ☐ ☐ ☐	4. Group theories		
☐ ☐ ☐ ☐	5. Psychodynamic theories		
☐ ☐ ☐ ☐	6. Behavioral, cognitive, and learning theories		
☐ ☐ ☐ ☐	7. Community development theories		
☐ ☐ ☐ ☐	8. Person in environment		
☐ ☐ ☐ ☐	9. Addiction theories and concepts		
☐ ☐ ☐ ☐	10. Communication theories		
☐ ☐ ☐ ☐	11. Defense mechanisms		
☐ ☐ ☐ ☐	12. Normal and abnormal behavior		
☐ ☐ ☐ ☐	13. Indicators of normal physical growth and development		
☐ ☐ ☐ ☐	14. Adult development		

[1] Items adapted from "Content Outlines and KSAs: Social Work Licensing Examinations" (Association of Social Work Boards, 2011) available at **www.aswb.org**.

4	3	2	1	Rating Statement
☐	☐	☐	☐	15. Effects of life crises
☐	☐	☐	☐	16. Impact of stress, trauma, and violence
☐	☐	☐	☐	17. Emotional development
☐	☐	☐	☐	18. Sexual development
☐	☐	☐	☐	19. Aging processes
☐	☐	☐	☐	20. Family life cycle
☐	☐	☐	☐	21. Family dynamics and functioning
☐	☐	☐	☐	22. Cognitive development
☐	☐	☐	☐	23. Social development
☐	☐	☐	☐	24. Child development
☐	☐	☐	☐	25. Basic human needs
☐	☐	☐	☐	26. Adolescent development
☐	☐	☐	☐	27. Human genetics
☐	☐	☐	☐	28. Gender roles
☐	☐	☐	☐	29. The impact of environment on individuals
☐	☐	☐	☐	30. The impact of physical, mental, and cognitive disabilities on human development
☐	☐	☐	☐	31. The interplay of biological, psychological, and social factors
☐	☐	☐	☐	32. The effects of family dynamics on individuals
☐	☐	☐	☐	33. The dynamics of grief and loss
☐	☐	☐	☐	34. The impact of economic changes on client systems
☐	☐	☐	☐	35. The effects of body image on self and relationships
☐	☐	☐	☐	36. Cultural, racial, and ethnic identity development
☐	☐	☐	☐	37. The strengths perspective
☐	☐	☐	☐	38. Abuse and neglect concepts
☐	☐	☐	☐	39. Indicators and dynamics of sexual abuse
☐	☐	☐	☐	40. Indicators and dynamics of psychological abuse and neglect
☐	☐	☐	☐	41. Indicators and dynamics of physical abuse and neglect
☐	☐	☐	☐	42. Characteristics of abuse perpetrators
☐	☐	☐	☐	43. Indicators and dynamics of exploitation
☐	☐	☐	☐	44. The influence of culture, race, and/or ethnicity on behaviors and attitudes
☐	☐	☐	☐	45. The influence of sexual orientation and/or gender identity on behavior and attitudes

				Self-Appraisal of Proficiency in the ASWB Master's Level Social Work Licensing Exam Knowledge, Skills, and Abilities
4	3	2	1	**Rating Statement**
☐	☐	☐	☐	46. The influence of disability on behaviors and attitudes
☐	☐	☐	☐	47. The effects of differences in values
☐	☐	☐	☐	48. The impact of cultural heritage on self-image
☐	☐	☐	☐	49. The impact of spirituality and/or religious beliefs on behaviors and attitudes
☐	☐	☐	☐	50. The effects of discrimination
☐	☐	☐	☐	51. Systemic (institutionalized) discrimination
☐	☐	☐	☐	52. Professional commitment to promoting justice
☐	☐	☐	☐	53. The impact of social institutions on society
☐	☐	☐	☐	54. The impact of diversity in styles of communicating
☐	☐	☐	☐	55. The influence of age on behaviors and attitudes
☐	☐	☐	☐	56. Psychopharmacology
☐	☐	☐	☐	57. The components of a biopsychosocial history
☐	☐	☐	☐	58. The components of a sexual history
☐	☐	☐	☐	59. Common prescription medications
☐	☐	☐	☐	60. The components of a family history
☐	☐	☐	☐	61. Basic medical terminology
☐	☐	☐	☐	62. Symptoms of mental and emotional illness
☐	☐	☐	☐	63. Symptoms of neurologic and organic processes
☐	☐	☐	☐	64. Indicators of sexual dysfunction
☐	☐	☐	☐	65. Indicators of psychosocial stress
☐	☐	☐	☐	66. Indicators of traumatic stress and violence
☐	☐	☐	☐	67. Indicators of substance abuse and other addictions
☐	☐	☐	☐	68. The use of collateral sources to obtain relevant information
☐	☐	☐	☐	69. Methods used to evaluate collateral information
☐	☐	☐	☐	70. The process used in problem identification
☐	☐	☐	☐	71. Methods used to assess the client's communication skills
☐	☐	☐	☐	72. The use of observation
☐	☐	☐	☐	73. Methods of involving clients in identifying problems
☐	☐	☐	☐	74. Indicators of client's strengths and challenges
☐	☐	☐	☐	75. The use of assessment/diagnostic instruments in practice

4	3	2	1	Rating Statement
☐	☐	☐	☐	76. Methods used to organize information
☐	☐	☐	☐	77. Current *Diagnostic and Statistical Manual* diagnostic framework and criteria
☐	☐	☐	☐	78. The components and function of the mental status examination
☐	☐	☐	☐	79. The process of social work assessment/diagnosis
☐	☐	☐	☐	80. Methods used in assessing ego strengths
☐	☐	☐	☐	81. Methods used to assess community strengths and challenges
☐	☐	☐	☐	82. Methods used in risk assessment
☐	☐	☐	☐	83. Indicators of client danger to self and others
☐	☐	☐	☐	84. Indicators of motivation and resistance
☐	☐	☐	☐	85. Methods used to identify service needs of clients
☐	☐	☐	☐	86. The use of interviewing techniques
☐	☐	☐	☐	87. The process of assessing the client's needed level of care
☐	☐	☐	☐	88. Factors used in determining the client's readiness/ability to participate in services
☐	☐	☐	☐	89. Criteria used in selecting intervention modalities
☐	☐	☐	☐	90. The components of an intervention or service plan
☐	☐	☐	☐	91. Human development considerations in the creation of an intervention plan
☐	☐	☐	☐	92. Methods used to develop an intervention plan
☐	☐	☐	☐	93. Techniques used to establish measurable intervention or service plans
☐	☐	☐	☐	94. Methods used to involve clients in intervention planning
☐	☐	☐	☐	95. Methods for planning interventions with groups
☐	☐	☐	☐	96. Methods for planning interventions with organizations and communities
☐	☐	☐	☐	97. Cultural considerations in the creation of an intervention plan
☐	☐	☐	☐	98. Client advocacy
☐	☐	☐	☐	99. Empowerment process
☐	☐	☐	☐	100. Methods used in working with involuntary clients
☐	☐	☐	☐	101. Psychosocial approach
☐	☐	☐	☐	102. Components of the problem-solving process
☐	☐	☐	☐	103. Crisis intervention approach
☐	☐	☐	☐	104. Task-centered practice
☐	☐	☐	☐	105. Short-term interventions
☐	☐	☐	☐	106. Methods used to provide educational services to clients

				Self-Appraisal of Proficiency in the ASWB Master's Level Social Work Licensing Exam Knowledge, Skills, and Abilities
4	**3**	**2**	**1**	**Rating Statement**
☐	☐	☐	☐	107. Methods of conflict resolution
☐	☐	☐	☐	108. The use of case management
☐	☐	☐	☐	109. Techniques used to evaluate a client's progress
☐	☐	☐	☐	110. The use of contracting and goal setting with client systems
☐	☐	☐	☐	111. The use of timing in intervention
☐	☐	☐	☐	112. Phases of intervention
☐	☐	☐	☐	113. Indicators of client readiness for termination
☐	☐	☐	☐	114. Techniques used for follow-up in social work practice
☐	☐	☐	☐	115. The use of active-listening skills
☐	☐	☐	☐	116. Techniques used to motivate clients
☐	☐	☐	☐	117. Techniques used to teach skills to clients
☐	☐	☐	☐	118. The use and effects of out-of-home placement
☐	☐	☐	☐	119. Methods used to develop behavioral objectives
☐	☐	☐	☐	120. Client self-monitoring techniques
☐	☐	☐	☐	121. Technique of role play
☐	☐	☐	☐	122. Assertiveness training
☐	☐	☐	☐	123. Role modeling techniques
☐	☐	☐	☐	124. Limit setting
☐	☐	☐	☐	125. Methods used to develop learning objectives with clients
☐	☐	☐	☐	126. Models of intervention with families
☐	☐	☐	☐	127. Couples intervention/treatment approaches
☐	☐	☐	☐	128. Interventions with groups
☐	☐	☐	☐	129. Techniques for working with individuals within the group context
☐	☐	☐	☐	130. The use of expertise from other disciplines
☐	☐	☐	☐	131. Approaches used in consultation
☐	☐	☐	☐	132. Processes of interdisciplinary collaboration
☐	☐	☐	☐	133. Methods used to coordinate services among service providers
☐	☐	☐	☐	134. A multidisciplinary team approach
☐	☐	☐	☐	135. Case recording and record keeping
☐	☐	☐	☐	136. Methods used to facilitate communication

4	3	2	1	Rating Statement
☐	☐	☐	☐	137. Verbal and nonverbal communication techniques
☐	☐	☐	☐	138. Techniques that explore underlying meanings of communication
☐	☐	☐	☐	139. Methods used to obtain/provide feedback
☐	☐	☐	☐	140. Methods used to interpret and communicate policies and procedures
☐	☐	☐	☐	141. Methods used to clarify the benefits and limitations of resources with clients
☐	☐	☐	☐	142. The use of case recording for practice evaluation or supervision
☐	☐	☐	☐	143. The use of single-subject designs in practice
☐	☐	☐	☐	144. Evaluation of practice
☐	☐	☐	☐	145. Interpretation and application of research findings to practice
☐	☐	☐	☐	146. Process used to refer clients for services
☐	☐	☐	☐	147. The use of cognitive-behavioral techniques
☐	☐	☐	☐	148. Culturally competent social work practice
☐	☐	☐	☐	149. Concepts of organizational theories
☐	☐	☐	☐	150. The impact of social welfare legislation on social work practice
☐	☐	☐	☐	151. Methods used to establish service networks or community resources
☐	☐	☐	☐	152. Techniques for mobilizing community participation
☐	☐	☐	☐	153. Techniques of social planning methods
☐	☐	☐	☐	154. Techniques of social policy analysis
☐	☐	☐	☐	155. Techniques to influence social policy
☐	☐	☐	☐	156. Techniques of working with large groups
☐	☐	☐	☐	157. The use of networking
☐	☐	☐	☐	158. Approaches to culturally competent practice with organizations and communities
☐	☐	☐	☐	159. Advocacy with communities and organizations
☐	☐	☐	☐	160. The impact of agency policy and function on service delivery
☐	☐	☐	☐	161. Professional values and ethics
☐	☐	☐	☐	162. Client self-determination
☐	☐	☐	☐	163. The intrinsic worth and value of the individual
☐	☐	☐	☐	164. The client's right to refuse service
☐	☐	☐	☐	165. Ethical issues regarding termination
☐	☐	☐	☐	166. Bioethical issues
☐	☐	☐	☐	167. The identification and resolution of ethical dilemmas

				Self-Appraisal of Proficiency in the ASWB Master's Level Social Work Licensing Exam Knowledge, Skills, and Abilities
4	**3**	**2**	**1**	**Rating Statement**
☐	☐	☐	☐	168. Ethics to practice issues
☐	☐	☐	☐	169. The responsibility to seek supervision
☐	☐	☐	☐	170. The use of professional development to improve practice
☐	☐	☐	☐	171. Professional boundaries
☐	☐	☐	☐	172. Legal and ethical issues regarding confidentiality, including electronic communication
☐	☐	☐	☐	173. The use of client records
☐	☐	☐	☐	174. Ethical and legal issues regarding mandatory reporting
☐	☐	☐	☐	175. How to obtain informed consent
☐	☐	☐	☐	176. Social worker–client relationship patterns
☐	☐	☐	☐	177. The concept of empathy
☐	☐	☐	☐	178. The process of engagement in social work practice
☐	☐	☐	☐	179. The concept of a helping relationship
☐	☐	☐	☐	180. The principles of relationship building
☐	☐	☐	☐	181. Professional objectivity in the social worker–client relationship
☐	☐	☐	☐	182. The concepts of transference and countertransference
☐	☐	☐	☐	183. The use of the social worker–client relationship as an intervention tool
☐	☐	☐	☐	184. Social worker–client relationships in work with communities and organizations
☐	☐	☐	☐	185. Social worker–client relationships in work with small groups
☐	☐	☐	☐	186. Methods used to clarify roles of the social worker
☐	☐	☐	☐	187. The social worker's roles in the problem-solving process
☐	☐	☐	☐	188. The client's roles in the problem-solving process
☐	☐	☐	☐	189. The influence of (my personal) values on the social worker–client relationship
☐	☐	☐	☐	190. Dual relationships
☐	☐	☐	☐	191. The influence of cultural diversity on the social worker–client relationship
				Total

This instrument can help you estimate your self-appraised proficiency in the knowledge, skills, and abilities addressed in the ASWB-sponsored master's-level social work licensing examination. Because it is based on your own appraisal, absolute scores are relatively unimportant. Rather, use the results as a stimulus to ask yourself questions concerning your knowledge, skills, and abilities, and to develop plans by which to improve your proficiency. You may complete the instrument at various points throughout the learning process. Increased proficiency may be reflected in changing scores over time. In considering your results, please remember that a higher rating suggests a higher level of appraised proficiency.

To score the Self-Appraisal of Proficiency in the ASWB Knowledge, Skills, and Abilities instrument, simply sum the total of your ratings to the 191 items. Your score should range somewhere between 191 and 764. In theory, a score of 573 (or an average of 3 on each of the 191 items) would indicate that, on average, you "agree" with statements suggesting that you are quite proficient. Please note, however, that such an average score does not necessarily indicate that you are proficient in all dimensions. You might obtain such a score by rating several items at the "4" or "strongly agree" level and an equal number at the "2" or "disagree level." Therefore, you should look carefully at your rating for each item, as well as the total score.

If all learners in your program share their item ratings and total scores, perhaps anonymously, with a professor or program administrator, responses can be aggregated. When analyzed, they may reveal areas where students believe they are proficient and areas that require additional study or practice. Comparison of pre- and post-test scores of individual students or those of student cohorts represents another way to use this self-appraisal to assess progress and promote learning.

Finally, you should recognize that this instrument reflects your own subjective opinions. You may consciously or unconsciously overestimate or perhaps underestimate your proficiency. Therefore, please use these results in conjunction with other evidence to establish a more balanced approximation of your current knowledge, skills, and abilities.